ᗡᑭ
6/14

# Roadfood

## Also by Jane and Michael Stern

The Lexicon of Real American Food

Confessions of a Tarot Reader
   (by Jane Stern)

500 Things to Eat Before It's Too Late

Roadfood Sandwiches

Two for the Road

Elegant Comfort Food from the Dorset Inn

The Loveless Cafe Cookbook

Southern California Cooking from the
   Cottage

Cooking in the Lowcountry

The Famous Dutch Kitchen Cookbook

Ambulance Girl (by Jane Stern)

Carbone's Cookbook

Harry Caray's Restaurant Cookbook

Louie's Back Yard Cookbook

The Durgin-Park Cookbook

The El Charro Cookbook

The Blue Willow Inn Cookbook

Blue Plate Specials and Blue Ribbon Chefs

Chili Nation

Two Puppies

Eat Your Way Across the USA

Dog Eat Dog

Happy Trails (with Roy Rogers
   and Dale Evans)

Way Out West

Jane & Michael Stern's Encyclopedia
   of Pop Culture

American Gourmet

The Encyclopedia of Bad Taste

Sixties People

A Taste of America

Elvis World

Real American Food

Roadfood & Goodfood

Where to Eat in Connecticut

Square Meals

Goodfood

Horror Holiday

Friendly Relations

Douglas Sirk (by Michael Stern)

Auto Ads

Amazing America

Trucker: A Portrait of the Last
   American Cowboy (by Jane Stern)

# Roadfood

The Coast-to-Coast Guide to 900 of the Best
Barbecue Joints, Lobster Shacks, Ice Cream Parlors,
Highway Diners, and Much, Much More,

Now in Its 9th Edition

# Jane and Michael Stern

CLARKSON POTTER/PUBLISHERS ✳ New York

Copyright © 2014 by Jane Stern and Michael Stern

Published in the United States by Clarkson Potter/Publishers, an imprint of the Crown
Publishing Group, a division of Random House LLC, a Penguin Random House Company,
New York.
www.crownpublishing.com
www.clarksonpotter.com

CLARKSON POTTER is a trademark and POTTER with colophon is a registered trademark
of Random House LLC.

This work was originally published in the United States by Random House LLC, New York,
in 1978. Subsequent revised editions were published in the United States by Random House
LLC, New York, in 1980, Alfred A. Knopf, a division of Random House LLC, New York,
in 1986, Harper Perennial, a division of HarperCollins Publishers, New York, in 1992,
Broadway Books, a division of Random House LLC, New York, in 2002, 2005, and 2008,
and by Clarkson Potter/ Publishers, an imprint of the Crown Publishing Group, a division of
Random House LLC, New York, in 2011.

Library of Congress Cataloging-in-Publication Data is available upon request.

ISBN 978-0-7704-3452-6
eISBN 978-0-7704-3453-3

Printed in the United States of America

Book design by Caroline Cunningham
Maps designed by Jeffrey L. Ward
Cover design by Daniel Rembert
Cover photographs: (ribs) Stephen Walls/iStock, (sky) soleg_1974/iStock, (sign) onepony/
iStock, (horizontal sign) chrispoundsphotography/iStock, (arrow) Car Culture/Getty

10 9 8 7 6 5 4 3 2 1

Second Clarkson Potter/Publishers Edition

# Contents

## Great Plains 527

## West Coast 563

It was almost forty years ago that we coined the term "roadfood" to describe local eats around America. At the time, we felt like crusaders, trying to get people to pay attention to what we considered a neglected national treasure: regional food. My, how times have changed! We now sometimes wish people didn't pay quite so much attention to it—particularly on those occasions when we must wait in line forty minutes to get a cheeseburger from a once-obscure diner that has been discovered by the media.

In the restaurant business, success isn't always a good thing, especially for humble places unprepared to handle it. You know the sad scenario: A quiet gem of a restaurant appears on TV. It gets so flooded with curiosity seekers that the regular customers who were a part of its personality can't get in. Business is so good, new cooks are hired. The menu is streamlined down to what the guy on TV talked about. Shortcuts are taken, the dining room is expanded. No doubt about it: Some of the charming one-of-a-kind eateries we have written about over the years are now multiple-location empires and their food has gone to pot. To the degree that we have set that process in motion, we apologize. Apparently our enthusiasm has been contagious. On the other hand, some favorite places have expanded with care and intelligence; their original locations are still listed in this book, along with notes about their expansion.

For all the media brouhaha about the subject, and food's seeming omnipresence in the blogosphere, the joy of traveling *Roadfood*-style hasn't changed all that much. As seen in the Roadfood.com "Trip Reports" forum, dedicated eaters plan their itineraries meal by meal and continue to enjoy the experience that we have enjoyed from the beginning: finding oneself in a restaurant very different from anyplace near home, eating food unique to the region, meeting local people—customers and staff—for whom the restaurant is part of their life, their community, their identity. This new edition of *Roadfood* includes an "Honor Roll" of the 100 restaurants that we believe epitomize that experience—the crème de la crème of regional dining all around the country.

    *Roadfood* is about finding good food, of course. But to us, that food in a cultural vacuum, however good it might taste, is not very interesting. What makes it really delicious is all of its connections—connections to the people who grow it, cook it, serve it, and eat it; connections to the places that have nurtured it and given it a regional identity; connections to the history from which it arises, which in America's case is an adventure of immigration, adaptation, invention, and audacity. Just as one man's diet can give you a vivid picture of who he is, America's diet is a grand national portrait.

We urge you to visit each and every one of the 900-plus restaurants in this book: We have included them because we think their food is great and the experience of eating in them is memorable. One hundred of those restaurants are starred with an asterisk to indicate that they are, to us, extra-special. We have come to love them because we believe that each is a unique expression of something wonderful about American food and foodways. A few are relatively new, but most have stood the test of time. This is the **Roadfood Honor Roll**.

## New England (11)

| | |
|---|---|
| Frank Pepe Pizzeria Napoletana | New Haven, CT |
| Super Duper Weenie | Fairfield, CT |
| Zuppardi's Apizza | West Haven, CT |
| Five Islands Lobster Co. | Georgetown, ME |
| Maine Diner | Wells, ME |
| Clam Box | Ipswich, MA |
| Hartley's Original Pork Pies | Fall River, MA |
| Polly's Pancake Parlor | Sugar Hill, NH |
| The Commons Lunch | Little Compton, RI |
| Blue Benn Diner | Bennington, VT |
| Up for Breakfast | Manchester, VT |

## Mid-Atlantic (11)

| | |
|---|---|
| Ben's Chili Bowl | Washington, DC |
| Faidley's | Baltimore, MD |
| Harold's New York Deli | Edison, NJ |
| Jimmy Buff's | West Orange, NJ |
| White House Sub Shop | Atlantic City, NJ |
| Aléthea's | Williamsville, NY |
| Katz's Delicatessen | New York, NY |
| Nick Tahou Hots | Rochester, NY |
| Schwabl's | West Seneca, NY |
| John's Roast Pork | Philadelphia, PA |
| Mama's | Bala Cynwyd, PA |

## Mid-South (13)

| | |
|---|---|
| Bon-Ton Mini Mart | Henderson, KY |
| Peak Bros. | Waverly, KY |
| Keaton's | Cleveland, NC |
| Lexington Barbecue #1 | Lexington, NC |
| Skylight Inn | Ayden, NC |
| Arnold's Country Kitchen | Nashville, TN |
| Cozy Corner | Memphis, TN |
| Prince's Hot Chicken Shack | Nashville, TN |
| Ridgewood Barbecue | Bluff City, TN |
| Metompkin Seafood | Mappsville, VA |
| Red Truck Bakery & Market | Warrenton, VA |
| Southern Kitchen | New Market, VA |
| Coleman's Fish Market | Wheeling, WV |

## Deep South (18)

| | |
|---|---|
| Niki's West | Birmingham, AL |
| AQ Chicken House | Springdale, AR |
| McClard's | Hot Springs, AR |
| Stubby's Bar-B-Que | Hot Springs, AR |
| O'Steen's | St. Augustine, FL |
| Whitey's Fish Camp | Orange Park, FL |
| Mary Mac's Tea Room | Atlanta, GA |
| Silver Skillet | Atlanta, GA |

| | |
|---|---|
| Brenda's Diner | New Iberia, LA |
| Café des Amis | Breaux Bridge, LA |
| Domilise's Po-Boys | New Orleans, LA |
| Johnson's Boucanière | Lafayette, LA |
| Morning Call Coffee Stand | Metairie, LA |
| Doe's Eat Place | Greenville, MS |
| White Front Cafe | Rosedale, MS |
| Bertha's Kitchen | North Charleston, SC |
| Bowens Island | Charleston, SC |
| Hominy Grill | Charleston, SC |

## Midwest (23)

| | |
|---|---|
| Hot Doug's | Chicago, IL |
| Johnnie's | Elmwood Park, IL |
| Poochie's | Skokie, IL |
| Rip's | Ladd, IL |
| Superdawg | Chicago, IL |
| Gray Brothers Cafeteria | Mooreseville, IN |
| Nick's Kitchen | Huntington, IN |
| Bob's Drive-Inn | Le Mars, IA |
| Coffee Cup Café | Sully, IA |
| The Cherry Hut | Beulah, MI |
| Jean Kay's | Marquette, MI |
| Hell's Kitchen | Minneapolis, MN |
| Lange's Cafe | Pipeston, MN |
| Snead's | Belton, MO |
| Stroud's | Kansas City, MO |
| Ted Drewes | St. Louis, MO |
| Al's Corner Restaurant | Barberton, OH |
| Camp Washington Chili Parlor | Cincinnati, OH |
| Henry's | West Jefferson, OH |
| Leon's | Milwaukee, WI |
| McBob's | Milwaukee, WI |
| Solly's Grille | Milwaukee, WI |
| Stockholm Pie Company | Stockholm, WI |

## Southwest (12)

El Guero Canelo .......................................................... Tucson, AZ
Pico de Gallo ...................................................... South Tucson, AZ
Woodyard Bar-B-Que ............................................ Kansas City, KS
Frontier ........................................................... Albuquerque, NM
La Posta de Mesilla ............................................ Old Mesilla, NM
Cattlemen's Steakhouse ..................................... Oklahoma City, OK
Van's Pig Stand ..................................................... Shawnee, OK
Bryce's Cafeteria ................................................. Texarkana, TX
Little Diner ........................................................ Canutillo, TX
Louie Mueller's ....................................................... Taylor, TX
Monument Cafe ................................................ Georgetown, TX
Taco Taco .................................................... San Antonio, TX

## Great Plains (3)

Hudson's .................................................... Coeur d'Alene, ID
Eddie's Supper Club ........................................... Great Falls, MT
Rosita's ......................................................... Scottsbluff, NE

## West (9)

The Cottage ....................................................... La Jolla, CA
Du-par's ....................................................... Los Angeles, CA
Hodad's ........................................................ Ocean Beach, CA
Swan Oyster Depot ........................................... San Francisco, CA
Bowpicker .......................................................... Astoria, OR
South Beach Fish Market ...................................... South Beach, OR
Waves of Grain ............................................... Cannon Beach, OR
Bakeman's .......................................................... Seattle, WA
Spud Fish and Chips .............................................. Kirkland, WA

✶ If you are planning a special trip to any restaurant in this book, we urge you to call ahead to make certain it is open and is serving what you want to eat. Hours of operation change over the course of the year and proprietors sometimes go fishing. Our notation of BLD (breakfast, lunch, and dinner) can mean different times in different places. For instance, many heartland restaurants do serve dinner, but dinner hours can end as early as seven o'clock. Also, some specialties are seasonal. (When calling, be aware that telephone area codes are changing all the time.)

✶ The vast majority of Roadfood restaurants require no reservations and are come-as-you-are. A few pricier ones do require a reservation. We've made note of which ones get insanely crowded, and what you can do about it. But again, if in doubt, please call ahead.

✶ We have given an approximate cost guide using dollar signs, but be aware that this can vary dramatically. Many Roadfood restaurants that offer $5 sandwiches for lunch also serve $50 dinners. Also, wine, beer, cocktails, and multiple desserts can seriously jack up prices. Our one-to-three dollar-sign rating describes the meal we talk about most in the review (breakfast, lunch, dinner):

* $ = one full meal is under $12
* $$ = one full meal is between $12 and $30
* $$$ = one full meal is over $30

* Just because a restaurant from a previous edition of *Roadfood* does not appear here does not mean it's out of business or that we don't like it anymore. Either circumstance might be true, but it also is possible that we excised it simply to make room for one of the two hundred new places we believe deserve your attention.

* We welcome tips for inclusion in future editions, comments, and even complaints. Please address any such correspondence to us c/o our publisher, Clarkson Potter. Or e-mail us: roadfood123@hotmail.com, or tell us what you think at our website: www.roadfood.com.

# New England

Connecticut

*

Maine

*

Massachusetts

*

New Hampshire

*

Rhode Island

*

Vermont

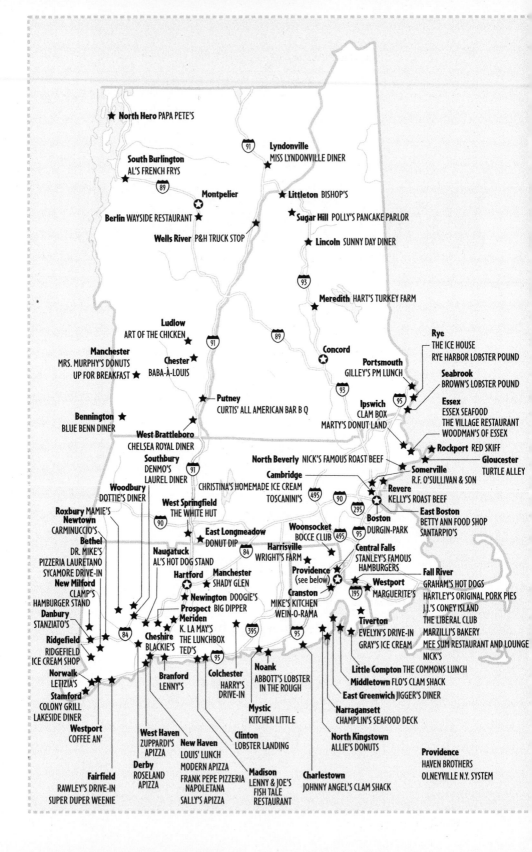

★ **North Hero** PAPA PETE'S

**Lyndonville**
MISS LYNDONVILLE DINER

**South Burlington**
AL'S FRENCH FRYS

**Littleton** BISHOP'S

**Montpelier**

**Sugar Hill** POLLY'S PANCAKE PARLOR

**Berlin** WAYSIDE RESTAURANT ★

**Wells River** P&H TRUCK STOP

★ **Lincoln** SUNNY DAY DINER

**Meredith** HART'S TURKEY FARM

**Ludlow**
ART OF THE CHICKEN

**Rye**
- THE ICE HOUSE
RYE HARBOR LOBSTER POUND

**Concord**

**Manchester**
MRS. MURPHY'S DONUTS
UP FOR BREAKFAST ★

**Chester** ★
BABA-À-LOUIS

**Portsmouth**
GILLEY'S PM LUNCH

**Seabrook**
BROWN'S LOBSTER POUND

★ **Putney**
CURTIS' ALL AMERICAN BAR B Q

**Ipswich**
CLAM BOX
MARTY'S DONUT LAND

**Essex**
ESSEX SEAFOOD
THE VILLAGE RESTAURANT
WOODMAN'S OF ESSEX

**Bennington** ★
BLUE BENN DINER

**West Brattleboro**
CHELSEA ROYAL DINER

★ **Rockport** RED SKIFF

**Southbury**
DENMO'S
LAUREL DINER

**North Beverly** NICK'S FAMOUS ROAST BEEF

**Gloucester**
TURTLE ALLEY

**Woodbury**
DOTTIE'S DINER

**Cambridge**
CHRISTINA'S HOMEMADE ICE CREAM
TOSCANINI'S

**Somerville**
R.F. O'SULLIVAN & SON

**West Springfield**
THE WHITE HUT

**Revere**
KELLY'S ROAST BEEF

**Roxbury** MAMIE'S
**Newtown**
CARMINUCCIO'S

**East Longmeadow**
DONUT DIP

**Woonsocket**
BOCCE CLUB

**Boston**
DURGIN-PARK

**East Boston**
BETTY ANN FOOD SHOP
SANTARPIO'S

**Bethel**
DR. MIKE'S
PIZZERIA LAURETANO
SYCAMORE DRIVE-IN

**Naugatuck**
AL'S HOT DOG STAND

**Harrisville**
WRIGHT'S FARM

**Central Falls**
STANLEY'S FAMOUS
HAMBURGERS

**New Milford**
CLAMP'S
HAMBURGER STAND

**Hartford**
★ **Manchester**
SHADY GLEN

**Providence**
(see below)

**Fall River**
GRAHAM'S HOT DOGS
HARTLEY'S ORIGINAL PORK PIES
J.J.'S CONEY ISLAND
THE LIBERAL CLUB
MARZILLI'S BAKERY
MEE SUM RESTAURANT AND LOUNGE
NICK'S

**Danbury**
STANZIATO'S

★ **Newington** DOOGIE'S
**Prospect** BIG DIPPER
**Meriden**

**Westport**
MARGUERITE'S

**Cranston**
MIKE'S KITCHEN
WEIN-O-RAMA

**Ridgefield**
RIDGEFIELD
ICE CREAM SHOP

**Cheshire**
BLACKIE'S

K. LA MAY'S
THE LUNCHBOX
TED'S

**Tiverton**
EVELYN'S DRIVE-IN
GRAY'S ICE CREAM

**Norwalk**
LETIZIA'S

**Noank**
ABBOTT'S LOBSTER
IN THE ROUGH

**Little Compton** THE COMMONS LUNCH
**Middletown** FLO'S CLAM SHACK
**East Greenwich** JIGGER'S DINER

**Stamford**
COLONY GRILL
LAKESIDE DINER

**Branford**
LENNY'S

**Colchester**
HARRY'S
DRIVE-IN

**Narragansett**
CHAMPLIN'S SEAFOOD DECK

**Westport**
COFFEE AN'

**Mystic**
KITCHEN LITTLE

**North Kingstown**
ALLIE'S DONUTS

**West Haven**
ZUPPARDI'S
APIZZA

**Clinton**
LOBSTER LANDING

**Providence**
HAVEN BROTHERS
OLNEYVILLE N.Y. SYSTEM

**Derby**
ROSELAND
APIZZA

**New Haven**
LOUIS' LUNCH
MODERN APIZZA
FRANK PEPE PIZZERIA
NAPOLETANA
SALLY'S APIZZA

**Madison**
LENNY & JOE'S
FISH TALE
RESTAURANT

**Charlestown**
JOHNNY ANGEL'S CLAM SHACK

**Fairfield**
RAWLEY'S DRIVE-IN
SUPER DUPER WEENIE

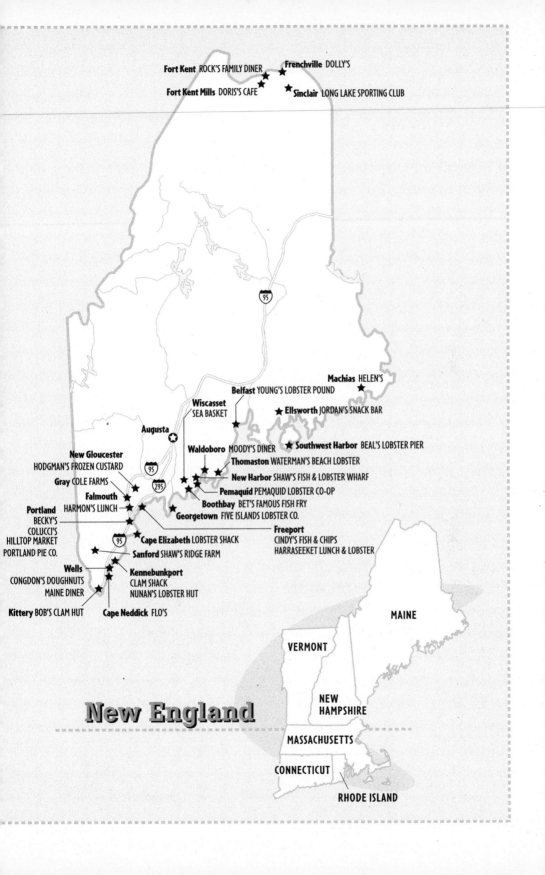

Fort Kent ROCK'S FAMILY DINER
Frenchville DOLLY'S
Fort Kent Mills DORIS'S CAFE
Sinclair LONG LAKE SPORTING CLUB

Machias HELEN'S
Belfast YOUNG'S LOBSTER POUND
Ellsworth JORDAN'S SNACK BAR
Wiscasset
SEA BASKET
Augusta
Waldoboro MOODY'S DINER
Southwest Harbor BEAL'S LOBSTER PIER
New Gloucester
HODGMAN'S FROZEN CUSTARD
Thomaston WATERMAN'S BEACH LOBSTER
Gray COLE FARMS
New Harbor SHAW'S FISH & LOBSTER WHARF
Falmouth
Pemaquid PEMAQUID LOBSTER CO-OP
HARMON'S LUNCH
Boothbay BET'S FAMOUS FISH FRY
Portland
Georgetown FIVE ISLANDS LOBSTER CO.
BECKY'S
COLUCCI'S
Freeport
HILLTOP MARKET
Cape Elizabeth LOBSTER SHACK
CINDY'S FISH & CHIPS
PORTLAND PIE CO.
HARRASEEKET LUNCH & LOBSTER
Sanford SHAW'S RIDGE FARM
Wells
Kennebunkport
CONGDON'S DOUGHNUTS
CLAM SHACK
MAINE DINER
NUNAN'S LOBSTER HUT
Kittery BOB'S CLAM HUT
Cape Neddick FLO'S

MAINE
VERMONT
NEW
HAMPSHIRE
New England
MASSACHUSETTS
CONNECTICUT
RHODE ISLAND

## Abbott's Lobster in the Rough

117 Pearl St.
Noank, CT

860-536-7719
www.abbotts-lobster.com
LD May to Labor Day, then weekends
through mid-Oct | $$

"In the rough" was never so agreeable. On an alfresco dining area perfumed by sea breezes and protected from marauding seagulls, one dines on lobster steamed to such perfect plumpness that meat erupts when the shell is broken. If cracking the carapace of a whole one seems too labor-intensive, the alternative is a hot lobster roll, which is hunks of lobster bathed in butter and sandwiched inside a warm bun. Cold lobster salad rolls are also available, as are hot and cold crab rolls.

While you can get excellent lobsters all up and down Yankee shores, one item you'll find only in this southernmost area is clear-broth clam chowder, of which Abbott's makes the best. Not nearly as creamy-dreamy as New England chowder, and lacking the cacophony of vegetables in Manhattan chowder, as well as the pink tomato blush of Rhode Island shore dinner-hall chowder, the clear-broth stuff is focused and intense. It is the essence of the ocean, and although it is dotted with bits of clam and little nuggets of potato, it is the liquid itself that commands attention. Unadulterated as it is, this is a dish strictly for seafood lovers. If you need something creamy, Abbott's lobster bisque is dramatically so.

## Al's Hot Dog Stand

248 S. Main St.                203-729-6229

Naugatuck, CT                  BLD | $

Relish steals the show at many of Connecticut's big-name hot dog joints, and you will find some of the best at Al's. There are two kinds: hot relish, which will make lips glow, and Hawaiian relish, which balances the formidable heat with a shot of sweet pineapple. The dogs themselves are pork-and-beef foot-longs served in a split-top bun that gets nicely grilled on both sides. They are long enough that if you are a first-timer, you can put regular hot relish at one end and Hawaiian relish on the other and you will have multiple mouthfuls of both to compare and contrast.

Hot dogs are not the only worthies at Al's. Fried seafood, softshell crab in season, and bacon cheeseburgers all are good drive-in fare. French fries are crinkle-cuts and worth ordering. Milk shakes are the real thing.

But in truth, what we like best about Al's is not the food. It is Al's itself, a personality-plus eat shack staffed for more than three decades by family who take what they do quite seriously but offer it up with humor and charm. Dining here is light-years away from dining at a common junk-food franchise. Accommodations include outdoor picnic tables and weird indoor desks with avocado-green office chairs.


## Big Dipper

91 Waterbury Rd.              203-758-3200

Prospect, CT                  www.bigdipper.com

                             (limited winter hours) | $

Inspired by the traditional Good Humor bar but infinitely more delicious, Big Dipper's toasted-almond ice cream delivers the luxury of marzipan and the euphoria of Independence Day. It is but one of a multitude of flavors that include plain vanilla, silky chocolate, silly cotton candy, and a shockingly sophisticated cinnamon-coffee Café Vienna. Because it is not cloyingly rich, Big Dipper ice cream begs to be eaten in large quantities, or in such indulgences as a triple-dip fudge sundae. The line stretches far out the door on a pleasant night, and the staff is famously fun to deal with.

One thing we especially like about this place is that you are not limited to scoops as a measurement of your serving. You can buy as much or as little as you want. Each customer is charged by weight (of the ice cream).

## Blackie's

2200 Waterbury Rd.
Cheshire, CT

203-699-1819
www.blackieshotdogs.com
LD (closed Fridays) | $

Hot dogs are so entirely the specialty of the house at Blackie's that regular customers walk in the door and simply call out a number, indicating how many they want. The dogs are boiled in oil to the point that their outside surface bursts apart from heat. One variation to consider is to add the suffix "well" to the integer you name. This means well-done, which adds extra crunch to the hot dogs' skin.

They are served plain in spongy buns, and it is up to each eater to spoon out mustard and relish from condiment trays that are set out along the counter. The mustard is excellent, and we recommend a modest bed of it applied to the top of each wiener, all the better for the relish to cling to. The relish is thick, luxurious, dark-green, and pepper-hot enough that the nerve endings on your lips will want to hum. Blackie's—and its devoted clientele—are happy enough with this formula for frankfurter perfection that the kitchen doesn't bother to offer sauerkraut or chili. Service is nearly instantaneous, so if your preference is *hot* hot dogs, it is entirely practical to order them one by one until you can't eat any more.

Blackie's (since 1928) has oodles of old-fashioned charm, although you ought not come if you feel like kicking up your heels. A sign on the wall warns, "No Dancing."

## Carminuccio's

76 S. Main St. (Rt. 25)
Newtown, CT

203-364-1133
www.carminucciospizza.com
LD | $

At the small array of bare-topped indoor tables or on the patio to the side of this inconspicuous yellow house by the side of the road, customers eat pizzas on a level with New Haven's best.

Patted out extra-thin, Carminuccio's crust has such a sturdy crunch that you can hold a hot slice by the circumference and the center will not wilt. Even with meat and vegetables on top it stays sturdy from the outer edge almost to the point, and no matter what ingredients you get, topping slippage is rare.

New Haven–made sausage, strewn edge to edge in countless little pinches, is cooked and well drained of fat before a sausage pie is assembled and baked, thus ensuring the cheese stays cheesy and the crust dry. Vegetables are pre-cooked in a convection oven, a process that not only saps crust-threatening moisture but dramatically intensifies the flavor of such toppings as spinach, onions, and tomatoes. Garlic especially benefits from the process, each whole clove caramelized to its soft, sweet essence. Before learning how it is done, we would have sworn the brilliant flavor of the kitchen's supple red pepper strips came from marinade and/or seasoning. But they are unadulterated, nothing but red peppers roasted to a sunny concentrate as vibrant as pumate. Combine the peppers with roasted garlic and sausage and you have a magisterial combo, one of the Earth's essential pizza-eating experiences.

## Clamp's Hamburger Stand

| | |
|---|---|
| Route 202 | No phone |
| New Milford, CT | LD Apr–Sept \| $ |

Despite its lack of a sign, street address, and telephone number, Clamp's is easy to find. Head north on Route 202 out of New Milford and when you see a crowd of cars on the right, you have arrived. Open from late April to early September from 11 a.m. to 2 p.m. and from 5 p.m. to 8 p.m., this little food stand has been a Litchfield County summertime ritual since 1939. (Those hours are exact. We arrived one day at 2:05 and got nothing to eat!)

Tables are arrayed on grassy groves on either side of the shack where you order, pay for, and pick up food. Hamburgers and cheeseburgers are the basis of Clamp's reputation. Made fresh daily and cooked the way you request, they are medium-size patties that leak enough juice to give the bun its own beefy appeal. Their edge slightly crisp, the fibers of the meat infused with a smoky taste that sings of summer afternoons, they are picnic food. All condiments are available; we highly recommend fried onions, which are cooked until caramel-sweet.

## Coffee An'

| | |
|---|---|
| 343 Main St. | 203-227-3808 |
| Westport, CT | BL \| $ |

A good donut is like a flower in bloom or a splendid sunset; the magic has something to do with the knowledge that its allure is fleeting. By tomorrow, even some of the best donuts might barely be edible. That's especially true of Coffee An's devilish devil's food sinker, which, when fresh, is as rich as expensive chocolate cake—crisp-skinned and with a roundhouse chocolate punch. Definitely one of the best chocolate donuts anywhere. The next day, when the infusion of hot oil has turned to cool fat and you sink your sorry teeth into it, you recoil as if from a hideous stranger that you find in your bed upon awakening. What possibly could have been this donut's allure?

Do return for a fresh one, and, once again, all is well with the world.

We also can recommend the plain cake and cinnamon-coated donuts, each of which has a memorably crunchy surface . . . but an equally ephemeral appeal.

## Colony Grill

172 Myrtle Ave.
Stamford, CT

203-359-2184
www.colonygrill.com
LD | $$

Pizza is the only food on the menu of this old neighborhood tavern, and it is available in one size, about a foot and a half in diameter, with crust as thin as a saltine. Aside from the wild crunch of its crust, Colony pizza is known for locally made sweet sausage and for the optional topping called "hot oil": peppery olive oil that imbues the pie with luscious zest unlike any other. Each slice is crisp and yet so sumptuously oily that your fingers are guaranteed to glisten, even if you forgo the wonderful hot oil. Postprandial wreckage on the table is a giddy bedlam of severely battered trays piled with countless balled-up and knotted paper napkins.

Note: Two new locations have recently opened, at 1520 Post Road in Fairfield (203-259-1989) and at 36–38 Broad Street in Milford.

## Denmo's

346 S. Main St.
Southbury, CT

203-264-4626
LD | $$

Denmo's snuck up on us. We've been going to this picnic-table-only drive-in for years, always leaving happy and well fed. The foot-long, natural-casing hot dogs are presented in Yankee-style split-top buns, and they are beauties: slightly gnarled from getting fried, crisp-skinned, and full of garlic. The dogs are good, but it's the relish that we love. Peppery, pickly, a little bit sweet, and very hot, this relish, along with a good line of zesty mustard, will clear your sinuses and make you sing hallelujah.

Hot dogs actually are a sideshow for what Denmo's is most proud of: fried seafood. Crunchy clams with just-right bellies, sweet shrimp, and silky scallops all are fine shoreline treats (although Denmo's is a good thirty miles inland). They even have hot lobster rolls at (relatively) bargain prices, and when they are good, they are wonderful: fresh and perfectly buttered hunks of claw and tail. On occasion, however, the meat isn't as bright and sweet as one wants, and can taste like it was picked a while ago.

Among non-fried foods, the sleeper on the menu is soup. Every day there are a couple of varieties. The chowder is swell, as one might expect, but so are chicken soup and lentil soup and beef barley soup.

It is a fun place, with a big public bulletin board that is a fascinating portrait of a community's skills, needs, wants, and preferences. The only reason we can think of for not having included it in earlier *Roadfood* editions is that, as so many locals do with restaurants they frequent, we took Denmo's for granted.

## Doogie's

2525 Berlin Tpk.          860-666-6200
Newington, CT             www.doogieshotdogs.com
                          LD | $

Doogie's boasts of being "Home of the 2-foot hot dog." It is an astounding piece of food, but don't let the circus size divert attention from the fact that it is delicious. Firm-fleshed and with a chewy skin that gets charred on the grill, it has a vigorously spicy flavor that holds up under any and all toppings, especially Doogie's superb homemade hot relish. For those of meek appetite, the same good frank is available in mere sixteen-inch and foot-long configurations too.

Doogie's hamburgers, cooked on the same charcoal grill where the hot dogs are made, have a delicious smoky flavor. The top-of-the-line hamburger is listed on the menu as the MOAB (Mother of All Burgers), and while not as awesome as the elongated hot dog, it is an impressive package: a big patty buried under lettuce, tomato, chipotle mayonnaise, thousand island dressing, pickle chips, sliced red onions, provolone and pepper jack cheeses, bacon, caramelized onions, and roasted peppers—all on a garlic toasted roll.

## Dottie's Diner

740 S. Main St.          203-263-2516
Woodbury, CT             BLD | $$

Dottie's is one of the few diners we know where you can still get an old-fashioned Connecticut chicken pie: savory crust loaded with nothing but warm, moist chicken meat served under a mantle of gravy. Dottie's also makes a more familiar chicken potpie that includes gravy, peas, and carrots. On the side, mashed potatoes are the genuine article.

As for donuts, which we have considered America's best since Dottie's was known as Phillips Diner and run by the Phillips family, they are, if possible, better than ever. Cinnamon donuts are creamy inside with a wickedly crunchy exterior (unless the humidity is really high that day); chocolate donuts come loaded with vast amounts of the glossy dark glaze that so perfectly complements the cake within.

Since her tenure began some four years ago, Dottie has spiffed things up with retro aqua upholstery in the booths and a new counter, and she's even gotten a liquor license and has begun serving dinners. The friendly community feeling so essential to the soul of a diner is thriving.

## Dr. Mike's

158 Greenwood Ave.      203-792-4388
Bethel, CT      (weekends only in winter) | $

Forget psychotherapy and medication! The best antidepressant we know is a visit to the good Dr. Mike of Bethel. The cones and cardboard cups dished out by this little shop are a miracle cure. As hopeless ice cream addicts, we must tell you that there is nothing quite like Dr. Mike's, and there are occasions when its ultra-richness is actually overwhelming. The longtime standard bearer, "rich chocolate," is only sweet enough to coax forth maximum cocoa flavor, its chalky chocolate and smooth butterfat body hypnotically fused. "Chocolate lace and cream" is another Dr. Mike's invention, made with wisps of refined chocolate-covered hard candy. The shards of candy are suspended in a pure white emulsion of sweetened cream: another dreamy experience, but in this case our warning is to get it in a cup. The crunch of the candy conflicts with the crunch of a cone.

We've named our two favorite flavors. Don't hesitate, though, if you find your personal favorite among the approximately eight varieties available any particular day. Each one is made the old-fashioned way, using cream from dairy buckets, in five-gallon batches, and we have fond memories of Dr. Mike's coffee, coconut, cinnamon, Heath Bar crunch, even prune, dazzling vanilla, and some real tongue-stunners made with fresh fruits in the summer.

Nota bene: Fudge sauce for sundaes is magnificent. Whipped cream is thick and fresh.

## *Frank Pepe Pizzeria Napoletana

157 Wooster St.                     203-865-5762

New Haven, CT                       www.pepespizzeria.com

LD | $$

Dating back to 1925, Frank Pepe Pizzeria Napoletana is a brash neighbor-hood joint on New Haven's pizza-parlor row that makes what we have long considered to be the best pizza on Earth. Any toppings are fine (pepperoni especially so), and the crust is sensational—brittle at its edges, ruggedly chewy where it puffs up, scattered on its crisp underside with burned grains of semolina from the oven's brick floor. The emblematic pizza is white clam, which Frank Pepe created midcentury after discussing the idea with a ven-dor selling littlenecks in a Wooster Street alley near the pizza parlor. It is an uncomplicated pie strewn with freshly opened littleneck clams and their nectar, a scattering of grated sharp Romano, a salvo of coarsely minced garlic, and a drizzle of oil.

In 2006, Pepe's opened a second store in Fairfield, Connecticut, and has since opened others in Manchester and Mohegan Sun, as well as in Danbury and in Yonkers, New York, with more on the way. Despite our skepticism of such proliferation, the pizzas we've had at the new places have been every bit as good as the original. Usually the wait for a table—which can be daunting in New Haven—is somewhat shorter.

## Harry's Drive-In

104 Broadway                        860-537-2410

Colchester, CT                      www.harrysplace.biz

LD (summer only) | $

A completely alfresco eat place with wood-slat picnic tables arrayed under groves of flowering trees, Harry's has been a favorite stop for people on their way to and from the beach for more than eighty years. One of the best things about coming here is waiting for a meal to be assembled. There is no curb service. Exit your vehicle and stand in line; place an order and pay, then slide sideways to the pickup window. The view is breathtaking: two dozen hamburgers lined up on a glistening hot grill, sizzling and sputtering and oozing juice. They are formed from spheres of meat that get slapped onto the grill and lightly squished so they flatten a bit; but the gnarled patties remain enormously juicy inside their rugged crust. With a mantle of melted cheese and a few strips of bacon, garnished with slices of summer tomato, lettuce, pickle, and mustard, sandwiched inside a fine bakery bun and held together with a long toothpick, this might be the best drive-in hamburger anywhere.

## K. LaMay's

690 E. Main St.  
Meriden, CT

203-237-8326  
www.klamayssteamedcheeseburgers.com  
LD | $

As national interest in regional American food has blossomed in the last several years, the steamed cheeseburger has been discovered. While it is no longer an obsession known only to denizens of central Connecticut, it remains an acquired taste, the acquisition usually quite difficult for those who did not grow up eating it. Unlike renowned hamburgers elsewhere, this patty has no crunch whatsoever to its surface. At its worst, it resembles a wet sponge. But at its best, it is all juiciness and flavor.

It most definitely is at its best at K. LaMay's. Kevin LaMay began work in the burger field at Ted's, which today is the grand old institution of steamers. When he opened his own place, he decided to improve upon the formula. His burgers are bigger—one-third pound, rather than one-quarter pound; they are generously draped with steamed-soft cheese, and they are insanely juicy. One burger with the works, which would be tomato, lettuce, mustard, ketchup, and/or a dollop of the Sweet Baby Ray BBQ sauce on each table, is a big, sloppy, delicious mess. On the side there are French fries and onion rings, interesting potato chips, and locally bottled Foxon Park sodas.

## Kitchen Little

36 Quarry Rd.  
Mystic, CT

860-536-2122  
www.kitchenlittle.org  
BLD | $

Kitchen Little got big. In the spring of 2012 it moved from its minuscule location on the road to Mystic Seaport and reopened in a spacious setting that overlooks docked boats at the Mystic River Marina. You now can order beer and wine to accompany your cheeseburger, BLT, or lobster roll (available hot and cold).

Breakfast still stars, and "AM Eggstasy" remains the house motto. Omelets are impeccable, as are a variety of benedicts (California = asparagus and crab; Portuguese = *chourico* sausage and a Portuguese muffin). We love the sizzled-crisp corned beef hash, especially when customized with jalapeño cheese, onions, and sour cream. Kitchen Little's chowder is exemplary

Southern New England–style: steel-gray and briny, with induplicable fresh clam flavor.

We've yet to try dinner, served in summer Thursday through Sunday.

## Lakeside Diner

| | |
|---|---|
| 1050 Long Ridge Rd. | 203-322-2252 |
| Stamford, CT | BL | $ |

A humble eat shop literally at the foot of the southbound Exit 34 ramp off the Merritt Parkway, the Lakeside Diner is set up just like countless other diners, with a counter and stools and a scattering of tables. But there is a big difference: One whole wall is a picture window that overlooks Holts Ice Pond, where waterfowl skim past while customers fork into dandy short-order meals.

Pancakes are very good—thin and buttery, and available loaded with blueberries. Donuts are Lakeside's main claim to fame. There is no variety; these are simple cake donuts stuck with massive amounts of coarse sugar, great for dunking or eating by the bagful once you are back on the highway.

The menu is huge: all kinds of omelets and pastries, and a full repertoire of lunches that range from wraps and sandwiches to such blue-plate specials as meat loaf with mashed potatoes and gravy—all made from scratch.

## Laurel Diner

| | |
|---|---|
| 544 S. Main St. | 203-264-8218 |
| Southbury, CT | BL | $ |

Hash house connoisseurs should ignore Laurel Diner's few tables and get a stool at the counter facing the pint-sized grill. Here you have a spellbinding vision of time-space management as two short-order chefs fry, scramble, and flip eggs, fold omelets, butter toast, pour pancakes, and squish down patties of the diner's legendary corned beef hash.

The hash is a coarse-cut mélange of spicy beef shreds and nuggets of potato cooked on the griddle until a web of crust begins to envelop the tender insides. If you ask, the grill man will cook the hash until it is brittle-crisp nearly all the way through, which is a great idea if textural excitement supersedes succulence in your hierarchy of culinary pleasure; but we personally enjoy it the regular way: forkfuls of corned beef that are brick-red and moist, their pickly zest balanced perfectly by the soft pieces of potato.

You have two choices of potato: chunky home fries, which are excellent, and hash browns, which are better. While the chefs regularly scrape debris into the grill's front gutter, their touch is light enough that the flavors of bacon, ham, sausage, and hash linger, ready to be sucked into heaps of shredded potatoes piled on the hot surface. A broad cake of three or four servings is flattened and remains untouched long enough for the underside to turn gold, then the still-soft top is crowned with a scoop of butter. As the butter melts, the potatoes are flipped and worried so that by the time they are plated, they have become mostly crunchy, but with enough tender white tips to sop up at least two sunny-side yolks.

## Lenny & Joe's Fish Tale Restaurant

| | |
|---|---|
| 1301 Boston Post Rd. (Rt. 1) | 203-245-7289 |
| Madison, CT | www.ljfishtale.com |
| | LD | $$ |

Lenny & Joe's opened as a roadside fried-clam stand in 1979. It has since become two large restaurants with menus that range from hot dogs to whole lobster dinners (summertime) to superior fried seafood. Whole-belly fried clams are big and succulent with golden crusts. We love the fried shrimp and scallops, even simple fried fish. All fried items are available in an ample regular size configuration as well as a "super" plate with double the amount of fish. This is one restaurant where the undecided customer who craves the crunch of fresh-fried seafood will be happy ordering a variety platter with some of everything. It is a gargantuan meal, including crinkle-cut French fries and a little cup of sweet coleslaw. The only other necessary item would be an order of fried onions; Lenny and Joe's are wicked good!

There are two other locations, with table service: at 86 Boston Post Road (Route 1), Westbrook, CT (860-669-0767) and 501 Long Wharf Drive, New Haven, CT (203-691-6619).

## Lenny's

| | |
|---|---|
| 205 S. Montowese St. | 203-488-1500 |
| Branford, CT | www.lennysnow.com |
| | LD | $$ |

A longtime fixture of the Indian Neck section of Branford's coast, this excellent restaurant is a neighborhood place with a menu that ranges from hamburgers and hot dogs to full shore dinners. The latter includes chowder (either creamy New England–style or clear-broth shoreline-style), cherrystone clams on the shell, a lobster, a heap of steamers, sweet corn, and a thick slice of watermelon for dessert.

Good as both kinds of chowder are, one should never begin a meal at Lenny's without "zuppa d'clams": steamed-open cherrystones in a bowl of spicy, lemon-laced broth, a half loaf of bread on the side for dunking. Delicious! Many of Lenny's best meals are fried: whole-belly clams, oysters, scallops, fish and chips, and huge butterflied shrimp. Crunch-crusted and clean-flavored, these are consummate fried seafoods, and proof that a crisp, clean crust can be the very best halo for seafood's natural sweetness.

Lenny's is a year-round destination. In the fall, every Sunday is turkey dinner day, featuring excellent mashed potatoes and gravy and stuffing. In the summer, diners top off meals with true Yankee strawberry shortcake, made from a sideways-split, unsweet biscuit layered with sliced berries in a thin sugar syrup, crowned with whipped cream.

## Letizia's

666 Main Ave.      203-847-6022
Norwalk, CT      www.letiziaspizza.com
     LD | $

While the strip-mall setting isn't much, Letizia's name is part of northeast pizza history, one of the first in the region to serve it—as a weekend-only item—when Joe Letizia opened his Italian restaurant down on Norwalk's Wall Street in 1937. Well after his death in 1962, Uncle Joe's was still known as a source of fine red-sauce meals at rock-bottom prices. The family sold the old place in 1985 (it is now in others' hands), but today's Letizia's, opened by grandson Dan in 1992, still offers baked ziti and manicotti, spaghetti with marinara, and hot-parm grinders on made-here rolls. But it's pizza that matters.

The crust is terrific. Baked on a screen, then further toughened on the oven's brick floor, it is medium-thin Neapolitan-style, chewy more than brittle, with a full, earthy taste. Traditional mozzarella and sauce—the same food-service brands the family has used since the beginning—meld into a creamy Italian-American slurry with veins of tomato tang. Add discs of pepperoni, weeping oil into the mix, and you've got a mighty bite that is outrageously juicy. It is best consumed the New York City way, by pulling one triangular slice from the circle and folding it in half along the radius—the crust is pliable enough to bend, not break—creating a trough that holds everything like an open-top calzone.

## Lobster Landing

152 Commerce St.                    860-669-2005
Clinton, CT                         L | $$

Although lobster is considered the king of North Atlantic seafood and tends to be priced accordingly, it usually tastes best when eaten in the least formal surroundings: at a picnic on the beach or overlooking a harbor, or in a place for which the term "restaurant" seems too grandiose: a shack. In this context, we present for your lobster appreciation an eatery called Lobster Landing.

Technically speaking, the dining area isn't even a shack. There is a tumbledown, hundred-year-old, wood-frame shanty by the water where you buy lobsters, oysters, and steamer clams to take home and cook. But to eat here, you sit at a plastic table in a sort of picnic area on a broken-clamshell deck that offers a makeshift tent for inclement weather. As for the choice of meals, there are hot dogs, sausage-pepper-onion subs, and lobster rolls.

The lobster roll is all that matters. It is very large—a heap of meat piled into a hollowed-out submarine loaf. The meat is bathed in butter but not swimming in it—all the better to savor the lobster itself. That's all there is to it: resilient, juicy, ocean-sweet lobster, drawn butter with a soupçon of lemon, and a toasted roll. What could be better?

## Louis' Lunch

261 Crown St.                       203-562-5507
New Haven, CT                       www.louislunch.com
                                    L | $

You don't have to be a hamburger historian to appreciate Louis' Lunch, which claims to have invented the hamburger. The burgers are unique. They are hand-formed and cooked in ancient metal broilers that let much of the grease drip away, yet they remain juicy enough to sop the toast that encloses them. Yes, toast. There are no buns at Louis' Lunch for the obvious reason that when Louis Lassen invented the hamburger about six score years ago, there were no hamburger buns. Nor is ketchup available. You can get a slice of tomato on your burger, but ketchup always has been taboo. Other options for the burger are onions, grilled into the burger as it cooks, and Cheez Whiz.

Louis' Lunch exudes history. The small brick building is outfitted with snug school-desk seats and an ancient wooden counter with years' worth of initials carved into it. Alas, its fame has made it maddeningly popular, so waiting for a place to sit has become part of the experience.

## The Lunchbox

620 E. Main St.  
Meriden, CT

203-238-0313  
www.theoriginallunchboxct.com  
BL | $

A few years ago, Lunchbox proprietor Anita Dufresne won the "Most Creative" award in a Meriden newspaper's Battle of the Burgers competition for her Military Burger topped with guacamole, blue cheese, Cheddar, bacon, onion, lettuce, tomato, and mushroom. It's monumental, but even her regular steamed cheeseburger, maybe adorned with a couple of strips of bacon, packs enough convincing savor to put it in the topmost echelon of central Connecticut steamers.

While burgers are the regional specialty that makes the Lunchbox a siren song to culinary explorers, the menu beyond them is pretty great. We particularly remember a bowl of chicken soup that was as homey as Grandma's, as well as a plate of well-made Texas-style *migas*. During a recent Roadfood.com eating tour of Connecticut, several world-class eaters were stopped in their tracks by the unbelievably cheesy steamed cheeseburger omelet.

It should also be mentioned that Anita and her crew infuse the Lunchbox experience with the joie de vivre of a dream diner. They love to chat about food and everything else in the world. Even an antisocial introvert will walk out of this place not just well fed but with spring in his step.

## Mamie's

162 Baker Rd.  
Roxbury, CT

860-210-0618  
www.mamiesrestaurant.com  
B (weekends only); LD (closed Tues) |  
$$

Mamie's is glorious on a sunny day. Not that there's anything wrong with the handful of tables inside the bakeshop café, where customers come to chat, read the paper, drink coffee, and eat a handsome meal. The indoor seating is snug, sociable, and relaxed. But the more wonderful seats are outside, on a patio and at picnic tables on a sweeping lawn, where diners look out upon achingly scenic Litchfield County.

As one wants in so bucolic a setting, it is a casual place—the menu lists sandwiches, salads, and a roster of breakfast dishes ranging from familiar (bacon and eggs) to swank (crème brûlée French toast). Silverware comes wrapped in thick linen napkins, and the service, while friendly and familiar, is extraordinarily polite. If you'd like wine with dinner, BYOB.

It's weekend breakfast (aka brunch) we like best. Perfectly poached eggs come either in a cup or perched atop Mamie's autumn-root-vegetable hash or summer-vegetable hash. Toast is made from rough-textured seven-grain bread. Other breakfast highlights include banana pancakes and a chorizo omelet and—occasionally available—Mamie's freshly made beignets. Even the granola is a cut above—served warm and accompanied by fresh fruits.

Among sandwiches, we are suckers for the BLT, made with plenty of thick, smoky bacon, good tomatoes, and fresh lettuce, all best on that seven-grain toast. Locally raised Greyledge Farm beef is used for the hamburgers, thick enough to pack obscene amounts of juiciness that destroys the elegant buns.

Mamie's began as a bakery, meaning the pastries command attention. Cases display kingly coconut layer cake, banana cake, and big, chewy brownies. From the cooler come Key lime and peanut butter pies.

## Modern Apizza

874 State St.          203-776-5306
New Haven, CT          www.modernapizza.com
                       LD | $$

While it is less famous than Pepe's and Sally's, Modern Apizza, a 1930s-era pizzeria on State Street in New Haven, is one of the Earth's best pizza parlors. Some savvy pizzaphiles consider it *the* best. "Our brick oven reaches temperature in excess of 700 degrees," Modern's menu warns. "Some pizzas may blacken around the edges, and even lose their perfect shape due to contact with the brick floor of the oven." OK with us! While a few patches around the edge may be charred, the whole pizza has a swoonfully appetizing smoky taste, and you see why when you devour slices off the paper on which the pizza rests atop its round pan. The paper appears strewn with charred little bits of semolina from the oven floor, most of which cling to the underside of the crust, creating a slightly burnt hot-bread flavor that no wussy metal-floored pizza oven could produce.

Modern's specialty toppings include broccoli, sliced tomato, artichoke, and clams casino. It is known for the Italian Bomb, which is a joy to eat despite the fact that it totally overwhelms its crust: sausage, pepperoni, bacon, peppers, onions, mushrooms, and garlic. There is also a Vegetarian Bomb, topped with spinach, broccoli, olives, peppers, mushrooms, onion, and garlic. As for the New Haven favorite, white clam pizza (hold the mozzarella, please), Modern uses canned clams, not fresh, meaning there is less soulful marine juice to infuse the pizza; nevertheless, it is delicious—ocean-sweet and powerfully garlicky, and built on a crust that puffs up dry and chewy around the edges but stays wafer-thin all across the middle.

## Pizzeria Lauretano

291 Greenwood Ave.        203-792-1500
Bethel, CT                www.pizzerialauretano.com
                          LD | $$

There are many excellent things on the menu of this gracious pizza parlor in the town that gave birth to P. T. Barnum: a just-right walnut-cranberry-gorgonzola salad dressed with lemony dressing, panini sandwiches at lunch, and pine-nut-dotted meatballs; but as the name suggests, pizzas are its glory. And glorious pizzas these are, in their own way every bit as soulful as those from Connecticut's funkier famous places. Imported flour and a wood-fired oven that proprietor Michael Lauretano brought from Naples create a crust with exquisite chewy-brittle balance. It puffs up along the edge so there may be a few spots that taste (quite deliciously) of carbon; the whole thing is insinuated with fire because just before the pizza is ready to be pulled off the oven's floor, the pizzaiolo slides his peel underneath and holds it at the very top of the oven directly over the smoldering wood pile for a few moments, making sure the top is fully cooked and at the same time giving it a smoky fragrance. We love the plain garlic pizza—really just a gilded flatbread; manna for crust lovers—as well as the mighty garlic and broccoli rabe white pizza; there are tradition-minded margheritas and puttanescas as well as occasional specials that include a ramp pizza in the spring and a fall harvest locavore's delight of multiple vegetables known as the garden pizza.

If you're lucky, when you dine here the kitchen will be passing out little lagniappes to each table to accompany salad or to munch while you wait for the pie to cook: thin strips of oven-hot crust, oh-so-ready to be dipped in seasoned olive oil.

## Rawley's Drive-In

1886 Post Rd.　　　　　　　　203-259-9023

Fairfield, CT　　　　　　　　LD | $

Rawley's opened in 1947 and defined a way of cooking hot dogs that has become gospel for many of the important frank emporia in southwestern Connecticut. Into the deep fryer goes a substantial natural-casing dog. When plump and darkened, it is pulled from the hot vegetable oil and rolled around on the griddle with a spatula—a finishing touch that strains off excess oil and gives the exterior a delectable crackle. The dog is then bedded in a high-quality roll that has been spread open, brushed with butter, and toasted on the griddle until its interior surfaces are crisp, in contrast to the outside, which remains as soft and pliant as an oven mitt. The kitchen does the dressing, the most popular configuration being mustard and relish topped with sauerkraut and garnished with a fistful of chewy bacon shreds. To our taste, it is a perfect combination, although "heavy bacon"—twice as much—is a popular option.

The restaurant is pint-sized: four booths, plus a six-stool counter on what used to be a front porch, where an open picture window provides a scenic view into the lively short-order kitchen. As plebeian as can be, it is known for attracting celebrities who live or summer in the area. We had our first Rawley's hot dog on the recommendation of Martha Stewart.

## Ridgefield Ice Cream Shop

680 Danbury Rd.　　　　　　　203-438-3094

Ridgefield, CT　　　　　　　　$

A former Carvel stand, the Ridgefield Ice Cream Shop makes soft-serve ice cream by using machines from Carvel's early days, when the formula was not pumped full of air. The resulting lick is not sinfully rich or weird-flavored or in any way surprising. But in our book, it is perfect: smooth, pure, and dense, and so perfectly balanced that it tastes right no matter what the weather or time of day. While it is available with all sorts of jimmies, sprinkles, coatings, and nuts, we like ours just the way it comes from the gleaming stainless-steel machine: a swirly mound piled up on an elegant wafer cone. For those who live nearby, there are extraordinary ice cream cakes made from the same frozen manna and layered with icing and crumbled cookies.

Although it has a sunny, summertime feel, Ridgefield Ice Cream is open year-round, rain or shine. In good weather, customers have their cones while leaning on their cars in the lot, or at one of the picnic tables out front.

## Roseland Apizza

350 Hawthorne Ave.      203-735-0494
Derby, CT      D Tues-Sun | $$$

Roseland Apizza (pronounce that second word the Neapolitan way, "AH-beets") started as a bakery in 1934. Today, it is a popular neighborhood restaurant that is a shining example of Connecticut's great Italian-American cuisine: ravioli, lasagna, and nightly specials featuring shellfish and pasta, as well as brick-oven pies of the highest order. The crust is New Haven–style: thin but not quite brittle, with enough brawn to support all but the weightiest combinations of ingredients and to allay the pizza-eater's primal fears: slice collapse and topping slippage.

The luxe of some pies is surreal. High rollers can get a lavish shrimp-casino pie topped with bacon, mozzarella, fresh garlic, and too many jumbo shrimp to count. We recently enjoyed one heaped with a mountain of cool arugula salad—a yin-yang adventure of hot and cool, bread and veg, sweet cheese and bitter greens. We love the Connecticut classic white-clam pizza made without tomato sauce or mozzarella, just a crowd of clams strewn across a crust glazed with olive oil and scattered with bits of basil, parsley, and oregano, thin-sliced garlic, a twist of cracked black pepper, and a scattering of grated Parmigiano-Reggiano.

Note: Prices at Roseland are high, and some items, such as a dreamy shrimp oreganate pizza we recently had, seem outrageous. That one was more than $40. However, take into account the fact that everything served here is huge; virtually nobody leaves without boxes and bags of leftovers. That pizza satisfied two healthy appetites at dinner and provided lunch for two the next day.

## Sally's Apizza

237 Wooster St.      203-624-5271
New Haven, CT      www.sallysapizza.com
     D | $$

Sally's has soul. The place glows with old-neighborhood feel: wood-paneled walls, booths with well-worn Formica-topped tables, ubiquitous images of Frank Sinatra (a fan of Sal's cooking) all over the walls. And the pizza packs a wallop. It is generously topped, well oiled, and built upon a thin crust that is smudged and gritty underneath. Of special note are summertime's fresh tomato pie and broccoli rabe pie, heaped with bitter greens when they are available at the produce market. Although it is not formally listed on the menu, Sally's multi-meat "Italian bomb" (sausage, pepperoni, bacon, plus lots of onions) is also significant.

Old friends of Sally's are treated like royalty. Newcomers and unknowns might feel like they have to wait forever, first for a table, then for their pizza, and they will likely endure a staff who are at best nonchalant; but no one comes to Wooster Street for polished service or swank ambience. It's great, thin-crust pizza that counts, and on that score, Sally's delivers the goods.

## Shady Glen

840 E. Middle Tpk.          860-649-4245
Manchester, CT               BLD | $

Shady Glen makes baroque cheeseburgers. On a high-temperature electric grill, each circular patty of beef is cooked on one side, flipped, then blanketed with several square slices of cheese. The cheese is arranged so that only one-quarter to one-third of each slice rests atop the hamburger. The remainder extends beyond the circumference of the meat and melts down onto the surface of the grill. At the exact moment the grilling cheese begins to transform from molten to crisp, the cook uses a spatula to disengage it from the grill and curl it above the meat like some wondrous burgerflower— still slightly pliable, but rising up in some kind of symmetry. The petals of cheese, which may be topped with condiments and are crowned by a bun, are crunchy at their tips but chewy where they blend into the soft parts that adhere to the hamburger. The same cooking technique is used on hot dogs, known as cheesefurters.

The restaurant originally was opened in 1948 by John and Bernice Reig in order to put something on the menu of their dairy bar other than homemade ice cream. The ice cream is fantastic, including such seasonal flavors as minced pie, cranberry, and pumpkin in the fall and the outstanding February specialty, Bing cherry and chocolate chip. Our personal flavor faves include Grape-Nuts and Almond Joy.

## Stanziato's

35 Lake Ave.

Danbury, CT

203-885-1057

www.stanziatos.com

LD | $$

In an ordinary-looking storefront on a drab commercial stretch of road, Matt Stanczak has set up an extraordinary wood-fired oven and goes to the trouble to make individual pizzas with real character. They are traditional Neapolitans, individually sized and baked ultrafast. It is hypnotic to stand at the counter and watch a pizza go from raw to done in less than two minutes. The crust puffs up around the edge and turns golden brown while the cheese melts in the middle and begins to spread. Matt removes the finished pie from the oven with his long-handled peel, spritzes on a bit of olive oil, and decorates it with a few fresh leaves of basil. Beautiful!

The toppings roster includes familiar ingredients such as sausage, pepperoni, and mushrooms—all excellent—but this is one place where it pays to venture into the unusual options. Roasted cauliflower pie, for instance, is a devastatingly rich invention gilded with Burrata cheese and truffle oil; a soppressata pie boasts spicy salami from Arthur Avenue and very hot chile peppers; El Diablo features lime-marinated shrimp.

Pizzas star, but salads are by no means second-class menu items. We are smitten with the "winter salad": chopped romaine, sliced apples, grapes, peppery-sweet roasted pecans, and gorgonzola cheese dressed with maple balsamic vinaigrette. Other worthy dishes (after you have eaten your way through the pizza menu) include chicken wings baked in the wood-fired oven and a marvelous "mac 'n' cheese" that actually is a mix of couscous and roasted cauliflower.

Although the oven and flour for dough are imported, Matt is a locavore chef, obtaining vegetables from surrounding farms, coffee from a nearby roaster, and ice cream from a neighborhood creamery. There always are interesting beers listed on the blackboard, and teetotalers will appreciate Sprecher's root beer served in a frosted mug.

## *Super Duper Weenie

306 Black Rock Tpk.

Fairfield, CT

203-334-DOGS

www.superduperweenie.com

LD | $

We've been on the Super Duper Weenie bandwagon since it was a food truck. It is now a restaurant, albeit an extremely casual one, and it has been featured on every TV show and in every publication that pays attention to hot dogs. In fact, several years ago when *Reader's Digest* asked us to name our single favorite drive-in eatery anywhere in America, this is the place to which we gave the nod. If you love hot dogs, it's a Holy Grail. (And if you don't love hot dogs, its hamburgers are terrific; from-scratch soups and sandwiches are first-rate too.)

The dogs are firm-fleshed franks made especially for SDW, which splits and grills them until their outsides turn a little crusty. They are sandwiched in fresh rolls and adorned with made-here condiments that include sweet onion sauce and hot relish. Chef Gary Zemola makes choosing easy with suggested basic configurations that include the New Englander (with sauerkraut, bacon, mustard, sweet relish, and raw onion), the New Yorker (sauerkraut, onion sauce, mustard, and hot relish), and the Chicagoan (lettuce, tomato, mustard, celery salt, relish, and a pickle spear). Whatever you get, you must get French fries: beautiful golden twigs served fresh from the fry basket and made extra-delicious by a perfect sprinkle of salt *and* pepper.

## Sycamore Drive-In

282 Greenwood Ave.
Bethel, CT

203-748-2716
www.sycamoredrivein.com
BLD | $

Hamburgers at the Sycamore Drive-In are golf-ball-sized spheres of meat that get slapped onto the grill, then spatula-flattened so intensely that edges are nearly paper thin and develop a lacy crunch. You can have one plain, doubled, sizzled with onions, topped with bacon and/or tomatoes, and if you still have questions, the menu offers "The Final Answer to the Hamburger." That's a Dagwood burger: two patties with cheese and every garnish known to mankind.

The Sycamore is rightly famous for root beer, made on premises and served in frosty glass mugs. It varies from sweet to dry, depending on where in the barrel the serving is drawn, but whatever its nature on any day, it always makes an ideal basis for a root-beer float.

The Sycamore is a genuine drive-in with carhop service (blink your lights) and window trays for in-car dining. Indoors, there are booths and a long counter. In the summer, on Saturday evenings, "Cruise Nights" attract vintage car collectors in their finest restored and custom vehicles. It's a true blast from the past!

## Ted's

1046 Broad St.  
Meriden, CT  

203-237-6660  
www.tedsrestaurant.com  
L | $

Central Connecticut is home to about a half-dozen restaurants that all make steamed cheeseburgers, a regional specialty so geographically focused that it does not exist in eastern or western Connecticut. A steamer, as served at Ted's (since 1959), is cooked not on a grill or grate, but in a steam cabinet, the meat held inside a square tin as it browns. Adjacent to the beef in the cabinet are tins into which are placed blocks of Vermont Cheddar. The cheese turns molten and is ladled atop the burger in a hard roll (preferably with lettuce, tomato, pickle, and mustard).

If you love crusty hamburgers that crunch before your teeth sink into the pillowy meat, beware: This one is soft, inside and out, and the cheese atop it is the consistency of custard. For many otherwise broad-minded burger fans, it's just too weird. But those who become addicted to steamed cheeseburgers know nothing else that delivers its squishy satisfaction. Curiously, the dish was created in the 1920s when eating steamed food was a health fad.

## *Zuppardi's Apizza

179 Union Ave.  
West Haven, CT  

203-934-1949  
www.zuppardisapizza.com  
LD | $$

Zuppardi's is a family-run neighborhood restaurant that has earned generations of loyal clientele since 1934. You might have to wait for a table on weekend nights, but given its location far from Wooster Street's famous pizzerias, it never gets insanely crowded. The pizza it serves is every bit as good as New Haven's finest. Or is it the best anywhere?

Crust: Neapolitan-style. Thin and crisp with a puffy circumference that tilts more toward crunch than chew, it lacks a raunchy underside (the oven floors are regularly vacuumed), but it resonates with yeasty savor. Available toppings include sausage that is made on premises in two-hundred-pound batches and strewn across the pizza in rugged clumps, fresh tomato, broccoli rabe, escarole and beans, hot peppers, and roasted peppers. Clam pizza is listed twice on the menu, as whole baby clams and fresh clams, the latter twice as expensive as the former. That is because the fresh ones really are fresh, opened when you order your pizza (you will wait) and spread about the pie in superabundance. One of the Zuppardi family told us that for years vendors have tried to get them to switch over to flash-frozen, cryonautic, or otherwise pickled clams, guaranteeing the embalmed ones are indistinguishable from fresh. "Frankly, I think even the canned ones are better," she scoffed.

But freshly shucked ones are best, and the star ingredient in a magnificent pizza. They are tender littlenecks, glistening with briny-sweet oceanic liquor, complemented by a surfeit of chopped garlic and herbs. "Some customers ask for mutz [mozzarella cheese]," the pizzaiolo shared with a disapproving frown, "but that just weighs it down." Mutzless, Zuppardi's fresh white-clam pie, however perspicuous, is overwhelmingly satisfying.

## Beal's Lobster Pier

182 Clark Point Rd.  207-244-3202
Southwest Harbor, ME  www.bealslobster.com
LD | $$

Picnic tables overlook the harbor; from them, you can see the mountains of Acadia National Park in the distance and listen to the water rippling against the hulls of berthed fishing boats. At sunset, Beal's is magic.

Inside, select a lobster from the tank. While waiting for it to boil, eat your way through a bucket of steamer clams or dip into a cup of chowder. Lobsters come pre-cracked for easy meat extraction, but it's still some work. If a handsome whole one is too challenging a proposition, have a lobster roll—tightly packed, with plenty of fresh, cool meat atop a cushion of shredded lettuce. Burgers and a few other non-lobster meals also are available.

## Becky's

390 Commercial St.  207-773-7070
Portland, ME  www.beckysdiner.com
BLD | $

Becky's has dramatically expanded since we first wrote about the little waterside diner many years ago, but it remains friendly, inexpensive, and delicious. Becky loves her varied clientele. "Side by side at my counter sit fishermen and captains of industry, college professors and paranoid schizophrenics," she boasts. They talk to each other and they talk to those who work here. We are all family."

The breakfast menu includes homemade muffins, French toast made from locally baked Italian bread, and "loaded" hash-brown potatoes, which are mixed with peppers and onions and blanketed with melted cheese. There is a full array of usual breakfast sandwiches, and one sandwich that isn't usual at all: peanut butter and bacon. "I guess it's a breakfast sandwich," Becky chuckles. We love the "Titanic omelet," loaded with all three breakfast meats, cheese, onions, and peppers, and accompanied, preferably, with Portland's favorite morning breadstuff, Italian toast. If you are in the mood for fruit, we highly recommend Becky's fruit salad, for which everything is fresh, and is fresh-cut to order.

Lunch and dinner are equally impressive. Becky's haddock chowder is a local legend. Dinners such as pot roast with boiled potatoes and roast turkey with sausage stuffing define comfort food. Desserts include Grape-Nuts pudding, Becky's blueberry cake with cream-cheese frosting, and a marvelous Whoopie Pie cake that is like the small snack, but layered and large.

## Bet's Famous Fish Fry

Route 27          No phone
Boothbay, ME      L Tues–Sat; D Tues–Fri (seasonal) | $

A tip of the hat to Holly Moore of hollyeats.com for directing us to this happy food truck just off Boothbay's town square. As its name says, fried fish is the dish to have—the only dish on the menu—either paired with chips (French fries) or in a gigantic sandwich or very large half sandwich. The fish is haddock, some of which is caught by Bet herself, the rest of which is secured from nearby boats. It is creamy-fresh, cased in fragile red-gold crust, and attains extra savor when dolloped with dill sauce. Get your beverage from the soda machine or bring your own.

Bet's a character, always gabbing with customers, her truck painted with a sign advertising FREE BEER TOMORROW.

## Bob's Clam Hut

315 US Route 1                    207-439-4233
Kittery, ME                       www.bobsclamhut.com
                                  LD | $$

Bob's motto is "Eat Clams." Fried clams, clam cakes, clam chowder, and clam burgers are all wonderful, but they are just the headliners on a long menu of excellent Downeast seafood.

Seafood rolls take center stage, and not just those piled with fried whole-belly clams or clam strips. You can have them loaded with scallops, shrimp, and oysters (all fried) or with crab, shrimp salad, or lobster. The high-ticket lobster roll is a beaut, served in a nice warm bun that is buttered and grilled until toasty golden brown on both sides; the lobster meat inside is faintly chilled, but not so much that any of the taste has been iced. On the side of most seafood dishes comes Bob's excellent tartar sauce, a perfect balance of richness and zest.

There is no table service. Either outdoors or at the indoor counter, read the posted menu, then place your order and pay in advance. You get a number, then dawdle around the pickup window (different from the order window) until the number is called. Dine either in your car, indoors at tables and counter, or at one of Bob's blue-checked picnic tables.


## Cindy's Fish & Chips

292 Route 1                       207-865-1635
Freeport, ME                      LD mid-May-mid-Sept | $

The fish and chips is terrific, the haddock dipped in batter and fried until a golden envelope of crust forms to secure the moistness of the fish. The same technique is used for whole-belly clams, yielding crunchy, dark-gold mouthfuls of marine manna. Onion rings, French fries, and scallops all benefit from the same technique.

To go with these expertly fried items are coleslaw and tartar sauce made here each morning, as well as a fine clam chowder that teeters at the exact sweet spot between briny and creamy. For dessert, there are seasonal fruit pies, strawberry shortcake, and molasses-sweetened hermit bars.

Roadside archeologists will have a field day at Cindy's, which is a mini amusement park of pop-culture detritus that ranges from Mickey Mouse effigies to a human-sized lobster trap that visitors can stand in for a photo, the setting titled "Real Maine Tourist Trap." Signs abound, including one that advises, "Helen Waite is our credit manager, so if you want credit . . . go to

Helen Waite!" Silly, silly stuff, but one sign has real significance: "We cook our food to order . . . and it takes time. But if you are unable to wait, please take the nearest exit, go to Rt. 1 north to Ketchup Corners." That takes you to the nearest McDonald's.

## Clam Shack

2 Western Ave.  
Kennebunkport, ME

207-967-2560  
www.theclamshack.net  
LD (summer only) | $$

The Clam Shack anchors one end of the bridge that connects Kennebunk to Kennebunkport. Fried clams, sold by the pint, are some of the best anywhere—crisp-crusted and heavy with juice. Lobster rolls are strato-spheric. Big hunks of fresh-picked meat are arrayed across the bottom of a round bakery roll. It is your choice to have them bathed in warm butter or dolloped with cool mayonnaise before the roll's top is planted. It is not a huge sandwich, dimensionally speaking, but its flavor is immeasurable: a Maine summer pleasure to make any lobster lover weak-kneed.

Whole lobsters are boiled and sold from an adjoining store that is also a seafood market and bait-and-tackle shop. Upon receiving a cooked lob-ster, and maybe a half pound of steamer clams, it is the customer's job to find a place to eat. There are benches on a deck in back and seats facing the sidewalk in front, where fish crates serve as makeshift tables. (Town zoning forbids proper seating here.) Potatoes? Rolls? Corn? Dessert? You are on your own. The store does sell bottles of beer and wine.

## Cole Farms

Route 100  
Gray, ME

207-657-4714  
www.colefarms.com  
BLD | $

Opened as a farmland diner in 1952, Cole Farms still can be relied on to serve such parochial arcana as boiled dinner and mince pie in the autumn, corn chowder every Wednesday, and a choice of sweet beverages that in-cludes both milk shakes (no ice cream, just milk and flavoring) and frappes (what the rest of the world knows as a milk shake, made with ice cream). It is not, however, preserved in amber. Remodeled and expanded at least a dozen times, the building is now huge and features a gift shop as well as a banquet room. Lunch choices include wraps and modern salads with fat-free raspberry vinaigrette dressing alongside such longtime kitchen specialties as clam cakes and chicken potpie. Even morning muffins aren't quite as dour as they used to be. "We've tweaked them over the years," says proprietor Brad Pollard. "People want their muffins sweeter. You have to keep up." Such changes notwithstanding, a Cole Farms muffin is demure, nothing like a cloying cake-batter pastry.

A good measure of Cole Farms' personality is American chop suey, a *déjuner maudit* listed on the menu right below baked beans (available with or without a hot dog). Like the shockingly red hot dogs, American chop suey is an archaic New England meal once popular in institutions and on the supper tables of frugal housewives: ground beef mixed with elbow macaroni and vaguely Italian tomato sauce. It is bland as can be—closet comfort for those of us who sometimes wax nostalgic for school lunch.

The enduring regional value we like best at Cole Farms is the importance of pudding. Indian pudding, the rugged cornmeal samp sweetened with molasses, is served hot under a scoop of vanilla ice cream. Grapenut pudding comes as a cool block of custard topped by a ribbon of sweetened cereal that has an amber crust reminiscent of a swanky crème brûlée. Swanky, it is not; Yankee, it is.

## Colucci's Hilltop Market

135 Congress St.          207-774-2279
Portland, ME             L | $

Portland, Maine, loves the sandwich known as an Italian. Although an Italian is similar to hoagies, heroes, grinders, blimps, zeps, wedges, and submarines elsewhere, the Downeast version has character all its own. Its uniqueness is not owed to the meats and cheeses, which are commonplace, but to the toppings and the bread. Thick-cut tomatoes, crunchy strips of pepper, briny olives, and a surfeit of spiced oil give the upper layer sparkle. The bread below, completely unlike the muscular, chewy lengths typical of Mid-Atlantic sub sandwiches, is soft and light, something like a gigantic version of the split-top buns in which Yankee wieners typically are served. The layers of salami or ham and cheese form a barrier between the bread and the oily vegetables above, but once that barrier is breached (generally at first bite), the bread quickly absorbs what's on top and loses its ability to hold anything. The experience is similar to eating a hot buttered lobster roll: midway through, the absorbent bun has transformed from a foundation into just one element among the stuff it originally contained.

The best Italian we found was at Colucci's Hilltop Market. As proprietor Dick Colucci expertly assembled one for us behind the counter of his corner store, he told us that his place has been making Italians since the end of World War II. It is also a source for blueberry muffins arrayed each morning in their tins, for cheeseburgers made from just-ground beef, and for such démodé hot lunches as mac 'n' cheese, beef chili, and chop suey. There is no place to eat in this family-run market; any meal you get is takeout.

## Congdon's Doughnuts

| | |
|---|---|
| 1090 Post Rd. | 207-646-4219 |
| Wells, ME | www.congdons.com |
| | BL \| $ |

Muffins are the reigning morning pastry throughout most of Maine, but since 1955, Congdon's has built its reputation on donuts. There is a full breakfast menu, and from what we've seen, it looks pretty good. (Who doesn't like a place that includes a pot of baked beans with the meal?) But when we come to this place, we aren't going to be using up any appetite on bacon and eggs or corned-beef hash. We'll be having maple cream donuts, sugar twists, cruellers (yes, that's how they spell "cruller" here), and apple fritters. Of the many varieties, the plain honey donut is probably the best: fluffy, fresh and rich, although not so heavy that three or four aren't a reasonable breakfast. If you buy six, you get the seventh free.

Seating is diner-style, counter and booths.

## Dolly's

| | |
|---|---|
| 17 US Route 1 | 207-728-7050 |
| Frenchville, ME | BLD \| $ |

Next to Dolly's cash register is a griddle about four feet square, sided by a pitcher filled with *ploye* batter. A *ploye* is an Acadian buckwheat pancake that gets cooked very briefly and never flipped. It comes off the hot iron with an underside that is slightly crisp and a top that is tender enough to beg for melting butter and maybe a dollop of molasses or maple syrup.

Unless you say otherwise at Dolly's, supper will come with *ployes* rather than rolls, and these *ployes* are memorable. They are butter-yellow with a faint green tinge created by the buckwheat (which is botanically an herb rather than a grain) and they arrive three-by-three straight off the griddle. They are a glorious companion for Dolly's Acadian chicken stew. More a curative soup than a casserole, the kindly bowl of schmaltz-rich, golden broth is crowded with large pieces of meat, nuggets of potato, and little freeform dumplings, plus a measured scattering of herbs.

Old-time Acadians ask for *creton* with their *ployes*. Creton is a crazy-fatty-good pork spread not unlike French rillettes. Dolly's version is bright and flowery, a refreshing burst of unexpected spices, including cinnamon, that harmonizes just right with a warm buckwheat crepe.

## Doris's Café

345 Market St.          207-834-6262
Fort Kent Mills, ME      BL | $

The Roadfood connoisseur will grin with joy upon entering Doris's Café, which shares a building with the Fort Kent Mills Post Office. On one wall hang patrons' coffee cups, which they grab upon entering (starting at 5 a.m.), then pour their own coffee while Linda Daigle (the late Doris's sister) makes sure the frying potatoes look good and the eggs are ready to crack.

With a couple of exceptions, the menu is unsurprising town-café fare, including stout toast made from baked-here bread and desserts such as pecan pie, chocolate cream pie, Boston cream cake, and "JJ apple pie," which is an obscure name for a sensational creation made from big, spicy apple chunks with a savory crust festooned with a ribbon of caramel. Hot meals come with homemade rolls, and just about anything should be sided by French fries. This is potato country, and Linda makes the most of it, producing irregularly cut, soft-centered fries from the deep fryer next to the griddle.

Fries are the foundation for the Québécois (and northernmost Maine) specialty known as *poutine*. Atop a heap of just-cooked potatoes goes a blanket of dark gravy and a big fistful of mozzarella cheese that melts from the heat of the spuds. Known in most local restaurants as "mix" or "fry mix," *poutine* delivers a roundhouse punch that makes it a nice dish to split among two (or four). The other unique treat is *ployes,* which are crepelike buckwheat pancakes cooked only on one side, resulting in a top that has a million holes can absorb massive amounts of butter and syrup or gravy from the hot turkey plate or boiled dinner, which here is made with ham.

## *Five Islands Lobster Co.

1447 Five Islands Rd.      207-371-2990
Georgetown, ME         www.fiveislandslobster.com
                         LD (summer only) | $$

You don't come to Five Islands, sit at a table, and get waited on. Securing dinner is part of the experience. First, go to the building with the sign above the door that says "Lobsters." Look in the tank and pick the one you want. Tell the people in here if you want clams, corn, or potatoes thrown into the net and boiled alongside the lobster. You can buy a soft drink (or bring your own wine or beer), although we had to convince one old salt to sell us a bottle of Moxie, which she promised was too bitter for travelers unaccustomed to the Yankee beverage that was originally marketed as nerve tonic. While the meal cooks, find a picnic table. If you are very hungry or for some reason don't want a lobster, go to the other building and pick up an order of fried clams, a lobster roll, fried fish, or even a hamburger or hot dog.

Good as all that other stuff is, you're crazy not to get a lobster. Proprietor Chris Butler told us that the water around here is the deepest and coldest on the coast, explaining why these lobsters yield meat that is so firm and radiant with clean marine flavor.

Tranquility reigns when you look out at the islands in the distance, even when all the picnic tables are crowded with happy eaters chattering with the joy of their sleeves-up meal. As we devoured our shore dinners, savoring the beautiful scene every bit as much as the food, a fishing boat glided into the harbor and tied up at the wharf a few yards from our table. We ate Maine blueberry cake while watching two lobstermen offload crates full of lobsters just trapped in the deep.

## Flo's

| | |
|---|---|
| Route 1 | 800-255-8401 |
| Cape Neddick, ME | www.floshotdogs.com |
| | L (closed Weds) | $ |

Flo's blubbery little pink weenies are not gourmet sausages, and the place itself feels like a crowded garage. Nonetheless, there are many tube steak connoisseurs who put this wacky little place on the short list of America's must-eat hot dogs.

Hot dogs are the one and only thing on the menu, so all you need to do to place an order is to call out a number to indicate how many you want and let the staff know how you want them dressed. As far as we are concerned, there are two basic ways to go: mustard and hot sauce or mayo and hot sauce. The sauce, which is technically optional but culinarily essential, is nothing like chili on a chili dog. It is a devilishly dark sweet/hot relish of stewed onions, glistening with spice and customarily finished with a sprinkle of celery salt. With mayonnaise, it makes for a rich little weenie. With mustard, you get a dog that barks. Nestled in steamed-soft buns, the franks are small enough that two are a mere snack; four to six make a meal.

It is our duty to inform you that visitations from TV food shows have made Flo's so popular that the wait to place an order can approach an hour.

## Harmon's Lunch

144 Gray Rd.                                207-797-9857

Falmouth, ME                                L | $

Doneness is not an issue at Harmon's. All hamburgers are grilled medium so they are moist but not oozing juice or pink inside. They get sandwiched inside soft Portland-bakery buns that are buttered and heated just enough that they become tender mitts for burger-holding. Among the options you do have when you order a hamburger is a slice of cheese melted on top and, better yet, grilled onions. The onions are fried until melting soft, and they add sweet vegetable savor to the little package. Also available are mustard and vivid red relish. Don't bother to ask for lettuce and tomato. They are unavailable, and if you don't like that fact, please reread the sign behind the counter that warns, "This is not Burger King. You don't get it your way. You take it my way, or you don't get the damn thing."

The only side dish is French fries, and they're super: thick-cut and delivered too hot to handle. However, when this little shop gets crowded, as it so often does, ordering French fries can delay delivery of the meal. The problem is that exactly fifteen hamburgers fit on the grill at one time, but the fry kettle has room only for four orders of potatoes. Therefore people who come only for burgers have their order put to the head of the line while potato-eaters wait.

The little wood-frame diner north of Portland was opened in 1960 by Marvin Harmon, and current boss Peter Wormell maintains the unforgiving attitude for which the place has become known over the years. He only reluctantly agreed to allow us to take pictures of the wonderful décor—row after row of old-fashioned glass milk bottles from long-gone Maine dairy farms—and he did not seem at all pleased when we started asking him about the source of his good-tasting beef. Nonetheless, after we paid at the press-button, non-digital cash register and walked out the front door heading for our car in the dirt parking lot, Mr. Wormell came running out behind us—leaving a griddle full of hamburgers sputtering—just so he could give us a small magnetic calendar, the kind you slap onto a refrigerator door, that featured the restaurant's name, address, and phone number, as well as the pacific motto, "Let's Get Harmonized!"

## Harraseeket Lunch & Lobster

36 Main St.  
South Freeport, ME

207-865-4888  
www.harraseeketlunchand  
lobster.com  
LD May–Oct | $$

They tell us that it does rain in Freeport, but every visit we have made seeking lunch at Harraseeket Lobster, the sun was shining and gulls were swooping overhead through the blue, blue sky. Picnic tables overlook the Freeport town harbor; meals are perfumed by the salt smell of the ocean and serenaded by the sound of an American flag flapping overhead.

The specialty is boiled-to-order lobsters (also available live, to go), but don't ignore the seafood baskets. Whole-belly clams are giants, hefty gnarled spheres of golden crust enveloping mouthfuls of ocean nectar. On the side, you want onion rings: puffy circles of brittle sweet batter around a hoop of onion that still has crunch. Clam cakes are good too, their puffy dough holding dozens of nuggets of marine goodness. Chowder is swell, as is the cool lobster roll, served splayed open in a broad cardboard dish and packed with briny-sweet chunks of meat. Have it with onion rings and conclude with a fudgy, hand-fashioned whoopie pie.

## Helen's

28 East Main St.  
Machias, ME

207-255-8423  
www.helensrestaurantmachias.com  
BLD | $

Helen's is deservedly famous for blueberry pie. A dense slurry of cooked and fresh tiny wild Maine blueberries—one-fifth the size of the big ones you buy by the pint at the supermarket—is piled onto a flaky crust and heaped with whipped cream. If all you know are the store-bought ones, the flavor of these berries is astonishing: intensely fruity, sweet but not sugary, bright as the sun. You can get Helen's blueberry pie year-round, but the best time to have it is late summer, when fresh-picked lowbush blues are abundant.

The same fine blueberries find their way into morning muffins, and pies made from raspberries, strawberries, and boysenberries should not be ignored, nor should brownies, cakes, and turnovers. But Helen's is not merely a pastry shop. It is a dandy small-town restaurant that serves a lunch of fried clams or fried haddock, broiled halibut, hot turkey and mashed potatoes or a simple bowl of fresh-picked lobster meat sopped with butter.

## Hodgman's Frozen Custard

1108 Lewiston Rd.
New Gloucester, ME

207-926-3553
Mother's Day to Labor Day (closed
Mon & Tues) | $

Hodgman's custard is dense, smooth, and creamy-rich, made in vanilla and chocolate flavors, plus one special flavor each week. We loved the peanut butter flavor we tried one day, but chocolate and vanilla are so purely perfect that exotic flavors are like gilt for the lily. You can have your custard in a cone or cup, as the foundation for a sundae, banana boat, frappe, float, or what is known here as a thunderstorm, for which the custard is swirled together with toppings. If you are heading straight to a picnic or a place with a refrigerator, be aware that Hodgman's also makes custard pie with a graham-cracker crust.

There is no indoor dining area, but facilities include picnic tables and a gazebo to the side of the stand, where you can sit and lick in the shade.

## Jordan's Snack Bar

200 Downeast Hwy.
Ellsworth, ME

207-667-2174
www.jordanssnackbar.com
LD Mar-Nov | $

For three decades now, Jordan's has been a favorite stop for locals and visitors in search of good burgers, hot dogs, fried seafood, and a selection of ice cream treats, from cones and cups to banana boats and fruited milk shakes. Much business is takeout for people on their way to Bar Harbor, but you can eat here at an outdoor picnic table, in an air-conditioned dining room, or under a covered gazebo. There is a playground, and every Wednesday, Jordan's hosts a vintage car cruise night with live country music.

Among the stars of the menu are toasty, lightly battered fried clams, shrimp, and scallops, each available as a roll (sandwich), as a lunch with fries, or as a dinner with fries and coleslaw. The dinners are huge—big enough to split. Crab rolls are made with sweet, fresh meat, as are lobster rolls, although the latter seemed a bit stingy and stringy—not among Maine's finest.

# Lobster Shack

225 Two Lights Rd.            207-799-1677
Cape Elizabeth, ME          www.lobstershacktwolights.com
LD (closed winter) | $$

Some foodies like to say that ambience doesn't matter all that much; what you put in your mouth is all that counts. If you are of that persuasion, you probably want to skip the Lobster Shack and move on up the coast. Not that the seafood here is bad. In fact, it's good; but there are better fried clams and lobster rolls elsewhere.

On the other hand, nowhere else will you find a setting like that of the Lobster Shack, located in Two Lights State Park. Outside, by a rockbound cliff overlooking Casco Bay, you can sit at a picnic table and eat a lobster that really is seasoned by salty sea air blowing in. Instead of piped-in music, you will be serenaded by gulls screeching overhead.

Aside from whole lobsters, we recommend the creamy lobster stew, perhaps accompanied by a clam cake or two, and whole-belly clams, which are good and crunchy. The lobster roll is a cool one, with plenty of meat and mayonnaise applied in a single dollop on top, allowing the eater to spread it or move it aside as desired. Desserts to know about are Grape-Nuts pudding and Maine's favorite snack cake, Whoopie Pie—or as it is spelled here, curiously, Whoopy pie.

# Long Lake Sporting Club

48 Sinclair Rd.              207-543-7584
Sinclair, ME                www.longlakesportingclub.com
D | $$

You wouldn't call the Long Lake Sporting Club blue-chip (swank restaurants do not exist in northern Aroostook County), but neither is it blue-collar. Set in a peaceful waterside location on Long Lake and accessible by auto, boat, or seaplane (or snowmobile in season), it is a north woods supper club to which locals and visiting outdoorsmen repair for cocktails and big-deal meals of prime rib, lobster, or fried chicken.

The chicken is especially good, pressure-fried so it develops a hard, toasty crust that shores in amazing amounts of juice. Alongside the chicken comes a ramekin of translucent red barbecue sauce with spices that give the chicken a welcome jolt. Whatever main course you choose, comes as part of a ritual meal that includes a finely chopped cabbage and carrot salad bathed in a spicy tomato dressing not unlike that used on barbecue slaw in the Mid-

South. Well-salted French fries are thick with a tough coat enclosing creamy insides. All meals include a plate of *ployes,* the thin buckwheat pancakes that are popular in this part of Maine in lieu of dinner rolls. The *ployes* arrive wrapped in a thick white napkin accompanied by bubble packs of butter and margarine and a pitcher of corn syrup. Two plates are provided so you can pour a pool of syrup into the second plate, peel a *ploye* from the stack on the other plate, butter it, roll it into a tight tube, then dab it in the syrup for between-meat bites.

## *Maine Diner

2265 Post Rd.                    207-646-4441
Wells, ME                        www.mainediner.com
                                 BLD | $

For us, no trip up Route 1 is complete without a visit to the Maine Diner, whether it's for a plate of homemade baked beans, the world's most delicious seafood chowder, or grandma's-recipe lobster pie. Truly special daily specials include New England boiled dinner every Thursday and red flannel hash . . . while supplies last. We are especially fond of the fried clams, which are vigorously oceanic, just a wee bit oily, so fragile the crust seems to melt away as your teeth sink into them. Serious clam devotees can get a "clam-o-rama" lunch, which includes clam chowder, fried whole-belly clams, fried clam strips, and a clam cake!

Seafood rolls are outstanding—split buns piled with clams, haddock, scallops, or shrimp. And the lobster rolls are not to be missed. Yes, we said rolls, plural; the Maine Diner offers two kinds—a lobster salad roll, of cool meat and mayo, or a hot lobster roll with plenty of melted butter to drizzle on it. Either one is terrific; for us, the hot lobster roll is heaven on Earth.

The menu is vast, including such all-American items as buffalo wings and a barbecued pork sandwich, plus a superb chicken potpie. In our book, the single mustn't-miss dish is lobster pie—a casserole containing plump sections of lobster claw and chewy tail meat, drenched in butter and topped with a mixture of cracker crumbs and tomalley. It is a strange, punk-colored dish, monstrous green and brown and pink, shockingly rich.

To sate that after-meal sweet tooth, there are homemade pies of the day, three kinds of pudding (Grape-Nuts, Indian, bread), blueberry-chip ice cream made especially for the diner, and strawberry shortcake.

## Moody's Diner

Route 1  
Waldoboro, ME

207-832-7785  
www.moodysdiner.com

BLD | $

Moody's no longer is open around the clock, but it remains one of the top spots along the coast route for pre-dawn breakfast. When the doors open at 4:30 (5 a.m. in winter), morning muffins have been out of the oven long enough that you can pull one apart without searing fingertips; through the cloud of steam that erupts, a constellation of blueberries glistens in each fluffy half.

Thrift is a pillar of traditional New England cooking and a big part of Moody's echt-Maine character. This is not the place you come to splurge on a full-bore shore dinner or a $15 lobster roll; in fact the restaurant's 208-page cookbook, *What's Cooking at Moody's Diner,* doesn't contain a single recipe for lobster. But it does offer "mock lobster bake" made with haddock fillets. Haddock, which costs less than just about any other edible fish, has been served with egg sauce every Friday for as long as any of the Moody family can remember. (At last count, more than two dozen Moodys have worked in the restaurant and at the motel and cabins just up the hill.)

The menu is a primer of Northeast diner fare: meat loaf and mashed potatoes, hot turkey sandwiches, a panoply of chowders, stews and soups, red flannel hash, baked beans with brown bread, and a fabulous selection of pies, including a legendary walnut pie that is actually a gloss on southern-style pecan pie but, as Alvah Moody proudly notes, "not sickening sweet."

## Nunan's Lobster Hut

9 Mills Rd.  
Kennebunkport, ME

207-967-4362  
www.nunanslobsterhut.com  
D (summer only) | $$

No frills at Nunan's will distract you from the goodness of the lobster (except maybe the view, when the panels on the sides of the dining room are raised to reveal a pleasant vista of Cape Porpoise marshlands). Each lobster is steamed in a couple inches of salty water for twenty minutes, emerging with silky tender claw meat, its knuckles and tail succulent and chewy. It comes to the table on a pizza pan with cups of drawn butter.

The Nunan family have been lobstering for three generations and running this restaurant since 1953, so by now they have the process of enjoying their catch down to its essence. In addition to whole lobsters, they serve lobster stew, lobster rolls, and lobster salad (plus a small assortment of hot dogs, hamburgers, and so on for those with lobster allergies). After supper, there are homemade brownies or a slice of pie, the recipes for which have been perfected over the last thirty years. Blueberry and apple are memorable, their subtly sweetened fruits encased in sugar-dusted crusts.

Should you desire to wash your hands before, during, or after eating, sinks are available in the open dining room, ready for immediate action. They are proletarian sinks like you'd want to have next to your workbench in the basement. For drying hands, Nunan's supplies rolls of paper towels.

## Pemaquid Lobster Co-Op

| 32 Co-Op Rd. | 207-677-2801 |
| Pemaquid, ME | www.pemaquidlobstercoop.com |
| | LD May-Oct \| $$ |

Lobster is deluxe food that many people like to eat in a primitive setting. If you're such a person, find your way to Pemaquid, Maine, and its Lobster Co-Op. And we do mean find your way: Pemaquid is not on the way to anywhere other than the famously scenic Pemaquid Lighthouse. But once you get here, you can eat some of the nicest lobster anywhere off picnic tables overlooking the harbor where co-op members berth their fishing boats.

A first-timer probably ought to have the basic shore dinner, which is a pound-plus lobster with meat that completely fills out its shell, steamer clams with broth and butter, corn on the cob, coleslaw, and a roll. Lobster options include a lobster salad roll in a split-top Yankee bun; the already-extracted lazy-lobster plate; and rich, hearty lobster stew. Fried seafood is also a specialty, and supposedly it all is local, including Maine shrimp, but we choose to devote our full appetite to lobster. BYOB.

## Portland Pie Co.

| 51 York St. | 207-772-1231 |
| Portland, ME | www.portlandpie.com |
| | LD \| $$ |

Pizza purists, move along; there is nothing for you to eat here. What you're going to find at the Portland Pie Company is nothing like the Neapolitan ideal of pizza pie. But for eaters of wide-ranging taste, and for those of us who rarely meet a style of pizza we don't like, it's a very interesting place.

Starting as a humble delivery service and now sporting four large, sit-down restaurants in and around town, the Portland Pie Company boasts of gourmet flavored pizza dough infused with basil, garlic, or beer. Available toppings are even less common. The pizza called Red Claws (named for Portland's NBA D-League affiliate of the Boston Celtics) is topped with a three-cheese blend, garlic, butter, and nice pink hunks of lobster meat. The Bar Harbor comes with scallops. Perhaps the most unusual pie is the Chamberlain. Why it's called that, we do not know, for its theme is Chinese cuisine with a Dixie accent: General Tso's sauce, diced peppers, carrots, toasted sesame seeds, and pulled pork!

## Rock's Family Diner

| | |
|---|---|
| 378 W. Main St. | 207-834-2888 |
| Fort Kent, ME | BLD \| $ |

Rock's is ambiguously located smack between two scenic markers, one declaring itself the beginning of Route 1—2,209 miles from Key West; the other saying it is the end of Route 1—2,390 miles from Key West. We've never measured, nor do we have an opinion about whether Route 1 starts or ends in Fort Kent; but we have eaten several meals at this diner in the northeasternmost corner of the United States and recommend it with no ambiguity at all.

Walk in, study the wall menu, place your order, and pay. Then find a seat at a table or booth or one of the communal counters. In a short while, out comes a member of the staff with your cheeseburger, chili dog, sandwich, or hot-lunch plate. The burgers are thin patties, squished hard on the grill but fatty enough to be plenty juicy. On the side, fried potatoes are the order of the day, available seven ways: jo-jo's, curly fries, plain fries, fries topped with gravy, hamburger or Italian sauce, or as a mix (the local version of *poutine*): potatoes heaped with mozzarella cheese and dark-brown gravy.

In August, when Fort Kent holds its annual Muskie Derby and Ploye Festival, Rock's hosts a contest to see who can eat the most *ployes* (buckwheat crepes). When we attended in 2009, they served a traditional Acadian meal that included some of the best pot roast anywhere, plus stacks of *ployes* to mop its gravy.

## Sea Basket

303 Bath Rd.  207-882-6581
Wiscasset, ME  www.seabasket.com
LD (closed Tues & all of Jan & Feb) | $

Sea Basket is a roadside café with eat-in-the-rough service: place an order and wait for your number to be called. We are huge fans of its lobster stew, which is loaded with hunks of knuckle and claw meat and is creamy but not heavy, gilded with a glistening butter slick on top. Fish chowder and clam chowder are similarly excellent, and the baskets of fried shrimp, clams, and haddock—made using a process the management calls "convection deep frying"—are all fresh and crisp. To our taste, Sea Basket scallops are especially delicious—sweet, tender, and veiled in a crust that virtually melts when bitten. We also sampled a lobster roll, which was filled with good pieces of meat bound in just enough mayonnaise, but packed into a sturdy bun similar to what you'd use for a hero sandwich—too much bun, we think.

The proper dessert for almost any Maine Roadfood meal is a whoopie pie, of which the Sea Basket has a whole selection: classic soft chocolate cakes surrounding white sugar filling, as well as raspberry crème whoopie pies made with white cookies, peanut butter cream whoopie pies, and thin-mint whoopie pies ("Tastes Just Like One!" a sign boasts).

## Shaw's Fish & Lobster Wharf

129 Route 32  207-677-2200
New Harbor, ME  LD mid-May–mid-Oct | $$

Perched on the second floor of a building that overlooks Muscongus Bay and a small commercial harbor, Shaw's has a million-dollar view and priceless fresh seafood. Unless you happen to be driving down toward Pemaquid Point (a worthy destination, scenery-wise), you'll never accidentally pass Shaw's, a good half hour due south of Route 1. If you are hankering for impeccably fresh lobsters (brought ashore within sight of the restaurant), buttery chowder, and handsome whole-belly clams, the detour makes perfect sense.

In addition to whole lobsters, Shaw's offers cool lobster rolls and lobster pie, which is a soupy bisque decorated with crumbled Ritz crackers. There is "lazy man's lobster" too: a bowl full of picked meat swimming in butter. If there happens to be any seafood frowners in your party, they can avail themselves of a hamburger, hot dog, or chicken-finger basket. Downstairs is a small bar where locals congregate and visitors are tolerated.

## Shaw's Ridge Farm

59 Shaw's Ridge Rd. (Rt. 224)        207-324-2510
Sanford, ME        LD (closed in winter) | $

A few years ago, when Roadfood.com's Stephen Rushmore, Amy Breisch, and Chris Ayers set out on a "Quest for the Best Ice Cream of New England," they gave Shaw's Ridge Farm five out of a possible five cones, declaring that this combination barbecue barn, miniature golf course, and creamery had "clearly perfected the art of ice cream making." Some of the flavors they liked best were coffee ("for coffee drinkers"), Indian pudding ("strong molasses flavor"), and native strawberry ("the standard by which all strawberry ice creams should be measured"). They also praised the hot fudge sauce as "thin, smooth, and slightly bitter . . . one of the greatest hot fudge sauces in the country!"

The native strawberry ice cream is not idly named: It really is made with fresh, handpicked strawberries. Likewise, blueberry, orange, lemon, and raspberry sing of the fruits at their core. Shaw's Ridge even brews its own coffee extract for the truly caffeinated coffee ice cream, which is made from a recipe developed long ago by Grammy Shaw. Among the more exotic flavors available are coconut pineapple, cashew caramel, mocha-macadamia, and that New England fave, Grapenut. Rococo cones, shrouded in chocolate, nuts, or jimmies, are available to hold the ice cream, but this is one place where we don't want anything distracting from the ice cream itself . . . except for a spill of that devilish hot fudge sauce.

We've heard very good things about the BBQ part of this operation but have yet to give it a try. Nor have we played the golf course.

## Waterman's Beach Lobster

343 Waterman's Beach Rd.        207-596-7819
Thomaston, ME        www.watermansbeachlobster.com
        LD Jun-Sept | $$

Waterman's Beach Lobster earned national fame in 2001 when it was presented a James Beard Foundation Award as one of America's Regional Classics. This came as no surprise to shore visitors who have been patronizing the traditional in-the-rough lobster shack since it opened in 1986, selling lobsters fresh off nearby fishing boats.

The menu is basic. No surprises. Choose what size lobster you want, usually between one and two pounds, and it is steamed to plump-meat perfection, then served on disposable trays and plates with corn on the cob, a bag of potato chips, coleslaw, and bread. Lobster salad rolls are made on circular buns rather than split-tops, as are crab sandwiches and tuna melts. For dessert, you want pie à la mode made with Maine's own Round Top ice cream. BYOB.

## Young's Lobster Pound

| | |
|---|---|
| 4 Mitchell St. | 207-338-1160 |
| Belfast, ME | LD \| $$ |

Many people come to Young's Lobster Pound as if it were a picnic, bringing just about everything except the lobster. Some even bring tablecloths, utensils, and plates (Young's serves everything on cardboard and in Styrofoam). Steamed with Penobscot Bay salt water to the point of perfect plumpness, served with a heap of steamer clams, and eaten off of picnic tables with a view of Belfast Harbor, this is one of Maine's top lobsters.

The staff will pre-crack the shell for those feeling weak. It is also possible to avoid all effort by ordering a lobster roll on a round bun, lobster stew, crab, haddock, grilled scallops, or fried clams.

Young's is a huge barn of a place with seating for five hundred and tanks that hold literally tens of thousands of live lobsters, mostly for the wholesale trade. Docking is available for those who arrive by boat.

## Betty Ann Food Shop

565 Bennington St.          617-567-1479

East Boston, MA            B (closed Mon) | $

Opened in 1931, Betty Ann Food Shop sells five kinds of donuts: crullers, yeast, cake, and Bismarcks filled with either raspberry or lemon jelly. There is nothing outlandish about any of them, and the word "artisan" would never apply to such humble pastries (each of which sells for under $1), but these handmade sinkers are among the Northeast's elite. We are especially fond of the double-risen yeast donuts: dense, cakey, and crisp-edged. What a wonderful companion for morning coffee!

Betty Ann, however, does not sell coffee: It is strictly a bakery. In addition to donuts, the inventory includes pies, cakes, and cookies. Note that Betty Ann opens at 7 a.m. but closes at 10 or 10:30 every morning.

## Christina's Homemade Ice Cream

1255 Cambridge St.         617-492-7021

Cambridge, MA             www.christinasicecream.com

                          $

Christina's has two strikes against it. First, seating is severely limited and because the place is so popular, it is not uncommon even in inclement weather for crowds to hover on the sidewalk licking cones and spooning into cups.

Second, it is virtually impossible to park anywhere nearby. Roadfood.com's Bruce Bilmes offered his solution to the latter problem, which was either to take mass transit or "move to within walking distance." If you love ice cream, housing near enough to walk for a cup of Christina's would be Millionaire's Row.

Take, for example, the flavor called burnt sugar, an alchemical combination of high-butterfat ice cream and sweet sugar that teeters on the edge of bitter-burnt. It is a flavor that stimulates appetite at the same time it sates it, inevitably causing return trips in twenty-minute increments and, finally, futile alcoholic-like promises to eat moderately the next time. Burnt sugar is only one of dozens of interesting flavors at the pinnacle of greater Boston's pantheon of great ice cream shops. Seasonal specialties include eggnog, fresh rose, and pumpkin. Among the occasional must-licks are honey lavender, cinnamon rice pudding, and banana-cinnamon.

Five or more nondairy sorbets also are available each day.

## *Clam Box

246 High St.                    978-356-9707
Ipswich, MA                     www.ipswichma.com/clambox
                                LD (summer only) | $$

It's hard to believe that we ever wondered where the best fried clams are made. One taste of those served at the Clam Box is irrefutable evidence that there are none better. The whole-belly clams are not overly gooey and not too large, offering a subtle ocean sweetness that is brilliantly amplified but not the least bit overwhelmed by the crusty sheath outside. A whole clam plate is a magnificent meal, including not only the native beauties sheathed in their fragile red-gold envelope, but also elegant onion rings, French fries, and bright, palate-refreshing coleslaw. The lobster roll is loaded with meat; Jane declares the clam chowder to be among New England's best; and our friends Bruce Bilmes and Sue Boyle wrote, "Clam Box's fried clam strips are perhaps the only strips we've ever eaten that don't seem like a compromise. They are as good as the bellies, in their own way."

The place itself is a gas, shaped like a clam box, the trapezoidal container in which fried-clams-to-go are customarily served. It is a genuine roadside attraction that dates back to the 1930s and would be of interest for its looks alone. There is indoor seating, but across the parking lot are choice seats whenever the weather is nice: sunny picnic tables for open-air dining. Throughout most of the summer, expect a wait in line at mealtimes. The Clam Box is famous, deservedly so.

## Donut Dip

648 N. Main St.           413-736-2224

East Longmeadow, MA       BL | $

"What foods these morsels be!" is the motto on the box in which your dozen is presented at the counter of a modest store that happens to be one of New England's premier donut shops. The box also boasts of forty-nine different varieties, including French crullers and long crullers, devil's-food-dark chocolate, butternuts, toasted coconut, and jelly-filled, plus fritters and fruit bars. The flagship donut is apple cider, which Roadfood.com's Chris Ayers and Amy Breisch described as "the finest we've ever eaten, the crunchy, cracked exterior bursting with cinnamon-y apple flavor."

A second shop is located at 1305 Riverside Street, West Springfield, MA.

## Durgin-Park

340 Faneuil Hall Marketplace    617-227-2038

Boston, MA                 www.arkrestaurants.com/
                                 durgin_park.htm

                                 LD | $$

Durgin-Park attracts hordes of tourists. It is noisy and can seem impolite. It is a pillar of Yankee gastronomy that twice a day clatters out expertly made plates of regional food, many of which are getting hard to find elsewhere. Seated at the long, red-checked communal table, you holler your order to a waitress, who soon slaps down some corn bread. You then move on to such old favorites as lobster stew, Boston scrod, fishcakes and spaghetti, roast turkey with sage dressing, pot roast, or pork loin. The house specialty is prime rib, a gargantuan cut that overhangs its plate. Side that with a mountain of mashed potatoes and a scoop of fresh apple sauce, and please, please, an order of superb Boston baked beans—firm, silky, not too sweet—and you've got a meal to nourish a nation.

The dessert list is tradition itself, featuring hot mince pie in the autumn, apple pandowdy, deep-dish apple pie, strawberry shortcake on a biscuit, and the world's best Indian pudding, which is a steaming gruel of cornmeal and molasses that traditionalists love. The downright weird alternative dessert is coffee Jell-O.

## Essex Seafood

143 Eastern Ave.          978-768-7233

Essex, MA          www.essexseafood.com

LD | $$

The sweetest, tenderest soft-shelled clams—perfect for frying—are harvested from the mudflats on Essex Bay, and here at Essex Seafood, they are expertly cooked and informally presented. This place boasts a lobster pound, where people come to buy them live to take home and boil, or boiled and ready to eat. Adjacent to the market and the holding tanks is a quiet dining room with a window to the kitchen. Here diners select from a menu of various-sized lobster dinners as well as boats, plates, sandwiches, and side orders of fried clams, scallops, and shrimp, plus excellent clam chowder and corn on the cob. The lobsters are swell, and the fried-seafood plates are beautiful to behold: a layer of French fried potatoes, topped with a layer of onion rings, topped with a heap of your seafood of choice.

Eat inside, at booths in the wood-paneled dining room that is decorated with nautical bric-a-brac, or choose a green-painted picnic table outdoors in back—a breezy retreat from Route 133 near the Essex-Gloucester town line. Unlike many of the seafood eateries in this area, Essex is open year-round.


## Graham's Hot Dogs

931 Bedford St.          508-678-9574

Fall River, MA          L | $

Franks 'n' beans are a time-honored combo almost everywhere, but there are few places where they come together as nicely as in Fall River, Massachusetts. Hot dog shops (of which the city has multitudes) offer them in a bun, the beans serving as a condiment either below or on top of the wiener. Graham's beans are especially good: brown-sugar-sweet, soft and goopy, laced with limp leaves of onion. The same good beans are available bunned with *chourico* sausage, with kielbasa, and with a hamburger. Or for all of $1.15, you can buy only beans in a bun.

Should you be interested in outfitting your hot dog with things other than beans, Graham's has a panoply: ground *chourico,* bacon, potato chips, Coney Island–style chili sauce, sauerkraut, onions sopped with hamburger juices (that one is known as a whimpy), and the moist grated Cheddar that is a local favorite.

Dating back to 1962, Graham's lacks the patina of culinary history that makes so many of the region's more ancient hot dog joints charming. Its school-desk seats along the wall are fairly modern and the façade is boring brickface. But the bean dogs and hot cheese sandwiches are exemplary.

## *Hartley's Original Pork Pies

1729 S. Main St.                     508-676-8605
Fall River, MA                       BL | $

Aside from its great food, we especially like Hartley's Original Pork Pies because its continued existence is incontrovertible evidence that regional specialties are thriving and ready to eat for anyone willing to look for them. This hundred-plus-year-old bakery continues to make and sell the meat pies introduced by British Isles immigrants as well as French Canadians who came to this region to work in the mills. The savory pies are made as family-sized nine-inchers and as individual units the size of a large cupcake. In addition to traditional ground pork with gravy, variations include chicken pie, chorizo pie, and even Buffalo chicken pie with hot sauce and blue cheese. Salmon pies are available on Friday and Saturday. The fillings are hearty and unmistakably artisan; the crust is sensational—melting-rich and flaky the way only a crust made with lard can be. In addition to meat pies, Hartley's makes stuffed quahogs and chorizo pizza. Local enough for you?

There are no dining facilities. Although infused with gravy, the pies are fairly tidy and manageable as dashboard eats with several napkins.

## J.J.'s Coney Island

565 S. Main St.                      508-679-7944
Fall River, MA                       BLD | $

One of the least known and underappreciated specialties of Fall River, Massachusetts, is the hot cheese sandwich. Hot cheese, a specialty? Yes, indeed. The item so listed on J.J.'s menu is anything but ordinary. The cheese itself is different: sharp Cheddar grated into a rugged hash similar to riced potatoes. J.J.'s keeps it warm in a steam-table tureen, where, miraculously, it does not clump or melt, and from which it is retrieved by the scoopful and put into a burger bun. In the world of interesting cheeses, it alone might not achieve stardom, but it assumes beguiling buttery luxe when topped with a measure of the chili-meat sauce used on Coney Island hot dogs plus a scattering of crisp raw onions and a squirt of yellow mustard.

Aside from hot cheese and Coney Island hot dogs, J.J.'s is a terrific source of such regional favorites as *chourico* pie and stuffed quahog clams, as well as an oddity locals know as a Wimpy Burger. That's a beef patty that is cooked, then steeped in gravy and bunned with a big, soft onion petal (and, preferably, some of that good hot cheese).

J.J's is an extraordinarily polite place for a joint where weenies star. Proprietor Albano Medeiros once told a reporter, "We want families to come here. . . . We wanted to offer a classier place." The large street-corner restaurant is accoutered with comfortable booths and tables and even an espresso machine for leisurely sipping. There are no counter seats. And the management explicitly forbids swearing.

## Kelly's Roast Beef

410 Revere Beach Blvd.  781-284-9129
Revere, MA  www.kellysroastbeef.com
LD | $

There are a couple of other Kelly's branches, but they do not compare to the charm of the Kelly's at Revere Beach, especially on a warm spring weekend when gulls screech overhead and occasionally panhandle from the sky over diners who don't closely guard their meals. The salty air of the ocean wafts in to add ineffable savor to the roast beef sandwiches, and the sun shines down making the roast beef's special sauce glisten. While there is no indoor dining at Kelly's, the pavilions at the broad beach across the street are one of the nicest dining areas a Roadfood devotee could hope for.

The beef sandwich is a North Shore paradigm. There are many toppings available, but the primary trio—and a fine combo—are cheese, sauce, and mayo. If the beef tends to be a little bit dry—and in our experience, sometimes it is—the sauce and mayo are superb compensation, and the cheese, of course, adds extra fatty luxury to beef that is fundamentally lean. We're also fans of the tender sesame seed bun.

Beyond the signature beef, Kelly's menu is mostly beach cuisine: fried clams, lobster rolls, scallops, shrimp, French fries, and onion rings.

## The Liberal Club

20 Star St.  508-675-7115
Fall River, MA  www.theliberalclub.com
LD | $$

The Liberal Club is more than a restaurant. It is a social club, function hall, and barroom to which regulars come for shots and beers every morning.

While the banquet rooms are capacious, the restaurant's dining room is modest, outfitted with Red Sox décor above unupholstered wooden booths.

The menu is South Coast Massachusetts Portuguese-American, ranging from prime rib and whole lobsters for Saturday-night feasts to marinated conch salad (what Rhode Islanders call snail salad) and shrimp Mozambique in a judiciously spiced garlic sauce. The Portuguese sausage known as *chourico* (similar to the Spanish chorizo) is huge in Fall River, available here either as *chourico,* the familiar nuggets of cased sausage presented in a bun, or *chourico* meat, something else altogether: broad, thin slices of marinated pork loin, moist and flamboyantly spiced, to be eaten with knife and fork.

When appetizers arrive—fried smelts and calamari, onion rings and stuffed quahogs—the waitress asks if we want oil and vinegar to go with them. "You do!" she says when we look puzzled by the mundane offering. Out comes a gravy boat full of marinade so crowded with herbs, minced garlic, and chopped green onion that each spoonful is a savory bouquet, delicious enough to spread like tapenade across pieces of dinner roll from the bread basket. All the seafood dishes we've tried are terrific, including fried shrimp and fried lobster tails (!), and magnificent day-boat scallops. Gilded with a translucent veil of bread crumbs and perched in a sizzling pool of garlic-charged melted butter that blends with fallen crumbs to create veins of wicked crunch on the bottom of the serving dish, the scallops are dense and cream-rich.

The Liberal Club began as a soccer club in 1915, when soccer was huge in Fall River among immigrants from the British Isles, and it continues to run the bar for the restaurant that occupies its kitchen and dining room. That means you place orders with two waitresses—one from the restaurant, one from the bar—and you pay two separate checks (cash only, please).

## Marguerite's

778 Main Rd.        508-636-3040
Westport, MA     www.margueritesrestaurant.com
                            BLD Mon-Sat; BL Sun | $

Walking into Marguerite's at noon on a rainswept winter day, the aroma in the dining room was the nicest kind of welcome: sweet clam chowder, buttery bisque ballasted with hunks of lobster, and hot crust on chicken potpie. A town lunchroom with no more than a dozen tables and a short counter, this is where folks come for honest shoreline food and the good company of waitresses who seldom stroll the dining room without a coffee pot in hand for instant refills. We love the fried bay scallops, veiled in the thinnest possible crust, and sweet-mussel billi-bi redolent of rosemary; but the dish that makes us loyal for life is stuffed quahogs: big clam shells piled with stuffing made from chopped clams, onions, and linguica sausage. Known as stuffies, these savories are found on many menus in southern New England; we've found none as good as Marguerite's. Dessert can be that New England specialty, Grape-Nuts custard.

## Marty's Donut Land

8 Central St.  978-356-4580
Ipswich, MA  B | $

Except for the fact that you can't have a smoke with your coffee anymore, Marty's seems never to change. Its big, hefty donuts are classics from long before recent donut fads, its "honey dew" a simple sinker with a substantial sweet cake texture that is perfect for dunking. On the lighter side are those that are "honey dipped"—airy, raised rounds that want to evaporate on your tongue. Chocolate-frosted donuts are weighty and crunch-skinned, and there are jelly-filled and powdered and coconut-spangled, too.

A simple storefront, Marty's has a counter where takeout dozens are sold and where customers sit and converse as life comes in and out. And there are counter seats in the front window that afford a view of passing traffic on Route 133. Years ago, after a really satisfying Marty's breakfast, we asked the cashier if she had a business card she could give us with the address, phone number, and so on of the establishment for our records. "This is Marty's, hon," she informed us. "We don't do business cards."

## Marzilli's Bakery

944 Bedford St.  508-675-5551
Fall River, MA  www.marzillisbakery.com
BL | $

The sign outside Marzilli's Bakery is subtitled "Grinder—Pizza," and its menu is similar to what you find in sleeves-up Mediterranean places throughout southern New England. But Marzilli's offers a distinct southeastern Massachusetts flavor. In this part of the world, calzones are known as *chourico* rolls, and they come filled with the crumbled Portuguese sausage locals like so much. You can eat stuffies (stuffed quahog clams) and Portuguese custard tarts. Along with familiar soups and chowders is kale soup, a Fall River standard.

Pizza at Marzilli's is offered bakery-style, known as a tray, made medium-thin like focaccia and generally bought by the individual piece, known as a square, and served at room temperature. Toppings other than *chourico* are a rarity. The meal for which loyal customers have enshrined this humble place for decades is its grinder (the regional New England term for a hero or hoagie). All sorts of fillings are available, from seafood salad to steak and onions, but the favorite is the classic Italian combo of cold cuts, cheese, and (optional) hot and/or sweet peppers on wonderful house-baked loaves. Grinders come in three sizes, the large one a handsome meal for two . . . and at about $10, a good deal indeed.

## Mee Sum Restaurant and Lounge

1819 S. Main St.          508-678-9869
Fall River, MA           LD | $

"Have you had our Fall River chow mein before?" asks Sue the waitress. It's a question she feels she needs to ask, because the chow mein in and around the old South Coast city is different from any other. That is why Mee Sum is such a significant Roadfood restaurant, despite the fact that most of its menu and décor are standard-issue, mid-twentieth-century faux Chinese.

What makes Fall River chow mein unique is the way it is served—as a sandwich—and the goodness of its noodles, which have been made since 1926 by the Oriental Chow Mein Company over on Eighth Street. Oriental Chow Mein, now run by the son and daughter-in-law of the founder, rolls out extremely thin sheets of noodle dough, cuts them into strips scarcely thicker than a shoestring, then fries the noodles to a vivid crisp. They are nutty-rich and more addictive than potato chips, the ideal balance for soft brown gravy laced with celery and onion. Ladle the gravy atop the bottom half of a burger bun, strew it with crisp noodles, then cap the whole thing with the bun's top and you have a chow mein sandwich—a fascinating swirl of soft and crunch, moist and brittle—unique to this small part of New England (and, oddly enough, Nathan's of Coney Island).

Novitiates and even most regular customers eat the sandwich with a knife and fork. But there are seasoned chow mein sandwich–eaters who know to ask for theirs wrapped, and who eat the whole thing without benefit of utensils, maybe with only a couple of napkins. Sue explained to us that when the sandwich is enclosed in wax paper for even a few minutes, the gravy begins to bind it together and the tight wrapper causes the noodles to steam soft, returning to a state that is something like lo mein.

Other curious Fall River sandwiches on the otherwise classic

Cantonese-American menu include egg foo yung (vaguely similar to the St. Paul of St. Louis) and a chop suey sandwich, which Sue rightly warned us was ridiculously wet, not benefiting from crisp noodles.

One of the fun things about dining at Mee Sum, aside from the unique sandwiches and ingenuously kitschy moo-goo-gai-pan repertoire, is that the menu offers exotic Polynesian potations served in tumblers shaped like the heads of Aku Aku and Fu Manchu. One drink dubbed Dr. Ming of Tahiti turned out to be a very rummy piña colada variant. After a few sips, we believed the promise on the menu, that Dr. Ming would "spin you to the island of Tahiti."

## Nick's

534 S. Main St.  
Fall River, MA

508-677-3890  
LD | $

Long known as Dirty Nick's, this little storefront may be the oldest weenie joint in Fall River, dating back to 1920, when Nicholas Pappas came to town with a hot-dog-sauce formula he learned in Philadelphia. Similar to the New York System weenies of adjacent Rhode Island, a hot dog at Nick's is small and pink with gentle flavor that begs to be doctored up. The standard "works" configuration is a squiggle of mustard, a thin line of the spicy, dark meat sauce, and a scattering of chopped raw onions, all loaded into a fleecy bun. No single ingredient is glorious (although an argument could be made for the sauce); nor is the whole package one of those swoonfully delicious things that induces love at first bite. No, the pleasure of these little things is more progressive, leading from taste-bud bafflement to intrigue to pleasure and, ultimately, to addiction. One is only the beginning. Two is a nice snack. Four would be a meal, except for the fact that if you buy five at Nick's ($1.26 each), you get the sixth one free. Nick's weenies are the foundation also for a Fall River delight known as the bean dog, a tube steak topped with a scattering of sweet baked beans.

Smoky *chourico* is huge in this region thanks to the Portuguese roots of so many citizens, and another local creation is the *chourico* and fry plate, which is sliced discs of sausage along with a few French fries in a bun surrounded by lots more French fries. Nick's makes its fries as needed: When you order them, someone grabs a potato, puts it in the French-fry cutter, then takes the little white spud logs and throws them into a vintage Autofry machine that automatically dispenses the cooked potatoes after their allotted cooking time.

One more local specialty not to miss: the melted cheese sandwich.

"Melted cheese?" you ask. "How boring is that?" Not. While Fall River's melted cheese sandwiches are by no means epicurean tours de force, they are irresistible. Other examples around town use Cheddar so finely shredded that it seems to have been through a ricer; Nick's makes its version using tiles of sharp Cheddar that melt but don't quite drip. With some of that magic hot sauce on top, sandwiched in a supersoft bun, it's a wonderful little sandwich.

What better place to eat these nostalgic treats than in one of the hundred-year-old school desks lined up along Nick's wall?

## Nick's Famous Roast Beef

139 Dodge St.                978-922-9075
North Beverly, MA            www.nicksfamousroastbeef.com
                             LD | $

Last we heard, Roadfood.com's Chris Ayers was engaged in a project to taste and evaluate all the roast beef sandwiches north of Boston. Although a common item everywhere in the United States, this particular sandwich is a passion hereabouts, and dozens of restaurants make it a specialty. Until Chris completes his monumental roastbeefathon, we'll be happy to maintain loyalty to Nick's of North Beverly.

Like most local roast beef houses, it is a simple, self-service sandwich shop. You can get a junior or large sandwich or a super beef sandwich on an onion roll. That last one is what we recommend. It is a hefty pile of thin-sliced, full-flavored pink beef inside a giant rectangular roll that is egg-yellow and studded with squiggles of onion. Among such add-ons as cheese, mayo, and mustard, the ones to which you should pay attention are barbecue sauce, which has a spicy sweetness, and horseradish sauce with a wicked sting. The two together are a magic halo for roast beef.

All sorts of other sandwiches and subs are listed on the menu, and there are platters that include your meat of choice (including roast beef) along with a salad, French fries, and onion rings. The onion rings are particularly good—golden brown and crunchy.

It has become a tradition for Nick's devotees who travel to take a bumper sticker with them and have their picture taken holding it. Nick's décor consists of hundreds of snapshots taken of roast beef fans all over the world.

## Red Skiff

15 Mt. Pleasant St.            978-546-7647
Rockport, MA                   BL | $

Remodeled several years ago by new owners, the Red Skiff remains a cozy café that attracts enough tourists and locals that you can expect to wait for a table or counter seat anytime after eight a.m., especially on weekends.

The most interesting item on the menu is anadama bread, which was supposedly invented in Rockport, when a fisherman grew so angry at his lazy wife, Anna, that he baked his own loaf of bread from wheat flour, cornmeal, and molasses . . . all the while muttering, "Anna, damn her." Whatever its origins, the Red Skiff makes a dark, sweet, and high-flavored anadama loaf that tastes just great when toasted and buttered. The unique bread is used to make interesting French toast, available plain or topped with strawberries, but in truth, we like simple toasted anadama bread better. The egg dip, frying, and strawberry topping tend to detract from the solid Yankee character of the bread itself. Other good breakfasts include plate-wide pancakes (buttermilk, blueberry, or chocolate chip) and a warm pecan roll that is served adrip with caramel frosting.


## R.F. O'Sullivan & Son

282 Beacon St.            617-492-7773
Somerville, MA            www.rf-osullivan.com
                          LD | $$

This popular, boisterous watering hole makes quintessential pub burgers, meaning extra-large mounds of beef with a crusty surface and juice-oozing insides. A plain one is pretty sloppy, and they get sloppier when you choose one of several dozen ways the kitchen has of tricking them out. Naturally, there are cheeseburgers and bacon cheeseburgers, but opportunities to go wild abound. How about a black-and-blue burger rolled in black pepper and draped with blue cheese? Or an Empire State burger covered with Italian sausage and mozzarella cheese and festooned with peppers and onions? Thick steak fries and sweet onion rings are superb on the side.

## Santarpio's

111 Chelsea St.   617-567-9871
East Boston, MA   www.santarpiospizza.com
LD | $$

Like so many of the great pizzerias of the Northeast, Santarpio's started as a bakery at the beginning of the twentieth century. It went to pizza in the 1930s. Arriving on battered metal trays carried by a staff of indomitable waitresses, Santarpio's Neapolitan pies are among the region's best. Their circumference is a masterful balance of crunch and chew, even if the inside has a tendency to melt like a Salvador Dalí image when ballasted with toppings. Strangely, the toppings that normally give pizza a flavor wallop, such as garlic and anchovies, even sausage, seem somewhat mild. That is a good thing because the personality of these pizzas is not overwhelming. They are pies of mild and creamy disposition, all about the interplay of tomato and cheese (and, of course, crust).

Other than pizza, you need to know about Santarpio's barbecue. Nothing like pit-cooked 'cue, this version is homemade Italian sausage, steak tips, or skewered hunks of lamb cooked over an open fire. The sausage is a taut tube with the flavor of charcoal insinuating its high-spiced insides. The lamb is quite ewey, with big flavor for lamb lovers only. Regular customers get barbecue as a pre-pizza hors d'oeuvre with hot cherry peppers and crusty Italian bread.

The second location of Santarpio's is at 71 Newbury Street in Peabody, MA (978-535-1811).

## Toscanini's

899 Main St.   617-491-5877
Cambridge, MA   www.tosci.com
$

First, let us say that the vanilla ice cream made by Gus Rancatore at Toscanini's is some of the best there is; pure, uncomplicated, satisfying. And the regional favorite, Grape-Nuts, is as good as it gets, the familiar breakfast cereal blended into sweet cream so it becomes flavorful streaks of grain. We love such flavors as cocoa pudding and cake batter as well as such extreme exotica as black pepper bourbon. But the true call to glory is burnt caramel. If you are one who enjoys the preciousness of the crust on a flawlessly blowtorched crème brûlée, you too will understand how a controlled sugar burn creates an ice cream that transcends sweetness and makes taste buds buzz.

## Turtle Alley

42 Rogers St.  
Gloucester, MA

978-281-4000  
www.turtlealley.com  
L | $

Mayans knew long ago what modern cooks only recently discovered, that flavoring chocolate with pepper has mouthwatering sex appeal. Our favorite way to appreciate the culinary collusion is candy made by chocolatier Hallie Baker at Turtle Alley. She creates turtles in white, dark, and milk chocolate; the stunner is an almond chipotle turtle in which the pepper's smoky bite surges through the caramel filling and around the nuts like edible adrenaline, all its excitement robed in a silky sweet chocolate coat that assures on-fire taste buds that all is well.

Not all of Hallie's vast school of terrapins are so exotic. There are plenty of normal turtles, all of which are abnormally delicious, each handmade piece as unique as a snowflake. You can get them with pecans, almonds, peanuts, and macadamias, as well as cashews, which she believes are the ideal nut, at least cosmetically, because cashews resemble turtle flippers.

Beyond turtles, the shelves are crowded with brittles, clusters and butter crunches, chocolate-robed candied fruits, nonpareils, and simple hunks of uncomplicated chocolate. Samplers are available by mail order.

There is a second Turtle Alley at 1 East India Square Mall, Salem, MA (978-740-0660).

## The Village Restaurant

55 Main St.  
Essex, MA

978-768-6400  
www.village-essex.com  
LD | $$

The Village has been a Cape Ann favorite since the 1950s. It is fun to read the early menus posted in the vestibule, not only for their deflated prices ($1 for a nice dinner) but because they show that the kitchen has maintained its character. For travelers in search of traditional North Shore meals, this place is a treasure trove. Here are excellent fried clams, of course, as well as chowders and seafood stews, lobster rolls and lobster pie, and first-rate examples of such regional desserts as baked Grape-Nuts custard, strawberry shortcake on a biscuit, and Indian pudding served piping hot under a scoop of fast-melting ice cream. A fancier dessert, but true to local character, is blueberry bread pudding, made of cornmeal and molasses bread and set afloat in a pool of sweet rum sauce.

Don't get the impression that the Village is hidebound. It has changed with the times too, and stylish twists on tradition include lobster mac 'n' cheese, shrimp scampi bruschetta, and seafood Provence. While you can't go wrong ordering seafood, know that this really is the town café, where the menu is broad enough to please everyone in the family. Fish frowners can enjoy steaks, Tuscan chicken, and a beautiful Village burger—eight ounces of beef complemented by bacon–blue cheese butter and melted mozzarella.

## The White Hut

| | |
|---|---|
| 280 Memorial Ave. | 413-736-9390 |
| West Springfield, MA | BLD \| $ |

You want a fast meal? Really, really fast? Stop in the White Hut around lunchtime, and you can be in and out—and very well fed—in less than five minutes. There are no more than a few counter seats, plus a couple of tables for eating while standing up, so it's not creature comforts that have drawn crowds to this little fortress near the Big E Fairgrounds since 1939. It is cheeseburgers. White Hut offers a modest-sized patty topped with standard American cheese. What puts it into the pantheon is the tangle of grilled onions that every regular customer knows to order as a garnish. In fact, if you forget to order onions, the waitress will ask if you want them anyway. And if you say *hamburger,* she'll shoot back, "You mean cheeseburger?" Meat, cheese, onions: It's the only way.

Sizzled on the grill alongside the hamburgers, hot dogs blossom under a mantle of mustard, relish, and raw onions (applied by the waitress, as you specify), and they are served in a bun that is soft on the inside, but buttered and toasted to a luxurious golden brown on the outside.

A second White Hut location is at 1A Boltwood Walk, Amherst, MA (413-835-0455).

## Woodman's of Essex

| | |
|---|---|
| 121 Main St. | 978-768-6451 |
| Essex, MA | www.woodmans.com |
| | LD \| $$ |

Overlooking a scenic marsh in the heart of the clam belt, where towns have bivalvular names like Ipswich and Little Neck, Woodman's epitomizes a whole style of informal Yankee gastronomy known as "eat in the rough." That means you stand at a counter, yell your order through the commotion, then wait for your number. The food is served on cardboard plates with plastic forks. Carry it yourself to a table (if you can find one that isn't occupied).

A chart we made several years ago comparing and contrasting the top clam shacks along the North Shore evaluated Woodman's clams as follows: Crust crunch = crusty. Chew = resilient. Belly goo = overflowing. Flavor = clamorama! Quantity = substantial. Whole platter presentation = merry jumble. In our experience, Woodman's clams tend to be somewhat larger and gooier than those served in other local places, sometimes a bit too large. Of course, all that depends on what the market has to offer at any given time. But whatever their size, there is no faulting the frying, which results in big mouthfuls that are shattering crisp. Also on the must-eat, fried-food roster are onion rings and French fries, and big, spherical clam fritters. Nor is clam chowder to be ignored.

Woodman's is open year-round.

## Bishop's

183 Cottage St.
Littleton, NH

603-444-6039
www.bishopshomemadeicecream.com
April–Columbus Day | $

Bishop's ice cream flavors range from the baroque—Bishop's Bash is chocolate chips, nuts, and brownie chunks in dark chocolate—to basic. Vanilla is pure and creamy-white; chocolate is like iced chocolate milk more than some ungodly-rich chocolate mousse cake; the coffee is reminiscent of HoJo's—smooth and creamy more than ultracaffeinated. Here too you can savor the old Yankee favorite, Grape-Nuts ice cream, in which the little specks of cereal soften into grainy streaks of flavor in pudding-smooth ice cream.

There is something unusually civilized about coming to Bishop's for ice cream. You'd think that such a happy-time product would stimulate yelps of exuberance and that the interior of the shop would ring with rapture. On the contrary, there is a reverential hush about it, even when Bishop's is jammed and every little table is occupied with ice cream eaters and a hundred are waiting to get inside. Perhaps it's due to the stately old house in which the business is located or the polite way of doing business—wooden cone holders are provided for parking the cone while you pay; or maybe the civilized demeanor is owed to the charm of the ice cream servers, who are extraordinarily solicitous as you choose between a S'mores sundae and a maple sundae, and who want to know, if you order a sundae with butter-crunch and coffee ice cream, which flavor you prefer on top.

## Brown's Lobster Pound

407 Route 286
Seabrook, NH

603-474-3331
www.brownslobsterpound.com
LD (weekends only from mid-Nov–Mar) | $$

For sixty-plus years now, Brown's has been a magnet for people on their way to or from the beach, hungry for all manner of Yankee seafood. It started as a lobster pound, and lobster remains its glory. Pick your own from among the tanks; it will be caught and cooked to order, preferably served with a pile of good Maine steamers. A terrific alternative to the work of a whole lobster is Brown's baked lobster pie: big chunks of meat in a savory crust. Another good lobster option: deep-fried, totally indulgent. The lobster roll is a lobster salad roll, the meat cool, bound in mayo.

Choose from among three types of chowder—corn, fish, and clam—or have a large lobster bisque. Fried seafood is double-dipped and cracker-meal-coated, so it is extra-crunchy—wonderful with big, whole-belly clams, but less wonderful around scallops, which the crust tends to smother.

Brown's is a sprawling place with a dining room reminiscent of an old-time shore dinner hall. Getting the food can be a bit confusing, as you order lobster and steamers at one window, fried food at another. BYOB.

## Gilley's PM Lunch

175 Fleet St.
Portsmouth, NH

603-431-6343
www.gilleyspmlunch.com
LD | $

Gilley's is an old-fashioned night-owl lunch wagon now anchored on Fleet Street in Portsmouth. It was named for Ralph "Gilley" Gilbert, an employee who slung hash here for over fifty years. If it is the wee hours of the morning and all the normal restaurants are closed and even the bars are shut, you can count on this joint to be serving up hamburgers with chocolate milk on the side to a rogues' gallery of city folk who range from derelicts to debutantes. Seven days a week, Gilley's closes at 2:30 a.m.

Many dine standing on the sidewalk, but there is limited indoor seating at a thin counter opposite the order area and galley kitchen. Gathered here under some of the most unflattering lighting on Earth are insomniacs, diehard partiers, and late-shift workers with no other place to eat, feasting on such quick-kitchen fare as chili dogs, French fries gobbed with cheese, and fried egg sandwiches with ultrastrong coffee on the side. The best dish in the house, or at least the one that seems most appropriate in this reprobate restaurant, is the hamburger; actually the cheeseburger . . . no, make that a double cheeseburger. House lingo is as follows. Works = mustard, relish, onion. Loaded = works + ketchup. Pickles and mayonnaise are available, but must be specified by name.

## Hart's Turkey Farm

233 Daniel Webster Hwy. (Route 3)    603-279-6212
Meredith, NH                         www.hartsturkeyfarm.com
                                     LD | $$

At Hart's Turkey Farm, it is Thanksgiving every day of the year except Christmas, when the place is closed. Hart's is not a cozy café, that's for sure—the restaurant is gigantic with a theme-park feel—but there is no faulting the moist, full-flavored meat on the turkey dinners (white, dark, or mixed) in sizes that range from a small plate (3.5 ounces of turkey) to the jumbo plate, which is more than a pound of meat. With the turkey you get stuffing, potatoes, gravy, and cranberry sauce, and a diner with a mighty appetite can pay $6.99 extra to augment the basic meal with beverage, soup, salad, and dessert.

If sliced turkey is not your style, alternatives include turkey tempura, turkey Parmesan, turkey nuggets, turkey livers, turkey croquettes, turkey pie, turkey marsala, and turkey Divan. Not to mention big slabs of prime rib and a full repertoire of pastas and seafood. For those entertaining at home, Hart's offers roasted and ready-to-carve birds up to thirty-six pounds.

## The Ice House

112 Wentworth Rd.           603-431-3086
Rye, NH                     www.theicehouserestaurant.com
                            LD mid-Apr-Oct (closed Mon) | $$

Many people like the Ice House for its ice cream: Richardson's-brand, ranging in flavors from vanilla to death-by-chocolate and rum-flavored frozen pudding. It is very good ice cream, especially when used as the base for signature sundaes such as the S'Mores (vanilla ice cream, crumbled graham crackers, hot fudge, and marshmallow) and the Kitchen Sink (with strawberry, fudge, marshmallow, and pineapple toppings, plus bananas and nuts).

In addition to dessert, there is a whole menu of burgers, hot dogs, baked and broiled fish, and a superb fried fish sandwich (haddock) served with big, hand-cut, battered onion rings. Chowder lovers can avail themselves of a weeklong rotation of different choices, including corn, scallop, and clam, as well as beef or chicken chili. Coleslaw, pickled beets, and three-bean salad are all made on the premises.

Dining facilities include booths in a pine-paneled dining room decorated with an assortment of license plates, as well as picnic tables out back.

## *Polly's Pancake Parlor

Route 117                       603-823-5575
Sugar Hill, NH                  www.pollyspancakeparlor.com
                                BLD (closed in winter) | $$

A few years ago when a documentary film crew from Germany wanted us to take them to a restaurant that was echt New England, we knew exactly where to go: Polly's Pancake Parlor. They were worldly folks and knew about maple syrup, but its celebration at Polly's was, for them, a wondrous experience. If you like pancakes and maple syrup and lovely log-cabin restaurants in the heart of the White Mountain sugarbush, you too may find a visit to Polly's wondrous. We sure do.

The pancakes are made from stone-ground flours or cornmeal, either plain or upgraded with shreds of coconut, walnuts, or blueberries. One order consists of half a dozen three-inchers, and it is possible to get a sampler of several different kinds. They come with the clearest and most elegant fancy-grade maple syrup, as well as maple sugar and mouthwatering maple spread (that last one the consistency of soft cream cheese, but pure maple). You can also get maple muffins, sandwiches made with maple white bread, ice cream with maple hurricane sauce (syrup and apples stewed together), and all sorts of maple candies to take home.

Polly's is surrounded by maple trees that get hung with taps and buckets in the spring, but the most wonderful time to visit is autumn, as the trees turn color. The dining room has a glass-walled porch that overlooks fields where horses graze, and its inside walls are decorated with antiques and tools that have been in the family since the late eighteenth century.

## Rye Harbor Lobster Pound

1870 Ocean Blvd.          603-964-7845

Rye, NH                LD (closed in winter) | $$

The management at Rye Harbor Lobster Pound bills its lobster roll as "infamous." For these parts, it certainly is anomalous: nine out of ten local lobster rolls are lobster *salad* rolls made with cool meat and mayo. This one is hot, and unlike the classic Connecticut-born hot lobster roll, the warm meat isn't just bathed in butter. It is sautéed in butter and sherry, giving it a perfumy twist. Per tradition, it comes in a toasted split-top bun.

Lobster also might play a part in your Rye Harbor chowder. You can have very good creamy clam chowder or ask for it "fluffy"—augmented with hunks of sherry-sopped lobster meat. Whole cooked lobsters and steamers also are available, as are lobster macaroni shells 'n' cheese and lobster gazpacho.

## Sunny Day Diner

Route 3              603-745-4833

Lincoln, NH          BL (closed Tues) | $

It's a sunny day indeed that starts with breakfast at the counter or in a booth at the Sunny Day Diner. A gleaming mid-twentieth-century streamliner that used to be known as Stoney's when it was parked in Dover, it was moved to Lincoln in the late 1980s, and it became the place it is today about ten years after that.

If we describe it as a diner with an elevated culinary consciousness, please do not expect a menu of striving dishes or service that's in any way pretentious. This is a heart-and-soul hash house, its goodness amplified by the fact that nearly everything is made from scratch. Corned beef hash is rich and luxurious, as are biscuits and gravy. You can have French toast made with banana bread and served, of course, with real maple syrup. On the side of eggs and omelets, the toast choice includes white, raisin, oatmeal, rye, and wheat—all made here. Bakery items are a specialty, and it would be wrong not to have at least one muffin or sticky bun. We've yet to have lunch at the Sunny Day, but its Reuben sandwich is legendary.

## Allie's Donuts

3661 Quaker Ln. (Route 2) · 401-295-8036
North Kingstown, RI      B | $

Allie's is so popular that it has two doors, funneling people to separate counters to place their orders. The waiting area is fairly small, but the open kitchen behind it is an immense workspace where powerful mixers whir and deep-fryers bubble. There is no indoor seating. A couple of picnic tables are available outdoors, but most people get their dozens to go or to eat in the front seat of their car. It is common to see people buy a boxful (to take to the office), plus a bag of two or three to eat in the parking lot on the way to the car, or behind the wheel on the way to the office, before the box is opened.

The variety of donuts made each morning is vast, including honey-dipped, glazed crullers, raised jelly sticks, plain cake donuts, coconut-glazed solid chocolates, and a rainbow of jimmie-topped extravaganzas. None are fancy-pants pastries; these are big, sweet, pretty things to eat, the cake variety boasting a crisp skin and creamy insides. In addition to donuts, there are fruit squares, turnovers, and giant donut cakes suitable for slicing into a dozen or more servings.

## Bocce Club

226 St. Louis Ave.                    401-767-2000
Woonsocket, RI                        D | $$

It was at the Bocce Club in the 1920s where the Rhode Island tradition of big, family-style chicken dinners began when the Pavoni family decided to serve meals to friends who came to their house to play bocce. Over the decades, the ad-hoc eatery grew and became a legend, known for rosemary-roasted chicken bathed in butter and olive oil. The main course is preceded by kale soup and/or an effulgent antipasto salad, accompanied by crusty bread, penne noodles in red sauce, and a motley heap of French-fried *and* oven-roasted potatoes.

Bocce Club is famous for chicken, but it has an extensive menu that includes Italian and Portuguese dishes as well as steaks. Our waitress looked crestfallen when we chose chicken for two. "Chicken is where we started," she explained, "but our chef is so good, there is so much more to try." That may be, but to come to the Bocce Club and not eat roast chicken would be like visiting Memphis and ignoring the pork.


## Champlin's Seafood Deck

256 Great Island Rd.                  401-783-3152
Narragansett, RI                      www.champlins.com
                                      LD (closed in winter) | $$

Champlin's is a seafood market and casual eatery at the entrance to Galilee Harbor. Cooked food comes on disposable plates and customers carry their own meals from the kitchen window to bare-topped tables, many of which are perched on a deck overlooking the harbor's boats.

Burgers, hot dogs, and chicken fingers are about the only non-seafood items on a menu that ranges from whole lobsters and raw cherrystones to baked stuffed shrimp and charbroiled swordfish. It is possible to buy your lobster from the retail store, then ask the kitchen to cook it. The cost is $3, including a supply of melted butter. If you come without your nutcracker, you can get one by leaving a $2 deposit with the staff. To accompany lobsters, there are buckets of steamers with broth and butter, and three kinds of chowder: creamy white, Rhode Island red, or South Coast clear broth.

You can get almost any fried seafood, including clams and really good flounder—a broad fillet of sweet, moist meat encased in unobtrusive crust. The flounder is available by the piece or as half of a fish and chips plate. While French fries are fine, we recommend substituting onion rings, which come enveloped in a hopsy batter, or boiled red potatoes, which are cream-textured with an earthy spud flavor.

The one thing we cannot figure out about Champlin's is the kitchen's apparent aversion to garlic. There seems to be none in the snail salad, a Rhode Island specialty that is customarily radiant with a garlic halo, nor in the linguine with white clam sauce.

## *The Commons Lunch

| | |
|---|---|
| 48 Commons | 401-635-4388 |
| Little Compton, RI | BLD | $ |

The Commons Lunch was ten years old when we came upon it in the mid-1970s. We were overjoyed to find so consummate an example of Ocean State roadfood, and for years it remained a favorite destination for square meals that reflected the foodways of southern New England. The place burned down in 2004 but reopened as it always was: a small-town café with authentic Rhode Island food and a clientele of authentic Rhode Islanders.

The state's signature cornmeal pancake, the jonnycake (listed on the menu as Johnny Cake), is always available. These jonnycakes are the elegant, thin variety with lacy edges and a faintly crisp surface sandwiching a fine ribbon of steamy fine yellow meal. Although they resemble pancakes and many people do eat them for breakfast with maple syrup on top, they are suitable as a side dish to lunch and supper as well. Jonnycakes are a good companion to a bowl of ocean-perfumed quahog chowder or a lobster-meat plate lunch of plump, pink claw and knuckle hunks bound in mayonnaise. The Commons Lunch menu is broad, ranging from simple sandwiches and mac 'n' cheese to plates of expertly fried shrimp, clams, scallops, and clam fritters, as well as meat pies that reflect the French heritage of some local citizens. Desserts include the Yankee stalwarts Grape-Nuts pudding and Indian pudding, plus some nice-looking pies.

## Evelyn's Drive-In

| | |
|---|---|
| 2335 Main Rd. | 401-624-3100 |
| Tiverton, RI | www.evelynsdrivein.com/Welcome .htm |
| | BLD (summer only) | $$ |

Most of Evelyn's regulars take a seat inside at tables or the counter, but for us travelers in search of local color as well as local food, picnic tables outside are the place to be. They provide a dreamy view of Sakonnet Bay, Newport shores, and pleasure boats skimming through the water. It is sleeves-up outdoorsy, but we have seen one couple spread a tablecloth across the weathered wood table and open their own wine to accompany lobster dinners.

Many of the locals order non-seafood meals from a broad menu of diner standards such as meat loaf, burgers, chicken pie, and the local oddity known as a chow mein sandwich. Using crisp, full-flavored noodles made by the Oriental Chow Mein Company in Fall River, Massachusetts, it is a plate of soy-sauced gravy and vegetables (and beef or chicken, if desired), made into a nominal sandwich by the addition of a hamburger bun.

Evelyn's is at its best being a seafood shack, so the chow mein is also available as lobster chow mein. But among more normal shoreline fare, you can count on good whole-belly fried clams, fish and chips, clam cakes and chowder (that's South Coast chowder, which is thin and briny), and two-pound seafood platters with some of everything.

Cocktails, beer, and wine are available, as are Grape-Nuts pudding, blueberry pie, and Buddha's chocolate—milk chocolate almond toffee.

## Flo's Clam Shack

4 Wave Ave.  401-847-8141
Middletown, RI  LD March 1-Thanksgiving | $$

Even if you don't come away with a souvenir T-shirt emblazoned with the cry, SMACK MY CLAM AND CALL ME FLO!, you will fondly remember a visit to this good old eatery for its excellent chowders, stuffies, clam cakes, and all manner of fried seafood.

Yes we did say "chowders," plural, because three types are available: creamy New England, South Coast clear, and Rhode Island pink. With an order of clam cakes, a bowl of any of these would make a nice meal. But it would be a shame to visit Flo's without also forking into a stuffie, which is a quahog clamshell loaded with chorizo-charged stuffing, or a serving of nice whole-belly clams or batter-coated fish and chips.

Service is clam-shack casual with tote-your-own trays and disposable dishware. The drink menu includes beer, wine, and mixed drinks. One of the listed specials is a pair of hot dogs and a bottle of Champagne, for $50.

Beware of long lines. You will especially wait for a table on the weekend.

## Gray's Ice Cream

16 East Rd. at Four Corners       401-624-4500
Tiverton, RI                      www.graysicecream.com
                                  $

On a summer day in Tiverton, Gray's parking lot is packed with people who come from miles around to indulge in the time-honored ritual of standing in line at the order window and getting ice cream that ranges from normal flavors to that Yankee oddity, Grape-Nuts. Gray's also is proof that Rhode Island is one of the most coffee-conscious places in the nation. Coffee ice cream here is robust and just-right sweet. The other great Gray's flavor is ginger, made with bits of fresh root that give the creamy scoops a sparkling spicy bite. In the fall, pumpkin and then eggnog join the flavor rotation.

## Haven Brothers

Fulton and Dorrance St. at        401-861-7777
    Kennedy Plz.                  D (late night) | $
Providence, RI

For anyone who thinks food-truck infatuation is a twenty-first-century phenomenon, we recommend a visit to Haven Brothers, an enterprise that has been dishing out street food from a truck since 1888. The short-order menu includes lobster rolls and steak and cheese on toast, but most orders are for hot dogs or hamburgers. The dogs are plump and pink, served in soft steamed buns, available with chili and all the usual condiments. The hamburgers are modest-sized patties, available from plain to deluxe (lettuce, tomato, mayo, and so on). Devotees of junk food will enjoy the triple Murder Burger, which is three patties topped with every condiment in the house, plus bacon, cheese, and chili. Side a Murder Burger with cheese-glopped French fries, and you have a sidewalk meal to reckon with.

The most popular beverage at Haven Brothers is coffee milk—like chocolate milk, but flavored with coffee instead. Or you can have a frappe made with ice cream, milk, and flavoring (what the rest of the world knows as a milk shake).

Honestly, the scene is more alluring than the food. From the time it pulls up to Kennedy Plaza alongside City Hall at 4:30 p.m. to its 5 a.m. closing, the Haven Brothers truck hosts a party of Providence characters who carry on a continuous conversation with the staff, with other customers, or—if no one will listen—with the voices inside their own heads. Dining facilities include two stools at a counter inside, and the steps of City Hall. Most customers eat standing on the sidewalk.

## Jigger's Diner

| | |
|---|---|
| 145 Main St. | 401-884-5388 |
| East Greenwich, RI | BL | $ |

Jigger's, a 1950 Worcester Dining Car with gleaming silver and enamel blue exterior and polished wooden booths, has had more than its share of ups and downs since we first wrote about it in *Gourmet* in the mid-1990s. At that time, it had been closed for a decade, finally reopened with brio in 1992 by Carol Shriner. But after Carol moved away eight years later, it went through a few owners and finally was padlocked once again in 2011. Diner lovers wept. Then, in early 2012, it was brought back to life.

Rhode Island cornmeal jonnycakes continue their role as the heart and soul of the breakfast menu. They are South County–style, meaning they are silver-dollar wide and quite thick (as opposed to the superthin, lace-edged ones typical of restaurants east of the Bay). With real maple syrup ($1.99 extra), they're a great meal unto themselves or a companion to any egg dish, preferably one accompanied by pit-smoked ham or brisket hash.

The lunch menu is salads, sandwiches, wraps, grilled paninis, and hand-pressed burgers—nothing uniquely Rhode Island except for a coffee cabinet, "cabinet" being the Queen State term for milk shake, and coffee being the locally loved flavoring for dairy drinks.

## Johnny Angel's Clam Shack

| | |
|---|---|
| 523 Charlestown Beach Rd. | 401-419-6732 |
| Charlestown, RI | LD (summer only) | $ |

A seasonal clam shack at Shelter Cove Marina, Johnny Angel's is a local fave that offers not only classic Yankee seafood but Wednesday-night pasta suppers. The good eats include New England–style chowder (thick and creamy), whole-belly clams fried to a crisp, and fish and chips. Clam cakes are superb: crisp-skinned, moist inside, and seductively oceanic. For dessert, there is good Windsor Dairy ice cream as well as a selection of donuts from Rhode Island's esteemed Allie's (p. 68).

No indoor seats, but there is a broad deck for picnic-style dining.

## Mike's Kitchen

170 Randall St. (at Tabor-Franchi  401-946-5320
VFW Post 239)  LD | $$
Cranston, RI

Mike's Kitchen serves excellent Italian/Portuguese/Rhode Island food in a VFW hall at reasonable prices. The heart of the menu is a roster of well-made standards such as chicken marsala, veal Française, and tortellini marinara. You can begin a meal with a stuffie (a stuffed quahog clam), a whole artichoke loaded with sausage stuffing, or the unique Ocean State appetizer known as snail salad. Seafood pastas are especially wonderful, offered with a choice of red or white sauce. The top of the line is seafood Diablo—lobster, scallops, and shrimp spread out across a bed of noodles. While most main-course preparations involve a degree of kitchen wizardry, it also is possible to have a simple plate of broiled scallops, swordfish, salmon, or sole. On the side of anything, you want polenta—a cream-soft block of steamy cooked cornmeal that is especially wonderful when accompanied by fennel-spiked sausage. Servings are immense. The chicken Parmesan we ordered provided one full meal in the restaurant and another big one at home the next day.

To drink with your meal, wine and cocktails are available from a bar at one side of the dining room. You will pay for these separately, as the bar is run by the veterans who own the building.

## Olneyville N.Y. System

20 Plainfield St.  401-621-9500
Providence, RI  www.olneyvillenewyorksystem.com
LD | $

Rhode Island's distinctive New York System hot dog, known also as a hot wiener, is a small, pink, natural-casing, pork-beef-veal frankfurter that gets grilled, then inserted in a steamed bun, topped with yellow mustard, chopped raw onions, and a dark sauce of ground beef, plus a sprinkling of celery salt. It's the sauce that makes the dog unique—spicy but not hot, the meat as fine as sand, the flavor vaguely sweet, reminiscent of the kaleidoscopic flavors that give Greek-ancestored Cincinnati Five-Way chili its soul.

Olneyville was opened in the 1930s by the Stevens family, Greek immigrants who came to Rhode Island by way of Brooklyn. It is still a Stevens-family operation, and countermen use the old-time wiener-up-the-arm technique of preparing the hot dogs, lining up six to eight bunned ones from wrist to elbow and spreading sauce, onions, and mustard on all of them in the blink of an eye. A sign posted outside announces the everyday special: "Buy ONE wiener for the price of TWO and receive the second FREE!" As of 2013, the Hot Wiener Challenge record holder was John Munroe, who ate eighteen in forty-five minutes.

One curious item on the short menu is beef stew, which is not beef stew at all. It is an order of salted French fries spritzed with vinegar and ribboned with ketchup. The beverage of choice is the Rhode Island favorite, coffee milk—like chocolate milk, but coffee-flavored.

Two other locations: 1012 Reservoir Avenue, Cranston (401-275-6031) and 1744 Mineral Spring Road, North Providence (401-383-4155).

## Stanley's Famous Hamburgers

535 Dexter St.       401-726-9689
Central Falls, RI       www.stanleyshamburgers.com
      LD Thurs–Sat until 2 a.m. | $

A swell blog called Small Bites ("spices and stories from local eateries in the smallest state") alerted us to the Stanleyburger, a crisp-edged patty customarily grilled with onions and served with pickle chips. While bigger than slider-sized, Stanleyburgers are small enough that we highly recommend a double or two, preferably with cheese, maybe also with bacon and tomato. French fries are crisp and flavorful, available plain, topped with cheese or chili, or Quebec-style, here meaning smothered with mozzarella shreds and dark gravy, a version of *poutine*. Stanley's offers milk shakes, including the Rhode Island preference, coffee shakes; for dessert, the local favorite is Grape-Nuts pudding.

## Wein-O-Rama

1009 Oaklawn Ave.       401-943-4990
Cranston, RI       BLD | $

"The best hot weiners anywhere!" crows the menu at Wein-O-Rama, and in a state crazy for little pink weenies topped with chili, that's a bold assertion. Unlike most wiener restaurants (all of which spell the word *ei* rather than *ie*), this one has a full three-meal-a-day menu, but when the waitress caught us actually reading it, she interrupted our study and demanded to know, "You are not going to try our wieners?!"

Although the term "New York System" appears nowhere at Wein-O-Rama, the dogs served here are exactly what is known by those terms throughout the Providence area. A Wein-O-Rama frank is a small, snappy one buried inside a soft bun, dressed with meaty, vividly spiced sauce, mustard, raw onion, and celery salt. It's a fine harmony in which the several ingredients, none of which is particularly great on its own, combine to make something quite delicious. To drink: Rhode Island's favorite non-alcoholic libation, coffee milk. Rice pudding is dense and fresh, the grains of rice offering a nice al dente resistance.

## Wright's Farm

84 Inman Rd.         401-769-2856
Harrisville, RI        www.wrightsfarm.com
                            D | $$

In the early 1950s, after hosting chicken-dinner picnics for local clubs, the owner of Wright's Chicken Farm opened a restaurant. Today it is the biggest of the Blackstone Valley's chicken dinner halls—one of the biggest restaurants anywhere, with seats for up to 1,500 eaters at a time in multiple dining rooms. On a Friday or Saturday night, you'll park a quarter mile away and you might wait an hour for your party's name to be called on the speaker system. While biding time, you can shop for toys, fudge, and kitschy bric-a-brac in the 4,000-square foot gift shop, try your luck at a window dedicated to selling lottery tickets, or play keno in one of the four bars. Tables are set up for groups of ten and twenty or more. Once seated, you will be waited on and served instantly. When you are done, you pay the waitress with cash. No credit cards are accepted (but there is an ATM machine in the lobby). Everything about the experience is so huge it is hallucinatory.

Once you are at a table, the meal comes quickly because everybody gets the same thing: hot rolls, cool salad, macaroni shells with red sauce, and fabulous thick-cut French fries all orbiting around bowls full of dripping-good roasted chicken enveloped in gossamer skin with booming flavor. What's so especially good about the chicken is that in addition to its fallapart-tender mouthfuls, there are significant surface areas where the skin has pulled away during roasting and the bare exterior of the meat itself turns firm, becoming chewy, moisture-beaded bark with flavor even more intense than the soft, juice-dripping parts within. Meals are all-you-can-eat. If ever a bowl is emptied, it gets replaced with a full one.

Chicken frowners do have an alternative: steak. It is ordered by fewer than 1 percent of Wright's customers.

## Al's French Frys

1251 Williston Rd.
South Burlington, VT

802-862-9203
www.alsfrenchfrys.com
LD | $

Guess what's the specialty at Al's French Frys! Available by the cup, pint, and quart, these spuds are handsome, irregularly cut sticks that are fried before your eyes until their skin turns golden-brown and the edges get crisp. They arrive lightly salted, and the choice of condiments on each table includes vinegar to sprinkle on for zest. The fries are available with cheese sauce or gravy, but why goop up such perfectly made potatoes?

The hamburgers and hot dogs available to go with these fries are perfectly all right, the buns for both griddle-toasted until crisp. If you have a craving for beef, get a double burger; the patties are slider-sized. Milk shakes are made from scratch.

Al's has been around since the late 1940s, when it was known as Al's Snack Bar. Even then, Al's advertised its specialty with the unconventional spelling.

## Art of the Chicken

1C Lemere Sq.  
Ludlow, VT

802-228-7180  
LD | $

Other than a vegetable sandwich, a few side dishes, and excellent apple pie, every dish in the house is chicken. You can start with wings, fingers, or chicken chowder, move on to a CLT sandwich, or a dinner of chicken that has been roasted, deep-fried, or stir-fried. It's not just a gimmick. Every dish we've tried is really good, the chicken impeccably cooked, and its accouterments first-rate: homemade bread, hefty French fries, macaroni salad, and house salad with maple-mustard dressing.

For such a homey place with handcrafted square meals, the location of Art of the Chicken is incongruous: next to a Tacos Tacos in a cluster of commercial enterprise known as Lemere Square.

## Baba-À-Louis

92 Route 11W  
Chester, VT

802-875-4666  
www.babalouisbakery.com  
BL (closed Apr & Nov) | $

While scarcely a restaurant—no hot meals are served in the morning, and only quiche, sandwiches, soup, and a salad bar at lunch—Baba-À-Louis in Chester is one of Vermont's most noteworthy breakfast stops. Since they opened a small storefront bakery in Chester in 1976 (moved to the current location in '97), John McLure and Ruth Zezza have won a reputation for masterful yeast breads. Stop in any day after 7 a.m., find a seat at one of the tables opposite the bakery shelves, and enjoy a cup of coffee while you tear off pieces from a warm baguette, anadama loaf, or sourdough rye. Morning-specific pastries are breathtaking, especially Mr. McLure's sticky buns. Ribboned with a walnutty brown-sugar glaze, these buttery cylinders are so fragile and fine that they verge on croissanthood.

Lunch is served cafeteria-style. There is pizza on the weekends, and Tuesday through Saturday, you can have a panini, open-face, or regular sandwich, quiche or soup or salad.

The place itself is beautiful: a sun-bathed cathedral with a full view of the open kitchen, where doughs are kneaded and breads pulled from ovens.

## *Blue Benn Diner

314 North St.                     802-442-5140
Bennington, VT                    BLD | $

In the morning, it is hypnotic to watch coffeepot-armed waitresses maneu-ver around the cramped confines behind the counter and among the short line of wooden booths of this creaky but ultra-energetic monitor-roof diner that got planted here on Route 7 in 1949. What a joy it is to slide a fork down into a steamy slice of corn-bread French toast or a stack of crunch-berry pancakes with crisp turkey hash on the side. The true-blue hash-house menu offers hearty soups and gravy-topped biscuits as well as more creative fare that includes grilled salmon Caesar salad, soya sausage, and Syrian roll-ups. Every available surface is festooned with handwritten signs advertising literally hundreds of specials, including many choices to please vegetari-ans . . . like a terrific no-meat enchilada.

## Chelsea Royal Diner

487 Marlboro Rd.                  802-254-8399
West Brattleboro, VT              www.chelsearoyaldiner.com
                                  BLD | $

Nestled at the foot of the Green Mountains, the Chelsea Royal (Worcester Dining Car #736) is like a culinary yacht: polished wooden booths and gracefully curving wood ceiling, tiny-check tile floor, everything old but oh-so shipshape. "What can we eat that's real Vermont?" we ask our wait-ress, who wears a "Good Food Fast" T-shirt.

"Blue Plate Special!" she shoots back. Lucky us, it is chicken potpie— comfort food supreme. We get macaroni and (Vermont) cheese and Yankee baked beans on the side and top it off with maple walnut pie and a bowl of that Yankee stalwart, Indian pudding—a luxurious hot cornmeal and mo-lasses cereal that arrives under a crown of vanilla ice cream.

Open every day of the year, and serving breakfast all day long, the Chel-sea Royal is a place to come for scrumptious corned-beef hash or French toast with real maple syrup ($1.25 extra) in the morning and meat loaf with a side of baked beans at supper . . . or such unexpected exotica as a Cajun skillet breakfast or Teriyaki chicken salad lunch. A full fountain offers milk shakes, sundaes, floats, and splits as well as homemade root beer and black cherry soda. The kitchen makes Mexican food Tuesday through Saturday and New England boiled dinner every Monday night. April through October, an ice cream stand offers soft-serve and hard-pack as well as burgers and foot-long hot dogs.

## Curtis' All American Bar B Q

7 Putney Landing Rd. (Exit 4 off I-91)  802-387-5474
Putney, VT                              www.curtisbbqvt.com
                                        LD April-Oct, Weds-Sun | $$

Curtis Tuff's barbecue is more a picnic than a restaurant. Orders are placed and food retrieved from a blue-painted school bus, one of several planted in a meadow outfitted with picnic tables. There is no indoor dining. Dishware is disposable. When you have finished, discard the dishes and drive away.

This rib-and-chicken joint has been around for more than three decades, starting in a time when decent barbecue was an extreme rarity in the Northeast. Now there are pretty fair smokehouse meals from New York to the International Boundary, but even with the growing competition, Curtis's ribs are outstanding. Available as slabs and half slabs, they are painted with a vinegar-tinted red sauce (mild or spicy) that does a fine job of underlining the piggy personality of the meat. Side dishes include corn on the cob, collard greens, baked potatoes loaded with garnishes, and saucy beans that taste especially good when topped with Vermont Cheddar cheese. We are less impressed with the chicken, which is perfectly all right but lacks the juiciness and flavor sparkle of good, smoky pork.

The picnic setting encourages strangers to share tables (especially on a really nice weekend day, when crowds come), making a meal at Curtis' a social as well as culinary event.

## Miss Lyndonville Diner

686 Broad St.                  802-626-9890
Lyndonville, VT                BLD | $

When you see it from the outside, Miss Lyndonville does not look like a classic diner. But there is a real Sterling dining car here, now surrounded by a half century's worth of additions and extra seating. In food and in spirit, Miss Lyndonville is 100 percent diner. You can count on change from a ten-dollar bill at breakfast and lunch; the most expensive dinner on the menu—steak and shrimp—is all of $11.99. True to hash-house tradition, portions are large, service is lightning-fast, and waitresses dish out sassy repartee and wield coffeepots with the aplomb of baton twirlers.

The multipage menu devotes maximum space to breakfast. Breads are baked on-premises, meaning that even standard toast is better than ordinary; cinnamon bread is outstanding, as is French toast (especially cinnamon bread French toast).

Featured lunches include hot turkey and hot pot roast sandwiches and a North Country Special: a one-third-pound hamburg (they drop the *er* at the end of the word hereabouts) with Vermont Cheddar and sliced tomato on grilled house-baked bread. For dinner, you can choose among such blue-plate stalwarts as pot roast, liver and onions, maple-cured ham steak with raisin sauce, and roast turkey with the works. Fresh blueberry and strawberry pie lead the summer dessert menu; there always is a cream pie of the day as well as good-old pudding. Even Jell-O.

## Mrs. Murphy's Donuts

374 Depot St. (Route 30)          802-362-1874
Manchester, VT                    BL | $

A counter stool at Mrs. Murphy's is a box seat in donut heaven. You can get deluxe ones—Boston creams, jelly-filled, iced and jimmie-sprinkled—but we'll take plain sinkers every time. They are the polar opposite of the frivolous fat puffs sold by Krispy Kreme in other parts of the country (but *not* in Vermont). These hefty boys have a wicked crunchy skin and cakey insides that love to sop a while in coffee.

The storefront café is a locals' favorite. It occurred to us one breakfast hour that most customers didn't tell Cheryl the waitress what they wanted; she brought them the usual. One banker-looking guy in striped suit and brogues left his sedan idling outside, stepped up to the takeout counter, grabbed a bag, and flapped it open for Cheryl to load with six sour cream donuts. As she rang him up, he nodded thanks to her and she nodded thanks to him, then he left and drove away; not a word was spoken between them.

## P&H Truck Stop

Exit 17 off I-91                  802-429-2141
Wells River, VT                   Always open (hot food available only
                                  from 6 a.m. to 10 p.m.) | $

P&H is a 24/7 truck stop, not for the fastidious epicure. You need to pass through the aroma of diesel fuel outside to get to the fresh-baked bread and pot roast blanketed with gravy in the dining room. Soups and chowders are especially inviting: tomato-macaroni soup is thick with vegetables, ground beef, and soft noodles; corn chowder is loaded with potatoes and corn kernels and flavored with bacon. We love any kind of sandwich using thick-sliced P&H bread, but the mashed potatoes (*purée de pommes de terre* on the bilingual menu, written for French-Canadian truckers) taste like they were made from powder, and the meat loaf is strictly for die-hard diner fans.

Given the on-premises bakery, breakfast is especially worthwhile. There are big, heavy donuts that demand a dunk in coffee; there are thick slices of swirly cinnamon-raisin bread that make divine buttered toast and even better French toast. Toasted maple-nut bread is another winner, especially when spread with apple jelly. Like everything else you will eat here, pies are hale and hearty: fruit pies, berry pies, custard pies, meringue pies, Reese's pie (a peanut-cream), and maple-cream pie thick as toffee and topped with nuts.

## Papa Pete's

35 Bridge Rd.  
North Hero, VT

802-393-9747  
LD (summer only) | $

As the crow flies, North Hero, Vermont, is practically a neighbor to Plattsburg, New York. But to get from Plattsburg to North Hero by car is nearly an hour's drive, out to Carry Bay in the middle of Lake Champlain. For anyone in search of Michigans, it is a worthwhile journey because it takes you to Papa Pete's and one mighty good Michigan.

In case you are not up on your tube-steak etymology, a Michigan is a style of chili dog unique to the area around northern Lake Champlain, especially Plattsburg (where, allegedly, it first was configured): a plump little dog in a large, soft roll that is closed off at its ends to hold maximum amounts of the meaty sauce. Mustard and raw onions are traditional condiments. Papa Pete's, a tiny snack shack with a walk-up window and picnic-table accommodations, offers not only classic Michigans but hamburgers enlivened by the same glowing Michigan sauce.

Beyond Michigans, this is a surprising little place, offering such non-snack-shack amenities as freshly baked rolls and hand-cut French fries. Less a surprise, considering its proximity to Canada, Pete's also serves *poutine*. On weekends, an on-premises smoker yields ribs and pulled pork.

## *Up for Breakfast

4935 Main St.                          802-362-4204

Manchester, VT                         BL | $$

It can be difficult to order pancakes at Up for Breakfast because the menu also beckons with red flannel hash, griddle-cooked muffins, Benedicts, frittatas, and French toast. But oh, those pancakes! Three kinds are available, with or without blueberries in the batter. Buttermilk pancakes are sunny-hued and fluffy, easy to eat; those made from buckwheat batter are dark and serious; the sourdough cakes are breathtaking. The first thing you notice about the sourdoughs is the sound they make when you press the edge of a fork to one of them. You hear a faint crunch as the tine breaks through a lacy crust. Inside the chewy web that encloses them, they are thin but substantial, with the vigorous disposition of an old sourdough starter that has had years to develop its tang. Pair this with a generous infusion of sweet-tart blueberries and some of that woodsy syrup—served warm, praise be—and maybe an order of Up for Breakfast's wild turkey hash, and you'll understand why Vermont can claim the title of America's Breakfast Destination.

You really do go *up* for breakfast—to a cozy, second-story restaurant with window views of Main Street. There is pleasant art on the walls, and if you sit toward the back, you can enjoy watching goings-on in the semi-open kitchen. Seats can be scarce, but if you are looking for something extra-special in the morning, Up for Breakfast is a gold mine worth the wait.

## Wayside Restaurant

1873 US Route 302                      802-223-6611

Berlin, VT                             BLD | $

Closing in on a century in business, the Wayside Restaurant remains an oasis of such true-Vermont fare as salt pork and milk gravy, fresh native perch, old-fashioned boiled dinner, and red flannel hash. Even if you are not on a mission to eat regional arcana, you can be sure of good food, priced right, in this cheerful town lunchroom. Meals start with glossy-topped dinner rolls, warm from the oven. How nice it is to tear off a piece of roll and dunk it into a bowl of Wayside beef barley soup—a hearty brew so thick with meat and pearly grain that a spoon literally stands up in it. What a feast the Wednesday chicken pie is, piled into a big crockery boat with dressing and a crusty biscuit, with a great heap of gravy-dripping mashed potatoes on the side. Pot roast comes piled high on a plate under a mantle of good gravy. Even franks and beans are a cut above: Quality sausages and good beans come with a square of crumbly, barely sweet corn bread.

In addition to such classic North Country sweets as Grape-Nuts pudding, mince pie, and homemade ginger snaps, the dessert repertoire includes apple pie made with densely packed hand-cut apples in a fork-crimped crust and maple cream pie. Low and flat, the filling of the maple pie is too delicious for words. Its radiant band of amber cream is complex, powerful, and elegant the way only pure maple can be, and it resonates on your taste buds after a Wayside meal like a Yankee cordial.

# Mid-Atlantic

Delaware

*

District of Columbia

*

Maryland

*

New Jersey

*

New York

*

Pennsylvania

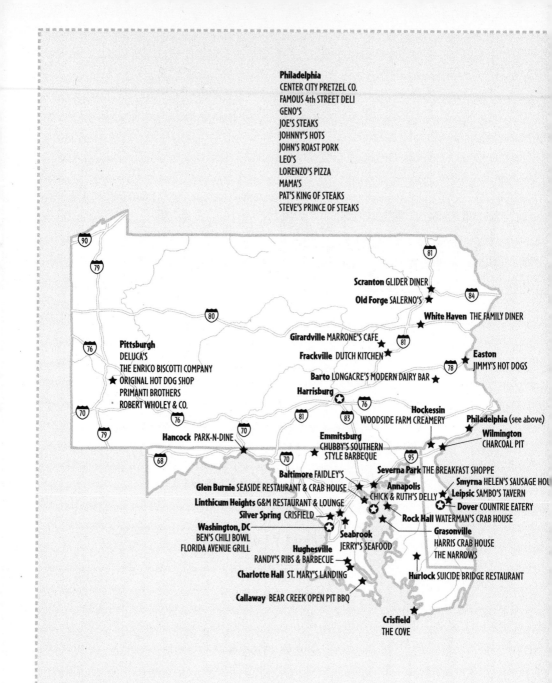

**Philadelphia**
CENTER CITY PRETZEL CO.
FAMOUS 4th STREET DELI
GENO'S
JOE'S STEAKS
JOHNNY'S HOTS
JOHN'S ROAST PORK
LEO'S
LORENZO'S PIZZA
MAMA'S
PAT'S KING OF STEAKS
STEVE'S PRINCE OF STEAKS

**Scranton** GLIDER DINER
**Old Forge** SALERNO'S

**White Haven** THE FAMILY DINER

**Girardville** MARRONE'S CAFE
**Frackville** DUTCH KITCHEN

**Easton**
JIMMY'S HOT DOGS

**Barto** LONGACRE'S MODERN DAIRY BAR

**Pittsburgh**
DELUCA'S
THE ENRICO BISCOTTI COMPANY
ORIGINAL HOT DOG SHOP
PRIMANTI BROTHERS
ROBERT WHOLEY & CO.

**Harrisburg**

**Hockessin**
WOODSIDE FARM CREAMERY

**Philadelphia** (see above)

**Wilmington**
CHARCOAL PIT

**Hancock** PARK-N-DINE

**Emmitsburg**
CHUBBY'S SOUTHERN
STYLE BARBEQUE

**Severna Park** THE BREAKFAST SHOPPE

**Baltimore** FAIDLEY'S

**Smyrna** HELEN'S SAUSAGE HOU
**Leipsic** SAMBO'S TAVERN

**Glen Burnie** SEASIDE RESTAURANT & CRAB HOUSE
**Annapolis**
CHICK & RUTH'S DELLY

**Linthicum Heights** G&M RESTAURANT & LOUNGE
**Dover** COUNTRIE EATERY

**Silver Spring** CRISFIELD
**Rock Hall** WATERMAN'S CRAB HOUSE

**Washington, DC**
BEN'S CHILI BOWL
FLORIDA AVENUE GRILL

**Seabrook**
JERRY'S SEAFOOD

**Grasonville**
HARRIS CRAB HOUSE
THE NARROWS

**Hughesville**
RANDY'S RIBS & BARBECUE

**Charlotte Hall** ST. MARY'S LANDING
**Hurlock** SUICIDE BRIDGE RESTAURANT

**Callaway** BEAR CREEK OPEN PIT BBQ

**Crisfield**
THE COVE

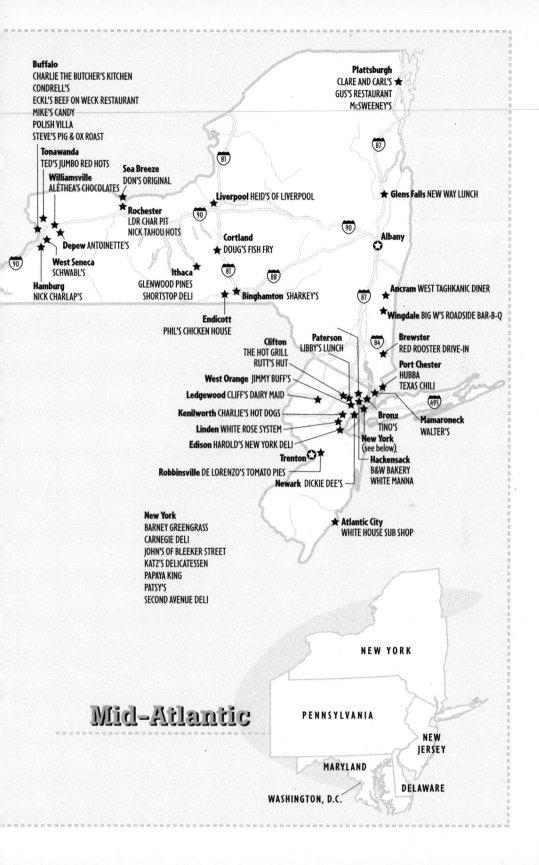

**Buffalo**
CHARLIE THE BUTCHER'S KITCHEN
CONDRELL'S
ECKL'S BEEF ON WECK RESTAURANT
MIKE'S CANDY
POLISH VILLA
STEVE'S PIG & OX ROAST

**Tonawanda**
TED'S JUMBO RED HOTS

**Williamsville**
ALÉTHEA'S CHOCOLATES

**Sea Breeze**
DON'S ORIGINAL

**Rochester**
LDR CHAR PIT
NICK TAHOU HOTS

**Depew** ANTOINETTE'S

**West Seneca**
SCHWABL'S

**Hamburg**
NICK CHARLAP'S

**Ithaca**
GLENWOOD PINES
SHORTSTOP DELI

**Liverpool** HEID'S OF LIVERPOOL

**Cortland**
DOUG'S FISH FRY

**Binghamton** SHARKEY'S

**Endicott**
PHIL'S CHICKEN HOUSE

**Plattsburgh**
CLARE AND CARL'S ★
GUS'S RESTAURANT
McSWEENEY'S

★ **Glens Falls** NEW WAY LUNCH

**Albany** ✪

**Ancram** WEST TAGHKANIC DINER

**Wingdale** BIG W'S ROADSIDE BAR-B-Q

**Clifton**
THE HOT GRILL
RUTT'S HUT

**West Orange** JIMMY BUFF'S

**Ledgewood** CLIFF'S DAIRY MAID

**Kenilworth** CHARLIE'S HOT DOGS

**Linden** WHITE ROSE SYSTEM

**Edison** HAROLD'S NEW YORK DELI

**Trenton** ✪

**Robbinsville** DE LORENZO'S TOMATO PIES

**Newark** DICKIE DEE'S

**Paterson**
LIBBY'S LUNCH

**Brewster**
RED ROOSTER DRIVE-IN

**Port Chester**
HUBBA
TEXAS CHILI

**Bronx**
TINO'S

**Mamaroneck**
WALTER'S

**New York**
(see below)

**Hackensack**
B&W BAKERY
WHITE MANNA

★ **Atlantic City**
WHITE HOUSE SUB SHOP

**New York**
BARNEY GREENGRASS
CARNEGIE DELI
JOHN'S OF BLEEKER STREET
KATZ'S DELICATESSEN
PAPAYA KING
PATSY'S
SECOND AVENUE DELI

**Mid-Atlantic**

NEW YORK

PENNSYLVANIA

NEW JERSEY

MARYLAND

DELAWARE

WASHINGTON, D.C.

## Charcoal Pit

2600 Concord Pike (Route 202)     302-478-2165
Wilmington, DE                    www.charcoalpit.net
                                  LD | $

Charcoal Pit's hamburger is a quarter-pound patty with a smoky taste, served on a big, spongy bun, either plain or in the deluxe configuration, which adds lettuce, tomato, and pickle. For those who crave extra meat, there is also a double-size eight-ounce hamburger, but in our opinion, that defeats the mid-twentieth-century charm of the meal. (The Charcoal Pit opened for business in 1956.) Fries on the side are savory, normal-size twigs with a nice tough skin and soft potato flavor. And the milk shakes are so thick that the long-handled spoon provided is much more useful than a straw. Crab cakes, while no competition for the Chesapeake Bay's best, are nice: hardball-shaped spheres with crusty outsides and a fair measure of crab. They're made here every Monday, Wednesday, and Friday.

We like this old-fashioned place with its comfy maroon booths and wall décor that includes vintage menus. Waitresses go about their job with aplomb and an attitude that make customers feel part of a cheap-eats ritual that has gone on forever.

Another Charcoal Pit is located in Prices Corner at Kirkwood Highway and Greenbank Road.

## Countrie Eatery

950 North State St.  
Dover, DE

302-674-8310  
www.countrieeatery.com  
BLD | $

The Countrie Eatery is especially notable for breakfast: buttermilk pancakes filled with blueberries or chocolate chips and topped with fruits, nuts, or syrup; creamed chipped beef on toast; and three-egg omelets served in a skillet. Among noteworthy side dishes are grits, corned-beef hash, and scrapple that is fried until crunchy on the outside, but moist and porky within.

At lunch you can have a half-pound hamburger, a hot sandwich made with turkey, meat loaf, or roast beef with mashed potatoes and gravy, or a cheese-topped crab melt on an English muffin. Desserts include rice pudding, bread pudding, an apple dumpling, layer cakes, and fruit pies.

Ambience is country-craftsy Colonial with primitive art and old-time farm implements on the wall.

## Helen's Sausage House

4866 N. Dupont Hwy.  
Smyrna, DE

302-653-4200  
www.helenssausagehouse.com  
BL | $

If you are hungry and rushing north toward the Delaware Valley Bridge anytime between four in the morning and lunch (or on Sunday, starting at 7 a.m.), call Helen's and place a sandwich order. That's the way the truckers do it, and in this case, the truckers are on to a very good thing. Helen's Sausage House is a roadside eatery with big sandwiches at small prices.

The sausages are thick and crusty giants with plenty of Italian zest. They spurt juice when you bite them, and a normal sandwich is two in a roll (although wimpy appetites can get a single). With fried green peppers and onions, it is a majestic arrangement—a little messy to eat but nevertheless one of the great sausage sandwiches anywhere.

Helen's offers all manner of breakfast sandwich on bread or rolls, made with eggs, bacon, scrapple, and fried ham; as well as lunchtime sandwiches of steak, cheesesteak, burgers, hot beef, and hot ham. Other than the sausage, the must-eat (and must-see!) meal is Helen's pork chop sandwich. When the menu says *jumbo* pork chop, you better believe it. This slab of meat is approximately three times larger than the puny pieces of white bread that are stuck on either side of it. It isn't all that thick a chop, but it is tender, moist, and mouth-wateringly spiced.

While most of Helen's clientele stop by for sandwiches to go, it is possible to dine here. Place your order at the counter and carry it to a table opposite the instant-order counter, or proceed into a dining room decorated entirely with pictures of Elvis. Roadfood extraordinaire!

## Sambo's Tavern

| | |
|---|---|
| 283 Front St. | 302-674-9724 |
| Leipsic, DE | LD April–Oct \| $$$ |

Bring plenty of money to eat at Sambo's, even though there is little in the way of décor and few frivolous amenities at the big waterman's tavern where cold beer goes best with just about everything. The full Mid-Atlantic seafood menu includes creamy crab soup, plush crab cakes, rockfish and chips, spiced shrimp, and fried fish of all kinds. Good as all that may be, newspapers on the table are a telltale sign that this is an establishment primarily devoted to the ritual of a crab feast. The disposable tablecloths, paper-towel napkins, hammers, and picks are at the ready to attack piles of hard-shelled crabs that radiate Old Bay spice. They're delicious, and the big ones will cost plenty; for crab fanciers, a meal like this is well worth the Benjamins.

Note: all customers must be of drinking age.

## Woodside Farm Creamery

| | |
|---|---|
| 1310 Little Baltimore Rd. | 302-239-9847 |
| Hockessin, DE | www.woodsidefarmcreamery.com |
| | (closed in winter) \| $ |

Woodside Farm is home of the Hog Trough Sundae. That's five flavors of ice cream—two scoops of each—topped with three different toppings, a fresh banana, whipped cream, and a cherry. For less gluttonous sorts, there are normal-sized cups, cones, and sundaes too, all featuring ice cream made the old-fashioned way, by taking high-butterfat milk and turning it into sweet cream. The sweet cream is mixed with fruit, flavors, and nuts and frozen in small batches to be sold at the farm's stand. Jim Mitchell, whose family settled here in 1796, likes to tell visitors, "Two weeks ago, our ice cream was grass." Mr. Mitchell credits the goodness of his ice cream to the fact that the milk's source is his herd of Jersey cows (superior to Guernseys), whom he keeps happy by grazing them on fields of sweet grass.

Flavors range from chocolate and coffee to pumpkin pecan and butter brickle toffee. It is wonderfully normal ice cream, by which we mean it is not sickeningly butterfatty or cloying with too many mix-ins. The ingenuous true-farm flavor is especially welcome in varieties made with fresh fruit: peach, strawberry, black raspberry, and black cherry.

## *Ben's Chili Bowl

1213 U St. NW
Washington, DC

202-667-0909
www.benschilibowl.com
LD | $

It is possible to get only chili at Ben's Chili Bowl, the landmark lunch counter on U Street in the nation's capital; but even the President of the United States (a Ben's customer when the wife isn't looking) knows that the best way to enjoy the mahogany-brown ground-meat stew is atop a half-smoke. That's the city's unique tube steak—a plump, gently smoked beef-and-pork sausage link that gets sizzled on a hot griddle until its skin turns snapping-crisp. Served in a bun with mustard and onions, it's swell without chili; but when smothered, it may well be the ultimate chili dog. Ben's half-smokes are presented in a red plastic basket and hopefully accompanied by the kitchen's fine French fries, then topped off with a slice of sweet-potato pie, sweet-potato cake, or strawberry layer cake.

Big as its reputation is, Ben's remains a relaxed and easygoing diner, part of the neighborhood since 1958, surviving urban unrest and economic ups and downs. In 2001, its founders, Ben and Virginia Ali, were inducted into the Washington, DC, Hall of Fame. Today the restaurant is run by their sons.

## Florida Avenue Grill

1100 Florida Ave.
Washington, DC

202-265-1586
www.floridaavenuegrill.com
BLD | $

America is overpopulated with subpar or merely adequate biscuits, which is why discovery of excellent ones is cause for joy. In the cool, pre-dawn hours at the counter or in a booth at the Florida Avenue Grill, they are served two by two, warm enough so you can only gingerly grab the top and bottom of one to pull it into halves, all the better for the fleecy interior to absorb a cascade of spicy, sausage-crowded, cream-thick gravy. A smothered pair is adequate breakfast for modest appetites or an awesome side dish with fried pork chops, grits, and stewed apples. Alternate breakfast meats include crisp-fried scrapple and bisected half-smoke sausages.

Breakfast is the best meal of the day, but lunch and supper are special too. It is possible to order such soul-food standards as pigs' feet and chitterlings, but unless you are already a feet or intestine aficionado, we suggest you begin with more familiar things to eat. Spare ribs, for example, glazed with breathless hot sauce, are rugged and satisfying. For a tender meal, how about meat loaf, served with a side of mashed potatoes and a heap of collard greens? True to southern custom, there are lots of sides to accompany the entrees: candied sweet potatoes, mac 'n' cheese, lavish potato salad, rice, beans, peas, and always sweet corn bread for mopping up a plate.

Long a favorite destination for Washington's power brokers as well as blue-collar folk, and just a quick cab ride from Capitol Hill, the Grill's walls are plastered with 8 × 10 photos of officeholders and sports stars who all are fans of the long-lasting soul-food diner. If you value honest eats, this humble restaurant with its sprung-spring booths, pink counter, and red plastic stools is choice. It is cheap, fast, and the motherly waitresses make even pale-faced strangers feel right at home.

## Bear Creek Open Pit BBQ

20294 Point Lookout Rd.　　　301-994-1030
Callaway, MD　　　　　　　www.bearcreekbarbq.com
LD | $

Over a capacious open pit, chef Curtis Shreve cooks pork and beef so tender that if you look at it hard, it falls apart. We are especially fond of the pork, either hand-pulled into shreds or sliced. It has a smoky flavor and a piggy richness that defies description. It is good enough to need no sauce whatsoever, all the better to savor the flavor of the meat. (Mr. Shreve's sauce, we should say, is excellent: sweet, gently spicy, and mildly addictive.)

Mr. Shreve originally hails from the Louisiana/Texas area, so his cooking reflects southwest roots too. Corn dogs are reminiscent of those at the Texas State Fair, and chili is the sleeper on the menu. It's a meat-and-bean stew with assertive but not incendiary spices, served under a mantle of grated cheese. Here also is that miraculous Texas twist on chili known as Fritos pie: a bed of crisp corn chips topped with chili and spangled with Cheddar cheese and chopped raw onions. Shreve remembered, "When I was a kid years ago, they used to take a scoop of chili and put it right in the bag of Fritos and you ate it just like that. Now the bags are made of plastic that does not withstand the heat. So we serve our Fritos pie in a dish."

## The Breakfast Shoppe

552 Ritchie Hwy.         410-544-8599

Severna Park, MD       www.thebreakfastshoppe.com

BL | $

Start with fresh OJ, then move on to buckwheat pancakes with molasses syrup, omelets and egg scrambles, eggs Benedict in various configurations (including one made with Nova Scotia lox), or a megameal known as the Backpacker. That's eggs, sausage, ham, bacon, potatoes, peppers, onions, spinach, broccoli, tomatoes, and jack cheese all loaded into a hot iron skillet that is set upon a trivet on the table.

Pancakes are terrific, available as tall stacks (five), normal stacks (three), short stacks (two), and singly. In addition to buckwheat, there are banana-nut cakes and pancakes topped with strawberry marinade. Creamed chipped beef, a fairly scarce Mid-Atlantic delight, is a house specialty, served on thick-cut challah bread with fried potatoes on the side.

The staff of swift waitresses makes life here friendly. Ours was always ready to refill coffee cups and to offer her own huzzahs about the menu items she likes best. When we told her how much we were enjoying our meal, she responded, "I know; it's so good. This is where I eat on my days off!"

## Chick & Ruth's Delly

165 Main St.          410-269-6737

Annapolis, MD       www.chickandruths.com

BLD | $

Being near the District of Columbia, Chick & Ruth's Delly has its own twist on the kosher-style restaurant theme of giving celebrity monikers to sandwiches. Here house specialties carry the names of politicians ranging from Sen. Barbara Mikulski (open-face tuna and cheese on a bagel) to Annapolis Fire Chief David Stokes (ham, turkey, Swiss, lettuce, and tomato on whole wheat toast). Traditional deli-meat sandwiches are swell and, satisfying as the regular-sized ones are, Chick & Ruth's has a separate category of novelty sandwiches dubbed "colossal," which means up to three pounds per sandwich. (You might want to accompany that with a colossal milk shake, which is all of six pounds and costs $17.95.)

Improbable specialties of the kosher-style (but definitely not kosher) eatery include barbecued ribs, fried shrimp, and crab cakes. "I know most people don't think of crab cakes when they think about good deli food," says

Teddy Levitt, whose father started the business in 1965, "but this is crab country. We get the best crab and I believe we make the best cakes." They are available on a surf 'n' turf platter with a T-bone steak or as a seafood combo with fried clams and shrimp. Levitt attributes their moistness to the fact that the meat is cooked quickly at a high temperature. "The longer you take, the greater the chance it will dry out," he explains.

As you may have ascertained by now, Chick & Ruth's is not the place to come for a quiet, private, or intimate conversation. It is fun and disheveled, full of life, and so cramped that if you sit in one of the booths opposite the counter, you will be within inches of the stranger next to you.

## Chubby's Southern Style Barbeque

16430 Old Frederick Rd.    301-447-3322
Emmitsburg, MD    www.chubbysbbq.net
LD | $$

A plain place in the beautiful countryside south of Gettysburg, Chubby's has become a destination dining spot for lovers of barbecued pork. Smoke-meister Tom Caulfield marinates and dry rubs ribs, cooking them low and slow until drippingly tender, serving them with a choice of sauces that includes South Carolina mustard–style, North Carolina vinegar-pepper, and the most familiar tomato sweet/tangy. Caulfield's pulled pork is soft and smoky, and baked beans are liberally laced with shreds of it. Side dishes are fine smokehouse standards such as collard greens, French fries (superb), corn bread, and in-season corn on the cob.

The menu is broad and also includes non-barbecued daily items that range from cream of crab soup to a fried bologna sandwich to a tilapia platter. Several years ago Washington Redskins lineman Randy Thomas made pig-out history by consuming six pounds of Chubby's food in less than an hour. His menu included a pound of brisket, two and a half pounds of ribs, a pound of shrimp scampi, a pound of chili, three-quarters of a pound of crab dip, cheese-garlic toast, cheesecake, and a pumpkin parfait. His beverage of choice was a gallon of iced tea. Anyone else seeking glory is invited to take the "Avalanche Challenge": Eat a pair of Avalanche Burgers (each of which is composed of four quarter-pound cheeseburgers, four hot links, and all the fixins on a triple-decker roll) in one sitting, in one hour, with no bathroom visits, and you get it for free, plus a $100 gift certificate, a T-shirt, and your picture on the wall of fame. If you fail, the meal will cost $39.95.

## The Cove

718 Broadway            410-968-9532
Crisfield, MD           LD | $$

Crisfield's water tower is emblazoned with the image of a crab, and while there are many seafood restaurants in town where the Chesapeake Bay crustacean stars, we like the Cove. A modest, somewhat threadbare place just off the main drag, it is worth knowing about if you like crab cakes. The Cove's are especially creamy, perhaps not as lumpy-luxurious as those of crab houses farther north, but rich and fresh and satisfying. They are available as full-sized cakes or as mini cakes on a bun, aka crab-cake sliders. The right way to have the full-sized cake is broiled, and we think that works just as well on the slider version, but it is possible to have the cake fried. The result is a crunchy crust with moist meat inside, the good ocean flavor of the crab somewhat muted by its hot-oil bath. The other items we have sampled from the Cove's seafood menu were all unremarkable.

Several cakes are available for dessert, including the local specialty (and official state dessert of Maryland), Smith Island cake. Resembling a Hungarian *dobos torte,* it is ten microthin layers of yellow cake interleaved with ribbons of fudgy chocolate frosting. While the cake itself is not dramatically excellent, its extravagant layering is a sugar-rush indulgence. Several mainland bakeries in Salisbury and Ocean City make Smith Island cake, but the Cove is proud of the fact that the slices it serves are the real deal, cut from cakes brought by ferry from a baker on nearby Smith Island.

## Crisfield

8012 Georgia Ave.         301-589-1306
Silver Spring, MD        LD | $$$

Crisfield's is expensive, but no-frills. The room you enter is like a bar, with a long counter running along both sides and stools where people sit to eat and drink. The adjoining dining room has walls covered with white tile and cinderblocks, with all the charm of a locker room. Service is brusque and efficient, yet dinner for two can eat up most of a hundred-dollar bill.

We'll happily pay the prices because some of the food served here is top-drawer. Crisfield is a fish house with regional specialties you simply don't find many places anymore: seafood Norfolk-style (that is, swimming in butter), and huge fillets of flounder, broiled or fried or heaped with fresh lump crabmeat, as well as oysters and softshell crabs in season.

We have found the "Crisfield special" (lump crabmeat mixed with a bit of mayo and baked until golden brown) to be erratic: one time fresh and sweet, another tired; but the crab-stuffed flounder has never been a disappointment. It is a gigantic, milky-white fillet covered with a full-flavored crown of crab. We also liked the "Combination Norfolk"—hunks of crab, whole shrimp, and pieces of lobster all crowded into a skillet up to their waistlines in melted butter. It's a simple preparation, but unbeatable.

## *Faidley's

203 N. Paca St.      410-727-4898
Baltimore, MD       www.faidleyscrabcakes.com
                    LD | $$

You may think you know what a great crab cake tastes like, but until you have eaten one at Faidley's, you cannot be sure. Forget all the spongy, bready, fishy blobs that pass as crab cakes in most other places; here is the paradigm: a baseball-sized sphere of jumbo lump crab meat held together with minimal crushed-saltine filler and a whisper of mayo and mustard that is just enough to be a foil for the marine sweetness of the meat. While Faidley's offers "regular" crab cakes, made from shredded claw meat, and backfin crab cakes, made from slightly larger strips of body meat, the one you want is the "all lump crab cake." It is significantly more expensive than the others, but the silky weight of the big nuggets, which are the choicest meat picked from the hind-leg area of the blue crab, is what makes these cakes one of the nation's most memorable local specialties.

Operated by the same family that started it in 1886—and who still form each jumbo lump cake by hand—Faidley's is fortuitously located on one side of the boisterous, centuries-old food emporium known as the Lexington Market. Amenities are minimal. Stand up to order, then stand up to eat at chest-high tables provided. You can down raw oysters at the oyster bar, and in addition to crab cakes, the menu includes both Maryland crab soup (red) and cream of crab soup, as well as the Baltimore fish cake known as a coddie, composed of cod, mashed potato, and onion. Whereas jumbo lump crab cakes are the top of the line at well over $10 each, a coddie costs less than $3.

## G&M Restaurant & Lounge

804 N. Hammonds Ferry Rd.          410-636-1777
Linthicum Heights, MD              www.gandmcrabcakes.com
                                   LD | $$$

G&M is practically the only restaurant where we would recommend ordering stuffed shrimp. Given the usual flaccidity of the dish, we were not inclined to do so until our waitress passionately recommended them, guaranteeing that the stuffing of these shrimp was all crab. We took the plunge and got a trio (at nearly $30; G&M is not cheap). Each of three big, buff shrimp was heaped with its own virtual crab cake—a pile of pearly white lumps separated by one-dimensional lines of spicy filler that do for crab what salt does for sirloin.

G&M's crab cakes, which come two to an order, sport the biggest possible lumps. You can count the pieces of meat in each one, those from the interior glistening, resilient and all white, those forked off the outside offering a browned facet with faint crunch. The crab is so regal that it is a perfect fit for crab imperial, the butter-rich casserole infused with a shot of Greek spice.

As noted above, G&M is at the high end of the Roadfood cost scale. A nice dinner for two with a few drinks easily can hit triple-digit prices. But if you are looking for a grand Baltimore meal in a dining room with such amenities as nondisposable flatware and white tablecloths, it's hard to beat. Beyond legendary crab meat, the menu is extensive, including such local specialties as broiled rockfish and fried oysters as well as yet-to-be-sampled temptations as Chesapeake chicken (stuffed with crab meat) and Baltimore's take on German sauerbraten—sour beef and potato dumplings.

## Harris Crab House

433 N. Kent Narrows Way           410-827-9500
Grasonville, MD                    www.harriscrabhouse.com
                                   LD | $$$

Long tables are covered with brown wrapping paper. The big, airy dining room and outdoor deck pulse with the beat of crab shells cracking and people slurping up sweet pink meat. Buy big ones by the dozen and feast, the Chesapeake Bay way. Alternatives to the full-bore crab feast include steamed spiced shrimp and fried shrimp, cherrystone clams by the pail, snow crab by the bucket, stuffed softshells, even steak and chicken and ribs. One appetizer known as Cajun mac 'n' cheese is not particularly Cajun, but is pretty damn wonderful: shrimp and crawfish plus bacon are mixed into the noodles along with sharp, smoky cheese. None of this food is inexpensive, but it tastes as rich as it costs.

Of the several profligate desserts (fudge brownie cake, Key lime pie, turtle cheesecake), one holds tremendous appeal to those of us who share a forbidden love of gas-station ice cream—those inexcusably bad but somehow alluring King Kones, Drumsticks, and so on. This is Harris's own Nutty Buddy, made with actual quality ice cream, crisp nuts, and decent chocolate.

## Jerry's Seafood

9364 Lanham-Severn Rd.  302-645-6611
Seabrook, MD  www.jerrys-seafood.com
L Mon-Fri; D Tues-Sat | $$$

Surefire tipster Joe Heflin described Jerry's Seafood to us as the "best overall Maryland seafood restaurant without a view." He warned that the ambience is nondescript—Jerry's is located in a strip mall—and we should expect long lines any evening, especially weekends.

No problem. We'll gladly wait for this extraordinary DC-area seafood treasure. Nor do we need to be soaking up ambience when we have one of Jerry's Crab Bombs on a plate in front of us. This is a fairly gigantic (ten-ounce) and expensive (more than $30) crab cake that is nothing more than fresh jumbo lump meat, Old Bay seasoning, and just enough mayonnaise to make it cling together, baked until a fragile crust develops all around the edges but the inside is still dripping-sweet. Even better for those with a yen for spice thrills is the firecracker crab bomb, to which mustard and pepper are added. Jerry's also makes a six-ounce Baby Bomb and ordinary-sized crab cakes about which the menu boasts, "Absolutely no filler!"

Mr. Heflin's other recommendation was crab soup, a virtuoso balance of creaminess, crabbiness, and sharp spice. You can also eat velvety crab imperial perked up with peppers, crab dip, and crab bisque made with sherry. Those who are anti-crab can revel in fried shrimp, scallops, and oysters, all with a light fragile crust, as well as good side dishes that the menu promises are from Jerry's mom's recipes: stewed tomatoes and coleslaw.

Jerry's has a second location at 15211 Major Lansdale Boulevard in Bowie, MD (301-805-2284).

## The Narrows

3023 Kent Narrows Way S.          410-827-8113
Grasonville, MD                   www.thenarrowsrestaurant.com
                                  LD | $$$

Here is an extraordinarily handsome Eastern Shore restaurant in a breath-taking setting overlooking the Kent Narrows at the eastern end of the Chesapeake Bay Bridge. The menu is broad, including $30+ steak dinners, sandwiches and salads, hamburgers, cioppino, and barbecued quail accompanied by Smithfield ham in a balsamic glaze.

Great stuff, what little of it we have sampled, but we likely wouldn't include this fairly pricey place in *Roadfood* if it weren't for two great local specialties, crab cakes and oysters. The crab cakes are the purest ever: jumbo lump crab piled into a mound and just barely kissed by a bit of spice in the ridiculously minimal filler. As your fork touches the cake, chances are good it will tumble into big lumps, their outside surfaces faintly brown and barely crisp, the interior nothing but moist, warm, and fragrant.

Oysters, breaded in cornmeal and fried, are known hereabouts as White Gold, and what's so magnificent about them is that although they have been cooked, the meat of the oysters retains all of its fluid sensuousness—as much as a raw one, but even more intense because of its warmth and the frail cornmeal crust with which the oyster melds. You can get a great big plate of them or have them as the ne plus ultra topping of a Caesar salad.

## Park-N-Dine

189 E. Main St.                   301-678-5242
Hancock, MD                       www.park-n-dine.com
                                  BLD | $

If you are traveling through the narrowest part of western Maryland in Hancock and find yourself hankering for meat and potatoes or a bountiful breakfast, pull up to Park-N-Dine. Located alongside I-70 and at the end of the bike trail from Indian Springs along the C&O Canal, this venerable establishment is a blast from the past (1946) where uniformed waitresses are pros and where the kitchen still practices the craft of from-scratch cooking.

Kudos to the old-fashioned roast turkey dinner with mashed potatoes, stuffing, and gravy. Sandwiches and hamburgers are available, but the charm of Park-N-Dine for us is its seven-day-a-week roster of Sunday dinner—that is, pork chops, meat loaf, and plates of corned beef and cabbage. Portions are big and prices are moderate.

# Randy's Ribs & Barbecue

7744 Leonardtown Rd.　　　301-274-3525
Hughesville, MD　　　www.randysribs.com
LD | $

Randy's opened in 1981 as a weekend-only roadside stand, and while its catering business has become large, the eatery remains charming. The sweet perfume of slow-smoking pork fills the air seven days a week throughout the year, and if you are one who considers barbecue foremost among the food groups, you will love what you find.

Sandwiches and platters are available: minced or sliced pork, ribs and ham, whole chickens, and slabs of ribs. "Slaw on that?" the order-taker will ask if you get a sandwich. "Yes!" we say, and then unwrap the foil around a big bun loaded with chunks of moist, full-flavored pork bathed in Randy's excellent sweet hickory sauce, with which sweet slaw sings happy harmony. Ribs are large and chewy, their meat infused with smoke.

Randy also offers a mighty fine half-smoke, which is a local variant of a hot dog: a plump sausage bisected lengthwise and smoke-cooked until its skin is taut and dark red, its insides succulent. All the usual hot dog condiments are available, but we recommend topping it with only one thing: Randy's sauce. That good sauce is available by the pint and gallon: an excellent investment in one's future culinary happiness.

# Seaside Restaurant & Crab House

224 Crain Hwy. N.　　　410-760-2200
Glen Burnie, MD　　　www.theseasiderestaurant.com
LD | $$

Beautiful steamed crabs (preferably jumbos, if available) come to the table stuck with a peppery, salty spice mix and too hot to handle. Grab your knife to pry away the outer shell, pick up the mallet to start pounding, and soon you will be rewarded with fat nuggets of sweet meat. Toss your shells into brown paper bags on the floor and hoist an ice-cold beer to quench the thirst that spicy crabs inevitably provoke.

Beyond blue crabs, the Seaside Restaurant has a menu of other specialties worth sampling, especially if crabmeat-extraction is too daunting a task: broiled shrimp, scallops, and flounder, and zesty crab cakes, plus fine crab soups, both Maryland-style (red, with vegetables) and creamy.

A busy place, especially on weekends. Expect to wait at mealtime.

## St. Mary's Landing

29935 Three Notch Rd.       301-884-6124

Charlotte Hall, MD       BLD | $$

St. Mary's County stuffed ham is a seasonal dish, generally served between Thanksgiving and Easter, but you can get it year-round at St. Mary's Landing. It's wonderful stuff: a corned ham packed with heaps of kale, cabbage, onions, and spice, served for breakfast on a plate with delicious potato cakes or for supper as a main course.

Lucky for us, they were out of stuffed ham when we came for supper. That meant we discovered the kitchen's good crab cakes, a plate of big, snapping-firm spiced boiled shrimp, and barbecued ribs that had a delicate crunch to their edges and meat that slid right off the bone.

This is a fascinating restaurant—a drinker's tavern as well as a family-friendly eatery—with a wall-mounted TV monitor that displays keno numbers and a countdown to the next game. One morning when we arrived at 7 a.m., we were the first customers to take seats in the restaurant, but bar stools in the taproom were already occupied by ladies and gentlemen having shots and beers to start their day.

## Suicide Bridge Restaurant

6304 Suicide Bridge Rd.       410-943-4689

Hurlock, MD       www.suicide-bridge-restaurant.com

LD | $$$

On two occasions, men shot and killed themselves on the bridge over Cabin Creek, then fell into the water. Another guy drove off the bridge. A subsequent jumper's body was fished from the creek and laid out on the wooden bridge, where his blood soaked into the boards, which stayed stained for five years. All this we learned from the takeout menu at this rather eerily named restaurant that is—bridge notwithstanding—extremely charming. Located on an Eastern Shore inlet from which paddlewheel boats glide into the Choptank River for dinner cruises, its broad windows offer views of the boats, the water, and the notorious bridge.

While the menu has a small section for "land lovers" that lists steaks, ribs, and chicken, the reason we recommend eating here is seafood—primarily broiled rockfish, fried oysters, cream of crab soup with a shot of sherry, and first-rate crab cakes. There are backfin cakes, available either fried or broiled, their fine and wispy meat humming with a devilish pepper glow, and there are the fancier (and more expensive) "Kool's Deluxe Crab Cakes" made with jumbo lump crab meat and available only broiled. Kool's Deluxe cakes also have some sharp seasoning, and their snowy hunks of meat are speckled with green herbs; nevertheless, the overwhelming goodness of those big pieces of crab puts all other seasoning into the background.

Suicide Bridge also makes a specialty of crab balls—peppery little orbs of deep-fried crabmeat, a crunchy pop-in-the-mouth bar snack or hors d'oeuvre.

## Waterman's Crab House

21055 E. Sharp St.          410-639-2261
Rock Hall, MD               www.watermanscrabhouse.com/home
                            LD | $$

A big, breezy eatery with a deck overlooking Rock Hall Harbor and shuttle service for those who arrive by boat at one of the nearby marinas, Waterman's is a good-time place. Blues, rock, and 1950s oldies bands perform on weekends, and at dusk merrymakers gather at the forty-foot-long bar to savor cocktails, beer, and a spectacular sunset.

Many regulars come for steamed crabs by the dozen, but the rest of Waterman's menu is broad and inviting. Other seafood temptations include crab soup served with a shot of sherry, crusty-creamy jumbo lump crab cakes (fried or broiled), stuffed flounder, spiced steamed shrimp, softshell crabs, and a gorgeous broiled rockfish available with or without a side of crab imperial. Even fish frowners will find plenty here: baby-back ribs, ten-ounce hamburgers, and one-pound "Admiral's cut" prime rib.

Recommended desserts: lemonade cake, Smith Island cake, and hot apple dumpling à la mode drizzled with caramel sauce.

## B&W Bakery

614 Main St.                          201-342-5383

Hackensack, NJ                        B | $

In a wide orbit around New York City, crumb cake is not just a generic term for coffee cake with some crumbs on top. It refers to a pastry that is significantly more crumb than cake. The benchmark version, as made by B&H Bakery, has so little cake that you might think of it as merely a conveyance mechanism to hoist streusel from plate to mouth. But that would be wrong. The cake provides creamy balance for the crumbs; the two elements together make a fine friend for morning coffee.

Whole cakes are huge, as are single slices; one of them will cover most of a nine-inch plate. Beyond the crumb cake, B&W makes a full array of regular pastries. Among the highlights are éclairs loaded with creamy filling, crumb-raisin buns, black-and-white cookies, and a killer banana cream pie.

There are no dining facilities on premises.

## Charlie's

18 S. Michigan Ave.          908-241-2627
Kenilworth, NJ              LD | $

While you can order what the menu calls a "push cart dog"—an ordinary street weenie on a blah roll with mundane condiments, Charlie's raison d'être is its Italian hot dog: one or preferably a pair of deep-fried, crisp-skinned, bursting-with-flavor franks stuffed into a half circle of what's known hereabouts as pizza bread. It's a round loaf that resembles a pita pocket with muscle. The bread is chewy, soulful, and absorbent, that last quality essential for engulfing the traditional garnishes that an Italian hot dog demands. These include fried peppers and onions and crisp-fried potato discs. The same ingredients can be used to accompany a sausage sandwich, also packed into pizza bread.

Service is do-it-yourself. There are tables but a majority of business is takeout.


## Cliff's Dairy Maid

1475 Route 46              973-584-9721
Ledgewood, NJ             www.cliffsicecream.com
                          LD | $

Cliff's is a great place to know about if you and your appetite are traveling along Route 80 through New Jersey. The 1975 drive-in is most famous for its ice cream but is also a worthy source for foot-long hot dogs and chili dogs (especially good when topped with a tangle of sautéed onions), hamburgers, and buckets of French fries.

Cliff's ice cream menu lists a few dozen "original homemade flavors," which range from utterly familiar chocolate and strawberry to bubble gum, cotton candy, and banana walnut chocolate chunk, plus another few dozen "fantasy flavors": sticky bun, holy cannoli, Bavarian cream raspberry truffle, and so on. In addition to these hard-pack ice creams, Cliff's boasts several soft-serves, which are dense and rich. There is always a flavor of the month—and it can be swirled together with one of the regulars. We very much enjoyed a twist of chocolate and the March flavor, mint.

No indoor seating at this drive-in, but there are picnic tables out back.

## De Lorenzo's Tomato Pies

2350 US-33                              609-341-8480
Robbinsville, NJ                        www.delorenzostomatopies.com
                                        LD | $$

De Lorenzo's makes what many connoisseurs consider to be America's best pizza. It is certainly among the top ten for its impeccable pizza harmony: crisp crust, creamy mozzarella, fruity crushed tomatoes, and zesty, fennel-laced Italian sausage. DeLo's calls them tomato pies, the old Napoli term, and one reason the toppings blend so well is that the pizza men first apply some cheese to the unbaked crust, then sauce and toppings, then another sprinkle of mozzarella. In the oven, they all swirl together just right.

For decades located in an extremely humble neighborhood storefront (so primitive that it had no restrooms!), De Lorenzo's moved to a modern place a few years ago, expanding its menu to include fine salads that include fresh berries and interesting cheese.

## Dickie Dee's

380 Bloomfield Ave.                     973-483-9396
Newark, NJ                              LD | $

No ordinary weenie, Dickie Dee's specialty is an Italian-style (aka Newark-style) hot dog, meaning one or a pair are deep-fried and stuffed into half a loaf of Italian bread along with fried peppers, onions, and big chunks of crisp-edge, soft-center fried potatoes. All the ingredients are cooked in the same vat of oil next to the order counter, and they are plucked from the oil and inserted directly into the bread (no draining!), making for a wondrously oily double-handful of food.

Be prepared for a faceful of attitude from behind the counter of this brash lunchroom. When it's crowded—it usually is—the line moves fast, and woe to he who hesitates when placing an order. As the sandwich is made, the cook will demand to know what you want on it in the way of condiments, and this is another time you don't want to be slow responding. (We suggest that a spritz of ketchup is a nice complement for the potatoes that go atop all the other ingredients in the sandwich.)

Carry your tray to a table and ease into a molded plastic chair. Lay out plenty of napkins and dig into a hot dog that is a true North Ward original.

## *Harold's New York Deli

3050 Woodbridge Ave.
Edison, NJ

732-661-9100
www.haroldsfamousdeli.com
BLD | $$$

Just because Harold's is comical doesn't mean it isn't seriously great. It may just be the best New York deli anywhere, even if it is in Edison, New Jersey. For intensely chickeny chicken soup with matzoh balls, for spice-edged pastrami that is melting-rich, for creamy blintzes and even creamier egg creams, for the best rugelach anywhere and a pickle bar to make the famous Guss' of New York blush, Harold's is the gold standard. The menu is vast, ranging from kosher hot dogs to triple-decker sandwiches, cold fish plates to hot suppers—all of it exemplary.

What's funny about the big, boisterous eatery is the size of its portions. While most New York delis offer sandwiches stacked extra-high and soup with very large matzoh balls, Harold's ups the ante to surreal proportions. A single matzoh ball is bigger than a softball, and yet, rest the edge of a spoon at its top and gravity is all that's needed to send the spoon sliding smoothly down into the ball's fluffy center. It is impossible not to gasp when you enter and see shelves of whole, wedding-sized cakes, each two feet tall. When a towering "large sandwich" gets carried past your table to a party of four (who will divvy it up, eat their fill, and each take home enough meat for more sandwiches the next day), no superlatives seem adequate to express the awe it inspires. Ridiculous, insane: the biggest food anywhere! While such protean portions of protein might seem wasteful and/or expensive, remember that everyone walks out with leftovers. On a recent visit, a single brisket sandwich provided a very filling lunch for one. Its remains became the basis of an excellent beef hash lunch for two the next day, and leftovers of the leftover hash became a pair of hearty breakfasts on day three.

## The Hot Grill

669 Lexington Ave.
Clifton, NJ

973-772-6000
www.thehotgrill.com
BLD | $

Texas weiners (spelled *ei,* not *ie*) are a big deal in this part of New Jersey, the word "Texas" being Northeast hash-house code for chili. One of the best places to sample this Garden State specialty is the Hot Grill of Clifton.

Step up to the order counter and order a pair. *Nobody* gets just one Texas weiner! The counterman will holler out to the back kitchen, "Two, all the way!" And within ninety seconds, a pair of handsome hot dogs will appear on the tray in front of you. Each is a deep-fried pup with rugged skin nestled in a too-short bun topped with mustard, onion, and sweet beef-chili sauce. On the side you definitely want gravy fries, or fries topped with gravy plus cheese and/or sauce.

Many customers come for hamburgers, in single or double configurations, served plain, all the way, or ultra all the way, which augments the onions-mustard-chili topping with a slice of grilled pork roll and a fried egg.

It's fun to dine in the Hot Grill's vast, modern dining room where, instead of music, you listen to the calls of the countermen back to the kitchen, and instead of sports, the overhead TV is tuned to "The Hot Grill Channel," which is a continuous program of hosannas to the hot dog.

## *Jimmy Buff's

60 Washington St.      973-325-9897
West Orange, NJ      www.jimmybuff.com
LD | $

James Racioppi, proprietor of Jimmy Buff's, believes it was his grandparents, James and Mary Racioppi, who created the Newark hot dog, in 1932. Mr. Racioppi says, "He played cards there every week. My grandmother served sandwiches to him and his associates. After a while, people started coming just to eat." As for the name of the store, James explains: "My grandfather Jimmy was an excellent card player. He was known for his talent to bluff, but with their Italian accents, they used to call him Jimmy Buff."

A Newark hot dog is built in a round of fresh, chewy Italian bread that is nothing at all like a flimsy, sponge-soft hot-dog bun. It *must* be tough to hold all the ingredients that get piled into it. The bread is cut in half, forming two half-circles. Each gets squeezed open to become a pocket like a robust pita. Into the pocket go a pair of all-beef hot dogs that have been fried in hot fat until crunch-crusted, a heap of onions and peppers that have been sautéed until limp, and a handful of crisp-fried potato discs. Options include ketchup and/or mustard and/or marinara sauce, and fire-hot onion relish.

A second Jimmy Buff's in Kenilworth is at 506 Boulevard (908-276-2833).

## Libby's Lunch

98 McBride Ave.                         973-278-8718

Paterson, NJ                            LD | $

Texas weiners were invented in New Jersey prior to 1920 by John Patrellis, who worked at his father's hot dog stand at the Manhattan Hotel in Paterson. According to hot dog historian Robert C. Gamer of Wyckoff, Mr. Patrellis devised the formulation of a deep-fried frankfurter in a too-short bun topped with mustard, onions, and spicy-sweet meat sauce, traditionally accompanied by French fries and a mug of root beer. In 1920 the hot dog stand was renamed the Original Hot Texas Weiner because Mr. Patrellis believed the sauce to be like Texas chili (and, presumably, because he wanted the spelling of weiner to set his invention apart from ordinary wieners). In fact, a Texas weiner is more Greek than Texan; but the Lone Star moniker has stuck, and today the region is rich with Texas weiner shops.

Libby's Lunch, since 1936, serves 'em with an impeccable pedigree, dishing out dogs all the way, meaning topped with mustard, chopped onions, and sauce. Good as the spicy chili sauce is (you can buy it by the pint), it is the hot dog itself that makes this a memorable eating experience. Its insides are tender and succulent, while the exterior is blistered and chewy because of its hot-oil bath. Extra-large dogs (and cheese dogs) are available, but we believe the original size works best. A pair of these tube steaks with a side of crisp French fries blanketed with gravy is a grand plate of food: true New Jersey, and uniquely American.

Beyond weiners, Libby's has a full short-order menu of burgers, sandwiches, and a homemade soup of the day.

## Rutt's Hut

417 River Rd.                           973-779-8615

Clifton, NJ                             www.ruttshut.com

                                        BLD | $

Rutt's Hut "rippers" are a cheap-eats legend among Garden State frank fanatics. They got their nickname because their skin tears and crinkles as they cook in a vat of hot oil and their exterior turns rugged and chewy. Weenie wimps can ask for an "in and outer," which gets plucked from the boiling fat more quickly and remains thoroughly pink and plump. Extremists get "cremators" (well-done), which are so porcine they remind us of fried pig skin.

The stellar condiment for a ripper is Rutt's spicy-sweet relish, a dense yellow concoction made from onions and finely chopped carrots and cabbage. Hamburgers and hot-from-the-kettle French fries are all right too, and we are fond of Rutt's chili: a chunky Mid-Atlantic brew of clods of ground beef with an occasional bean among it, suspended in a vividly spicy tomato emulsion. With crumbled crackers on top, it's a formidable meal.

Rutt's serves hot-lunch meals as well as real drinks in an adjoining taproom with a separate entrance. Here, amid wood-panel décor, one can quaff many beers with platters of such blue-plate fare as chicken croquettes, stuffed cabbage, Jersey pork chops, and that Garden-State favorite, Taylor Ham on a bun. Prices are low, and the food we have tasted is satisfying. But if you are coming to Rutt's only once, eat hot dogs at a counter. It's a Roadfood experience to remember: Dine in a wide-open mess hall with high counters that provide a view of the parking lot. Stand and eat off paper plates, and enjoy the calls of the countermen as they sing out, "Twins, all the way," meaning a pair of rippers with mustard and relish.

## *White House Sub Shop

| | |
|---|---|
| 2301 Arctic Ave. | 609-345-1564 |
| Atlantic City, NJ | www.whitehousesubshop.net |
| | L \| $ |

What makes a White House sub so good is more than superb bread and quality cold cuts. Its virtue is imparted by the artistry of its builders—the profusion of cold cuts without a hint of glut, the symmetry of ingredients, the spring of the lettuce applied in all the right places, the perfect splash of oil. And there's the astounding size. One whole sub is close to a yard long, requiring a string of paper plates to hold it. Even a half sub will challenge all but the healthiest appetites. Ingredients range from fancy white tuna fish to meatballs and sauce, and the Philly cheesesteak (arguably a sub corollary) is excellent. The traditional favorite is an Italian special or its big brother, the White House Special—Genoa salami, ham, capicola, and provolone cheese all rolled and tightly packed inside the loaf, lubricated with olive oil, and decorated with lettuce and bits of sweet pepper.

The White House is a landmark for sandwich connoisseurs, and like the cheesesteak shops of Philadelphia, it boasts of a glitterati clientele. Pictures of famous customers line the walls, inscribed with praise for the excellence of the cuisine. News clippings tell of the time the astronauts came to scarf down subs, and of Frank Sinatra once having a bunch of them shipped from New Jersey across the world to a movie location. For all its stardust, the White House remains a humble Naugahyde-and-neon eatery with a row of booths along the wall and a counter up front. The lighting is harsh, the napkins are paper, and the service is lightning fast: It would be a sin to sell subs any other way. Expect a long wait at noon.

## White Manna

358 River St.                          201-342-0914
Hackensack, NJ                         BLD | $

With good reason, New Jersey is famous for its vibrant hot dog culture; but here is one great hamburger joint that earns high marks from cheap-eats devotees. White Manna's burgers are paradigmatic sliders: little balls of freshly ground chuck that get slapped down onto a greasy griddle, preferably along with a handful of thin-sliced onions, mashed with a spatula, flipped, topped with cheese if requested, then crowned with the top of a tender potato roll. The roll is soft enough to sop up massive amounts of protein nectar that oozes from the beef as well as sweet perfume from the steamed onions, and its yeasty blandness is just what the forceful ingredients need to hit their peak. Heaps of thin-sliced pickle chips come alongside. Four or six of these make a nice meal.

The place is a minuscule diner with hardly more than a dozen seats and minimal counter space. We've never been to White Manna when it isn't very crowded, meaning that although the hamburgers are definitive fast food, you might wait a while to get some.

## White Rose System

1301 E. Elizabeth Ave.                 908-486-9651
Linden, NJ                             www.whiterosediner.com
                                       BL | $

Roadfood pillars Bruce Bilmes and Sue Boyle referred to pork roll, egg, and cheese on a bun as the "unofficial state sandwich of New Jersey," the context for which was their review of White Rose System. Now, these two know New Jersey like nobody else in the state, so when they said this sandwich is the best, we were on our way.

We're the first to admit that we are not connoisseurs of pork roll (aka Taylor ham), but we do have high appreciation for this tremendously fatty, salty loaf of pork products that is sliced thin and usually fried. Together with egg and cheese in a hard roll or, better yet, as per Bruce and Sue's advice, in a hero roll, and maybe with some fried potatoes added to the sandwich, it makes up virtually an entire day's recommended intake of just about everything we're supposed to be afraid of eating. In diner slang, the combo is known as a triple bypass.

White Rose System provides the ideal ambience for ingesting pork roll. It is a sassy diner with counter seats that provide a view of short-order cooks at work. The menu includes such other Garden State delights as an Italian hot dog (with fried potatoes, onions, and peppers), an Italian cheesesteak (also with potatoes), a super-hot sausage sub, greasy little oniony sliders (here known as little bullets), and—of all things—fish and grits!

## *Aléthea's Chocolates

8301 Main St.                               716-633-8620
Williamsville, NY                           www.aletheas.com
                                            $

Aléthea's is a top-tier source for such Buffalo specialties as sponge candy (chocolate-coated spun sugar) and Charlie Chaplins (marshmallow, coconut, cashews, and chocolate). Here too you will find fudge, turtles, barks, and chocolate-covered ginger and chocolate-covered raspberries to die for. All these can be purchased in the impeccably clean showroom in front of the large area in which everything is made, or via mail order.

The Roadfooder passing through who wants to sit down and have something more than bonbons needs to know about Aléthea's adjoining ice cream parlor, where truffled hot fudge, dark-amber caramel sauce, freshly made marshmallow topping, and crunchy-crisp, well-salted nuts crown luxurious ice cream. Have a classic "Mexicano" (chocolate sauce and Spanish peanuts) or a Delphi Maiden of chocolate chip and coffee ice cream topped with marshmallow, chocolate sauce, and toasted almonds. Or just a regular sundae topped with devilishly chocolaty hot fudge.

# Antoinette's

5981 Transit Rd.　　　　　　　716-684-2376
Depew, NY　　　　　　　　　www.antoinettesbuffalo.com
　　　　　　　　　　　　　　　$

There are two Antoinette's in greater Buffalo: the original on Transit Road and a second, around the corner from Schwabl's Restaurant at 1203 Union Road in West Seneca. Either one demands attention from the devotee of ice cream and/or masterfully made chocolates. Simply walking into the store will make you smile: The air is cocoa-scented. Watching a sundae being constructed is enchanting gastronomic foreplay. Starting at the top, nuts are fresh and crunchy. Whipped cream is, in fact, cream that is whipped. Nothing else, not even sugar, is added. It gets piped onto the ice cream from a pastry tube in thick, luxurious swirls. Fudge sauce? Caramel sauce? Better yet, fudge and caramel and pecans on cream-pure vanilla ice cream to make a turtle sundae? It doesn't get better than this.

Spend enough time here and you will earn an advanced degree in soda-fountain mixology. Sundaes are available with twenty different toppings, including six different chocolate variations: cinnamon-chocolate, chocolate-mint, hot fudge, French chocolate pudding, bittersweet chocolate, and regular chocolate. "Classic sundaes" include a rum-n-butter frappe, cara-mallow, a crunchy coffee special, and French chocolate nutty nut. There's a variety of sodas, milk shakes, floats, and fancy frappes.

The candy selection is magnificent, including Buffalo's own sponge candy and Charlie Chaplin logs as well as an assortment of barks, clusters, molasses pops, truffles, cordials, chocolate pretzels, and chocolate popcorn.

# Barney Greengrass

541 Amsterdam Ave.　　　　　212-724-4707
New York, NY　　　　　　　　www.barneygreengrass.com
　　　　　　　　　　　　　　　BL | $$

The food that put Barney Greengrass on the map is smoked fish. In the glass case of this restaurant and takeout store between 86th and 87th streets, you will find lean and silky sturgeon, salty cured salmon (known as lox), not-so-salty cured salmon (novie), snow-white whitefish, and luscious sable. In the dining room adjacent to the takeout counter, the fish are available on platters, with bagels and/or bialys, cream cheese, onions, tomatoes, and olives. These are the makings of a grand New York breakfast, and there isn't a restaurant in town that does it with the aplomb of bare-tabled Barney Greengrass.

## Big W's Roadside Bar-B-Q

1475 Route 22
Wingdale, NY

845-832-6200
www.bigwsbbq.com

LD | $$

Big W's began as a food truck and roadside smoke pit but subsequently moved to permanent quarters in a small cluster of buildings by the side of the road. While the new accommodations are more commodious and the place is able to stay open year-round, the move in no way diminished the in-your-face authenticity of this excellent barbecue.

When we say "excellent barbecue," we do not feel the need to qualify our kudos with such phrases as "for New York" or "for the Northeast." This is good meat by any standard. We are particularly impressed by the brisket, which is fatty enough to outrage a prim cadet from the nutrition police, and therefore dripping flavor. You can get it by the plate along with side dishes, by the pound, or in a sandwich, of which the menu lists three sizes: Truly Sensible (one-third pound meat), Sensible (one-half pound meat), and Roadside (one and one-third pounds meat). Pulled pork also is available in all those configurations, and it is handsome pig meat—shreds and hunks meticulously separated from their fat. Other smokehouse choices include spare ribs, chicken, and burnt ends. On the side, you can have sweet corn pudding that is as dense as bread pudding, mac 'n' cheese, greens, hush puppies, or mashed potatoes. If you're lucky, the potatoes will be garnished with porky cracklins.

Part of the fun of dining at Big W's is the presence of pitmaster Warren Norstein, who seems always busy carving meat, pulling things from the oven, and kibitzing with customers like a loquacious deli man.

## Carnegie Deli

854 7th Ave.
New York, NY

212-757-2245
www.carnegiedeli.com

BLD | $$

Rude, loud, uncomfortable, overrun with tourists, and ridiculously over-priced, the Carnegie Deli is an only-in-New-York eating experience. Its pastrami and corned beef are among the best anywhere; the kaleidoscopic menu of sandwiches, coffee-shop hot lunch, and Jewish comfort food is definitive. Merely walking in from Seventh Avenue is a gastronomic blast as the aroma of cured deli meats and sour pickles assaults your nose. A host points you to the back, and as you walk toward the tables, you pass a counter full of meats and smoked-fish salads behind which sandwiches are made. Salamis hang like a curtain over the counter, adding their garlicky perfume to the air. At the back of the restaurant, or in the adjoining dining room, you will be directed to a place at a table where you sit elbow-to-elbow with strangers.

Although purists gripe that the cured meats no longer are available hand-sliced, we have no complaints about the Carnegie's machine-sliced pastrami. It is mellow and not too zesty, tender and infused with fatty savor. A sandwich of it is ridiculously large—so tall that the top piece of rye bread appears to be merely an afterthought applied to the tower of meat. In fact, it is difficult to eat the ordinary way, by picking it up in your hands and taking a bite. Many customers go at it by piece-by-shred, directly from the plate. To accompany the monumental sandwiches, the Carnegie supplies puckery accouterments—half-sour and sour dill pickles arrayed in silver bowls along the tables. Beyond sandwiches, culinary highlights include blintzes and potato pancakes, gefilte fish and pickled herring, borscht, and kreplach soup.

## Charlie the Butcher's Kitchen

1065 Wehrle Dr.  716-633-8330
Buffalo, NY  www.charliethebutcher.com
LD | $

According to Charlie Roesch, proprietor of Charlie the Butcher's Kitchen, it was beer that inspired the invention of beef on weck. He believes that back in the 1880s a now-forgotten local tavern owner decided to offer a sandwich that would induce a powerful thirst in his patrons. He had plenty of coarse salt on hand for the pretzels he served, so he painted a mixture of the salt and caraway seeds (*kummelweck*, in German) atop some hard rolls, cooked a roast and sliced it thin, and piled the meat inside the rolls. As a condiment, he served hot horseradish. Slaking the thirst these sandwiches induced, beer sales soared. And Buffalo's passion for beef on weck was born.

Charlie's father was a butcher, as was his grandfather (their slogan: "You Know It's Fresh if It Comes from Roesch"). To honor the family trade, he wears a white hard hat and a butcher's smock and necktie as he carves beef in the open kitchen at the center of his restaurant. The beef on weck sandwiches are protein ecstasy, the rolls delicate but tough enough to sop up gravy and still stay strong.

Charlie's menu extends well beyond beef on weck, and everything else we've sampled is first-rate: Buffalo-made hot dogs and sausages grilled over coals, chicken spiedie (a boneless breast that is marinated and grilled), full-flavored roast turkey, and such daily-special sandwiches as meat loaf, double-smoked ham, and prime rib. The beverage list includes the local favorite, loganberry juice, as well as Charlie's personal favorite, birch beer.

## Clare and Carl's

4731 Lake Shore Dr.          518-561-1163
Plattsburgh, NY              LD (summer only) | $

A newspaper story posted on the wall at Clare and Carl's says that the region's unique weenie, the Michigan, owes its name to a Michigander named Eula Otis, who came to work for Clare Warn in the early days of the drive-in (it opened in 1943) and went around to area restaurants saying, "I'm from Michigan. Would you like to try one of our chili dogs?" The state's name clung to the hot dog topped with Warn's sauce, which she had invented because New York–style hot dogs with mustard and sauerkraut weren't selling well. The Michigan became a passion of New York's North Country between the Adirondacks and Lake Champlain, served at summer-time stands, in grocery stores, and even in the cafeteria at the Champlain Valley Physicians Hospital Medical Center.

Clare and Carl's presents its Michigans in a cream-soft bun that is similar to the Northeast split-top, but is thicker at the bottom and closed at both ends, forming a trough to shore in the sloppy topping. The chili is thick with meat, intriguingly spiced, not at all sweet, and just barely hot.

There is another Clare and Carl's at the marina in town, but the original is a wonderful vision of long-gone roadside Americana, its clapboard walls so old that they appear to have settled deep into the earth. Carhops attend customers in a broad parking lot, and there is a U-shaped counter with padded stools inside. A menu posted above the open kitchen lists Michigans first; signs outside advertise the house specialty as Texas red hots.

## Condrell's

2805 Delaware Ave.          716-877-4485
Buffalo, NY                 www.condrells.com
                            LD | $

We're not sure if the formal name of this place is Condrell's or King Condrell's; both are used on menus, on signs, and when employees speak of it. No matter, because what's important here are sundaes—some of the best on the planet. Atop locally made Perry's ice cream you can have basso profundo hot fudge, warm French chocolate sauce that is lighter-flavored than fudge and more pudding-like, or traditional chocolate sauce that is thin and innocent. Marshmallow topping is smooth as cream, caramel is extra-buttery, whipped cream is utterly fresh, and nuts are crisp and salted just enough to be a perfect foil for everything sweet. Portions are big.

Do not neglect Condrell's candies. There are exemplary sponge candies and Charlie Chaplins (Buffalo faves), as well as more universally known delights, including molasses paddles and molasses chips enrobed in dark or light chocolate, truffles of every kind, cashew or pecan turtles, chocolate-covered chunks of candied orange, pineapple, and ginger, dozens of varieties of cream centers, nut barks, chocolate-covered pretzels, and malted milk balls. To shop at Condrell's is truly to be a kid in a candy store. No metaphor exists to express the bliss of a Condrell's sundae.

## Don's Original

4900 Culver Rd.
Sea Breeze, NY

585-323-1177
www.donsoriginal.com/seabreeze
LD (summer only) | $

Say "New York hot dog" and most people will conjure up a street-corner dirty-water dog or a kosher frank from an urban deli or Nathan's of Coney Island. But culinarily, as in every other aspect of its culture, New York has two personalities: downstate and everything else. Hot dogs on the far side of the Southern Tier are a food group unto themselves, known as hots. There are two primary subcategories: white hots and red hots.

The white hot, as served by Don's Original at the Lake Ontario summer playground known as Sea Breeze, is an all-pork tube steak (which locals call a porker) that wants to spurt juice when teeth sink into it. Split and grilled to sputtering succulence, a white hot is dressed with mustard and diced onions. Don's red hot, known as a Texas hot, is firmer and looks more like a traditional weenie and is dressed with finely ground chili.

Frankfurter frowners love this happy Rochester landmark (since 1945) because of its one-third-pound hamburger, known here as a "ground steak sandwich." It is cooked to order and brought to its best self by an application of bright-red hot sauce. Big, fat onion rings are made here, as is custard, available inside or at the walk-up window.

## Doug's Fish Fry

3638 West Rd.
Cortland, NY

607-753-9184
www.dougsfishfry.com
LD | $$

Doug's is a fish-and-chips lover's dream. Your choice is either a sandwich, a fish dinner, or a fish onion dinner. The titles are misleading because the sandwich is in fact two or three large hunks of fried fish piled in and around a modest bun that is in no way large enough to hold even half its ingredients. Like a tenderloin from the southern Midwest, the presentation pushes the envelope of what defines a sandwich. A fish dinner adds chunky French fries to the pseudo-sandwich; a fish onion dinner means onion rings.

The fish is Atlantic cod, bought fresh in Boston five times a week. It is moist, sweet, and meek-flavored, encased in a sandy crust with just the right amount of crunch. It comes with pickly tartar sauce that is surprisingly unsweet. Sweetness comes in the form of Doug's superb coleslaw, which is finely chopped and fetchingly spicy. And then there is sweet dessert: excellent soft-serve custard, dense and alabaster-pure. Throughout summer the custard is a foundation for warm fruit sundaes. The available compote, made right here from the fruit of the season, begins with strawberries and blueberries early in the summer, then moves to peaches and finally to apples in the fall. Glorious!

Service is eat-in-the-rough-style: Place your order at the stand-up counter (from which you have an appetizing view of fish and fries coming out of the hot oil), pay for the meal, and wait for your name to be called. Fetch your own utensils from a table in the center of the dining room that holds plastic forks and knives, ketchup and mustard, and malt vinegar for spritzing on fries.


## Eckl's Beef on Weck Restaurant

4936 Ellicott Rd.
Orchard Park, NY

716-662-2262
LD | $$

Eckl's is an old-fashioned supper club where the star attraction is beef on weck. To watch one of these magnificent sandwiches being prepared (as you can do from a seat in the bar or nearest dining room) is to fully understand how different beef on weck is from any ordinary roast beef sandwich. The custom at Eckl's is for the carver to slice it thin, by hand, of course, piling up enough slices for a sandwich—an inch thick, at least. He then dunks the whole mound of meat into a pan of natural gravy, placing the soaked beef upon the bottom of the *kummelweck* roll. You tell the waitress what degree of doneness you prefer and that is how you get it, from dusky outside flaps to rose-red slices from the inside of the roast.

Beyond first-rate beef on weck, a meal at Eckl's can include bacon-rich potato salad, French onion soup topped with a thick layer of juice-laden caraway rye bread, and a whiskey sour that is textbook-right.

## Glenwood Pines

1213 Taughannock Blvd.              607-273-3709
Ithaca, NY                         www.glenwoodpines.com
                                   LD | $

The primary attraction of this friendly roadhouse overlooking Cayuga Lake is a Pinesburger. That's a six-ounce beef oval topped with a couple of slices of cheese wedged into a length of Ithaca Bakery French bread with lettuce, tomato, onion, and your choice of Thousand Island dressing or mayonnaise. Connoisseurs told us that we had to have it with the Thousand Island; the sweetness of the dressing is a grand complement for the smoky meat and all its dressings. On the side, good companions include ultra-crunchy fried onion rings and creamy coleslaw. Anyone who eats four Pinesburgers in less than an hour gets their picture on Glenwood Pines' Facebook Wall of Fame.

We said the Pinesburger was the primary reason to visit. The secondary one is the fish fry. A huge, thick length of haddock is breaded and fried crisp and served with either tartar sauce or cocktail sauce. It is sweet, moist, flavorful fish, and a giant meal.

Ambience at the 1946-vintage Glenwood Pines is old-time tavern. When you walk in, you see a few pinball machines and a bowling game on the right, a pool table ahead of you, and, beyond that, the bar where folks sit and imbibe beers with (or without) their Pinesburgers.

## Gus's Restaurant

3 Cumberland Head Rd.              518-561-3711
Plattsburgh, NY                    BLD | $

In the same phylum as the Coney Islands of the heartland and New York Systems of Rhode Island, the Michigans of New York's North Country are primarily summertime food. They are little porkers that come nestled in a soft bun and topped with a fine-grained, mildly spicy meat sauce.

Gus's serves Michigans year-round. It started as a dog stand in 1951, but it has grown to a three-meal-a-day restaurant with a full menu that boasts, "The restaurant features just about everything [even Lake Champlain perch], including their famous 'Michigan red hot,' which they invite you to try while dining." Each Michigan you order arrives in a cardboard boat. The heft of the sauce contrasts with the fluffy bun and fatty frank, and while each separate ingredient is inarguably loutish, the combo achieves a satisfying dignity—especially when topped with a judicious line of yellow mustard and a scattering of crisp, chopped raw onions.

## Heid's of Liverpool

305 Oswego St.  
Liverpool, NY

315-451-0786  
www.heidsofliverpool.com  
LD | $

Heid's has been around as long as the hot dog, and for as long as any living human can remember, hot dogs have been its claim to fame. For a while there were branches of the original, but today only one remains: a fast-food dog house with some tables inside and picnic tables outdoors under a tent.

The menu is wienercentric. German franks, Texas hots (red wieners), or Hofmann brand white hots made of beef, pork, and veal are quickly grilled, a process you can watch after placing your order. These are handsome sausages with a delicate casing and dense insides. In the old days the one and only available condiment was mustard. But since John and Randall Parker started running Heid's back in 1995, the topping choices have expanded to include chili, onions, sweet onion relish, and ketchup.

As always, the beverage list is a short one, including milk shakes, sodas, beer, and chocolate milk.

## Hubba

24 N. Main St.  
Port Chester, NY

914-939-7271  
BLD | $

In southeastern New York, central New Jersey, and western Connecticut, the word "Texas," when used to modify the words "hot," "hot dog," or "weiner" (yes, *ei*), means chili. A Texas hot is a chili dog. The long-standing chili dog king of Port Chester is Hubba, formerly known as Pat's Hubba Hubba and, before that, Texas Quick Lunch. While there is a full menu written in permanent marker on white paper plates tacked to the wall, nine out of ten meals served are the same: two, four, or six split and grilled weenies blanketed with no-bean, ground-beef chili and garnished with crisp chopped onions. It is a wanton combo—hot, greasy, and messy—but with a personality so intense that when the yen for one strikes, not even prime filet mignon will cut the mustard. Those who need more sustenance than a brace of chili dogs get chili cheese fries on the side. To drink: Hubba water, which is tap water tinted pink by a dash of Hawaiian Punch.

Hubba's chili dogs are famous as the kill-or-cure conclusion to a night of heavy drinking. The restaurant stays open until just before dawn on weekends. No wider than an apartment hallway, with only about a dozen counter seats, it is known also for its eye-boggling décor: every available piece of wall and ceiling is papered with dollar bills.

## John's of Bleecker Street

278 Bleecker St.
New York, NY

212-935-2895
www.johnsbrickovenpizza.com
LD | $$

There are nearly as many John's pizza shops in New York as there are Ray's, but the one to know about is John's of Bleecker Street. It looks well lived-in and well eaten-in, its walls and the wooden backs of its rickety booths covered with a thicket of graffiti that represents the countless enthusiastic visitors who have dined here since 1929. At the back of the front dining room, photographs of famous fans are displayed. They include former Mayor Rudy Giuliani and former Chairman of the Board Frank Sinatra.

Pizzas come large (eight slices) or small (six slices). There are no surprises on the ingredient list, except taste-wise: the sausage is especially delicious, the mushrooms are fresh, and the mozzarella has a creamy goodness that makes magic with the brightly herbed red sauce. What makes John's pizza taste important is its crust. Cooked in a coal-fired wood oven at 850 degrees, it has a dough that turns almost brittle at its outer edges in places where it blisters and blackens from the heat, and yet just fractions of an inch inside that circumference, it has a wondrous chew. Flip over a slice—you can do this, for the toppings cling well and each slice has enough structural integrity to stay together as it's handled—and gaze upon the bottom. It is crunchy from its stay on the floor of the old oven. For serious bread-and-pizza lovers, this crust verges on a spiritual experience.

# *Katz's Delicatessen

205 E. Houston St.  
New York, NY

212-254-2246  
www.katzsdelicatessen.com  
BLD | $$

Katz's has been about to be demolished for a half-dozen years, but until that happens, it's one of New York's Lower East Side relics, remaining as it was a century ago. It is a gymnasium-sized eating hall with lined-up tables, the air filled with the noise of shouted orders and clattering carving knives and the aroma of the odoriferous garlicky salamis hanging along the wall. Pictures of happy celebrity customers ranging from comics Jerry Lewis and Henny Youngman to former Police Commissioner Ray Kelly are everywhere.

Ordinary table service by waiters is available, and quite easy. But the better way to do it is to personally engage with a counterman. Here's how: Make eye contact with one of the white-aproned carvers who is busy hand-slicing meats and making sandwiches behind the glass. Once you've gotten his attention, be quick and tell him what you want: pastrami on rye or on a club roll, or corned beef or brisket. They portion out meat and assemble sandwiches with the certainty and expertise of a Dutch diamond cutter.

King of Katz's sandwiches is pastrami—not the hugest in the city, but very possibly the best: three-quarters of a pound, expertly severed into pieces so chunky that the word "slice" seems too lightweight to describe them. Each brick-red, glistening moist hunk is rimmed black, redolent of garlic, smoke, and pickling spices, as savory as food can be. You can pay a dollar extra to have it cut extra-lean, but that would be sad.

Beyond superb cured meat: Katz's hot dogs just may be the city's best all-beefers; omelets are made deli-style, meaning open-face and unfolded; there are tender-souled matzoh ball soup and chicken noodle soup as well as potato latkes and blintzes; and to drink you can have a classic New York egg cream, chocolate or vanilla.

## LDR Char Pit

4753 Lake Ave.  
Rochester, NY

585-865-0112  
www.ldrcharpit.com  
LD | $

When you first see an LDR steak sandwich, you will likely be suspicious. The single, broad cut of meat in its bun looks like a challenging chew, especially considering the bargain price of $6.25 and the fact that the LDR Char Pit is a booth-and-counter diner, as far from a prime steak house as a restaurant can be. But when you take a bite, the preconception vanishes. This slim steak, which is maybe a quarter of an inch thick and cooked to order, is tenderness incarnate, oh-so-easy to chew and a joy to savor, as buttery-beef-flavored as a KC strip: a miracle sandwich.

It arrives completely unadorned. Condiments, including a meaty hot sauce, are available at a help-yourself counter; but we highly recommend you forgo them. The beauty of this steak sandwich is its simplicity: meat and bread. Anything else is only a complication.

LDR's menu also lists red hots and white hots—traditional upstate New York frankfurters—as well as grilled chicken and ham steaks, none of which we've tried. The steak is too compelling. When you are finished, walk a half block toward Lake Ontario and you will find an Abbott's custard shop. Creamy, dense, dairy-pure, it is wonderful dessert. Our favorite flavor is chocolate almond.

## McSweeney's

535 N. Margaret St.        518-562-9309
Plattsburgh, NY           www.mcsweeneysredhots.com
                          LD | $

A style of chili dog unique to New York State's Northland, the Michigan goes back to the early 1940s. Each place that makes Michigans in and around Plattsburgh has its own formula, but the basic idea is a piggy-pink wiener in a split-top bun, topped with dark-orange chili sauce in which the meat is sandy smithereens.

McSweeney's, which bills itself as Plattsburgh's Red Hot Car Hop Stop, is a relative newcomer to the area, opened in 1991 and now boasting three locations. We visited the one on Route 9 North (Margaret Street), which features old-time carhop service and an inside counter as well as comfortable sit-down tables indoors. Its sauce is especially beefy, flecked with pepper that kindles a nice glow on the tongue. The package is substantial enough that Michigans come with a fork. Looking around the dining room and at people eating off trays hung on car windows, it appeared to us that most customers forgo the utensil. A few people we observed had perfected a technique of hoisting the entire cardboard boat to chin level with one hand, then using the other hand to ease the Michigan from boat to mouth, bite by bite.

McSweeney's sells Michigan sauce by the pint ($11.50) and offers a Michigan without the hot dog: mustard, onions, and plenty of sauce in a hollowed-out bun. This configuration is known as a sauceburger, and as much as we like the sauce, we much prefer it in concert with a weenie.

## Mike's Candy

2110 Clinton St.
Buffalo, NY

716-826-6515
www.mikescandies.com

$

Of Buffalo's several claims to culinary fame (wings, beef on weck, char-cooked hot dogs), one of the lesser-known stars is sponge candy. Made of sugar that is cooked and spun and leavened to a state of desiccated near-weightlessness, then cut into diaphanous, double-bite-sized hunks and sheathed in dark chocolate (or milk chocolate, if you prefer), it is similar to candy known in some parts of the Midwest as seafoam or fairy food.

We well remember our first bite at Mike's, a Buffalo chocolate shop where everything is made from scratch in a small backroom kitchen, and where sponge candy is an obsession. We stood at the counter and sampled a piece, remarking that the molasses interior seemed actually lighter than air, as if it would float upward without the ballast of its thick chocolate coat. As soon as it was bitten and slightly moist, it evaporated into pure flavor with no cor-poreal residue at all. Susan Walter, daughter of founders Mike and Anastasia Melithoniotes, listened to us, but not to our words. "It sounds a little crisp today," she said, noticing the faint crunch it made when our teeth first met the sponge underneath its chocolate sheath. "It's breaking hard." The subtlety of her evaluation was lost on us, for it seemed absolutely perfect. Susan also clued us in to the uniquely Buffalonian favorite the Charlie Chaplin, which is a log of freshly made marshmallow laced with coconut and rolled with cashews and chocolate. Neither she nor any other confectioner in town had a convincing explanation for how the Buffalo obsession got its name.

Sponge candy is almost always available in-store at Mike's, as well as for mail-order throughout the year except in the hottest months of summer, when heat and humidity preclude shipping.


## New Way Lunch

54 South St.
Glens Falls, NY

518-792-9803
BL | $

New Way Lunch, which longtime residents know as Dirty John's, has a sign outside boasting that it has been world famous since 1919, and although it now occupies a new, modern building, its way with hot dogs (or, as locals call them, dirt dogs) is timeless. They are slim, non-kosher franks that are griddle cooked and slipped into soft, warm buns. The fundamental dressing formula is a trio of mustard, diced onions, and a finely textured beef sauce that has a peppery tang. It is a small package, costing just over a dollar. Takeout customers come in for dozens.

There's a brief menu of other items too: char-cooked burgers, a Philly cheesesteak, fried fish and chicken, and a Greek salad. For a quick lunch not far from the New York Thruway, New Way is an easy detour.

## Nick Charlap's

7264 Boston State Rd.      716-312-0592

Hamburg, NY 14075      LD | $

"Vat pasteurization is the key," Mr. Charlap told us, explaining that most ice cream makers pasteurize their product as quickly as possible for efficiency's sake. But he holds his at 180 degrees for a full twenty minutes. The result is flavor that tastes deep rather than superficial, cooked-in rather than added-on. You can savor it easily in plain vanilla, but the depth is there too in chocolate and coffee, as well as in more complicated flavors such as cashew caramel crunch, raspberry chocolate chip, deep-dish apple pie, burgundy cherry, cinnamon, and caramel brownie overload. Charlap's hard ice cream is scooped and served at a temperature that makes it nearly as soft as custard, meaning the flavor glows.

Dine outside at a picnic table, or inside, where the ambience is 1950s retro with neon signs, glass-brick counter, and checkered tile floor. Adjoining is a grill serving hot dogs, hamburgers, sandwiches, and fries.

## *Nick Tahou Hots

320 W. Main St.      716-436-0184

Rochester, NY      www.garbageplate.com

                           LD | $

Don't confuse a Rochester Garbage Plate with junk food that is tossed willy-nilly into a paper bag or bucket. At Nick Tahou Hots, where it was invented, a Garbage Plate is a carefully assembled meal. It demands a table and utensils, not to mention a big appetite and courage.

Construction of a Garbage Plate begins with your choice of two items from among home fries, French fries, macaroni salad, and baked beans. The duo is marshaled half-and-half onto a carton-weight cardboard plate. Atop the foundation of starches are positioned a brace of hot dogs, hamburgers or cheeseburgers, Italian sausage or steak, or fried eggs. Piled onto the protein layer are meaty hot sauce and onions, and bread comes alongside to push, mop, and scoop.

The Garbage Plate was created by Nick Tahou during the Great Depression, when it was known as hots and potots—"hots" being the upstate New York term for hot dogs. The maximum-food/minimum-cost meal was renamed by happy customers and has been embraced by Rochesterians as a hometown specialty as dear as wings in Buffalo.

To its loyal clientele, Nick Tahou's is more than a restaurant. It is home, it is family, it is a spirit of ragtag generosity with which Nick's son Alex Tahou feeds needy kids at Christmas and takes care of neighbors and friends as well as newcomers all year-round.

## Papaya King

179 E. 86th St.        212-369-0648
New York, NY          www.papayaking.com
                      LD | $

Incredibly, Papaya King began as a health-oriented juice store. That was 1932, when original proprietor Gus Poulos hired waitresses to do the hula on the sidewalk and lure people inside to taste "nature's own revitalizer." You still can have papaya juice, which is frothy and sweet if not necessarily salubrious, but it's for the hot dogs this popular street-corner eatery has earned its stripes. A sign boasts that they are "tastier than filet mignon." They do pack a booming garlic taste inside natural casing that pops when you bite it. Available toppings include chili, sauerkraut, even coleslaw; the essentials are New York–style stewed onions and good ol' mustard.

Dine at an eating shelf that affords a nice view of the passing scene along Third Avenue and 86th Street.

## Patsy's

2287 1st Ave.         212-534-9783
New York, NY          LD | $

New Yorkers think nothing of picking up a slice of pizza for eating on the go. Patsy's is the Italian landmark in the midst of Spanish Harlem where street slices first were served back in the 1930s. To this day, customers stand around on the sidewalk or lean on an open-air counter facing First Avenue wolfing down slices of pizza, which is the only thing on the menu. These are some of the most elegant slices you'll find in the city: wafer-thin charcoaled crust, minimal tomato, and just enough cheese to make it rich.

Whole pies are served at tables and booths inside. While all sorts of toppings are available, we like the most basic tomato-cheese combo: easy to hoist slice by slice, built on that marvelous fragile crust. Two versions of plain cheese pizza are available: fresh mozzarella, with thin pools of creamy sliced cheese spread out within the microthin layer of tomato sauce, and regular mozzarella on which saltier, slightly oilier shredded cheese is spread evenly all across the surface.

## Phil's Chicken House

| | |
|---|---|
| 1208 Main Rd. | 607-748-7574 |
| Endicott, NY | www.philschickenhouse.com |
| | B(weekends)LD \| $ |

Phil's Chicken House was opened a half century ago by Phil Card, who learned his skills at Endicott's Chicken Inn. His folksy wood-paneled restaurant is decorated to the hilt with country-crafty knickknacks (souvenir plates, angel statuettes, lighthouse miniatures) and it attracts customers that range from local families to well-armed state police SWAT teams (who practice marksmanship nearby).

As you might suspect by the name of this restaurant, its featured attraction is chicken—slow cooked, and relentlessly basted on a rotisserie until the skin is glazed gold and the meat drips juice. The breast meat is velvet soft; thighs and drumsticks pack a roundhouse flavor punch; wings, which carry maximum marinade, reverberate with exclamatory gusto. The marinade is the classic Cornell chicken formula, devised by a professor by the name of Dr. Robert Baker in 1946—a tomato-free vinaigrette, enriched with eggs and shot through with poultry spice, now used as a marinade and/or basting sauce by cooks throughout the region.

While nine out of ten customers come to Phil's for a half or a quarter barbecued chicken, square meals of all kinds are available, including pot roast, meat loaf, grilled ham, and steak. There's a lunch buffet every day and a breakfast buffet on weekends.

## Polish Villa

| | |
|---|---|
| 2954 Union Rd. | 716-683-9460 |
| Cheektowaga, NY | BLD \| $ |

One of the chief culinary assets of America's heartland is its bounty of Eastern European restaurants. Polish Villa is one of the best. Look, for example, at the pierogies, stuffed with sauerkraut, their soft and tangy filling robed in dough that gets quick-sautéed to a crisp just before being served: magnificent! Sweet-and-sour cabbage—available as a side dish for any meal—is soft but not mushy, balanced perfectly between sugar and tang. Other menu highlights include *czarnina* soup, kielbasa, *golabki,* and fruit crepes for dessert. One course after another, everything you eat is Mom's-home-cooking good: slightly sticky potato pancakes served with either sour cream or applesauce (but you must pay extra if you want both); firm-fleshed, smoky sausages; crisp wiener schnitzel sided by creamy mashed potatoes, *kluski* noodles topped with chicken and mushrooms.

Such a welcoming restaurant! It's informal, but so polite. At the door, you are greeted by a hostess who seems genuinely grateful you have arrived. Waitresses are able to explain anything that needs explaining. And the room's tone is that of a huge family reunion, where nearly everybody present seems very happy to be plowing into such exquisite Old World meals.

## Red Rooster Drive-In

| | |
|---|---|
| 1566 Route 22 | 845-279-8046 |
| Brewster, NY | LD \| $ |

Although a roadside archeologist would categorize the Rooster as a drive-in, there is no car service and there are no carhops. Still, plenty of people eat in their cars, and the service, cuisine, and ambience are *Happy Days* incarnate.

The hamburgers are not too big, not odd in any way, just pleasant handfuls fashioned by proprietor Jack Sypek or Andy the grill chef and sizzled on a charcoal grill. We are particularly fond of cheeseburgers gilded by onions that have been grilled until limp and slippery. They are served on tender buns—deluxe, please, with lettuce and tomato—and accompanied by French fries, milk shakes, ice cream floats, or egg creams.

In nice weather, customers can choose to eat at one of several picnic tables spread across the lawn in back. Adjacent to this open-air dining room is a miniature golf course where kids and carefree adults while away pleasant evenings in the Red Rooster's afterglow.

## *Schwabl's

| | |
|---|---|
| 789 Center Rd. | 716-674-9821 |
| West Seneca, NY | www.schwabls.com |
| | LD \| $$ |

Now operated by former waitress Cheryl Staychok and her husband, Gene, Buffalo's best-known beef house didn't miss a beat when the Schwabl family left the business. Here is the benchmark version of that glorious Buffalo specialty, beef on weck. The beef itself is superb: thin slices (preferably rare) severed from a center-cut round roast just before the sandwich is assembled. The pillow of protein is piled high inside a *kummelweck* roll heavily crusted with coarse salt and caraway seeds, the roll's top momentarily dipped in natural gravy before it sandwiches the meat. The only thing this package could possibly want is a dab of horseradish, which is supplied on each table.

Of the several side dishes, mashed potatoes are very good (and topped with excellent gravy), but tangy-sweet German potato salad is our pick. That is all you need to know about Schwabl's, except for the nice hot ham sandwich on white bread in a pool of tomato-clove gravy. The ham is an interesting alternative to the beef, although it has none of the clout.

Schwabl's is a casual, well-aged eatery, attended by businesspeople at noon and families at suppertime. While liquor is served, the best beverage to pair with beef on weck is birch beer, which is available here on draft: a local brew with the faint twang of spearmint.

## Second Avenue Deli

162 E. 33rd St.  
New York, NY

212-689-9000  
www.2ndavedeli.com  
BLD | $$

The Second Avenue Deli has moved closer to Third Avenue, on Thirty-Third Street, but it remains one of the ever-scarcer true Jewish delicatessens. You can smell its culinary character the moment you walk in and inhale the swirling perfume of sour pickles, aged salami, hot chicken broth, steamy corned beef, and pastrami. Where else can you begin a meal with *gribenes,* which are the leftovers from rendering chicken fat? The Second Avenue Deli makes them in big batches, so they aren't as refined or as delicate as you might find on the kitchen counter at Grandma's house, but they are nonetheless irresistible: squiggles and nibbles of skin along with limp caramelized shreds of onion that have been fried in the full-flavored oil. Dangerous to munch before a meal because they are so addictive and so corpulent, *gribenes* are the world's best complement to chopped liver, which here is smooth-flavored but ragged enough for textural excitement, rich the way only organ meat can be, and yet fresh and sparkling the way liver so seldom is.

Smoked fish platters are silky luxury, soups—especially the legendary mushroom barley—are some of the city's best, and deli sandwiches are delightful. While the sandwiches are not gargantuan, they are piled high enough that they are barely pickupable. Pastrami is especially excellent, more smoky than spicy, and unless you pay $2 extra for lean meat, it comes just-right fatty. Our only complaint is the rye bread, which, as in so many otherwise first-rate delis nowadays, is second-class, pale and flabby.

Meals are topped off with a complimentary shot-glass chocolate phosphate ("Bosco and seltzer," explains the waitress). Second Avenue's kitchen actually is kosher, meaning you can't get cheese on a sandwich.

## Sharkey's

56 Glenwood Ave.      716-729-9201
Binghamton, NY        LD | $$

Larry Sharak's father started making spiedies at a cookfire in the window at the family's tavern over sixty years ago. Skewered, marinated hunks of lamb were cooked on a charcoal grill and served with broad slices of bread. The custom was to grab the bread in one hand and use it as an edible mitt to slide a few hunks off the metal rod, thus creating an instant sandwich. Spiedies are still served and eaten this way at the bar and tables of Sharkey's. Lamb has grown too expensive, however, so today's spiedies are made from either pork or chicken. When you bite into a piece, it blossoms with the flavorful juice of a two-day marinade that tastes of garlic and vinegar, peppers and oregano and, according to Larry Sharak, for whom the recipe is a family heirloom, "a lot of pinches of many spices."

Sharkey's is a local institution to which families have come for generations. Old-timers know to enter through the back door rather than the front. Here, you walk into a dark dining room outfitted with ancient wooden booths and long family-style tables formed from pushed-together dinettes. Between courses, the young folks get up to play a few lines on the old Tic Tac Strike game, a pre-electronic diversion that seems at home in this historic tavern.

## Shortstop Deli

204 W. Seneca St.     607-273-1030
Ithaca, NY            www.shortstopdeli.com
                      Always open | $

Any hearty eater who attended Cornell University in Ithaca in the last half century knows about Hot Truck, the mobile food wagon that invented French bread pizzas in the early 1960s. As served every night starting at 11 p.m. during the school year, these fusions of pizza and submarine sandwich are piled with ingredients then baked open-face until the bread is shatteringly crisp, the cheese bubbles, and the meats sizzle.

The Hot Truck's hours are extremely limited, which is why we love the Shortstop Deli, which features Hot Truck cuisine and never closes. More a big convenience store than a sit-down eatery, the Shortstop features shelves of snack foods, countless varieties of coffee, and a counter where you write down your order. There are no tables and chairs, just some concrete benches outside the front window to bring your wrapped sandwich and your cup of soda (10¢ with a meal!) and dine alfresco with a view of the parking lot.

The pizza subs are made on loaves of Ithaca Bakery French bread, and they range from the basic PMP (Poor Man's Pizza), which is nothing but bread, sauce, and cheese, to the extravaganza known as a Suicide (garlic, sauce, mushrooms, sausage, pepperoni, and mozzarella). These sandwiches have inspired a language all their own. For example, a "Triple Sui, Hot and Heavy, G and G" is a full Suicide with three extra homemade meatballs, a sprinkle of red pepper, extra garlic, mayonnaise, and lettuce. (G and G = grease and garden—that is, mayo and lettuce.) A Flaming Turkey Bone (which contains no turkey and no bones and is not served on fire) includes chicken breast, tomato sauce, cheese, onions, extra hot and heavy, plus "spontaneous combustion" (double-X hot sauce).

### Steve's Pig & Ox Roast

951 Ridge Rd.  716-824-8601
Lackawanna, NY  LD | $

Here is one of the Buffalo area's more interesting beef on weck sandwiches. The beef is not sliced thin into rose-red slices like at most local beef houses. It is thicker and cooked through, tender like pot roast. It comes with a cup of natural gravy for dipping or pouring into the sandwich and a mountain of French fries. The spuds are long and thin with lots of crunchy squiggles throughout. Bruce Bilmes and Sue Boyle, who tipped us off to this neighborhood roaster-café, warned that unless we specifically asked for a *kummelweck* roll, sandwiches are served on regular buns. Weck is the way to go.

At $5 each—for pork, lamb, or turkey, as well as for beef—these mountainous sandwiches are a great bargain, available with Buffalo's beloved loganberry juice to drink. Meats are cooked on an impressive rotisserie adjacent to the dining room. If you arrive early, chances are you will see the meat still in motion.

# Ted's Jumbo Red Hots

2312 Sheridan Dr.
Tonawanda (Buffalo), NY

716-836-8986
www.tedshotdogs.com

LD | $

Ted's began as a horse-drawn hot dog cart in Buffalo in the 1920s. It became a permanently anchored hot dog stand under the Peace Bridge in 1927 and opened as a bigger store on Sheridan Drive in 1948. There are now eight Ted's in western New York, and one in Tempe, Arizona; but the one to which we always want to return is Ted's of Tonawanda. It has modernized since 1948 and is as clean and sanitary as any fast-food franchise, but the hot dogs are like no others. Natural-casing Sahlen's-brand franks, available regular-length or foot-long, are cooked on a grate over charcoal that infuses each one with pungent smoke flavor and makes the skin get crackling-crisp. As they cook, the chef pokes them with a fork, slaps them, squeezes them, and otherwise abuses them, thus puncturing the skin and allowing them to suck in maximum smoky taste.

In consultation with a person behind the counter known as "the dresser," you decide how you want to garnish your tube steak. The standout condiment is Ted's hot sauce, a peppery concoction laced with bits of relish. You also want onion rings, sold as tangled webs of crisp fried batter and limp onion. The beverage of choice in these parts is loganberry juice, which is a kind of grand cru Kool-Aid.

# Texas Chili

8 S. Main St.
Port Chester, NY

914-937-0840

BLD | $

Although Texas Chili is neat, clean, and well-lit, it delivers all the funky soul you expect in a chili-dog joint. Opened in 2009 by two partners who had worked down the street at the legendary greasy spoon Hubba (p. 123), it has a three-meal-a-day menu on which nearly everything, from omelets at dawn to wieners at 4 a.m. on Saturday night, features chili. It is a beanless, ground-beef brew glistening with oil, so peppery that it is not listed on the menu as a stand-alone—although serious chiliheads do get it solo. It is best as an eyebrow-raising complement for little tube steaks that are split and grilled until their edges get crusty. Atop the chili on the hot dog, chopped onions are the standard garnish. Crisp, cool, and refreshing, they are a marvelous counterbalance for the chili dog, doing what onions so seldom do:

carrying the banner for an actual vegetable. It is traditional for hot dogs in this area to be served in little white-bread buns; Texas Chili grills its buns in butter (or maybe buttery-flavored grease), adding a note of opulence to a package that is unctuous in so many other ways.

While a full array of soda pop is available to drink, the connoisseur's choice is what's known here as Texas water: plain water turned pink by an infusion of Hawaiian Punch.

## Tino's

| | |
|---|---|
| 2410 Arthur Ave. | 718-733-9879 |
| Bronx, NY | www.tinosdeli.com |
| | L | $ |

The Bronx originally was part of Westchester County, so it makes sense that when you go to Tino's for a chicken parm hero, you'll hear some fellow eaters refer to it by its Westchester moniker, a wedge. Whatever you call it, this mighty log of lunch is authoritative. First, there's the bread. Many sandwiches of chicken parmigiana (and eggplant parmigiana) are built upon a toasted loaf. Not that there's anything wrong with that, but all too often toasting is simply a way of disguising a stale or inferior length of bread. Tino's doesn't toast, but if you want that crunch, get yours on a crisp-crusted Italian roll that is impeccably fresh and Arthur-Avenue soulful. Soft club rolls also are available. Then there's the chicken itself, a cutlet that's lightly breaded and glazed with fantastic sauce that tastes like it's really made from tomatoes, all of this crowned with creamy-fresh mozzarella. We nominate Tino's handsome hunk as king of hot Italian sandwiches.

If you are in the market for a cold-cut sandwich that is super-hot, we recommend what Tino's calls Bocca di Fuoco: hot soppressata, hot capicola, and hot peppers with mozzarella cheese. Tino's combo is a classic Italian sub of salami, ham, mortadella, and provolone with lettuce, tomato, and roasted peppers, and the only proper condiments: oil and vinegar.

## Walter's

| | |
|---|---|
| 937 Palmer Ave. | No phone |
| Mamaroneck, NY | www.waltershotdogs.com |
| | L | $ |

Even if you have another weenie you love more, it is hard to deny that Walter's belongs on any list of America's top dogs. Each begins as a beef-pork-veal frank made exclusively for Walter's, as they have been since 1919. The frank is bisected lengthwise and cooked on a grill coated with secret-formula sauce. It's a buttery sauce with an ineffable spice that insinuates flavor into the cut-flat surface of the weenie and gives it a faint crunch that is a joy to bite, especially inside a soft bun that has been toasted on an adjacent grill. Some customers ask for their hot dog well-done and therefore more crisp than usual (not a bad idea) and others get a double dog (in our opinion, an imbalance of dog and bun), but whichever way you like it, please have it with mustard. It is Walter's own mustard, grainy and dotted with pickle bits. To drink? Walter's makes a fine malted milk shake.

The place is a vernacular-architecture hoot, designed to evoke a pagoda, complete with lanterns and a sign that spells out WALTER'S in letters that look vaguely like Chinese brushstrokes from a distance but turn out to be images of hot dogs strung together. On a pleasant day, you can dine in a grove of picnic tables suited to devouring multiple hot dogs; but in inclement weather, you are on your own. Walter's has no inside seats.

## West Taghkanic Diner

Route 82 & Taconic Pkwy.       518-851-7117
Ancram, NY                     www.taghkanicdiner.com
                               BLD | $

When we first walked into the West Taghkanic Diner, a beautiful streamliner from 1953, we passed two women dressed in business suits in the silver vestibule. They stopped, blocking our way, and one furtively whispered a single word: "jitterbug." Then they let us pass.

When the waitress came to take our order, we mumbled, "Um, er, 'jitterbug'?" We said the secret password, having no idea if it was a clue or the ranting of a crazy woman. "Fine," she said. "You want your bread toasted?" We said no, wondering what exactly we had ordered. The jitterbug, it turns out, is a mid–Hudson Valley specialty of a hamburger between two pieces of bread or toast, sided by potatoes and covered with gravy. The burger is juice-laden, the gravy thick, the mashed potatoes lumpy-good and tinged with garlic.

The rest of the menu is vast and inviting, a wide array of sandwiches, salads, and hot dishes. Among daily specials written on a board above the counter are homemade stuffed cabbage, pot roast, chicken Parmesan, and tuna noodle casserole. A bowl of chili is not huge, but it is dense and thick, loaded with chunks of meat that taste like (and may be) broken-up meat loaf. It's a Northeast classic, slightly sweet and just a bit spicy, thick with meat and beans and onions and peppers.

Despite its age, the West Taghkanic is spanking-clean and like new: boomerang-pattern Formica tabletops, baby-blue upholstered stools that match the blue tiles in the floor and arched blue ceiling, and a counter where you can watch the waitress mix an egg cream (chocolate or vanilla).

## Center City Pretzel Co.

816 Washington Ave.          215-463-5664
Philadelphia, PA             www.centercitypretzel.com
                             $

Bad-tasting water = good-tasting food. There is no other logical explanation for the excellence of Philadelphia soft pretzels. There is a brackish tang to the flavor of the pretzel, especially to its tan skin, that puts it a cut above pretzels from any other city. If it's morning when you get one—or, preferably, a bag of several—it likely will still be oven-warm, the absolute freshness bold-facing its dense, chewy nature. Some pretzel lovers like to have a little mustard as a condiment. As far as we're concerned, these big softies need nothing to attain street-food perfection.

Notes: Center City pretzels are all-natural (nothing but flour, yeast, water, and salt), made in a nut-free environment, and are kosher-certified.

## DeLuca's

2015 Penn Ave.              412-566-2195
Pittsburgh, PA              BL | $

If you crave maximum breakfast in Pittsburgh, visit DeLuca's. There are frittatas, pumpkin pancakes, extra-large egg sandwiches, and a showstopper called mixed grill: sausage or ham sizzled with a huge heap of peppers, onions, tomatoes, mushrooms, and zucchini, crowned with a couple of eggs (optional) and sided by home-fried potatoes and a couple of slabs of toast. Among the available varieties of toast are cinnamon-raisin, rye, wheat, and white.

For many visitors, DeLuca's is an opportunity to indulge in one of the really outrageous breakfast items, such as the chocolate chip hotcake sundae, which is a stack of pancakes chockablock with melted and melting chocolate chips, topped with ice cream and strawberries. We are fond of blueberry French toast made with that sweet-smelling raisin bread.

Expect to wait for a seat at peak mealtime hours, especially on weekends when Pittsburghers throng to the Strip on a kind of eaters' holiday. For us, the choice place in DeLuca's is at the counter, with a good view of the short-order chefs flipping eggs and hotcakes at lightning speed.

## Dutch Kitchen

433 S. Lehigh Ave.       570-874-3265
Frackville, PA           www.dutchkitchen.com
                         BLD | $

The Dutch Kitchen is really convenient. At Exit 124B off I-81, it always seems to be just where we need it when hunger strikes south of the I-80 junction. It is a big, friendly place, a former dining car to which has been added a whole dining room decorated to the max with country crafts, speckleware, homily plaques, and souvenirs of Pennsylvania.

In some ways, the Dutch Kitchen is a traditional diner where you can come for bacon and eggs or a nice hamburger or sandwich. But beyond good versions of standard fare are such hearty Keystone State dishes as smoked pork chops, turkey croquettes, and a stupendously good potpie with homemade noodles, chicken and turkey, potatoes, and vegetables. One of our favorite daily specials is a stew of ham, cabbage, and potato sided by a block of brown-top corn bread nearly as sweet as cake. For dessert, we like shoofly pie—a ribbon of molasses filling topped with a crumbly top—or shoofly cake, a dark spice cake that is a supreme coffee companion and easy to eat while driving.

## The Enrico Biscotti Company

2022 Penn Ave.                      412-281-2602
Pittsburgh, PA                      www.enricobiscotti.com

BLD | $

One of the fringe benefits of coffee's ascendance in recent years is the discovery of biscotti, the firm, twice-baked Italian cookie that dunks so well. Alas, like coffee itself, there are a lot of lame versions around. We didn't even think we liked them . . . until we visited the Enrico Biscotti Company in Pittsburgh's historic Strip District. Here baker Larry Lagattuta makes them by hand using the finest ingredients, turning out such flavors as anise-almond, apricot-hazelnut, and pineapple-vanilla with white chocolate. They are firm enough that you'd never call them soft, but they do offer a tooth-pleasing resistance completely different from the desiccated, cellophane-wrapped variety.

Attached to the bakery is a European-style café where you can eat individual-sized brick-oven pizza, *torta rustica* (quiche), beans and greens, soup, or a "big fat salad." Here too is the espresso machine, as well as a handful of tables both inside and outdoors in a makeshift patio along the sidewalk. We know of no nicer place to start the day with strong coffee and biscotti, or to have a leisurely lunch of true Italian food. Bring your own wine.

## The Family Diner

302 Main St.                        570-443-8797
White Haven, PA                     BL | $

Interstate 80 through Pennsylvania is a challenging route for people who like to eat. There are truck stops and restaurants at nearly every exit, but most are mediocre. That is why we like the Family Diner, just a few minutes' detour from the highway. There is something for everyone in this friendly place, from blue-plate liver and onions or meat loaf and mashed potatoes to a fourteen-ounce burger (preferably with cheese and bacon) that eclipses both its bun and the plate it comes on.

As in so many diners, breakfast is deeply satisfying, served here from dawn until the middle of the afternoon. Pancakes, while not what you'd call elegant, are colossal. To add ballast, have them blanketed with gooey hot apple or blueberry topping. The Pennsylvania favorite, creamed chipped beef, comes sided by home fries or bite-sized potato cakes. Eggs are available any way (including soft-boiled and poached) with bacon, ham, sausage, pork roll, or scrapple. Scrapple is a Mid-Atlantic passion—thin slices from a loaf of ground pork and cornmeal that are sizzled in a pan until crisp.

## Famous 4th Street Deli

700 S. 4th St.  
Philadelphia, PA  

215-922-3274  
www.famous4thstreetdelicatessen.com  
LD | $$

Since it opened in 1923, the Famous 4th Street Deli has had its ups and downs, but today it is a consummate kosher-style eatery: glass cases up front full of smoked fish, wrinkly salamis hanging from the ceiling, colossal sandwiches of cured meat, and a vast menu of such classic Jewish fare as matzoh ball soup, noodle kugel, and chicken-in-the-pot.

Sinatra and Sammy Davis Jr. croon on the sound system in the background. A plate arrives with crisp coleslaw and a half-sour pickle. Dr. Brown's soda comes in a can along with an immense tumbler full of ice. And finally—ta-da!—the sandwich arrives. You can have it regular-sized, which is quite large, or zaftig, meaning cartoon-large. We love the pastrami, which is only modestly spiced even at its blackened edges. It is rich enough to feel like wanton indulgence, but not obscenely fatty.

While not cloyingly so, décor truly is nostalgic: an ancient black-and-white tiny-tile floor, vintage mirrored cabinets at the back of the dining area, and walls crowded with press accolades and pictures of the still-famous and long-forgotten personages who have eaten here.

## Geno's

1219 S. 9th St.  
Philadelphia, PA  

215-389-0659  
www.genosteaks.com  
LD | $

Whichever of Philadelphia's cheesesteak shops we happen to consider our favorite at any particular time, we have always appreciated Geno's classicism. This is the cheesesteak as it originally was served (by Pat's [p. 150], virtually across the street). It seems that here the meat is cut a little thicker than at other places (although it's still thin enough to be cooked through almost instantly when it hits the griddle), the rolls are sturdy, and the cheese choice includes Provolone, American, and Whiz. Open into the wee hours of the morning, Geno's is a magnet for night owls who eat standing under carnival-colored neon lights, leaning forward at the waist so shreds of beef that fall from the sandwich hit the sidewalk rather than their shoes.

Be sure to order your steak properly: First give your choice of cheese, then say the word "with" or "without," indicating your decision on whether or not you want onions. In other words, "Whiz without" means a cheesesteak made with Cheez Whiz but no onions. Red sauce is another option, but for most aficionados, sauce is not an essential cheesesteak ingredient. On the other hand, you must have fries—or cheese fries—on the side.

## Glider Diner

890 Providence Rd.          570-343-8036
Scranton, PA                www.gliderdiner.com
                            BLD | $

Named because it originally was built from the packing crates that held a glider airplane, the wood-sided Glider Diner was replaced by a shiny silver Mountain View dining car in 1952. A large annex known as the Fireside Lounge was added in the early 1960s, but for blue-plate traditionalists, the old silver streamliner is the place to be. Here breakfast is served 'round the clock. Lunch and supper specialties include Gliderburgers and milk shakes and hot sandwiches of roast beef, meat loaf, Virginia ham, and turkey.

Roadfood stalwarts Bruce Bilmes and Sue Boyle clued us in to the real specialty of the house, listed on the menu as roasted porketta and available in a toasted hard roll as the centerpiece of a hot platter, accompanied by mashed potatoes and blanketed with gravy. Porketta is well-seasoned roast pork, sliced thin and dripping moisture: delish!

## Jimmy's Hot Dogs

2555 Nazareth Rd.          610-258-7545
Easton, PA                 LD | $

We're not cheapskates, but we must confess that there is something irresistibly alluring about a decent meal that costs considerably less than coffee at Starbucks. Maybe *decent* isn't the exact right term to describe what's served at Jimmy's Hot Dogs, for these skinless dogs are sinful little steamers—piggy and juicy and priced under one dollar each. This means you can have two hot dogs, dressed, of course, the Jimmy's way—with mustard, onions, and pickle spears—along with a bag of potato chips and a Coke or chocolate milk for about three dollars. If you've got a big appetite, you might want three or four hot dogs; but even if you and a friend indulged in four apiece, you could still walk out with change from a ten-dollar bill.

Want something other than a hot dog and chips? Too bad, because that is the extent of Jimmy's menu. There is no extra charge to kibitz with members of the Apostopolous family, who have run the joint for decades . . . and who have perfected the art of freezing and overnight-shipping their beloved weenies to ex-Eastonites desperate for a taste of home.

Note: There are no seats. Business is takeout only.

## Jim's Steaks

400 South St.  215-928-1911
Philadelphia, PA  www.jimssteaks.com
LD | $

Opened in 1939, Jim's is Philadelphia's second-oldest cheesesteak shop (after Pat's [p. 150]), and it is definitely the sharpest-looking with its deco black-and-white tile décor. It's a very popular place, which is a good thing, because your wait in line will provide ample time for deciding how you like your steak garnished—"wit" or "witout" (onions), and whether you want the standard Cheez Whiz or optional American or provolone. The wait takes you past the back of the store, where an automatic slicer produces heaps of rosy-colored beef ready to be fried.

The steaks are made by hacking up the meat on the grill so it becomes hash. If you get sliced cheese, it is layered in the roll before the meat and melts underneath it. Whiz is ladled atop the meat. The bread is excellent, the fried onions are appropriately slippery, and the optional hot peppers are breathtaking.

## Joe's Steaks

6030 Torresdale Ave.  215-535-9405
Philadelphia, PA  www.chinksteaks.com
LD | $

Joe's Steaks (formerly Chink's) is an old-fashioned cheesesteak shop staffed by young women who delight in what they do, which includes building banana splits supreme and blending chocolate milk shakes thick enough that trying to suck one up a straw will cause serious hollows in your cheeks.

The open kitchen—little more than a griddle—is up front at a picture window that allows pedestrians to watch the cooks fry meat, scoot sizzling onions around, layer on slices of cheese, then hoist the jumble into a long, chewy, toasty-edged roll. The result: a well-balanced, buttery confluence of meat and dairy and weeping sweet onion that welcomes a spill of sharp yellow peppers and pickle chips, arriving on a square of butcher paper.

Joe's interior is vintage Americana: old wooden booths and a short, five-stool counter. A sign up front reads "Please do not lean on the counter. This is our work space. Thank you."

## Johnny's Hots

| | |
|---|---|
| 1234 Delaware Ave. | 215-423-2280 |
| Philadelphia, PA | BL \| $ |

The name of this restaurant refers to a tube steak that is similar to a half-smoke or Georgia hot: finely ground pork and plenty of spice packed into a taut casing. While it is not brutally hot, your tongue will glow, and if you like that glow, get your hot with hots, long hot peppers with exclamatory punch.

Johnny's is known for top-ranked cheesesteaks and breakfast sandwiches that include eggs along with the hot sausage, but the one item that most deserves attention if you are a devotee of recherché local taste is what wiseacres know as Philly surf 'n' turf: a hot dog and fish cake sandwich. Yup, snugged into a single sturdy roll is a split hot dog (or hot sausage, if you prefer) with a fish cake smooshed right on top of it. We got ours with that ever-rarer local condiment, pepper hash. The hash is wonderful. The fish cake and wiener combo demands more culinary mercy than we can muster.

Located on the Fishtown waterfront, Johnny's has no indoor dining room or tables and chairs. Place your order and pay for it at one window, pick it up at a window a couple of yards to the right, then marshal the meal onto one of the metal counters provided at chest level against the shop's stone block wall and on the pillars in front. When finished—ten, fifteen minutes at most—gather crumbs in the papers in which the food was wrapped, dispose of your refuse in a garbage can, and drive away.

## *John's Roast Pork

| | |
|---|---|
| 14 E. Snyder Ave. | 215-463-1951 |
| Philadelphia, PA | www.johnsroastpork.com |
| | BL \| $ |

John's roast pork sandwich is one of Philadelphia's culinary treasures, made from "Pop Pop's original recipe," cooked and boned on premises. The slices of pale, sweet meat are forked from a drippy trough and piled into a superb Carangi Bakery seeded roll, then preferably supplemented by clumps of spinach sautéed in olive oil with plenty of garlic. While the tonic shot of spinach is a welcome addition, we recommend forgoing optional cheese toppings. They detract from the essential piggy pleasure of the pork itself.

John's cheesesteak, ordered from a separate station at the walk-up counter, also is one of the city's best. John Bucci Jr., whose family started the place, explains why he thinks the steaks are so good. "When you order one, there is nothing on the grill. We start clean," he says. "Onions are not precooked; every steak is made for the person who orders it. I am a cheese fanatic. We put five slices on every sandwich, eight if you order extra." There is so much meat in a John's sandwich that the server tears out some of the roll's insides to make room. The onions are sweet, the beef juicy, the cheese abundant, the roll fresh: Is there a better formula for cheesesteak perfection?

John's original customers were shipyard personnel who went home for dinner, so it closes midafternoon. Heavy industry no longer dominates the neighborhood, which has become a Monopoly board of big-box stores, strip malls, and discount warehouses that dwarf the modest sandwich shop and its patio picnic tables. There is no indoor dining; but heat lamps and shutters are set up for cool weather.

## Leo's

| | |
|---|---|
| 1403 Chester Pike | 610-586-1199 |
| Folcroft, PA | LD \| $ |

A full-sized Leo's cheesesteak is enough for two normal appetites. A half yard of excellent Amoroso Bakery bread is split open and loaded with an incalculable amount of sliced-thin beef that has been sizzled and trowel-cut on the griddle, interlaced with caramelized onions, and saturated with melted cheese. Steaks are available without cheese, as hoagies (meaning lettuce and tomato added), as well as in the configuration known as a pizza steak: with sauce. But there is no improving on the classic configuration, plus a scattering of peppers and pickles to add a bit of sparkle.

Leo's offers no indoor seating. It is a counter where you place your order and can watch the grill man cook it. Picnic tables are provided outside.

## Longacre's Modern Dairy Bar

| | |
|---|---|
| 1445 PA Route 100 | 610-845-7551 |
| Barto, PA | www.longacresicecream.com |
| | BL (closed Sun) \| $ |

The rolling land of eastern Pennsylvania, dotted as it is with black-and-white bossies roaming farm fields, is a perfect appetizer for one of Longacre's excellent milk shakes or malts, or an old-fashioned ice cream soda in a tall tulip glass. If you need an ice cream dish that is more substantial, choose a sundae made from your choice of more than a dozen flavors of ice cream and nearly two dozen toppings, including the usual fudge and marsh-mallow and butterscotch as well as such old-time fountain oddities as wet maple walnuts and crushed cherries. The supreme concoction is known as the Longacre Special Garbage Sundae and features ten scoops of ice cream, ten toppings, whipped cream, and a cherry.

It is also possible to come to Longacre's for a hamburger, a double ham-burger, or a California burger (all dressed-up); a hot dog; or a tuna salad sandwich. Side dishes include red beet eggs and mac 'n' cheese.

Longacre's little eating area—a short counter and a handful of booths and tables (plus picnic tables outside)—opens at 7:30 a.m., when customers come for eggs with bacon, ham, or pork roll. But the waitress assured us that it is not uncommon for the doors to open at dawn for customers to order up a cookie-dough sundae or a CMP (chocolate marshmallow pea-nut sundae) for breakfast. Humankind's fundamental need for excellent ice cream is a craving that cannot be controlled by the hands of a clock.

## Lorenzo's Pizza

900 Christian St.
Philadelphia, PA

215-922-2540
www.phillyitalianmarket.com/market/
lorenzos_pizza/index.htm
LD | $

Located on a corner near the Italian Market, Lorenzo's is a real neighbor-hood place with little tourist traffic. Its cheesesteaks are superb, made from frozen sheets of lean meat, which is not really a bad thing—after all, we are not talking about prime beef here. Anyway, the frozen sheets get thrown onto the grill along with a pile of raw onions. As the meat and onions sizzle together, the chef hacks away at them with a spatula, winding up with a hodgepodge of meat and soft-cooked onions. The aromatic combo is shaped into an oval about the length of the Italian bread for which it's destined and infused with molten Cheez Whiz.

The pizza is street food–style, not artisan in any way, available by the whole pie or slice, thin crust or Sicilian. White pies and cheeseless tomato pies frequently are available, as are Stromboli, hoagies, and burgers.

# *Mama's

426 Belmont Ave.
Bala Cynwyd, PA

610-664-4757
www.mamaspizzeria.com
LD | $

Although the cheesesteak was invented in the hubbub of Philadelphia's Italian Market, the best one we've ever eaten is far from the urban core, in the suburb of Bala Cynwyd. In fact, the cheesesteak made at Mama's might be too good. Although the place is a modest pizza parlor and sandwich shop, one local we know contends that Mama's cooking is too masterly and that its refined cheesesteak defies the proletarian nature of a street-food sandwich most commonly made from stringy beef and Cheez Whiz. OK, then, let's call this the übercheesesteak.

Chef Paul Castellucci's beef is thin-sliced, lean, and scarlet, hitting the hot griddle in clumps that get hacked up with a trowel as they brown. He then applies a great mound of what looks like shredded mozzarella but is in fact a proprietary mix that, incredibly, does not stick to the hot iron surface. The beef and cheese are worked over so thoroughly that cheese nearly disappears into the finished product, but its luxury saturates every bite. The onions are not cooked on the grill among the shreds of beef, which is the customary way steak chefs do it. Instead, Castellucci sautés them separately until they tip from sharp to sweet and crisp to limp. They are added after the loose log of meat and cheese is hoisted from the griddle into the jaws of a length of muscular Italian bread. Long hot peppers, roasted in Mama's pizza oven, add brilliant red and jade green hues as well as hot sparkle to the earthy combo.

Mama's standard cheesesteak weighs a pound and a half. The mini is three-quarters of a pound.

# Marrone's Cafe

31 W. Main St.
Girardville, PA

570-276-6407
LD | $

Marrone's of Schuylkill County serves its own unique variation of Old Forge pizza. Presented on a thin sheet of paper in a metal pan, it is rectangular with a lightweight crust that is about a half-inch thick and crisp around the edges but chewy-bready toward the middle. Most regular pizza toppings are available in addition to the standard gobs of cheese, and on the side comes a plastic cup full of bright-red, crushed-pepper hot sauce. A plastic spoon is provided to spread the sauce atop the pizza, and it is a brilliant addition.

The pizza is mild-mannered; the sauce packs a punch. Beyond pizza, the Italian-American menu includes lasagna that Roadfood.com's Buffetbuster deemed "the best I have had, with a dark, sweet, and chunky sauce."

Marrone's is a seventy-plus-year-old, brick-front tavern where many people come only to drink in the bar next to the dining room. The ideal beverage to accompany its distinctive pizza is locally brewed Yuengling beer, known here in coal country as Pottsville Punch.

## Original Hot Dog Shop

3901 Forbes Ave.          412-621-0435
Pittsburgh, PA            www.theoriginalhotdogshop.com
                          LD (late night) | $

The Original Hot Dog Shop, aka the O or the Dirty O, has quite a large menu, including pizza, hoagies, fish sandwiches, and hamburgers; but if the name of the place doesn't clue you in to what's good, the view behind the counter will. There on a broad grill are row upon row of hot dogs—pale pink ones barely warm, and darker ones cooked through and ready to be bunned. Regular or all-beef, these are fine franks with a loud meaty flavor, available plain or gooped with cheese or in a "Super" configuration with cheese and bacon, and with a full array of condiments that include ketchup, mustard, relish, onion, pickle, chili, mayo, and kraut.

On the side of whatever hot dog suits your taste, you must get French fries. O fries are legendary, twice-fried to a crisp with clean flavor and a wicked crunch that makes them such a good companion for just about any sandwich. Even a small order is a substantial dish.

Aside from great fast food and post-midnight hours, one reason Pittsburghers are so fond of the Original Hot Dog Shop is that it can trace its heritage back to the Original Famous Sandwich Shop, where the foot-long hot dog was introduced in 1928. Syd Simon, who opened the Original Hot Dog Shop in 1960 (just as the Pirates won the World Series in Forbes Field across the street), worked fifteen years at the old Famous.

## Pat's King of Steaks

1237 E. Passyunk
Philadelphia, PA

215-468-1546
www.patskingofsteaks.com
Always open (except Thanksgiving and
Christmas) | $

Street-food historians believe that Pat Olivieri invented the cheesesteak in Philadelphia in 1933. His family continues to operate the restaurant he began, and while aficionados of the cheesesteak enjoy debating the merits of the city's many cheesesteak restaurants there is no denying the absolute authenticity of Pat's sandwich, which is oily, salty, and meaty—in other words, everything nutrition prigs dislike. Thin flaps of less-than-prime beef are sizzled on a grill alongside onions and hefted into a roll (with or without onions), then a trowel of melted Cheez Whiz is dripped on top. Peppers, mushrooms, pizza sauce, and double cheese are all extra-cost options, and if you wish to dude it up further, there are big glass jars with hot sauce and peppers near the takeout windows.

The combination of plebeian ingredients adds up to something that is certainly not aristocratic but carries a distinction all its own. Side your sandwich with a cup full of cheese fries (more of that melted Whiz), and eat standing on the sidewalk under harsh lights. Observe the splattered hot sauce and dropped French fries crushed underfoot. Listen to the rumble of trucks going past on their way to or from the Italian Market. Smell the mingling of cheap aftershave lotion and fancy fragrances on customers in line—both aromas overwhelmed, as the line approaches the takeout window, by the powerhouse aroma of steak and onions sizzling on a hot grill.

## Primanti Brothers

46 W. 18th St.
Pittsburgh, PA

412-263-2142
www.primantibros.com/home.htm
Always open | $

When we first wrote about Primanti Brothers, it was one of a kind. Now with twenty-one locations, including three in Florida, and more on the way, we're hard-pressed to justify its inclusion in a book devoted to unique eateries. Nevertheless, a Primanti's *sandwich* is unique, and while we've never had one anywhere else, we do highly recommend having one in the original eatery in the Strip District of Pittsburgh.

The astonishing sandwiches were designed in the 1930s for truckers who hauled produce to the nearby wholesale market. While their trucks were being unloaded, they dashed over to Primanti Brothers with a big appetite but little time to eat a Dagwood, slaw, and potatoes separately. The solution was to load hot French fries directly into the sandwich atop the customer's meat of choice, then top the fries with Pittsburgh-style (no mayo) coleslaw and a few slices of tomato: an all-in-one meal. The sandwiches are assembled at the grill behind the bar at the speed of light, so when delivered, the fries and grilled meats are still steaming hot, the slaw and tomato cool. The barely hoistable meal is presented wrapped in butcher paper.

## Robert Wholey & Co.

1501 Penn Ave.            412-261-3377
Pittsburgh, PA            www.wholey.com
                          LD | $

Located in Pittsburgh's appetite-inducing Strip District, Robert Wholey & Co. seems more like a culinary amusement park than a mere store. It has a toy train running around and singing mechanical pigs to amuse children and an extensive kitchenware department to amuse recipe-obsessed adults.

Once strictly a wholesale fish market, Wholey now carries a vast inventory of foodstuffs that range from baked ham by the haunch to sides of tuna that are cut into steaks to order. For those of us who demand immediate gratification, there are a few makeshift tables for sit-down meals at the end of a cooked-food line, and more tables upstairs in the Pittsburgh Room. While you can order crab cakes, shrimp, and even chicken, the meal most people come to eat is a fish sandwich on a tender, butter-rich bun. Whiting and cod are both available, the king of sandwiches being the Wholey Whaler: a pound of whiting sizzled crisp in the bubbling fry kettles toward the front. If that's not enough to sate you, simply ask the staff to fry (or broil) as much fish as you want to eat and they will charge you by the pound.

## Salerno's

139 Moosic Rd.            570-457-2117
Old Forge, PA             LD | $$

Salerno's is a tavern where many people come only to drink. We recommend a visit for Old Forge pizza, a style of pie unique to the area around Scranton. An Old Forge pie is squared off rather than round, airy-crusted, and topped with sweet marinara sauce and a mild blend of Italian and American cheese. It's an easy-to-eat pizza, simple and friendly.

At lunch Salerno's serves only red pizza, which is a twelve-slice pie big enough for two healthy appetites. At dinner, the better-known creation is a white pizza—a double-cruster made with a blend of several cheeses between the crusts. BTW, a slice of this pizza is called a cut, and a whole pie is a tray.

There is a broad menu beyond pizza in this neighborhood tavern: spaghetti and meatballs, sausage and peppers, chicken Parmesan sub sandwiches, *pasta e fagiole*. Many customers take their food at the bar, where they can knock back draft beers and watch the wall-mounted TV.

## Steve's Prince of Steaks

7200 Bustleton Ave.  
Philadelphia, PA

215-338-0985  
www.stevesprinceofsteaks.com  
LD | $

"The perfect balance of flavors and textures" is how Roadfood.com's Bruce Bilmes and Sue Boyle described the cheesesteak at Steve's Prince of Steaks in northeast Philadelphia. Unlike steak places that chop their meat into hash on the grill, Steve's slices it into flaps and sizzles the pieces in the traditional Italian Market way. The meat is not prime cut, that's for sure, but its flavor is a welcome, oily blast of beefy protein. Combine that with a load of Cheez Whiz and a heap of fried-soft, sweet onions all piled into a chewy tube of fresh bread and you've got a picture of cheesesteak perfection.

Here are the choices you'll need to make when you dine at Steve's: plain steak, cheesesteak, pizza steak (with sauce), or steak hoagie (with lettuce and tomato); normal weight or double-meat. If you choose cheese: American, Whiz, provolone, or mozzarella. Extras? They include pizza sauce, mushrooms, and house-roasted hot red and green peppers. Dill pickles, relish, cherry peppers, yellow peppers, and hot sauce are available as garnishes. The French fry selection features cheese fries and pizza fries. Soft drinks include birch beer; or you can have a chocolate soda, which is nothing but chocolate syrup mixed with seltzer water.

The dining experience is unequivocal street food. Read the menus posted on the wall, place your order at two different windows (one for sandwiches, the other for fries and drinks, each paid for separately), then dine at the easy-wipe silver counter that runs along the wall.

Steve's two other locations are at 2711 Comly Road in Philadelphia (215-677-8020) and 1617 East Lincoln Highway in Langhorne (215-943-4640).

# Mid-South

Kentucky

＊

North Carolina

＊

Tennessee

＊

Virginia

＊

West Virginia

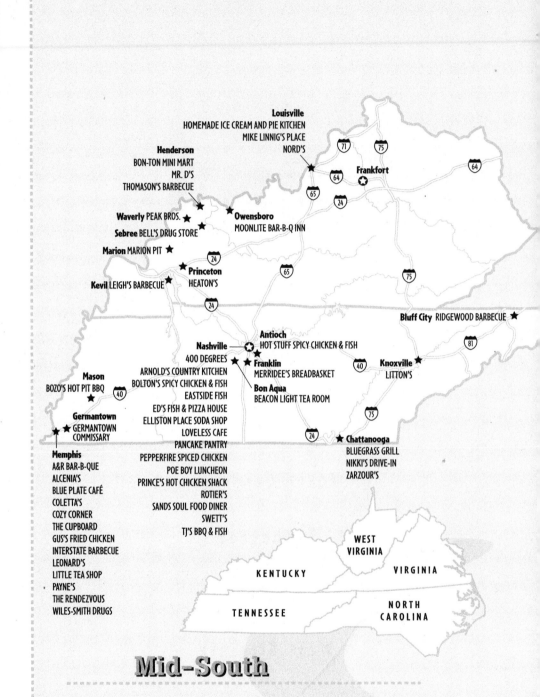

**Louisville**
HOMEMADE ICE CREAM AND PIE KITCHEN
MIKE LINNIG'S PLACE
NORD'S

**Henderson**
BON-TON MINI MART
MR. D'S
THOMASON'S BARBECUE

Frankfort

**Waverly** PEAK BROS.

**Sebree** BELL'S DRUG STORE

**Owensboro**
MOONLITE BAR-B-Q INN

**Marion** MARION PIT

**Kevil** LEIGH'S BARBECUE

**Princeton**
HEATON'S

**Bluff City** RIDGEWOOD BARBECUE

**Antioch**
HOT STUFF SPICY CHICKEN & FISH

**Nashville**
400 DEGREES
ARNOLD'S COUNTRY KITCHEN
BOLTON'S SPICY CHICKEN & FISH
EASTSIDE FISH
ED'S FISH & PIZZA HOUSE
ELLISTON PLACE SODA SHOP
LOVELESS CAFE
PANCAKE PANTRY
PEPPERFIRE SPICED CHICKEN
POE BOY LUNCHEON
PRINCE'S HOT CHICKEN SHACK
ROTIER'S
SANDS SOUL FOOD DINER
SWETT'S
TJ'S BBQ & FISH

**Franklin**
MERRIDEE'S BREADBASKET

**Bon Aqua**
BEACON LIGHT TEA ROOM

**Knoxville**
LITTON'S

**Mason**
BOZO'S HOT PIT BBQ

**Germantown**
GERMANTOWN
COMMISSARY

**Memphis**
A&R BAR-B-QUE
ALCENIA'S
BLUE PLATE CAFÉ
COLETTA'S
COZY CORNER
THE CUPBOARD
GUS'S FRIED CHICKEN
INTERSTATE BARBECUE
LEONARD'S
LITTLE TEA SHOP
PAYNE'S
THE RENDEZVOUS
WILES-SMITH DRUGS

**Chattanooga**
BLUEGRASS GRILL
NIKKI'S DRIVE-IN
ZARZOUR'S

WEST
VIRGINIA

KENTUCKY

VIRGINIA

TENNESSEE

NORTH
CAROLINA

# Mid-South

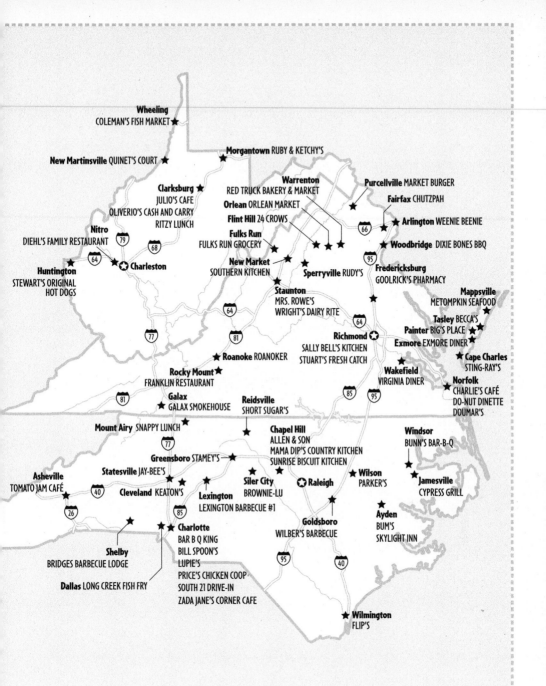

**Wheeling**
COLEMAN'S FISH MARKET ★

**New Martinsville** QUINET'S COURT ★

**Morgantown** RUBY & KETCHY'S

**Clarksburg** ★
JULIO'S CAFE
OLIVERIO'S CASH AND CARRY
RITZY LUNCH

**Warrenton**
RED TRUCK BAKERY & MARKET

**Orlean** ORLEAN MARKET

**Flint Hill** 24 CROWS

**Purcellville** MARKET BURGER

**Fairfax** CHUTZPAH

**Arlington** WEENIE BEENIE

**Nitro**
DIEHL'S FAMILY RESTAURANT

**Fulks Run**
FULKS RUN GROCERY

**Woodbridge** DIXIE BONES BBQ

★ Charleston

**New Market**
SOUTHERN KITCHEN

**Sperryville** RUDY'S

**Fredericksburg**
GOOLRICK'S PHARMACY

**Huntington**
STEWART'S ORIGINAL
HOT DOGS

**Staunton**
MRS. ROWE'S
WRIGHT'S DAIRY RITE

**Mappsville**
METOMPKIN SEAFOOD

**Tasley** BECCA'S

**Painter** BIG'S PLACE ★★

**Exmore** EXMORE DINER ★

**Richmond** ✪
SALLY BELL'S KITCHEN
STUART'S FRESH CATCH

★ **Cape Charles**
STING-RAY'S

**Roanoke** ROANOKER

**Rocky Mount** ★
FRANKLIN RESTAURANT

**Wakefield**
VIRGINIA DINER

**Norfolk**
CHARLIE'S CAFÉ
DO-NUT DINETTE
DOUMAR'S

**Galax**
★ GALAX SMOKEHOUSE

**Reidsville**
SHORT SUGAR'S

**Mount Airy** SNAPPY LUNCH

**Chapel Hill**
ALLEN & SON
MAMA DIP'S COUNTRY KITCHEN
SUNRISE BISCUIT KITCHEN

**Windsor**
BUNN'S BAR-B-Q

**Greensboro** STAMEY'S →

**Statesville** JAY-BEE'S

**Siler City**
BROWNIE-LU

**Asheville**
TOMATO JAM CAFÉ

**Cleveland** KEATON'S

**Lexington**
LEXINGTON BARBECUE #1

✪ **Raleigh**

**Wilson**
PARKER'S

★ **Jamesville**
CYPRESS GRILL

★★ **Charlotte**
BAR B Q KING
BILL SPOON'S
LUPIE'S
PRICE'S CHICKEN COOP
SOUTH 21 DRIVE-IN
ZADA JANE'S CORNER CAFE

**Goldsboro**
WILBER'S BARBECUE

**Ayden**
BUM'S
SKYLIGHT INN

**Shelby**
BRIDGES BARBECUE LODGE

**Dallas** LONG CREEK FISH FRY

★ **Wilmington**
FLIP'S

## Bell's Drug Store

7107 Kentucky Route 56
Sebree, KY

270-835-7544
www.bellsdrugstore.wordpress.com
L | $

As we drove into the small town of Sebree on a backroads eating tour in the company of Kentucky-food authority Louis Hatchett IV, Louis suddenly called out, "Orangeade!" We pulled up at the sturdy old brick-facade building that is Bell's Drug Store. It is a working pharmacy with shelves of patent medicines for sale and a short soda fountain counter up front.

We placed our orangeade orders and then a moment later, the soda jerk turned to us with a tragic look on his face. "We have run out of oranges," he lamented. But there was still a good supply of lemons, so we ordered lemonade made with an extra lemon (50¢ surcharge): what a mighty sweet/tart wallop that delivered! Then there is lemon ice, a Bell Drug specialty: nothing but fresh lemon juice poured over crushed ice and seasoned with a dash of salt. When the mixologist handed it to us, he pointed to a large sugar dispenser that had been filled with salt (and conspicuously so labeled!). "There's more salt if you'd like," he said. To our taste, it was just right as presented, the sprinkle of salinity enriching the pure citrus power.

## *Bon-Ton Mini Mart

2036 Madison St.                   270-826-1207
Henderson, KY                      L | $

West of Louisville is fried-chicken country. Nearly every restaurant, plain or fancy, has its own special version. One of the most humble—and the best— is the Bon-Ton Mini Mart. In this former convenience-store snack shop, white and dark meat are marinated before getting fried, resulting in pieces that are wickedly crunchy, dripping-moist inside, and fairly exploding with flavor. With the chicken come savory biscuits, French fries, and coleslaw.

The chicken is so incredibly good that it is all too tempting to eat until appetite has become only a distant memory. But the Bon-Ton demands you save room for dessert. Banana pudding is a big bowl of comfort, coconut cream and chocolate pie are deeply satisfying, and the chess pie just may be the best one we have ever tasted. It has a buttery richness that goes beyond sweetness. What a brilliant dessert!

## Heaton's

495 Marion Rd.                     270-365-3102
Princeton, KY                      BL | $

We admit to getting perverse pleasure from dining at a table opposite shelves of motor oil and other automotive necessities. Located in a Marathon ser- vice station, Heaton's resembles a thousand other quick-stop, quick-eat mini-marts around rural America. But the barbecue it serves is superb. It is real Kentucky 'cue—in this case pulled pork, served in a sandwich, large or small, as a plate with two side dishes, by the pound, and whole shoulder. It is hickory smoked, rugged-textured, and comes with a fascinating sauce that is slightly sweet with a bright citrus flavor. Ribs also are available, as are breakfast sandwiches and hamburgers.

## Homemade Ice Cream and Pie Kitchen

2525 Bardstown Rd.                 502-459-8184
Louisville, KY                     www.piekitchen.com
                                   $

Because we visit Louisville only for short periods of time, coming to this place is inevitably frustrating. There is no way two people or even five people can sam- ple a significant fraction of the tempting desserts available on any one day. The good news is that nearly every pie and cake is available by the slice, maximizing opportunity to taste the most number of things. All the usual suspects are available, from red velvet cake to Key lime pie, and several desserts are little known outside the South: chess pie that is purity itself; hummingbird cake sweet enough to please a nectar-crazed avian, sweet-potato pie, Italian cream cake (a Kentucky favorite), and praline ice cream. In addition to regular chess, which is little more than cream, sugar, and eggs, there are lemon chess and chocolate chess.

Many of the handsome layer cakes come swirled with sweet buttercream icing, but our favorite variety is yellow cake with caramel icing. Or perhaps Georgia cake, which features mandarin oranges and pineapple whipped topping. Among pies, the one not to miss is Dutch apple blanketed with molten caramel.

Note: There are a handful of other locations around Louisville.

## Leigh's Barbecue

| | |
|---|---|
| 9405 US Route 60 | 270-488-3434 |
| Kevil, KY | L (closed Weds) \| $ |

Not for barbecue milquetoasts, Leigh's pork packs punch—even before the application of vinegar-pepper sauce. Sandwiches come light, medium, or heavy, referring to the amount of sauce desired. The 'cue itself is of the ridiculously tender sort—cooked in the hickory haze of an open pit for a full twenty-four hours, emerging smoky-sweet the way only long-cooked pork can be. Regulars know to ask for inside or outside pieces, or a mix of both; the pork is chopped when a sandwich is ordered. On the side, you definitely want Leigh's potato salad and maybe baked beans too. Coleslaw is good, in or out of the sandwich.

Opened in 1950 and now in a third generation of the Leigh family, Leigh's is a stark cinder-block bunker by the side of the road just west of Paducah. Seating is at a curved counter, or at the picnic table outside. Note that Leigh's is open only for lunch, and closes when the day's meat supply runs out (sometimes before 2 p.m.).

## Marion Pit

| | |
|---|---|
| 728 S. Main St. | 270-965-3318 |
| Marion, KY | www.marionpitbbq.com |
| | LD \| $ |

Marion Pit, known also as Jack's By the Tracks, has been around nearly four decades, long enough to become a Crittenden County institution. Proprietor Jack Easley said that he usually cooks an especially large number of pork shoulders on Saturday because so many local churches purchase meat by the pound for Sunday suppers. His place is the oldest smokehouse around, and certainly the most unpretentious—a hut on the outskirts of town with a few picnic tables for dining outdoors or inside a screened patio.

Place your order at a window in the small building, to which hickory-cooked shoulders are brought from an adjoining cookhouse and readied for eating. Mr. Easley told us that he cooks his meat for seventeen hours, using no seasonings and no sauce. The long smoke at low temperature results in pork that is unspeakably tender, so soft that it cannot be sliced, because it would fall apart. You can buy it by the pound to go, by the sandwich, or by the plate (billed here as a "big pile of bar-b-q"). It is some of the best Q anywhere, served with a delicious sauce, the recipe for which is known only to Mr. Easley, his wife, and his son.

## Mike Linnig's Place

9308 Cane Run Rd.  
Louisville, KY

502-937-9888  
www.mikelinnigsrestaurant.com  
LD (closed Mon) | $$

Mike Linnig's opened some ninety years ago as a fruit and vegetable stand on the Linnig family farm. It is now a big restaurant with beer-garden accommodations outside and cavernous dining rooms indoors. The menu includes just about every kind of seafood that can be fried, including sea scallops, crawfish, and salmon, but its highlights are such heartland fish-camp specialties as catfish, whitefish, and frog legs—all served in immense portions. We are especially fond of the spicy fish nuggets and the freshly breaded shrimp. The frog legs, the scallops, and the oysters have a nice crunch to their crust but are not otherwise memorable.

Onion rings are a specialty. They are big chunky things, extremely brittle, and mostly crust with just a hint of onion flavor emanating from the slick ribbon within. By the way, the tartar sauce and cocktail sauce, while served in the sort of individual cups typical of institutional meals, are Mike Linnig's own recipe, and both are outstanding.

Among the beverage choices are iced tea (sweet or not), lemonade (which tastes a lot like the tea), and genuine Kool-Aid, listed as fruit punch.

## Moonlite Bar-B-Q Inn

2840 W. Parrish Ave.      270-684-8143

Owensboro, KY      www.moonlite.com

LD | $$

There is a printed menu of dinners and sandwiches at the Moonlight Bar-B-Q, but nearly everyone who isn't crippled avails themselves of a spectacular buffet that occupies one large room with salads and desserts on one side, vegetables and meats on the other. There are barbecued chicken, ribs, pulled pork, spectacularly succulent beef brisket, and even a pan of non-barbecued sliced country ham that is firm and salty, as well as a tray of ready-made ham biscuits. And there is western Kentucky's favorite barbecue meat, mutton. Cooked until pot-roast tender, it is set out on the buffet two ways: chopped or pulled. Chopped mutton is pulverized to nothing but flavor: tangy lamb and woodsmoke in a bold duet. The pulled version is a textural amusement park—rugged and chunky with a lot of hard outside crust among soft, juicy chunks of interior meat. Apply your own sauce at the table from the pitchers the waitress brings. One is a dark orange emulsion with gentle vinegar-tomato zest; the other is known as "mutton dip," an unctuous gravy that is used to baste the mutton as it cooks. For those who need heat, Moonlite also supplies bottles of "Very Hot Sauce," which is brilliantly peppered and will set your lips and tongue aglow.

An impressive deployment of vegetables: cheesy broccoli casserole, creamed corn niblets, and butter-drizzled mashed potatoes, plus the western Kentucky soup/stew of mutton and vegetables known as burgoo (pronounced BUR-goo). Other notable sides: crusty corn muffins, mac 'n' cheese, baked apples, and ham and beans. We also sampled a silly but intriguing banana salad made with Miracle Whip and chopped nuts, plus a couple of tables of terrific Kentucky pies. On Thursday and Friday nights, shrimp and catfish are added to the buffet.

## Mr. D's

1435 S. Green St.      270-826-2505

Henderson, KY      LD | $

A fiberglass chicken as tall as a grizzly bear stands outside of Mr. D's, beckoning customers to drive in. While Mr. D's is a full-menu drive-in with a repertoire of hamburgers, hot dogs, and sandwiches, the chicken rules. It is made from a recipe popularized decades ago by a legendary chicken man named Colonel Jim, and like the chicken at the nearby Bon-Ton Mini Mart

(p. 158), it has a wickedly crunchy crust spicy enough to make your eyes water.

Because Mr. D's is a quick-service drive-in with car-service only, the chicken you order will be delivered to your window in five minutes or less, meaning that the kitchen cooks it ahead of time rather than to order. This is good if you are really, really hungry, but not so good if you are a crisp-skin connoisseur, because the crust loses its crunch. Make no mistake: This is four-star fried chicken, and puts just about any non-Kentucky fried chicken to shame. But the next time we order some, we are going to do as Henderson tipster Louis Hatchett IV advises: request that it be cooked to order. If that twenty-minute wait means crust that cracks when bitten, we'll happily endure it.

## Nord's

2118 S. Preston St.          502-634-0931
Louisville, KY              www.nordsbakery.biz
                           B | $

Nord's is a full-service bakery with a vast menu of pastries that will send sweets fanciers into orbit. Among the highlights are iced sugar cookies in the shape of Kentucky, long johns frosted with maple spread and topped with crisp bacon, donuts shaped like pretzels, glazed bear claws, knobby apple fritters, plump Boston creams filled with luxurious custard, and ooey-gooey cinnamon-veined pecan rolls. Even if you are not a buttercream fan, we suggest you try at least one cream puff filled and topped with buttercream. The word "buttercream" attains full meaning here, as that's what the stuff tastes like: butter and cream (and just enough sugar).

While most business is takeout, there are a handful of tables up a flight of stairs in back. A sign posted above the little dining area proclaims, "It's all good!" Amen to that.

## *Peak Bros.

5363 US Hwy. 60            270-389-0267
Waverly, KY               LD | $

Peak Bros., which had become a legend among western Kentucky barbecue parlors since it opened in 1948, burned down in 2006. It has been rebuilt and is as good as ever. Originally guided here by Kentucky tipster Louis Hatchett IV, who referred to Waverly as "the western edge of barbecued muttonland," we began our Peak Bros. love affair with chipped mutton sandwiches. Chipping, a local term for intensive chopping, turns the meat into a hash sopped with the potent natural gravy known as dip.

Debbie Britt, whose father and uncle started the restaurant, assured us that chipped is good, but sliced is even better. At her urging, we got some slices and they were really good, although our preference is chipped. Peak Bros.' ham, edged with pepper, was a sweet harmony of pork and smoke, luxuriously tender; the sliced mutton was moist and mellow with none of the rank bite typical of mature lamb elsewhere.

Come November, Peak Bros. becomes a favorite source among locals and fans from around the country for Thanksgiving and Christmas hams. They are sweet and smoky with a hugely savory blackened crust all around their vast lode of pink meat. Lady Bird Johnson once declared Peak Bros. ham to be the best "this side of Texas."

## Thomason's Barbecue

701 Atkinson St.　　　　　270-826-0654
Henderson, KY　　　　　　LD | $

Thomason's barbecued beans are magnificent—rich and smoky, laced with shreds of meat and so vividly spiced that they taste like Kentucky Christmas. The barbecue itself is worth a trip too.

Thomason's barbecues everything: pork, mutton, beef, spare ribs, baby-back ribs, chicken, ham, and turkey. You can get your choice of meat on a plate, which includes pickle, onion, bread, and beans; on a tray, which includes only pickle, onion, and bread; or in a sandwich. Like all other sandwiches in this area, Thomason's can scarcely be picked up by hand because juice from the meat saturates the lower piece of bread, causing it to disintegrate. The pork is velvet-soft, moist, and seductively smoky; the mutton is sopped with gravy and gentle-flavored.

A simple, freestanding eatery with an order counter and a scattering of tables, Thomason's does a big carry-out business, selling its specialties by the pound and gallon. On a shelf below the order counter are for-sale bottles of dip, which is a sauce with natural "au jus" character.

## Allen & Son

6203 Millhouse Rd.                    919-942-7576
Chapel Hill, NC                       LD | $

Cinder-block walls, plastic tablecloths, and pork slow-smoked over hickory coals: Here is a consummate North Carolina barbecue parlor. Sandwiches are available, but we recommend getting Allen's meat on a plate, which includes a pile of sparkling coleslaw and about a half-dozen spherical, crisp-skinned hush puppies. Meat is served just barely moistened with sauce, but you can boldface it with further applications of Allen & Son's butter-rich, vinegar-based hot sauce loaded with spice and cracked pepper.

If you get the combination plate known to some locals as "stew and que" (highly recommended), the pile of good smoked meat is supplemented by a bowl of Brunswick stew, another traditional companion to smoked pork in these parts. Unlike the meatier Brunswick stews of southern Virginia, this luscious stuff is mostly vegetables with a few shreds of meat, all cosseted in a tomato-rich sauce. It is a hearty, rib-sticking food that makes a wonderful contrast to the exquisite pork. On the side: sweet, sweet tea.

## Bar B Q King

2900 Wilkinson Blvd.          704-399-8344
Charlotte, NC                 www.barbqking.com
                              LD | $

Bar B Q King is an American drive-in par excellence, complete with a vintage "Servus-Fone" ordering system whereby you study the menu, then press a button to speak with the kitchen, and place your order. Meals are brought to the car on blue plastic trays.

Our first visit, we made the mistake of asking for a "pork sandwich." What we got was a perch sandwich. We ate it anyway, and it was marvelous—moist, sweet white meat so satisfying it reminded us of the best pork, but encased in a golden crust. In fact, the perch was so good, we subsequently ordered trout, shrimp, and oysters—all fried in that only-in-the-South soulful way that's guaranteed to convert even a diehard fish frowner.

What we learned from our experience—other than to recommend BBQK as a fried-fish restaurant—is that if you want smoked pork hereabouts, you don't say "pork"; you say "barbecue." Of course it is pork, available sliced or minced, and it too is a winner—tender, succulent, veiled in a vinegar sauce that does not overwhelm the meat's fundamental fineness and always paired with a layer of coleslaw in the bun. Fried chicken also is barbecued: first fried, then quickly dipped in hot sauce long enough to get hot, but not so long that it doesn't stay crisp.

## Bill Spoon's

5524 South Blvd.             704-525-8865
Charlotte, NC                www.spoonsbarbecue.com
                             L | $

A sign on the front of Bill Spoon's announces, "We cook the whole pig. It makes the difference." That's no lie. As swell as slow-smoke-cooked shoulders and butts may be, they cannot match the rousing diversity of hacked-up whole hog, from creamy to crunchy, which you can have here with a couple of side dishes or packed into a bun and crowned with bright mustard slaw.

Spoon's Brunswick stew is so dense with meat and vegetables that you can clean the bowl using only a fork, and tubular hush puppies with vivid onion punch provide a cornmeal counterpoint to the spice of barbecue or barbecue-laced beans. If there is a pork frowner at your table, Spoon's chicken, cooked ultra-tender and encased in succulent skin, is a fine alternative.

To drink: sweet tea, refilled approximately every ninety seconds by roving waitstaff. For dessert: banana pudding. It all adds up to an archetypal barbecue meal, just what you'd hope for in a place that's built a grand reputation pit-cooking pig since 1963. Founder Bill Spoon learned the barbecue trade from John Skinner, who learned his craft at North Carolina's first sit-down barbecue restaurant, opened by Bob Melton in Rocky Mount in 1924.

## Bridges Barbecue Lodge

| | |
|---|---|
| 2000 E. Dixon Blvd. | 704-482-8567 |
| Shelby, NC | www.bridgesbbq.com |
| | LD (closed Mon & Tues) \| $ |

Bridges has no written menu, just the slip of paper used by the waitress to take orders: sandwich, tray, or plate. A tray is barbecue and barbecue slaw; a plate also holds French fries, lettuce, tomato, and pickle. Both are accompanied by hush puppies, and whether you select sandwich, tray, or plate, you must decide if you want your meat (pork shoulder) minced, chopped, or sliced. It is a major decision, for they are almost like three different foods. Bridges is one of the few places that offers minced barbecue, an old-time configuration from traditional pig-pickin's. It is pulverized into moist hash with some little shreds of darkened, chewy crust among the distressed pork. The mound is held together by a good portion of uniquely North Carolinian sauce with a strong vinegar punch. Chopped is the more typical way modern North Carolinians like it—chunky and easily chewable, and with only a smidgen of sauce. Sliced barbecue comes as big, soft flaps. With the pork comes a Styrofoam cup of warm sauce for dipping.

Tubular hush puppies, some of the best in the South, sport a sandy-textured crust and creamy insides. Bridges' slaw is *barbecue* slaw, meaning finely chopped cabbage bound together with—what else?—barbecue sauce! It's got a brilliant flavor and a pearly-red color that handsomely complements your pork of choice. The small tray, by the way, is only about three by five inches and an inch and a half deep, but it is astounding how much meat and slaw get packed into it.

Bridges' dining room is plain and soothing, with the kind of meditative atmosphere unique to the finest pork parlors of the Mid-South. Square wooden chandeliers cast soft light over green-upholstered booths and a short counter up front where single diners chat quietly among themselves as they sip buttermilk or iced tea and fork into barbecue. During our first meal here, five police officers with gleaming nickel-plated pistols occupied a table toward the back. Even they spoke in hushed tones, as if it would be sacrilegious to be raucous in this decent eat place.

## Brownie-Lu

919 N. 2nd Ave.                           919-663-3913
Siler City, NC                            BLD | $

Brownie-Lu, which opened in 1960, earned the Golden Chicken Award from the Broaster Company, which makes equipment that simultaneously fries and pressure cooks the bird. The result is meat so tender that it barely clings to the bone, encased in crunchy-brittle skin. It has a full but mellow flavor, like something an ideal grandma might make. At Brownie-Lu, a counter-and-booth diner loved by locals, it is served with such laudable side dishes as black-eyed peas, genuine mashed potatoes, and butter beans cooked with ham. There are enough good vegetables on the menu that a health-food type could come here and have a totally meatless, delicious meal. A full breakfast is served—country ham is a must—and lunch and supper demand a slice from one of the kitchen's homemade cream pies.

## Bum's

566 3rd St.                               252-746-6880
Ayden, NC                                 BL | $

Many people think of Bum's as a barbecue restaurant, and that in itself is a high compliment, considering its "competition" in Ayden is the Skylight Inn (p. 175), which any sane person must agree is one of the best barbecue restaurants on Planet Earth. Some others think of it as a chicken restaurant. You'll wait a good twenty minutes for the bird to fry, but the reward for your patience is crisp-crusted chicken on a par with North Carolina's finest. We love Bum's most for its vegetables and side dishes.

It's a small torture to go through the cafeteria line and have to choose among corn sticks, corn bread, porky boiled cabbage, pieces of crisp pork skin, butter beans, and collard greens. The last, those greens, are actually grown by proprietor Latham "Bum" Dennis in his home garden (Ayden is the collard capital of the world), and they are cooked to a point of supreme tenderness. There are a few desserts from which to choose; warm banana pudding is the one not to be missed.

Breakfast features excellent biscuits (with or without gravy) and a choice of pig meats that includes homemade sausage, pork tenderloin, and fried ham.

## Bunn's Bar-B-Q

127 N. King St.

Windsor, NC

252-794-2274

L | $

Bunn's building started life in the mid-1800s as a doctor's office. It became a filling station in 1900, and in 1938 barbecue was added to the menu. There's still an old Texaco pump outside, and the place is decorated with vintage signs, ads, and ephemera. The atmosphere is vaguely similar to what the Cracker Barrel chain aims to create; but in this case, it is real.

You eat pork, with or without Brunswick stew, accompanied by crisp, fresh coleslaw. The pork is chopped ultra-fine, a mix of soft white meat from the inside of the shoulder laced with chewy brown bark from its surface. It comes ever-so-lightly sauced with what the locals like: vinegar and spice; but if you want it moister or hotter, other sauces are provided. Each plate is topped with a square of thin, unctuous corn bread that has a serious chew and is the ideal medium for pushing around Brunswick stew on the plate. Two slices of this corn bread stand in for normal bread on Bunn's barbecue sandwich, which also contains a measure of slaw.

## Cypress Grill

1520 Stewart St.

Jamesville, NC

252-792-4175

D Jan-Apr | $$

For those of us who grew up thinking of herring as a pickled hors d'oeuvre, North Carolina river herring is a shock. For one thing, it looks like a fish. Second, it tastes like fish, not the least bit like chicken or anything else. There is no better place to get to know it than at the Cypress Grill on the banks of the Roanoke River. Here is the last of the old-time herring shacks, quite literally a cypress wood shack, open only for the herring run, mid-January through April. (In recent years, even in those months, herring de-population has sometimes meant a no-herring menu early in the year.)

There is no meal on the Cypress Grill menu other than fish. Other than herring, you can have rock (striped bass), perch, flounder, shrimp, oysters, devil crab, clam strips, trout fillet, or catfish fillet. Side dishes include a choice of vegetables, which are fine but not particularly interesting: boiled potatoes, fried okra, or slaw.

The herring are served with their heads lopped off, each one's flesh scored with notches and veiled in the thinnest possible sheath of cornmeal, so that when it was tossed into the boiling oil, it cooked quickly deep down to the bone. The big issue among river herring lovers is degree of doneness.

Some ask for it sunny-side up, meaning minimal immersion in the fry kettle, resulting in a fish from which you can peel away the skin and lift moist pieces of meat off the bones. The opposite way to go is to ask for your herring cremated: fried until hard and crunchy and so well cooked that all the little bones have become indistinguishable from the flesh around them. The meat itself is transformed, its weight lightened so the natural oiliness is gone, but the flavor has become even more intense. The crust and the interior are melded, and they break off in unbelievably savory bite-sized pieces, finally leaving nothing but a herring backbone on the plate.

While herring-crazed patrons fill up on four, five, six, or more of the plush fish, we advise first-time visitors to the Cypress Grill to leave appetite for dessert. That's the one non-fish item on the menu worth singing about. Every morning, proprietors Leslie and Sally Gardner make pies. When we stopped to visit one day around 10 a.m., Mr. Gardner led us right over to the pie case—a wooden cupboard built by a neighbor to be so sturdy, he says, "you could dance on it." He insisted we feel the bottom of a pie pan, still nearly too hot to touch. We sat down then and there and forked up a piece of chocolate pie that was modest-sized but intensely fudgy.

## Flip's

5818 Oleander Dr.                910-799-6350
Wilmington, NC                   LD | $

Smoke-infused and as rich as pork belly, hacked into a fine hash that is mostly cream-soft but speckled with chewy little nubbins, Flip's barbecue is a Cape Fear treasure. Mustard-tweaked coleslaw is optional on sandwiches; a plate includes crunchy long hush puppies and two side dishes from a list that includes baked beans, green beans, French fries, Brunswick stew, deep-fried corn nuggets, fried okra, fried squash, boiled potatoes, and little triangular hunks of fried mac 'n' cheese!

Flip's sauce, available to take home, is more hot than sweet—thinner than western North Carolina tomato-based sauce, but thicker than the mostly vinegar sauces common in the eastern part of the state.

Dessert? Banana pudding is a creamy swirl of custard, Cool Whip, banana slices, and softening vanilla wafers: the denouement for a just-right meal.

## Jay-Bee's

320 Mocksville Hwy.  704-872-8033

Statesville, NC  LD | $

The brash personality of this drive-through (or dine-in) eat place is hard to resist. "This Ain't No Fast Food Joint!" a sign outside brags. "We Proudly Make All Our Menu Items to Order and It Takes a Little More Time." That would be about a three-minute wait until you are presented with a bacon-Cheddar dog, a Northerner's Fancy with sauerkraut and mustard, or a Prairie Dog topped with barbecue sauce, chopped onions, and melted cheese. They come all-beef or not, in regular and foot-long sizes. You can also get a double—two in one bun. Hamburgers are less impressive, although their institutional blandness is overcome by adding sautéed onions to the package.

The beverage menu ranges from sweet tea and milk shakes to Dr Pepper and Mountain Dew, and if you dine inside, a refill of any soda is free. Don't tell Mayor Bloomberg of New York, but thirty-two-ounce drinks are available at the drive-through window.


## *Keaton's

17365 Cool Springs Rd.  704-278-1619

Cleveland, NC  www.keatonsoriginalbbq.com

  L Tues & Weds; LD Thurs-Sat | $

A cinder-block bunker in North Carolina cattle land between the High Country's natural beauty and High Point's unnaturally low-priced furniture outlets, Keaton's serves some of the best fried chicken you ever will eat.

Step up to the counter and order an upper or a lower (the polite country terms for breast and wing or thigh and drumstick). Pick side dishes from a soulful repertoire of mac 'n' cheese, baked beans, hot-sauce slaw, or white-mayo slaw; choose iced tea (sweet, of course) or beer; then go to your assigned table or booth, to which a waitress brings the food.

In Keaton's kitchen, the chicken is peppered and salted, floured and fried, at which point it is simply excellent country-style, pan-cooked chicken. Then comes the distinctive extra step: just-fried pieces are immersed in a bubbling vat of secret-formula red sauce, a high-spiced, opaque potion similar to what graces High Country barbecued pork. This process takes only seconds, but the throbbing sauce permeates to the bone. You eat this chicken with your hands, pulling off crisp strips of sauce-glazed skin, worrying every joint to suck out all the flavor you can get.

## *Lexington Barbecue #1

101 W. Center St. Ext.
Lexington, NC

336-249-9814
LD | $

"Monk's Place," as locals know it (in deference to founder Wayne "Honey" Monk), looks like a barn with six smelters attached to the back. From their tall chimneys issues the scent of burning hickory and oak wood and slow-cooking pork, one of the most appetite-arousing perfumes in the world. Honey Monk's is a straightforward eatery with booths and tables and carhop service in the parking lot. Much business is takeout.

There are no complicated techniques or deep secrets about Lexington Barbecue. After about ten hours basking in smoke, pork shoulders get chopped into a hash of pieces that vary from melting soft (from the inside) to chewy (from the "bark," or exterior). Nothing like pyrotechnical barbecue of the Midwest or balls-out beef from the pits of Texas, this is subtle stuff, a graceful duet of pork and smoke, full appreciation of which demands a well-honed palate. The meat is served on a bun with finely chopped coleslaw or as part of a platter, on which it occupies half a small yellow cardboard boat, with slaw in the other half. Like the meat, the slaw is flavored with a vinegar/sweet red barbecue sauce. As part of the platter you get terrific, crunch-crusted hush puppies. For dessert, there's peach cobbler and, on rare occasions, berry cobbler too. Cheerwine is available on draught.

## Long Creek Fish Fry

1425 Lower Dallas Hwy.
Dallas, NC

704-922-3998
LD (closed Mon & Tues) | $

If you are only a little bit hungry, go somewhere else. Long Creek Fish Fry is all about eating large, even if you order the "small" plates that are available for most entrees. But it's not just quantity that marks this out-of-the-way fish camp as a worthy destination. It is simple and delicious food. Since the mid-twentieth century, Long Creek has drawn crowds of locals—very large crowds on weekends—for its crisp-crusted fried catfish (whole or filleted), green shrimp (small and crunchy), oysters, and salt-and-pepper flounder, accompanied by French fries or onion rings, tubular hush puppies, slaw, and sweet iced tea. Tartar sauce that comes alongside is bright and pickly.

Dining is fish-camp casual. Find a place to park, maybe along the road. Dine off disposable dishware at unclothed tables.

## Lupie's

2718 Monroe Rd.                    704-374-1232
Charlotte, NC                      LD | $

Lupie's is the sort of place locals love but outsiders seldom discover. It's been part of the Elizabeth neighborhood since 1987, and it has unvarnished charm that is increasingly rare in a world of corporate restaurants. Prices are in the single-digit range. Sweet tea is served in mason jars. Décor includes odes to Elvis as well as portraits of the waitstaff from years past. Lupie's isn't just a restaurant; it is a part of its community.

Much of the food is true South. The four-vegetable plate is a meat-and-three benchmark. We had one with painfully tender discs of yellow squash and sweet onions, green beans (non-canned, well cooked) saturated by waves of pork flavor, large hunks of carrot sweetened with brown sugar, and super-cheesy mac 'n' cheese. On the side came a square of corn bread. The menu lists three kinds of chili: Texas, vegetarian, and Cincinnati-style. We've enjoyed them all. Burgers too are beautiful: thick and craggy, all the better to hold massive quantities of melted Cheddar cheese. You get your choice of Kaiser or onion roll, potato chips or coleslaw.

For dessert, we've yet to go beyond banana pudding, which is thick with crumbled vanilla wafers. One portion will feed two or three.

## Mama Dip's Country Kitchen

408 W. Rosemary St.                919-942-5837
Chapel Hill, NC                    www.mamadips.com
                                   BLD | $$

"Mama Dip" is Mildred Council, founder/owner/chef at Chapel Hill's beloved soul-food restaurant. Ms. Council, nicknamed "Dip" by her siblings because she was tall with long arms that enabled her to dip water from the very bottom of the rain barrel, wrote *Mama Dip's Kitchen* in 1999, a valuable cookbook that includes many of the restaurant's recipes.

Three meals a day are served in Dip's nouveau rustic quarters. Lunch and dinner offer great southern classics—fried chicken, chitlins, Brunswick stew; at breakfast, you can't go wrong with eggs, pork chops and gravy, and regular or sweet-potato biscuits. The morning menu also includes trout fillets, whole catfish, and fried salmon cakes.

Later in the day, what we like best about Dip's meals, aside from the lumpy, crunchy, brightly salty crust of the fried chicken, are the vegetables. The daily list includes long-cooked greens, black-eyed peas, crunchy nuggets of fried okra, mashed potatoes and gravy, porky string beans, okra stew with tomatoes, corn-dotted coleslaw, always a sumptuous vegetable casserole, and cool sweet-potato salad. For mopping and dipping, there are buttermilk biscuits, corn bread, and yeast rolls.

## Parker's

2514 Hwy. 301 S.     252-237-0972
Wilson, NC           LD | $

Parker's goes back to the 1940s when Wilson was the place tobacco farmers sold their crop. A big barbecue meal was how they celebrated the harvest; buyers ate here and spread the word up and down Highway 301, which was the main north-south road prior to I-95. Still, the interstate is only seven miles away, making Parker's an extremely convenient stop.

It is a spacious eating facility with multiple dining rooms. Customers crowd the lined-up tables for family-style combo platters of chopped pork, fried chicken, Brunswick stew, boiled potatoes, corn sticks, and sweet coleslaw with a mustard tinge. Cooked in hardwood smoke and chopped into hash, the pork is moist and scarcely sauced. If you do want to doll it up, tables are set with plain vinegar and a hot sauce that has a vinegar base. As for the Parker's chicken, we like it even better than the pork. Its brittle crust encloses juice-dripping meat, the dark pieces especially luscious. Family-style dinners, including all-you-can-eat barbecue, two pieces of fried chicken per customer, and all the fixins are available for under $10 per person.

From the moment it opens each day, Parker's always seems to bustle. As you enter, it's an adventure maneuvering your way to a table as waiters zoom past toting platters piled high with food.

## Price's Chicken Coop

1614 Camden Rd.     704-333-9866
Charlotte, NC        www.priceschickencoop.com
                     LD (takeout only) | $

Once inside the door of this little South End storefront, two-thirds of which is dedicated to cooking and one-third to ordering (no dining facilities), you pick your place in one of six or seven lines leading to a counter with three cash registers, each of which is flanked by white-uniformed servers. The cinder-block room thunders with kitchen clatter undershot by the syncopation of bubbling oil, and everything happens double-fast.

Order a quarter or half, white or dark, wings, gizzards, or livers, and it will all be assembled by the time you draw your wallet. Box of chicken in hand, you exit and find a place to eat: back at work, in your car, or on the pleasant grassy berm of the light rail line across the street.

Amenities are minimal, but the fried chicken is maximal. There is nothing dramatically unusual about it. It is cooked in peanut oil, and while brothers Steve and Andrew Price keep their seasonings a secret, it is not spice that makes it unforgettable. What's so great is the surfeit of crunchy skin imbued with the silky goodness of chicken fat. The skin is substantially chewy and you can hear its juices when you apply your teeth to it—just before it dissolves into a flood of chicken flavor on your tongue. Expectedly, the meat of the dark parts oozes savory juice. Not so predictably, even the breasts are moist and big-flavored in a way that white meat seldom is.

We love the express guarantee on Price's menu: ALL FOOD GUARANTEED SATISFACTORY.

## Short Sugar's

1328 S. Scales St.          336-342-7487
Reidsville, NC              BLD | $

At the tap of a horn, carhop service is still available at Short Sugar's, which opened as a hamburger joint in 1949. It now serves three meals a day, and the menu is vast, including breakfast, sandwiches, and a burger roster with a "teenage burger" (a double cheeseburger). Chili dogs are raunchy little things topped with chili so fine that it is more paste than hash. Barbecue is the featured attraction, a point that is obvious if you walk in the door that leads to the takeout counter, for here you have a view of quarter hogs on the grate, soon to be chopped and served on a plate (with fries, slaw, and hush puppies), on a tray (with just slaw and hush puppies), or as a sandwich. The meat is sweeter than most, due to Short Sugar's fascinating sauce, which is mixed in and also available on the table if you want more. The slaw is brilliant, fresh as can be, and the hush puppies provide a welcome crunchy counterpoint for the tender pork. Our only disappointment was a bland ham biscuit.

A big restaurant with a long counter, booths, and tables, Short Sugar's has the patina of a place that has been around many decades. Most of the clientele are regulars, but the staff treats strangers as welcome guests.

## *Skylight Inn

4618 S. Lee St.  
Ayden, NC

252-746-4113  
www.skylightinnbbq.com  
LD | $

Hickory-smoked, whole-hog barbecue, unaffected by time or trends, has made the Skylight Inn a legend. Unlike pyrotechnical kick-ass Q's, Skylight's marriage of smoke and pork is a subtle nuptial, elegantly abetted by the addition of a little vinegar and Texas Pete hot sauce, salt and pepper—nothing more—as it is chopped with cleavers on a hard-rock maple cutting board. Beyond exquisite flavor, what is most striking about whole-hog barbecue is the texture. Along with soft shreds from the interior are chewy strips from the outside as well as shockingly crunchy nuggets of skin. The cooked skin conveys terabytes of lusciousness, its firmness adding drama that is lacking in barbecue made only from upscale hams or shoulders. Any sauce beyond the vinegar and Texas Pete is anathema. There are two and only two ways to have meat at the Skylight Inn: in a cardboard tray or on a bun. Other than a tile of unleavened corn bread and some coleslaw, there is nothing else on the menu.

Sandwiches are a twentieth-century addition to the Jones family repertoire, but their pairing of barbecue and corn bread goes back to 1830 when ancestor Skilton M. Dennis, who cooked whole hogs in pits dug in the ground, brought some of the meat to sell at a nearby Baptist convention. "As far as we know, that was the first time barbecue was served to the public in North Carolina," says Samuel Jones, Dennis's seventh-generation descendant, who operates the Skylight Inn along with his father, Bruce. Sam is the grandson of Pete Jones, the longtime pitmaster who started in the business with his uncle, Emmett Dennis, when he was six years old. Pete built the current Skylight Inn in 1947, and in 1988 he put a jumbo replica of the Capitol Dome atop the building after a journalist declared his place the Barbecue Capital of America.

## Snappy Lunch

125 N. Main St.  
Mount Airy, NC

336-786-4931  
www.thesnappylunch.com  
BL | $

As Yankees, we'd never heard of a pork-chop sandwich until we traveled south. Even in Dixie, it is not all that common. One of the very best is the boneless beauty at Snappy Lunch. It is a broad slab of meat that is breaded and fried similar to the tenderloins of the Midwest, but with more pork, and battered rather than breaded. It is soft and juicy, as tender as a mother's love.

Few customers of Snappy Lunch get a plain pork-chop sandwich. The ritual here in Mount Airy (Andy Griffith's hometown, and the inspiration for TV's Mayberry) is to have it *all the way,* which means dressed with tomato, chopped onion, mustard, meaty/sweet chili, and fine-cut cabbage slaw speckled with green peppers and onions. The total package is unwieldy in the extreme. Served in booths or at the counter in a wax-paper wrapper, this is a sandwich that requires two hands and a meaningful grip. There are no side dishes available other than a bag of potato chips, and the beverage of choice is tea—iced and pre-sweetened, of course.

There are, however, other items on the menu, including a weird Depression-era legacy known as the breaded hamburger, for which ground beef is extended by mixing it with an equal portion of moistened bread. The result is a strange, plump hamburger that resembles a crab cake. There's an all-beef burger too; but the pork-chop sandwich is what you want.

## South 21 Drive-In

3101 E. Independence Blvd.    704-377-4509
Charlotte, NC                 www.south21drivein.com
                             LD | $

If you like classic American drive-ins and don't already know about Charlotte's South 21, allow us to introduce you to your new best friend.

When South 21 Drive-In boasts that its Super Boy burger is a meal in itself, that's only partially true. It's a lot of food, for sure: two good-sized patties with the works in a sesame bun crowned with a quartered pickle spear and sided by a heap of French fries. While that may indeed be a meal, all aficionados of this vintage 1955 drive-in know that no meal is complete without an order of onion rings. They are individual hoops that arrive so greaseless that they first appear to have been baked, not fried. But after a few bites, the lavishness of the fry kettle becomes apparent. With some salt added, these are four-star O-rings. The other thing necessary to complete the meal is either cherry-flavored lemon Sundrop (a tradition hereabouts) or one of South 21's excellent milk shakes, blended to order.

While we love this old-fashioned drive-in with its articulated window-side trays and Servus-Fone ordering equipment at every car slip, we do believe the hamburgers need doctoring up; they tend to be dry enough to beg for extra condiments. That's why many regulars prefer the heftier and juicier hamburger steak platter or fried chicken.

## Stamey's

2206 High Point Rd.         336-299-9888
Greensboro, NC          www.stameys.com

LD | $

Stamey's dates back to 1938 and pretty much defined what is now known as Lexington-style North Carolina barbecue: pork shoulder pit-cooked over smoldering hickory coals until eminently tender, then chopped or sliced. Chopped means nearly pulverized. Slices are more like shreds of varying sizes, some soft, others crusty. The sauce is peppery with a vinegar twist, and thin enough to permeate the soft pork rather than blanket it. If you get a platter (as opposed to a sandwich), it will be accompanied by a powerfully zesty red coleslaw and odd-shaped, deep-fried corn squiggles that are Stamey's version of hush puppies. This is a Piedmont meal that connoisseurs put in the top tier of a state that is fanatical about barbecue. Be sure to leave room for dessert: the peach cobbler is nearly as famous as the barbecue.

There is a second Stamey's at 2812 Battleground Avenue (US 220 North) in Greensboro (336-288-9275).

## Sunrise Biscuit Kitchen

1305 E. Franklin         919-933-1324
Chapel Hill, NC          BL | $

If you have a cramped and uncomfortable car, you might find Sunrise Biscuit Kitchen problematic. It is drive-through only, offering no place to eat. But if you are a biscuit lover, you will want to come here even if you're the filling of a Smart Car. Sunrise biscuits are big and buttermilky with an outside surface that is golden-crisp. The kitchen pulls them into halves and loads in resounding slices of grilled country ham, pork tenderloin, or pillows of expertly fried white-meat chicken. Coffee is available, but so is sweet tea, which is a good biscuit's soul mate.

There is another Sunrise Biscuit Kitchen at 208 S. Bickett Boulevard in Louisburg (919-496-2609). It has indoor seating.

# Tomato Jam Café

379 Biltmore Ave.                    828-253-0570
Asheville, NC                        www.tomatojamcafe.com
                                     BL Mon-Fri | $

Biscuits earn Tomato Jam Café high standing on the Roadfood honor roll—Cat's Head Biscuits in particular, so named because they are closer to the size and shape of a big cat's knobby noggin than they are to a smooth and symmetrical hockey puck. Made using whole-grain flour, they are biscuits of color rather than the more familiar lily-white ones. Yet there is nothing cloddish about them and they are seriously flavorful. They are probably best enjoyed with nothing but butter and a schmear of the café's wonderfully fruity tomato jam, but they are sturdy enough to be a great mitt for a breakfast BLT that includes apple-smoked bacon and broiled tomato. You even can have a biscuit topped with vegan-sausage gravy!

Vegetarian items are not an afterthought at TJC, and if you can forgo an order of creamy, buttery, stone-ground grits, it's possible to eat vegan. At lunch, in addition to hamburgers made from grass-fed cow meat, the menu lists a black-bean burger and a pseudo-burger made of a marinated portabella cap. There are lots of different grilled cheese options as well as pimiento cheese, available hot or cold, with or without roasted tomato, and with the option of that good apple-smoked bacon.

Side dishes not to be missed include chunky cinnamon-spiced applesauce, griddle-crisped potato cakes, and slow-roasted tomatoes (heirloom tomatoes in the summer). Desserts that demand attention include banana pudding, red velvet cake, and cashew-studded brownies.

Tomato Jam is fun and funky with thrift-shop-retro décor and a cavalcade of characterful customers, especially at breakfast, who make eavesdropping on other diners' discussions irresistible. The proprietors are so dedicated to using local groceries that they have a chalkboard listing their suppliers, farms, and bakeries. Their mission statement is to make food "a rich part of daily being," and their philosophy avows, "We at Tomato Jam consider our customer's health and well being as important as our own."

## Wilber's Barbecue

4172 US Hwy 70 E.  919-778-5218
Goldsboro, NC  www.wilbersbarbecue.com
BLD | $

Pilots who take off from Seymour Johnson Air Force Base have flown the fame of Wilber's far and wide, and legends abound regarding the pounds of barbecue carried aboard strategic flights. Even if it weren't at the end of the runway, Wilber's reputation for serving first-class Lexington-style North Carolina barbecue could never have remained merely local. This place is world-class! Since 1962, when Wilber Shirley stoked the oak coals in old-fashioned pits, he has been known for whole-hog barbecue, chopped and shrewdly seasoned with a peppery vinegar sauce. After eight hours over coals, the meat is soft as a sigh, its natural sweetness haloed by hardwood smoke. It is served with potato salad, coleslaw, Brunswick stew (a pork hash with Veg-All type vegetables), and squiggly hush puppies.

Beyond terrific barbecue, the original Wilber's has the added attraction of serving breakfast, in the form of a buffet with smoked sausages, thick-cut bacon, cracklins, biscuits and gravy, grits, and sweet muffins. By late morning, chopped barbecue reigns, and it is served until about nine at night . . . or until the day's supply runs out. When that happens, the management locks the door and hangs up a sign that advises, OUT OF BARBECUE!

## Zada Jane's Corner Cafe

1601 Central Ave.  704-332-3663
Charlotte, NC  www.zadajanes.com
BLD | $$

When the old Coffee Cup bit the dust, we despaired about the dearth of great breakfast in Charlotte, but a visit to Zada Jane's restored our faith. Not that the two places are similar. Zada Jane's is fashionable and modern, with a menu that includes gluten-free pancakes as well as soysage and tofu for non-carnivores. Situated in the same once-shabby, now upwardly mobile neighborhood as the old Penguin, the stylin' eatery is a favorite of local foodies. It is small and cozy, making it a sociable dining experience whether or not you want to socialize. Expect to wait for a seat, at table or counter, especially on weekends.

Buttermilk biscuits come with apple jam and multiberry jam obtained from a small farm outside of Asheville. Hash, made from sweet potatoes, is like the tenderest home fries but with a spicy-sugary edge. It shines in the

Booker T's East Side Hasher breakfast, where it is topped with a couple of eggs cooked frittata-style and topped with cheese and sausage, plus green onions. (That last ingredient is inspiration for the dish's name.) Among the sausage choices is beautifully seasoned, locally made Grateful Grower's pork. Thick slices of challah-bread French toast are dipped in batter flavored with amaretto and are served with orange butter. Coffee is served in an assortment of kitschy souvenir mugs.

## 400 Degrees

319 Peabody
Nashville, TN

615-244-4467
www.400degreeshotchicken.com
LD | $

At 319 Peabody in Nashville, Tennessee, is a Quizno's food court with a difference. The difference is that in addition to the mass-market sub shop, it contains 400 Degrees, which is one of the premier sources for Nashville hot chicken. Here you will find mercilessly spiced leg-quarter sandwiches, quartets of wings, and pork chops sided by sweet baked beans.

The menu item titled "400 Degrees" is the hottest chicken you can order. It is taken from the fry basket and painted with a thick pepper impasto that is as dark as antique bronze. "200 Degrees" chicken is brighter red and still sinus-clearing. "100 Degrees" is just a bit spicy, and there is "Zero," which is fried but not at all peppered. What's truly grand about the hot chicken is how the pepper paste fuses with its fried skin, forming a coat that you can lift away in bite-sized masses of pure, hot savor.

Proprietor Aqui Simpson originally opened for business in a two-table dive out on Clarksville Highway, but success eventually led her to this incongruously bland location, where there is plenty of seating at laminate tables under bright, mall-like lights. Aqui reminded us that regular customers call ahead so their chicken is ready when they arrive. Hot chicken is always made to order, meaning a twenty-minute wait is mandatory.

## A&R Bar-B-Que

1802 Elvis Presley Blvd.          901-774-7444
Memphis, TN                       www.aandrbbq.com
                                  LD | $

At the counter where you stand and place your order at A&R you can hear a blissful smokehouse lullaby coming from the kitchen: chop-chop-chop on the cutting board, as hickory-cooked pork gets hacked into mottled shreds and pieces for plates and sandwiches. The sandwich is Memphis-style: pork mixed with tangy red sauce piled in a bun and crowned with coleslaw. The slaw in a Memphis barbecue sandwich is as important for its texture as for its taste. The cabbage adds nice little bits of crunch to velvety pork.

Beyond pig sandwiches, the A&R menu is full. You can have pork or beef ribs, catfish dinner, hot tamales, smoked sausage, a turkey-leg plate, and that only-in-Memphis treat, barbecue spaghetti. That's a mound of soft noodles dressed not with ordinary tomato sauce, but with—what else?—barbecue sauce, laced with shreds of pork. For dessert, you want fried pie, warm, with ice cream.

The ambience of A&R is unadulterated BBQ parlor: quiet enough so you can hear the chopping in the kitchen. It is a big place with a lot of elbow room. Raw brick walls and fluorescent lights set a no-nonsense mood, and however hot it is outside, you can count on the air-conditioning system to be running so high that it's practically like going into hibernation. Or is the trance we experience a result of hypnotically good food?

There are three other A&Rs in Memphis.


## Alcenia's

317 N. Main St.                   901-523-0200
Memphis, TN                       www.alcenias.com
                                  L | $

Everyone who eats at Alcenia's gets a hug from proprietor B. J. Lester-Tamayo, either on the way in or out, or both. "I feel so guilty if I haven't hugged you, I'll chase you down the street when you leave," she says with a laugh. Her restaurant, named for her mother and granddaughter, is a modest lunchroom decorated in a style that is an intriguing mix of 1960s psychedelic beaded curtains, primitive folk art, odes to African American culture, and white wedding-veil lace strung up across the ceiling over the large table.

B.J. learned to cook from her mother, who lives in Meridian, Mississippi, but comes to visit and makes tea cakes and egg custard pie and coaches B.J. on the phone when she is making chowchow or pear preserves. B.J.'s turnip greens are extraordinary, flavored not with pork but with what she calls turkey "tails." Even more wondrous is cabbage, which we first assumed was steamed with greens because dark leaves were laced among the white ones. B.J. explained that those are the cabbage's outer leaves. "The best part!" she declared. "Most people throw them away because they are tough. They need an hour extra steaming; that makes them soft and brown." Flavored with a hail of spice that includes jerk chicken seasoning and lots of pepper, this is cabbage with tongue-searing punch. On the side comes a basket of hot-water corn bread: cushiony-moist, griddle-cooked cakes that are the perfect foil for ecstatically seasoned vegetables.

Aside from Alcenia's vegetables, dining delights here include a fried pork chop that is crisp and dripping with juice, crunchy fried chicken, and bread pudding that the Memphis *Commercial Appeal* declared to be one of the ten best desserts in the city.

## *Arnold's Country Kitchen

605 8th Ave. S.                       615-256-4455
Nashville, Tennessee                  L | $

If you have time to experience just one meat-and-three restaurant in Nashville (perish the thought), please consider Arnold's Country Kitchen. Service is cafeteria-style, tables are shared by strangers when the place is crowded (it always is), and the food is beautiful. Not beautiful in a glossy-magazine sense, but beautiful the way plate lunch ought to be: messy, colorful, bread-crumb-crusted, cheese-dripping, hog-jowl-flavored soulful. The meats include moist and mighty meat loaf, exemplary fried chicken, pulled pork, and catfish; among the side dishes that command attention are greens, squash casserole, and most especially that distinguished "vegetable," mac 'n' cheese. Two kinds of corn bread are available, both essential: muffins and skillet-cooked cakes, the latter especially useful for mopping gravy, sopping the liquor under porky green beans, and dipping into the creamy emulsion in which black-eyed peas are suspended.

If only for its banana pudding, we would put this place on any hit list of great Music City destinations. But if by choosing pudding you neglect the pies, you will be sorry, because Arnold's pies are some of the best anywhere. Especially the chess pie: smooth, simple, butter-rich, and sugar-sweet.

## Beacon Light Tea Room

6276 Hwy. 100
Bon Aqua, TN

931-670-3880
www.beaconlighttearoom.com
D Tues-Thurs; BLD Fri-Sun | $

Opened in 1936 by Lon Loveless, who went on to open the renowned Loveless Cafe (p. 195) in Nashville, the Beacon Light Tea Room is a lesser-known gem of Tennessee country cooking. Longtime Loveless fans will have déjà vu upon opening the menu, for it is the same as the Loveless's used to be. Fried chicken and country ham with red-eye gravy are the entrees to know about, and among essential sides is the sumptuously rich midcentury Home-Ec triumph, hash brown casserole. Potato shreds are mixed with cheese, sour cream, and—you guessed it—a can of chicken soup, then baked until bubbly with a crust on top.

Meals are sided by biscuits with homemade peach and blackberry preserves. They are set out on the table in spoon-it-yourself crocks. There are soft hunks of peach in the amber one, and the blackberries have a sultry flavor that is a brilliant counterpoint to supersalty country ham.

Although it was originally named for the revolving spotlight that directed planes flying mail between Memphis and Nashville, the term "Beacon Light" now has another meaning. For the proprietors, the beacon is Jesus, and his image is everywhere in art on the old wood-paneled walls. Each table, which is clad with a leatherette cloth, is outfitted with a "Scripture Bread Box," a small plastic loaf hollowed out to contain cards about the size of fortune-cookie fortunes, but with scriptural advice on each side.

## Bluegrass Grill

55 E. Main St.
Chattanooga, TN

423-752-4020
www.bluegrassgrillchattanooga.com
BL | $

We get lots of suggestions about where to eat. Some pan out, others don't. Ever since John Reed tipped us off to Zarzour's (p. 203), we have learned to put full faith in any of his suggestions. That is how we came upon the Bluegrass Grill, to which Mr. Reed directed us for "heavenly muffins, granola, cinnamon rolls, biscuits and breads all made from scratch starting at 3:30 a.m. by Father Jonas." Fr. Jonas Worsham, along with his family, including wife Joan Marie, have created a beckoning breakfast destination that also is open for lunch.

Big, squared-off biscuits, given extra character by the inclusion of whole wheat flour, arrive hot enough to melt butter pats. Add gravy on top and get a bottomless cup of coffee, and you will have a mighty morning meal for under $6. French toast is made from a choice of house-baked breads, including multigrain; superb home fries—red potatoes sautéed with onion and garlic—are offered as a side dish to omelets or as a bed for toppings that range from gyro meat to chorizo to beans and cheese. Muffins, cinnamon rolls, whipped-cream-topped brownies: all first-class!

The lunch menu is soup, chili, sandwiches, and salads. If you have a party of fifteen or more and want dinner, the Worsham family also offers a "Greek feast" for which you consult about the menu. For that, of course, advance notice is required.

## Blue Plate Café

| | |
|---|---|
| 5469 Poplar Ave. | 901-761-9696 |
| Memphis, TN | BLD \| $ |

In this cheery café that was once a private home built by Holiday Inn inventor Kemmons Wilson, breakfast is served anytime and it is good enough to draw crowds on the weekend. Omelets are good, French toast is better, pancakes are best. (Waffles stink; Blue Plate has gone from thin, elegant ones to fat-ass Belgians.) We are fond of the kitchen's banana pancakes, with fruity sweetness complemented by crunchy peanut syrup. Flavorful knobby-top biscuits are served with cream gravy dotted with bits of sausage.

Lunch is good ol' meat-and-threes, with such entrees as pot roast, baked pork chops, chicken and dumplings, and fried shrimp (that last one is every Friday). The "and-three" roster is about twenty items long, including real mashed potatoes, turnip greens, creamed corn, mac 'n' cheese, and so on and so forth. If you want something simpler than meat-and-three, there are salads, soups, and sandwiches, including a fried peanut butter and banana sandwich. Apparently, that one is health food: It is served on whole wheat bread.

## Bolton's Spicy Chicken & Fish

| | |
|---|---|
| 624 Main St. | 615-254-8015 |
| Nashville, TN | LD \| $ |

Bolton's manager Dolly Graham once said, "Our chicken is hot, but it won't cause you to lose your composure." That depends. If you are leery of high-capsicum fare, Bolton's chicken might be reason for a meltdown, especially if you ask for it hot. Those who do like inflammatory food love it because the heat is deep in the meat, right down to the bone itself. It is much more spicy than it is salty, making for a meal's worth of taste-bud kicks.

It is beautiful chicken with a thin, red-gold crust that flakes off in delicate strips. You can get breast, leg, or wings, and side dishes include turnip greens, sweet coleslaw, strangely soupy mac 'n' cheese, and that Nashville soul-food favorite, spaghetti. In addition to chicken, Bolton's sells a whiting sandwich that is available garnished in the locally favored way, with mustard, onion, pickles, and enough hot sauce to make your tongue glow.

A tiny East Nashville shop with a carry-out window to its side and a dining room with a handful of tables (oilcloth-covered), Bolton's is a vital stop for anyone in search of a true taste of Music City.

## Bozo's Hot Pit BBQ

342 Hwy 70       901-294-3400
Mason, TN       LD Tues-Sat | $$

Since it opened in 1923, Bozo's has earned a sterling reputation for barbecue. Slow-smoked shoulder is served white or dark, the former unspeakably tender shreds, the latter more chewy and crusty outside meat. (Many savvy eaters get a combination of the two.) You can have it the classic Memphis way, in a sandwich with slaw (although here the slaw has a more pronounced vinegar tang), or on a plate with beans and/or onion rings. Sandwiches are immense, loaded with more meat than any bun could possibly contain. Tables are armed with three sauces: mild, sweet, and hot. Hot is very hot.

Although barbecue is the must-eat meal, Bozo's menu also includes steaks, shrimp, and pies made by Ms. Perry, known for years among Bozo's aficionados as the Pie Lady. Named for founder Thomas Jefferson "Bozo" Williams, the restaurant was engaged in a trademark battle with Bozo the Clown back in the 1980s. *Bozo v. Bozo* went all the way to the US Supreme Court, which refused to hear it. So Bozo's is still Bozo's, its well-worn Formica tables showing only sixty-four years of use. (The original Bozo's was destroyed by fire in 1950.)

## Coletta's

1063 South Pkwy E.       901-948-7652
Memphis, TN       www.colettas.net
                                LD | $

At Coletta's Restaurant, a medium-thick-crust pizza pie with a glaze of melted mozzarella is topped not with Italian sauce and sausage or pepperoni, but with a bouquet of barbecued pulled pork in a zesty cinnabar pit sauce. No, it is not one of the world's great pizzas; nor is it in the highest echelon of Mid-South barbecue; but it is a specialty worth noting—and eating—for all who want to savor America's rules-be-damned cuisine.

Coletta's also serves barbecue salad, which is like any ordinary salad (iceberg lettuce, carrot shreds, tomatoes) but adorned with barbecue—the same moist mix of fine shreds and a few chewy nuggets as on the pizza. The meat on the salad is unsauced. Dressing is the customer's choice, and it makes all the difference. Italian vinaigrette nudges it in the direction of minimally sauced eastern North Carolina 'cue; thousand island or Russian is more like mountain smokehouse meals; ranch dressing brings it close to that strange Alabama variety of sauce that is based on mayonnaise.

Barbecue pizza and salad are just two items on a full-range menu of familiar Italian-American fare, including more universally known pizzas, house-made sausage, ravioli, and spaghetti and meatballs.

Around the corner from Graceland, Coletta's has a sad look from the outside, but red-checked tablecloths in the dining room, which sport paper place mats that explain Italy's many charms, set a hospitable tone. The cognitive dissonance of barbecue pizza defines the ambience as well: a vintage Italian-American dining room where the wood-paneled walls hold massive amounts of Elvisiana and where waitresses speak in syrupy southern drawls.

## *Cozy Corner

745 North Pkwy.          901-527-9158
Memphis, TN              www.cozycornerbbq.com
                         LD | $

In America's premier barbecue city, the number one barbecue restaurant is the Cozy Corner. The house specialty in this family run storefront is Cornish hen, a plump little bird that emerges from its long smoke bath with fragile, burnished skin wrapping meat that throbs with spicy flavor. Cozy Corner's sauce-glazed spare ribs pack huge sweet-pork punch; baby-backs boast meat that slips from the bone in glistening ribbons; thick discs of barbecue bologna are a revelation; and whatever meat you get, you can side it with that delightfully monomaniacal Memphis side dish, barbecued spaghetti. There are two wonderful desserts: sweet-potato pie and banana pudding.

Despite its reputation among barbecue connoisseurs, the Cozy Corner remains humble, its front room clouded with haze from the Chicago-style aquarium smoker behind the self-service counter. It was established back in

1977 by Raymond Robinson, who, until his death early in 2001, oversaw his empire from a seat behind the order counter, haloed by the glow of his smoke pit. Today his widow, Desiree, keeps up the high culinary standards and the friendly air that has always made this such a happy place to visit.

## The Cupboard

1400 Union Ave.      901-276-8015
Memphis, TN      www.thecupboardrestaurant.com
     BLD | $

The Cupboard is a hugely popular restaurant in what used to be a Shoney's, where a sign outside boasts, "Freshest Veggies in Town." Proprietor Charles Cavallo is a fresh-food fanatic, a joy he credits to his uncle, who sold watermelons. He drove a produce delivery truck for ten years, and in 1993 bought the Cupboard (then, a much smaller place) with the goal of making it a showcase for vegetables. Tomatoes direct from the field in Ripley, local squash, crowder peas, onions, cabbage, and sweet potatoes appear not only on the menu (which features a four-vegetable, no-meat meal), but also on the floor of the restaurant, in the vestibule, and around the cash register, from which they are sold by the peck and bushel when they are in season.

One of the best-cooked vegetables here is the simplest: a whole baked sweet potato, starchy-sweet and soft as pudding. Corn pudding is stellar; ditto the baked apple. The Cupboard's full-flavored turnip greens are made without pork or poultry, just boiled and seasoned. "My greens taste like greens," Charles says, stating the obvious. "Sometimes I have people who come in and say, 'You've changed the recipe. These are different.' Yes, they are different, I say: maybe younger, maybe winter greens, which have a softer taste, maybe they are from Georgia instead of Tennessee. Every bunch has a flavor of its own."

Non-vegetable notables include corn bread gem muffins and yeast rolls, warm fruit cobbler, and brilliant lemon icebox pie.

## Eastside Fish

2617 Gallatin Pike      615-227-8388
Nashville, TN      www.eastsidefish.com
     LD | $

The Giant King, signature dish at Eastside Fish, is immense. A pair of whiting fillets, each at least half a pound, are dredged in seasoned cornmeal and crisp-fried, then sandwiched between four slices of soft supermarket white bread. The fish is cream-moist and delicate, its brittle crust mottled with splotches of four-alarm Louisiana hot sauce and enveloped in a harmony of crunchy raw onion, dill pickle chips, and smooth yellow mustard. Standard companions for the fish are white bread, hush puppies, coleslaw, and, strangely enough, meat-sauced spaghetti.

The small storefront tucked back from Gallatin Pike has minimal seating for those who need a place to eat, but Eastside's business is virtually all takeout. The brown paper bags in which customers receive their fish out the order window are steaming hot and splotched with oil, the sandwich inside wrapped in wax paper and held together with toothpicks.

## Ed's Fish & Pizza House

| | |
|---|---|
| 1801 Dr. D. B. Todd Jr. Blvd. | 615-255-4362 |
| Nashville, TN | LD \| $ |

Fried fish has been a staple at soul-food restaurants for as long as there have been soul-food restaurants, but Nashville has a very specific way of serving it: the hot fish sandwich. A couple of crisp-fried whiting fillets—often totaling a pound, spritzed with hot sauce—are arranged between two to four slices of white bread with sliced raw onion, pickle chips, and mustard. Various accompaniments are available, including coleslaw and fried potatoes, but the classic companion is a serving of sweet-sauced spaghetti noodles.

The goodness of a hot fish sandwich depends to a large degree on its being eaten within moments of the fish being pulled from the fry kettle. We are happy to report that at Ed's we waited a good fifteen or twenty minutes for our sandwich to be presented, the fish still sizzling hot.

What a magnificent sandwich: plump, moist fillets in a golden crust, splotched with only enough hot sauce to tease forth their flavor. The spaghetti we ordered on the side left its al dente character long behind, and its chunky red sauce was nearly chutney-sweet. The bright innocence of these noodles is just the right partner for hot and funky fish.

## Elliston Place Soda Shop

| | |
|---|---|
| 2111 Elliston Pl. | 615-327-1090 |
| Nashville, TN | BL \| $ |

It bills itself as a soda shop, and a fine one it is; but we like Elliston Place more for meat-and-three lunch. Choose sugar-cured ham, salt-cured country ham, southern-fried chicken (white or dark meat), a pork chop, or liver and onions, then select three vegetables from a daily roster. On Mondays and

Thursdays the house special is turkey and dressing, a casserole of shredded roasted white and dark meat with steamy corn-bread dressing: delicious! If you want to skip meat altogether (Elliston Place vegetables are so good, such a strategy makes sense), there is a four-vegetable plate, accompanied by hot bread, for about $5. The vegetable repertoire includes whipped potatoes, turnip greens, baked squash, fried rounds of okra, black-eyed peas, and congealed fruit salad (the Dixie name for Jell-O). Banana pudding, streaked with fluffy veins of meringue, is exquisite.

Breakfast biscuits are crunchy brown on the outside with a soft interior that begs to wrap itself around a slice of salty country ham. On the side comes a bowl of firm, steamy white grits—a mild-mannered companion for full-flavored breakfast meat.

A city fixture since 1939, this is a restaurant with personality! Its tiny-tile floor is well weathered and its tables wobble. Above the counter, vintage soda fountain signs advertise banana splits, fruit sundaes, sodas, and fresh fruit ades. Each green-upholstered booth has its own jukebox with selections that are, suitably enough, country classics.

## Germantown Commissary

2290 S. Germantown
Germantown, TN

901-754-5540
www.commissarybbq.com
LD | $$

The most exalted barbecue often is served in the lowliest dives, but here is fine smokehouse fare in decorator-rustic surroundings. Give your car to the valet and enter dining quarters, where barnboard walls sport collectible old tin signs, wind-up telephones, and vintage advertisements . . . and the air is filled with the unmistakably seductive aroma of real barbecue.

It is best known for ribs, which truly are first-rate: crusted with sauce, scented by hickory, meaty as hell with enough chew to provide maximum flavor. You can order them by number of bones, from five to twelve (a full rack), or as part of a combo plate with one to three other meats. We suggest the sampler, because it would be a crime to come to the Commissary and *not* have pulled pork. It is shoulder meat, pulled into slightly-more-than-bite-sized strips and hunks, some edges crusty, some parts velvet-soft. You can also get the meat chopped, which is OK but deprives your tongue of the pleasure of worrying those long strips of meat you get when it's pulled.

For dessert, we like banana pudding with softened vanilla wafers in the custard, tongue-soothing lemon icebox pie, and caramel cake.

## Gus's Fried Chicken

310 S. Front St.          901-527-4877

Memphis, TN          LD | $

The sign outside Gus's says that it is world-famous. The menu says its fried chicken is hot. Both claims are debatable: Gus's certainly is known among chicken connoisseurs, but it has yet to gain fame on the order of other Road-food shrines such as, say, Arthur Bryant's or Pepe's Pizzeria. As for hot, it is not ferocious like hot fried chicken in Nashville. Having now said what it is not, let us say what Gus's is: one of the best fried chicken restaurants anywhere. Each piece, dark and white, is encased in a zesty envelope that vigorously crunches then offers plenty of rewarding chew, all the while radiating the ecstatic flavor combo of chicken fat and pepper.

Other than catfish a couple of nights a week, chicken is Gus's only entree; any pieces are available in any combination; side dishes include baked beans, coleslaw, fried rice (!), fried okra, and spiced French fries. Even those who aren't fans of fried green tomatoes and fried dill pickles should consider ordering some of Gus's to start the meal. No novelty in this kitchen, the pickles maintain nice al dente firmness inside their crunchy coat, which, like the batter on the chicken, is an elegant balance of spice and lusciousness.

To call the restaurant casual underestimates its humility. On a crappy street the wrong side of Beale, it regularly posts a security guard on the side-walk so that visitors will feel safe between car and front door. The interior, where mismatched chairs are arranged around a couple dozen tables topped with easy-wipe tablecloths, seems like a chaotic madhouse as customers mill around near the door waiting for their turn to sit. Once seated, you will deal with a staff who are nothing but courteous and efficient.

## Hot Stuff Spicy Chicken & Fish

1309 Bell Rd., Ste. 218      615-712-6100

Antioch, TN          www.hotstufftn.com

                           LD | $

Fast food this is not. The kitchen starts cooking only after an order is placed, and since there is no jiffy way of frying chicken right, time passes while appetite builds. The twenty minutes spent waiting is the best argument you'll ever know in favor of the slow food movement. What you get, served in a Styrofoam clamshell with white bread, French fries, and pickle chips, is Nashville hot chicken at its finest.

Compared to some of the other chicken shacks around town, the heat levels at Hot Stuff seem relatively sane. Hot is very hot but not killer. Even X-hot is more pleasure than pain. As for XX and XXX . . . we'll leave them to the asbestos-tongue crowd. Hot Stuff also offers Li'l Spice, Mild, Lemon Pepper, Cajun, and Sweet Heat versions that will not set taste buds on fire.

The chicken is ravishing red-gold. Press it gently with fork or finger and juices start oozing. Dark meat is especially luscious, but Hot Stuff's breasts drip savor too. The crust is crisp and thin, radiant with that magic combination of palliative chicken fat and incendiary spice.

When we placed our order, co-owner Kiki Montgomery suggested house-made sweet tea to deal with the chicken's heat, and in one way, she was right. It is so sweet that it manages to divert attention from tongue fires. But it does little to actually tamp them down. A thick piece of mocha layer cake, made by local baker Spencer D. Middlebrooks and available by the slice at Hot Stuff's counter, was more effective (and really delicious) relief.

## Interstate Barbecue

2265 S. 3rd St.                        901-775-2304
Memphis, TN                          www.interstatebarbecue.com
                                            LD | $$

Interstate's Jim Neely is a master barbecue man, and in the city of Memphis, to be a respected pitmaster is to be a god. His restaurant is a modest pork house serving ribs, shoulder meat, sausages, and bologna with all the proper fixins, including barbecue spaghetti (soft noodles in breathtaking sauce).

Each rib exudes the perfume of woodsmoke; chewing it generates massive infusions of flavor that literally exhaust taste buds after a while. Chopped pork shoulder is a medley of shreds, chunks, wisps, and ribbons of smoky meat, all crowned with Neely's spicy-sweet red sauce. A chopped pork sandwich is the most Memphian dish on the menu, made with a layer of cool coleslaw atop the well-sauced meat. And true to Memphis's Q obsession, Neely's also offers barbecue salad and barbecue nachos.

A second location is at 150 West Stateline Road, Southhaven, Mississippi (662-393-5699).

## Leonard's

5465 Fox Plaza Dr.
Memphis, TN

901-360-1963
www.leonardsbarbecue.com
L Sun–Weds; LD Thurs–Sat | $

In 1922 Leonard Heuberger configured the barbecued pork sandwich that has become a regional icon: shreds of smoked shoulder meat topped with tomato-sweet, vinegar-tangy sauce, festooned with creamy coleslaw. It is a mesmerizing confluence of sugar and spice, meat and bread and sauce.

Choices at Leonard's include slabs of ribs, platters and plates, barbecued bologna, and even a roster of Italo-Dixie combo plates that include spaghetti with ribs and barbecue with ravioli. Big eaters avail themselves of the lunch buffet Sunday through Friday and the evening buffet Friday and Saturday.

Leonard's is worth visiting not only for its pork but for its sign, which is one of the great images in porklore: a neon pig, all decked out in top hat and tails, captioned "Mr. Brown Goes to Town." Years ago, a waitress explained its significance: "Mr. Brown was the term used for brown-meat barbecue. It is the outside of the shoulder that gets succulent and chewy from the sauce and the smoke in the pit. The inside part of the roast, which is moist but has very little barbecue flavor is known as Miss White. People in Memphis used to ask for plates and sandwiches of 'Mr. Brown and Miss White.'"

## Little Tea Shop

69 Monroe
Memphis, TN

901-525-6000
L | $

Memphis is our favorite place to eat pork, but there's none served at the Little Tea Shop down by old Cotton Row. Proprietor Suhair Lauck is Muslim, and yet despite her religion's prohibition against pigs, she serves some of the most soulful eats in the city. We were aghast when Sue told us that her greens were in fact completely meat-free. It had always seemed to us that the opulent "likker" in which they wallow in their serving bowl—a spruce-green broth retrieved from the pot in which they have boiled—gets its intoxicating character at least as much from the hambone as from the collard, turnip, or mustard leaves that the boiling process turns soft and mellow.

But tasting is believing, and let us tell you that a serving of pork-free turnip greens with pot likker at the Little Tea Shop is positively tonic. If a flavor can be verdant, here it is: the heady soul of a plant with leaves that marinate in sunlight. Turnip greens are the centerpiece of Sue's most popular lunch, on the printed-daily menu every day of the week. It is a bowl filled with sultry dark greens sodden in their likker, the once-tough leaves cooked so limp that you can easily separate them with a soup spoon and gather it up with plenty of the liquid. Atop the greens are slices of raw onion, leaching pungent bite into the leaves, and atop the onions are bright red slices of tomato, which are shockingly sweet compared to everything below. On the side are crisp-edged, cream-centered corn sticks well suited for crumbling into the bowl.

The process for ordering food is do-it-yourself. Every customer gets a one-page printed menu of the day with a little box next to each item. Like voting with an old-fashioned ballot, you put a check mark in the box next to each dish you want to elect for your lunch. Other than pot likker, some of the outstanding choices are the Lacy Special (named for a cotton trader), in which corn sticks sandwich a chicken breast topped with gravy, and such vegetables as sliced candied yams, fried corn, baked squash, black-eyed peas, and scalloped tomatoes. The longtime favorite dessert is a frozen pecan ice cream ball topped with hot fudge.

## Litton's

2803 Essary Dr.
Knoxville, TN

865-688-0429
www.littonsburgers.com
LD | $

With a catalogue of hamburgers that range from minimalist beef patties to a "Thunder Road" burger (named for the movie about moonshining in the Appalachians) topped with pimiento cheese, onions, and hot peppers, Litton's is a burger lover's paradise. Freshly ground meat is formed into a patty that is nearly half a pound and it is cooked to order, then sandwiched in a made-here bun, preferably with at least lettuce, tomato, and onion and, at most, bacon, pickles, or chili.

At least as famous as the hamburgers are Litton's desserts: coconut cream pie, chocolate chess pie (Tuesday only), old-fashioned red velvet cake, banana pudding, and cream-cheese-frosted Italian cream cake, a buttery concoction that goes perfectly with a cup of after-meal coffee.

## Loveless Cafe

8400 Hwy. 100
Nashville, TN

615-646-9700
www.lovelesscafe.com

BLD | $

Eating at the Loveless Cafe isn't only a matter of fried chicken and biscuits. It is all about the South, Tennessee in particular, and Nashville, heart and soul. Three or four decades ago, when it was known only to cognoscenti and accidental tourists, the Loveless could get crowded; if you knew you were coming during peak mealtime, you could call and make a reservation. When you did, you said whether you were planning on having fried chicken or ham. That was pretty much the extent of the menu . . . along with the immemorial companions: biscuits, cream gravy, red-eye gravy, peach preserves, blackberry preserves, honey, and sorghum syrup. Now the kitchen's repertoire has grown—although country ham and fried chicken remain the anchor meals—and the Loveless Cafe has itself become a national celebrity. Among luminaries who have visited in recent years are Britain's Princess Anne (in the neighborhood for a horse show) and Sir Paul McCartney (who spontaneously sang "Happy Birthday" to a sixteen-year-old customer who had come to celebrate with friends).

Despite its renown, the Loveless remains faithful to its roots, and like a true-hearted singing star who hits the big-time, it has never strayed from the fundamental good things that led to its original success. First among them is fried chicken . . . the original meal served by Lon and Annie Loveless back in the early 1950s when they began offering picnic suppers to passersby along Highway 100. The major alternative to chicken is country ham, and the newly expanded menu includes the likes of pulled pork, green tomato BLTs, and what is perhaps the most elegant banana pudding anywhere.

## Merridee's Breadbasket

110 4th Ave. S.
Franklin, TN

615-790-3755
www.merridees.com

BL | $

Merridee's is a casual bakery-café where people come early in the day to buy breads and pastries to take home or to sit down for breakfast or lunch. Place an order at the counter and they'll call your name when it is ready, by which time, hopefully, you will have found a seat. The repertoire includes hot breakfasts and a vast array of oven-fresh rolls (almond swirl, cinnamon twist, sticky bun, muffins, biscuits, scones, and so on) as well as lunch of sandwiches, salads, and crescents ("No, not croissants!" says the menu), which are homemade bread doughs wrapped around turkey and honey mustard, spinach and feta cheese, or roast beef and Swiss.

Pimiento cheese, a Mid-South passion, is the essential sandwich. It is not dramatically different from ordinary cheese spread, but subtle difference is just the point. Pimiento cheese is all about nuance: the slight zip of chopped pimientos and sweet relish and their red and green sparkle in the gentle-flavored cheese. While hearty and satisfying, it has a refined character that sings of ladies' lunchrooms, afternoon tea, and Dixie finesse.

For dessert: cake, pie, fudge brownies, and sugar tea cakes, available with espresso coffee drinks.

## Nikki's Drive-In

| | |
|---|---|
| 899 Cherokee Blvd. | 423-265-9015 |
| Chattanooga, TN | BLD \| $ |

Although carhop service no longer is available, Nikki's remains a timeless mid-twentieth-century drive-in, complete with long counter, jukebox at every booth, and Coke served in glass bottles. Signs atop the brick building do not boast of hamburgers (although the burgers are very nice lunch-counter patties); they advertise the house specialties: Gulf Coast shrimp and southern fried chicken. The fried shrimp are relatively pricey (over $20 for a dozen), but meaty enough that six of them, with salad, fries, and hush puppies, make a fine meal. We thank tipster John Reed for telling us we had to have bacon-wrapped, deep-fried chicken livers (oh, Mama, are these ever rich!) as well as Nikki's justifiably famous big-hoop battered onion rings. We topped things off with very good pecan pie.

## Pancake Pantry

| | |
|---|---|
| 1796 21st Ave. S. | 615-383-9333 |
| Nashville, TN | www.thepancakepantry.com |
| | BL \| $ |

We suffer from anxiety at the Pancake Pantry. First we worry about getting in. There is almost always a line of hungry Nashvillians waiting for a precious seat in this singular restaurant that transcends generic pancake-house dining. Second, simply choosing from the menu induces paroxysms of indecision. If we order sweet-potato pancakes that are so good drizzled with cinnamon cream, then it doesn't make sense also to eat onion-laced potato pancakes. And if we get stacks of pancakes, how much appetite can possibly remain to enjoy what are surely the best hash browns in the South? We don't know if they're cooked on the same griddle as the pancakes, or if it's just pancake scent in the air, but Pancake Pantry potatoes are as buttercream fluffy as the best flapjack. Fried to a golden crisp, they are counterpoise for the salty punch of a brick-red slab of griddled country ham.

A few other favorites from the broad and inviting menu: Smoky Mountain buckwheat cakes, which appear dark and somber, but are featherlight, arriving as a stack of five with plenty of butter and a pitcher of warm syrup to pour on top; Caribbean buttermilk pancakes; and thin and eggy Swedish pancakes wrapped around lingonberry preserves.

The Pancake Pantry is a big restaurant with plenty of space among the tables and a high-spirited ambience throughout the dining room. It is impossible to imagine being in a bad mood when eating here.


## Payne's

1762 Lamar Ave.      901-272-1523
Memphis, TN      L | $

As in most barbecue parlors of the Mid-South, the counter man at Payne's will not ask if you want coleslaw when you order a pulled pork sandwich. It is automatic: tender pork shoulder is hacked with a cleaver on a wooden block and piled into a bun with hot or mild sauce, and to balance the meat's smoky profundity, pickly sweet, mustard-tinged slaw goes on top. This configuration, formally known as a pig sandwich, is a brilliant, wide-spectrum presentation that combines warm meat with cool slaw, spicy sauce with creamy dressing, piggy pork with crunchy cabbage.

Expect no frills in this fundamental place, where accommodations are just a few scattered tables to which you carry your own food, presented ready-wrapped. The menu is posted on a moveable-letter board above the order counter, where the short list includes beef barbecue, sausages, rib tips, and bologna, with sides of beans, slaw, and French fries. In our experience none of these is stellar; but the pig sandwich is.


## Pepperfire Spiced Chicken

2821 Gallatin Pike      615-582-4824
Nashville, TN      www.pepperfirechicken.com
     LD | $

Isaac Beard opened Pepperfire in the fall of 2010 and is currently the one white man among Nashville's hot-chicken purveyors. (About ten years ago, Caucasian country-music couple Lorrie Morgan and Sammy Kershaw briefly operated a place called Hotchickens.com, which has since gone under.) Although a native of Nashville, Beard wasn't all that impressed with hot chicken until a revelatory moment some five years ago when he visited Prince's (p. 199) and suddenly was struck with its glory, becoming a two-times-a-day extra-hot eater. Despite its built-in inefficiencies, he is convinced hot chicken has potential to become popular all over the country, just as its profile in Nashville has gone from being a strictly black-neighborhood specialty to a source of citywide pride and inspiration for an annual hot-chicken festival every Independence Day. "I believe I was born to do something with hot chicken," he says. "I am a hot-chicken evangelist."

He makes what is perhaps the most beautiful hot chicken in the city: cinnabar-red, glistening with fat and heat, oozing juice at the slightest poke. In addition to breast quarters and leg quarters, as well as half and whole chickens, Pepperfire offers jumbo hot wings and tenders. Side dishes are mere palate-salve: crinkle-cut fries, potato salad, coleslaw, baked beans, and green beans.

Pepperfire used to be a drive-through junk-food joint, and although much business remains take-away, a weather-protected area was recently established for dining on premises.


## Poe Boy Luncheon

3000 Dickerson Pike       615-226-1957
Nashville, TN       LD | $

Poe Boy's motto is "Food for the Soul," but we suggest expanding the sentiment to say "Meal for the Soul." It is not only the good food but the place itself and the people who run it that make coming to this somewhat forlorn building on Dickerson Pike a dining experience that is rich and heartening and bottom-line delicious. Despite bars on the windows and door of the cinder-block building (which, we assume, was at one time a place where bad people congregated), the moment we walked in, we felt a hospitable warmth and knew we were in for a Roadfood meal to remember.

Poe Boy is a stone's throw from Prince's Hot Chicken Shack (see below), but here the chicken is roasted, not fried. A breast quarter is painfully tender, presented boneless, sopped with zesty barbecue sauce and laced with limp onions. Alongside comes mac 'n' cheese that is sticky and chewy and enthusiastically peppered, and cabbage cooked long and slow with enough pig meat that it has been reborn as a luxury dish. Meals are accompanied by a slab of griddle-cooked hot-water corn bread with crisp outsides and a moist interior.

There is one and only one dessert to consider: caramel cake. A bundt-shaped loaf of creamy yellow cake is enrobed with a thick coat of golden-brown caramel frosting that is as rich as butter, with a toasty aura and just-right sweet. Eat it right and each forkful will be about three-quarters cake and one-quarter caramel. There is nothing fancy about it, but if we were to list the ten best cakes we've ever eaten, this would be among them.

## *Prince's Hot Chicken Shack

123 Ewing Dr.  615-226-9442
Nashville, TN  LD Tues-Sat | $

Pay attention to the name: Prince's *Hot* Chicken Shack. Available mild, medium, hot, and extra-hot, be forewarned that even mild packs a punch. We tried hot and it had us tearing up . . . with joy! What's great about this crisp-fried wonder is that it isn't merely hot. It is radiant with flavor; its chewy skin has soulful character; the meat is moist and luxurious. To say it is addictive is not hyperbole: We have met devotees who told us they come to Prince's five times a week (it's closed Sunday and Monday), and any day they didn't get their extra-hot was a sad one.

Chicken is all you need to know, except for French fries, which are terrific too. The chicken comes in halves and quarters. It is delivered in a paper bag near the window where you placed your order and paid. There are a handful of tables in the restaurant and many people simply step outside to dine on the walkway of the small strip mall where Prince's is located. Beverages are sold from vending machines inside.

## The Rendezvous

52 S. 2nd St.  901-523-2746
Memphis, TN  www.hogsfly.com
D | $$

Famous as they are as a symbol of Memphis barbecue, the Rendezvous's ribs technically are not barbecued; they are charcoal broiled. Instead of being bathed in sauce, which is the more typical Memphis way, they are dry. Dry, but not drab. Indeed, these are some of the most flavorful ribs you will eat anywhere. Instead of sauce, the meaty bones arrive at the table encased in a crust of powerful spice. The spice accentuates the sweetness of the pork and also contains and concentrates its succulence. Rendezvous ribs are the juiciest.

With its semi-subterranean dining room where the décor is antique bric-a-brac and thousands of business cards left by decades of happy customers, the Rendezvous is more reminiscent of a beer hall in *The Student Prince* than a Mid-South barbecue. To accompany the beer you must drink before (as well as during) any meal, there are plates of sausage and cheese that are a merry hors d'oeuvre. Sound like a lot of food? Eating large is part of the Rendezvous experience; of all the restaurants in town, we nominate this one as the worst to visit on a diet.

## *Ridgewood Barbecue

900 Elizabethton Hwy. (Old 19E)    423-538-7543
Bluff City, TN    LD | $$

When we first came upon the Ridgewood Barbecue in Roadfood's earliest days, we knew we had found a benchmark. The food was sensational, and Mrs. Proffit, who ran the place, along with her good ol' girl staff, were a vision of no-bull country hospitality. The queenly Mrs. Proffit and her gals are gone, but the place is pretty much the same, as are its priceless recipes.

Hams are hickory-cooked in a pit adjacent to the restaurant, sliced into fairly thin pieces, then reheated on a grill when ordered. The meat is souped with a tangy, dark-red, slightly smoky sauce (available by the pint and quart near the cash register) and served as a platter with terrific dark-gold French fries, or in a sandwich that spills out all sides of the bun. We like the platter because it allows one to fork up a French fry and a few flaps of sauced meat all at the same time, making for one of the world's perfect mouthfuls. Prior to the arrival of the platter, you will be served a bowl of coleslaw—cool, crisp, sweet—surrounded by saltine crackers. We also recommend ordering a crock of beans. They are laced with meat and have a fetching smoky flavor.

A word of warning: If you arrive at a normal mealtime, expect to wait. Despite its fairly remote location, Ridgewood's excellence has earned it fame. It attracts barbecue pilgrims from far and near.

## Rotier's

2412 Elliston Pl.    615-327-9892
Nashville, TN    www.rotiersrestaurant.com
LD | $

A longtime favorite of Vanderbilt students, Rotier's is a blast from the past, its burger one-of-a-kind. A thick, irregularly shaped patty of ground beef is grilled to glistening perfection and stacked with lettuce, tomato, pickle, and hopefully a layer of bright-orange cheese and a good squirt of mustard between two handsome tiles of toasty French bread. The package is tall enough that it arrives stuck together with a toothpick.

Although everyone in town knows Rotier's as the hamburger place, it also happens to be one of Nashville's premier hot-lunch restaurants, where you can choose from a menu of such entrees as pork barbecue, country-fried steak, fried chicken, and meat loaf. On the side, pick two vegetables from a list of southern classics: black-eyed peas, turnip greens, fried okra, baked squash casserole, crowder peas, white beans, and more. Or, it is possible to get a plate of nothing but vegetables—an excellent strategy if for some reason you are going meatless. With the vegetables come good rolls or warm corn bread, and if you don't want to drink beer, the menu lists milk shakes, chocolate milk, sweet milk, and buttermilk. And, of course, sweet tea.

## Sands Soul Food Diner

937 Locklayer St.          615-742-1652
Nashville, TN              BL | $

Breakfast and meat-and-three lunch are portioned out from a short cafeteria line that gives Sands customers a view of what's to eat as well as the opportunity to discuss options with one of the team of servers behind the counter: What's good with smothered pork steak? (Answer: stewed apples and fried potatoes with onions.) Don't be surprised if the helpful gals dipping plates refer to you as honey, darlin', sweetheart, or baby.

We recommend the country ham, but a good fallback meat is fried bologna, served under a tangle of sweet, soft fried onions. Grits are thick, full-flavored, and especially wonderful when ladled with plenty of butter. Huge chicken wings are dished out with a mantle of brown gravy, and among the worthy vegetables at lunch are greens, green beans, and macaroni and cheese (in the South, mac 'n' cheese is a vegetable).

Sands, which used to be called Silver Sands, is a low-slung cinder-block building tucked into an otherwise residential neighborhood just west of the Farmers Market in North Nashville. There are about a dozen tables—much business is carry-out—and despite circulating overhead fans, air in the cream-colored dining room is thick with the homey aromas of good cooking.

## Swett's

2725 Clifton Ave.          615-329-4418
Nashville, TN              www.swettsrestaurant.com
                           LD | $

Swett's is a visible success story: opened in 1954 as a small soul-food meat-and-three café, it became a large, modern cafeteria, burned down, and was built again. Portraits of the founding Swetts adorn the walls, and their legacy is reflected by a kitchen serving hearty southern meals at reasonable prices.

Like so many cafeteria lines, this one starts with dessert: pie ranging from low-profile chess to lofty meringues, plus a couple of hot fruit cobblers. Beyond the sweets are the meats: masterful fried chicken, spice-encrusted baked chicken, sausages, country steak, and beef tips. Now comes the real fun: vegetables. Swett's repertoire is a symphony of steamed or fried okra, fried corn, squash casserole, candied yams, mashed potatoes, mac 'n' cheese, stewed cabbage, candied apples, baked beans, turnip greens, rice and gravy, et cetera. Most customers get one meat and two or three vegetables. Some fill their tray with nothing but four or five vegetable dishes . . . accompanied, of course, by corn bread, either baked as a loaf and sliced or in the more typical local formation, as a cake fried on a griddle.

Draw your own tea (sweet or unsweet) at the end of the cafeteria line.

## TJ's BBQ & Fish

1104 Ed Temple Blvd.          615-329-1200
Nashville, TN                 LD | $

A few years back, Jim Myers of *The Tennessean* declared the hot fish sandwich at TJ's BBQ & Fish to be one of the best in Nashville. The same story noted that TJ's pitmaster happened to be the son-in-law of the pitmaster at Joe's Bar-B-Que & Fish, and that the two places' fish sandwiches were remarkably similar. We came to the same conclusion during an eating expedition of Nashville. Now that Joe's is gone, TJ's stands alone.

The menu lists whiting and catfish, and we do love the whiting. But it's TJ's pork for which we'll make return visits. It is lasciviously tender and plays crazy chords of flavor all over one's tongue. Sauce is available hot or not; the former is a little sweet and a lot hot. Griddle-cooked corn bread makes a wonderful companion. Other available sides include turnip greens, fried okra, mac 'n' cheese, and spaghetti.

As it was at Joe's, service is strictly drive-through (no indoor seating). Once you place an order, you pull around to an adjacent parking lot and when it is ready, someone from the kitchen runs it out to the car.

## Wiles-Smith Drugs

1635 Union Ave.

901-278-6416

Memphis, TN

BL | $

Just up the road from the Sun Records studio, where Elvis made his first recording, is a drugstore that opened when the King was nine years old. Wiles-Smith has been remodeled, so it doesn't look ancient, but its culinary values are tradition itself. You can sit at the boomerang-pattern Formica counter and enjoy a nice breakfast or lunch sandwich or meal-sized beef stew for under $5. Ice cream concoctions are classic, including perfectly blended sodas, cherry and chocolate sundaes, and milk shakes that come in tall silver beakers so you can refill your glass approximately one and a half times. When Memphis sizzles in the summer, this is the place for an icy fruit freeze.

## Zarzour's

1627 Rossville Rd.

423-266-0424

Chattanooga, TN

L Mon-Fri | $

When you walk into Zarzour's, you will be greeted by chef Shannon Fuller, who wants to know, "Are you having a cheeseburger, or dining off the menu today?" The burgers are not to be slighted: hand-pattied, thick and juicy and satisfying. But the menu, a 5×7 piece of paper with three entrees handwritten every day above a printed list of vegetables, is irresistible. If turnip greens are on it, they're a must: murky, pork-sweet, as tender as long-steamed cabbage, and heavy with tonic pot likker. We adore the antediluvian baked spaghetti, which is toothless pasta laced with crumbled beef, chewy shreds of cheese scraped from the edge the casserole, and a web of hardened noodles from the top. No hot meal is more popular than the every-Wednesday salmon croquettes (known to some fans as "redneck crab cakes"). "I make twenty-five or thirty plates of them," Shannon says, showing how she forms each one from a mix of salmon, egg, onion, flour, and milk, then pan-fries it so the pink mash inside is encircled by a good crunch.

Shannon's mother-in-law, Shirley (granddaughter of the man who first opened Zarzour's in 1918), developed the recipes for dessert. Her glories include lemon icebox pie, peach ice cream in season, banana pudding, and the amazing millionaire pie. That's pineapple chunks, walnut pieces, green grapes, and mandarin orange slices suspended in a mix of frozen Cool Whip and sweetened condensed milk.

## 24 Crows

650 Zachary Taylor Hwy.          540-675-1111

Flint Hill, VA                   BL | $$

While it looks like a humble sandwich shop–café (and in some ways, it is), 24 Crows has masters in its kitchen.

Look at the "club trout" sandwich: Long fillets of pan-fried trout, moist and creamy inside their crisp coats, are complemented by thick strips of apple-smoked bacon, plus lettuce, tomato, and spiced mayonnaise, all heaped into a handsome challah roll. Four stars! For the chicken sandwich, roast chicken and sharp Vermont Cheddar cheese are dressed with fig chutney and creamy mustard on thick slices of toasted whole-grain bread. One more temptation from the sandwich board: the Italian roast pork sandwich with sun-dried tomato, pesto, and arugula on toasted olive bread.

House-made ice cream is reason enough to make a pilgrimage to 24 Crows. Each flavor pops like its namesake with an exclamation mark. Apricot hits a sweet spot of dairy luxury in balance with musky-tart fruit. Belgian chocolate is all about equanimity: deep, dark chocolate; bright, fresh cream; and just enough sugar to create profound harmony.

Note: the dining area is a veritable museum of local (and some faraway) crafts: all for sale.

## Becca's

24399 Lankford Hwy.
Tasley, VA

757-789-3686
www.beccascakesandmore.com
BL | $

Becca's is a bakery-café by the side of Highway 13, which threads Virginia's Eastern Shore from the Chesapeake Bay Bridge-Tunnel to the Maryland state line. The specialty of the house is Smith Island Cake, which is the official dessert of Maryland, named for one of the Chesapeake Bay's two inhabited islands. It is an impressive multiple-layer stack cake, made at Becca's in more than a dozen flavors, including banana with cream-cheese icing, banana with caramel icing, coconut, coconut/lemon, Oreo, red velvet, chocolate cherry, carrot, and caramel. The fluffy layers are iced while still warm—a practice that amplifies their tenderness.

While a lot of Becca's business is whole cakes to go (as well as catering), you can sit down here for a slice of cake or a very nice little meal: sandwiches, burgers, soups accompanied by sweet-potato biscuits (sweet potatoes are a prize produce grown on the Eastern Shore), and Rebecca's dandy crab melt, which is lump crab meat topped with melted Havarti cheese.

## Big's Place

35044 Lankford Hwy.
Painter, VA

757-442-5535
LD | $

Big's is a comfortable former art gallery, happily disheveled and immensely friendly. It's the most likely restaurant along Virginia's Eastern Shore to have swelling toads on the menu. An unluckily named but accessibly flavored specialty found in this region, swelling toads ("puffers") are tiny blowfish that get cut into little fillets and fried in a pan full of butter. Their flesh is firm and moist, similar to flounder.

In addition to puffers, Big's Place offers more familiar shore fare such as soft crabs, shrimp and grits, speckled trout, and fried seaside oysters. Or you can have a nice peppercorn-crusted steak or spaghetti and meatballs. Drink some good sweet tea on the side, and pray that Grandmother's Coconut Sour Cream Cake is available when you come. If it isn't, Mother-in-Law's Ultra-Tall Lemon Meringue Pie is a fine sweet-tart consolation. Chocoholics can hope for Death by Chocolate Cake, which is layered with Amaretto mousse, iced with fudge, and drizzled with Amaretto.

## Charlie's Café

1800 Granby St.          757-625-0824
Norfolk, VA              BL | $

When we asked locals for Roadfood suggestions in Hampton Roads, many recommended Charlie's Café, describing it as a great greasy spoon. The wood-frame house does have a well-worn feel and cheap-eats accommodations: bare tables, counter with stools, unbreakable heavy-duty china. And the menu is hash-house cuisine par excellence. But if Charlie's is a greasy spoon in ambience, it is a cut above in food and service. Even the walls are interesting: a gallery for strange and intriguing paintings that are a far cry from standard-issue diner décor.

There is a full lunch menu with burgers of all kinds, sandwiches, salad, and homemade soup, as well as daily specials that always include a full turkey dinner every Thursday; but it's breakfast that is the big draw (very big on weekends; prepare to wait for a table). Omelets are notable. Ingredients are not unique—choices range from fajita chicken or chili filling to vegetarian specials—but the eggs from which they're made are grand. I sat at the counter and watched my potato omelet made (at the suggestion of regional food savant Patrick Evans-Hylton, a potato omelet topped with "habinaro salsa") and didn't see the cook do anything special; yet the fluffy cloud of eggs that arrived on my plate was sheer elegance. In concert with a filling of crisp-fried potatoes and melted jack cheese, it was one splendid breakfast. Potential accompaniments include biscuits, corn bread, Texas toast, and butter-gobbed grits. Coffee is bottomless and tea is sweet.

## Chutzpah

12214 Fairfax Towne Center      703-385-8883
Fairfax, VA                     www.chutzpahdeli.com
                                BLD | $$

Located at the far end of a nondescript Fairfax shopping center, Chutzpah is a modest-sized storefront with an immodest personality. Billing itself as a *real* New York deli, it features gigantic sandwiches, smoked fish platters, bagel plates, hot or cold borscht, and a full repertoire of Dr. Brown's sodas. While it is in no way regionally unique, it's a good spot to know about if you want authentic deli food on Interstate 66 west of DC.

Meals begin with bowls of sour and half-sour pickles and creamy coleslaw. We spooned into matzoh ball chicken noodle soup, which was as homey as can be, then feasted on wiener schnitzel—a big, thick slab of juicy meat in an envelope of crunchy, dark-brown crust. It is served with lemon wedges and a large side dish of serious meaty gravy. We thought the gravy superfluous; but the latke (potato pancake) on the side was excellent. Of course, we also had to have a sandwich, but which to choose? Pastrami (annotated on the menu with the advice "Please don't embarrass yourself and ask for mayonnaise"), hot brisket, or chopped liver? We went for a Reuben, which is an extremely unwieldy tower of steamy corned beef, sauerkraut, melted Swiss cheese, and Russian dressing between two crisp-grilled slabs of rye bread. It comes with thick-cut steak fries and it is delicious!

For dessert, we walked out with a nice black-and-white cookie, forgoing the seven-layer cake, carrot cake, and genuine New York cheesecake.

## Dixie Bones BBQ

13440 Occoquan Rd.         703-492-2205
Woodbridge, VA             www.dixiebones.com
                           LD | $$

Cooked at least a dozen hours over smoking hickory logs, Dixie Bones pork is velvet-soft and gentle-flavored, served in sandwiches heaped on a platter with such side dishes as Laura's favorite creamy-lush macaroni salad, French fries, baked beans, limp greens, and a terrific item known as muddy spuds. That last item is chopped-up baked potato dressed with barbecue sauce.

There are three heat levels of Carolina-style sauce (tomato-sweet/vinegar-tangy), the hottest of which is not incendiary. In addition to boneless pork, there are ribs sold by the rack and half-rack, pork sausage, beef brisket, pulled chicken breast, and fried catfish fillets.

Pies are made here, and we found the individual fried apple pie endearingly soulful—well-sweetened and cooked long enough that the pieces of apple inside were as tender as the barbecued pork. Thursday is lemon pie day. Saturday's pie is sweet potato. Bread pudding with caramel sauce is always available.

## Do-Nut Dinette

1917 Colley Ave.           757-625-0061
Norfolk, VA                BL | $

On an unlikely corner in Norfolk's rather trendy Ghent neighborhood, Do-Nut Dinette is the real deal. Early one morning, we were thoroughly entertained by the back-and-forth palaver among stool-sitters and staff; the topics covered including tattoos gotten while drunk and why hash brown potatoes are good for you. As the name suggests, donuts are the specialty: raised and glazed, light enough that three or four or even a half dozen doesn't seem like too many for a healthy appetite. They are vaguely like Krispy Kreme; quality donuts that are good even if they're not hot from the fryer.

You do want to get to Do-Nut Dinette early in the day when the donuts are fresh. Only one batch is made each morning, and it can be gone by noon. The rest of the menu is a repertoire of Mid-South diner classics including sizzled country ham and well-buttered grits. If grits are not your thing, do consider the hash browns. They are good and greasy, brightly seasoned—the sort of spud that seems just right in a dinette.

Note the eccentric hours of operation: open every day from 6 a.m. to 2 p.m., plus Friday and Saturday nights from midnight to 2 p.m. the next day.

## Doumar's

20th St. & Monticello Ave.          757-627-4163
Norfolk, VA                          www.doumars.com
                                     BLD | $

Doumar's has been at the corner of 20th Street and Monticello Avenue in Norfolk since 1934, but it was thirty years before that and in the city of St. Louis that the Doumar name first gained fame. At the World's Fair of 1904, Mr. Doumar introduced a novel way of serving and eating ice cream: the cone. The cone made it possible for fairgoers to walk and eat ice cream at the same time—surely one of the great ideas in culinary history.

Today's Doumar's of Norfolk is marked by a sign with two big ice cream cones on either side, but it's known also for pork barbecue, double-meat hot dogs, burger-and-French-fry plates, and flat grilled cheese sandwiches. As for ice cream, if you choose not to get a traditional waffle cone (still made the old-fashioned way), you can order what is here known as a Reggie (a chocolate milk shake with crushed cone chips), a June Bride (chocolate ice cream topped with strawberry sauce), or a Kingston Flat (strawberry short-cake with bananas). Milk shakes are served in glasses made of . . . glass!

There's plenty of indoor seating, but Doumar's also delivers its classic fare on trays that hang on the window of your car.

## Exmore Diner

4264 Main St.

Exmore, VA

757-442-2313

www.exmorediner.com

BLD | $

The Exmore Diner is a wood, tile, and stainless-steel streamliner just off the main highway on Business Route 13 heading into town. It's the sort of place Roadfooders prize not just because it has good things to eat but because it is an ad-hoc community center—the gastronomic version of what now takes place mostly in cyberspace: human interaction. Counter and booths arrayed beneath the curving monitor roof are close enough that unless you speak very quietly, your conversation is open to the public. We first had breakfast here shortly after a fluke blizzard and the place was buzzing with tales of shoveling, busted pipes, frozen gas lines, and treacherous backroads snowdrifts.

Breakfast is an especially good time to come to the Exmore Diner, not just for local color but for such Mid-Atlantic signatures as creamed chipped beef, sausage gravy biscuits, and scrapple with grits. Fried chicken, along with such soulful sides as collard greens, mac 'n' cheese, and braised cabbage, are everyday winners, and the kitchen is known for its seafood, including pancake-flat, griddle-cooked blue crab cakes ("shell is possible," the menu warns); beautiful fried butterflied shrimp; and a platter of all the seafoods in the kitchen, which is, the house boasts, the "largest plate anywhere." Extremely local dishes frequently offered as specials include swelling toads (little panfish that taste great sautéed in butter) and fried ribs from the black drumfish.

You can top things off with rice pudding or bread pudding, but we'll always go for sweet-potato pie. Sweet potato crops are especially bounteous on Virginia's Eastern Shore.

## Franklin Restaurant

20221 Virgil H. Goode Hwy.

Rocky Mount, VA

540-483-5601

BLD | $

Traveling from Roanoke toward Winston-Salem along the Virgil H. Goode Highway (Route 220) early one morning, we spotted a bunch of vehicles with local license plates pulled into the parking lot at the Franklin Restaurant in Rocky Mount. Upon opening the car door, we were suddenly intoxicated by the smell of sizzling country ham. This is the real stuff, salt cured to a concentrated essence-of-pig flavor that no other meat can match. You can get a big serving as part of a meal with eggs and such or have it more simply sandwiched in one of Franklin's tender, crumbly, homemade biscuits, which have enough body to sop up a full charge of ham essence.

A return trip confirmed that breakfast may be the most important meal of the day, but it's not the only good one in this friendly diner. Supper of turkey with all the trimmings was glorious. It is nothing out of the ordinary: a meal where the much-abused saw "home cooking" would seem to fully apply, except for the fact that salad is retrieved from a (very nice) salad bar. We only wish the wonderful warm peach cobbler that came for dessert had been served alongside the full-flavored ham steak that was our other main course. There aren't too many taste sensations more thrilling than the sweet-salty punch of these two.

## Fulks Run Grocery

11441 Brocks Gap Rd.  540-896-7487
Fulks Run, VA  www.turnerhams.com
$$

As its name suggests, Fulks Run Grocery is a grocery, not a restaurant. Other than Friday-only ham sandwiches on a makeshift table in back, you can't eat here. But you can buy out-of-this-world Turner Ham. Available with or without the bone and even by the slice or as trimmings for flavoring soups and vegetables, it is cured with brown sugar as well as flake salt, which makes for a ham that is nut-rich, mellow, and memorable. Other highlights of shopping here: pimiento cheese, Virginia peanuts, Red Rooster barbecue sauce, and raspberry-Dijon ham glaze.

Many people who know Turner Hams never even go to Fulks Run; it has been a thriving mail-order business for years. But there is a special pleasure in visiting the wood-floor market and inhaling its smoky perfume. Whole hams, wrapped in nets, are displayed in shopping carts. Merely finding the place is a pleasure. Located along the North Fork of the Shenandoah River just south of the West Virginia border, it is surrounded by nothing but countryside.

## Galax Smokehouse

101 N. Main St.  276-236-1000
Galax, VA  thegalaxsmokehouse.com
LD | $$

A sign on the front of this friendly corner storefront announces "Genuine Pit Barbecue," and that is a promise you can believe. Ravishing ribs, available in slabs from four to twelve bones, come with hush puppies, corn on the cob, sauce-absorbent bread, and such other sides as barbecue beans, fried potatoes, corn nuggets, and smoked mashed potatoes. Brunswick stew, generally served as a side dish but also available by the bowl, is a fork-thick gallimaufry of hunky vegetables. No less than seven different barbecue sauces are available, from Tennessee Sweet to South Carolina Mustard.

If ribs are not your dish, the Smokehouse also offers pulled pork, brisket, and chicken (white or dark), as well as handsome half-pound hamburgers and all-beef hot dogs. Big smoked potatoes are available with just butter and sour cream or loaded with your choice of barbecued meat. Smokehouse banana pudding is some of the best anywhere: big-flavored and soulful.

## Goolrick's Pharmacy

901 Caroline St.  540-373-9878
Fredericksburg, VA  L | $

Goolrick's is a vintage pharmacy lunch counter where shakes are still assembled from ice cream, syrup, and milk, whirled by wand, and served in the tall aluminum beaker in which they were mixed. Not only are the shakes great, so is the lemonade, which is freshly squeezed. And while nothing on the lunch menu will win huzzahs on the Food Network, we love a roster of nice, modest sandwiches such as BLT, chicken salad, grilled cheese, cream cheese and olive, and even peanut butter and jelly. If a shake or lemonade doesn't suit your fancy, how about a cherry Coke, vanilla Coke, or chocolate Coke—each made by squirting fountain syrup into the bottom of the glass before the Coke is drawn.

Accommodations are limited to counter stools and a handful of tables along the wall. In back, a compounding pharmacist can actually fill prescriptions the old-fashioned way, by customizing medicines.

## Market Burger

145 W. Main St.  540-751-1145
Purcellville, VA  www.marketburger.net
LD | $$

Market Burger is a Main Street storefront that sells proudly priced hamburgers. Paper menus are available in a little holder as you walk in the front door so you can peruse them and make some decisions while waiting in line to place an order at the counter between the dining area and the open kitchen. Find a table and not too long after you get comfortable, your name will be called. Fetch dinner and dig in!

If two people in a party each order a burger and French fries, both meals will be piled onto a single tray, making for a really impressive mountain of food. While they are nothing like minimalistic sliders, the burgers are small enough that two in a bun makes sense. Even a three-patty stack can be hoisted in two hands, as we found when we ordered the posted daily special, dubbed the Ian-Ate-R after a hungry customer named Ian. It was three patties, three slices of cheese, lettuce, tomato, pickle, and mayo all layered inside a nice bun from Lyon Bakery in Washington, DC. These burgers will thin your wallet: $7 for a single, $8.50 for a double. The Ian-Ate-R, with fries, was $13. French fries are hand-cut irregulars and very delicious.

The condiment menu offers such interesting complimentary choices as house-made pickles, cranberry mayo, and curry mayo, and for $1 each, what the menu calls "not-so-complimentary toppings" that include Cherry Glen goat cheese, Vermont Cheddar, smoked bacon, and sautéed mushrooms.

Everything you order at Market Burger comes from somewhere near and good, as noted on a blackboard above the order counter that gives current sources for beef, produce, cheese, and buns. Milk shakes, made from scratch, come with both spoon and straw, and the drink selection includes familiar national brands, artisan sodas, and Cheerwine.

## *Metompkin Seafood

14209 Lankford Hwy.   757-824-0503
Mappsville, VA    Tues–Sat 9-6 (closed winter) | $

Cruising along Highway 13 between Temperanceville and Modest Town on Virginia's Eastern Shore, there is no ignoring Metompkin Seafood. Brightly painted yellow sign boards set up by the roadside like a flurry of vintage Burma-Shave ads are emblazoned with red script calling out "soft crabs," "steamed shrimp," "fried fish," "oysters," and "homemade crab cakes." The place is a shack with a wooden crab mascot hung on its clapboards overlooking picnic tables and handwritten menus posted on the wall. Inside is a seafood market and takeout counter, along with a single round table and a couple of rocking chairs where customers who have placed their orders can sit and wait for them to cook.

Fast food this is not. When owner Ellen Hudgins takes your order at the counter, she writes it on a slip of paper and carries it to the back room where the fish is fried, oysters opened, and shrimp steamed. While you wait, you can peruse raw seafood in the case, shop for seasonings and hush-puppy mix on the wall shelves, and watch TV at the single table that is outfitted with paper towels, hot sauce, a local real estate guide, and a Bible. After about fifteen minutes, Ellen announces, "I've got some orders here." Hungry hopefuls listen to see if their time has come. Platters come in Styrofoam clamshells, sandwiches are wrapped in foil; serve yourself canned beverages from the cooler, then dine at a picnic table or in your car.

## Mrs. Rowe's

74 Rowe Rd. (Exit 222 off I-81)    540-886-1833
Staunton, VA    www.mrsrowes.com
    BLD | $

Mrs. Rowe's is not what it used to be, but that doesn't mean you won't enjoy its freshly baked biscuits and sticky buns, crunchy fried chicken with mashed potatoes and/or mac 'n' cheese on the side, the pork chop and stewed apple plate, and creamy, meringue-crowned banana pudding. Opened by the late Mildred Rowe decades ago as a mom-and-pop café, the once-homey eatery has become a big roadside enterprise. Its long-lasting fame and its location at the end of a highway exit ramp attract crowds on busy travel weekends (a million people per year!) and sometimes it can seem like an assembly-line eatery. But we've never found the staff less than courteous, and once the food starts coming we easily drop prejudice engendered by Mrs. Rowe's conspicuous success and eat hearty.

## Orlean Market

6855 Leeds Manor Rd.    540-364-2774
Orlean, VA    BLD | $

The Orlean Market really is a market, with an inventory that ranges from mousetraps and 30-weight motor oil to Cheerios and Jell-O. Above the counter up front, a blackboard menu offers ham biscuits, barbecue, and sandwiches, plus such daily specials as Cuban paninis and chili. Place your order, grab a drink from the cooler and maybe a bag of Mama Zuma's Revenge potato chips, and find a seat at one of the sundry tables scattered around the store or in an adjoining dining room.

We very much enjoyed the crisp-grilled Cuban sandwich and made-to-order house salad with its balsamic reduction decoration, and the hamburgers are first-rate, but the one thing for which we will forever love Orlean Market is coconut layer cake. Made by a local baker, it is fresh and sunny, the frosting extra-thick and sweet but not cloyingly so. The lady who makes it regularly bakes cakes for the Market, about one every other day, her specialties also including caramel cake and hummingbird cake.

## *Red Truck Bakery & Market

22 Waterloo St.

Warrenton, VA

540-347-2224

www.redtruckbakery.com

BL | $

The Red Truck Bakery & Market is mostly a takeout place with a large mail-order business and a regular output of such palate-boggling creations as moonshine double-chocolate cake, real suet-rich mince pie, and bourbon cake . . . not to mention the best granola on Earth.

While it is not by any means a full-service restaurant, there is a sit-down option for hungry travelers. Between the bakery cases and the kitchen is a room with a single large table for whoever happens to be eating in. Draw your own coffee from the urn, select a cranberry orange walnut muffin or a slice of Shenandoah apple cake, and you have a simple but memorably delicious breakfast. For lunch, choose from a selection of sandwiches such as chicken salad made from local chickens, egg salad made with eggs laid by local chickens, ham, cheese, and vegetarian "beetloaf"—all, of course, made on Red Truck's freshly baked bread or focaccia. There is soup, a full assortment of Route 11 potato chips, and a different kind of cookie every day. Many of the spectacular cakes and pies are available only whole, and granola is sold only by the bag, so unless you have a really big appetite, much of the Red Bakery's best stuff is not practical for eating here. Also, we should warn you that the supply of sandwiches can run out by midday.

## Roanoker

2522 Colonial Ave.

Roanoke, VA

540-344-7746

www.theroanokerrestaurant.com

BLD | $

When we first came across the Roanoker while researching the first edition of this book, it was a snug little downtown café with a front window full of burlap-wrapped country hams. When it moved to its present location in 1982, it became a sanitary middle-class lunchroom and lost its vintage ambience. But breakfast of ultrathin "wafer-sliced" country ham with red-eye gravy, fried apples, and biscuits remained the menu headliner. The ham still is terrific, as is the large variety of southern-style side dishes that accompany lunch and dinner: crunchy corn sticks, candied yams, peppery boiled cabbage, congealed salads (aka Jell-O), and always several highly seasoned greens and beans. Of course, there is fried chicken, and a dinner-thick country ham steak also is available, served with red-eye gravy.

Dessert pies include sweet potato, egg custard, peach, and apple.

## Rudy's

3710 Sperryville Pike
Sperryville, VA

540-987-9494
www.thorntonrivergrille.com/#/
rudys-pizza

LD | $

Living in the Northeast, where excellent pizza is commonplace, we tend to be snobbish on the subject. But every once in a while we are surprised by good pizza in an unlikely place. "Not bad pizza for the middle of nowhere," boasted one of the pizzaioli at Rudy's in Sperryville, Virginia, just east of Shenandoah National Park. We say it's better than that. Rudy's makes pretty darn good pizza by any standard, and while it isn't going to knock Pepe's, Zuppardi's, or Pizzeria Bianco off anybody's top-ten list, it is a very worthy Rappahannock County destination.

Located in a vintage grocery store, the pizza parlor offers a scattering of tables and stand-up viewing of the pizzas being made. They are handsome pies, Neapolitan-thin with a puffy collar. The mozzarella is creamy, the crust is chewy, and the locally made sausage is pig-perfect.

All the usual toppings are available, plus fancier items such as artichoke, sun-dried tomato, and prosciutto. Build your own or choose from a roster of house specialties that includes Skyline BBQ Chicken (feta cheese, barbecue sauce, and a balsamic vinegar glaze), Maui Wowi (pineapple, ham, onion, jalapeño, and teriyaki glaze), and Rappahannock Veggie.

One thing we like about Rudy's, other than the fact that the pizza is good, is its prices. What is here known as a "personal pizza" is sized for one very hungry person. Costing all of $5, plus 75¢ per extra topping, it is a tremendous bargain. A large pie, which will easily satisfy three normal appetites, goes for $13, plus $1.75 per extra ingredient.

# Sally Bell's Kitchen

708 W. Grace St.
Richmond, VA

804-644-2838
www.sallybellskitchen.com
L Mon-Fri | $

Sally Bell's Kitchen was conceived in 1924 as a bakery, and that is what it is today—a charming relic from the past, with Sally Lunn muffins, pies, tarts, and that nearly lost icon of the Old South kitchen, beaten biscuits. The biscuits are crisp, tan rounds with silky tops that are an ideal companion for bisque or Sally Bell's tomato aspic. Cupcakes are notable because they are iced all over, not just on top. We love the strawberry cupcakes, so pretty in pink.

There is no place to eat on premises, but boxed lunch is a specialty. Inside a white cardboard box, inscribed with the trademark feminine silhouette, you will find a sandwich on a made-here roll or bread, a cup of macaroni or potato salad, a cupcake . . . and this marvelous thing called a cheese wafer. Topped with a single half pecan, it is delicate and fragile—a couple of bites and it is gone—a taste of a more refined era long before supersizing. Among available sandwich ingredients are chicken salad, egg salad, Smithfield ham, cream cheese with nuts or olives, and, of course, pimiento cheese.

# *Southern Kitchen

9576 S. Congress St.
New Market, VA

540-740-3514
BLD | $

If you want something genuine to eat, something genuinely southern, bypass the junk-food restaurants clustered near I-81 and find a seat in the dining room, at the counter, or in one of the old booths of the Southern Kitchen. Here you will find country ham at breakfast and Virginia peanut soup at lunch. The soup is the consistency of light cream, nutty-flavored but not like liquid peanut butter, and laced with fetching onion sweetness. A little goes a long way; it is an Old Dominion specialty whose svelte character is a perfect hors d'oeuvre before a supper of powerhouse country ham.

If a thick slice of that good ham is just too intense for dinner, consider fried chicken, encased in a succulent golden crust, or even fried oysters, which, considering the location hundreds of miles from seawater, are surprisingly bright. Among noteworthy sides are stewed tomatoes made the traditional southern way—extra-sweet; a welcome balance for the ham. Pies are homemade and worth saving appetite for—especially coconut meringue.

## Sting-Ray's

26507 Lankford Hwy.
Cape Charles, VA

757-331-1541
www.cape-center.com
BLD | $$

Located on Virginia's Eastern Shore and known to locals as Chez Exxon, Sting-Ray's shares space with fuel pumps, a pottery shop, and a boat-storage facility. Instead of the familiar gas station repertoire of corn dogs and cellophane-wrapped honey buns, it is a source of superb local cuisine.

Oysters and shrimp are expertly fried (marinated shrimp are gorgeous too). A not-to-be-missed kitchen specialty is sweet-potato biscuits. Made from a recipe that is decades old, they are particularly good sandwiching thin slices of country ham, which, being Virginia ham, isn't all that brackish. Regional highlights also include ultra-luxurious crab imperial and flounder stuffed with crab imperial as well as a creamed crab dish that isn't really a stew but is too thick to pass as a soup.

Deluxe though some dishes may be, service at Sting-Ray's is down-home. Place your order at the counter and pay. Find a seat (which can be difficult on weekends) and your food will be brought out by one of a staff of professional waitresses. One named Etta turned out to be a fount of Sting-Ray's history as well as a top-notch adviser when it came to ordering, steering us toward the sweet-potato pie for dessert. Its creamy goodness was accented by a dollop of bright-flavored damson plum preserves.

## Stuart's Fresh Catch

2400 Mechanicsville Tpk.
Richmond, VA

804-643-3474
www.stuartsfreshcatch.com
LD | $

Stuart's is a storefront seafood market with no place for customers to eat. Everything is sold fried (or grilled), either ready to eat by the tray, dinner, piece, and sandwich, or ready to take home and cook. We accompanied our sandwich of cream-fleshed fried lake trout, fried oysters, and fried shrimp with individual orders of exemplary collard greens, fried okra, macaroni and cheese, and, best of all, spoonbread. A rarity in any other region and ever more difficult to find even in the South, this billowy corn pudding has a kind of gaiety that tastes as much of corn as any outside sweetener. It is earthy but elegant, and even though it does require a spoon, it makes an ideal companion for hunks of golden-crusted lake trout with its dense meat and crisp golden crust that is so right to pick up and eat with fingers.

## Virginia Diner

408 County Dr. N.

Wakefield, VA

757-899-3106

www.vadinerrestaurant.com

BLD | $

The sign outside Wakefield's Virginia Diner declares it to be the Peanut Capital of the World. Here you can buy pounds of Virginia peanuts, which are 100 percent better than any other peanuts: big, crunchy, dark, and rich. They come salted or unsalted, spiced with Old Bay seasoning or Cajun pepper, butter-toasted, in the shell or shelled, and as the foundation for a truly aristocratic peanut brittle.

Curiously, there are not a lot of peanuts served in the restaurant, although it used to be that Virginia ham had to be made from peanut-fed pigs (no more). This diner's ham is terrific, available baked or fried. Fried chicken, having nothing to do with peanuts, is also mighty good, sheathed in a brittle crust. With these fine southern entrees, you can choose turnip greens, candied yams, spoonbread, black-eyed peas, or stewed tomatoes.

For dessert, you definitely want peanut pie. Served warm, it is a simple dish similar to pecan pie but not so plush.


## Weenie Beenie

2680 S. Shirlington Rd.

Arlington, VA

703-671-6661

BLD | $

Weenie Beenie is the sole survivor of a small Washington-area chain of drive-ins specializing in half-smokes. No one knows for sure how the half-smoke got its name (perhaps because it's only half-smoky or because many places, like Weenie Beenie, bisect them horizontally before they are grilled), but it is unique to the area around the District of Columbia. Here you can have one at lunch dressed with chili (known as a chili smoke), mustard, onions, and relish. At breakfast your half-smoke will be matched with a fried egg and a slice of bright orange cheese.

Regular hot dogs also are available, but they look pretty boring to us. You also can order barbecue pork or just a bowl of beef chili. Picnic tables are arrayed along the side of the takeout-only restaurant for those who choose not to eat in their cars.

## Wright's Dairy Rite

346 Greenville Ave.
Staunton, VA

540-886-0435
www.dairy-rite.com

LD | $

The star of the menu is a Superburger: two beef patties with cheese and lettuce, topped with special sauce and layered in a triple-decker bun. First served in 1952, it is still served as it was then, by carhops at the window of your vehicle in a car slip at the side of the restaurant. Wright's added a dining room in 1989, so it is also possible to eat inside, where décor includes a Wurlitzer jukebox and vintage Wright's menus from the 1950s and 1960s. In 1958, the Superburger cost 55¢.

Handsome as the Superburger is, we prefer a Monsterburger (a half-pound patty) or a Carolina burger (with cheese, chili, slaw, and onion); they tend not to lose their juice, which can be a fault of the smaller ones. On the side, you want Wright's homemade onion rings. Milk shakes are the real thing, available in chocolate, strawberry, or vanilla, as well as with bananas or strawberries, with or without malt powder for additional richness. It is, after all, Wright's *Dairy* Rite, so don't hesitate to have a banana split, a float, or a flurry (candy and/or cookies blended into soft-serve ice cream).

Wright's menu goes well beyond burgers. There are regular and foot-long hot dogs, corn dogs, pork barbecue on a bun, sandwich baskets, sub-marines, chili with beans, even a veggie wrap with fat-free dressing. In addition to milk shakes and soda pop, the beverage list includes freshly brewed iced tea (sweet or not) served in twenty-ounce cups.

## *Coleman's Fish Market

2226 Market St.                     304-232-8510

Wheeling, WV                        LD | $

Coleman's fish sandwich is simplicity itself: two pieces of soft white bread holding a cluster of steaming-hot fried-fish fillets. It is delivered across a counter, wrapped in wax paper. Find a table on the broad floor of the renovated century-old Wheeling Centre Market House, unwrap, and feast!

The crust on the North Atlantic pollock fillets is made of cracker meal, thin as parchment. When you break through it, your sense of smell is tickled by a clean ocean perfume, and as the pearl-white meat seeps warm sweetness, you taste a brand-new food, like no other fish sandwich ever created.

After you've eaten several dozen over time, you might want to branch out and try some of the many other excellent foods Coleman's makes: a Canadian white sandwich (a bit blander and "whiter"-tasting than the regular fish), shrimp boats and baskets, fried clams, oysters, deviled crabs, and Cajun-spiced catfish. Coleman's really is a fish market, and if you wait in the "Special Line" (as opposed to the "Regular Sandwich Line"), you can ask the staff to cook up just about any raw fish in the case, and pay for it by weight. On the side of whatever fish you get, there are good French fries and Jo-Jo potatoes, and onion rings every day but Friday (when the deep fryers are totally devoted to making only fish sandwiches).

## Diehl's Family Restaurant

152 Main Ave.                              304-755-9353

Nitro, WV                                  LD | $

Now run by a third generation of the Diehl family, this gem of a restaurant seems never to have heard of convenience cooking. Everything is made from scratch. "Do you know?" asks the paper placemat, and several bulleted points give you the facts, including, "We make our own Thousand Island dressing," "Cornbread and hot rolls made daily," and "Special hot bologna sauce since 1960." Whether you come for a $5 pulled-pork sandwich or a $7 twelve-ounce cheeseburger, we guarantee that you will be whistling a happy tune when you are finished. Big-deal dinners, selling for about $10, include bone-in country ham, roast beef and mashed potatoes with gravy, and huge plates of spaghetti with meat sauce or marinara. On the side come such country veggies as creamed tomatoes, buttered corn, fried apples, and sage dressing.

Whatever you eat, save room for dessert. Creamy-sweet graham-cracker pie is the highlight, but when Roadfood.com's Dale Fine visited in 2011, he reported that the chocolate peanut butter pie was not to be missed, describing it as "moist, rich, and truly decadent."

Interior décor consists of enthusiastic odes to NASCAR and local sports teams, including model cars, pennants, and a fender that came off Dale Earnhardt's car when he hit the wall at Bristol Motor Speedway.

## Julio's Cafe

501 Baltimore Ave.                         304-622-2592

Clarksburg, WV                             LD | $$

Across from the train station in the old Elk Point section of Clarksburg, Julio's is a first-rate Italian restaurant with a tin ceiling, carved wooden bar, and plush leather booths. While the food is prepared by a chef with culinary expertise and prices are fairly high, service is neighborhood-friendly.

The bill of fare includes four different versions of *pasta e fagiole*—with cream sauce, with marinara, with potatoes and kale, and *en brodo* that twinkles with fennel. There are Italian-American standards such as lasagna, spaghetti with meatballs, and pasta primavera made with uncooked vegetables in red sauce. Waitresses recite what is available for any given meal.

For an hors d'oeuvre, we love the "paisano salad," a cold antipasto plate topped with the kitchen's jade-green garlic-basil dressing, and roasted pepper–gorgonzola bruschetta. Other favorite dishes include red peppers stuffed with hot ground sausage atop a bed of al dente spaghetti noodles and a stylish plate of tuna pomodoro. Meals commence with a basket of garlic toast and conclude with an outrageously rich house-made éclair loaded with French cream and blanketed with chocolate.

## Oliverio's Cash and Carry

427 Clark St.      304-622-8612
Clarksburg, WV      $

"This was once *the* spot in Clarksburg," Angela Oliverio told us several years ago as she slid a long length of pig gut onto the spout of her hand-cranked sausage-making machine. "We had everything here in Elk Point [the Clarksburg neighborhood where her grocery is located]: prostitution, gambling, big business, street-corner business, thriving industry."

While not by any means a bustling metropolis, Elk Point is coming back and, most important, Oliverio's is as wonderful as ever: a vintage, family-run grocery store where Angela sits in back and with the help of her brother John cranks out lengths of Italian pork sausage seasoned with paprika, fennel seed, and hot pepper. She also prepares bowls full of peppered green and black olives that she will sell you by the pint.

Note that Oliverio's is not a restaurant. It is a little grocery store, and unless Angela takes a liking to you and you happen to arrive just when she's cooked up a batch of her sausage for tasting, you cannot eat here.

## Quinet's Court

215 Main St.      304-455-2110
New Martinsville, WV      www.quinets.com
     BLD | $

"We use the area's finest hobby chefs' recipes often," boasts the printed menu of Quinet's Court, where the choice of items on multiple buffet tables is cornucopic. Although presented in big institutional pans on room-length steam tables, most of the dishes seem like home cooking at its finest—from cake-smooth corn bread to stuffed peppers to cream pies, cobblers, cookies, and pudding.

To accompany baby-back ribs, kielbasa, chicken casserole, or ham loaf with pineapple glaze, customers avail themselves of a side-dish smorgasbord to make even a devoted vegetarian smile. Silk-tender butter beans, sweet hunks of carrot, scalloped potatoes, homemade noodles, five-cheese mac 'n' cheese, and baked beans can fill a plate.

The buffet rule is that you pay one price and help yourself to as much as you want. A sign at the beginning of the first table does warn, however, that a $2 surcharge will be added to the bill of anyone who wastes food. Our waitress was especially generous. As we walked in the door, early during lunch hour, we noted a couple of beautiful sticky buns in a pan leftover from breakfast. When we asked her if we could have one, she brought it, no charge, and told us simply to consider it part of our lunch buffet.

Accommodations are appropriately vast: big tables in several spacious dining rooms. Décor includes an awesome picture of prizefighter Jack Dempsey (who ate here in the 1940s) and thousands of pictures of town history and local citizens. It is possible to dine non-buffet-style: breakfast, lunch sandwiches, and a selection of hot meals listed on the menu under the heading "Great Specials for Our Not-So-Hungry Friends."

## Ritzy Lunch

456 W. Pike St.
Clarksburg, WV

304-622-3600
www.ritzylunchwv.com
BL | $

Hot Dog John Selario's parents opened Ritzy Lunch in 1933. "Ritzy Lunch has always been known for hot dogs," he tells us. "Clarksburg itself is an important hot dog town, not so much because of the weenies but because of the way we make our chili. There are so many immigrants and sons and daughters of immigrants—Greeks and Italians, mostly—that when we spice up our chili, we know how to do it right!" He will get no argument from us. His dogs are lovely little puppies, buried deep inside a steamed-soft bun and topped with a zesty ground-beef sauce that is lightly peppered and earthy-flavored. If you want to add a sweet note, get a layer of coleslaw atop the chili—a popular configuration throughout West Virginia.

Note also the Giovanni, a burger topped with melted cheese and roasted peppers served between two slices of butter-and-garlic-infused toast. Excellent!

Ritzy Lunch is an immensely happy place, a sort of non-alcoholic tavern where old friends and town characters hang out on the ancient counter stools to kibitz back and forth among themselves and the waitresses and where, on any pleasant day, two or three wiseacres are likely to be found out on the sidewalk making friends with newcomers.

## Ruby & Ketchy's

2232 Cheat Rd.                     304-594-2004
Morgantown, WV                     BLD | $

Ruby and Ketchy's is an out-of-the-way diner in the Cheat Lake area east of Morgantown. It's open for three meals a day, and its knotty-pine booths and counter are usually occupied by locals who come for good eats and conversation. Opened by Ruby Nicholson in 1958, who was soon joined by husband Ketchy, it's still run by their descendants, and many of the recipes, including the vegetable soup, chili, and every-Tuesday meat loaf, are Ruby's.

Hot meals range from crab cakes to sirloin steak, and such lunch specials as bean soup and corn bread (every Thursday) and salmon patties with mac 'n' cheese on Friday. We enjoyed our ham dinner, of which the menu boasts "served over 30 years." The ham was pan-sizzled and had a rewarding chew. Hot roast beef was also good: pot-roast tender and accompanied by a sphere of mashed potatoes covered with gravy. If you come for dinner on Friday, you can order stuffed cabbage, which Roadfood.com's Buffet-buster has declared his favorite Ruby & Ketchy's dish.

Blackberry pie is the go-to dessert. It is dark purple and winey, with a rugged berry texture. The crust could have been flakier, but the filling was first-rate.

## Stewart's Original Hot Dogs

2445 5th Ave.                      304-529-3647
Huntington, WV                     www.stewartshotdogs.com
                                   LD | $

With countless stands and storefronts that specialize in spicy little weenies topped with chili and coleslaw, West Virginia considers itself the hot dog capital of the universe. The best place to test that claim is Stewart's, a curb-service drive-in since 1932. The formula includes local Logan hot dogs and Heiner's buns and, most important, all the trimmings: onions, mustard, and—drum roll, please—Stewart's secret-recipe chili sauce. The sauce is thick and pasty, not too hot. West Virginia hot dog connoisseurs believe the picture is not complete unless it also includes coleslaw as part of the trimmings constellation; Stewart's is creamy with a bit of pickle bite.

To drink, nearly everybody swills renowned Stewart's root beer, available in quantities that range from a four-ounce mug for kids to a thirty-two-ounce drink to a gallon jug. Or you can enjoy it as the basis of an ice cream float.

Note: There are three other Stewart's locations in the Huntington area: First Street and Adams Avenue in West Huntington; 1025 Oak Street in Kenova; and 205 Towne Center Drive in Ashland, Kentucky.

# Deep South

Alabama
✦
Arkansas
✦
Florida
✦
Georgia
✦
Louisiana
✦
Mississippi
✦
South Carolina

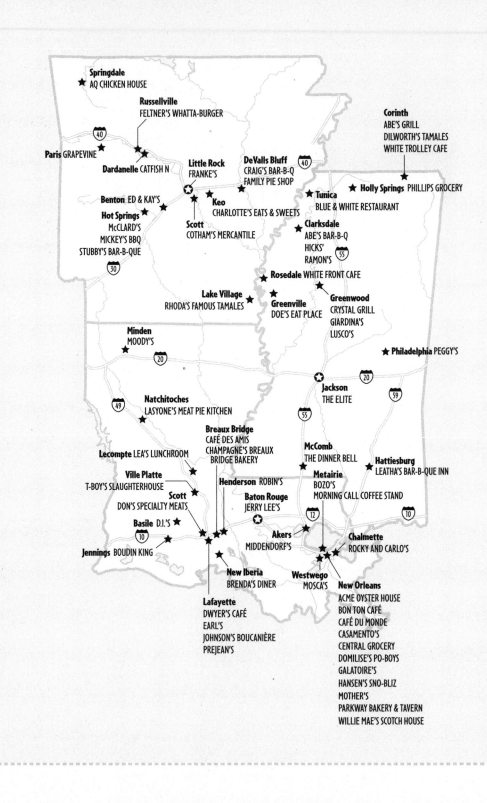

**Springdale**
AQ CHICKEN HOUSE

**Russellville**
FELTNER'S WHATTA-BURGER

**Corinth**
ABE'S GRILL
DILWORTH'S TAMALES
WHITE TROLLEY CAFE

**Paris** GRAPEVINE

**Dardanelle** CATFISH N

**Little Rock**
FRANKE'S

**DeValls Bluff**
CRAIG'S BAR-B-Q
FAMILY PIE SHOP

**Holly Springs** PHILLIPS GROCERY

**Benton** ED & KAY'S

**Keo**
CHARLOTTE'S EATS & SWEETS

**Tunica**
BLUE & WHITE RESTAURANT

**Hot Springs**
McCLARD'S
MICKEY'S BBQ
STUBBY'S BAR-B-QUE

**Scott**
COTHAM'S MERCANTILE

**Clarksdale**
ABE'S BAR-B-Q
HICKS'
RAMON'S

**Rosedale** WHITE FRONT CAFE

**Lake Village**
RHODA'S FAMOUS TAMALES

**Greenville**
DOE'S EAT PLACE

**Greenwood**
CRYSTAL GRILL
GIARDINA'S
LUSCO'S

**Minden**
MOODY'S

**Philadelphia** PEGGY'S

**Natchitoches**
LASYONE'S MEAT PIE KITCHEN

**Jackson**
THE ELITE

**Breaux Bridge**
CAFÉ DES AMIS
CHAMPAGNE'S BREAUX
BRIDGE BAKERY

**McComb**
THE DINNER BELL

**Hattiesburg**
LEATHA'S BAR-B-QUE INN

**Lecompte** LEA'S LUNCHROOM

**Metairie**
BOZO'S
MORNING CALL COFFEE STAND

**Ville Platte**
T-BOY'S SLAUGHTERHOUSE

**Henderson** ROBIN'S

**Scott**
DON'S SPECIALTY MEATS

**Baton Rouge**
JERRY LEE'S

**Basile** D.I.'S

**Akers**
MIDDENDORF'S

**Chalmette**
ROCKY AND CARLO'S

**Jennings** BOUDIN KING

**New Iberia**
BRENDA'S DINER

**Westwego**
MOSCA'S

**New Orleans**
ACME OYSTER HOUSE
BON TON CAFÉ
CAFÉ DU MONDE
CASAMENTO'S
CENTRAL GROCERY
DOMILISE'S PO-BOYS
GALATOIRE'S
HANSEN'S SNO-BLIZ
MOTHER'S
PARKWAY BAKERY & TAVERN
WILLIE MAE'S SCOTCH HOUSE

**Lafayette**
DWYER'S CAFÉ
EARL'S
JOHNSON'S BOUCANIÈRE
PREJEAN'S

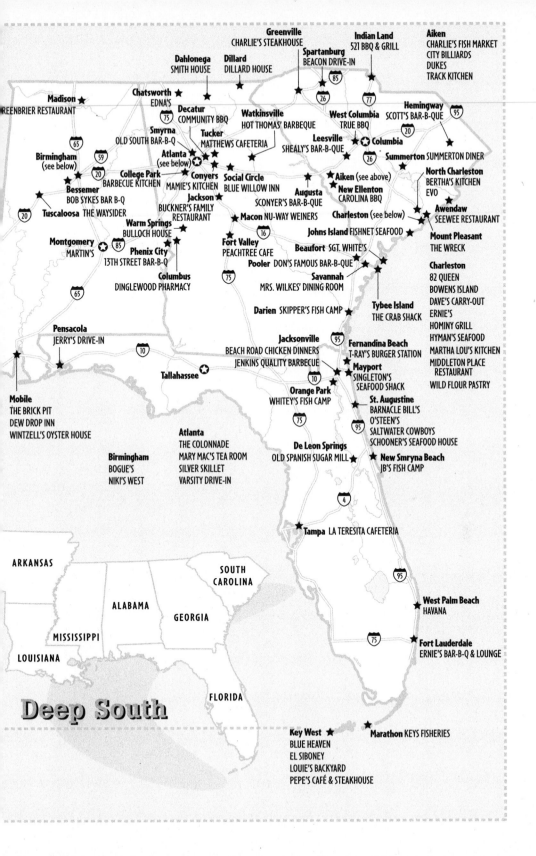

Greenville CHARLIE'S STEAKHOUSE

Spartanburg BEACON DRIVE-IN

Indian Land 521 BBQ & GRILL

Aiken
CHARLIE'S FISH MARKET
CITY BILLIARDS
DUKES
TRACK KITCHEN

Dahlonega SMITH HOUSE

Dillard DILLARD HOUSE

Madison ★
REENBRIER RESTAURANT

Chatsworth ★
EDNA'S

Decatur COMMUNITY BBQ

Watkinsville HOT THOMAS' BARBEQUE

West Columbia TRUE BBQ

Hemingway SCOTT'S BAR-B-QUE

Smyrna OLD SOUTH BAR-B-Q

Tucker MATTHEWS CAFETERIA

Leesville SHEALY'S BAR-B-QUE

Columbia

Birmingham
(see below)

Atlanta
(see below)

Summerton SUMMERTON DINER

Bessemer BOB SYKES BAR B-Q

College Park BARBECUE KITCHEN

Conyers MAMIE'S KITCHEN

Social Circle BLUE WILLOW INN

Aiken (see above)

New Ellenton CAROLINA BBQ

North Charleston
BERTHA'S KITCHEN
EVO

Tuscaloosa THE WAYSIDER

Jackson BUCKNER'S FAMILY RESTAURANT

Augusta SCONYER'S BAR-B-QUE

Charleston (see below)

Awendaw SEEWEE RESTAURANT

Warm Springs BULLOCH HOUSE

Macon NU-WAY WEINERS

Johns Island FISHNET SEAFOOD

Mount Pleasant THE WRECK

Montgomery MARTIN'S

Phenix City 13TH STREET BAR-B-Q

Fort Valley PEACHTREE CAFE

Beaufort SGT. WHITE'S

Charleston
82 QUEEN
BOWENS ISLAND
DAVE'S CARRY-OUT
ERNIE'S
HOMINY GRILL
HYMAN'S SEAFOOD
MARTHA LOU'S KITCHEN
MIDDLETON PLACE RESTAURANT
WILD FLOUR PASTRY

Columbus DINGLEWOOD PHARMACY

Pooler DON'S FAMOUS BAR-B-QUE

Savannah MRS. WILKES' DINING ROOM

Tybee Island THE CRAB SHACK

Pensacola JERRY'S DRIVE-IN

Darien SKIPPER'S FISH CAMP

Jacksonville
BEACH ROAD CHICKEN DINNERS
JENKINS QUALITY BARBECUE

Fernandina Beach T-RAY'S BURGER STATION

Mayport SINGLETON'S SEAFOOD SHACK

Tallahassee

Orange Park WHITEY'S FISH CAMP

St. Augustine
BARNACLE BILL'S
O'STEEN'S
SALTWATER COWBOYS
SCHOONER'S SEAFOOD HOUSE

Mobile
THE BRICK PIT
DEW DROP INN
WINTZELL'S OYSTER HOUSE

Atlanta
THE COLONNADE
MARY MAC'S TEA ROOM
SILVER SKILLET
VARSITY DRIVE-IN

De Leon Springs
OLD SPANISH SUGAR MILL

New Smryna Beach JB'S FISH CAMP

Birmingham
BOGUE'S
NIKI'S WEST

Tampa LA TERESITA CAFETERIA

ARKANSAS

SOUTH CAROLINA

ALABAMA

GEORGIA

West Palm Beach HAVANA

MISSISSIPPI

LOUISIANA

Fort Lauderdale ERNIE'S BAR-B-Q & LOUNGE

Deep South

FLORIDA

Key West
BLUE HEAVEN
EL SIBONEY
LOUIE'S BACKYARD
PEPE'S CAFÉ & STEAKHOUSE

Marathon KEYS FISHERIES

## 13th Street Bar-B-Q

3869 US Hwy. 80W  
Phenix City, AL

334-291-1855  
LD | $

We've eaten a few memorable pork chop sandwiches around the country, from Helen's Sausage House in Delaware to Pork Chop John's in Montana and, of course, the hallowed Snappy Lunch in Mount Airy, North Carolina. Here's a real beauty, in an inconspicuous smokehouse that bills itself as "Home of the Original Pork Chop Sandwich." You get a pair of thick, boneless slabs dressed with a measure of slaw and you choice of mild or (very) hot mustard sauce. The sandwich arrives in a tender, poppy-seeded roll that serves not only as a good mitt for lifting the chop but as a quiet bready counterpoint for the succulent meat and spicy sauce.

The full barbecue menu also includes ribs crusted with vivid glaze as well as barbecue sandwiches and plates: chipped, chopped, or sliced. 13th Street also makes its own version of the scrambled dog, which here is two hot dogs topped with chili, cheese, onions, and coleslaw. Yet to be sampled: a five-pound "Hawg Dog," selling for $24.95.

## Bob Sykes Bar B-Q

1724 9th Ave. N.              205-426-1400
Bessemer, AL                 www.bobsykes.com
                             LD | $$

Bob Sykes opened in 1956, and at one time there were fourteen Bob Sykes barbecues in northern Alabama, but in 1977 the Sykes family decided to concentrate on one location in Bessemer, southwest of Birmingham. Since then, this smokehouse, now run by a third generation of Sykeses who still uses the original recipes, has been a smoke signal of good eats.

Cooked over smoldering hickory wood, the pork is finely chopped and succulent; ribs are beautiful burnished mahogany with great hefty ribbons of meat around each bone; chopped beef is particularly flavorful. "Big Bob" specials include your barbecued meat of choice with baked beans, coleslaw, and French fries or potato salad, plus rolls. For those with a lot of hungry mouths to feed, Sykes's menu lists extra-large orders for five or ten (the latter is based on two and a half pounds of barbecue and comes with a gallon of tea). Carry-out meals and big feeds for twenty-five people and more are sold at a drive-through window. Pies are excellent, sold by the slice, whole pie, or junior pie. You can get chocolate, pecan, and coconut. The one that must be sampled is the meringue-topped lemon pie: sweet, creamy, and southern to its soul.

## Bogue's

3028 Clairmont Ave.          205-254-9780
Birmingham, AL               BLD | $

Despite the motto "It's Vogue to Eat at Bogue's," you won't have to worry about those bothersome paparazzi when you dine here. If you seek an epicurean breakfast, obsequious service, or the trendy restaurant where fashionistas dine, Bogue's is all wrong. If, on the other hand, you want a cheap, rib-sticking breakfast featuring grilled country ham, buttered grits, and biscuits so richly endowed with cooking grease that your fingers glisten after you split one in half, this is where you want to be. If for some reason you don't want biscuits, we highly recommend the caramel sweet rolls.

All the usual subjects are available as breakfast meat, plus flavorful boneless pork chops that look especially right sandwiched between biscuits.

## The Brick Pit

5456 Old Shell Rd.                  251-343-0001
Mobile, AL                          www.brickpit.com
                        LD | $$

Pitmaster Bill Armbrecht operates a room-sized pit into which he piles hickory and pecan logs and cooks meats at the lowest possible temperature for the longest possible time. Pork shoulder basks in smoke for some thirty hours; ribs for twelve; chicken for six. During the process, the meats' natural fat becomes their basting juices; by the time they are done, each piece of pork and chicken is virtually fatless, yet moister than moist.

We're especially smitten with the pulled pork. It is presented as a pile of motley chunks and shreds—some as soft as warm butter, others with a crunchy crust. Ribs are blackened on the outside but extravagantly tender, with many areas so gentled by their tenure in the smoke pit that the lightest finger pressure causes pieces of meat to slide off the bone.

The low-slung dining room at the Brick Pit is painted white and completely covered in signatures, tributes, and other happy graffiti. Orders are taken at a back window; once you've said what you want, you find a seat, and in no time a waitress brings the meal in a partitioned plate that holds the meat of choice separate from the beans and coleslaw that come with it.

## Dew Drop Inn

1808 Old Shell Rd.                  334-473-7872
Mobile, AL                          LD | $

South Alabamians put ketchup on their hot dogs—an anomaly in most places, a criminal act in most of the Midwest. But talk to any wiener lover who grew up in Mobile, and you will see eyes mist with nostalgia for the unique joy of their hometown hot dog as dished out by street vendors during Mardi Gras and as served at the Dew Drop Inn year-round. They are bright-red steamed franks of medium size, their presentation a work of art. The wiener, nestled in a toasted bun, is topped with cool sauerkraut and a layer of warm, beefy chili with spicy-sweet zest. Standard condiments include mustard and pickles as well as ketchup. Aesthetes order them upside down (the dog sits atop the condiments) and others like them "shaved" (without kraut).

A comfy, wood-paneled roadhouse that opened in 1924 and introduced hot dogs to southern Alabama, the Dew Drop Inn also offers a full menu of po' boys, gumbo, Gulf shrimp, and hot dinners accompanied by such of po' boys, gumbo, Gulf shrimp, and hot dinners accompanied by such vegetables as turnip greens and rice and gravy. Coca-Cola is served the true-South way, in its shapely bottle alongside a glass full of ice. Banana pudding is the choice dessert. Service is speedy; checks are delivered with meals.

## Greenbrier Restaurant

27028 Old Hwy. 20          256-351-1800
Madison, AL                oldgreenbrier.com
                           LD | $

Mike Stroud, the Roadfooder who pointed the way to this fine old country café, warns, "Beware of confusing this place with 'Greenbrier Bar-B-Que.' . . . It has a similar menu but nowhere near the charm and spaciousness." The spaciousness to which Mr. Stroud refers is at least as much outside as in. Surrounding Greenbrier are endless acres of cotton fields.

Inside, there is elbowroom aplenty; walls are corrugated metal and hand-hewn wooden tables are covered with easy-wipe cloths. The two big main edible attractions are pork shoulder and catfish fillets—available separately or on a combo platter with pickle-topped, tart coleslaw and spuds (baked or fried)—preceded, always, by a basket of squiggly hush puppies. Within moments of one's sitting down, the pups arrive hot from the fryer. Some visitors consider them to be bland as-is, and so bring them to life by applying one of the barbecue sauces on the table: traditional vinegar-pepper hot sauce or the Alabama-only curiosity, white sauce, based on mayonnaise and containing a rousing shot of pepper.

The menu also includes barbecued chicken, on which that white sauce sings, and ribs, which benefit from a third, tomato-based sweet sauce. Pork and catfish frowners can order fried or boiled shrimp.

## Martin's

1796 Carter Hill Rd.       334-265-1767
Montgomery, AL             LD | $

Oh, such biscuits begin supper at Martin's! Warm with gossamer insides, they would be insulted by the use of butter. The only thing better than biscuits is corn bread, in the form of soft-textured muffins, also warm.

The dinner menu offers such main-course choices as whole fried catfish, stuffed deviled crabs, and fried chicken livers. At lunch, there are daily specials: catfish fillets, smoked sausage, country-fried steak, chicken and dumplings. You always can count on a roster of side dishes that honor the southern way with vegetables: velvet-soft cooked cabbage, pot-likker-sopped collard greens, pole beans, buttery mashed potatoes, plus, of course, Jell-O salad in rainbow hues. The standout meal is fried chicken. Its crisp crust has a nice jolt of spice, it is easy to handle (that is, grease-free), and it is dripping moist inside. One serving includes a meaty white breast and a dark-meat thigh. With biscuits, mashed potatoes, and greens, it makes a memorable meal, especially when followed by Martin's coconut meringue pie.

A wood-paneled, colonial-themed restaurant in a strip mall, Martin's is busier at lunch than at supper. At noon, you will likely have to wait as early arriving customers devour their plates of fried chicken with hedonistic gusto.

## *Niki's West

233 Finley Ave.
Birmingham, AL

205-252-5751
www.nikiswest.com
BLD | $

In the Deep South, vegetables are grown nearly year-round; and many of those vegetables are trucked to the produce center in Birmingham, where they are then shipped to destinations all over the East. Niki's West, surrounded by warehouses and loading docks, is where the produce-haulers come to eat. We counted more than three dozen vegetables along the steam-table line—far too many to even contemplate sampling some of each; so prepare yourself to make some hard choices among the likes of yellow squash casserole, fried green tomatoes, black-eyed peas, and three different kinds of seasoned greens (turnip, collard, and spinach). Some items from the market are austere enough to please even the strictest dieter: unadorned sliced tomatoes, raw vegetable vinaigrette, and baby lima beans. But the more tempting segment of Niki's produce repertoire is prepared according to voluptuous southern-café tradition. Broccoli is mixed with cheese and rice in a crazy-rich mélange; tomatoes are stewed with sugar and shreds of torn white bread until they become as sweet as cobbler; bright-orange yams are infused with sugar; crunchy-fresh okra is sheathed in a deep-fried crust.

The decorative theme at Niki's is the Aegean Sea (fishnets, scenic art of fishing boats), and when it comes to choosing an entree, we recommend baked fish Creole, broiled mackerel, and grilled amberjack. For fish frowners, there is always a selection of beef and pork as well as a terrific baked Greek chicken.

We used to not like dessert here, but recent visits have made us happily eat our words. Lemon meringue pie is lofty and light, lemon icebox pie is vibrant, and banana pudding, as rich as caramel, is one of the South's best.

## The Waysider

1512 Greensboro Ave.      205-345-8239
Tuscaloosa, AL      BL | $

For decades now, the Waysider has been the breakfast spot of choice in Tuscaloosa, especially well known for its airweight biscuits, served with honey and, preferably, a slab of country ham with red-eye gravy and a side of hearty cheese grits. On weekends, the place is breakfast-only, but during the week you can count on lunch of such Dixie café fare as fried chicken with fried okra, field peas, collard greens, squash soufflé, candied yams, or fried corn. Warm fruit cobbler and cream pies top things off with a super-sweet exclamation mark.

## Wintzell's Oyster House

605 Dauphin St.      334-432-4605
Mobile, AL      www.wintzellsoysterhouse.com
     LD | $$

Wintzell's used to be one-of-a-kind. There now are six of them in Alabama and one in Hattiesburg, Mississippi. We've heard mixed reviews about the others, but have only good things to say about the original in downtown Mobile. Aside from impeccable, opened-as-you-watch raw oysters, grilled oysters, oysters Bienville, and oysters Rockefeller, you can sample such definitive Gulf Coast specialties as seafood gumbo and crisp-fried crab claws, po' boys, and crusty-fried catfish. This is a good place to eat the unique Mobile specialty, West Indies salad. It's nothing more than crab meat marinated in oil and vinegar with grated onions. If the crab is good—and you can count on that here—it is a dish that is rich and ocean-sweet, so good that many customers forgo it as an appetizer (its usual role) and get a couple of large orders for their main course, accompanied by saltine crackers.

The restaurant itself is heaps of fun. Opened by Oliver Wintzell as a six-stool oyster bar in 1938, it has survived hurricanes and floods, and has been rebuilt and expanded into a big place. There still is an oyster bar where you can sit and knock 'em back by the dozen, and the ongoing contest continues to see who can eat the most raw oysters in one hour. The walls are plastered with thousands of little signs offering bons mots and rules of life put there by the late Mr. Wintzell, starting in the 1950s. For example: "If you want to save face . . . keep the lower half shut." *Bits of Wit and Wisdom (The Signs at Wintzell's Oyster House)* and *Oysters and Politics,* Mr. Wintzell's self-published books, are available for sale at the cash register.

# *AQ Chicken House

1207 N. Thompson
Springdale, AR

479-751-4633
www.aqchickenhouse.net
LD | $

Fried chicken? There is none better. Charcoal-cooked chicken? AQ's is the best. Barbecued chicken? These crusty pieces, sticky with dark-red, spicy-sweet sauce, will never get kicked off our plate. The point is: If you like chicken, you need to come to Springdale (or AQ's second location on Highway 71B in Fayetteville) and test this fine bird for yourself. Fried is juice-spurting tender, encased in a chewy-crisp envelope of well-seasoned crust. Charcoal-cooked is nearly as indulgent, its spicy skin imbued with the flavor of smoke and a vigorous lemon-pepper smack. If you can't make up your mind, the menu does offer a sampler platter of three pieces, each cooked a different way. An all-you-can-eat plan is available for $11.99 per person.

Meals at this big, family-friendly restaurant begin with glossy-topped cloverleaf rolls hot from the oven, and among essential side dishes are sweet-potato casserole, batter-dipped French fries, seasoned green beans, baked beans, and mashed potatoes. Unless you have a note from your doctor, you must order fried peaches for dessert: slices of al dente peach are battered and fried and served hot under a pile of ice cream.

## Catfish N

210 Dardanelle Dam Rd.
Dardanelle, AR

479-229-3321
www.catfishn.com

D | $$

Catfish N is an eating barn above the Arkansas River where you can pile your plate with whole mudcats or fillets (and, if you wish, fried chicken and boiled shrimp), along with hush puppies (regular or jalapeño-spiked), fried biscuits, assorted vegetables, and salad fixins. Help yourself to as much as you want; everything is set out in an open-access buffet. Beneath its thick, golden crust, the whole catfish is moist and sweet, the fillets somewhat less so. For dessert, there are usually a couple of cobblers from which to choose. They are sweet and gooey, equal amounts crust and cooked-soft fruit.

## Charlotte's Eats & Sweets

290 Main St.
Keo, AR

501-842-2123
L | $

One of the most prolific contributors to Roadfood.com is a gent who goes by the screen name Buffetbuster. There is no food or food group Buffetbuster doesn't like, but of all the good eats a traveler can discover along the American road, pie is his special field of expertise. So when Buffetbuster declares the pies at Charlotte's Eats & Sweets to be "world-class," pastry lovers among us pay serious attention. In his words, "They are such masters of the meringue. . . . The filling of the chocolate pie is deep, dark, and fudgy, while the silky smooth, rich custard of the caramel pie is unmistakably homemade. The delicate meringues are a brilliant white and reach an impressive five to six inches high."

The quality of Charlotte's pies is no secret to the people who live around Keo (population 235). They know to come at 11 a.m., when the restaurant opens, or even earlier to avoid a line. If you come too late in the lunch hour, chances are your favorite kind of pie will be all eaten up.

Pre-pie soups and salads include very nice garlic cheese biscuits, but most people who don't go directly to dessert avail themselves of a grill-toasted Keo Klassic, which is smoked turkey, Monterey Jack cheese, tomato, onion, and avocado on sourdough.

## Cotham's Mercantile

5301 Hwy. 161 S.               501-961-9284

Scott, AR                   www.cothams.com

                                   L Mon-Sat; D Fri-Sat | $

In the Grand Prairie southeast of Little Rock, Cotham's Mercantile is perched on stilts above a slow-flowing river. Built in 1917, it has been a general store, a jail, and a military commissary. Since 1984, Arkansans have come to know it as a plate-lunch destination.

The old wood building is fronted by a broad porch. Enter a swinging door into a dining room packed literally to the ceiling with vintage house and farm bric-a-brac, from garden tools to primordial television sets. Remote the restaurant may be, but it is rare to see an empty chair. Bare wood tables are surrounded by customers who come for meals built around catfish, chicken-fried steak, or chicken-fried chicken, and such daily lunch specials as fried pork chops (Monday), chicken and dumplings (Tuesday), meat loaf (Wednesday), and southern-fried chicken (Thursday). Side dishes include corn fritters, hush puppies, collard greens, and fried green tomatoes.

Cotham's calls its burger a Hubcap Hamburger. It is an immense circle of cooked ground beef—close to a foot in diameter and half an inch thick—that comes in a bun that nearly fits, dressed with a salad's worth of mustard, lettuce, tomato slices, pickles, and hoops of onion. The outlandish specialty has earned such renown that the store's pushpin map of the United States has no room left to show where Hubcap-loving customers have come from; business cards from visitors around the globe are tacked up all around it.

Desserts include Arkansas fried pies and peach or blackberry cobbler.

## Craig's Bar-B-Que

Hwy. 70 W.               870-998-2616

DeValls Bluff, AR        LD | $

Craig's pork is deeply smoked and brushed with thick, orange sauce that is big on spice and nearly sugarless, with a twist that tastes vaguely like citrus. To balance the devilish sauce, which is available ultra-hot if specially requested, sandwiches are constructed with a layer of sweet coleslaw inside the bun. That bright slaw sings a fine tune when it dresses one of Craig's Polish sausages, also lined with mustard and topped with hot sauce. Dinner plates include beans and slaw; the only other available side dish is a bag of chips. The proper thing to drink is iced tea—very sweet tea, of course.

Ambience is hunting-lodge rustic. Pinned to the walls are business cards and hand-penned ads who-knows-how-old: lost dogs, pre-owned shotguns, beauty salons, deer processing, and taxidermy. Diners' attire ranges from still-wet camouflage waders to pressed pinstripe suits and well-worn over-alls. Although the dining room is bisected (a legacy of segregation days), quarters are close enough that conversations are wide open among seated eaters as well as takeout customers hovering around waiting for their food.

## Ed & Kay's

15228 I-30         501-315-3663
Benton, AR         BLD | $

Best known for its showstopping pies, Ed & Kay's also happens to be a good stop for a hamburger with onion rings or a satisfying plate lunch. There may be only one or two hot entrees any day—stuffed peppers, fried chicken, ham, pork chops—but the list of side dishes is awesome, including mac 'n' cheese, purple hull peas, creamed corn, and skillet fried potatoes. Most people get an entree and two or three vegetables, but it is possible to neglect a main altogether and have a wonderful meal of four different sides.

Meringue pies are amazing-looking, their tops a perfect volcano shape that is two or three times the height of the filling itself. Of course there are chocolate cream, coconut cream, and lemon meringue. Our personal favorite from this phylum is peanut butter cream. But neither should one ignore the non-meringue pies. Pecan is masterful, and the one known as PCP is the ultimate, its initials standing for pineapple, coconut, and pecan.

## Family Pie Shop

Hwy. 70 W.         870-998-2279
DeValls Bluff, AR      Erratic hours; call ahead | $

Mary Thomas, who long ago was a barbecue cook for Mr. Craig at Craig's Bar-B-Que on the other side of Route 70 (p. 240), opened her little bakery in 1977, and while it is merely a cinder-block garage hidden from easy view, aficionados consider Mary's the finest pie stop in the state: high honor here-abouts, where pie consciousness is as elevated as Iowa's.

Mary's dining facilities are virtually nonexistent other than a couple of stools and a random kitchen chair in a disheveled storage room next to the kitchen. Most people get whole pies or small ones for two to eat in the car or at home. Mary told us that when Bill Clinton lived in Little Rock, he stopped in all the time and ate pie at the counter with his friends and family. He didn't have a favorite. "He liked them all!" she confides. She also advised that former governor Mike Huckabee used to love her pies too. But then he went on a diet.

Mary's simple egg custard pie is nothing short of perfect, as are the luxurious "Karo nut," aka pecan, and sweet-potato pie. Crust lifts them all heavenward. Honey-brown, ready to flake with slight pressure from a plastic fork, it is as fine as a Viennese sugar cookie. The crust's savor is amplified in Mary's version of the Arkansas favorite, fried pie—apple, peach, or apricot filling inside a crescent of deep-fried brittle pastry dough.

## Feltner's Whatta-Burger

1410 N. Arkansas          501-968-1410
Russellville, AR           LD | $

There are Whatta-Burger shops throughout the Southwest, but none like this one, where the "custom made hamburgers," served with crisp French fries and thick milk shakes are a cut above.

In addition to big and good meals, Feltner's offers the kick of an only-in-America experience that is fast food at its finest. The instant you enter the low-slung brick building, an order taker virtually accosts you at the door to find out what you want. At the head of the line, you convey the precise details of your order, from a simple Whatta-Burger (a quarter-pound patty on a five-inch bun) to a Whatta-Burger with double meat and double cheese. At the end of the line, you pay and receive your meal on a tray in a white bag. Find a booth in the big dining room, where the walls are lined with humorous and inspirational homilies: "We guarantee fast service no matter how long it takes"; "The hurrier I go, the behinder I get"; "Cherish yesterday, dream tomorrow, live today."

Feltner's is *the* town burger joint, a favorite for families, teens on dates, and Arkansas Tech students. We well recall our first visit, when we shared the dining room with a happy stampede of approximately three dozen fresh-faced six-footers attending basketball camp at the college, each of whom carried a tray with a brace of double-doubles and a heap of French fries.

## Franke's

11121 N. Rodney Parham      501-225-4487
Little Rock, AR            www.frankescafeteria.com
                                    LD | $

Where to begin? As is the custom in bountiful cafeterias, let us begin with dessert. Custard pie in particular is a study in culinary clarity: egg-rich and cream-smooth, it fairly floats in its fine, flaky crust. There are cobblers, hot custard and banana pudding, cheesecake, and brownies—not a clinker among them—but pie is king at Franke's. If not custard, then coconut cream, Karo nut (pecan), chocolate, or apple.

As you might extrapolate from the pie selection, Franke's is a Dixie classic. In fact, it's the oldest restaurant in Arkansas (since 1919). The only bad thing to say is that there are too many wonderful items to eat on any one day, forcing those of us passing through to leave town longing for all the good stuff we did not taste. For example, if you come on a Thursday, the day's special entrees will include chicken and dumplings, fried chicken livers, and fried chicken in addition to such everyday items as baked pit ham and roast beef. Choosing vegetables is an even more daunting task; Thursday's are fried okra, rice pilaf, okra and tomatoes, Brussels sprouts, and pinto beans. Every day there are mac 'n' cheese, greens, candied yams, from-scratch mashed potatoes, and an absolutely sensational eggplant casserole that includes tomatoes, onions, bread crumbs, and a layer of melty cheese on top. Breadstuffs? Choose from white rolls, whole wheat rolls, biscuits, garlic toast, and hush puppies.

We were clued in to this grand place by tipster Michelle Little, a New Orleans resident who grew up in Little Rock. Michelle wrote, "Franke's is the best. This is a part of my childhood that makes me happy—good food, lots of tasty vegetables, fluffy rolls, sweet tea, and most of all, those cream pies at the end of the line. . . . Even though I live in a food heaven here in New Orleans, I still miss those meat-and-threes (plus cream pies) from home."

There is another location of Franke's at 400 Broadway in Little Rock (501-372-1919).

## Grapevine

105 E. Walnut
Paris, AR

479-963-2413
www.thegrapevinerestaurant.com
BLD | $

The Grapevine defies categorization. It is a worldly restaurant in a country town. Its repertoire ranges from catfish to coconut shrimp, veggie plates to surf 'n' turf, sweet tea to chocolate milk to wines from France and Arkansas. The staff is folksy and down-home but able to walk you through the menu with the savvy of a learned gastronome. It's the finest food for miles around, and you will be hard-pressed to spend more than $10 for a meal.

You know you are in for something special when the bread basket arrives. Crisp-crusted tawny loaves with a slightly sweet edge are cut into irregularly sized slices and served with a ramekin of honey butter. Hamburgers are one-third-pound beauties; the salad selection includes Greek, Cobb, and a "Santa Fe" concoction topped with unbelievably tender grilled chicken and served with creamy avocado dressing. Full dinners, including barbecued beef, chicken-fried steak, and house-smoked brisket, come with such sides as fried okra and mac 'n' cheese.

Bread pudding is huge: physically and flavorfully, a dense block of bread that has become custard, served floating in a pool of sweet praline sauce.


## *McClard's

505 Albert Pike  
Hot Springs, AR

501-623-9665  
www.mcclards.com  
LD | $$

Pork is king in this legendary smokehouse, the pulled pork ineffably tender, its smoky sweetness especially radiant when spread with hot sauce. The standout dish is a rib and fry plate. The ribs are a meat-heavy slab with a sticky glaze of peppery red sauce. They are presented under a tangle of gorgeous honey-brown French fried potatoes and sided by coleslaw to create what may be the most perfectly balanced barbecue meal anywhere.

A whole section of McClard's menu is devoted to tamale plates, ranging from plain tamales with beans to a full "spread"—a pair of tamales topped with sauce-sopped chopped smoked meat, beans, crisp Fritos chips, raw onions, and shredded orange cheese. Spreads remind us of the locally favored Fritos pie, but with the added zest of genuine pit barbecue.

The neon-lit 1942 stucco building that houses McClard's once offered toot-your-horn carhop service but now hordes of happy eaters line up to fill the booths inside. The recipe for its sauce supposedly dates back to 1928, when a customer at the McClard family trailer court couldn't pay his bill and so offered his barbecue sauce recipe instead.


## Mickey's BBQ

1622 Park Ave.  
Hot Springs, AR

501-624-1247  
www.mickeysbbq.net  
BLD Tues-Sat | $

Hot Springs is a barbecue hot spot, its highlights including not only ribs and pulled pork but also great beans and pit-cooked potatoes. You'll find all of the above at Mickey's, a snug hut where the "Hickory Nut" dining room features napkin holders carved from tree limbs, as well as wood paneling branded with scenes deer, ducks, and pheasants. The beef and pork are terrific, ham is exemplary, and Mickey's hot, complicated sauce infuses each of them with a delicious glow.

And what fine side dishes. The potato, slow cooked over hickory smoke just like the meats, has a leathery skin and cream-soft center. You can have it gobbed with butter or, even better, stuffed with the barbecue meat of your choice (beef, pork, or ham) then heaped with just-right spicy-sweet barbecue sauce, coleslaw, and beans. That treatment is more of a meal than a side. Beans, by the way, are also top-drawer, larded with shreds and chunks and chewy debris off the good ham roast.

## Rhoda's Famous Tamales

714 Saint Mary St.    870-265-3108
Lake Village, AR     BL | $

Rhoda Adams's tamales deserve the fame they have earned throughout the Mississippi Delta. Made with a mixture of beef and chicken, they emanate an irresistibly appetizing aroma and are a joy to eat any time of day.

Beyond tamales, the menu at James and Rhoda Adams's little eat place by the side of the road is a roster of soulful regional specialties. For fried chicken or pigs' feet, pork barbecue or catfish dinner, you won't do better for miles around. Early one morning Rhoda made us a breakfast of bacon and eggs with biscuits on the side. Rhoda is one of those gifted cooks who makes everything she touches something special.

We've always considered Arkansas one of America's Big 7 pie states (along with Iowa, Wisconsin, Minnesota, Virginia, Texas, and Maine). Rhoda's pies are proof. She makes small individual ones as well as full-size pies. Sweet-potato pie, lemon pie, and pecan pie are world-class.

## *Stubby's Bar-B-Que

3024 Central Ave.    501-624-1552
Hot Springs, AR     www.stubbysbbq.com
            LD | $$

Chris Dunkel, whose family bought Stubby's from founder Richard "Stubby" Stubblefield Sr. in 1977, is known now to regulars as "Stubb" because he carries on the traditions that have made this place a hallowed barbecue destination since 1952. "There are three things that mark a good barbecue," Chris told us. "A wood pile, mismatched chairs, and high-quality meat."

Stubby's has all of those, and is delicious. Ribs, pork, and ham each in its own way presents the magical duo of swine and smoke; even the brisket is Texas-tender and dripping juice. Chicken, which in our book of barbecue tends to be a secondary consideration, is not to be dissed in this place; its skin is nearly blackened by smoke exposure in the pit, its meat is moist and ludicrously tender. No matter what your meat preference, two side dishes are essential. The smoked pit potato is a pound-plus spud that emerges from a long, slow heat bath with insides that are fluffy and delicious even before butter and sour cream are applied. Stubby's pot-o-beans is laden with smoky ham and a blanket of sauce. That sauce, made in the back room daily, is so beguilingly spiced that we find ourselves dipping plain old white bread in it after the beans are gone and the meat on our plate is a glowing memory.

## Barnacle Bill's

14 Castillo Dr.
St. Augustine, FL

904-824-3663
www.barnaclebillsonline.com
LD | $$

Barnacle Bill's is not an undiscovered Roadfood hole in the wall. It is big and popular and in fact there are two of it, the second location (dinner only) at 451 A1A Boulevard in St. Augustine, phone: 904-471-2434. (But these two are no relation to the other Barnacle Bills found along the Atlantic coast.)

Shrimp brought in on boats to nearby Mayport are the main attraction: They are firm, juicy butterflies available simply fried in an envelope of melting-crisp crust, in a coconut crust or, most exciting of all, in a crust enhanced by the heat of locally grown datil peppers. The pungent datil, which seems to be a sport variety of the habanero, has become St. Augustine's signature flavor agent.

For first-timers and those who have a hard time making up their mind what kind of shrimp they want, there are plates of a dozen, four of each variety. You can get stuffed shrimp, blackened shrimp, teriyaki shrimp, shrimp scampi, and steamed peel-your-own shrimp. The menu offers all sorts of other seafood and even a selection of "landlubber fare," but we agree with tipster Meg Butler, who first clued us in to this restaurant: "I can't say much other than fried shrimp, fried shrimp, fried shrimp."

## Beach Road Chicken Dinners

4132 Atlantic Blvd.          904-398-7980

Jacksonville, FL          www.beachroadchickendinners.com

LD | $

Jacksonville is America's shrimp central, but don't let that make you disregard Beach Road Chicken Dinners. Fried shrimp indeed are on the menu, and we suspect they are good, a suspicion based on the fact that the fried chicken is first-rate. Served family-style with biscuits and gravy and honey, corn nuggets, fried okra, French fries, coleslaw, and creamed peas, white and/or dark parts come encased in a crisp, red-gold crust and drip with flavorful juices. Adventurous chicken eaters can get livers, gizzards, or hearts, and should there be someone with an allergy to fried food, baked chicken is available (if you are willing to wait forty-five minutes).

A low-slung building that has expanded in all directions since opening day in 1939, Beach Road offers little in the way of polite amenities (when the staff isn't feeling gruff, they'll call you hon), and chances are you will wait in line for a table.

## Blue Heaven

729 Thomas St.          305-296-8666

Key West, FL          www.blueheavenkw.com

BLD | $$

Off the beaten path in the Bahama Village area of the sunny neverland known as the Conch Republic, Blue Heaven is a breakfast lover's dream. Dining is *en plein air* on a broad outdoor patio under a canopy of opulent banyan trees, where your companions include the café's flock of hens and roosters who hop and peck around tables and chairs. Their cock-a-doodle-doing is a natural companion for hefty omelets, but our favorite dishes are the tropical-tasting banana pancakes and seafood benedict built upon ocean-fresh fish and topped with lime hollandaise. To drink? Who can resist a mimosa made with fresh-squeezed OJ? Lunch items include wonderful barbecued shrimp, fresh local fish, and jerk chicken.

An incredibly colorful place to eat, Blue Heaven has been the home of a boxing ring (Ernest Hemingway sparred here), a bordello (the tiny rooms upstairs are now part of an art gallery), a bookmaking parlor, and a cock-fighting pit (heroic roosters are buried in a little graveyard behind the dining area), as well as inspiration for Jimmy Buffett's song "Blue Heaven Rendezvous."

# El Siboney

900 Catherine St.  305-296-4184
Key West, FL  www.elsiboneyrestaurant.com
LD | $$

When you consider El Siboney is just ninety miles from Cuba itself—closer to Havana than to Miami—you understand why its Cuban food tastes so right. This is the best place we know on Key West to taste grilled garlic chicken, a half bird with a crisp skin and meat so tender that going at it with utensils feels like overkill. Plantains on the side are slightly crusty and caramelized around their edges. And yuca, served with roast pork, beans, and rice, is a revelation. Soft and glistening white hunks, reminiscent of a well-baked potato but more luscious and substantial, are served in a bath of heavily garlicked oil and garlanded with onion slices.

The Cuban mix sandwich is a beaut, made on a length of fragile-texture toasted bread cut in half at a rakish angle and loaded with ham, roast pork, salami, and cheese with pickles, lettuce, and tomato. Conch chowder is thick with conch meat, and provides a great opportunity for dunking shreds of the buttered Cuban bread that comes with every meal. The grandest dish in the house is paella Valenciana for two (call ahead; it takes an hour to prepare), a vast fisherman's stew served with rice, black beans, and plenty of Cuban bread for mopping juices. Dessert choices include Key lime pie, flan, and rice pudding, accompanied of course by espresso or café con leche.

El Siboney is a clean, pleasant place with red-striped tables topped with easy-wipe plastic and silverware presented in tidy little paper bags. If you don't speak Spanish, the waitresses do their best to help you. The name of the place is a variation of the word Ciboney, who were occupants of Florida and the Caribbean region since the Stone Age. The restaurant was established in 1984.

# Ernie's Bar-b-que & Lounge

1843 S. Federal Hwy.  954-523-8636
Fort Lauderdale, FL  BLD | $$

Conch chowder is served throughout Florida, but none is so fully satisfying as that served at Ernie's, where the menu declares, "Conch Is King." It is potent stuff, vividly peppered, thick with sweet bits of nicely clammy conch and chopped vegetables, with sherry available to add a whole other layer of intoxicant to the heady Caribbean classic. Ernie's version delivers maximum ocean flavor and is hearty enough to be a meal or, in a smaller portion, a sturdy companion to one of Ernie's fine barbecue sandwiches, constructed on thick-sliced Bimini bread and accompanied by a bowl of barbecue sauce for dipping. Even if you don't have a sandwich, get some of that bread to go with the chowder. It looks pretty much like white bread but is soft and cake-like, with alluring sweetness that partners nicely with the briny flavor of mollusk. Conch fritters and conch salad also are featured on Ernie's menu. As for the barbecue, you can do better elsewhere.

## Havana

6801 S. Dixie Hwy.  561-547-9799
West Palm Beach, FL  www.havanacubanfood.com
LD | $

There is something especially right about a *media noche* from the walk-up window of Havana restaurant because the window is open 'round the clock. *Media noche* means midnight, which traditionally is when this unique variant of the Cuban sandwich is the snack of choice. It is suitable for late-night eating because it is somewhat lighter than a dinner-sized Cuban . . . but only somewhat. The ingredients are the same—roast pork, ham, and Swiss cheese—but instead of a hearty Cuban loaf, it is made on sweet, eggy bread. When grilled, the sweet bread develops a light crunch that is completely different from the chewier nature of the traditional baguette.

In addition to the twenty-four-hour walk-up window, Havana is a full-service, sit-down restaurant with a king-sized Cuban menu ranging from white bean soup on Sunday to guanabana milk shakes and café con leche. The *media noche* and classic Cuban are supplemented by an "Especial de West Palm Beach"—a similar Dagwood but with a full deck of ham, turkey, Swiss cheese, bacon, lettuce, and tomato. Note: Pickles are a standard Cuban sandwich ingredient, but here they must be requested.

## JB's Fish Camp

859 Pompano Ave.  386-427-5747
New Smyrna Beach, FL  www.jbsfishcamp.com
LD | $$

The cracker fish camp is a vanishing species, its unapologetic rural nature out of step with twenty-first-century life in general and with the ever-denser population of waterside Florida in particular. Nowhere is the culture clash more apparent than on the road to JB's Fish Camp at the southernmost end of Turtle Mound Road (Route A1A) outside New Smyrna Beach. Other than by boat along the Intracoastal Waterway, the only way to get to JB's is to drive past miles of new high-rise housing and recently built shopping malls. The bourgeois landscape shifts dramatically the moment you pull onto Pompano Avenue and find the white-sand parking lot that surrounds the helter-skelter restaurant and its annex trailer selling T-shirts that depict the mosquito as the Florida state bird. A bumper sticker plastered to the dining room door announces, "Slow Down. You're Not on the Mainland," and shows a slovenly catfish who appears to be drunk or hungover.

The menu offers every kind of Florida seafood, including rock shrimp and pompano. Capt. John A. Bollman III, who runs the place, is a passionate crabber. The restaurant nabs its own, a fact evident in the snowy crab cakes and a "Crabulous Sandwich," which is nothing more than cool, fresh crab meat, mayo, and a sprinkle of spice. Blue crabs are sold by the dozen, infused with whatever degree of JB's spice mix you specify, and there are softshells, stone crab claws, and snow crab clusters. There's also a full array of fresh oysters, scallops, pink shrimp and rock shrimp, and clams.

JB's really is a fish camp, offering kayak rentals, bait to catch redfish, and slips for arriving boaters. Located along the Canaveral National Seashore between the Mosquito Lagoon and the Atlantic Ocean, it does have indoor dining, but the choice seats are outside on a broad deck by the water, where lucky ones glimpse manatees and porpoises cavorting nearby. Private and commercial fishing boats come and go and ever-present sunshine muffles even the high-spirited chatter of JB's raucous clientele. Among those eating at the breezy picnic tables are local anglers, tourists, and road-tripping bikers, as well as a large number of people for whom Florida is a second home and who come here to enjoy what the state was like before they arrived.

## Jenkins Quality Barbecue

830 N. Pearl St.          904-353-6388
Jacksonville, FL          www.jenkinsqualitybarbecue.com
                          LD | $

Jenkins smokes beef, pork, and chickens in a pit fired by oak logs, then serves them with sauce made from a recipe that is a long-held family secret. The sauce is unusual stuff, peppery but not ferocious, mustard-orange and as thick as Thanksgiving gravy—a righteous companion especially for Jenkins's superb roast chicken, but also swell on ribs or beef and delicious soaked up straight with the white bread that is used for sandwiches.

The sandwiches are sandwiches in name only. The spare rib sandwich is four slices of white bread surrounding four or five big spare ribs, the whole thing drenched with enough sauce that picking it up whole is impossible. Instead, one folds back the thick butcher paper in which it is presented and alternately gnaws a rib and peels off pieces of sauce-drenched bread. Very good! On the side, you want an order of corn nuggets, which are creamy-centered corn fritters. For dessert, there is fine red velvet cake.

The store on Pearl Street, in a fairly desolate part of downtown Jacksonville, is the main location. There are a few other Jenkins around the city. Dining facilities include a handful of booths and a couple of picnic tables outside.

## Jerry's Drive-In

| | |
|---|---|
| 2815 E. Cervantes | 850-433-9910 |
| Pensacola, FL | BLD \| $ |

Jerry's opened for business in 1939 and, frankly, it doesn't look like it's changed much since then. It is a Formica-counter café with a few tables and booths and help-yourself rolls of paper towels for customers to use as needed. The walls are decorated with college pennants, silly homilies, and beer ads going back decades. Jerry's has character to spare . . . but it also has important hamburgers—good-sized, juicy patties of beef beautifully dressed with lettuce, tomato, chopped onions, mustard, and mayo, served with sweet coleslaw and crisp French fries. Not gourmet burgers, not unusual burgers: just good, satisfying hamburgers . . . in a classic lunch-counter setting.

Although many visitors to the "Redneck Riviera" know Jerry's as the hamburger place, regulars come for three square meals a day. The breakfast menu features all the usual configurations of eggs and luncheon meat (with grits and/or hash browns), plus an extraordinarily luxurious chicken liver omelet. At lunch, you can have such regional delights as smoked mullet, deviled crab, and broiled grouper, as well as big deep-fried oysters with hush puppies and cold beer on the side.

## Keys Fisheries

| | |
|---|---|
| 3502 Gulf View Ave. | 866-743-4353 |
| Marathon, FL | www.keysfisheries.com/restaurant |
| | LD \| $$ |

The most famous place to eat stone crabs is Joe's Stone Crab of Miami, and there is something right about eating the regal food in so fancy a setting. On the other hand, it's also good to get stone crabs at a bargain price (relatively speaking), fresh off the boat, and eat them at a picnic table.

If you like the sound of the latter and are traveling the Overseas Highway, pull over in Marathon and have a meal at Keys Fisheries. In contrast to ordering from one of Joe's formally attired waitstaff, the process of getting crabs at Keys Fisheries is purposely goofy. The custom is to place your order at a counter and give the order taker a celebrity name, not yours, to call out when it's ready. Plates and utensils are disposable, dining is virtually outdoors (with plastic sheeting to keep out wind and rain, if necessary), and the view is fishing boats coming or going and a nightly ooh-and-ahh sunset. The menu is replete with local seafood dishes from conch chowder to Key West pink shrimp, and many habitués swear by the lobster Reuben, a locally loved grilled sandwich of lobster meat, Swiss cheese, sauerkraut, and thousand island dressing on rye. But it's stone crabs that steal the show. Nowhere will you find them cheaper or more perfectly fresh.

## La Teresita Cafeteria

3248 W. Columbus Dr.

Tampa, FL

813-879-4909

www.lateresitarestaurant.com

BLD (open all night Fri & Sat) | $

A Cuban sandwich is a beautiful thing: ham, roast pork, and cheese, along with mustard, mayonnaise, and pickles encased in elegant bread that is toasted to a crisp. There is no better place to eat one than Tampa, especially at the neighborhood café called La Teresita.

While La Teresita is a full-scale restaurant and banquet hall, the Roadfooder's choice will likely be in the lunch-counter part of the operation, where choice seats (and swift service) are at a sweeping serpentine counter at which whole families line up on the rows of stools, dawn to dark. Regulars come for breakfast of buttered Cuban bread and café con leche; lunch favorites include carne asada, *ropa vieja, vaca frita,* and the best black beans and rice in town. Throughout the day, you'll see groups of happy gents gathering in the street after dining at La Teresita. Here they fire up big made-in-Tampa cigars and look like kings who have just enjoyed a royal feast.

## Louie's Backyard

700 Waddell Ave.           305-294-1061
Key West, FL           www.louiesbackyard.com
                                LD | $$$

Louie's is not cheap or in any way typical. It is one of a kind. But when we visit Key West and think about dinner, our thoughts immediately take us to a table at Louie's Backyard, where the best seats are located on a multi-leveled terrace overlooking the Atlantic. Here you dine while pleasure boats sail past and pelicans graze the waves.

The gracious pink classic-revival house could serve TV dinner and it would be irresistible on a moonlit night, but it happens to be one of the innovators of Key West cuisine, known for such tropical delights as Bahamian conch chowder with bird-pepper hot sauce, grilled local shrimp with salsa verde, and cracked conch with pepper jelly and ginger daikon slaw. The Louie's supper forever etched in our book of great culinary memories was our first: a pair of lovely grilled strip steaks glazed with hot chipotle chile sauce, sided by garlic mashed potatoes and red onion corn relish. To top things off, we had fancy coffee and feathery Key lime tarts. Soft island breezes made hurricane lamps flicker. Bulbs strung among branches in overhead trees formed a radiant canopy above the patio. The ocean glowed cobalt blue when distant, lightning storms ignited over the horizon.

## Old Spanish Sugar Mill Grill

Ponce de Leon Blvd.           904-985-5644
De Leon Springs, FL         www.planetdeland.com/sugarmill
                                BL | $

Cook your own pancakes at the Old Spanish Sugar Mill Grill in De Leon Springs State Park. Tables have griddles built into their center. The staff brings two pitchers from the kitchen—a milled-here, stone-ground, buckwheat-style batter as well as more traditional buttermilk batter—plus whatever mix-ins you need (bananas, blueberries, pecans, apple chunks, peanut butter, chocolate chips, and apple sauce are all available for a slight extra cost). You pour and flip the flapjacks as you like them. Sausage, bacon, and ham are also available . . . but cooked in the kitchen.

It's fun to punctuate the process of eating pancakes by cooking them at your speed and in your size; you can keep pouring batter until you bust. At $4.95 per person (plus the park entrance fee and obligatory 18 percent tip), this is one of the bargain breakfasts of the South. The pancakes are served from morning until midafternoon, but if you're not in the mood to cook, the kitchen also will make a fine sandwich on house-made whole-grain bread (the BLT is extremely well endowed with bacon) or a salad.

The restaurant is located in an old mill building in the beautiful area where explorers once sought the Fountain of Youth. The park around it is an idyllic recreation area with boat rides and picnic tables and opportunities to hike and bird-watch. It is a popular destination and the restaurant is a small one, so almost any time of day you will likely wait for a table.

## *O'Steen's

205 Anastasia Blvd.  904-829-6974
St. Augustine, FL  www.osteensrestaurant.com
LD | $$

With about a dozen tables and a six-stool counter, O'Steen's is a minimalist kind of place: no credit cards, no tablecloths, no cocktails, no wine or beer. A sign on the wall reads "If you have reservations, you are in the wrong place." It is so popular that there always is a wait, even at 11:30 a.m. and 5 p.m. There's good reason for the crowds. The north Florida coast is the center of America's shrimping industry, a fact immediately apparent when you bite through the crunchy veil that encloses the dense pink flesh of O'Steen's fried shrimp, which are as rich as nutmeat and ocean-sweet. O'Steen's sells them by nine, twelve, eighteen, or twenty-four; they are medium-sized and each butterflied to resemble the lines inside a peace symbol.

"Have you been here before?" the waitress asks as she sets down a plate of them. When we say no, she points to a plastic ramekin that holds the kitchen's special pink sauce for dipping. She then hoists a Grolsch beer bottle. "And this is the datil pepper sauce we make. Don't start with it alone. Mix it with the pink." O'Steen's hot sauce, turbocharged with datil peppers, is bright and fragrant and even when prudently blended with the milder pink stuff engenders a back-of-the-throat roar that rumbles forward with inexorable titillation.

## Pepe's Café & Steakhouse

806 Caroline St.  305-294-7192
Key West, FL  www.pepescafe.net
BLD | $$

Breakfast at Pepe's, from 6:30 every morning, is heaps of fun, always featuring a bread of the day in addition to omelets, pancakes, homemade granola, and creamed chipped beef on toast. Later in the day, Apalachicola Bay oysters make Pepe's a destination for oyster lovers who consume them raw, baked, or roasted Mexican-style. Weekly traditions include a Sunday-night barbecue that features steak, pork ribs, tenderloin, chicken, salmon, and mahimahi. The lunch menu offers both a blue-collar burger and a white-collar burger. (The former is six ounces, the latter four.)

Pepe's boasts that it is "the eldest eating house in the Florida Keys," and it sure does have the feel of a place that's seen it all. The well-burnished dining room is covered with knickknacks as miscellaneous as Grandma's attic, including pictures of famous people and nobodies, a nude painting, nautical bibelots, and scenes of old Key West. Each varnished wooden booth is outfitted with a shelf that holds about a dozen different hot sauces for oyster eating. Out back is a bar where locals congregate. (The bar opens at 7 a.m.) And to the side on an open patio strewn with mismatched tables, illumination is provided by an array of fixtures that includes a crystal chandelier, green-shaded billiard lamps, and year-round Christmas lights.

## Saltwater Cowboys

Dondanville Rd.
St. Augustine, FL

904-471-2332
www.saltwatercowboys.com
D | $$

Named for founder Howard Dondanville, who was affectionately called Cowboy, and designed to look like a salt-marsh fish camp from long ago, this way-too-popular restaurant serves excellent Minorcan clam chowder (a St. Augustine specialty) and a slew of southern seafood: freshly opened oysters and fancy-cooked ones, boiled crawfish with Cajun vibes, snapper, deviled crabs, softshells, and shrimp. A whole portion of the menu is headlined "Florida Cracker Corner" and is devoted to frog legs, cooter (soft-shelled turtle), catfish, alligator tail, and even fried chicken with a vividly flavored bread-crumb crust. We suggest starting a meal with oysters Dondanville, served on the half shell glistening with a mantle of garlic, butter, wine, and finely chopped onions, then moving on to Cowboy's jambalaya, which is a profusion of shrimp, oysters, chicken, ham, and sausage on a pile of seasoned rice.

Fish-camp-fare frowners can have open-pit barbecue, including ribs, chicken, and shrimp. What we saw on other people's plates looked good, but the opportunity to indulge in so much inviting seafood precluded a sample.

When we wrote "too popular," we meant that chances are good you will wait for a table at any normal suppertime. It's a big place with four dining rooms, but reservations are not accepted. Waiting facilities are an open-air deck where cool frozen drinks (and sweet tea in mason jars) are served. The place exudes ramshackle beauty, occupying a restored old home with its bentwood chairs and walls decorated with antique fishing gear, snakeskins, and cracker memorabilia. Windows look out over marshland and dusk on the Intracoastal Waterway.

## Schooner's Seafood House

3560 Ponce De Leon　　　　904-826-0233
St. Augustine, FL　　　　www.schooners-seafood.com
　　　　　　　　　　　　LD | $$

Pilau, which has twins and cognates known variously as *perloo, perlau, pilaw,* and *purlieu* from America's Low Country to the Middle East, is always based on rice. The common history of all of them is that of cooks making something bountiful out of what they happened to have on hand. Pilau can be a side dish or a meal, pyrotechnical or bland. Familiar as it is to so many cooks, it tends to be fairly rare on restaurant menus.

In St. Augustine, while looking for Minorcan clam chowder, we came across a lovely chicken perloo while sitting at the counter of Schooner's Seafood House. It was not a regular menu item but the daily special. "This here pilau is good but needs a kick in the you-know-what," suggested a cologne-scented customer in beltless high-pocket slacks and a torso-hugging, no-iron short-sleeved shirt. He threw his tie back over one shoulder and poured dark red datil pepper sauce atop the old-time coastal casserole of chicken and rice, then forked into it with a madman's glee.

"Excuse me," the waitress piped in. "It is *perloo,* not pilau!"

"Says who?" said he.

The waitress pointed both thumbs at her chest. "Cracker, here; born and bred. Do not question authority."

Schooner's perloo, served with candied yams and stewed okra, proved to be a welcoming tableau for the locally favored datil pepper sauce, which transformed it from palliative comfort food into a meal so exhilarating that a cool piece of Key lime pie became a necessary conclusion.

Everyday menu items include very good local shrimp, fried oysters, scallops, crab cakes, and clam strips, as well as catfish, gator, and frog legs.

## Singleton's Seafood Shack

4728 Ocean St.                  904-246-4442
Mayport, FL                     LD | $$

Singleton's is a delightfully déclassé nautical wreck with a low ceiling, listing wooden floors, bare wood tables, and hard benches. Everything is served in Styrofoam. Utensils are plastic. Waitresses reward customers with such appellations as hon, babe, and dear. And the cuisine is North Coast seafood in all its glory. Yes, there are burgers and barbecue and slaw dogs on the menu, but they are immaterial. What matters is fried shrimp that fairly burst with flavor, briny oysters sheathed in fragile crust, and devil crab that is moist and seasoned with eye-opening panache.

Dinners come with a pair of hush puppies, clad in a red-gold crust that surrounds insides that are as moist as cake. Collard greens are vaguely sweet, limp leaves, as earthy-tasting as tobacco and yet deliriously healthful. You also can have a good bowl of Minorcan clam chowder, a St. Augustine specialty that is like Manhattan clam chowder but kick-ass hot.

The entrance to the restaurant features a large case full of raw seafood, and seats afford a view of fishing boats rocking in their berths. Nautical bric-a-brac is everywhere, and there is a large annex that is a makeshift museum of wooden model ships.


## T-Ray's Burger Station

202 S. 8th St.                  904-261-6310
Fernandina Beach, FL            BL | $

As the name suggests, burgers are what's to eat. They come in two sizes and dressed in many ways. We like the Big T Bacon Burger—extremely juicy and full-flavored. For beef frowners there is a portobello mushroom burger. Beyond burgers, T-Ray's offers salads and fried chicken and delicious cheese grits too. Locals know it as the place to get superb chicken and dumplings every Thursday as well as banana pudding for dessert every day. They flock here in the morning for masterful hot-from-the-oven biscuits.

It's easy to drive right past. It looks like every other Exxon station, except for the cars circled every day around it at breakfast and lunchtime. Dine at the counter or one of the mismatched tables. Ray's the guy who does the cooking. His father, Terrell, runs the gas station.

# *Whitey's Fish Camp

2032 CR 220            904-269-4198
Orange Park, FL       www.whiteysfishcamp.com
                      LD | $$

We came upon Whitey's Fish Camp researching the first edition of this book more than thirty years ago. We ate wild-caught catfish, which was so delicious it made us instant fans. Subsequent encounters with farm-raised catfish revealed that the flavor of genuine, bottom-feeding river cats is something special. Pond-raised are fine—mild and polite, receptive to all kinds of character-building treatments such as blackening and Cajun-spicing. But farmed fish are no comparison to the wild ones at Whitey's, where the menu and the place have expanded dramatically but where catfish still reigns.

Served AYCE (local fish-house shorthand for All You Can Eat), the cats vary from three inches to over a half-foot long. Unless you specify what size you want, each plate delivered to the table will hold one or two big ones and two or three little ones. The tiniest are so fragile that experienced diners eat even the tender rib bones, leaving nothing but vertebrae. Big ones, with a skeleton that demands respect, provide easy access to meat. Simply poke the tines of a fork through the sandy cornmeal girdle just below the backbone, then pull downward. A nice mouthful slips cleanly off the ribs. Atop the patch of brittle crust on your fork is dense meat as luxurious as prime beefsteak but with a freshwater sparkle that evokes vacation campfires and balmy summer nights. We have never eaten anything so indisputably outdoorsy in a normal cloth-napkin restaurant. (In lieu of napkins, Whitey's supplies each table with a roll of paper towels.)

It wasn't only the robust character of the fish that impressed us when we first found Whitey's. It was the place itself, which today remains a community center as much as it is a restaurant: boat launches, bait-and-tackle shop, oyster bar and beer bar, and a campground and RV park complete with hair-styling salon. With its out-of-fashion video games for kids and two-dollar claw machine that grabs a live lobster rather than a stuffed toy, Whitey's is not quaint like some bucolic farm-town café or vintage diner. It is a taste of what locals like to call cracker culture, meaning it evokes the old, pre-air-conditioned Florida that had its own special brand of sporting lifestyle long before the great influx of retirees. A blatant patch of cracker living such as Whitey's is a good reminder of the old saw that the farther north you go in this state, the deeper south you are.

## Barbecue Kitchen

1437 Virginia Ave.      404-766-9906
College Park, GA      BLD | $

Atlanta's Hartsfield Airport is surrounded by ho-hum strip-mall cafés and fast-food franchises, but those who crave an authentic Dixie meal have another choice: the Barbecue Kitchen. It's an old-time restaurant practically around the corner from the airport, right next to a Waffle House. And while barbecue is its name and, rightfully, its fame, a sign outside boasts of fresh vegetables. These are superb, nutritious southern kitchen classics: collard greens, rutabagas, speckled butter beans, pole beans, simple sliced tomatoes, and stewed squash. On a slightly less salubrious note, choices include fried okra, baked potato casserole, creamed corn, and baked apples.

Each item arrives in its own little bowl atop a partitioned unbreakable plate, the largest section of which can be filled not only with hickory-smoked barbecue (the real deal) but with such items as fried chicken, grilled ham, or corned beef hash. On the side come corn muffins and/or biscuits, the former not the least bit sweet (a perfect companion for those greens), the latter a good moppin' sop for barbecue. Of course, the libation of choice with such a model meat-and-three meal is sweet tea. For dessert: coconut layer cake.

## Blue Willow Inn

N. Cherokee Rd.
Social Circle, GA

404-464-0599
www.bluewillowinn.com
LD | $$

"We have two rules," says the waitress when you are seated at a table and receive your sweet iced tea (known here as the Champagne of the South). "Rule one is that no one goes home hungry. Rule two is that everybody has to have at least two desserts." Each guest is given a plate and invited to go to the serving tables as often as possible to help himself. Every day here is Sunday supper, southern-style. The beautiful, bounteous buffet is located in a room that includes far more dishes than any one appetite can sample in a single meal. A few of the must-eats are fried chicken, fried green tomatoes, collard greens that are long-cooked to porky tenderness, chicken and dumplings, and, of course, biscuits. Using a recipe from Sema Wilkes's legendary boardinghouse in Savannah (p. 268), the Blue Willow kitchen creates tan-crusted domes with fluffy insides and a compelling fresh-from-the-oven aroma. Their tops are faintly knobby because the dough is patted out rather than rolled.

For dessert, there are pies, cakes, cookies, and pudding, but the one we recommend (assuming you have an inkling of appetite by the end of the meal) is warm fruit cobbler. The Inn provides rocking chairs on its broad front porch for postprandial snoozing. It is a magnificent place, a grand mansion that is said to have inspired Margaret Mitchell to conceive of Tara in *Gone With the Wind*. Although meal service is help-yourself, the serving staff couldn't be more gracious.

## Buckner's Family Restaurant

1168 Bucksnort Rd.
Jackson, GA

770-775-6150
www.bucknersfamilyrestaurant.com
LD Wed-Sun | $$

The full name of this restaurant is real in many ways. First, it really has been family-run, by the Buckners, since it opened in 1980. More important, the food is cooked from family recipes and served family-style. Seating is at banquet-sized round tables with lazy Susans in the middle, on which are placed platters of fried chicken, barbecue, and at least a dozen side dishes. These likely will include Brunswick stew, corn-bread dressing, whipped sweet potatoes and hunks of yam, black-eyed peas, and speckled butter beans. Plus, of course, corn bread and yeast rolls. Spin the lazy Susan, and keep helping yourself until you've had enough. Then dig into fruit cobbler. It's a consummate southern-comfort feast, shared with family, friends, and perfect strangers with whom you likely will share a table.

Note: On Friday and Saturday nights, after-dinner entertainment (included in the prix fixe) includes live bluegrass and/or gospel music from 7 p.m. to about 9 p.m.

## Bulloch House

47 Bulloch St.

Warm Springs, GA

706-655-9068

www.bullochhouse.com

L daily; D Fri & Sat | $

Benjamin Bulloch's home, built in 1893, became a restaurant in 1990. The menu reflects both vintage and modern taste. Twenty-first-century types can come for fruit in a shell (that's a tortilla shell), a turkey burger (or beef burger), a veggie wrap, or a grilled chicken panini. Classicists come for the buffet, available at lunch every day and at dinner Friday and Saturday. While the specifics of the buffet change, depending on which vegetables look good at the market, you can always count on fried chicken, biscuits, and corn bread, as well as fried green tomatoes and fried apples, plus soufflé-light mac 'n' cheese. Desserts, ordered from the waitress, include to-die-for caramel cake, a six-layer chocolate cake, pecan pie, and banana pudding.

Bulloch House still looks very much like a private house, with seating in several small dining rooms as well as on an enclosed porch.

## The Colonnade

1879 Cheshire Bridge Rd.

Atlanta, GA

404-874-5642

www.colonnadeatl.com

LD | $$

It is unlikely one of television's food showboats will soon be reporting on the Colonnade. There is nothing about this vintage eatery that's outrageous, outlandish, outsized, or in any way vulgar enough to succeed on the boob tube.

On the other hand, people with a honed Roadfood sensibility will find a meal at the Colonnade to be pulse-quickening nurture for the spirit as well as for the appetite. In this polite place, a bastion of square meals since 1927, waitresses speed trays of southern comfort food to families who have been customers for generations. The specialties, which never change, include fried chicken, pork loin, pot roast, and roast turkey breast, served with your choice from a roster of over two dozen soulful southern vegetables, including sweet-potato soufflé, turnip greens, rutabagas, and fried okra. The whole wonderfully predictable experience begins with a lovely bread basket piled with corn muffins, yeast rolls, and whole wheat rolls, and perhaps a Waldorf salad or tomato aspic. Our next meal will be the one Roadfood .com's Dale Fine, who goes by the screen moniker Wanderingjew, reported on back in 2012. He called it "spruced up" liver and onions: calves' liver smothered with not only bacon and onions but with sautéed-soft Granny Smith apples, all in a rich demiglace.

Among the flawless desserts are strawberry shortcake, hot fudge cake (with ice cream, of course), and an only-in-the-South coconut icebox pie.

## Community BBQ

1361 Clairmont Rd.          404-633-2080
Decatur, GA                 www.communityqbbq.com
                            LD | $

"We cook fresh every day . . . that means we have to guess how much we will need . . . Please understand that we will run out of meat occasionally." Fair warning from the Community menu. Do plan to arrive early, because this is one barbecue you do not want to miss. It is among Atlanta's best; maybe it is the best, since Harold's hit the skids and finally closed.

Pulled pork is a mélange of velvety strips and chewy bits of bark, brought to full flower by the application of vinegar-pepper sauce (or a sweeter, more tomato-based sauce). Dry-rub ribs ooze juice as soon as tooth pressure is applied. Strangely enough—this being the Deep South—Community brisket delivers beefy satisfaction reminiscent of the benchmark Q's of Texas. Brunswick stew is hearty enough that it easily could be a meal. Sandwiches come on buttery Texas toast. Among side dishes, mac 'n' cheese, made with penne noodles, is a standout: chewy, gooey, cheesy, and greasy.

Our only disappointment was a rather monotone banana pudding at dessert. Next time, we'll try the cobbler or bread pudding.

## The Crab Shack

40 Estill Hammock Rd.       912-786-9857
Tybee Island, GA            www.thecrabshack.com
                            LD | $$

It may not be the most romantic come-on in the restaurant world, but what Roadfooder could resist the Crab Shack's catchphrase, "Where the Elite Eat in Their Bare Feet"? Need we say that this is not a formal dining room? Park among heaps of oyster shells and eat off paper plates at picnic tables to the sound of Jimmy Buffett tunes. The deckside view of the broad tidal creek is lovely—a true waterside picnic—but even lovelier are the great heaps of sloppy, hands-on seafood that Savannahians come to gobble up with beer and/or frozen margaritas.

The fundamentals include boiled shrimp (served the Lowcountry way with corn, potatoes, and sausage), steamers by the bucket, oysters on the half shell, crawfish in season, and your choice from a list of several crabs: Alaskan, blue, Dungeness, snow, and, when available, stone crab (claws only, of course). In addition to these simple seafoods, the Crab Shack offers deviled crabs, crab stew, and shrimp and crab au gratin. Couples and groups of three or four can opt for a seasonal shellfish feast, accompanied by corn, potatoes, and sausage.

## Dillard House

768 Franklin St.
Dillard, GA

706-746-5348
www.dillardhouse.com
BLD | $

Dillard House isn't really a boardinghouse, but it serves its meals boardinghouse-style. Everything is set out on the table on platters and in bowls. Friends, family, and strangers reach, pass, and grab for what they want. There is no fixed menu; the meal consists of everything the kitchen is offering at the time you sit down, the blackboard list changing hour by hour as new dishes are cooked and others are eaten up. It is essential to come to Dillard House with a big appetite; it would be wrong to practice moderation. And be prepared to grab what you like. At a boardinghouse feed like this, nobody wants to waste time being polite.

Fried chicken always is on the table, and it's crunch-crusted gold. Country ham, prime rib, and barbecue chicken are the other entrees. But it's the vegetables we like best at a Dillard House feed. They are lavish, ultra-flavored, stars-and-bars Dixie vegetables such as acorn squash soufflé loaded with coconut and raisins, creamy vanilla-scented yams streaked with mini-marshmallows, and limp-leaf collard greens pungent with the smack of a salty hambone. Plus dinner rolls and biscuits and, of course, iced tea in mason jars. The dessert to eat is peach cobbler. Breakfast is awesome too, with eggs a minor note in a repertoire that includes sausage, ham with red-eye gravy, bacon, and pork tenderloin, fried potatoes, grits, stewed apples, biscuits with sausage gravy, cinnamon rolls, and blueberry muffins.

The Dillard House dining room is huge and boisterous, just one part of a vast good-time complex in the scenic mountains that includes a hotel and cottages, hiking trails, and opportunities to whitewater raft, fish, and golf.

## Dinglewood Pharmacy

1939 Wynnton Rd.                706-322-0616

Columbus, GA                    L | $

The Northeast, where we live, has plenty of excellent hot dogs of all kinds, but nothing like a scrambled dog. When you sit at Dinglewood's counter (or at one of a few tables and booths) and receive your dog, you will not recognize it as a member of the wiener family. A shallow rectangular dish comes with the handle of a spoon sticking out from below a pile of oyster crackers, meat-and-bean chili, pickle slices, and chopped raw onions. Use the spoon to poke around a bit and you soon will discover the hot dog, a neon-red weenie already cut into bite-sized pieces, buried underneath everything else. The spoon, of course, is essential. This take on the scrambled dog cannot be picked up. It doesn't even pretend to have a bun. The movable-letter menu above the counter lists a few other sandwiches, a chili dog and a bun with nothing but chili in it, as well as milk shakes, sundaes, and fresh lemonade.

## Don's Famous Bar-B-Q

217 E. US Hwy. 80              912-748-8400

Pooler, GA                     LD | $

"I'm most certainly a barbecue snob," wrote Meg Butler in her recommendation of Don's, which she described as a "tiny shack, great for lunch." If, indeed, one were a Deep South barbecue snob, Don's might prove disconcerting, as the meat served here is more North Carolina–style—pulled pork hacked to smithereens, dressed with a thin, tangy pepper sauce, and best eaten in a bun. On the side you want onion rings and the thing to drink is sweet tea, served as per local custom in gigantic portions.

Don's is a minuscule place with barely room for a dozen people inside. But there is plenty of room at outdoor picnic tables.

## Edna's

Hwy. 411 S.                    706-695-4968

Chatsworth, GA                 LD | $

Every day Edna's puts out a short list of entrees and a long list of vegetables from which you choose one main course and three side dishes. In many

many meat-and-three restaurants, it is the vegetables that matter, and some customers forget the meat altogether, getting a four-vegetable plate for lunch. At Edna's the all-vegetable strategy would be a big mistake. We don't know about the meat loaf or the country-fried steak, but we can tell you that the fried chicken is delicious, a fact that becomes apparent if you look around the restaurant and note that probably half the clientele chooses it. Edna's logo is a chicken wearing a chef's toque with the proclamation, "Our chicken dinners are worth crowing about."

The side dishes include not only vegetables such as mashed potatoes, fried potatoes, green beans, pole beans, and so on, but also mac 'n' cheese and Jell-O salads. Whatever you get comes with a corn-bread muffin that crumbles very nicely over cooked greens. For dessert, there is no better choice than one of Edna's pies—peanut butter and coconut cream preferred.

## Hot Thomas' Barbeque

| 3753 Greensboro Hwy. | 706-769-6550 |
| Watkinsville, GA | LD Tues-Sat \| $ |

Hot Thomas' used to be a peach orchard. It grew into a country store in the middle of fruit-growing country, then a barbecue restaurant. The peach trees are no more, but the barbecue is well worth a trip.

Step up to the counter inside the sunbleached white building, order a plate of 'cue, and nab yourself a Coke or Mr. Pibb from the cooler. Find a seat and fork into moist hickory-cooked pork, hacked to smithereens with a good measure of "Mr. Brown" (crusty dark meat from the outside) laced among the supple, sweet pieces from the center of the shoulder. Side dishes to accompany this lovely entree include Brunswick stew, sweet coleslaw, and soft, white bread suitable for dunking in the stew and mopping up hot sauce. There are ribs too, as well as hamburgers, chili dogs, and chicken mull (a creamy stew), but chopped pork is what you want.

## Mamie's Kitchen

| 1294 S. Main St. NE | 770-922-0131 |
| Conyers, GA | BL \| $ |

Jack Howard started in the biscuit business in 1962 when he opened an eat shack in an industrial section of Atlanta. Named for a skillful cook in his employ, Mamie's Kitchen has since expanded to four locations east of the city. "In the early days, I used to go to the mountains and buy big cakes of butter from the farmers," Jack recalls. "I brought jars of preserves they made and put them on my tables. My slogan was 'I Am Rolling in Dough.'"

Anytime you order a biscuit at Mamie's, it comes hot from the oven. Its knobby golden surface has a gentle crunch, and although the inside is fleecy, it is not fragile. It is delicious plain or simply buttered, as well as topped with sausage gravy or sandwiching streak o' lean or fried chicken. Its greatest glory is to be pulled into two circular, gold-topped halves so it can sandwich a slice of deliriously flavorful country ham grilled until its rim of fat becomes translucent amber and the brick-red surface starts to turn crisp. The power of the ham—its complexity, its salty punch, its rugged, chewy texture—is perfectly complemented by the fluffy gentleness of the biscuit.

## *Mary Mac's Tea Room

224 Ponce de Leon Ave.        404-876-1800
Atlanta, GA                   www.marymacs.com
                              LD | $$

Originally opened in 1945, Mary Mac's is an old-fashioned urban lunchroom in the heart of Atlanta that offers a broad menu of Dixie cooking. You can start a meal with pot likker—that's soft turnip greens wallowing in a bowl with their flavorful cooking liquid—sided by a corn-bread muffin. Entrees include baked chicken with corn-bread dressing, pork barbecue with Brunswick stew, and country-fried steak with gravy. Fried chicken is crust-crunching, moisture-spurting delicious.

Many customers come only for vegetables. Stand-outs include sweet-potato soufflé that is spiced Christmas-sweet, mac 'n' cheese in which the noodles are suspended in an eggy cheese soufflé, tomato pie that is fruity and cheese-enriched, hoppin' John, and crisp-fried okra.

An airy place with soothing pastel yellow walls and tables covered with white oilcloth, Mary Mac's offers old-style tearoom service, which is great fun. When you sit down, you are given an order pad and menus. Once you've made your decisions, you write your own order and hand it to your waiter or waitress who, in the meanwhile, has brought you an immense tankard of what the menu lists as the table wine of the South—sweet iced tea.

## Matthews Cafeteria

2229 Main St.  
Tucker, GA

770-939-2357  
www.matthewscafeteria.com  
BLD | $

Matthews Cafeteria is 100 percent Roadfood. To fully understand its appeal, you need a deep appreciation of *cuisine maudite* cues such as ancient walls painted institutional beige, a raucous cafeteria line where food is marshaled upon the steam table with little regard for beauty, vegetables that are purposely overcooked, creamed corn that is crazy-creamy to the point where the kernels are a minor element, mac 'n' cheese with macaroni so soft that it is inseparable from the cheese, and strawberry shortcake sweeter than a Twinkie. Yes, we actually do like all these things . . . and, more important, we love Matthews's fried chicken, for which no apology need be made. It bears a fine, fragile crust, just salty enough to enhance the meat, which ranges from dripping-moist to chewy bark.

You can argue that there are better vegetables and fried chicken around Atlanta, but you will not find another place with the unvarnished charm of Matthews Cafeteria. We hesitate even to call it charming, because most common markers for charmingness are lacking, but if you check it out and fall in love with it as we did, you will have earned your Roadfood colors.

## Mrs. Wilkes' Dining Room

107 W. Jones St.  
Savannah, GA

912-233-8970  
www.mrswilkes.com  
L | $

West Jones Street is a boulevard of antique brick houses with curving steps and graceful cast-iron banisters. At eleven o'clock each morning a line begins to form at #107. At 11:30, the doors open and the lunch crowd finds seats at tables shared by strangers. And so begins Mrs. Wilkes' daily feast, boardinghouse-style.

The tabletops are crowded with platters of fried chicken and corn-bread dressing, corn muffins, and biscuits. As at any southern banquet worth its cracklin' corn bread, there are constellations of vegetable casseroles: great, gooey, buttery bowls full of mac 'n' cheese, candied yams, butter beans, squash casserole, okra and tomatoes, rice and gravy, and Savannah red rice. The food comes fast, and everybody eats fast in a joyful camaraderie.

When the late Mrs. Wilkes first started serving meals in this dining room in 1943, there were many similar places throughout the region, where boarders as well as frugal local citizens gathered to enjoy the special pleasure of a meal shared with neighbors and strangers. Now, the take-some-and-pass-the-bowl style of the old boardinghouse is a rarity. Mrs. Wilkes' is a prized opportunity to indulge in the delicious dining style of a culinary tradition that values sociability as much as a good macaroni salad.

## Nu-Way Weiners

428 Cotton Ave.    912-743-1368
Macon, GA          www.nu-wayweiners.com
                   BLD | $

There are other Nu-Way Weiner shops in central Georgia, but the one on Cotton Avenue in Macon is the original, established in 1916 by James Mallis and now run by his descendants. It is a shoebox-shaped restaurant with tables and a counter, instantaneous service, and addictive hot dogs. They are bright-red little private-label links that are grilled and bedded in a steamed-soft bun. Nu-Way's glory is having it "all the way," which means topped with mustard and onions and a fine-grained chili that is sweetened with porky-rich barbecue sauce. One other good topping is coleslaw, which is creamy-sweet. Or, you can order that peculiar Georgia configuration, a scrambled dog, which is a splayed-open bun topped with a hot dog and smothered with chili and beans.

A chocolate malt is the only reasonable alternative to soft drinks that are served extra-cold over Nu-Way's famous flaky ice.

Breakfast at Nu-Way features biscuits either on the side of eggs or sandwiching eggs along with bacon, sausage, regular or country ham, or Spicy Dog hot links. And of course there are bowls of grits.

## Old South Bar-B-Q

Windy Hill Rd.    770-435-4215
Smyrna, GA        www.oldsouthbbq.com
                  LD | $$

We first ran into barbecue salad in Memphis, but have since seen a claim for its invention in Alabama and found the exemplary one in Georgia, at Old South Bar-B-Q, a family-run eatery that's been slow-smoking meats since 1968. No paradigm exists telling exactly what such a salad should be; there are more ways to make it than there are to spell the word "barbecue." Some are regular green salads topped with barbecue sauce and/or salad dressing; Jim Neely's in Memphis adds bacon bits but no other meat; others pile dressed salad greens on top of sauced barbecue.

Old South calls its version a "chef's bar-b-q salad." It is a big plate of cold, crisp lettuce and grated orange cheese topped with pork (pulled, chopped, or sliced), beef brisket (chopped or sliced), or chicken, the whole meal-on-a-plate accompanied by your choice from a selection of eight salad dressings and four sauces (original, sweet, hot, or sweet-hot). Pour or dip: It's up to you. Our first-timer recommendation is pulled pork with hot or hot-sweet sauce and honey mustard dressing. Purely speaking, it's neither salad nor barbecue. But what it is is weirdly satisfying.

If you are a traditionalist, be assured that the regular barbecue plates and sandwiches are first-rate, the latter available on either bun or garlic toast.

## Peachtree Cafe

| | |
|---|---|
| Lane Packing Company | 800-277-3224 |
| 50 Lane Rd. | www.lanesouthernorchards.com |
| Fort Valley, GA | L \| $ |

The Peachtree Cafe at the Lane Packing Company, which farms over 2,500 acres of peach trees, has a nice lunch menu of barbecue, sandwiches, and salads; but it's dessert that is compelling. That is especially true during summer peach season, when over two dozen different varieties ripen, week by week, on company trees. Peach muffins and peach ice cream are swell, as are warm peach cobbler and butter pecan ice cream made from Lane Company nuts. Best of all is pecan pie, crowded with Lane Company nuts that are sweet and just-cracked crunchy. Top this with fresh peach ice cream, and your taste buds will be humming "Georgia on My Mind."

## Sconyer's Bar-B-Que

| | |
|---|---|
| 2250 Sconyers Way | 706-790-5411 |
| Augusta, GA | www.sconyersbar-b-que.com |
| | LD Thurs-Sat only \| $$ |

Sconyer's is an immense barbecue complex with seating for hundreds in multiple dining rooms, plus drive-through service. Hams are cooked a full twenty-four hours over oak and hickory, resulting in meat that is ridiculously tender and sopping in its own smoke-perfumed juices. Curiously, it is a lot like Lexington-style barbecue, but with a sauce that has more of a pepper punch. It comes on a plate along with hash and rice, pickles and coleslaw, and plenty of nice soft white bread for mopping, or in a sandwich or à la carte by the pound.

For people afraid of their food, Sconyer's offers 97 percent fat-free turkey as well as something called T-loin, which is billed as 96 percent fat-free, low sodium and low cholesterol "choice pork." We have yet to try it. Ribs, chopped beef, turkey, and chicken are also available off the pit. Wine is served in addition to sweet tea and Coke.

## *Silver Skillet

| 200 14th St. | 404-874-1388 |
| Atlanta, GA | www.thesilverskillet.com |
| | BL \| $ |

The Silver Skillet diner is a charismatic blast from the past, its glass windows tilting outward like midcentury tailfins. Booths are upholstered in green and orange Naugahyde, tables topped with boomerang-pattern Formica, and the clientele ranges from blue-collar boys in overalls to visiting celebrities with an entourage in tow.

Breakfast is fine: skillet-cooked ham afloat in a pool of dark, red-eye gravy with biscuits on the side; plate-wide pancakes; fried pork chops with grits. At lunch, there is meat loaf or fried chicken and always a list of southern-style vegetables from which you can make a bounteous four-vegetable plate.

And for dessert? Ah, dessert. The banana pudding is dandy, as is peach or blackberry cobbler, and the lemon icebox pie is stellar. Cool, creamy, and neatly poised between sugar-sweet and lemon-zesty, it is a superlative exclamation point after any meal, but especially after a slab of country ham.

## Skipper's Fish Camp

| 85 Screven St. | 912-437-FISH |
| Darien, GA | www.skippersfishcamp.com |
| | LD \| $$ |

Unlike most fish-camp restaurants, Skipper's is refined, its walls decorated with handsome nautical décor and a whole stuffed alligator. Service is solicitous; meals come on non-disposable plates. There is a boat launch next door that dates back to the time this place really was more like a fish camp; but now Skipper's is adjoined by a prestigious waterside condominium development where no worms are sold.

The handsomest meal here is crisp-fried flounder, a fish so big that it hangs over both ends of a good-sized plate. The plateau of meat below its craggy orange-gold crust is moist and sweet, easy to lift in bite-sized nuggets right off the skeleton. Fried shrimp, caught locally, are firm and fresh, accompanied by red-crusted hush puppies in which the cornmeal is infused with a beguiling swirl of sweetness and garlic. By comparison to the muscular shrimp, fried oysters are shockingly fragile, so tender that they virtually melt in the mouth. Excellent sides include brown-sugary sweet-potato casserole and bitter greens. Brunswick stew is available as a formidable hors d'oeuvre or entree companion.

The essential dessert is Georgia peach cobbler, a one-two punch of fruity sweetness and buttery crust. It is served hot, making a globe of vanilla ice cream perched on top melt fast.

## Smith House

84 S. Chestatee St.

Dahlonega, GA

706-867-7000

www.smithhouse.com

LD | $$

Did you know that Dahlonega, Georgia, had a gold rush in 1828? Proprietors of the Smith House like to say their building sits atop an untapped vein, but today's treasure is in the form of puffy yeast rolls, cracklin' corn-bread muffins, fried chicken, ham with dumplings, and vegetables that range from candied yams to chestnut soufflé.

Since 1922, when Henry and Bessie Smith turned the old house into an inn, service has been family-style: Pay one price and eat your fill. There is no menu to look at; there are no choices to make. Everything the kitchen has prepared that day is brought to the communal tables in large serving dishes. Local folks and visitors all behave as though they were at a family party, passing platters back and forth, chattering happily about the good ol' southern food they are eating.

## Varsity Drive-In

61 North Ave.

Atlanta, GA

404-881-1706

www.thevarsity.com

BLD | $

Like a nation unto itself, the Varsity is a teeming, overpopulated place that has its own language. If you order "a heavyweight, a ring, and a string," you will receive a hot dog with mustard and extra chili, onion rings, and

French fries. Although curb service is an option, full and true communion with the V requires that you get out of your car and stand in line at the inside counter. Here, as you go eye-to-eye with an order taker, he will bark out "What'll ya have?" with all the urgency of a Marine drill sergeant. The food will appear before you have a chance to reach for your wallet.

To drink, there's a full menu of reliable southern favorites: ice-cold buttermilk, gigantic cups full of Coke, PCs, and FOs. PC is Varsity lingo for chocolate milk ("plain chocolate") as opposed to a chocolate milk *shake* (with ice cream). FO means frosted orange, reminiscent of a Creamsicle. With or without chili dogs, frosted oranges are one heck of a way to keep cool.

Lest you have any doubts, this is health food. Varsity founder Frank Gordy, who lived well into his seventies, once proclaimed, "A couple of chili dogs a day keep you young."

## Acme Oyster House

724 Iberville St.
New Orleans, LA

504-522-5973
www.acmeoyster.com
LD | $$

As Roadfood.com contributor Anne Ritchings put it, when you get to Acme Oyster House, "you have found paradise." The only problem is that you are not the only one who wants admittance. In the heart of the French Quarter, this place overflows with customers. Expect an extended wait to be seated.

The rewards for patience include impeccable raw oysters, char-grilled oysters cooked with butter and grated cheese, overflowing oyster po' boys, even an oysters Rockefeller soup. Beyond bivalves, Acme offers gumbo, jambalaya, red beans and rice, and fine-crusted softshell crab.

Note: Seats at the oyster bar itself are especially precious, providing a view of master shuckers at work.

## Bon Ton Café

401 Magazine St.
New Orleans, LA

504-524-3386
www.thebontoncafe.com
LD | $$$

Magazine Street was laid out in 1788; the building holding the Bon Ton Café is slightly newer, going back to the 1840s. The restaurant opened in

1953. Its menu is old-time Louisiana cuisine that is *not* kicked up a notch, not overspiced or overhyped or blackened or infused, but simply delicious. This is the place to know the joy of crawfish étouffée, an unspeakably luscious meal especially in the spring, when crawdads are plumpest. You can have étouffée as a main course or as one part of a monomaniacal meal of bisque, étouffée, Newburg, jambalaya, and an omelet, each of which is made with crawfish. Or you can start dinner with fried crawfish tails. They look like little fried shrimp but taste like shrimp's affluent relatives.

Dinner begins with the delivery of a loaf of hot French bread, tightly wrapped in a white napkin. When the napkin is unfurled, the bread's aroma swirls around the table. Then comes soup—either peppery okra gumbo made with shrimp and crab or turtle soup into which the waitress pours a shot of sherry. Other than crawfish in any form, the great entree is redfish Bon Ton, which is a thick fillet sautéed in butter until just faintly crisp, served under a heap of fresh crabmeat and some gigantic fried onion rings. For dessert, you want bread pudding, which is a dense, warm square of sweetness studded with raisins and drenched with whiskey sauce.

A big, square, brick-walled room with red-checked tablecloths, Bon Ton is soothingly old-fashioned. There is no music, just the sounds of knife, fork, and spoon and happy conversation. Service, by a staff of uniformed professionals, is gracious and Dixie-sweet. As we prepared to take a picture of our redfish, a waitress rushed over and insisted on taking the picture herself, so she could include the two of us along with the lovely meal.

## Boudin King

906 W. Division St.    337-824-6593
Jennings, LA          BLD | $

Yes, the boudin at Boudin King is wonderful—densely packed, spicy, and deeply satisfying. Buy it mild or hot, by the link; it is a Cajun classic. Here also is fine gumbo, smoky-flavored and thick with sausage and big pieces of chicken. And speaking of chicken, we would rate the fried chicken served by Boudin King as some of the most delicious in southern Louisiana, a part of the world where frying chicken is a fine art. Other specialties include crawfish and fried pies.

The late Ellis Cormier, who founded this place back in the 1970s, once told us, "Nowhere else in America, except perhaps where the Mexicans live, is food properly spiced." Monsieur Cormier was one of the leading lights in America's rediscovery of its regional food, of Cajun food in particular. It was primarily thanks to his good cooking that in 1979 the Louisiana state legislature proclaimed Jennings "the Boudin Capital of the Universe."

## Bozo's

3117 21st St.

Metairie, LA

504-831-8666

www.bozosrestaurant.com

LD | $$

Metairie's time-honored, family-run tavern is a plain-looking place that is a bonanza of south Louisiana seafood: redfish, trout, shrimp remoulade, daily-delivered oysters either on the half shell or fried up for a fully dressed po' boy on fragile French bread, wild-caught cornmeal-crusted catfish with succulent sweet meat, and insanely luxurious barbecued shrimp that loll in a pool of garlicky, buttery juices.

Those allergic to seafood can have a plate-wide stuffed artichoke, red beans and rice with smoked sausage, or some of the finest chicken and andouille sausage gumbo in south Louisiana. Meals begin with crisp-crusted, fluffy-center bread that comes toasted and buttered. Dessert? Bread pudding, of course—topped with pecan praline rum sauce.

## *Brenda's Diner

409 W. Pershing

New Iberia, LA

337-367-0868

BLD | $

Brenda's brought tears of joy to our eyes. "It doesn't get better than this," we agreed out loud halfway through a lunch of fried chicken, fried pork chops, red beans with sausage, rice and gravy, candied yams, and smothered cabbage. Each dish Brenda Placide had cooked was the best imaginable version of itself. The pork chop was audibly juicy with a tender taste that had us gnawing to the bone. The chicken's fragile crust shored in juice-dripping meat. The red beans were New-Iberia *hot,* crowded with thick discs of sausage; smothered cabbage, speckled with nuggets of garlicky sausage, brought high honor to the vegetable kingdom.

We had to ask Brenda how she cooks such magnificent food, but we weren't surprised when she had no satisfactory answer. "It's from my mama's kitchen," she said. "I cannot tell you how to do it because she never taught me to measure anything. You add seasoning and spice until it's right." It occurred to us that even if we studied Brenda as she cooked, taking scrupulous notes about every grain of every ingredient she used, we couldn't in a lifetime make food like this. It would be like watching Isaac Stern play the violin, then copying his every move.

## *Café des Amis

140 E. Bridge St.
Breaux Bridge, LA

337-332-5273
www.cafedesamis.com
B Fri-Sun; LD daily | $$

A sign in the window of Café des Amis boasts that it is "The essence of French Louisiana." It's the real deal, all right, a French-accented mix of South and soul, with a dash of Caribbean spice and Italian brio.

At breakfast, it is beignets, crisp-edged twists of fried dough under an avalanche of powdered sugar; it is "Oreille de Couchon," a strip of fried dough that resembles a pig's ear, available plain or filled with boudin. It is biscuits topped with crawfish étouffée, omelets filled with tasso ham, and cheese grits with andouille sausage.

The menu for lunch and supper is a veritable encyclopedia of local favorites, including turtle soup, andouille gumbo, barbecue shrimp, corn bread filled with crawfish tails, softshell crab, and crawfish pie. Desserts include bread pudding with rum sauce, which is more of a New Orleans thing than a Cajun one, and gateau sirop, which is extremely local. Made from sugar cane—grown and processed all around here—it is a block of moist spice cake with the distinctive smoky sweetness of cane sugar.

A friendly old brick-wall storefront that has been renovated to serve as an art gallery and live-music venue (check out the Saturday-morning Zydeco breakfast) as well as a restaurant, Café des Amis is a gathering place for locals and an easy destination for passersby. If you are looking for a full, joyous taste of Acadian Louisiana, make Breaux Bridge your destination.

## Café Du Monde

813 Decatur St.
New Orleans, LA

504-581-2914
www.cafedumonde.com
Always open | $

Café Du Monde is a New Orleans institution, serving café au lait and beignets to locals and tourists for more than a century and a half. It is always open, and the characters you'll meet here—any time of day, but especially at odd hours in the middle of the night—are among the Crescent City's most colorful.

There is not much to the menu: chicory coffee, either black or au lait (with a lot of milk), white or chocolate milk, orange juice, and beignets. Beignets are dense, hole-less donuts, served hot from the fry kettle and so heaped with powdered sugar that it is not possible to eat one without getting white powder all over your hands, face, and clothes.

After leisurely coffee-sipping and beignet-eating, you can buy New Orleans souvenirs inside the restaurant, then stroll across Decatur Street to the place where fortune-tellers, tarot-card readers, and palmists set up shop every evening and, for the right price, reveal your future.

## Casamento's

4330 Magazine St.
New Orleans, LA

504-895-9761
www.casamentosrestaurant.com
LD (closed in summer) | $$

Oyster loaves are served throughout New Orleans and Cajun country, and it is rare to find one that's bad. But for many loaf lovers, Casamento's is the ultimate. Oysters aren't the only dish of note in this spanking-clean neighborhood oyster bar that closes for a long summer vacation when oysters aren't in season. You can also have fried fish and shrimp and springtime softshell crabs, and there's even a plate of that arcane Creole Italian meal, daube, which is pot roast in gravy on spaghetti noodles. (Need we mention that shucked-to-order raw oysters by the dozen are a specialty too?)

Casamento's oyster loaf is nothing short of magnificent: a dozen crackle-crusted hotties piled between two big slabs of what New Orleans cooks know as pan bread, aka Texas toast. Each single oyster is a joy, its brittle skin shattering with light pressure, giving way to a wave of melting-warm, briny oyster meat across the tongue. When we asked proprietor Joe Gerdes what made his oysters so especially good, he modestly replied that his method is "too simple to call a recipe." Of course, he uses freshly shucked local oysters, and he does recommend frying in lard, but the real secret is ineffable. "Everything is fried by feel and sound," he said. "It requires a lot of personal attention and experience."

## Central Grocery

923 Decatur St.
New Orleans, LA

504-523-1620
LD | $

The name "muffuletta" once referred to a round loaf of chewy bread turned out by Italian bakeries in New Orleans. Grocery stores that sold muffulettas got the fine idea to slice them horizontally and load them with salami, ham, and provolone, then top that with a wickedly spicy mélange of chopped green and black olives fragrant with anchovies and garlic. The place that claims to have done it first is the Central Grocery on Decatur Street.

While it has become a tourist attraction and muffulettas are now the only sandwich on the menu, the Central Grocery still feels like a neighborhood store, its yellowed walls decorated with travel posters, the air inside smelling of garlic and sausage and provolone cheese, its shelves stocked with such imported canned exotica as sardines, kippered snacks, hearts of palm, and octopus. There is no table service. Step up to the counter and order a whole or half. Whole sandwiches are cut into quarters (enough for four modest appetites) and wrapped, at which point you can take it to a counter toward the back of the store to unwrap and eat it.

## Champagne's Breaux Bridge Bakery

105 Poydras            337-332-1117
Breaux Bridge, LA      www.champagnesbakery.com
                       L | $

This charming nineteenth-century one-room bakery in the crawfish capital of the world caused us to stomp the brakes as we drove past early in the morning. The smell of just-baked bread was irresistible. Inside the door, a small card table was arrayed with loaves. They are the familiar-looking south-Louisiana torpedoes, like French baguettes but about half the weight. Some are wrapped in paper, the others in plastic bags. "You want soft, you get the plastic," advised the gent behind the counter. "For crisp, paper." Our paper-wrapped loaf had a refined crunch to its crust and feathery insides. It's delicious just to eat, but oh, how well this would scoop out to become a seafood boat filled with fried oysters or shrimp!

Cooked meat pies were displayed along the bakery counter, and good as they looked, we hesitated about getting one because who wants a cold meat pie? "We have a microwave," said the woman behind the counter, and although a regular oven is kinder to the crust, the pies she warmed for us were nothing short of spectacular: rich, moist, and vividly spiced.

## D.I.'s

6561 Evangeline Hwy.          337-432-5141
Basile, LA                    www.discajunrestaurant.biz
                              LD | $$

Set back from the two-lane in the middle of nothing but rice fields and craw-fish ponds, D.I.'s is a brimful measure of Acadian pleasure. If it hadn't been for Sulphur policeman and good friend Maj. Many McNeil, we never, ever would have come across it. When we told Many we were on the lookout for a true Cajun eating experience, he said D.I.'s was it.

Daniel Isaac ("D.I.") Fruge has been known to neighbors for his well-seasoned crawdads since the 1970s. He was a rice and soybean farmer who began harvesting the mudbugs, boiling and serving them on weekends to friends and neighbors. They were served in his barn the traditional way, strewn in heaps across bare tables with beer to drink on the side.

D.I. and his wife, Sherry, now run a restaurant with a full menu that includes steaks, crabs, oysters, frog legs, flounder, and shrimp, but vividly-spiced crawfish are the draw. The classic way to enjoy them is boiled and piled onto the beer tray—a messy meal that rewards vigorous tail pulling and head sucking with an unending procession of the vibrant sweet-water richness that only crawdads deliver. You can have them crisp-fried into bite-sized morsels, and there are crawfish pie, étouffée, and bisque.

No longer a makeshift annex to Monsieur Fruge's barn, D.I.'s is a spacious destination with multiple dining rooms and a dance floor. The Cajun music starts at seven.

## *Domilise's Po-Boys

5240 Annunciation St.         504-899-9126
New Orleans, LA               L | $

You won't likely come upon Domilise's bar/sandwich shop by accident, for it is located in an unscenic blue-collar neighborhood, and if you did accidentally drive by, you might not guess that it is the source of great New Orleans sandwiches. It looks like a small, no-frills neighborhood tavern, and in some ways, that is what it is. We guess it would be possible to walk in, sit at the bar, and have nothing but a liquid diet of longnecks or boilermakers. To do so, you'd have to have no sense of smell, for the air of this tavern is wildly perfumed with shrimp, oysters, and catfish hoisted from the fry basket.

You may have to take a number before you can place your order. At the height of lunch hour, Domilise's is packed, for its superior po' boys attract eaters from all over the city; table space is precious (strangers often share); and the house phone rings unanswered.

For the newcomer, delay provides an opportunity to read the menu on the wall and to observe the sandwich makers constructing different combos before you decide which is the right one for you. Hot smoked sausage with gravy is the one we recommend above all others. Get it "dressed," meaning topped with tomato, lettuce, and grainy Creole mustard. A large one is assembled on a length of bread so long that it must be cut in thirds. While the sandwich is being made, buy your drink at the bar and hope that by the time you are ready, space at a table is available.

## Don's Specialty Meats

730 I-10 (S. Frontage Rd.)          337-234-2528
Scott, LA                                   www.donsspecialtymeats.com
                                               L (butcher shop is open daily from
                                               6 a.m. to 7 p.m.) | $

A big modern building located just off the intestate, Don's is a destination for boudin and cracklins, hot lunch, po' boys, fried pork chops, fried chicken, hot meat pies, and just about any kind of Cajun-butcher fixins you need for cooking at home. There is a large indoor dining room as well as picnic tables outside. Service is do-it-yourself.

Weekends are an especially good time to eat at Don's. Saturday, the smoked pork chop draws fans from Lafayette Parish and beyond. Slices of white bread hold a giant, bone-in chop that oozes juice at first bite and is even messier if you have it dressed with barbecue sauce. Sunday, the place is thronged with locals who come for pork steak, stuffed brisket, and ribs.

## Dwyer's Café

323 Jefferson St.                      337-235-9364
Lafayette, LA                          BL | $

No one makes lunch sound as good as Mike Dwyer does. You will hear his pitch as you approach the cafeteria area of Dwyer's Café, where he enumerates the day's choices, one by one, with pride and exuberance to make appetites growl. In fact, this food needs no hard sell. The proof is in the tasting.

Dwyer's is a meat-and-three affair, the daily meats including such expertly cooked stalwarts as smothered pork chops, lengths of pork sausage, roast beef with dark gravy, and chicken-fried steak with white gravy. When we visited, Mike was pitching crawfish fettuccine, a fabulous cross-cultural

Franco-Italian-Cajun noodle casserole loaded with high-flavored crawdads. Among the notable sides are dirty rice, eggplant casserole, red beans, and sausage jambalaya. On cold days, you can get gumbo or chili.

Dwyer's is also a notable breakfast opportunity. We love the tender sweet-potato hot cakes with their faintly crisp edge (which Mike says he added to the menu for low-carb dieters!). When you order pancakes, the waitress will ask what kind of syrup you want: cane or maple. Sugar cane is a major crop around here, and the pancake syrup made from it is thick, dark, and resonantly sweet . . . very different from white-sugar sweet.

## Earl's

510 Verot School Rd.       337-247-7633
Lafayette, LA       www.earlscajunmarket.net
      L | $

West of New Orleans from Baton Rouge to St. Charles and from the swamps of Avery Island to the prairies of Evangeline Parish, hundreds of places sell boudin sausage. Among the best of them is Earl's, which sells it by the link from a hot box near the cash register. Customers buy it to take home or to eat in the car. There are no dining tables on premises.

Earl's boudin is ideal for off-the-dashboard dining, the links so dense that once their casing is breached with a sharp knife, you can fork out pieces in tidy clumps. Each bite is a country-style symphony of pork and rice, pepper and onion, needing only beer (or Barq's root beer) on the side.

Earl's also offers plate lunch, including fried chicken, po' boys, red beans and rice, and catfish on Friday—again, all on a takeout basis.

## Galatoire's

209 Bourbon St.       504-525-2021
New Orleans, LA       www.galatoires.com
      LD | $$$

Galatoire's is more formal than any other Roadfood restaurant—no jeans allowed, jackets are required for men. And at $50+ per person, it is beyond this book's normal price range. But if Roadfood is all about finding unique regional meals, meals that reflect the culture that gave birth to them, Galatoire's goes to the top of the list. It is the definitive Creole dining experience. With its mirrored walls, bright lights and dark woodwork, white linen tablecloths and black-tie waiters, it is a crystalline image of a bourgeois dining room from the turn of the nineteenth century: solid, dependable, with a bounteous larder of the highest quality. The staff is polite but not obsequious. They are able to clearly and appealingly describe every item on the multipage menu without making the description a grocery list or trying too hard to sell it. Nor will these pros offer the ridiculous "Good choice!" if you happen to select something of which they approve.

A surfeit of options makes deciding sweet agony. Do you like crab meat? You can have it au gratin, ravigote, Sardou, Saint-Pierre, maison, or Yvonne. There's shrimp Clemenceau, Creole, Marguery, au vin, étouffée, deep-fried, and the remoulade (which bears little resemblance to remoulades anywhere else). There are seven kinds of potato, nine omelets and egg dishes, and a choice of soups that includes oyster-artichoke, Creole gumbo, and turtle.

We've sampled only a fraction of what Galatoire's offers. Not once have we been disappointed; more often, we rave that the plate before us holds the paradigm of whatever it's supposed to be. Highest on our honor roll are the shrimp remoulade, trout amandine, crab Sardou (with spinach, artichoke hearts, and hollandaise sauce), softshell crabs (the tenderest, ever!), and the inconspicuous but conspicuously potent garlic green salad.

Meals begin with warm loaves of the fragile-skinned, fluffy bread found nowhere outside of southern Louisiana and, if you're a tippler, the classic New Orleans aperitif, a Sazerac. And they can end with a fiery climax: *café brûlot* for two, flamed tableside.

(Guys: House jackets are available if you come without yours.)

## Hansen's Sno-Bliz

4801 Tchoupitoulas St.  
New Orleans, LA

504-891-9788  
www.snobliz.com  
$

The shave ice served by Hansen's Sno-Bliz resembles a snow cone but is a world apart. Yes, it is ice and flavoring, but rather than being chopped and clumpy, shave ice is as fluffy as freshly fallen snow. Whereas the ice and syrup in a normal snow cone never quite blend, shave ice literally sops up its flavor and delivers such compelling refreshment that brain freeze is a near-certain side effect.

With historical antecedents in Asia and in Hawaii, shave ice had always been a time-consuming product to make, requiring that the ice actually be shaved from a block with knives. That changed in 1934 when Ernest Hansen of New Orleans invented a machine that shaves ice. Five years later he opened Hansen's Sno-Bliz, where homemade tropical syrups were applied to the ice in layers. Now run by Hansen's granddaughter, the little shop continues to set the gold standard, offering shave ice with such special flavors as cream of peach and cream of coffee, tart satsuma and limeade, as well as luxury toppings that include condensed milk, marshmallow, crushed pineapple, and whipped cream.

Expect to wait in line. Service is meticulous and therefore slow. Other than a few benches outside, there are no dining facilities.

## Jerry Lee's

12181 Greenwell Springs Rd.  
Baton Rouge, LA

225-272-0739  
www.jerryleescajunfoods.com  
L | $

Like most of the boudin makers in southern Louisiana, Jerry Lee's is a store rather than a restaurant. It is common to see customers sitting in their trucks or cars and dining off the dashboard or, on a nice day, eating off the tailgate. A neon sign in Jerry Lee's window shows a boiling pot (presumably where the pork is cooked) with this legend underneath: "If it's not Jerry Lee's, it's not Boudin." While a lot of Cajun boudin is fire-hot, Jerry Lee's is only haloed by pepper . . . all the better to savor the flavor of the rice that is its dominant ingredient, along with the luxe of ground pork that is its soul.

In a heated case near the cash register, you will find the boudin already extracted from its casing and piled into rolls along with cheese. In our opinion, the cheese is all wrong, completely overwhelming the refined flavor play of the sausage. The better choice is to forgo the fixins and get a couple of links, which cost about $1.75 each. Their casing is really tough, virtually impossible to cut with teeth alone, but once it is opened up with the plastic knife provided by the management, out wafts a balmy aroma that is unique to southernmost Louisiana. Grab a bag of Zapp's potato chips and a Barq's root beer and you have the makings of a five-dollar feast.

## *Johnson's Boucanière

111 St. John St.  
Lafayette, LA

337-269-8878  
www.johnsonsboucaniere.com  
L | $

*Boucanière* means smokehouse in Cajun, and smoking pork and beef is what the Johnson family has done since they opened up a grocery store in Eunice in 1937. Today they live above their smokehouse in Lafayette, making it easy for them to come downstairs about 3:30 in the morning to get meat on the grate, where it cooks low and slow. The results compose a lunch menu featuring pillowy pulled pork, beef brisket, tasso ham, and sausage made from pork or turkey. There's even a barbecue salad of your choice of pork, brisket, or chicken combined with lettuce, onions, tomatoes, and shredded cheese, dressed with Johnson's barbecue sauce.

Finally, but by no means the least of Johnson's accomplishments, is boudin sausage, the savory Cajun treat that may be eaten with a fork or hand-squeezed directly from its natural casing. The authoritative website boudinlink.com gave Johnson's Boucanière an A+ rating, declaring it to be the ideal blend of rice and meat with an overall flavor that is complex but clean. Boudin balls are crumbled and sandwiched with cheese in a grilled bun for a signature Parrain's Special, about which Stephen Rushmore wrote, "If the Cajuns were to create a cheesesteak, this would be it."

Much business is takeout. A covered porch provides casual accommodations for those who come to eat plate lunch.

## Lasyone's Meat Pie Kitchen

622 2nd St.  
Natchitoches, LA

318-352-3353  
www.lasyones.com  
BLD | $

When we surveyed visitors at the first annual Louisiana Roadfood Festival of 2009 to find out what food they liked best from among the several dozen specialties sold by street vendors, the winner by a landslide was the meat pie dished out by Lasyone's. Second place was Lasyone's crawfish pie. Lasyone's has returned to the festival every year and it always wins a unanimous thumbs-up.

Half-circle pastry pockets about the size of tacos with a rugged crimp around their edges, these deep-fried pies have golden crust that is brittle and crunchy near the crimp, pliant near the mounded center. Inside each flaky sheaf is a good-sized portion of deftly seasoned ground beef, moist enough to make gravy irrelevant. Spicy but not fire-hot, complex and succulent, it is an honest piece of food that satisfies in an old-fashioned way. Lasyone's serves them for breakfast, accompanied by eggs and hash browns, but most customers come midday to get a pair of them for lunch, with soulful dirty rice on the side, darkened with plenty of gizzards and topped with zesty gravy.

## Lea's Lunchroom

1810 US 71

Lecompte, LA

318-776-5178

www.leaslunchroom.com

BL | $

Many of Lea's biggest fans and most devoted customers never eat on premises. They come for ham and pies to take home. Luckily for us travelers, there is seating inside and a limited menu that includes chicken and cornbread dressing, red beans and rice, and, on Sunday, southern fried chicken and turkey. Dough-baked ham is the main attraction—the dough wrap ensuring that the pink meat stays super-juicy. A balance of sweet, spicy, and salty, the ham is available on platters, but the signature specialty is a ham sandwich. Served in a lightly toasted bun, it contains a surfeit of ham, along with mayonnaise, lettuce, tomato, and pickles.

Lea's is equally famous (since 1928) for its daily baked pies: soaring meringues, double-crusted fruit pies, insanely sweet pecan pie, and—in season—blueberry, blackberry, sweet potato, and pumpkin.

## Middendorf's

75 Manchac Way

Akers, LA

985-386-6666

www.middendorfsrestaurant.com

LD Wed-Sun | $$

Middendorf's has been remodeled with a waterfront deck and air-conditioned kitchen, but it remains the casual, noisy, and fun place it has been for eighty years. There is nothing like its catfish, whether you get thick or thin. Thick is a meaty cross-section of fish, similar to a steak wrapped in breading. It is sweet-smelling and has resounding vim that is unlike any seawater fish. Thin catfish is more elegant. Sliced into diaphanous strips that are sharply seasoned and quickly fried, thin cat fillets crunch loudly when you sink your teeth into their brittle crust, which is sheer enough to let the rich flavor of the fish resonate.

Beyond catfish, just about any seafood on the menu is worth eating. We have had some great gumbo here, made with shrimp and crab meat, which was surprisingly delicate compared to the more overpowering versions sold in NOLA's best gumbo houses. There are fabulous barbecued shrimp and oysters, sautéed softshell crabs, po' boy sandwiches, and Italian salads loaded with olives and spice.

## Moody's

601 Martin Luther King Dr.      318-377-5873
Minden, LA                       L | $

If you are traveling through Webster Parish along Interstate 20 east of Shreveport, we highly recommend taking Exit 47 and driving five minutes to the north. Here in Minden (where Hank Williams married his Billie Jean in 1952) you will find Moody's, where heavy-duty partitioned plates carry some of the highest-quality, lowest-priced meals in the South. Expertly made fried chicken, pork chops, or meat loaf is accompanied by such soulful vegetables as turnip greens, cheese-enriched broccoli, and candied yams. Filling out the plate are cylinders of hot-water corn bread—baked, then fried to a crisp. Peach and blackberry cobblers compete for your dessert vote with coconut pie and strawberry cream pie.

## *Morning Call Coffee Stand

3325 Severn Ave.          504-885-4068
Metairie, LA            www.morningcallcoffeestand.com
                          Always open, except Christmas | $

Crisp-edged and nearly as light as air, Morning Call beignets arrive three to an order, hot from the fry kettle. It is the diner's job to apply powdered sugar. This can be an arduous task if you prefer a thick blanket of the white stuff, because Morning Call offers it in shakers that have to be vigorously shaken to extract maximum sugar. Long ago, the restaurant supplied broad bowls full of powdered sugar so customers could simply sweep their hot beignet right through it. Worrying about the hazards of double dipping, health department authorities forbade that practice.

Café au lait is the time-honored beignet companion, and here is the best anywhere. What joy it is to look to the back of the dining room and watch it being concocted. The waitress holds a big pitcher full of ink-dark chicory coffee in one hand, pouring it into a cup in a long, flowing stream. When the cup is about half full, she takes a smaller pitcher in her other hand, hoists it high, and adds warm milk so that both streams swirl together, filling the cup to its top and creating a frothy head.

Morning Call has a second location at City Park Casino. It is always open, except on Christmas Day.

## Mosca's

4137 US 90 W.       504-436-8950

Westwego, LA     www.moscasrestaurant.com

D | $$$

Despite catastrophic hurricanes and cataclysmic changes in the American diet, Mosca's never seems to change. All the great things about this legendary destination still deserve legendary status, especially Oysters Mosca—a festival of garlic, olive oil, Parmesan cheese, and bread crumbs all cosseting little nuggets of sweet oyster meat.

The parking lot remains a gravel wreck; the outside is dark and nefarious. In fact, on a recent trip to New Orleans, we were told that Mosca's for many years was the hangout of the region's chief mafioso. If it's your first time, we guarantee you will think you are lost when you make the drive. And even when you find it, you will wonder: Can this two-room joint with the blaring jukebox and semi-secret kitchen dining area really be the most famous Italian roadhouse in America? Inside, conviviality reigns, and we saw only friendly sorts of folks eating; no one looked like a cast member of *The Godfather* or *The Sopranos*.

Aside from the setting and location, the primary thing you'll notice upon arriving at Mosca's is the sweet, provocative smell of roasting garlic. There are whole cloves of it in Chicken à la Grande—painfully tender pieces that arrive in a pool of rosemary-perfumed gravy. Thank God for spaghetti bordelaise, which is little more than a heap of thin noodles bathed in oil, butter, and garlic. It is an ideal medium for rolling up on a fork and pushing around in extra chicken gravy or the last of the Oysters Mosca bread crumbs.

Go with friends: The bigger the group, the more different dishes you can sample, and you do need also to taste Mosca's sausage, chicken cacciatore, and Louisiana shrimp. Everything is served family-style.

## Mother's

401 Poydras      504-923-9656

New Orleans, LA   www.mothersrestaurant.net

BLD | $

Mother's began in 1938 as a family-run diner specializing in po' boy sandwiches for a clientele that included working men from the waterfront as well as lawyers and newspaper reporters who had business in the nearby courthouse. Today it attracts hordes of tourists as well as locals who come for heroic sandwiches available in full-sized and two-thirds-sized portions, with fillings like smoked or hot sausage, shrimp, oysters, softshell crabs, and catfish. Most famous is called a Ferdi Special, after the local merchant who asked to have ham added to his roast beef po' boy, along with a spill of debris (meat scraps) and gravy. What a wonderful mess!

During World War II, Mother's became such a favorite haunt of US Marines that they named it "Tun Tavern—New Orleans" after the old Tun Tavern of Philadelphia, where the Marine Corps recruited its first members in 1775. The original mother, Mary Landry, who opened the restaurant with her husband, Simon, passed it on to her sons, who in 1986 sold it to Jerry and John Amato. The Amatos kept Mother's menu of effulgent po' boys, adding a repertoire of New Orleans classics such as filé gumbo, jambalaya, red beans and rice, black ham, and, of course, bread pudding for dessert. Today, there is probably no other restaurant in the city that so completely defines blue-collar Creole cuisine.

## Parkway Bakery & Tavern

538 Hagan Ave.                    504-482-3047
New Orleans, LA                   www.parkwaypoorboys.com
                                  LD (closed Tues) | $

After much arduous research, it is our opinion that the best roast beef po' boy in New Orleans (a city that takes its roast beef po' boys very seriously) is made by the Parkway Bakery & Tavern, overlooking Bayou St. John. The sandwich is presented tightly wrapped in a tube of butcher paper that already is mottled through with gravy splotches when you pick it up at the kitchen window. Unwrap it and behold a length of fresh, brawny bread loaded with beef so falling-apart tender that it seems not to have been sliced but rather hand-pulled, like barbecued pork, into myriad slivers, nuggets, and clumps. It is difficult to discern where the meat ends and gravy begins because there is so much gravy saturating the meat and so many carving-board scraps, known as debris (say DAY-bree), in the gravy.

That meaty gravy makes the city's ultimate dining bargain. At $4.85 for a full-length sandwich, and $3.65 for an eight-incher, Parkway's gravy po' boy is a minimalist sandwich of the good, chewy bread filled only with gravy. The bread is substantial enough to absorb massive amounts of the liquid and a booming beef scent, becoming the most appetizing savory loaf imaginable, its surface crowded with the concentrated essence of roast beef.

Parkway has a full repertoire of po' boy fillings, including oysters, crunchy fried shrimp (a fabulous partner with roast beef in the surf 'n' turf po' boy), and a brunch version that includes sausage, bacon, eggs, and cheese and is served with a side of syrup!

Note about the restaurant name: The original Parkway on this site indeed was a bakery, so beloved that lines of customers would stretch out the door at times when it was known fresh bread would be coming out of the brick oven. The bakery closed in the early 1980s and today's Parkway does not make its own, but the name lives on.

## Prejean's

3480 I-49 N.                  337-896-3247
Lafayette, LA                 www.prejeans.com
                              LD | $$

Prejean's is big and noisy (the live music starts every night at 7, and be sure to wear your dancing shoes), and the food is classic Cajun. In some other part of the country, a restaurant this brash might seem too "commercial" to qualify for Roadfood—walls hung with Acadiana, a stuffed alligator in the center of the dining room, a gift shop with tacky souvenirs—but for all its razzle-dazzle, Prejean's is the real thing, a fact about which you can have no doubt when you dip a spoon into the chicken and sausage gumbo or the dark andouille gumbo laced with smoked duck.

The menu is big and exotic, featuring dozens of dishes you'll not find on menus outside Louisiana, from crisp-fried crawfish boudin balls and catfish Catahoula (stuffed with crawfish, shrimp, and crab) to eggplant *pirogues* ("canoes" of bread) hollowed out, fried, and filled with crawfish and red snapper fillet, drizzled with buttery lobster sauce. It is possible to get a monomaniacal all-crawfish meal of crawfish bisque, fried crawfish, crawfish étouffée, crawfish pie, crawfish boulettes, and a salad dotted with crawfish. There are two significant desserts: red velvet cake and bread pudding with Jack Daniel's sour mash sauce.

## Robin's

1409 Henderson Hwy.           337-228-7594
Henderson, LA                 LD | $$$

Lionel Robin cooks some of the most distinctive restaurant meals in swamp country. Year-round, but especially in crawfish season from early in the year through spring, this is the place to have it either simply boiled or in all the ways Cajun chefs like to celebrate it. A crawfish dinner starts with smoky bisque. You then move on to a few boiled and fried ones, étouffée over rice, boulettes, stuffed pepper, and a superior pie in which the little crustaceans share space with vegetables and plenty of garlic in a translucent-thin crust.

The one crawfish dish we might not recommend here is gumbo—not because it isn't good (it is), but because the shrimp and okra gumbo is even better. And chicken and sausage gumbo, while containing none of the seafood for which Robin's is renowned, is wonderful—brilliantly spiced, thick with sausage you will remember for a long time.

For dessert: how about some of Monsieur Robin's Tabasco ice cream?

## Rocky and Carlo's

613 W. St. Bernard Hwy.     504-279-8323
Chalmette, LA               LD | $

Way out in St. Bernard Parish, Rocky and Carlo's opened in 1965 and has since survived hurricanes, floods, and a devastating fire in 2012. In this spacious eating hall you will find meals that reflect that essential trinity of south Louisiana cuisine—Italian-Cajun-Dixie. Walk along the cafeteria line and select from a hot-lunch menu that includes pork chops with greens, braciola, veal parm, stuffed peppers, muffulettas, fried shrimp or oysters, and gorgeous baked chicken. Rocky and Carlo's seafood gumbo, loaded with shrimp, crab, and crawfish and thickened with okra, just may be the best in or out of New Orleans. The blackboard menu also lists wop salad, the locals' politically incorrect term for garlicky iceberg lettuce with green olives, and many customers come for the excellent roast beef po' boys. Platters of wispy, deep-fried onions adorn almost every table.

No matter what you eat at Rocky and Carlo's, the single dish that you likely will remember best is the inconspicuous menu listing "macaroni." There is none better. Very different from typical mac 'n' cheese made with elbow noodles, this mountain of baked pasta is built from substantial perciatelli tubes that come plastered with orange cheese—tender gobs from the heart, chewy strips from the top, and crisp webbed bark from the casserole's edge. It is fine as it is, but some people get it topped with sweet red marinara sauce or glistening mahogany brown gravy.

## T-Boy's Slaughterhouse

2228 Pine Point Rd. (Hwy. 104)     337-468-3333
Ville Platte, LA                   L | $

The trip from the swamplands of the South to T-Boy's Slaughterhouse winds through Evangeline Parish prairies, where cattle and horses graze and native zydeco music sets the cultural beat. Once you arrive, you are in for a true taste of country life. As its name suggests, this place is not a restaurant. It is a from-scratch butcher and convenience store selling sausages and meats from the smokehouse, including paunce (stuffed stomach) and tasso ham. For those just passing through, it is a premier source of the moist and visceral Cajun sausage known as boudin. In the spring crawfish season, especially during Lent, crawfish boudin is a Friday special. It is moist, sweet, and swampy, with a slow-rolling pepper kick.

Boudin is sold hot by the long link, which proprietor T-Boy Berzas is happy to scissor into pieces two or three inches long, making it easy simply to squeeze the luxuriant filling from casing to mouth without the trouble of utensils. We strongly suggest accompanying boudin with some of T-Boy's fabulous hot cracklins, which are assertively seasoned, pop-in-the-mouth chunks and squiggles of deep-fried pig skin, fat, and shreds of meat that shatter when you bite into them, then dissolve into an ethereal slurry of pork and pepper—the flavor of Cajun Louisiana in bite-sized pieces.

T-Boy's has a second location in Eunice.

## Willie Mae's Scotch House

| | |
|---|---|
| 2401 St. Ann St. | 504-822-9503 |
| New Orleans, LA | LD \| $$ |

Willie Mae's, a formerly obscure eatery in New Orleans' Lower Ninth Ward has, over the years, become a destination for fried-chicken devotees. It was raggedy before Katrina's devastation, but the reborn restaurant is bright, clean, and welcoming. And the chicken really is something special—moist and luscious inside an amber crust so fine and fragile that it tends to flake into savory shards when you bite into it. The same luxurious envelope is available on what the menu lists as a chicken-fried pork chop, the chop's meat far chewier than chicken, but in its own way a grand crust companion.

If you are allergic to boiled-in-oil food (why are you here?), you can order a simple grill-cooked pork chop. There is no crust or batter. It is just a hunk of pork plastered with an intensely flavorful coat of seasonings.

Side dishes are noteworthy, especially the butter beans, which are large, silky pods with creamy flesh in garlic-rich gravy. Red beans are blander, leaner, but a rich and welcome starch alongside spicy meats. We even like the potato salad with its pickle smack and crunch.

## Abe's Bar-B-Q

616 State St.  
Clarksdale, MS

662-624-9947  
www.abesbbq.com  
LD | $

Folklore designates the crossroads of Highway 61 and 49 in Clarksdale as the spot Robert Johnson sold his soul to the devil in exchange for music mastery. In 1924, when Johnson was thirteen, Abraham Davis began selling sandwiches in Clarksdale. After World War II, he opened Abe's Bar-B-Q at the crossroads, and today his grandson Pat Davis runs the place, which is known for pecan-smoked pork and hot tamales.

Abe's barbecue is Boston butt that is cooked over pecan wood, cooled overnight, then sliced and heated again on the griddle when it is ordered. While on the grill it gets hacked up. The result? Pork hash with lots of juicy buzz in its pale inside fibers and plenty of crusty parts where it has fried on the hot iron of the grill. You can have it on a platter or in a sandwich, the latter available in two sizes—normal and Big Abe, which is twice the pork loaded into a double-decker bun. Clarksdale is close enough to Memphis that it is served city-style—that is, with the slaw inside the bun.

Abe's sauce is dark red and tangy, with the resonance of pepper and spice—a sublime companion for the meat. Pat Davis told us that it is made from the original recipe his grandfather developed, except for one ingredient, which he swears he doesn't use anymore. We wondered aloud if that secret ingredient might be opium, considering its addictive qualities. Pat denied it with a sly smile.

Served three to an order, with or without chili on top, Abe's tamales are packed into cayenne-red husks, their yellow cornmeal moist with drippings from a mixture of beef and pork. The recipe is Abe Davis's, unchanged. "No doubt Granddaddy got it from someone in town," Pat suggests, reminding us that Abe had come to the United States from Lebanon, where tamales aren't a big part of the culinary mix. Why Abe thought they would sell well in his barbecue place is a head-scratcher. "There were no Mexican restaurants here then," Pat says. "And as far as I know, not many Mexicans."

## Abe's Grill

803 Hwy. 72 W.           662-286-6124
Corinth, MS            BL | $

A tip of the hat to Michael Medley, whom we met in Salt Lake City, where he slipped us a tempting list of eateries in northern Mississippi. Otherwise, we might never have traveled out Highway 72 to Abe's Grill. What to eat at Abe's? "Breakfast!" Michael said, and sure enough, if you are looking for hot biscuits made the true-South way with Martha White flour, for country ham and eggs, or even for a plate of pork brains, you must stop at this colorful roadside attraction that is plastered inside and out with vintage advertising signs, license plates, postcards, calendars, and old-time photographs.

No praise is too high for Abe's biscuits, which are lightweight but substantially savory, and especially delicious when oven-fresh. Sawmill gravy is a well-known classic to top them, but, curiously enough, chocolate gravy is a classic too. (Ari Weinzweig of Zingerman's Deli [p. 374] did the research on this.) While it takes some getting used to, the chocolate makes a seductive alternative to ordinary biscuit companions. Split and buttered or sandwiching sausage or bologna is good too. Coffee is included with most breakfasts, but if you eat enough pig meat to rouse a powerful thirst, consider Abe's iced tea, served in a one-quart frosted mason jar.

We have yet to have lunch at Abe's, but we do look forward to a hamburger, which Abe's makes from beef ground here daily, as well as to Abe's "original recipe" corn dog along with fresh-cut French fries.

## Blue & White Restaurant

1355 US Hwy. 61 N.      662-363-1371
Tunica, MS      www.blueandwhiterestaurant.com

BLD | $

Tunica has gone from cotton fields to gamblers' paradise, but out on Highway 61, the old Blue & White Restaurant is operating pretty much the same as it's been since opening here in 1937 as a Pure service station. The gas pumps are gone, but if you are looking for good southern food at reasonable prices in an atmosphere that is more down-home than high-stakes, this is the place to go.

"You have ten more minutes to order breakfast," our waitress warned. "Then the lunch buffet will open." We started with a country ham plate, the vigorous, well-aged slab of pig accompanied by eggs, biscuits, chunky sausage cream gravy, coffee-flavored red-eye gravy, and a bowl of stout, buttery grits. What a great morning meal!

When the buffet opened up, we helped ourselves to chicken and dumplings, which was superb: powerfully chickeny, loaded with meat, and laced with free-form mouthfuls of tender dough. On the side, we spooned up black-eyed peas, creamed corn, escalloped potatoes, and some of the most amazing turnip greens we've ever eaten. These greens were oily, salty, luscious, and rich, more like the pork used to flavor them than the green vegetable they appear to be. On the side came a sweet-dough yeast muffin and a crisp corn stick, both oven-hot and delicious.

We paid extra for an order of that weird specialty invented several decades ago in the Delta, fried dill pickles. Blue & White's are ultrathin slices with a veil of crust, nearly weightless, served with ranch dressing as a dip. Light as they are, the pickles have a resounding brine flavor that induces a mighty thirst. If you are a beer drinker, you will have instant cravings.

## Crystal Grill

423 Carrollton Ave.      662-453-6530
Greenwood, MS      www.crystalgrillms.com

LD | $$

Years ago, the Crystal Grill was known for a neon sign that glowed NEVER SLEEP. Open from 4 a.m. until midnight, it hosted the locals for their pre-dawn coffee klatch as well as C&G Railroad men who'd stop their train on the tracks just across the street for late-night supper. Breakfast no longer is served; at lunchtime, townsfolk flock here with the gusto of celebrants arriving at a church picnic. Multiple remodelings have created a labyrinth of small dining rooms that can seat over two hundred people.

The menu is an eccentric spectrum of local treasures (peppery Delta tamales, Biloxi flounder, Belzoni catfish) and such saccharine Dixie oddities as pink velvet frozen salad (crushed pineapple, Cool Whip, cherry pie filling, and condensed milk). Proprietor John Ballas said that spaghetti sauce is made from a recipe that his father obtained years ago by writing a letter to Heinz. Our favorite dishes on the menu are shrimp and crab Newburg, fried oysters, turnip greens, and sweet, sweet tea. And pie.

Oh, what pie! Mile-high slices are significantly taller than they are wide, the great meringue triangle on top about twice the height of the ribbon of cream it surmounts. It's an adventure to ease the edge of a fork onto the top of the fluffy white crown and allow nothing more than gravity to carry it through to the filling, where its downward progress slows but doesn't stop. Finally the fork hits lard-laced savory crust that shatters under an ounce of pressure. Not to slight coconut cream, which is fantastic, but chocolate cream is Crystal Grill's crowning glory. It is like Swiss milk chocolate, its creamy soul as prominent as its chocolate flavor. It reminds us of fine chocolate pudding, all the more delicious for being sandwiched between a cloud of delicate meringue and a stratum of meltingly flaky crust.

## Dilworth's Tamales

702 Wick St.          662-665-0833

Corinth, MS          L | $

At $3 per dozen, Dilworth's tamales are a terrific bargain. You actually can eat a dozen, maybe even two dozen if you're hungry, for they are panatela-thin. Wrapped in parchment, they are a simple mixture of beef, cornmeal, and spice steamed in a parchment wrapper long enough to become a single, pleasing chord. Dilworth's sells them hot or mild, the former bright but not incendiary, the latter sheer Miss-Mex comfort.

All business is drive-through, and while your dozen will come well wrapped inside a brown paper bag, we advise being armed with napkins when you open up the butcher paper that contains them.

These tamales have a long history in Corinth. Proprietor Lisa Edmond's father used to ride through town on a three-wheel bike with a large basket, hawking tamales. The house motto is: "Dilworth's Are the Best Yet."

## The Dinner Bell

229 5th Ave.                     601-684-4883
McComb, MS                       www.thedinnerbell.net

L | $$

The Dinner Bell's reputation has gloriously unfurled since it opened in 1945. Now run by the Lopinto family, who took over in 1981, it is the place to go in Mississippi to experience revolving-table dining.

The tables are large and circular, and in the center of each is a lazy Susan that those seated at the circumference can set in motion. It is piled with a lavish array of food. Spin it and take what you want. When a serving tray starts getting empty, out comes a full one from the kitchen. Grab as much as you want and eat at your own speed.

It isn't only quantity and convenience that make Dinner Bell meals memorable. This is marvelous food: chicken and dumplings, catfish, ham, corn sticks, sweet-potato casseroles, black-eyed peas, and fried okra. The dishes we cannot resist are the flamboyant vegetable casseroles and the house specialty, fried eggplant. Spinach casserole enriched with cream cheese and margarine and cans of artichoke hearts is good for the soul . . . not to mention scrumptious. To drink, the right stuff is sweet tea.

## *Doe's Eat Place

502 Nelson                       662-334-3315
Greenville, MS                   www.doeseatplace.com

D | $$$

Located on the wrong side of town in the back rooms of a dilapidated grocery store, Doe's does not look like a restaurant, much less a great restaurant. Its fans love it just the way it is. Mississippians have eaten here since 1941, when segregation was a way of life. Back then, blacks entered through the front door for meals of fried fish and tamales; white patrons came in the back door and ate in the kitchen. Today, many dining tables still are located in the kitchen, spread helter-skelter among stoves and counters where the staff fries potatoes in big iron skillets and dresses salads. Plates, flatware, and tablecloths are all mismatched. Newcomers may be shocked by the ramshackle surroundings, but Doe's is easy to like once the food starts coming.

Begin with tamales and a brilliantly garlicked salad made of iceberg lettuce dressed with olive oil and fresh-squeezed lemon juice. Shrimp are usually available, broiled or fried, and they are very, very good. It is steak, however, for which Doe's has earned its reputation. "Baby Doe" Signa, son of the founder, told us that it is merely "US Choice" grade, which, frankly, we don't believe. Booming with flavor, oozing juice, tender but in no way tenderized, it is the equal or better of any expense-account chain restaurant steak. Choices range from a ten-ounce filet mignon up to a four-pound sirloin. Our personal preference is the porterhouse, the bone of which bisects a couple of pounds of meat that is very different in character on either side of the bone. The tenderloin side is zesty and exciting; the other side seems laden with protein, as deeply satisfying as beef can be. With steak come delicious French fries—dandy to eat "neat," even better when dragged through the oily juices that flow out of steaks onto the plate.

Note: Please do not confuse this great eat place or its family-run sibling in Little Rock with franchised Doe's throughout the South.

## The Elite

| | |
|---|---|
| 141 E. Capitol St. | 601-352-5606 |
| Jackson, MS | BLD \| $ |

Despite its name, the Elite is a restaurant for people of every social class: white-collar downtowners at breakfast, white and blue collars at lunch, whole families and even starry-eyed couples on dates for supper. A Jackson fixture now for one hundred years, it belongs to a little-acknowledged genre of the southern restaurant: the square-meals café with a Greek accent.

Most of what you'll eat is textbook southern-comfort fare: country-fried steaks and veal cutlets with gravy, Delta-style tamales, fried crab claws from the Gulf, Mobile Bay West Indies salad, crisp-fried shrimp, and a choice of vegetables from simple sliced tomatoes to elaborate casseroles. The Elite also offers a selection of Mexican food, including an enchilada plate that Roadfood.com's Bruce Bilmes and Sue Boyle described as "simply as good as it gets: gooey, laced with raw chopped onions, topped with a mantle of orange cheese." Breakfast biscuits are delicate; yeasty dinner rolls are famously good. There is excellent house-made baklava for dessert, but do not ignore the intense lemon chess pie.

## Giardina's

| | |
|---|---|
| 314 Howard St. | 662-455-4227 |
| Greenwood, MS | www.thealluvian.com/restaurants.php |
| | D \| $$$ |

Opened in 1936, Giardina's started as a fish market but soon became a restaurant popular among cotton growers, who dined in private, curtained booths where bootleg booze could be drunk in secrecy. As King Cotton lost its economic hegemony late in the twentieth century, Giardina's fortunes waned, along with those of Greenwood, the South's cotton capital. But then the Viking Range Corporation came to town in 1989 and turned everything around. The Mississippi Heritage Trust Awards that Viking has won for rehabilitation of local properties include the transformation of the historic Irving Hotel from a ratty embarrassment to a stylish boutique hotel called the Alluvian. What we like about the Alluvian, beyond its feather beds, is the fact that it is the new home of Giardina's (pronounced with a hard G).

Giardina's is stylish, modern, and expensive. Service is polished. Tables are outfitted with thick white cloths and snazzy Viking cutlery. The wine collection—stored in state-of-the-art Viking wine cellars—is impressive. And yet for all that, dinner is down-home Delta. You still sit in a private dining compartment. The menu is upscale cotton-country fare, including hefty steaks and elegant pompano, hot tamales, and a bevy of dishes that reflect the powerful influence of Italian immigrants on Greenwood's cuisine. These include garlicky salads and a marvelous appetizer called Camille's bread, which our waiter described as "like a muffuletta but without the meat"—a hot loaf stuffed with olives, sardines, and cheese.

## Hicks'

| | |
|---|---|
| 305 S. State St. | 662-624-9887 |
| Clarksdale, MS | LD \| $ |

"I am sixty-one years old, and I made my first tamales at age sixteen," Eugene Hicks told us years ago when we asked him why the ones he makes are so especially good. Laced with a hard kick of pepper spices, each one is hand-shucked, and they are available by threes, sixes, and twelves. A plate is served with chili and cheese, baked beans, and Italian-seasoned coleslaw.

Tamales are what put Hicks' on the map, but there is a whole menu of ribs, rib tips, and chopped pork shoulder cooked over hickory and topped with house-made sauce. In addition, there are Hicks-made pork sausages, fried catfish, and a "Big Daddy" sandwich that is made with a combination of sliced barbecued pork and smoked turkey.

## Leatha's Bar-B-Que Inn

6374 US Hwy. 98                    601-271-6003
Hattiesburg, MS                   LD | $

There's a sign for Leatha's on Highway 98, but it can be a challenge to see it behind the RV sales lot. In this case, your nose is more useful than your eyes, because if you roll down the windows you will smell it before you see it. The air is threaded by wisps of smoke puffing from the pit located next to a rickety building that is the restaurant.

Beautiful baby-back ribs come heavily painted with warm red sauce. Pulled pork is more lightly glazed, available on a plate or in a sandwich. Side dishes are de rigueur alongside any meat: There are sweet, soupy beans, mustard-powered coleslaw, and potato salad, and if you arrive before it's all sold out, memorable pecan pie. Tea is sweeter than sugar itself.

Everyone we know who has gone to Leatha's comes back raving not only about the food but about the kindness of the staff. Disheveled it may look from the outside, but you will feel extremely well taken care of.

## Lusco's

722 Carrollton Ave.               662-453-5365
Greenwood, MS                     D | $$$

To occupy one of Lusco's backroom private dining booths and to hear the plaint of blues musicians that floats from the sound system above the partitions that segregate each party of diners is a weird and compelling taste of cotton-country history. Planters around Greenwood came to know Charles "Papa" Lusco as a grocer in the 1920s. His wife, Marie "Mama" Lusco, sold plates of her spaghetti at the store, and Papa built secret dining rooms in back where customers could enjoy his homemade wine with their meals.

Mama and Papa were Italian by way of Louisiana, so the flavors of the kitchen they established are as much Creole as they are southern. Gumbo, crab, and shrimp are always on the menu, and oysters are a specialty in season—on the half shell or baked with bacon. The menu is best known for its high-end items. Lusco's T-bone steaks are some of the finest anywhere: sumptuous cuts that are brought raw to the table for your approval, then broiled to pillowy succulence. Pompano has for many years been a house trademark (when available, usually the spring), broiled and served whole, bathed in a magical sauce made of butter, lemon, and secret spices.

Lusco's is also known for its New Orleans–style salad of iceberg lettuce dolled up with anchovies, capers, and olives and liberally sopped in a fragrant vinaigrette; but third-generation Lusco Karen Pinkston is a serious salad buff who has made it her business to concoct more modern alternatives. One evening's choices included Mediterranean salad, made with feta cheese; traditional Caesar salad; and a salad billed as Gourmet Delight, made with arugula, radicchio, endive, red lettuce, and spinach. "Andy [Karen's husband] likes to tease me about that one," Karen said about the latter. "He tells me it's just weeds I've picked by the side of the highway. But the fact is that the Delta is different now than it used to be, and the new people have more educated palates. Even this place has to change with the times."

## Peggy's

| | |
|---|---|
| 512 Bay St. E. | 601-656-3478 |
| Philadelphia, MS | L (closed Monday) \| $ |

Peggy's started in the 1950s as a private home serving lunch to friends and passersby. You helped yourself and put some money in the cigar box. It is now officially a restaurant, but the folksy informality and down-home food scarcely have changed. The place is still an old house, the day's dishes set out on a card table in the hallway near the kitchen, where you grab a plate and dip your own. Chances are good you will share a table with strangers.

There are always a couple of entrees, such as pork chops, baked ham, and chicken and dumplings, but if you come on Tuesday, Wednesday, or Friday, you will have a chance to sample what is Peggy's culinary pennant: fried chicken. It's soulful chicken, with plenty of crunch and juice and chicken fat dripping down your chin when teeth sink into a thigh. Sides are classic Dixie fare: greens, butter beans, vegetable casseroles, corn sticks, and yeast rolls. Desserts include sheet cakes and lemon icebox pie.

Payment for lunch is on the honor system: Put your money in the bowl near the door as you leave.

## Phillips Grocery

| | |
|---|---|
| 541-A E. Van Dorn Ave. | 601-252-4671 |
| Holly Springs, MS | L \| $ |

Located in a two-story wood-frame house that was a saloon in the nineteenth century, Phillips became a grocery store in 1919 and has built its reputation on hamburgers since the 1940s.

The menu is written on a blackboard that lists side dishes, including fresh-from-the-freezer tater tots and morsels of deep-fried, bright-green okra enveloped in a golden crust. Corn nuggets are something special—

bite-sized fritters with lots of kernels packed inside a sweet hush-puppy-like jacket. You can get spicy or regular French fries. And if a MoonPie off the grocery shelf isn't your dish for dessert, Phillips also offers fried pies for a dollar apiece: a folded-over half-circle of dough fried until reddish brown and chewy, enclosing a heavy dollop of sugary peach or apple filling.

Hamburgers are presented wrapped in yellow wax paper. When you peel back the wrapping, particularly on a one-third-pound Phil-Up Burger, you behold a vision of beauty-in-a-bun: a thick patty with a wickedly good crunch to its nearly blackened skin, adorned with two kinds of cheese, bacon and ham, lettuce, tomato, and mayonnaise. The meat itself is smooth-textured and moist enough to ooze juice when you gently squeeze the soft bun wrapped around it. The flavor is fresh, beefy, and sumptuous: an American classic.

## Ramon's

| | |
|---|---|
| 535 Oakhurst St. | 662-624-9230 |
| Clarksdale, MS | D \| $$ |

We thank Roger and Jennifer Stolle, infallible tipsters for all things relating to food and culture in the Mississippi Delta, for taking us to Ramon's. "I wouldn't tell everyone to eat here," Roger said, pointing at the water-damaged acoustical ceiling tiles and explaining that local lore blames a lax landlord for the decomposition that makes the place a bona fide dump. Still, Thomas and Barbara Ely, the couple who run Ramon's, valiantly create a pleasing milieu in the form of empty fifths of Jack Daniel's and three-liter jugs of Taylor Chablis that have been made into decorative lamps, and they serve magnificent butterflied fried shrimp nearly as big as MoonPies. "We were taking bets in the kitchen if y'all would be able to finish," the waitress admitted when we left two of his dozen shrimp uneaten on the plate.

Roger said his favorite thing to eat was a plate of chicken livers and spaghetti. The livers are sensational: unspeakably rich and luxuriously crunchy. They are so filling that we barely forked into the heap of noodles that came alongside them.

## *White Front Cafe

| | |
|---|---|
| 902 Main St. | 662-759-3842 |
| Rosedale, MS | L \| $ |

Joe Pope is gone, but the little wood-frame house still attracts pilgrims from miles around for tamales—the one and only meal on the menu. Many people buy them to take home, but customers are welcome to sit at one of four kitchenette tables in the front room. Order three or four and they are served tightly wrapped in their corn husk. You can eat them one of two ways: pick up a tamale and squeeze out a mouthful of the succulent insides or peel away the husk and use a saltine cracker to scoop some up.

Mr. Pope once told us that he got his recipe from the daughter of John Hooks, who learned how to cook tamales from a Mexican from Texas who traveled through the Delta back in the 1930s. We believe they are some of the very best: all-beef (no pork), a well-nigh perfect blend of meat, cornmeal, and just enough peppery spice to excite but not overwhelm your tongue.

## White Trolley Cafe

1215 Hwy. 72 E.      662-287-4593
Corinth, MS      BL | $

The "slugburger" originally was configured in Corinth, Mississippi, during the first World War. The pint-sized patty, sometimes called a doughburger, was formed by mixing ground beef with potato flakes and flour. At first it was called a Weeksburger because the man who invented it was a diner owner named John Weeks. Over the years, grits have become the meat-extender of choice for the oddball blimpy, which gets deep-fried to a crisp and garnished with mustard, pickle chips, and onions. The name slugburger came about during the Great Depression, when you could buy one for a nickel and the five-cent piece was known as a "slug." The belief that the recipe calls for ground-up garden snails is a culinary canard.

With its dozen counter stools, mostly male clientele, and in-your-face hash-house ambience, the White Trolley Cafe is an ideal place to confront a slug. White Trolley's is thicker than most, with a crust that's tough or—if you ask for yours well done—brutally crunchy. The interior, however it's cooked, is soft but not too juicy. (Many years ago, the custom was to briefly dip the bun in cooking grease, thus adding succulence.) Native Corinthians adore them; for those accustomed to a red-meat hamburger that oozes juice, the slug is a demanding dish. The White Trolley also offers all-beef burgers, but if you don't say beef when you order, you get a slug.

Much business at the White Trolley is takeout, hence it makes sense that the popular dessert is a Mrs. Sullivan's pre-wrapped individual pie—pecan, coconut, or chocolate. Mrs. Sullivan's pies are another old-time inamorata, invented during the Depression in Jackson, Tennessee.

## 82 Queen

82 Queen St.
Charleston, SC

843-723-7591
www.82queen.com
LD | $$$

82 Queen is not typical Roadfood. At a good $50+ per person, maybe it isn't Roadfood at all. But if you want to eat some of the most inspired versions of coastal Carolina's regional specialties, it is a destination to treasure. For instance, there are good versions of shrimp and creamy grits throughout the Lowcountry, but 82 Queen chef Brad Jones enhances the formula by making his with barbecued shrimp—muscular sweeties whose coat of fire is dramatic balance for the earthy grits below. Enriched with cheese, sprinkled with a bounty of crisp bacon pieces and chopped green onions, this is an unforgettably good meal. The same good grits serve as a pedestal for grilled mahimahi, adorned with pumate butter and crisp fried green tomatoes. If you need to wait at the bar for your table, the not-to-be missed plate is fried oysters, little lodes of marine meat encased in crisp, Tabasco-charged crust, served with crushed red pepper marmalade.

A whole section of the menu is devoted to "Lowcountry Specialties": crab cakes with hoppin' John, Frogmore stew (a hearty gallimaufry of shrimp, sausage, corn, okra, and potatoes), and good ol' buttermilk fried chicken served with skillet corn bread and a luxurious portion of mac 'n' cheese. Sunday brunch features a spiced shrimp boil, crab Benedict, French toast casserole, and a BLT that promises a quarter pound of apple-smoked bacon. Desserts include bourbon pecan pie, peach praline cobbler, raspberry glazed Key lime pie, and outrageously indulgent Toll House pie.

## 521 BBQ & Grill

7580 Charlotte Hwy.   803-548-7675
Indian Land, SC    www.521bbqandgrill.com/521bbq
         LD | $

An inconspicuous storefront in a commercial strip by the side of the two-lane, 521 BBQ & Grill is a conspicuously worthy barbecue destination. Not that there's anything wrong with the menu's extra-thick fried bologna sandwich, but it would be a crime to come here and not eat chopped pork and/or ribs. The former—Boston butt that is slow-smoked for fourteen hours—becomes rough-hewn hash that is served sauceless. Please, savor some unadorned forkfuls for full appreciation of the refined synergy of swine and smoke. But then, bring on the sauce. Two kinds are arrayed in squeeze bottles on every table (next to the roll of paper towels): a thin, pepper-powered vinegar dressing that adds an exclamation mark to the flavor, and a thicker, sweeter, and extremely tangy tomato sauce. Both are winners.

The ribs are just about the meatiest baby backs we've ever run across. Huge amounts of juice-sopped meat slide off the bone at the slightest provocation. Like the pork butts, the ribs are slow-smoked so the woodsy flavor of the pit completely insinuates itself into every fiber of the meat. Then they are painted with some of that tangy sauce and grilled until the sauce begins to caramelize and hug the pork.

We haven't yet mentioned what some people consider to be the very best thing on the menu, included on every plate: hush puppies. Irregularly shaped with dark, red-gold skin that offers both crunch and chew, their interiors are moist and sweet-corn sweet, laced with perfumy onion. Neither are the baked beans to be ignored. They fairly vibrate with barbecue zest.

And finally we need to mention the staff: a corps of waitresses who are as much fun as they are efficient, eagerly replacing a couple of hush puppies that accidentally tumbled into the baked beans and taking great joy when a customer is caught licking every bit of sauce off his fingers. In short: If you like barbecue, put 521 on any short list of must-visits in the Carolinas.

## Beacon Drive-In

255 Reidville Rd.         864-585-9387
Spartanburg, SC        www.beacondrivein.com
                              LD | $

Drive-in service at the Beacon is swell, but any newcomer must avail himself of the serving line inside. Here, you enter a fourth dimension of restaurant-going, unlike anywhere else. As you approach the counter, an employee will demand, *"Call it out!"* Give your order quickly, or else stand back and allow other, swifter folks to say their piece. On a good weekend day, the Beacon serves five thousand people.

Once you give an order, it is shouted back to the huge open kitchen, then you are asked in no uncertain terms to *"Move on down the line!"* Grab a tray, and by the time you have moved twenty paces forward, there your order will be—miraculously, exactly as you ordered it, with or without extra barbecue sauce, double bacon on the burger. A bit farther down the line, you get your tea, lemonade, or milk shake and pay the cashier, then find a seat. Total time from entering to digging in—maybe two minutes.

The menu is big, ranging from gizzard plates to banana sandwiches. We recommend Pork A-Plenty, which is chopped and sauced hickory-cooked hot barbecue on a bun that also contains cool coleslaw. The "A-Plenty" designation, applied to burgers and even pimiento cheese sandwiches, indicates the addition of intertwined deep-fried onion rings and French fries. The only correct libation is sweet tea, served in a tall tumbler over crushed ice so cold that gulpers run the risk of brain-freeze headache. The Beacon sells more tea than any other single restaurant in the USA.

## *Bertha's Kitchen

2332 Meeting St. Rd.      843-554-6519
North Charleston, SC     L | $

Bertha's Kitchen, an out-of-the-way, soul-food eatery now in its fourth decade, is small enough that the cafeteria line isn't so much a line as it is a counter where you stand and tell one of the several kitchen staff if you want your pork-rib niblets on rice, which parts of the fried chicken you prefer, and if you're having just lima beans or lima bean dinner. The beans alone are a soupy, khaki-colored side dish. Dinner pairs them with hunks of neck from which weighty nuggets of meat are easily detached by probing with a fork. With the neck, or in place of it to accompany the beans, you also can choose pig tails, which are little more than cylinders of glistening, warm pork fat that melts as it hits your tongue. Who knew a menu item called lima beans could be so mighty a meal?

Beyond those great beans, the menu is a primer in Lowcountry soul food: red rice with sausage, fried chicken encased in fissured red-gold crust, pork chops with meat as wanton as gravy itself, turkey *prileau* (a doppelgänger of pilau), hoppin' John, and mac 'n' cheese with shards of crunchy-chewy crust. Every meal is prepared exactly as you order it. Do you want more pig tails or less in the limas? Will you have red rice, white rice, or hoppin' John—on the side or underneath? How much gravy will you have with your stewed gizzards? For all the precision ordering, meals come on disposable plates and it is difficult for one person to spend more than $10 for a tray-filling feast.

## *Bowens Island

1870 Bowens Island Rd.          843-795-2757
Charleston, SC                  www.bowensislandrestaurant.com
                                D | $$

Bowens Island oysters are hideous to see, all gnarled and splotched with pluff, which is the oysterman's term for the fine silt that is stuck on them when they are harvested and clings to them when they are roasted so that merely touching a cooked cluster will smudge your fingers. Experienced customers, who come for the all-you-can-eat deal ($20+), bring their own oyster-eating gloves. Amateurs, who might eat only a cafeteria tray's worth, are given a clean-looking washcloth, along with a dull knife for prying the shells open (an easy task on roasted oysters) and cutting the meat loose. However you do it, eating pluff is an inevitable part of the meal, and while it has what proprietor Robert Barber calls "a unique stinky smell," it is a good stink, an oceany aroma that adds mineral salubrity to the flavor. On the door of the hut where you go to place your order, a bumper sticker reads "Pluff Mud: The Goo That Holds the Earth Together."

"Most people who aren't from around here think of oysters as cold on the half shell, all wet and slimy," Barber told us. "They've never had them steamed, hot and juicy." The cooking process infuses the meat of the oyster with its own juices, concentrating the flavor, and while it takes nothing away from the sensual mouthfeel of a raw one, the lick of fire adds balmy bliss.

Oysters are the reason to come to Bowens Island, but they are not the whole story. You can eat expertly fried shrimp or fish or hearty Frogmore stew (a Lowcountry slumgullion of sausage, shrimp, corn, and potatoes).

The hush puppies served alongside are among the best anywhere, their dark-red, spherical surface hard and crunchy, their insides creamy rich.

Ambience is fish-camp rough-and-tumble, tables outfitted with holes in the center where you conveniently can throw shells after you have extricated the meat from the inner tidal bivalves that are shoveled onto the table hot from the roaster. (The verb "shovel" is not a metaphor; a garden shovel actually is used to serve the oysters.) The heavy kerplunk of emptied shells is the backbeat of dining at Bowens Island; the melody is the slurp of sucking slippery nuggets of marine meat straight off the oyster knife, then drinking down warm, salty liquor from the shell.

## Carolina BBQ

109 S. Main St.               803-652-2919
New Ellenton, SC              L Weds–Sat; D Thurs–Sat | $

The name Carolina BBQ is the truth, but not the whole truth. This restaurant is *South* Carolina barbecue, faithful to the likings of the south-central area of the Palmetto State. For one thing, it is open only Thursday through Saturday (plus Wednesday lunch); for another, service is buffet-style, all-you-can-eat. While neither trait is unique to South Carolina, both are true of nearly every great South Carolina barbecue. Most important, of course, is the food. This is all-about-the-hog barbecue, featuring a rugged mélange of meat that is smoky and sweetly piggy, ranging from velvet-soft hunks to shreds to crunchy shards. Alongside are trays of white rice and pork hash, the latter a South Carolina favorite comfort food that packs pure pork satisfaction.

And, oh, what side dishes! Most are familiar southern staples: crisp-fried okra; sweet and oniony hush puppies; mac 'n' cheese that is wildly funky-textured, from leathery top to soft elbow noodles stuck with cheese; greens and beans and candied yams. One jaw-dropper is fried squash—a simple dish, just discs of yellow squash that are fried up in a thin, well-seasoned batter, becoming the essence of vegetable with a crisp, warm halo. The big surprise among sides is sweet-potato tater tots, which look something like fried okra but are rolled in sugar, the yam inside the breading melting-soft and sweet. We returned for seconds, then thirds.

At the table, dress the pork with either red barbecue sauce or a true South Carolina mustard sauce that delivers a slow-rolling heat that is just what this subtle-flavored pork wants. Pitchers of iced tea are included with the price of the buffet, which is $9 for anyone ages eleven to sixty, $8.50 for those older, $6.25 for children ages six to ten, and $2.50 for ages three to five. Customers under three years old eat free.

## Charlie's Fish Market

813 Richland Ave. E.
Aiken, SC

803-649-2131
L | $

There are a few tables at Charlie's Fish Market, but hardly anybody eats here. Some come to buy raw fish—bream, whiting, mullet—for cooking at home; others have their fish fried and wrapped, ready to eat. It's a bare, no-frills sort of place with nothing by way of decorative charm, but the cook, Maria Kye, is warm and hospitable, informing us, when we ask her advice, that mullet is definitely the best-tasting of the bunch, so good that she has it almost every day for breakfast.

Mullet it is—two pieces. Maria goes to the case where the fish have been semi-filleted (with easy-to-eat-around bones remaining), picks a couple of hunks, briefly dredges them in cornmeal, then tosses them into a huge black skillet full of boiling oil. While discussing the big pieces of pineapple upside-down cake on the counter, which she says she accidentally made with chocolate cake rather than yellow (how can such an accident occur?), she uses long tongs to poke at the frying mullet and roll it over in the oil, and pretty soon it is done. She hoists out both pieces at once, gives them a quick shake for excess oil to drain, then lays them down on a sheet of butcher paper, which has been placed atop a large page of newsprint. "Mustard?" Yes, indeed. She squirts the fish with zesty yellow sauce. "Hot sauce?" Yes, that, too. Atop the sauced fish go two slices of white bread. The package is gathered up in the butcher paper, then in the newspaper, and it is ready to take to a table, the car dashboard, or somewhere else to eat.

The mullet is oily and unctuous, a very rich fish, but also mild-tasting, scarcely fishy. It is much more about the delectable contrast of creamy meat and crunchy crust than it is about overwhelming flavor. It makes for an extremely messy and very satisfying sandwich. And that chocolate pineapple upside-down cake? We prefer the traditional yellow-cake version, but next time we visit, we'll be happy to eat a few pieces of the chocolate one if Maria has once again made her baking mistake.

## Charlie's Steakhouse

18 Coffee St.
Greenville, SC

864-232-9541
www.charliessteakhouseonline.com
D | $$

Dinner at Charlie's is built upon time-honored rituals that citizens of Greenville (and their parents and grandparents) have come to know and appreciate since 1921: apply-your-own dressing service for salad or slaw, a bottle of Charlie's own steak sauce on every table, thick china plates rimmed with a pattern of magnolias, silver wrapped in thick linen napkins, and tables cushioned so well that highball glasses wobble as you slice into a steak.

The arrival of any steak is a celebratory event, for it comes on a hot metal plate (resting on a wood pallet), sizzling and sputtering so loud that all conversations stop in wonderment. It is nice meat, dense and juicy, although it lacks the delirious beef taste of a good old prime cut. Still, who could resist a menu that boasts "All beef shipped direct from Waterloo & Des Moines, Iowa; St. Joe & Kansas City, Mo"? The roster includes a T-bone, a filet mignon, and a porterhouse for one, but many groups opt for a jumbo sirloin cut into portions for two, three, or four people.

Charlie's is a low-key sort of place—polite, but not overly impressed by itself and not ridiculously overpriced like the national prime-steak chains. Waitresses are friendly as can be but also real pros, constantly positioning and repositioning the dressings, sour cream bowl, bread plate, and butter-pat dish on the table so everything is arrayed for maximum convenience.

## City Billiards

208 Richland Ave.
Aiken, SC

803-649-7362
www.citybilliardsaikensc.com
LD | $

City Billiards' sign boasts of "the best cheeseburger you'll ever eat." If not quite that, it is a mighty good one: velvety ground beef, thickly pattied and griddle-fried, plush enough to ooze rivers of savory juice into a steamed-soft bun, its condiments including mayonnaise, mustard, shredded lettuce, sliced tomato, and onions. Eighteen different burgers are listed on the menu, including ones topped with blue cheese or jalapeño cheese, with bacon or mushrooms or barbecue sauce or Jamaican jerk seasoning. We haven't tried the oddities but can vouch for the basic cheeseburger.

You also can get chili on your burger, which we find redundant, since it is a thick, beefy chili. But this same chili is the star ingredient in what may not be the best chili dog you'll ever eat, but one that will give the best of them a run for the money. The sauce, which the menu touts as "made from a 50-year-old recipe," is dense, sweet, and spicy, pairing beautifully with cheese, chopped raw onions, and yellow mustard. (Coleslaw is another good optional topping.) The dog itself is a blubbery pale pink one. At first sight of it, you might wish for a better class of wiener, but a fancy frank would be as wrong here as Luciano Pavarotti covering the Dead Kennedys. Its pallid cheapness is an ideal palette for the pyrotechnics that go atop it. The bun, too, is soft and squishy; an artisan roll would be sacrilege.

## Dave's Carry-Out

| | |
|---|---|
| 42 Morris St. | 843-577-7943 |
| Charleston, SC | LD \| $ |

Not to disregard Tuesday's jumbo turkey wings and red rice or Thursday's melting-tender Cornish hen with hoppin' John, but it is Dave's everyday shrimp that must be eaten. These taut pink crescents are veiled in a film of elegant crunch reminiscent of the legendary frying done by the long-gone Edisto Motel. It is hypnotic to watch the cook bread them one by one, then toss them into a fry basket that gets dropped into hot oil above the pieces of fish and pork chop that sizzle down below. Yes, everything goes into the same soup and comes out with its own flavor—pork, fish, chicken—complicated by a multi-flavored zest that is the hallmark of Lowcountry cooking.

Dave's is a tiny corner storefront with only two tables for eating on premises and a reputation for staying open long into the morning when everything else in town has closed. A few years ago it moved from its original oil-saturated disreputable location to the current corner storefront, which is freshly painted and shipshape. While purists bemoan the cultural elevation, the current Dave's is a restaurant where anyone will feel welcome, any time of night. As the name suggests, it is designed mostly for the takeout trade. Still, when it's crowded, as it inevitably is late at night, you can wait up to an hour for your food to be cooked and plated (in Styrofoam). Everything is cooked to order, order by order.

## Dukes

| | |
|---|---|
| 4248 Whiskey Rd. | 803-649-7675 |
| Aiken, SC | LD Thurs–Sat \| $ |

There are Dukes barbecues throughout South Carolina's Midlands and Lowcountry, named for the Dukes family that opened the first of them in the 1950s. None are part of any sort of chain, but they all specialize in the barbecue meal that has become a culinary signature of the Palmetto State: the grand, hog-centered, all-you-can-eat buffet.

Pulled pork is a dazzling jumble of light and dark, soft and chewy meat that is slightly smoky and intensely piggy. It is wonderful with no adornment whatsoever, but South Carolina mustard sauce, bright and tangy-sweet, is oh-so-right. The buffet line includes a pan that is full of fried chicken parts, freshly fried extra-thick potato chips, and lots of little squiggles and ribbons of fried chicken skin that really do melt in your mouth.

Among the more than two dozen available side dishes are rice and hash (a savory pork-products stew), squash casserole, macaroni with yummy cheese impasto, hush puppies, fried okra, and deep-fried corn nuggets. Beyond the buffet is a separate table that holds white bread and a bin full of cracklins—large and small, chewy and melty, indescribably piggy. For dessert, choose from among warm peach cobbler that is as dense as bread pudding, cool banana pudding streaked with cookie crumbs, and that seldom-seen legacy of the 1970s, Watergate salad, which is a Frankenstein-green pistachio pudding that includes mini marshmallows and pineapple.

Dukes' phone number, by the way, can be dialed as 803-649-PORK.

### Ernie's

64 Spring St.                      843-723-8591
Charleston, SC                     L | $

Charleston is filled with restaurants that are famous, most of them deserving the acclaim. It also has a number of superb eateries that aren't famous but are treasured by locals as sources of four-star soul food. Ernie's is one of the greats, well known enough to regulars that there is no sign outside.

One of the most satisfying low-cost meals anywhere is Ernie's lima bean dinner, a huge presentation that arrives on one plate (for rice) and in two bowls, one for beans, the other for an impossible amount of brick-red neck-bone meat dripping with hammy flavor. Cost: $6. Ernie's offers both okra soup and okra soup *dinner,* the latter poured over rice and supplemented by great chunks of meat. This soup has a dense vegetable flavor that is at once hugely satisfying and salubrious. Even the white rice that accompanies Ernie's fine fried chicken isn't plain: It is laced with soft wisps of cooked onion, it glistens with chicken fat, and bristles with grains of hot pepper.

A few other items that are favorites: turkey wings (gargantuan), turkey necks either as a dinner or simply with rice, gizzards, red rice with pork chops, hoppin' John, and huge, heavy hunks of stupendous bread pudding.

## Evo

1075 E. Montague Ave.        843-225-1796
North Charleston, SC         evopizza.com
                             LD | $$

While the Palmetto State is not famous as a source of great pizza, Lowcountry cooks are famously talented. And Evo—an acronym for "extra-virgin oven"—is evidence that those creative juices combined with local products and a wood-fired oven can equal outstanding pizza.

But before we get to the pizza, may we dally at hors d'oeuvres? . . . There's a peak-of-summer panzanella salad, starring big chunks of boomingly delicious heirloom tomatoes and significant house-made croutons along with pickled red onion, crumbles of creamy local blue cheese, and basil, all dressed with bright balsamic vinaigrette. For a simpler starter, you can get something called an olive plate. It is more than a plate. It is a big, fragrant bowlful of black and green ones—many dozens—along with a bunch of whole garlic cloves that have been roasted until they are soft and sweet, the gorgeous cornucopia marinated in oil rich with basil.

Now, about the pizza. Cooked briefly in a roaring wood-fired oven, it comes out with a crust that is thin and lightweight, easy to chew. Toppings range from basic margherita to such inventions as pistachio pesto topped with mozzarella (made here daily) and just enough crème fraîche to elevate the eating experience into wanton excess. We have enjoyed a special of locally made feta along with fresh okra and a purée of roasted garlic and corn as well as the oh-so-southern "pork trifecta" of house-made sausage, pepperoni, and smoked bacon.

For dessert, it is hard not to indulge in a sampler of Sweet Teeth brand chocolates (made by a former employee) that includes a salted caramel heart and a peach cobbler bonbon; but you should also consider reserving a significant amount of appetite for the outsized blueberry calzone—a pocket of pizza dough filled with dark chocolate melting around local blueberries and drizzled with South Carolina honey.

## Fishnet Seafood

3832 Savannah Hwy.          843-571-2423
Johns Island, SC            LD | $

A fundamental rule for finding good things to eat while traveling is to look for restaurants located in former gas stations. We don't know why, but they're some of the best Roadfood stops. To wit: Fishnet Seafood. It isn't really a restaurant at all; it is a fish market with no tables, not even provisions for stand-up eating. But if you point to just about any fish in the house, the staff will bread it and fry it to order, and in this part of coastal South Carolina, cooks know how to fry things. Flounder is particularly wonderful, sheathed in a brittle gold crust, its sweet white meat dripping moisture. If you order it as a sandwich, you get one huge, falling-apart-tender fillet with two token slices of white bread: finger food, for sure!

Another fine dish is Jesus crab, which is the management's name for what other places refer to as devil crab. A woman behind the counter explained that the dish was simply too good to be named for the prince of darkness. Indeed, Fishnet is a very religious place, its décor featuring signs reminding guests of Jesus's ultimate importance. We've seen a lot of barbecues where religion is a fundamental aspect of the dining experience, but not so many seafood places. This is one where the original fisher of men is the star of the menu.


## *Hominy Grill

207 Rutledge St.            843-937-0930
Charleston, SC             www.hominygrill.com
                          BLD | $$

Our first meal at the Hominy Grill was breakfast, and it was spectacular. The sausage patties that came alongside our sunnyside-up eggs were rugged and crusty and brilliantly spiced—a joy when pushed through some yolk or sandwiched inside a tall biscuit. Bacon was excellent too—double-thick, crisp, and full-flavored, just begging to be cosseted in that biscuit or eaten in alternating mouthfuls of smooth-textured grits. A great breakfast option, even if a bit biscuit-redundant, is house-made bread, either pumpkin-ginger or banana-nut, both of which are moist, full-flavored, and elegant.

We were equally impressed when we returned for lunch and plowed into thick shrimp gumbo and Brunswick stew. We love the distinctly southern BLT made with crunchy discs of fried green tomato. Buttermilk pie is the perfect dessert, surpassed only by what we both agree is the best chocolate pudding anywhere. And did we mention caramel layer cake, the hugely wonderful Charleston fave?

The Hominy Grill building was at one time a barber shop, and striped poles still flank the inside of the front door. It's a spacious room with an old stamped tin ceiling, wood-slat walls, and slow-spinning fans overhead. There also is an outdoor patio. You can expect to wait for a table, especially on weekends. It is no secret that this place serves some of the best Lowcountry food anywhere, and at very reasonable prices.

## Hyman's Seafood

213 Meeting St.
Charleston, SC

843-723-6000
www.hymanseafood.com
LD | $$

What we didn't eat one evening at Hyman's Seafood: amberjack, cod, flounder, mahi, mako, monkfish, snapper, hokie, salmon, tilapia, trout, tuna, and black drum. Those were the fish of the day on the blackboard, and below them were grouper, stuffed wahoo, and fried lobster tails, which we didn't sample either. Local oysters were coming in and available on the half shell or fried, and we didn't even have appetite enough for them. The point is that Hyman's has a big, big menu—mostly seafood, with a few token meats and pastas—and it's a little frustrating to pass up so many good things.

What we *did* have was swell: she-crab soup that is ridiculously thick, rich as cream sauce itself and loaded with meat; a broad dish with thirty steamed spiced shrimp; and a house specialty, crispy flounder. This is one large, beautiful fish that has been scored in a diamond pattern and broiled so the fork-sized sections of meat get a crusty edge and seem to virtually lift off the bone: one of the East Coast's top fish-eating experiences.

Hyman's is a tremendously popular place, frequented by tourists and locals alike. If you're looking for a romantic restaurant or an undiscovered hole in the wall, Charleston and vicinity have plenty, but for large-party ambience and impeccable local seafood, Hyman's is a good choice.

## Martha Lou's Kitchen

1068 Morrison Dr.
Charleston, SC

843-577-9583
BLD | $

We have driven past Martha Lou's Kitchen a few times when it was supposed to be open, but was not, so we suggest calling ahead. Persistence will pay off, for this place is a gem in the rough. The word "casual" doesn't begin to describe how casual it is. The window air-conditioning unit is propped up by a pepper dispenser; framed encomia from the press hung helter-skelter on the walls have not recently been dusted; a television is tuned to an evangelical station to which no one pays attention. And yet Debra Gadsden, who runs the place with her mother, Martha Lou, greets customers with genuine hospitality offered by few formal maître d's.

Debra guides newcomers through a menu that includes fried chicken every day and such specials as fried fish, pork chops, ribs, and chitterlings. Sides are Lowcountry paragons: mac 'n' cheese, red rice and white rice, collard greens, lima beans, okra soup, and corn bread.

Subtlety is not Martha Lou's culinary signature. Everything she cooks is boldly flavored. Even iced tea is supersweet and superlemony. Mac 'n' cheese is less comfort food than exciting food, the creamy cheese vibrant with pepper punch. The crust on fried chicken and fish is big-flavored salty; okra soup smacks you with a one-two punch of tomatoes and okra. Bread pudding, chockablock with fruit cocktail, is as sweet as candy.

We liked our first lunch in this place so much that we returned the next day. Debra offered suggestions of what we ought to eat so that we would get a full taste of her mother's skills, and she led us to one of the other tables so that this day's meal would provide a fresh point of view.


## Middleton Place Restaurant

4300 Ashley River Rd.          843-556-6020
Charleston, SC                 www.middletonplace.org
                               LD | $$$

It costs a lot of money to have lunch at the Middleton Place Restaurant: You easily can spend $20 for the food, plus you will pay $25 just to get on the grounds where the restaurant is located. It is part of a vast interpretive environment built on the plantation that once was the home of Henry Middleton, president of the First Continental Congress. If you have a taste for Colonial history, the cost of admission is money well spent, providing access to sweeping terraces, gardens, walks, and artificial lakes that proffer beauty from a bygone age. Attractions include "Eliza's House," a freedman's dwelling that shows what life was like for African Americans who stayed on the plantation after the Civil War, and the stable yards where blacksmiths, potters, and coopers demonstrate their eighteenth-century skills. Mounted trail rides (right past sneaky-looking alligators) are available at the nearby Equestrian Center, and the mansion itself is full of priceless antique furniture.

The restaurant is very much part of the effort to honor the Lowcountry's cultural heritage. When it opened as a tearoom run by the Junior League in 1928, its specialties were okra soup and sandwiches. In more recent times, southern cook Edna Lewis came on board with recipes that provide a sampler of beguiling southern specialties. We don't know any other restaurant in town that continues to serve Charleston's own Huguenot torte, a sticky-gooey apple dessert that is something like cobbler, but more intense. Peanut soup, thickened with sweet potatoes, is smooth and smoky, the earthy duet becoming a single note rather than two. Even the more ordinary dishes tend to be extraordinarily good. Fried chicken is hugged by thin buttermilk batter that is radiant with spice, its skin succulence incarnate. Greens are totally tender, not limp but pungent with tonic punch. Pulled-pork barbecue—smoke-cooked on premises—has simple authenticity that puts it right up there with South Carolina's best.

The dining room overlooks green grass and grazing sheep.

## Scott's Bar-B-Que

| | |
|---|---|
| 2734 Hemingway Hwy. | 843-558-0134 |
| Hemingway, SC | www.thescottsbbq.com |
| | LD \| $ |

Whole-hog pork, cooked all night over smoldering oak and hickory coals, is pulled into shreds and served with hunks of pig skin and servings of peppery, just-barely-sweet sauce for dipping. Two kinds of skin are available—either fried to a crisp or stripped off the hog, the latter as chewy as they are crunchy. White bread comes alongside, and you can get boiled peanuts for munching. Chicken and steak, also slow-smoked, are sometimes available.

Founded in 1972 by Ella and Rosie (short for Roosevelt) Scott, and now presided over by the Scotts' son, Rodney, this much-loved local place was anointed as authentic by the national press a few years ago and thereafter declared itself world-famous. Add to the fame Scott's proximity to Myrtle Beach and the result is big crowds, especially on weekends. Tourists notwithstanding, the meal on the plate and the place itself are the real deal.

## SeeWee Restaurant

| | |
|---|---|
| 4808 US 17 N. | 843-928-3609 |
| Awendaw, SC | B (only Sat); LD \| $$ |

A former grocery north of Charleston along US 17, SeeWee is now a hugely popular restaurant that includes an outdoor patio for alfresco dining. It still looks a bit like a roadside store—shelves stocked with supplies, higgledy-piggledy décor of nautical bibelots.

Daily specials are chalked up on a board: country-fried steak, whole catfish, Jamaican jerk chicken, Buffalo shrimp or oysters (fried in a spicy Buffalo-wing style), fish stew by the cup or bowl. We are partial to the regular menu and its roster of fried seafood. You can get a platter or a sandwich with very good extra-large French fries and coleslaw on the side. Our shrimp were snapping-firm and veiled in a fine, crisp crust.

One of the great only-in-the-South meals to get here is an all-"vegetable" plate. Choose four from a list of more than a dozen available, including such local likes as red rice, butter beans, fried squash, fried okra, and rice and gravy. We went for fried green tomatoes (deliciously al dente with a tangy smack), sweet-potato casserole (super spicy), mac 'n' cheese (dense and thick with cheese), and collard greens (salty, oily, luxurious).

As you walk into the restaurant you will see a shelf of the day's layer cakes, and desserts are listed on a blackboard. When we saw chocolate cake with peanut butter icing, we knew we had to have a piece. So we ordered it as we ordered lunch. The cake came before the meal. "I cut this for you because I was worried there wouldn't be any left by the time you were ready," our waitress kindly explained as she set it down with our sweet teas. We are so grateful she was watching out for us, because this cake was superb . . . as was our caramel layer cake and goober pie.

No bill arrives after the meal. When you're done eating, the waitress will instruct you to go up to the cash register and tell the man your table number. He's got your check and will tally it up and get you squared away.

## Sgt. White's

1908 Boundary St.     843-522-2029
Beaufort, SC       LD | $

Upon entering this little restaurant, you are faced with the steam table from which the server puts together your plate. While it is possible to order off a menu—and the fried chicken and shrimp therefrom are excellent—we cannot resist the array of barbecue and side dishes in the trays. You get either pulled pork, which is a medley of velvet-soft shreds from inside and crunchy strips from the outside of the roast bathed in the Sergeant's brilliant tangy-sweet sauce, or ribs, which are crusty and unspeakably luscious, also caked with the good sauce. Each side dish is a super-soulful rendition of a southern classic: smothered cabbage richer than ham itself, broccoli gobbed with cheese, brilliantly seasoned red rice, a vivid mix of collard and turnip greens, *real* mashed potatoes, candied yams, and so on. A normal meal is one meat and two sides, served with a block of corn bread. Even that corn bread is extraordinary: rugged-textured and sweet as cake.

## Shealy's Bar-B-Que

340 E. Columbia Ave.          803-532-8135
Leesville, SC                 www.shealysbbq.com
                              LD (closed Weds & Sun) | $

We found out about Shealy's thanks to tipster Paul McCravy, who wrote that "the vegetables surpass any I've had at the three family reunions I attend each year in Pickens County." Greens and beans, boiled, fried, and mashed, served plain and in elaborate casseroles, the array of vegetables is awesome. And they are merely the side dishes to outstanding fried chicken with cream gravy, including pulley bones for those who are feeling lucky.

For us, the main attraction is pork barbecue, which is presented at the buffet with all the folderol of a traditional South Carolina barbecue feast, meaning you will find just about every part of the pig from the rooter to the tooter. That includes meat, ribs, hash, skin, gravy, and a rather bizarre creamy/spicy mush apparently quite popular in these parts known as liver nips. Of special interest on the tender shreds of smoked pork is Shealy's sauce (available by the bottle), an alluring mustard-tinged sweet-and-sour condiment unique to the South Carolina Midlands.

## Summerton Diner

33 Church St.                 803-485-6835
Summerton, SC                 BLD (closed Thurs) | $

Since Lois Hughes opened it for business in 1967, this little café on the outskirts of town has been a favorite of locals and a beacon for travelers along I-95. After Lois's daughter Lynelle Blackwell took over in 1987, she enlarged and remodeled it, but the diner has the feel of an ageless eatery: well-worn Formica counter, blond wood-paneled walls, each table set with bottles of hot vinegar peppers for brightening up orders of collard greens.

There's a full menu, and such items as fried chicken or steak and quail are always available, but at lunchtime the thing to order is the special. For well under $10, you get an entree, three vegetables, dessert, and tea, plus corn bread and biscuits. We love baked chicken supreme, which is crusty and fallapart tender; the waitress asks if you want white or dark meat. Like all entrees, it comes on a partitioned plate along with two of the vegetables. (The third vegetable comes in its own bowl.) As you might expect in a true-South café such as this, the side dishes are superb: earthy fresh rutabagas, spicy stewed apples, porky sweet greens with an al dente oomph to their leaves, mashed potatoes blanketed in gorgeous, beef-shred gravy, hefty blocks of mac 'n' cheese with crusty edges and creamy insides, rice infused with soulful gravy. Et cetera!

## Track Kitchen

420 Mead Ave.                  803-641-9628
Aiken, SC                      B (closed in summer) | $

To the side of a rutted red-dirt road, Track Kitchen is a café in an old wood-frame building. It barely looks open for business. Inside, the menu is written with marking pen on a board above the order counter and tables are unceremoniously lined up like in a mess hall. If you want coffee, go back to the kitchen, grab a mug, and pour your own. Into this extremely humble dining room come trainers, riders, owners, and aficionados of some of the finest horseflesh on Earth. Aiken has long been a vacation destination for the horsey set—until 1954 train service direct from New York served wintering horses, horse owners, and their staff—and this is where a large number of them come for breakfast. If you get here much after 8 a.m., when it opens, most seats will be occupied by people who all seem to know one another and table-hop continuously.

Everybody is friends with Carol Carter, who runs the place with her husband, Pockets. (Pockets used to be a groom for King Ranch horses.) Carol commands the kitchen and does all the cooking. There is no fast food here: Service is deliberate, and you can be sure that each plate that comes from the kitchen is scrupulously prepared. Even the simplest meal of bacon and over-easy eggs gleams with that buttery, good-cook luster that makes the yolks taste extra sunny and the baked bacon break just right. Pancakes are fluffy, omelets are cooked through but never dried out, and country ham is a big, fibrous slab that requires (and rewards) serious chewing.

The restaurant is named because about twenty-five yards behind it is a training track where thoroughbreds are exercised. If you like watching these athletes work out, it's a great bonus of eating here.

## True BBQ

1237 D Ave.                    803-791-9950
West Columbia, SC              www.true-bbq.com
                               LD | $

The sign outside advertises "Best hash & rice in SC." If that claim is accurate, True BBQ probably could boast of the best hash and rice on Earth, since South Carolina is the only state where hash and rice is a common and significant menu item at nearly every place that slow-smokes swine. It is a side dish that comes with just about every meal: white rice topped with a finely chopped gravy made from the lowlier parts of the hog, but in some ways the most deliciously piggy—slightly sweet, a little bit tangy, a seductive food that both appeases and teases the appetite.

Along with the likes of collard greens, mac 'n' cheese, and baked beans, hash and rice is just one companion to well-crafted meats cooked in a smoker right in front of the restaurant. Available in large and small sizes, dinner choices include baby-back ribs and spare ribs, hacked-up pork, chicken, pork chops, and turkey wings. No matter which meat you get, we suggest first tasting it as it comes. It needs no sauce. On the other hand, the three sauces True BBQ serves are intriguing: Sexy Lady, which is tomato-based; Pretty Lady, which has a mustard twang; and Vinegar Red.

## Wild Flour Pastry

73 Spring St.  
Charleston, SC

843-327-2621  
www.wildflourpastrycharleston.com  
BL | $

Roadfood pathfinders Chris Ayers and Amy Breisch told us that the one thing we mustn't miss when visiting Wild Flour Pastry was the sticky bun. We *did* miss it because baker Lauren Mitterer makes sticky buns only on Sunday. But after morning visits on Wednesday and Thursday, we hardly feel deprived. We ate what may be the best turnover anywhere—a fine, flaky pastry, served warm, radiant with butter flavor, and filled with a mix of Nutella and fresh raspberries. Lauren's coffee cake muffin is packed with crunchy pecan halves; her raspberry scone strikes an ideal biscuity balance of savory and sweet; and her red velvet cupcake should be a lesson for lesser bakers who try their hand at the red velvet fad but wind up with duds.

Traveling gourmands intent on tasting the most different dishes will love Wild Flour because so many of the specialties are offered in single-serving sizes. Not just cupcakes and morning pastries, but lemon chess tarts, Key lime pies, milk chocolate crème brûlée, and passion-fruit pot de crème. Lauren's whole repertoire is not available every day, but count on enough selections to sate the most voracious appetite.

## The Wreck

106 Haddrell Pt.         843-884-0052
Mount Pleasant, SC   www.wreckrc.com
                             D | $$

The docks at Shem Creek in Mount Pleasant, just north of the city, are lined with seafood restaurants, all quite pleasant-looking and with similar shoreline menus; but if you meander farther along the water, out Live Oak Road to Haddrell Point, you will find a Roadfood jewel in the rough. And we do mean *find,* for the restaurant known as the Wreck (formally named the Wreck of the Richard and Charlene, for a boat hit by Hurricane Hugo) has no sign outside, and we also mean *in the rough,* for it is located in a former bait locker, and décor is mostly piles of cardboard beer cartons. Seats are plastic lawn chairs at tables clothed with fish-wrapping paper (but romantically lit by candles at night). If the weather is cool, you are warmed by a couple of fireplaces in the concrete-floored dining room. The view of docked shrimp trawlers couldn't be more appetizing. And the food is impeccable.

Place your order by using a marking pen to circle what you want on the paper menu. Meals begin with a bowl of soft-boiled peanuts. She-crab soup is served in the traditional manner with a shot of sherry to pour on top just before spooning in. Then come crunchy fried shrimp, scallops, oysters, or broiled fish accompanied by zesty slaw and tubular hush puppies. Depending on your appetite, you can get a meal either "Richard-sized" (copious) or "Charlene-sized" (normal portion). Everything is presented on cardboard plates with plastic utensils; beer comes in the bottle. Dessert is a choice of Key lime pie, Key lime bread pudding, or banana pudding.

If you are a fish frowner, the Wreck offers London broil. However, the menu warns, "This is a seafood house claiming no expertise in the preparation of red meat. So, when you order red meat it is yours . . . No returns!!!!!"

# Midwest

Illinois

✳

Indiana

✳

Iowa

✳

Michigan

✳

Minnesota

✳

Missouri

✳

Ohio

✳

Wisconsin

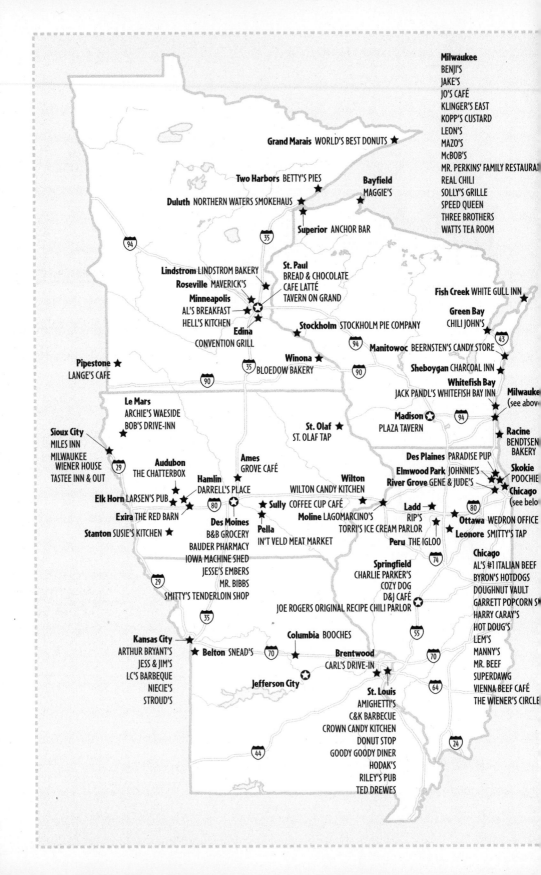

**Milwaukee**
BENJI'S
JAKE'S
JO'S CAFÉ
KLINGER'S EAST
KOPP'S CUSTARD
LEON'S
MAZO'S
McBOB'S
MR. PERKINS' FAMILY RESTAURA...
REAL CHILI
SOLLY'S GRILLE
SPEED QUEEN
THREE BROTHERS
WATTS TEA ROOM

**Grand Marais** WORLD'S BEST DONUTS ★

**Two Harbors** BETTY'S PIES

**Bayfield**
MAGGIE'S

**Duluth** NORTHERN WATERS SMOKEHAUS

**Superior** ANCHOR BAR

**Lindstrom** LINDSTROM BAKERY
**Roseville** MAVERICK'S

**St. Paul**
BREAD & CHOCOLATE
CAFE LATTÉ
TAVERN ON GRAND

**Fish Creek** WHITE GULL INN

**Minneapolis**
AL'S BREAKFAST
HELL'S KITCHEN

**Green Bay**
CHILI JOHN'S

**Edina**
CONVENTION GRILL

**Stockholm** STOCKHOLM PIE COMPANY

**Manitowoc** BEERNSTEN'S CANDY STORE

**Winona** ★
BLOEDOW BAKERY

**Sheboygan** CHARCOAL INN

**Pipestone** ★
LANGE'S CAFE

**Whitefish Bay**
JACK PANDL'S WHITEFISH BAY INN

**Milwauke**
(see abov...

**Le Mars**
ARCHIE'S WAESIDE
BOB'S DRIVE-INN

**St. Olaf** ★
ST. OLAF TAP

**Madison** ✪
PLAZA TAVERN

**Sioux City**
MILES INN
MILWAUKEE
WIENER HOUSE
TASTEE INN & OUT

**Racine**
BENDTSEN'S
BAKERY

**Audubon**
THE CHATTERBOX

**Ames**
GROVE CAFÉ

**Des Plaines** PARADISE PUP

**Elmwood Park** JOHNNIE'S
**River Grove** GENE & JUDE'S

**Skokie**
POOCHIE'

**Hamlin**
DARRELL'S PLACE

**Wilton**
WILTON CANDY KITCHEN

**Chicago**
(see belo...

**Elk Horn** LARSEN'S PUB ★

★ **Sully** COFFEE CUP CAFÉ

**Ladd** ★
RIP'S

**Exira** THE RED BARN

**Moline** LAGOMARCINO'S
TORRI'S ICE CREAM PARLOR

**Ottawa** WEDRON OFFICE

**Stanton** SUSIE'S KITCHEN ★

**Pella**
IN'T VELD MEAT MARKET

**Leonore** SMITTY'S TAP

**Des Moines**
B&B GROCERY
BAUDER PHARMACY
IOWA MACHINE SHED
JESSE'S EMBERS
MR. BIBBS
SMITTY'S TENDERLOIN SHOP

**Peru** THE IGLOO

**Springfield**
CHARLIE PARKER'S
COZY DOG
D&J CAFÉ
JOE ROGERS ORIGINAL RECIPE CHILI PARLOR

**Chicago**
AL'S #1 ITALIAN BEEF
BYRON'S HOTDOGS
DOUGHNUT VAULT
GARRETT POPCORN S...
HARRY CARAY'S
HOT DOUG'S
LEM'S
MANNY'S
MR. BEEF
SUPERDAWG
VIENNA BEEF CAFÉ
THE WIENER'S CIRCLE

**Kansas City**
ARTHUR BRYANT'S
JESS & JIM'S
LC'S BARBEQUE
NIECIE'S
STROUD'S

**Columbia** BOOCHES

★ **Belton** SNEAD'S

**Brentwood**
CARL'S DRIVE-IN

**Jefferson City** ✪

**St. Louis**
AMIGHETTI'S
C&K BARBECUE
CROWN CANDY KITCHEN
DONUT STOP
GOODY GOODY DINER
HODAK'S
RILEY'S PUB
TED DREWES

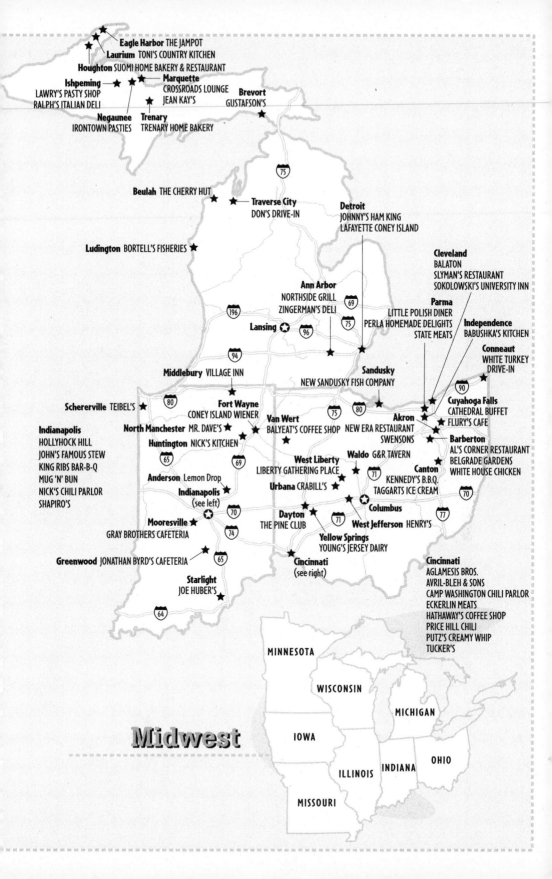

**Eagle Harbor** THE JAMPOT
**Laurium** TONI'S COUNTRY KITCHEN
**Houghton** SUOMI HOME BAKERY & RESTAURANT
**Ishpeming**
LAWRY'S PASTY SHOP
RALPH'S ITALIAN DELI
**Marquette**
CROSSROADS LOUNGE
JEAN KAY'S
**Brevort**
GUSTAFSON'S
**Negaunee** **Trenary**
IRONTOWN PASTIES TRENARY HOME BAKERY

**Beulah** THE CHERRY HUT
**Traverse City**
DON'S DRIVE-IN
**Detroit**
JOHNNY'S HAM KING
LAFAYETTE CONEY ISLAND

**Cleveland**
BALATON
SLYMAN'S RESTAURANT
SOKOLOWSKI'S UNIVERSITY INN

**Ludington** BORTELL'S FISHERIES

**Ann Arbor**
NORTHSIDE GRILL
ZINGERMAN'S DELI
**Parma**
LITTLE POLISH DINER
PERLA HOMEMADE DELIGHTS
STATE MEATS
**Independence**
BABUSHKA'S KITCHEN

**Lansing**

**Conneaut**
WHITE TURKEY
DRIVE-IN

**Middlebury** VILLAGE INN
**Sandusky**
NEW SANDUSKY FISH COMPANY

**Schererville** TEIBEL'S
**Fort Wayne**
CONEY ISLAND WIENER
**Van Wert**
BALYEAT'S COFFEE SHOP
**Akron**
NEW ERA RESTAURANT
SWENSONS
**Cuyahoga Falls**
CATHEDRAL BUFFET
FLURY'S CAFE

**North Manchester** MR. DAVE'S
**Huntington** NICK'S KITCHEN
**Waldo** G&R TAVERN
**Barberton**
AL'S CORNER RESTAURANT
BELGRADE GARDENS
WHITE HOUSE CHICKEN

**Indianapolis**
HOLLYHOCK HILL
JOHN'S FAMOUS STEW
KING RIBS BAR-B-Q
MUG 'N' BUN
NICK'S CHILI PARLOR
SHAPIRO'S

**Anderson** Lemon Drop
**West Liberty**
LIBERTY GATHERING PLACE
**Urbana** CRABILL'S
**Canton**
KENNEDY'S B.B.Q.
TAGGARTS ICE CREAM

**Indianapolis**
(see left)

**Columbus**

**Mooresville**
GRAY BROTHERS CAFETERIA
**Dayton**
THE PINE CLUB
**West Jefferson** HENRY'S

**Greenwood** JONATHAN BYRD'S CAFETERIA
**Yellow Springs**
YOUNG'S JERSEY DAIRY

**Starlight**
JOE HUBER'S
**Cincinnati**
(see right)
**Cincinnati**
AGLAMESIS BROS.
AVRIL-BLEH & SONS
CAMP WASHINGTON CHILI PARLOR
ECKERLIN MEATS
HATHAWAY'S COFFEE SHOP
PRICE HILL CHILI
PUTZ'S CREAMY WHIP
TUCKER'S

MINNESOTA

WISCONSIN

MICHIGAN

**Midwest**

IOWA

ILLINOIS INDIANA OHIO

MISSOURI

## Al's #1 Italian Beef

1079 W. Taylor St.

Chicago, IL

312-733-8896

www.alsbeef.com

LD | $

Al's, which claims to have invented the Chicago Italian beef sandwich, started as Al's Bar-B-Q in old Little Italy with no seats for dining, just waist-high counters along the wall. Some thirty years ago *Chicago* magazine named it the city's best beef, at which point it became Al's #1 Italian Beef. In 1999, Chicago Franchise Systems got involved and there now are more than a dozen around the city, as well as branches as far as California. The original Al's is especially worth visiting because it is directly across the street from Mario's Italian Ice.

Al's sandwich is thin-sliced, gravy-sopped, garlic-charged beef piled into a chewy length of Italian bread. You can ask for big beef (about twice as much) or have your sandwich double-dipped, which means totally immersed in a pan of natural gravy so the bread is soaked through. "Beef with hot" is a request for the relish known as *giardiniera,* an eye-opening garden mélange of finely chopped marinated vegetables, capers, and spice that is roast beef's perfect complement. "With sweet" is what you say if you prefer the popular alternative to *giardiniera:* big, tender flaps of roasted green bell pepper with a charcoal taste.

"Combo!" or "Half and half!" is a call for a sandwich that contains not only beef but also a plump, four-inch length of Italian sausage, retrieved from the appetizing haze that hovers over the hot metal grate just behind the order counter. Taut-skinned, succulent, and well spiced, the sausage is itself a major lure for many customers who sidestep beef altogether and order double-sausage sandwiches, hot or sweet.

## Byron's Hotdogs

1017 W. Irving Park Rd.
Chicago, IL

773-281-7474
www.byronshd.com
LD | $

As plump Polish sausages sizzle on the grill, the counterman dips a ladle into the fryolator to get some hot fat to pour over the grilling tube steaks. The grease helps give them a blackened, crisp skin; it also produces a look of glistening, sinfully swollen plumpness. These are some of the burliest Polish sausages in a city where Polish sausages, along with their all-beef brothers, hot dogs, are matters of serious culinary consideration. If you are a Polish sausage fanatic, it isn't likely you will be blasé about the big, charred tubes they serve up at Byron's dog haus; you will love them or hate them.

The hot dogs are more civil; we recommend them to all who appreciate a substantial, all-beef frank. They are Vienna brand, steeped to full succulence, with a faint crackle as you sink your teeth into them. Our only complaint is about the buns. They are a bore—small, plain (no poppy seeds), forked straight from their plastic-wrapped container (not warmed).

But Byron's condiments are fine: eleven different toppings that include strips of green pepper, cucumber discs, piccalilli, squeeze-on yellow mustard, onions, and sport peppers (hot!). And resting atop your hot dog and its condiments is one tomato, not quite still round, because it has been cut into slices. But because the slices don't go all the way through, it stays in one piece . . . until you try to eat the dog, at which time everything falls into a splendid mess. The tomato is customarily gilded with a sprinkle of celery salt.

Alongside this good specimen of frankfurter pulchritude, you want French fries. They are skinny and crisp—a suitable spuddy companion to the highly seasoned sausages that are this restaurant's specialty. Unless you really love French fries, one order is plenty for two.

A second Byron's is at 1701 Lawrence Avenue (773-271-0900).

## Charlie Parker's

700 North St.                    217-241-2104
Springfield, IL                  www.charlieparkersdiner.net
                                 BL | $

Don't rely on your GPS if you come hunting for Charlie Parker's, an out-of-the-way trackside Quonset hut that has a sense of scale as out of whack as its lat-long coordinates. One single pancake is the size of a large pizza—flipped on the griddle with a pizza peel and served in a pizza pan. No one ever has been able to eat a Four Giant Stack (but if you do, they're free). Even a single one is enough for two to four people. What's most amazing is that it's very good, made from a fresh, farmy batter and griddle-cooked so that it develops a faintly crisp skin.

Charlie's is also an appropriate place to eat a horseshoe, that outrageously huge Springfield specialty that is basically a pile of everything on a plate. Breakfast 'shoes are especially awe-inspiring: big oval mountains built upon a foundation of white bread. Atop the bread are eggs, breakfast meats, hash browns, and cream gravy and/or hot cheese sauce.

## Cozy Dog

2935 S. 6th St.                  217-525-1992
Springfield, IL                  www.cozydogdrivein.com
                                 BLD | $

Invented during World War II by Ed Waldemire when he was in the Air Force stationed in Texas, the corn-clad, deep-fried Cozy Dog was originally called Crusty Cur and was a big hit with flyboys at the Amarillo PX. After the war, Waldemire's wife convinced him that his wiener needed a more appealing name, and in 1946, they opened Cozy Dog (so christened because no one eats a single, lonely one). You don't have to be a street-food connoisseur to savvy the difference between a Cozy Dog and an ordinary corn dog. The cozy's batter jacket has a vivid crunch and earthy corn flavor; the dog within is plump with juice. Family baskets include four Cozy Dogs and a large order of (freshly-cut) French fries.

## D&J Café

915 W. Laurel St.                    217-753-1708
Springfield, IL                      BLD | $

The horseshoe is one of the most regionally restricted of all local specialties, found nowhere beyond Springfield, where it was first devised at the Leland Hotel back in 1928. It is one of America's most outlandish meals, in a class with the Rochester Garbage Plate (p. 128) and super nachos. Historians say it was named because it originally resembled a horse's shoe (a slice of ham) on an anvil (a hot metal plate) with farriers' nails (French fries) scattered around. But over the years, 'shoes have been supersized to the point that they no longer bear any resemblance to equine footwear. Drizzles of cheese have become gobs; a few French fries have become mountains. The original ham-and-cheese configuration has been augmented by 'shoes based on burgers, sausage, Buffalo-sauced chicken, and even vegetarian combos.

And, naturally, there is now the breakfast 'shoe, which may or may not contain ham (or bacon or sausage patties), and which will more likely be heaped with hash browns than French fries. It will contain two to four eggs. Cheese sauce may be supplemented by or replaced by cream gravy.

At the humble D&J Café, everything on the breakfast 'shoe is completely blanketed by hash browns that have a crisp outside coat and enough thickness that below the crunch is plenty of plush spuditude—essential for mopping eggs if you like runny yolks. What's notable about this particular 'shoe is its balance—a magnificent harmony of gravy, cheese, meat, and potatoes.

## Doughnut Vault

400 1/2 Franklin St.                 No phone
Chicago, IL                          B | $

So small that it needs a fraction for its street address, the Doughnut Vault shows just how cruel the law of supply and demand can be. About 1,000 donuts are made each morning and 10,000 Chicagoans want them. So the line forms before opening at 8:30 and the donuts can be gone before noon.

The buttermilk donuts are dense and cakelike, eminently suitable for dunking. Glazed donuts are lighter, and generally available in such flavors as chestnut, chocolate, and vanilla. While these donuts are big enough so that one will satisfy a modest appetite, you also can get stacks of three smaller ones. Daily specials include double-chocolate old-fashioneds, powdered sugar stacks, mocha glazed toasted almond, and pistachio.

## Garrett Popcorn Shop

625 N. Michigan Ave.      312-943-4200
Chicago, IL               www.garrettpopcorn.com
                          $

Most candy-coated popcorn is frivolous junk food. CaramelCrisp—Garrett's name for caramel corn—is serious and soulful. It scarcely tastes candied. The popcorn is an earthy note within a deeply buttery caramel sheath and has dark flavor that teeters at the edge of tasting burnt. Like singed crust atop a crème brûlée, the corn's coat smacks of fire as much as sugar.

Another thing that makes it good is that it is served hot and fresh. Once mixed with caramel it is spilled into a trough against the front wall, where a woman worries it with two large scoops, ensuring the caramel corn doesn't clump into pieces larger than three or four popped kernels. As it achieves perfect consistency, it is shoveled into the other end of the trough, where it is scooped into bags that are weighed out for customers. Almost equally excellent is Garrett's cheese corn, which is impossible to eat without your fingers turning bright orange from the cheese that coats and infuses the hot popped kernels. The cheese immeasurably enhances the starchy corn flavor of the puffy kernels, making a savory snack that is almost unimprovable.

But it can get better. Instead of ordering either CaramelCrisp or cheese corn, you can ask one of the women working the counter for a "mix," also known as the Chicago Mix. She fills a bag half full with caramel corn, tops it off with cheese corn, and then shakes. The combo is a giant taste sensation that seems to cover the whole spectrum of what a tongue can appreciate: salty, sweet, buttery, earthy, crisp, and chewy. Even a mini-mix, which is a mere eight ounces, exhausts our ability to eat anything else for hours.

Note: There are Garretts elsewhere; none we have tried can compare to those in Chicago, of which there are ten. The Michigan Avenue location is best of them all.

## Gene & Jude's

2720 N. River Rd.        708-452-7634
River Grove, IL          LD | $

Gene & Jude's has no tables or chairs. As is Chicago custom, it offers a counter to which you may bring your meal, unwrap it, and eat standing up. When finished, use the wax paper in which the food was served to gather up scraps and heave them into one of the garbage cans. The arrangement is comfortable and practical for eating extremely messy food; however, many customers choose to dine in their cars.

You get a hot dog or a double dog. The natural-casing, all-beef Vienna brand links are slim and snappy; they are inserted into soft buns and dressed with mustard, onions, piccalilli, and sport peppers. Tipster Glen Stepanovic told us that some hot dog historians consider this the "original" Chicago-style dog, before the more baroque garnishes of pickle spear, tomato slice, and celery salt. Whatever toppings are included, each dog gets heaped with a large fistful of freshly made French fries.

## Harry Caray's

33 W. Kinzie St.　　　　　312-828-0966
Chicago, IL　　　　　　　www.harrycarays.com
　　　　　　　　　　　　LD | $$$

Beyond his antics in the broadcast booth, especially as the voice of the Chicago Cubs, Harry Caray was known as a man who loved to eat. The place he opened is testimony to that passion. It is fancier and pricier than most Roadfood, but we include it here because it is the essence of edible Chicago. For example, there is not a better prime steak in town. We like the sirloin best, grilled in a coat of cracked peppercorns. Other highlights include such Italian specialties as lasagna, veal parmigiana, and a risotto of the day.

Among the "Italian" dishes is one that we've found only in Chicago, and it is magnificent: chicken Vesuvio. Chicken Vesuvio is several bone-in pieces of chicken, sautéed then baked to utmost succulence, encased in a dark, red-gold crust of lush skin that slides from the meat as the meat slides off its bone. The dark meat in particular sets new standards for chicken tenderness. Piled among the chicken are wedges of potato, long-sautéed in a bath of white wine, garlic, olive oil, and spice until they are soft as mashed inside, but with crunchy edges. Even if you don't get chicken Vesuvio, Vesuvio potatoes are available as a side dish to go with any steak or chop. The only problem about ordering them is that you likely won't also be ordering the superb garlic mashed potatoes.

The setting is vintage: an 1895 Dutch Renaissance–style limestone building now on the National Register of Historic Places, its interior a luxuriously muscular space of mahogany woodwork and broad tables covered by thick white napery. Although an opulent place to which many customers come in pinstriped business suits, there is a democratic feel about this dining room that makes any decently dressed customer feel right at home. Harry Caray was a people's hero, and that's the way he liked it.

# *Hot Doug's

3324 N. California Ave.          773-279-9550
Chicago, IL                     www.hotdougs.com

L | $

Chicago is a city of great hot dogs, and while opinions differ about which eatery makes the best Windy City red hot, Hot Doug's stands out above them all. Yes, you can get a paradigmatic Chicago dog at Hot Doug's Encased Meats Emporium and Sausage Superstore, but that is just a glimpse of a dining experience that is in a class by itself. The restaurant is informal and easygoing the way so much memorable Roadfood is, yet its menu is awesomely inventive and the sausages it serves are worthy of a four-star chef.

Several years back, Doug's got lots of media attention for its foie gras hot dog, which defied Chicago's ban on foie gras, and while that ridiculously rich weenie (a Sauternes duck sausage ribboned with truffle aioli and topped with large circles of foie gras mousse) is the headliner, there are other, less outrageous hot dogs that cry out to be tasted. Among the regular offerings are Polish and Italian sausages, andouille sausage, Thüringer, corn dogs, and a vegetarian dog. Specials include the likes of Thai chicken sausage, curried pork sausage, and Jamaican jerk sausage. Whatever you order, you can ask to have it char-grilled, steamed, or deep-fried. On Friday and Saturday, Doug's offers duck-fat French fries.

Word of warning: Hot Doug's is hugely popular. Plan to wait in line, sometimes an hour or more, before telling Doug Sohn what you want to eat. Doug, by the way, was the recipient of the 2012 Blue Plate Award at the Roadfood.com-sponsored New Orleans Foodfest.

# The Igloo

2819 4th St.                    815-223-0848
Peru, IL                        www.igloodiner.com

LD | $

Generations of Peruvians know and love the Igloo for hamburgers, chili, and pork tenderloins. Rich Decker, who, along with his brother Chris, bought the seventy-five-year-old drive-in in 2010 from the family who started it, explained that he serves "true tenderloin, not a chop, not just some loin, but the really good part." The wavy cutlet does have a regal bearing—thin and rich, offering just the right amount of succulent meat hugged by brittle crust, garnished with onion, pickles, and ketchup. Ketchup is an unusual tenderloin condiment, but it sings a sweet song with the tangy pickles, crunchy onion, sandy crust, and dense, moist pork. French fries are medium-thin, good lunch-counter potatoes, nothing unusual, but just right. Mid-sandwich they tend to soften, but the fresh potato flavor remains.

Even better than the tenderloin is a double tenderloin—two cutlets in one sandwich, accentuating the crispness—a sandwich that is as thrilling to bite as it is to taste. Igloo regulars do not order "tenderloins." They ask for a "pork," or a "double pork," and then for a malt.

"Is the malt real?" we ask Chris.

"I've got malt, I've got ice cream, I've got syrup," he answers, enumerating a flavor choice that includes vanilla, chocolate, root beer, cherry, and papaya. The malt comes with a broad straw, but even so, its thickness demands so much cheek-hollowing suction that we forwent the straw and gulped.

## Joe Rogers Original Recipe Chili Parlor

820 S. 9th St.        217-522-3722
Springfield, IL      www.joerogerschili.com
                L | $

Springfield chili, as made at Joe Rogers, is wild stuff, definitely not for the fastidious epicure. Cooked ground beef, which resembles loosemeats, comes afloat in grease—known more politely as hot oil—and is almost always accompanied by beans. It is possible to ask for the oil to be skimmed off when you order a bowl, but that would negate the purpose of the little oyster crackers that come alongside. They are a nice sponge for the oil, sopping up its chili-pepper zest. The chili comes in six different degrees of hotness, from mild to Firebrand, the latter known as the J. R. Special. If you eat a bowl of Firebrand, your name will be inscribed on the honor roll posted on the wall so that your survivors can come and salute your daredevil spirit.

Note that Joe Rogers spells chili the normal way, with a single L. That is unusual in Springfield, Illinois, because in 1993, when the state legislature formally declared the downstate capital to be the "Chilli Capital of the Civilized Universe," it purposely used the rare double-L spelling of the word, ordained by force of Senate resolution.

# *Johnnie's

| | |
|---|---|
| 7500 W. North Ave. | 708-452-6000 |
| Elmwood Park, IL | LD \| $ |

We do not eat Italian beef often enough to anoint one place the best. Chicago (and Chicago alone) has so many good ones, and as a native, Michael gets too sentimental at the very sight (and smell) of shaved-thin, garlic-sopped beef loaded into a brawny length of bread and crowned with pickly-hot *giardiniera* to make any sort of reasoned judgment. But the last time we were at Johnnie's and had a combo sandwich (that's beef plus sausage), we found it hard to believe that Chicago's great signature sandwich can get any better than this. The beef is soft and fairly softly seasoned—just garlicky enough to halo its protein magnitude—and the char-cooked sausage is dense, taut, and chewy. This glorious duo, plus Johnnie's vibrant *giardiniera* compose a taste-bud epiphany. To accompany Italian beef or to savor its afterglow, Johnnie's makes delicious Italian ice, a tantalizing balance of sweet and tart.

# Lagomarcino's

| | |
|---|---|
| 1422 5th Ave. | 309-764-1814 |
| Moline, IL | www.lagomarcinos.com |
| | LD \| $ |

Started as a Moline, Illinois, candy store in 1908, Lagomarcino's is still renowned for hand-dipped chocolates. You won't find better sponge candy anywhere, here known as sea foam (not available in hot summer months). Turtles, aka pecan dainties, are superb. In addition to familiar chocolate barks, Lagomarcino's offers lemon bark and peppermint bark.

What we like best is the hot fudge sundae, its fudge made from a recipe acquired in 1918 from a traveling salesman for the princely sum of twenty-five dollars. It is a bittersweet, not-too-thick elixir that just may be the best hot fudge in this solar system or any other. When you order a sundae, the great, dark stuff is served in a manner befitting its distinction: in a small pitcher alongside the tulip-glass full of ice cream and whipped cream, so you can pour or spoon it on to taste. This serving technique provides a fascinating demonstration of how soda-fountain habits reflect one's personality. Do you pour on all the fudge at one time, willy-nilly, risking that some will spill over the sides of the serving glass? Do you pour it on spoonful by spoonful, carefully ensuring that every bite will have just the proper balance of ice cream and fudge? Or do you eat all the ice cream, with maybe just a dash of fudge poured on, so you can then conclude your snack by downing all the hot fudge that remains in one dizzy chocoholic binge?

## Lem's

311 E. 75th St.

Chicago, IL

773-994-2428

www.lemsque.com

LD | $$

Lem's is a South Side barbecue that dates back to 1954, when brothers Bruce and Myles Lemons created the aquarium smoker, named because its tempered glass walls show the meat as it slow-cooks. This type of barbecue pit has since become a signature of Chicago's South Side, along with the rib tips that Lem's introduced as a less expensive but succulent alternative to whole racks.

The rib racks are sensational: big, meaty bats with all the lascivious fatty flavor and satisfying chew that baby backs simply cannot deliver. Also not to be missed are Lem's hot links—plump, rugged-textured sausages served with barbecue sauce, French fries, and white bread for sopping up the last of Lem's kaleidoscopic sauce.

Note: There are no dining facilities at Lem's. All business is takeout.

## Manny's

1141 S. Jefferson St.

Chicago, IL

312-939-2855

www.mannysdeli.com

BL | $$

We usually return to our favorite Chicago cafeteria-style deli with the vow to *not* eat corned beef sandwiches. There are so many other good-looking things to eat: kasha and bowtie noodles, short ribs of beef, oxtail stew, and pierogies, not to mention matzoh ball soup, blintzes, and potato latkes. But all too often, the beauty of the warm corned beef, thin-sliced before one's eyes and piled between slices of glossy-crusted rye bread, wins out and that's what we eat, sided by potato latkes.

Gino Gambarota, Manny's corned beef man for more than a quarter century, will cut the meat the way you like it—lean, fatty, or regular—but he will not cut it thick. "The art of cutting corned beef is to cut it as thin as possible, and against the grain," Gino says. His slices are shaved so thin they verge on disintegration, but they stay intact and miraculously succulent.

At the edge of Chicago's Loop, not far from where the everything-goes bazaar known as Maxwell Street once thrived, Manny's remains a magnet for Chicagoans of every stripe. Dining-room tables are occupied by politicians and other crooks, captains of industry and university professors, and cured-meat lovers from distant suburbs. When a newspaper photographer joined us at a recent meal, a nearby cop couldn't resist coming over to investigate. When he saw the lensman focusing on a corned beef sandwich, he beamed with understanding and gave us the high sign.

## Mr. Beef

666 N. Orleans
Chicago, IL

312-337-8500
www.mrbeefonorleans.com
LD | $

Mr. Beef is a premier source for the Second City's #1 street food, Italian beef. Great heaps of ultra-thin-sliced, garlic-infused beef are piled into a length of muscular Italian bread that gets soft as beef juices soak into it, but retains the oomph to stay in one piece even if you order your sandwich "dipped," which means double-soaked in gravy. An important choice you'll need to make is if you want your sandwich topped with roasted peppers or the peppery vegetable mélange known as *giardiniera,* which is crunchy, spicy, and a brilliant contrast to the full-flavored beef.

Sausages are excellent as well—cooked on a grate until they sweat juice. You can get a sausage sandwich in similar configurations as beef, and it is also possible to have a combo, a length of both sausage and beef.

Accommodations are minimal. There is an adjoining dining room, ironically titled the Elegant Dining Room, with actual tables at which to sit as well as a counter up front with stools, but the Italian beef connoisseur's choice is to stand at the chest-high counter that rims the perimeter of the main room. Here, the wax paper that wraps the sandwich can catch all the spillage and keep it at handy plucking distance.

## Paradise Pup

1724 S. River Rd.
Des Plaines, IL

847-699-8590
L | $

The name is Paradise Pup and the hot dogs are excellent—Chicagoland classics that are available topped with a wheelbarrow's worth of condiments. Italian beef sandwiches are top-tier. But the Pup's primary attraction is its cheeseburger. A hefty patty charcoal-grilled to crusty succulence, all the more delicious with a sheaf of bacon on top or perhaps raw or grilled onions, it comes on a seeded Kaiser roll. You get your choice of cheese—

American, mozzarella, or the connoisseur's choice: Merkt's, a tangy Cheddar from Wisconsin that matches perfectly with the beef.

Seasoned French fries are excellent too, whether you order them plain or loaded, which means heaped with cheese, bacon, and sour cream. To drink: a cream-rich milk shake.

Dining accommodations are virtually nonexistent—a handful of counter seats and outdoor tables with umbrellas—and the small eat shack is almost always crowded. Expect to wait.

## *Poochie's

| | |
|---|---|
| 3602 Dempster | 847-673-0100 |
| Skokie, IL | www.poochieshotdogs.com |
| | LD \| $ |

Poochie's red hots are the best. Standard hot dogs are all-beef Vienna franks, boiled to perfect plumpness and served in tender, seeded Rosen's-brand buns. Char dogs, cooked over coals, are crusty, blackened versions thereof. Polish sausages are plumper, porkier variants slit in a spiral pattern to attain maximum crunchy surface area. If one in a bun of any of these tube steaks is insufficient for your appetite, you can get either a jumbo dog or a double. Our personal favorite meal is a jumbo char dog with Cheddar fries (superb fries!) on the side.

Poochie's is proud of its char-cooked hamburgers, and we like them very much, especially piled high with those sweet grilled onions. But if you are passing through Chicago and stop at Poochie's with time for only one street-food indulgence, make it a red hot with the works and a side of fries. It is an only-in-Chicago meal, and a jewel in the Roadfood crown.

## *Rip's

| | |
|---|---|
| 311 N. Main Ave. | 815-894-3051 |
| Ladd, IL | www.ripschicken.com |
| | D \| $ |

In matters of food, as in politics, the state of Illinois gets eclipsed by the city of Chicago. But when it comes to fried chicken, Chicago cannot hold a candle to LaSalle and Bureau Counties. If you are a fried-chicken pilgrim, this big-sky prairie belongs on the essential itinerary right along with Nashville, Kansas City, and western Kentucky.

The region boasts literally dozens of good chicken places, nearly all of them taverns, most serving only supper. Rip's is the best—so good that fans don't mind an hour's wait for a table on weekends. Waiting in line with beer or cocktail in hand and telling other devotees how far away you live and how often you come is part of the experience.

Rip's is all about chicken (plus fish on Friday), and amenities are minimal: dishware is disposable, forks are provided only when requested. Rip's quarters, light or dark, are encased in a significant crisp crust. While much surplus skin has been trimmed away, there are places on each piece, such as the underside of the breast, that carry brittle little clumps of batter infused with chicken-fat flavor—some of the most sumptuous bites anywhere. Below the crunch is impeccable meat, bursting with juice all the way to the bone, thanks in large part to a prep process that includes brining. Pieces are served on a pallet of white bread, but the bread remains surprisingly dry and intact. As lubricated as this chicken is—it *is* all about deep-frying—it does not shed surplus grease.

One big reason for loyalty to Rip's is a unique item known as crunchies. Every table gets a cardboard boat full of them while waiting for quarters to fry. Hot morsels of batter retrieved from the cooking oil with a broad, long-handled screen, they are reminiscent of southern cracklins or, more to the point, Jewish *gribenes,* glowing with the silky luxury of fried chicken fat. Pure shattering flavor, crunchies are an item virtually impossible to stop eating once you start. They are served with a cup of tart dill pickle chips. Rip's bartender, Betha, demonstrated that the custom is to fold a pickle chip around a little cluster of crunchies, creating what regulars call a finger taco. She explained that the puckery pickles are an important part of the meal because their pungency gives the tongue endurance to eat more fried food.

## Smitty's Tap

308 Gary St.                               815-856-2030
Leonore, IL                                LD | $

Among the several Illinois River Valley restaurants known for good fried chicken, Smitty's Tap is listed among the top contenders, but when we came to this friendly crossroads tavern one Thursday, we ate none. Smitty's serves its chicken, which is broasted, only on Wednesday and Friday nights.

It was a good stop anyway, because Smitty's offers tenderloin every day. And oh, what a tenderloin: a foot across, piled with lettuce, tomato, and onion, and sandwiched—if that is the right word for it—in a ridiculously little-looking (but actually normal-sized) burger bun. The pounded-thin pork is sweet and moist, its crust a blond halo of crunch. For most folks, it is knife-and-fork food, but the waitress assured us that there are people who manage to fold the cutlet over on itself a few times so they can hoist it off the iron skillet in which it is served, using the bun in a normal way.

## *Superdawg

| | |
|---|---|
| 6363 N. Milwaukee Ave. | 773-763-0660 |
| Chicago, IL | www.superdawg.com |
| | LD | $ |

Many savvy Chicagoans believe Superdawg's all-beef tube steaks are the city's best. If not, they are surely among the top two or three. Contrary to Chicago custom, these proprietary franks are skinless, and yet they are burstingly juicy. And while they do have the garlic edge that defines red hots hereabouts, their dominant flavor is quality beef. Condiments are impeccable. Buns are fresh and soft, spangled with sesame seeds. Other super menu items include Superfries, Superonionchips, Superburgers, and Supershakes. Or you can have a Whoopskidog (the house name for a Polish sausage).

It is easy to spot Superdawg as you approach a pair of ten-foot statues of a male and female wiener (Flaurie and Maurie) wear leopard-skin togas and stand high atop the roof, winking electrically. Opened in 1948, this Roadfood landmark still features the once-modern "Suddenserver" automated order system and serves its dogs in cardboard boxes that announce, "Your Superdawg lounges inside contentedly cushioned in Superfries, comfortably attired in mustard, relish, onion, pickle, and hot pepper."

## Torri's Ice Cream Parlor

| | |
|---|---|
| 115 N. Main Ave. | 815-894-9316 |
| Ladd, IL | BL | $ |

Tom Torri, who opened his first business, the Fruit Store, in Ladd, Illinois, in 1911, became so well known for the ice cream he made that people traveled from Chicago and the Quad Cities to buy gallons of it to take home. Heidi Templeton, who bought what had become known as Torri's Ice Cream Parlor in 2004, no longer makes her own (she gets Sisler's ice cream from Ohio), but maintains a vintage sweetshop charm that makes this old place worth a visit. The wall behind the counter is occupied by a big 1950s wooden menu that lists hamburgers for 25¢ and banana splits for 35¢.

For years, the house slogan has been "Where Friends Meet." Torri's is the only place around serving breakfast (from 6 a.m.), so its tables and booths are where locals come to share morning conversation and to drink coffee served in a diverse collection of mugs. (We got ours in a Kinetico

Water Systems mug and a Harley-Davidson Happy Holidays mug.) Torri's also is the only place in town with a dessert menu.

As much as we enjoyed spooning into a classic banana split, it was even more fun sitting at the counter watching it being carefully constructed. The woman who made it offered a running commentary about each step of the process, explaining how the two halves of the lengthwise-sliced banana were supposed to form a trough, damming up ice cream and sauce. She was crestfallen when, just before presenting her creation, the dam was breached by a spill of chocolate. Available ice cream flavors include all the usuals, plus black cherry, cotton candy, mango, and moosetracks.

The breakfast menu boasts that biscuits are made from scratch. Heidi said that they are indeed homemade, but not made here. We were puzzled but didn't pursue the question, as Heidi had her hands full, being both waitress and chef on the morning shift. Wherever it comes from, the biscuit is bland, a deficiency that can be remedied by having it split, buttered, and cooked on the grill, where it absorbs savory bacon-sausage-ham-and-eggs perfume. Ours came on the side of "loaded hash browns," which, calorie-wise, provide momentous bang for the buck: a pallet of crisp-fried potatoes topped with peppers, onions, mushrooms, and a mantle of cheese, all for $3.25.

## Vienna Beef Café

2501 N. Damen Ave.
Chicago, IL

773-435-2309
www.viennabeef.com/cafemenu
BL | $

Chicago hot dogs, aka red hots, are famous for the splendor of their condiments, but if the dog itself doesn't cut the mustard, condiments mean nothing. Most of the city's best are dense, garlicky, all-beef tube steaks made by Vienna Beef Company. Glory be, Vienna Beef happens to run its own factory-store café, where you won't find a more perfect version of the Chicago classic: a wiener steamed to bursting plumpness, the tenderest poppy seed roll, crisp pickle spears, tomatoes, and brilliant spicy-sweet piccalilli. Even the bright yellow mustard tastes like it was made that morning.

That's not all. Vienna Beef also makes superior corned beef, Polish sausages, pastrami, hard and soft salami, and Italian beef, all of which are on the lunch menu. The flagship item is a 3XL corned beef sandwich, nine ounces of spicy beef piled between slices of very good rye bread.

## Wedron Office

2005 N. 35th Rd.        815-433-2974

Ottawa, IL        LD | $

If you are driving along Thirty-Fifth Road north of Ottawa, you can't miss Wedron Office because there is absolutely nothing else to see other than acres of cornfields. A cool, dark, insulated haven of hospitality, it is as much a tavern as it is a restaurant. There is a pool table up front and overhead televisions are tuned to TruTV. As we dined, we watched a show titled *Busted in the Buff,* featuring criminals apprehended while naked.

Terrific fried chicken. Encased in a thin envelope of crust with trailing squiggles of crunchy batter all about, each piece oozing juice. Tasty as the meat may be, it is tempting to eat only crust, like having all the bacon off your breakfast plate but leaving behind the eggs, spuds, and toast.

While fried chicken is a staple of many LaSalle County restaurants, blue gill is not. In fact, it is a rarity because a large fish produces only a small fillet, and you need up to a dozen to make a meal. Wedron Office serves a plateful of little curls of the flaky white fish in a nutty, toasty crust—just salty enough to tease all the natural sweetness from this freshwater prize.

## The Wiener's Circle

2622 N. Clark St.        773-477-7444

Chicago, IL        LD | $

The name of the Wiener's Circle is etymological hijinks typical of Chicago, but there is nothing silly about the red hots served here. They are among the city's best, presented in steamy-soft Rosen-brand poppy-seed buns and topped with flawless condiments.

The mustard is classic yellow, the piccalilli is brilliant green and vividly pickly, the tomatoes are small and flavorful—four or five whole, fresh-cut discs per dog. And there are grilled onions or raw, sport peppers (hot!), and a sprinkle of celery salt. Have your frankfurter as you like it, from naked to loaded, and you will not be disappointed. The major decision to make is how you want your hot dog cooked: boiled, which yields plump, taut skin, or charred, which gives the dogs rugged crunch and smoky savor.

Don't get a hot dog without French fries. These are beauties: hand-cut, freshly fried, served in ridiculously large amounts that totally overflow their cardboard boat and fall all over the wax paper on which the boat is pushed toward you out the order window.

Dining is either at counter space inside or picnic tables overlooking

Clark Street. Orders are taken and food delivered by one of several gals at the open-kitchen window. "Char Dog!" one calls out to a customer, using what he ordered as his name, then continuing her conversation as the bill is paid by calling him sweetheart, honey, and darling. On other occasions, it is not unheard-of for the staff to speak to customers the way Cubs fans yell at umpires who have made a controversial call. Such personality is an extra condiment that helps make Wiener's Circle hot dogs something special.

## Coney Island Wiener

131 W. Main St.

Fort Wayne, IN

260-424-2997

LD | $

Coney Island wiener shops abound throughout the heartland, "Coney Island" being the old term for hot dog, which once was a signature dish of New York. Fort Wayne's Coney Island, a Main Street storefront formally known as the Famous Coney Island Wiener Stand, was established in 1914, and has built its reputation on the classic Greek-American frankfurter: a modest-sized bright-pink weenie nestled in a steamed-soft bun and topped with Coney sauce, which is a fine-grind chili with a rainbow of seasonings and fetching sweetness. Although all condiments are technically optional, everyone orders their hot dogs with Coney sauce, as well as a line of mustard and a sprinkle of chopped raw onion. The only other things on the menu are baked beans, chili (more a soup than a stew), and hamburgers. Coke comes in classic small bottles.

Seating is at small tables along the wall and at counter stools. Stools up front offer a nice view not only of the doings behind the counter and between staff and customers, but also through the big window out onto Main Street.

Tipster Brett Poirier, who encouraged us to seek these fine weenies, pointed out that Fort Wayne makes a great way station for anyone traveling America's original coast-to-coast thoroughfare, the Lincoln Highway.

## *Gray Brothers Cafeteria

555 S. Indiana St.                      317-831-5614
Mooresville, IN                         www.graybrotherscatering.com
                                        LD | $

Gray Brothers is a gigantic cafeteria with deluxe décor. Expect it to be crowded, but this is one time when a slight delay is worthwhile. It gives you time to study the dozens of food items from which you will soon be choosing.

Among the most memorable dishes are chicken and homemade noodles, meat loaf with mashed potatoes, smoked sausage with baked beans, and roast pork with corn bread dressing. Tell the server what entrée you want; she puts it onto a flower-patterned plate then slides the plate to the vegetable area, where it is weighted with whatever sides you desire. Mac 'n' cheese, au gratin potatoes, cheesy broccoli and cauliflower, and melted-marsh-mallow yams all are standouts. The salad selection includes carrot-raisin-marshmallow, creamy pea, three-bean, and, of course, Jell-O.

Desserts are dazzling, whole pies arrayed on shelves below the individual slices (many pies get bought and taken home). Fruit pies abound, and there are swell butterscotch, banana cream, and pumpkin flavors, but the Indiana favorite, and a specialty of Gray's, is sugar-cream pie . . . as simple and pure and good as the name suggests.

## Hollyhock Hill

8110 N. College Ave.                    317-251-2294
Indianapolis, IN                        www.hollyhockhill.com
                                        D | $$

Big chicken dinners once were a signature of Indianapolis, a fact easy to believe when you visit Hollyhock Hill. Originally opened in 1928 as the Country Cottage, it offers a feast, served family-style in bowls and on platters that diners pass around the table. You start with innocuous pickled beets, cottage cheese, and a head lettuce salad. Then comes the chicken, skillet fried until crunch-crusted, served with pan gravy. Whipped potatoes, green beans, buttered corn niblets, and warm biscuits with apple butter come alongside and are replenished as long as the table keeps eating. They're fine, but it's the chicken that will make you want to return to Hollyhock Hill. (Chicken frowners can choose from among shrimp, fried cod, broiled orange roughy or haddock, and steak.)

For dessert, make your own sundae. Sauces of butterscotch, crème de menthe, and chocolate are provided. The normal flavor is vanilla, but true Hoosiers opt for the state favorite, peppermint.

## Joe Huber's

2421 Engle Rd.
Starlight, IN

812-923-5255
www.joehubers.com
LD | $$

Joe Huber's is not a charming little town café. It is a tourist attraction. But we defy you to sink your teeth into the crust of the fried chicken, or gather a silky dumpling from its chicken broth, or fork up some of those real mashed potatoes and not concur with Joe Huber's many fans that it is a worthy Roadfood destination. And the fried biscuits? Inspired! Roadfood.com contributor Cecif described them as "similar to beignets . . . but a bit less greasy and very fluffy and light." With or without the apple butter that comes alongside, they are impossible to stop eating. And that's a problem, because as soon as your biscuit basket looks empty, you will be served more.

There are other items on the menu, including pork chops, steak, and catfish, and groups of people can have the chicken served family-style along with slices of honey ham and a constellation of slaw, potatoes, gravy, green beans, corn and, of course, biscuits. Desserts include fruit cobblers and cream pies as well as miniature versions thereof for those of us without remaining appetite but with a demanding sweet tooth.

## John's Famous Stew

1146 Kentucky Ave.
Indianapolis, IN

317-636-6212
www.indysfamousstew.com
BLD | $

A few years ago, Roadfood.com team members Bruce Bilmes and Sue Boyle noted that stew happened to be an especially popular dish in Indianapolis, where more than a few taverns and sandwich shops make it a specialty. When we arrived at John's Famous Stew midafternoon, Pauline, who has been a waitress in this dark, adults-only tavern for a few score years, had some time to chat. She clued us in to the difference between stew and goulash (the latter has more vegetables) and told us that John's stew is available ladled on top of a stuffed pepper or a fried pork tenderloin. She also warned us that we did *not* want the hottest of the three degrees of stew available.

"We like hot," we insisted.

Pauline shook her head pityingly, insisting ours be medium, but she advised her sister in the kitchen, Phoebe, to elevate the heat level a few notches.

"How do you do that? Add more hot sauce?" we inquired.

"I can't tell you that!" Pauline answered, taken aback by our nerve even in asking. Apparently the stew recipe goes back to the original John, long since passed away, and imparted only to cooks who can be trusted.

Pauline spoke with authority about barbecue, fried chicken, and southern vegetables, and as we forked into a gigantic bowl of just-a-bit-hot comfort food, praising the big, lovely butter beans on top of the hugely meaty stew, she admitted that they normally do not appear on stew; they crown John's almost equally famous goulash.

## Jonathan Byrd's Cafeteria

100 Byrd Way          317-881-8888
Greenwood, IN         www.jonathanbyrds.com
                      LD | $

As immense as Jonathan Byrd's is, with its eighty-eight-foot serving line and seating for hundreds, the food it serves is humble and homey. Here you will find comfort in turkey potpie or a bowl of chicken and noodles, roast beef with gravy, meat loaf and mashed potatoes, or just a tray full of vegetables and side dishes. Highlights among the latter include pork-rich greens, buttered corn, twice-baked potato casserole, and corn bread dressing. Buttermilk drop biscuits are a must with any meal, and you have your choice of regular or sweet corn muffins. Many regular customers swear by the Toll House pie, which is great if your hunger for sweetness is insatiable; the desserts we like best are caramel bread pudding and hot fruit cobbler.

## King Ribs Bar-B-Q

3145 W. 16th St.      317-488-0223
Indianapolis, IN      www.kingribsbarbq.com
                      LD | $

King Ribs' house motto is "Fit for a King." The ribs are regal. They are tender enough so that the meat pulls from the bone in heavy strips, barely glazed with sauce but chewy enough that the pork flavor resonates forever. It is a pure, sweet flavor, just faintly tingling with smoke. The house sandwich is known as pork on a bun, and that is what it is: an outlandishly messy load of hacked-up pork dripping with sauce and surrounded by a bun too messy to be hoisted by hand. The sleeper on the menu is chicken: slow-cooked to fallapart tenderness, its meat moist and smoky.

Side dishes include mac 'n' cheese that is as thick as pudding and intensely cheesy, with noodles so soft they are almost indistinguishable from the cheese. Also: baked beans, fine-cut slaw, and white bread for mopping. For dessert, there is a choice of sweeties: chess pie or sweet-potato pie.

## Lemon Drop

| | |
|---|---|
| 1701 Mounds Rd. | 765-644-9055 |
| Anderson, IN | LD \| $ |

Roadfood stalwart Cliff Strutz (aka Buffetbuster) pointed the way to the oldest restaurant in Anderson, Indiana—the Lemon Drop—where the citrus theme includes bright yellow paint on the outside walls, lemon drop candies at the cash register, and lemon milk shakes.

Headliners are the toasted cheeseburger, sandwiched between tiles of buttered grilled toast instead of a bun (buns also are available) and the onionburger, which is made by folding onions right into the ground meat before it gets fried. Cliff noted that most customers get their onionburger on grilled toast too; he suggested that those with a big beef craving get a couple of burgers, as these patties are fairly thin, pressed flat on the grill.

If for some reason you don't want a lemon milk shake (you do!), Cokes are available doctored-up with chocolate or vanilla syrup.

## Mr. Dave's

| | |
|---|---|
| 102 E. Main St. | 260-982-4769 |
| North Manchester, IN | LD \| $ |

The tenderloin, formally known as a breaded pork tenderloin sandwich, sometimes abbreviated BPT, is a slice of pork pounded flat and wide, breaded and fried, and sandwiched in a bun, preferably with pickle slices and mustard. There are few restaurants as proud of this heartland treasure as Mr. Dave's, where the tenderloins are neither too thin nor ridiculously wide (as so many are). Four-ounce boneless pork medallions are cut and pounded out so there is still good heft to the meat; they are breaded in cornmeal and fried, coming out crunchy, tender, and piggy-sweet—just right inside a bun with lettuce, tomato, and mustard.

Although tenderloins have been its glory since "Mr. Dave" Clapp opened up in 1962 (the business is now run by his son Kevin), there is a full menu to make all but a strictly kosher traveler happy. You can get your pork tenderloin grilled rather than fried, and there is pulled-pork barbecue as well. Cheeseburgers, broasted chicken, and corn dogs fill out the menu.

Mr. Dave's used to do a brisk mail-order business selling breaded, frozen, and ready-to-fry tenderloins to homesick Hoosiers but a dozen years ago elected officials protected us against such evil by ruling that pork cannot be shipped without federal inspection.

## Mug 'n' Bun

| | |
|---|---|
| 5211 W. 10th St. | 317-244-5669 |
| Indianapolis, IN | www.mug-n-bun.com |
| | LD \| $ |

The mug is root beer, the bun a Hoosier tenderloin; together they are a paradigmatic Midwest drive-in meal. This timeless joint not far from the Indianapolis Motor Speedway gives customers a choice of eating off the dashboard or at outdoor picnic tables umbrella'd by radiant heaters for cold weather. In-car diners blink their lights for service and food is presented by carhops on window trays. People seated at tables summon the kitchen by using a buzzer that adjoins the posted menu.

We were tipped off to Mug 'n' Bun by writer Dale Lawrence, who described its root beer as "legitimately creamy, yes, but also smoky, carrying hints of vanilla fudge and molasses, as rich and smooth as a dessert wine." In other words, not your average soda pop! It is served in thick, frosted mugs and in sizes that include small, large, giant, quart, half gallon, and gallon. As for the tenderloin, it too is big, if not the juiciest in town. We were more fond of the Super Burger, which is two patties, cheese, and bacon, served triple-decker-style: bun halves on top and bottom, a slice of toast separating the two burgers. Onion rings are very good: thick, crisp, and sweet.

## Nick's Chili Parlor

| | |
|---|---|
| 2621 Lafayette Rd. | 317-924-5005 |
| Indianapolis, IN | www.nickschiliparlor.com |
| | LD \| $ |

Thanks to Ben Morton and Rick Garrett for alerting us to this happy chili parlor on a rather unhappy stretch of recession-blighted shopping centers. For anyone on a budget, it is an especially worthwhile place, offering good, filling meals for $5 or less. These include five-way chili, chili dogs with cheese, burgers with and without chili, hot tamales, and fillet o' fish.

While Nick's hot dogs themselves are nothing special, the chili does add panache that makes them into the sort of food that never makes one say, "Wow, this is delicious" but nevertheless somehow completely vanishes from the plate, inducing temptation for just one more.

Service is cafeteria-style, giving customers an opportunity to kibitz with the high-spirited guys behind the counter. While the staff all are African Americans, the clientele when we dined at Nick's was a racial rainbow that included youth in hip-hop uniforms and geriatric couples with matching walkers.

## *Nick's Kitchen

506 N. Jefferson St.  
Huntington, IN

260-356-6618  
www.nickskitchen.net  
BLD | $

With a history dating back to 1904, when Nick Freienstein started frying breaded pork cutlets to sell in sandwiches from a street cart in Huntington, Nick's Kitchen claims with some authority to have invented the tenderloin—a sandwich of crisp-fried pork. Whether or not the history is accurate, this is certain: Nick's twenty-first-century tenderloin is stupendously good. It is built around a wavy cutlet that extends a good two to three inches beyond the circumference of a five-inch bun, virtually eclipsing its plate. Soaked in buttermilk that gives a tangy twist to the meat's sweetness and tightly cased in a coat of rugged cracker crumbs (not the more typical fine-grind cracker meal), the lode of pork inside the crust fairly drips with moisture. Proprietor Jean Anne Bailey tells us she buys the meat already cut and cubed, then pounds, marinates, breads, and fries it.

Nick's Kitchen isn't only a tenderloin stop. It's a wonderful three-meal-a-day town café with big breakfasts and a noontime blackboard of daily specials. We loved our plate of ham, beans, and corn bread, and we have been bowled over, time and again, by Jean Anne's pies. Made using a hand-me-down dough recipe that incorporates a bit of corn syrup, her fruit pies have a flaky crust that evaporates on the tongue, melding with brilliant-flavored rhubarb or black raspberries. Butterscotch pie—which she learned to cook from her grandmother—is more buttery than sweet, nothing at all like cloying pies made from pudding filling. Sugar-cream pie, an Indiana signature dessert, is like cream candy in a savory crust.

## Shapiro's

808 S. Meridian St.

Indianapolis, IN

317-631-4041

www.shapiros.com

BLD | $

Shapiro's serves deli meals cafeteria-style. In addition to a full repertoire of traditional kosher-style fare such as gefilte fish, matzoh ball soup, and piled-high smoked-meat sandwiches, its menu includes specialties unique to the Midwest: perch plates every Friday, Hoosier sugar-cream pie, and Vernor's ginger ale. The corned beef sandwich is one of the best anywhere, the meat cut lean but not too much so. Each slice is rimmed with a halo of smudgy spice and is so moist that it glistens. The beef is mounded between slabs of Shapiro's own rye bread that has a shiny, hard, sour crust. Slather on the mustard, crunch into a dill pickle to set your taste buds tingling, and this sandwich will take you straight to deli heaven.

Get some latkes (potato pancakes) too. They are double-thick, moist, and starchy: great companions to a hot lunch of short ribs or stuffed peppers; Shapiro's supplements ordinary latkes with cinnamon-scented ones—wonderful with sour cream. And soup: bean, lentil, split pea, and chowder are daily specials; you can always order chicken noodle or borscht.

## Teibel's

1775 Route 41

Schererville, IN

219-865-2000

www.teibels.com

LD | $$

Teibel's is one of a handful of restaurants that continues to serve the favorite big-eats Sunday-supper sort of meal so beloved in northern Indiana: boned and buttered lake perch. When it opened in 1930, it was a mom-and-pop café, and today it is a giant-sized dining establishment (run by the same family), but the culinary values that made it famous still prevail.

The feast starts with a relish tray—scallions, olives, celery, and carrots—followed by a salad (superfluous), then a plate piled high with tender fillets of perch glistening with butter. It is a big portion, and this fish is full-flavored; by the time our plate was empty, we were more than satisfied. Our extreme satisfaction was due also to the fact that we ate an order of Teibel's fried chicken too. Perhaps even more famous than the perch, this chicken is made from a recipe that Grandma Teibel brought from Austria many years ago. It is chicken with a crumbly, red-gold crust and juicy insides, in a whole other league from the stuff that comes in a bucket from fast-food franchises. Some other interesting items from Teibel's menu: frog legs (another local passion), walleye pike, and shrimp de Jonghe. For fish and frog frowners, there is a turkey dinner.

After a family-style feed, what could be nicer than a hot apple dumpling? The flake-crusted, cinnamon-scented dumpling is served à la mode with caramel sauce on top.

## Village Inn

107 S. Main St.          574-825-2043

Middlebury, IN           BL | $

If you are looking for a meal fitted to the mighty caloric needs of the Amish farmers who live around Middlebury, we recommend a booth at the Village Inn. Of course you can have eggs and potatoes and toast, just as in any regular town café, but you can also plow into a vast plate of cornmeal mush, accompanied by head cheese. Lunches are huge too: chicken and noodles or meat loaf or beef stew and mashed potatoes, smothered steaks and stuffed peppers, all served with richly dressed slaws and salads and well-cooked vegetables fattened up with bread crumbs, butter, and cheese.

The chief reason to come to the Village Inn is pie. If you really love pie of all kinds, three times a day, this place is the Promised Land. A typical day's selection includes Funeral Pie (made of raisins), OF Cream (meaning "old-fashioned" cream, made of little more than brown sugar and cream), cherry, peach, pineapple, banana cream, custard (white sugar and milk), and peanut butter/powdered sugar. One time several years ago, we felt a little gluttonous ordering four pieces for the two of us. But then we noticed two giant-sized bearded gents in overalls topping off their hearty chicken-and-noodles lunch with an entire funeral pie, split half-and-half between them.

## Archie's Waeside

224 4th Ave. NE
Le Mars, IA

712-546-7011
www.archieswaeside.com
D | $$$

A steak-eaters' destination since Archie Jackson started it in 1949, Archie's is now run by grandson Bob Rand, who is a fanatic for excellence and produces some of the best steaks anywhere in America. They arrive a little crusty on the outside, overwhelmingly juicy and bursting with the resonant flavor of corn-fed, dry-aged beef. Even the filet mignon, usually a tender cut that is less flavorful, sings with the authority of blue-ribbon protein. Bone-in rib eye is deliriously succulent. And an off-the-menu item called the Benny Weiker (named for a good customer of years ago who was a famous cattle buyer in the old Sioux City stockyards) is simply the most handsome piece of meat we have ever seen presented on a plate: an eighteen-ounce, center-cut, twenty-one-day dry-aged filet mignon.

Archie's is a sprawling restaurant with wood-panel décor that seems not to have changed since the 1970s. Its capacious booths are filled with happy customers who come from miles around to enjoy the beefy pride of Siouxland.

## B&B Grocery

2001 SE 6th St.
Des Moines, IA

515-243-7607
www.bbgrocerymeatdeli.com
BL | $

At Des Moines's B&B Grocery, you will enjoy insanely wide tenderloins while dining elbow-to-elbow with lunching locals. When we ate here, a group of police officers took great delight in demonstrating how to fold the meat over once or even twice inside the bun to make it easier to handle. Although this is a relatively thin tenderloin, inside its crisp, golden crust is a vein of pork that remains sweet and juicy.

B&B also is known for heroic "killer sandwiches," such as the Dad's Killer, which is roast beef, turkey, ham, and corned beef with three kinds of cheese, lettuce, tomato, pickles, mustard, Miracle Whip, and Italian dressing. The burger selection ranges from one-third-pounders to multilayer burgers, all the way up to a four-patty Quadzilla with the works.

For ambience, B&B can't be beat: It is an old grocery store with a make-shift eating annex of counter and stools. The butcher is the real deal, offering everything from a pound of ground chuck to halves of cows and hogs cut into steaks, chops, ribs, and roasts.

## Bauder Pharmacy

3802 Ingersoll Ave.
Des Moines, IA

515-255-1124
www.bauderpharmacy.com
BL | $

Many Iowans who have never been to Bauder Pharmacy know and love its ice cream because it is a regular attraction at the annual state fair, where peppermint ice cream bars, made with an Oreo crust, are a highlight of the endlessly good grazing grounds near the show pavilion. In addition to its own ice cream, Bauder's serves such nostalgic soda-fountain treats as a cherry Coke, a Green River, and a lime phosphate. There are fine sundaes, shakes, malts, sodas, and floats of every stripe. Summer is an especially good time to visit when the ice cream flavor rotation includes fresh strawberry and peach.

The savory menu includes classic lunch-counter sandwiches such as grilled cheese and a hot Reuben, as well as a "Roosevelt Special" of turkey, Swiss, and mustard grilled on a long roll.

Bauder Pharmacy was founded in 1922 by Carolyn Bauder, a pharmacist whose motto was "Cleanliness. Order. Service." Ice cream became part of the pharmacy repertoire shortly after World War II.

## *Bob's Drive-Inn

| | |
|---|---|
| Highway 75 S. | 712-546-5445 |
| Le Mars, IA | L \| $ |

You will not find loosemeats listed on the menu that hangs above the order window at Bob's Drive-Inn. That is because it goes by one of its several aliases, a "tavern." The dish is so heralded hereabouts that Bob's doesn't even offer a hamburger. If you want beef, you get loosemeats. Browned, strained of fat, then pressure-cooked with sauce and spice, this meat is moist, full-flavored, and deeply satisfying. Each sandwich is made on a good-quality roll that proprietor Myles Kass secures from Le Mars's own Vander Meer Bakery.

If for some reason you don't want loosemeats, or if you want to sample every good hot dog, get a couple of franks. They are natural-casing Wimmer's-brand beauties made in Nebraska. In the best-of-both-worlds department, have a Bob Dog, which is one of these snappy franks topped with loosemeats. The preferred side dish is cheese balls, which are deep-fried cheese curds.

Root beer is house-made, and fruit shakes are made from real summer fruit.

## The Chatterbox

| | |
|---|---|
| 120 N. Division St. | 712-563-3428 |
| Audubon, IA | BLD \| $ |

What an awesome tenderloin, one of Iowa's finest. It overhangs its bun, but it is neither fun-house wide nor parchment thin. It is a perfectly balanced combo of tender pork and crunchy crust. It comes accoutered with pickle chips and a slice of white onion. Apply your own mustard and/or ketchup. We appreciate the audacity of the Chatterbox's "hamberloin," which piles a hamburger atop the fried pork patty in a bun, but as much as we like burgers in nearly every form, the combo doesn't do beef justice. Compared to the pork it crowns, the red meat is cloddish, adding only avoirdupois to what is, without the burger, a rather elegant sandwich.

The Chatterbox is open for three meals a day, and many regulars come to have coffee and conversation throughout the day.

## *Coffee Cup Café

616 4th St.       641-594-3765

Sully, IA       BLD | $

If you are southeast of Des Moines looking for the sort of town café where locals come to eat and schmooze, here's the place. Breakfast is dandy—plate-wide golden pancakes and big rounds of sausage; there are eggs and potatoes of course, and sticky pecan rolls and cinnamon buns with a translucent sugar glaze, served warm with butter. Menu pillars at lunch include hot beef sandwiches (on made-here bread), tenderloins, meat loaf, and roast pork. And there is one square-meal special every day—we have fond memories of baked ham with mashed potatoes and apple salad. Dutch lettuce is a unique concoction of crisp, cold iceberg leaves bathed in a warm sweet-and-sour creamy mustard dressing with pieces of bacon and hard-cooked egg.

No matter what meal you eat, or what time of day you eat it, you must have pie at the Coffee Cup Café. Iowa is major pie country, and it is in just such inconspicuous small-town cafés that some of the very best are eaten. Looking for a good cream pie? Have a wedge of Coffee Cup banana cream. It quivers precariously as the waitress sets it down on the table, the custard jiggling like not-quite-set Jell-O below foamy white meringue. The crust doesn't *break* when touched with a fork; it *flakes*. The whole experience of cutting a mouthful, raising it to one's mouth, and savoring it is what we imagine it would be like to eat pastries on the moon or some planet where gravity is only a fraction of Earth's, for the word "light" barely does justice to the refinement of this piece of pie.

## Darrell's Place

4010 1st St.       712-563-3922

Hamlin, IA       LD | $

Darrell's Place looks more like a large utility shed than a restaurant; but aficionados of the tenderloin know that it is a culinary gem. Winner of the 2003 Iowa Pork Producers Association Award for the best tenderloin in the state, Darrell's serves tenderloins that are thick and juicy, enveloped in a wavy, thousand-facet crust that hugs the luscious lode of pork within. The band of meat is a good half-inch thick, making for an ultra-opulent eating experience. Unlike many of Iowa's best tenderloins, which are ridiculously large, this crisp-edged patty barely extends beyond the bun, meaning you can easily pick it up, even with one hand.

Darrell's rhubarb pie, made using stalks from customers' gardens, is peerless, piled into a master-class crust, its tantalizing sugar-tart filling balanced by a cascade of soft-serve vanilla ice cream.

## Grove Café

124 Main St.         515-232-9784

Ames, IA           www.grovecafe.com

                           BL | $

When you say "pancake" at the Grove Café, you might want to separate the word. In this place, a pancake is a *pan cake*—a good-sized layer of cake that has been cooked in a pan, or in this case, on the grill. Nearly an inch thick in its center, it is as wide as its plate—a round of steamy cooked batter that has an appealing orange hue. It comes with butter and a pitcher of syrup (all of which this cake can absorb with ease). With some peppery Iowa sausage patties, one of these cakes is a full-sized meal. Two of them, listed as a "short stack," are a breakfast for only the tallest of appetites.

Grove Café also offers omelets with hash browns and happy little slices of French toast for breakfast, as well as hamburgers, hot beef, and meat loaf at lunch. But for many of its longtime fans, including hordes of Iowa State alumni who have consumed tens of thousands of calories in these baretabled booths and at the low stools at the counter, pancakes are all that matter. To its most devoted fans, Grove Café is a pancake parlor.

## In't Veld Meat Market

820 Main St.         641-628-3440

Pella, IA           L | $

Most customers come to In't Veld to shop for meat rather than to eat, and even those of us who are just passing through will find such good travel companions as summer sausage, dried beef, and wax-wrapped cheeses. For those in search of regional specialties, the meat to eat is ring bologna, also known as Pella bologna because this town is the only place it is made. It is a tube of sausage about as thick as a pepperoni stick, curled into a horseshoe shape—cured, smoked, cooked, and ready to eat. It is delicious sliced cold with a hunk of cheese and a piece of bread; it's even better when you can warm it up and cut it into thick discs like kielbasa.

For travelers, what is especially good about In't Veld Market is that you can sit down right here and have a hot bologna sandwich: several thick slices on a fresh bakery bun . . . pass the mustard, please! In fact, a whole menu of meat-market sandwiches is available for eating here (or taking out) until midafternoon each day. In addition to the famous bologna (wonderful when paired with Gouda cheese), you can have house-dried beef on a bun, homemade bratwurst with sauerkraut on a hoagie roll, ham and Swiss, Reubens, and wraps. For dessert, we suggest a walk across the square to Jaarsma Bakery, a Dutch-accented shop with beguiling pastries, sweet cakes, and the alphabet-shaped cookies known as "Dutch letters."

## Iowa Machine Shed

11151 Hickman Rd.    515-270-6818
Urbandale, IA        www.machineshed.com/des-moines
                     BLD | $

The handful of Machine Shed restaurants in and around Des Moines are scrupulously planned to evoke idealized twentieth-century farm life. The one in Urbandale, at the edge of the city, is huge, its dining-room walls crowded with vintage farm implements, seed bags, and advertisements for country-style products. The staff dresses in farmhand attire (but clean!). While the menu has something for everyone, its highlights are big-food bonanzas that theoretically provide enough calories for a long day's work but, in fact, make us need to take a nap.

Hamburgers are a nice eight ounces each, and the chicken potpie is a beauty; but the meat to eat is pork: crisp-fried tenderloins made into sandwiches, stuffed loin of pork, and best of all, the Iowa pork chop. Iowans make an issue of pork chops, differentiating between ordinary pork chops and Iowa chops, the latter cut so thick that the meat takes on the character of a roast. At the Machine Shed, we ate the thickest pork chop we have ever seen . . . and topped it off with mighty hunks of pie and cake.

Breakfast is hugely hearty, featuring cinnamon rolls as big as a bread box and fruit-filled sweet rolls dripping with frosting. The variety of pig meat to accompany eggs is complete, and pancakes are plate-sized.

Unlike most Roadfood restaurants, the Machine Shed is a highway-exit tourist attraction with an entire front room devoted to selling rustic-themed souvenirs and snacks. Don't expect small-town charm, but do expect a true Iowa meal as big as the outdoors.

## Jesse's Embers

3301 Ingersoll Ave.  
Des Moines, IA

515-255-6011  
theoriginaljessesembers.com  
LD | $$

Jesse's Embers is the sort of supper club you don't find much anymore: dark and cool, home of expertly made cocktails and high-quality meat-and-potatoes meals. Ensconce yourself at a comfy table and start with a pile of kettle-hot onion rings and an iceberg lettuce salad topped with creamy garlic dressing and croutons.

Although the menu lists fish and chicken, Iowa pork chops, and baby-back ribs, it seems wrong not to get red meat: a sirloin, rib eye, or shockingly flavorful filet mignon. Beef is what has made Jesse's a beloved destination since the early 1960s. Seared over an open flame, steaks have a succulence that satisfies hunger with great waves of flavor. On the side, you want cottage-fried potatoes or a baked spud loaded with butter and sour cream.

## Larsen's Pub

4206 Main St.  
Elk Horn, IA

712-764-4052  
LD | $

Winner of the 2007 Iowa Pork Producers Association Award for the state's best tenderloin, Larsen's Pub makes one that is approximately a half pound of meat, pounded tender so that it extends beyond its bun in all directions, but still so thick that the big vein of pork within the golden crust spurts juice when you sink your teeth into it. Spread with mustard and bunned with lettuce, tomato, and pickle chips, this fine sandwich is a good explanation for why the tenderloin has earned such stalwart devotees.

Larsen's is an extremely inconspicuous storefront tavern in a Danish-ancestored town known also for its authentic Danish windmill, the Danish Inn (*frikadeller* meat balls, *medisterpolse* sausage, and *smørrebrød* sandwiches), and its annual end-of-May Tivoli Fest, featuring folk dancers, a costumed parade, and Danish-themed food vendors.

## Miles Inn

2622 Leech Ave.          712-276-9825

Sioux City, IA           LD | $

In northwest Iowa, taverns (also known as loosemeats) are more popular than hamburgers. Dozens of restaurants serve them, and each has its own twist on the basic formula, which is ground beef that is gently spiced and cooked loose so it remains pebbly when put upon a bun. The meat is generally garnished with pickle chips and mustard, often with cheese, and the sandwich is almost never served on a plate.

Miles Inn calls its taverns Charlie Boys after Charlie Miles, who was founder John Miles's son. Served in a wax paper wrap, taverns are well fatted with a concentrated beef flavor that even a sirloin steak cannot match. (Raise your hand if you agree with us that the one meal that most fully satisfies the deepest hunger for beef is a great burger, even more than a great steak.) Two or three Charlie Boys make a hearty lunch, and the right libation is a schooner of beer from the tap.

Built in 1925, the Miles Inn is a sturdy neighborhood gathering place that sells suds by the case as well as by the draught. Seating is at tables or the bar, and if the Hawkeyes are playing, you can be sure the game will be on all house TVs. Charlie Boys are the only available hot food.

## Milwaukee Wiener House

One block east of 309 Pearl St.    712-277-3449

Sioux City, IA                 BLD | $

Milwaukee Wiener House specializes in Coneys, formally known as Coney Island hot dogs, which are franks blanketed with chili. You see them marshaled on the grill by the window as you walk in. The formation is impeccable: row upon row, side-by-side, identical in shape, not one out of place. All condiments are available, but connoisseurs know there is only one way to go: mustard, chili, and chopped raw onions. Each dog comes fitted in a warm bun so soft and fresh that it shows finger-mark impressions from the gentlest grasp. The hot dogs themselves are pale pink tube steaks well complemented by the cinnamony zest of the house-made fine-grind beef chili. Three or four such steamy babies make a nice meal. Hamburgers and loosemeats are available for wiener frowners.

The Milwaukee Wiener House is a big rectangular dining room with rows of booths to which you tote your own meal after ordering at the counter. It opens at six in the morning, as it has done for nearly a century (its original location was nearby on 4th Street). Old advertising posted on the wall boasts that it has served 4 million hot dogs, but about eight years ago we were told that the tally had already topped 10 million.

## Mr. Bibbs

2705 6th Ave.                           515-243-0929
Des Moines, IA                          L | $

Mr. Bibbs lacks all the usual markers for charm, even those one might apply to a diner. It is no-frills stark, a kind of neighborhood miniature mess hall with booths lined up like desks in a humorless teacher's classroom. But check out these onion rings: hot from the fry kettle, each individual hoop is a circle of luscious crust that melts on the tongue. And the chocolate malt is terrific, just thick enough to make straw-sucking seem like athletic activity.

The main reason you want to come to Mr. Bibbs is its tenderloin. Four kinds are offered: regular (undressed), unbreaded, chili-topped, and deluxe. Deluxe is the way to go: a thin, double-wide loin garnished with lettuce, pickle chips, chopped raw onions, sliced tomato, mustard, and ketchup. It's a winning combo of crunch and oink, all the condiments tickling the taste buds the way only a fully dressed tenderloin can do.

## The Red Barn

613 W. Washington St.                   712-268-2645
Exira, IA                               BLD | $

We arrived at the Red Barn at three o'clock one August afternoon. Inside the low-slung eatery, which is the size of a modest house trailer, three of its four tables were occupied, but the only thing available was coffee. ("We're always open for coffee," the waitress chirped). We returned the next day at 11 a.m. for lunch and had what might be our favorite Iowa tenderloin. It is superwide but also mighty thick, really juicy, and snug inside a savory crust, garnished with pickles, onions, and summer tomatoes. The tenderloin is just one item on a Hawkeye State menu that also includes pea salad with shredded cheese bound in Miracle Whip, a loosemeats sandwich, nutmeg-dusted custard, and rhubarb crisp that the waitress recommended we order à la mode so as to offset the natural tartness of the pie plant.

By 11:45, every seat in the Red Barn was occupied and we were sharing our six-chair table with four strangers. Whereas habitués may linger when they come for coffee midmorning or in the afternoon, country-café courtesy at mealtime demands freeing up a seat as soon as one has finished eating.

We quickly polished off dessert and paid our check. We couldn't help but worry that we had appropriated two seats from a rotation of customers that rarely includes anyone from out of town.

## Smitty's Tenderloin Shop

| | |
|---|---|
| 1401 SW Army Post Rd. | 515-287-4742 |
| Des Moines, IA | www.smittystenderloins.com |
| | LD \| $ |

"Home of the REAL Whopper" says a cartoon on Smitty's wall, and if you know the taste of Iowa, you know that in this case "Whopper" does not refer to a hamburger. It means a tenderloin: pork tenderloin, pounded thin and plate-wide, breaded and fried crisp and sandwiched in a bun. Smitty's Tenderloin Shop has been a tenderloin lovers' destination since 1952.

Like all top tenderloin tenderers, Smitty's is a humble setting. It has a scattering of tables and a friendly counter where locals sit and shoot the breeze at lunch hour. Although the menu includes a handful of other lunch-counter meals—hamburgers, double hamburgers, Coney Island hot dogs—"King Tenderloin" is the dish to eat. Available in small or large sizes (small is large; large is nearly a foot across), Smitty's tenderloin is served on an ordinary burger bun, which it dwarfs. Even a person with abnormally long fingers could not pick it up like a normal sandwich, but it is brittle enough to easily tear off and eat pieces from the circumference until the bun is reachable. Twice breaded with cracker meal, then cooked in soybean oil ("for the flavor," says third-generation chef Ben Smith), Smitty's King is all about the crunch that envelops a slim ribbon of juicy pork.

## St. Olaf Tap

| | |
|---|---|
| 106 S. Main St. | 563-783-7723 |
| St. Olaf, IA | LD \| $ |

A sign outside the St. Olaf Tap advises, "Put Something Big Between Your Buns." It refers to the one-and-a-quarter-pound hunk of pork tenderloin that gets pounded out until it becomes a ragged-edged circle larger than a dinner plate, then breaded and fried crisp. The colossal hunk of food is presented between two halves of a hamburger bun that appears so relatively small that it reminds us of a tater tot. You can ask for it between halves of two buns, or three or four. Even a quartet is dwarfed by the meat within.

Without question, St. Olaf Tap serves the biggest of all tenderloins in the southern Midwest's tenderloin belt; it is also one of the most delicious: a savory balancing act of crunchy crust and succulent white pork, beautifully abetted by jumbo onion rings and/or corn fritters. Half-size and quarter-size versions also are available, but if you are more than one person (or if you have an insatiable appetite), we highly recommend getting the super jumbo; it's an only-in-Iowa dining experience.

## Susie's Kitchen

404 Broad Ave.      712-829-2947
Stanton, IA      BL | $

Susie's Kitchen is also known as Susie's Kök to honor the Swedish heritage of Stanton. Many people come here only for pie, of which there is always a wide variety. The one to eat is Fruit of the Forest, an extravaganza of apple, rhubarb, strawberry, blueberry, and raspberry heaped into a golden crust that is light, flaky, and flavorful thanks to its inclusion of lard. Susie's other pies are not made with a lard crust, and not nearly as good.

Susie's décor has a Swedish theme—painted woodwork, *Välkommen!* stenciled on the wall—and the lace-thin Swedish pancakes with lingonberries are a memorable breakfast. The lunch menu is more all-American, including a big hot beef sandwich and a nice Iowa tenderloin served on Susie's rye.

## Tastee Inn & Out

2610 Gordon Dr.      712-255-0857
Sioux City, IA      www.tasteeinnandout.com
     LD | $

Tastee Inn & Out is strictly takeout. Meals are procured at either a walk-up or drive-through window, and they are eaten either in the car or at a picnic table in the parking lot. Run by the Calligan family for over a half century now, this ingenuous eatery specializes in what it calls a Tastee sandwich, known elsewhere in northwest Iowa as a tavern or a loosemeats: made with finely ground beef that is seasoned and barely sauced, it is steam-cooked then shoveled into a bun with a slice of bright orange cheese, pickle chips, and onion. It is sloppy and unjustifiable by Cordon Bleu standards but hard not to like. Its only possible companion is an order of onion chips, which are bite-sized, crisp-fried petals of sweet onion, served with a creamy dip that eaters in the Plains farther west would recognize as a variant of fry sauce.

## Wilton Candy Kitchen

310 Cedar St.

Wilton, IA

319-732-2278

www.wiltoncandykitchen.com

$

We've never sampled Hadacol, the high-proof patent medicine that Colonel Tom Parker used to hawk before he became Elvis Presley's manager. But we do endorse the teetotaler's version of it made at the Wilton Candy Kitchen—an essential stop for anyone in search of small-town America the way it used to be.

Fiz-biz historians trace a fountain on this spot to the mid-1880s; today's Candy Kitchen dates back to 1910, when a young immigrant named Gus Nopoulos came to town and rented the place to make candy and sell soda and ice cream. Now run by grandson George Nopoulos and family, the Candy Kitchen is a trip back to a world of long-forgotten concoctions such as a pink lady (strawberry, cherry, and vanilla flavoring), an oddball (strawberry and vanilla), and a dipsy doodle (six different flavors). Cokes and cherry Cokes are mixed to order, using water carbonated on-premises and Coke syrup. Mr. Nopoulos told us that Coke syrup, once a fountain staple in every American town, is getting hard to find. "We've got to go all the way to Cedar Rapids for it now," he lamented. That syrup is half of the formula for the Nopoulos family version of the Hadacol (cola plus root beer), the name of which George explained to us thusly: "They 'hada call' it something."

## Bortell's Fisheries

5528 S. Lakeshore Dr.          231-843-3337
Ludington, MI                  L (summer only) | $

You catch it, they'll cook it at this 116-year-old fish market and smokehouse that has all the exterior charm of a roadside garage. If you do not BYO seafood, you'll have a choice of walleye, smelt, catfish, trout, and whitefish from nearby waters. Bortell's also imports ocean perch and Alaskan salmon. Smoked fish is sold by the piece or pound; fried fish comes picnic-ready with French fries or onion rings and coleslaw. Step up to the counter, place your order, and pay. There is no dining room and business is strictly takeout. Once you get your fish, find a picnic table just outside or across the road at Summit Township Park on the Lake Michigan shore.

## *The Cherry Hut

211 N. Michigan Ave.           231-882-4431
Beulah, MI                     www.cherryhutstore.com
                               LD Memorial Day-mid-Oct | $

Opened as a farm stand in 1922, the Cherry Hut moved to its present location in 1937. It has since become a restaurant with a repertoire of terrific comfort food: turkey with dressing, meat loaf with mushroom gravy, roast pork, and a different homemade soup every day. Cherry-centric dishes include turkey salad brightened up with cherries, a cherry jelly and peanut butter sandwich, and a cherry sundae. But it is pie that is the destination dish. A single serving is one-quarter of a full-sized pie; spilling out its sides are bright red, locally grown cherries with a sweetness balanced by a beguiling tart undertone. The crust is melt-in-the-mouth savory. Topped by a scoop of creamy vanilla ice cream, it's a perfect, all-American dessert.

Dining facilities include outdoor as well as indoor tables, and part of the Cherry Hut experience is buying things to take home. The restaurant shop sells not only whole fresh pies but also jellies, jams, and a wide array of Cherry Jerry, the Happy Pie-Faced Boy souvenirs.

## Crossroads Lounge

900 County Rd. 480          906-249-8912
Marquette, MI              BLD | $

Crossroads Lounge opens at 7 a.m. and serves food until 10 p.m. (after which the bar stays open). It is locally famous for its Friday-night fish fry, but it also hosts a regular clientele of breakfasters who come for big omelets served in a skillet. Yoopers (that's people of the Upper Peninsula, aka the UP) come for half-pound hamburgers, pizzas, sandwiches, and a bargain lunch of bottomless soup-salad-breadsticks for $6.99. But the real deal here is the pasty.

It was on a pasty hunt that we were directed to this sociable outfit on the outskirts of the city by a man up Houghton way who told us that Crossroads' pasty was the best in the UP. We do not agree that it's the best, but it's definitely *one* of the best, packed with both beef and pork, as well as carrots in addition to the customary rutabaga, potato, and onion. While a common fault of inferior pasties is that they can be bland and/or dry, this one sings with spice and is moist enough that gravy is redundant.

Crossroads Lounge is all set up for takeout pasties: hot and ready to eat, cool and ready to heat, or frozen and ready to bake.

## Don's Drive-In

2030 N. US Hwy. 31          231-938-1860
Traverse City, MI          LD | $

Don's opened the year Elvis joined the army. Selections on its jukebox evoke days of American midcentury car culture at its prime, and the ambience is vintage rock-and-roll: hubcaps and album covers decorate the walls and you can dine inside or in your car, where meals are served on window trays. The menu is basically burgers and fries, featuring the old-fashioned "basket" presentation, meaning a sandwich sided by French fries and coleslaw.

The tough decision to make at Don's is whether to get a hamburger or a brace of Coney Island hot dogs. The burger is thick and juicy; a Coney, topped with chili sauce, is a Midwest paradigm. Whatever you get to eat, there should be no question about the beverage. Make it a milk shake. Don's blends its shakes to order, either large or small, both big enough to fill at least a couple of glasses, and both thick enough to require powerful suction with a straw. Chocolate and vanilla shakes are good all the time; in the summer, order a cherry shake—it is made with fresh local cherries.

## Gustafson's

4321 US-2                            906-292-5424
Brevort, MI                          L | $$

Michigan's Upper Peninsula lends itself to waterside picnics. A few chaws of beef jerky, a hunk or two of smoked freshwater fish, a stack of saltine crackers, a bag of cheese curds, and a few beers, plus the scenic beauty of Lake Michigan: What's better than that? And where better to get them than at Gustafson's, a gas station and party store that has it all ready-to-eat but does not offer full-service meals.

Even with your eyes closed, you'll find Gustafson's as you cruise along the shore road (we don't recommend driving this way) because a sugar maple haze from a quartet of smoldering smokers outside clouds the air with the unbelievably appetizing smell of whitefish, trout, menominee, chub, and salmon turning gorgeous shades of gold. Inside, coolers are arrayed with the firm-fleshed beauties, which you can buy by the piece, wrapped in butcher paper. Utensils and plates are unnecessary; it's a pleasure to use one's fingers to pick flavorful chunks of fish straight from the paper.

The beef jerky is top round, cut into strips, marinated, then slow-smoked over maple. You can get it Cajun-spiced, barbecue-flavored, or traditional smoky-sweet. Jerky is available through the mail, by the pound.

## Irontown Pasties

801 N. Teal Lake Ave.                906-475-6828
Negaunee, MI                         www.irontownpasties.com
                                     LD | $

On the exterior wall at the back of Irontown Pasties is a very old sign, partially gone now to make way for a new window. Its only completely legible letters are the last three: I-E-S, but you don't have to be a professional semi-ologist to know that the first four letters are P-A-S-T. This sign out of the past is a reminder that the building that now houses Irontown Pasties has purveyed the Upper Peninsula's favorite meat pies for a long, long time, its most recent prior incarnation being Grandma T's Pasty Shop. The current owners, John and Lori Cizek, bought Grandma T's, along with the recipes; then, as Mr. Cizek jokes, they "changed everything."

You still can get a typical pasty here, and it is a dandy: beefy comfort food in a lovely tender crust—satisfying plain, but exciting when decorated with one of the three degrees of hot jalapeño ketchup Irontown offers. Other pasty choices include vegetarian with cheese, vegan with no lard or suet, spicy beef, and chicken potpie pasties. When served on premises, they come with a fork, but Irontown's pasties would be easy to eat with your hands.

For dessert, have either Cedar Crest ice cream (a northern Midwest brand) or fruit turnovers that look a lot like pasties but are filled with com-pote of blueberry, raspberry, apple, or cherry.

## The Jampot

6559 State Hwy. M-26　　　　　　No phone
Eagle Harbor, MI　　　　　　　　www.societystjohn.com/store
　　　　　　　　　　　　　　　　L mid-June–mid-Oct | $

In a fairy-tale hut in the Eagle Harbor forest of Michigan's Upper Penin-sula, monks of the Society of Saint John make cookies, muffins, cakes, and breads. Simply stepping out of the car in the Jampot parking lot can be dizzying from the warm smell of Jamaican black cake soaked with liquor and filled with fruits marinated in wine and rum. As its name suggests, this place also is renowned for jams and jellies made from Keweenaw's wild fruits: thimbleberry, strawberry, raspberry, bilberry, blueberry, dewberry, cokecherry, pincherry, sugarplum, blackberry, and apple.

There is no place to eat at the Jampot, other than one of the most beau-tiful dining spaces on the planet: the great outdoors of Michigan's Upper Peninsula. We grabbed a big, muffin-shaped banana-walnut bread packed with blueberries, a bag of molasses-powered gingerbread cookies, and a lemon-frosted pumpkin muffin, then drove to a nearby snacking spot over-looking achingly beautiful Lake Medora. Gazing at the opposite shore, where autumn trees were perfectly mirrored on the still blue waters, we were in heaven, thanks in no small part to the monks.

## *Jean Kay's

1635 Presque Isle
Marquette, MI

906-228-5310
www.jeankayspasties.com
LD | $

Having had its ups and downs, Jean Kay's pasty shop currently is flying high. It was started by the Harsch family in 1975 in Iron Mountain and, as Jean Kay's Sweet Shop, its specialty was donuts. But then Mr. Donut came to Iron Mountain. Tourists favored the franchise, and when donut sales plummeted, Jean Kay Harsch suggested they make pasties. She felt the Upper Peninsula could use a place that made the British Isles meat pies the way her grandmother used to do it back when they were a staple in the diet of the region's Cornish settlers, who were known as Cousin Jacks and Cousin Jennies.

If you want to know what Grandmother's pasties were like, visit Jean Kay's of Marquette, a restaurant started by Jean Kay's son Brian, sold to someone else, then rebought by Brian when he came to believe that his successor's pasties were not up to snuff. Here you will savor a classic, made with steak (not burger meat) and suet (not lard). Although rutabaga-free pasties are available, Brian explained the value of rutabagas in the filling—an ingredient frequently ignored by Jenny-come-lately bakers. "It is an amazing vegetable," he enthused. "Aside from its own flavor, it works with whatever else is in there to keep the moisture flowing. It is a conduit."

While Jean Kay's is a small storefront with a few tables inside and out, the pasty-making part of the operation is big. Being USDA-approved, it can FedEx half-baked, frozen pasties coast-to-coast, anytime between September and May. Varieties include steak, veggie with cheese, and mini pasties that make wonderful hors d'oeuvres.


## Johnny's Ham King

2601 W. Fort St.
Detroit, MI

313-961-2202
BL | $

Now that Motor City muscle has atrophied and Motown is ancient history, we suggest Detroiters find pride in their ham. Thanks to a truck driver named Joe, who tipped us off to what he called "out of this world" ham, we discovered that this is a city where little diners make a big deal of ham at low prices. Mike's Famous Ham Place in Corktown and Johnny's Ham King at the Ambassador Bridge are the Big Two, where the pinkest part of the pig

is sliced to order and sizzled on the griddle, served on the side of eggs for breakfast or sandwiched, still warm, in soft onion rolls for lunch.

Gearjammer Joe, who especially recommended Johnny's four-egg omelet with ham and buttery, extra-crisp potatoes, noted that a swivel stool at the long counter was the place to sit. Here is where you get to watch Pete, a short-order cook with a quarter century of experience, wield his spatula like a samurai sword and entertain customers with impassioned political soliloquies. In addition to the Ham King, ham and bean soup is a must.

## Lafayette Coney Island
118 W. Lafayette Blvd.                313-964-8198
Detroit, MI                          LD | $

Although the term Coney Island comes from the Brooklyn beach resort where the hot dog supposedly was invented in 1867, you will find nothing called a Coney Island hot dog in the New York area. And the Coneys you do find nearly everywhere else in the nation bear only scant resemblance to the hot dogs of New York. While Coneys vary, their common denominator is chili topping, which never was part of the boardwalk formula. About 99 percent of them also are served with mustard and chopped raw onions.

Nowhere is the passion for Coneys more intense than Detroit, where an adjoining pair of rival storefront doggeries known as American Coney Island and Lafayette Coney Island serve franks that might look pretty much alike to the casual observer but are cause for adamant partisanship. We like them both, but last time we compared, Lafayette won.

Make no mistake, Lafayette's Coneys are not aristocratic; they are plebeian. But the harmony of spicy hot dog, soft white bun, smooth chili, bright yellow mustard, and crisp onions (and maybe shredded cheese too) is culinary magic. When the craving for one (or, more likely, four) of them strikes, Kobe beef wouldn't satisfy. It is possible to order one with "heavy chili," but we believe that throws the precious balance off. Better to have your extra chili blanketing French fries or cheese fries. The appropriate beverage with Detroit Coneys is a can of Vernor's ginger ale.

## Lawry's Pasty Shop

2381 US 41 W.
Ishpeming, MI

906-485-5589
www.lawryspasties.com
BLD | $

The sweet roll at Lawry's Pasty Shop is among the nation's pastry behemoths, approximately six inches square with enough white icing for a birthday cake. It's pretty good for that kind of thing, but heaven forbid you
expend all of your appetite eating one. A healthy appetite is essential for
enjoying Lawry's real specialties: pasties and *cudighi.*

One look at the semi-open kitchen behind the order counter provides
evidence of the menu's claim that "We still make our pasties with pride
every day just like our grandmother did when she started this business
in 1946." They are fine, hefty, hand-formed pastry pockets packed with
suet-saturated beef, potato, onion, and rutabaga. Succulent as it is, Lawry's
pasty is portable enough that a half-eaten one can be put back into the paper
bag in which it's served for a nice car snack later in the day.

Lawry's also makes an amazing *cudighi,* which is the sandwich made
from pattied Italian sausage by the same name. A passion in the central UP,
*cudighi* (the sausage) is distinguished by its use of such floral spices as nutmeg, clove, and allspice. Put between slices of flatbread along with onions,
peppers, mushrooms, Italian sauce, and grated cheese, it is a colossal meal.

## Northside Grill

1015 Broadway St.
Ann Arbor, MI

734-995-0965
www.northsidegrill.com/hom
BL | $

The Northside Grill is not a pancake house. The popular pine-paneled café
has a full menu for breakfast and for lunch, but other than drinking lots of
its really good coffee, we've not been able to get much beyond the superb
pancakes. Best of the bunch may be the apple–oat bran 'cakes with their
rugged, apple-chunk texture and cinnamon twist. A similar configuration is
available with blueberries. Plain buttermilk pancakes are too dairy-delicious
to be called plain. Potato pancakes are crunchy on the outside but creamy
within, and sparkling with herbs and spices, topped with grilled red onion
and accompanied by ramekins of sour cream and applesauce.

We loved our Big Easy Omelet made with andouille sausage and a
full measure of Cajun spice, and did manage to sample a piece of masterful apple pie, but there are so many subjects for further study, includ-

ing cinnamon-swirl French toast and breakfast burritos, not to mention a good-looking lunch repertoire of burgers, chili, Mexican plates, and salads.

## Ralph's Italian Deli

601 Palms Ave.  906-485-4557

Ishpeming, MI  www.ralphsitaliandeli.com

LD | $

Across the street from the US Ski & Snowboard Hall of Fame and catty-corner from a boring Pizza Hut, you will find Ralph's Italian Deli. It is anything but boring; it is an Upper Peninsula gem.

From the house bakery come sweet rye, cardamom loaves, and Italian breads, as well as enormous frosted apple-cinnamon rolls for breakfast. The butchers in back make sausage of all kinds, including the local fave, *cudighi*. Pronounced cud-a-gee with a hard *g,* it is such a specialty of Ralph's that there is a map posted on the back wall of the dining room where pushpins indicate all the places in the United States and beyond to which the butchers have shipped their sausage, titled "Where Has All the Cudighi Gone?"

A *cudighi* (sandwich) is available with a grilled patty of mild, medium, or hot sausage on a house-made white or whole-wheat roll. Standard dressing at Ralph's is mozzarella, mustard, ketchup, and onion. It's a strange combination of condiments, but somehow on this dense, crusty-edged sausage with perfumy seasoning, it works. For those interested in reducing their calorie intake, Ralph's also makes turkey *cudighi*.

## Suomi Home Bakery & Restaurant

54 Huron St.  906-482-3220

Houghton, MI  BLD | $

More people of Finnish descent live in Michigan's Upper Peninsula than anywhere outside of Europe, so it is hardly affectation that the menu of the Suomi Home Bakery & Restaurant lists dishes in Finnish with English translations. You can get familiar *voileivät* (sandwiches) for lunch, and rice pudding or banana cream pie for *jälkiruoat* (dessert), but we recommend *aamiainen* (breakfast—served all day), for which *nisu* bread, perfumed with cardamom, is made into Finnish French toast, and *pannukakku* is the star attraction. Described as a Finnish pancake, *pannukakku* puts us in mind of a crustless egg-custard pie—sweet, creamy, fundamental. One large cake, about a half inch thick, is baked in a glass tray and served in sunny yellow four-by-four-inch squares along with warm raspberry sauce. The sauce is wonderful, but we used it on *nisu* toast, unwilling to modify the pancake.

In some ways, Suomi is a classic American town café, where locals come to share morning coffee and regulars are well known by the staff. But the chatter, like the unusual food, lets you know you are someplace different. On our first visit one morning, it took a while to realize that cross-table conversations in the spacious dining area actually were in English rather than some Scandinavian language. It was the dialect known as Yooper, from UP (Upper Peninsula), a curiously musical blend that sounds Finnish and German and a bit Canadian and is especially strong northwest of Marquette.

The bill of fare at this handsome place, decorated with vintage photographs of copper-country history, is not all exotic. You can get bacon and eggs for breakfast (better yet, sausage and eggs; the dense, herby sausage links are made across the Keweenaw Waterway in Hancock) and hamburgers and ordinary sandwiches at lunch. And of course you can have a pasty filled with rugged clumps of beef and little irregular nuggets of potato and rutabaga. For a Finnish finish, end a meal with a bowl of cooked, cooled dried fruit known as *visku vellia*.

## Toni's Country Kitchen

| | |
|---|---|
| 79 3rd St. | 906-337-0611 |
| Laurium, MI | BLD \| $ |

Toni's is a few blocks off US 41, the main road leading up through the Keweenaw Peninsula. We likely never would have found it if an enthusiast we met in Houghton hadn't told us that his wife used to make *nisu* and saffron bread until they discovered Toni's, where the bread is so good that his wife hung up her apron. Those loaves, made by many Finnish bakeries in northernmost Michigan, are just two of the memorable eats.

Sticky buns: We smelled them the moment we walked in the front door. Three big round clusters of pull-apart buns were set on a rack atop the glass bakery case to cool. Each roll severed from the motherloaf was modest-sized but big-flavored. Just inside the front door, to the left, we peeked into the semi-open kitchen, where bakers were rolling dough on a floured table and another woman was plowing forearm-deep to hand-mix a big pan full of ingredients destined to be the filling of pasties. Toni's pasties are handsome fellas, light and elegant yet profoundly beefy.

It was late fall when we stopped in. The modest, one-room café was buzzing with conversations among locals who were reminiscing about the summer and anticipating the snows to come. When we ordered pasties, the waitress beamed with pride and exclaimed, "The best, ever!" We left with bags full of oven-warm molasses cookies and a loaf of *povitica,* a nut-rich sweet bread of central European heritage.

Note: Toni's closes just before Christmas and reopens at the end of January.


## Trenary Home Bakery

E2918 State Hwy. M-67      906-446-3330
Trenary, MI               www.trenarytoast.us
                          B | $

Like biscotti and zwieback, Trenary Toast is a brittle, twice-baked bread that is ideal for dunking. But unlike the first two, both of which literally mean twice-baked in their countries of origin (Italy and Germany), Trenary Toast is named for the one and only small-town bakery that makes it: Trenary Home Bakery in Trenary, Michigan. Available plain, sugared, or cinnamon-sugared, it is—like Vernor's ginger ale and Detroit-style square pizza—treasured by those who grew up with it.

Trenary Toast can be found in markets and delis throughout the central Upper Peninsula, as well as at a few places in lower Michigan. Although it virtually never gets stale, it is a special pleasure to get some straight from the source—a charming little bakery-café that also offers breads, cinnamon rolls, and cookies, along with coffee for sit-down snacking on the spot.


## Zingerman's Deli

422 Detroit St.           734-663-3354
Ann Arbor, MI             www.zingermansdeli.com
                          BLD | $$

It started small, but Zingerman's has become a culinary colossus that includes a mail-order business, creamery, bakehouse, coffee shop, and estimable full-service roadhouse (at 2501 Jackson Ave.). While not every success proves the adage that they must be doing something right, the fact is that Zingerman's doesn't merely do something right; it does everything fantastically well.

Sandwiches are our favorite things, made with such top-notch ingredients as Nueske's bacon, Amish free-range chicken, Niman Ranch pastrami, Michigan-grown vegetables, Italian salami, Arkansas ham, and smoked salmon from Maine. They are assembled on the best bread in the Midwest:

world-class baguettes, the best old-fashioned double-baked Jewish rye in the nation, sourdoughs, chile-Cheddar, pecan raisin, or challah. And let's not even get into such peripheral *(not!)* items as excellent pickles, olive tapenade, smoked fish salads, and multiple cheese spreads, including pimiento cheese that competes with anything in the South.

Obtaining lunch can be confusing. You enter the surprisingly small deli, which is a retail operation selling meats, breads, cheeses, and so on, and browse a menu posted all over the wall. While you are figuring out what you want, a server will approach to take your order and your name. Find a seat (lots of nice ones outdoors for fair-weather dining), to which your food will soon be brought. The staff is extremely friendly and patient, and they are full of helpful recommendations if you can't decide between, say, halloumi and Muenster cheese.

Zingerman's is more expensive than an average sandwich shop. A BLT is $9.50–$10.99, depending on size; grilled cheese is $6.50–$7.99. But what you get is far superior to, and considerably bigger than, an average sandwich. Roadfood omnivores will find it frustrating because a single visit, no matter how much you order, will provide only a glimmer of all the good things there are to eat . . . and to see and to smell.

# Al's Breakfast

413 14th Ave. SE

Minneapolis, MN

602-331-9991

BL | $

Al's is open year-round, but the coziest time to eat in this pint-sized diner near the University of Minnesota is from October through April, when the windows cloud with breakfast-scented steam from the well-seasoned griddle where pancakes, eggs, hash browns, and corned beef hash sizzle. It is impossible to convey the joie de vivre at Al's, where a patron once rhapsodized to us, "Al's is an organism. It is not some soulless concept restaurant that a corporate idea man at a drawing board designed. Good things happen here; people's lives change. If you want a car, or an apartment, or a sweetheart, come in and sit at the counter. Come in, have coffee, and chat a while. Pretty soon, I promise, you will get what you need. Al's has a life of its own, above and beyond any of us. I truly believe it is a crossroads of the universe."

OK, then, how about those buttermilk pancakes? They are broad, thin, and slightly sticky inside, with a good, sour smack. Rivulets of butter and sweet syrup complete their flavor perfectly; or you can get them made with blueberries or giant blackberries. The other basic batter variation is whole wheat, which has a wholesome, earthy flavor; either batter can be studded with corn kernels or walnuts as the pancakes cook. For garnishing these distinguished flapjacks, you can choose extra-cost maple syrup, sour cream, or bowls of berries. Beyond pancakes, Al's offers perfectly poached eggs, well-oiled corned beef hash, omelets, and crunchy hash browns.

## Betty's Pies

1633 Hwy. 61
Two Harbors, MN

218-834-3367
www.bettyspies.com
BLD | $

Betty's sports a full menu of walleye sandwiches, hamburgers, wraps, salads, and Upper Peninsula pasties, but its reputation was earned by pies. Pies still are the reason to visit. Fruit pies are heavyweights, cream pies thick and creamy, and a few years ago Betty's introduced an item called a pie shake. Yes, it is what it sounds like. One entire piece of pie of whatever flavor you choose is blended with ice cream and milk! Our waitress dissuaded us from getting one made with fruit pie, as it would have too grainy a texture, so we chose banana cream, which made us think of pie à la mode in a tall glass. Pieces of banana and bits of crust inevitably clogged the straw, making it a drink that must be gulped or spooned.

Betty's is famous enough that it can get crowded in the summer when travelers come to enjoy the beauty of Lake Superior's North Shore. Although remodeled since its opening in 1956, and now under new management with Betty retired, it remains a charming place with blue-and-white kitchenette décor and waitresses who are outspoken in the best diner tradition.

Note: Betty's has limited hours in winter months; be sure to call ahead.

## Bloedow Bakery

451 E. Broadway
Winona, MN

507-452-3682
B | $

Minnesota foodlore tells the story of the little, home-grown bakery (in business for some eighty years) that ran Krispy Kreme out of town. It was back in '03 that the national chain moved in, setting up its products throughout town in groceries and convenience stores. But the interloper donuts did not impress Minnesotans who knew better. In less than two years, KK had vanished from the shelves and Bloedow reigned supreme.

It's a sweet story for those of us who prize eateries with genuine character and the glazed and cake donuts, sweet rolls, maple-frosted long johns, and cookies at Bloedow (rhymes with Play-Doh) deserve their renown. Tipster Vanessa Haluska recommended Bloedow's peanut butter roll—a big, circular pastry made with sweet dough and swirled with peanut butter where you might expect cinnamon.

Note: In a 2012 poll conducted by Minneapolis's WCCO-TV, viewers elected Bloedow Bakery the Best Donut Shop in Minnesota.

## Bread & Chocolate

867 Grand Ave.
St. Paul, MN

651-228-1017
www.cafelatte.com/bread_chocolate.
htm
BL | $

Across the street from its parent eatery, Cafe Latté (below), Bread & Chocolate is an informal bakery and espresso shop open early every day for breakfast. There is lunch, which is mostly sandwiches on Cafe Latté bread, but it's the morning pastries that draw us near. Big croissants are available plain or filled; they are as flaky as possible, lightweight yet luxurious. It's astonishing how many blueberries get packed into the blueberry muffin, which is made from creamy batter that is an ideal medium for the fruit. Scones are moist and tender, like cake but not as sweet; tart lingonberries are an inspired inclusion, especially when the scone is topped with slivered toasted almonds.

A squared-off pastry called a "cinnamon swirl" is what you want a Cinnabon to be, but Bread & Chocolate's is no dyspepsia-inducing disappointment. The soft dough is butter-fresh and swirled with thick veins of cinnamon; the fine-textured icing makes sugar seem like health food. Best of everything is the sticky caramel roll: crisp-edged, enrobed in amber glaze, and studded with pecan halves.

Bread & Chocolate espresso is especially delicious: opaque and earthy. Next visit, we need to try the turtle latte listed on the coffee menu. The Twin Cities, after all, are in the running for Turtle Capital of America.

## Cafe Latté

850 Grand Ave.
St. Paul, MN

651-224-5687
www.cafelatte.com
LD | $$

There isn't anyplace in America that can top Cafe Latté when it comes to cake temptation. Triple-layer beauties include orange blossom, German chocolate, and turtle—an intense mountain of the moistest possible cake interleaved with fudge, caramel, and meaty pecan halves. Among notable double-layer cakes are très leches, pumpkin pecan, lemon blueberry, and pear ginger. And there are cheesecakes, bundt cakes, tortes, and tarts.

Pre-cake, Cafe Latté is a great place for soup, sandwiches, and salads. There are all kinds of Caesar salad variations—the classic version as well as a Caesar supplemented by artichoke hearts, Greek olives, or sliced tomatoes. Or how about a chicken Caesar pasta salad? Each individual one is made to order (service is cafeteria-style), so you can specify if you want a little more of this or that. In the adjoining wine bar, you'll find beautiful pizzas, from classic margherita to barbecue chicken potato.

## Convention Grill

3912 Sunnyside Rd.      952-920-6881
Edina, MN      LD | $

A Convention Grill hamburger won't win kudos from the nutrition police, but for us it inspires hash-house rapture. Sizzled to crisp-edged succulence on an oil-glistening grill, it oozes juice, and is complemented by melted cheese, lettuce, tomato, and mayonnaise (known as California-style). Fries are picture-perfect honeytone brown, a satisfying mix of crunch and spuddy creaminess. You also can order a Plazaburger with sour cream, chives, and chopped onions in a dark bun, as originated at the Plaza Tavern in Madison, Wisconsin.

Such a classic American meal demands a thick malt. Flavor choices include chocolate, wild blueberry, butterscotch, strawberry, coffee, banana, vanilla, caramel, honey, hot fudge, Butterfinger, mint, and Reese's Peanut Butter Cup. For 50¢ extra, you can have fresh banana added. If one of these malts doesn't satisfy your ice cream cravings, have a hot fudge sundae. It is served with a good portion of fudge underneath the ice cream, plus more fudge in a pitcher to pour on as you plow through.

## *Hell's Kitchen

80 S. 9th St.      612-332-4700
Minneapolis, MN      www.hellskitcheninc.com
     BLD | $$

Our first visits to Hell's Kitchen were for breakfast—some of the best breakfasts anywhere. Every table is supplied with chef Mitch Omer's magnificent preserves and marmalade and extra-luxurious chunky peanut butter, which are themselves a compelling reason to eat at this downtown hot spot. Among the stars of the morning menu are huevos rancheros of the gods—a huge plate of food that includes spicy beans, eggs, cheeses, sour cream, and fresh salsa on a crisp flour tortilla. Rosti potatoes come alongside too, and they are available as a dish unto themselves. Chef Omer's rostis are less like the Swiss spuds that are their namesake than they are glorified hash browns, shreds of potato mixed with bacon, onions, chives, and scallions and grilled in sweet cream butter. A few other breakfast specialties: lemon ricotta hotcakes, maple-glazed bison sausage, and a quarter-pound caramel pecan roll with a refined glaze that is a sweet tooth's dream.

No one should have breakfast at Hell's Kitchen without a serving of Mahnomin Porridge, a recipe that the promethean Mr. Omer came up with from reading trappers' accounts of native Cree Indian meals that featured wild rice. He supplements the Native meal of rice, hazelnuts, cranberries, and maple syrup with a full measure of warm, heavy cream, making this the most lavish hot cereal imaginable.

The lunch menu is every bit as inviting. How about a walleye BLT made with cornmeal-dusted fillets and lemon tartar sauce instead of the homemade mayo the kitchen uses on its regular BLT? Who cannot love the ham and pear crisp sandwich on sourdough bread, draped with a mantle of Swiss and fontina cheeses? We instantly became addicted to the house Bread Bucket, which is all the chewy, freshly made baguette you can eat, served along with sweet cream butter, Omer's preserves, and peanut butter.

We once were asked: "If you had time for only one meal in Minneapolis, where would it be?" Our immediate response was Hell's Kitchen. But the more we thought about it, the more we didn't like that answer. Only one meal would be insanely frustrating—there are too many fabulous things to eat.

### *Lange's Cafe

110 8th Ave. SE, Rt. 23          507-825-4488
Pipeston, MN                     Always open | $

The moment we walked into Lange's Cafe, we looked at the case of caramel rolls and knew we had hit pay dirt. Sure enough, as we ate our way through as much of the menu as possible, we swooned with pleasure over and over again. Roast beef is the entree not to miss. It is pot-roast tender, available with mashed potatoes, green beans, and gravy, or as "hot beef," which is a sandwich with mashed potatoes on top and gravy all over. Mashed potatoes are the real thing; dinner rolls are freshly baked.

The caramel rolls that so many people eat for breakfast must be sampled any time they are available. They are immense blocks of sweet, yeasty dough—about three inches square—and they are bathed in buttery warm caramel syrup that has a burnt smack to its sweetness.

Sour cream raisin pie, a specialty of bakers in Minnesota, Wisconsin, and Iowa, is at its best at Lange's. The custard base is dense, packed with raisins, creamy and sweet with the sour-cream edge that makes its sweetness all the more potent. The meringue is air-light; the crust flakes when poked by a fork. It was our supremely lucky day, for we walked into Lange's at about 10 a.m. and the pie was out of the oven only a short while. Our pieces were faintly warm, like baby food, and we declared this the best sour cream raisin pie ever made . . . 10 on a 1-to-10 scale.

## Lindstrom Bakery

12830 Lake Blvd.          651-257-1374
Lindstrom, MN             B | $

A Lindstrom Bakery Scandinavian donut is similar to a regular donut, but eggier, oilier, darker, and with a crisp tan surface. Proprietor Bernetta Coulombe, known to all as Bernie, said that her late husband endlessly fussed and fiddled with the recipe until he got it right. When he died, regular customers were concerned that his secrets went with him, but Bernie quickly assured them that she has what it takes to continue his legacy.

We wonder: "Why are they called Scandinavian?"

She answers: "Because I am Scandinavian and I make them."

In any case, they are pretty much the opposite of sissy donuts such as Krispy Kreme. Nothing wimpy or dainty about these sinkers. They come plain and glazed, coated with cinnamon sugar or drizzled with chocolate. In addition, Lindstrom makes donut holes and all sorts of more ordinary (that is, less substantial) donuts as well as Swedish white bread, caraway limpa bread, raisin rye, caramel rings, cookies, and coffee cakes. Lindstrom also makes a breakfast toast that is similar to Michigan's Trenary Toast (p. 374): baked-hard slices dusted with cinnamon sugar, ideal for soaks in morning coffee.

## Maverick's

1746 N. Lexington      651-488-1788
Roseville, MN      www.mavericksroastbeef.com
         LD | $

Maverick's doesn't look like much—an inconspicuous storefront in a strip mall—but its roast beef sandwich is extraordinary: pink, velvety slices cut to order and piled into a soft white bun while the meat is still hot and moist. Rick Nelson of the *Minneapolis Star-Tribune* told us that the restaurant concept was inspired by the proprietor's desire to improve on Arby's. If that was the goal, he has more than succeeded, for this is a super roast beef sandwich—simple, pure, and satisfying.

It is served cafeteria-style, along with a short menu of other beefy things, including brisket (offered on a dark pumpernickel bun) and barbecued beef, plus pulled pork, ham, chicken, and fish fillets. When we stopped by, open-face roast beef sandwiches were the day's special: the same good beef piled on a plate with the roll on the side and a couple mounds of mashed potatoes. While the beef in this one was the same as in the simple sandwich, we much preferred Maverick's crisp French fries to the ersatz mashed potatoes.

Once you get your food, stop by a condiment bar, where the choices range from horseradish and horseradish cream to hot peppers, ketchup, mustard, and pickles. Find a place at one of the four-tops along the side of the room or at the long banquet table in the middle. We walked out happy and satisfied.

## Northern Waters Smokehaus

394 Lake Ave. S., Ste. 106      218-724-7307
Duluth, MN      www.northernwaterssmokehaus.com
         L | $

Before he came to Duluth, Eric Goerdt was a fisherman in Sitka, Alaska, where he perfected his techniques for smoking fish as well as meats. When you listen to him talk about the firm luxury of a hunk of salmon that has been hand-trimmed, marinated, and smoked over maple wood, you are hearing a man on a mission to make delicious smoked food. Mission accomplished! His little smokery in the DeWitt-Seitz Marketplace in Canal Park is a culinary gem for passersby as well as lovers of smoked fish and meats who wish to mail-order their favorites.

It is a tiny retail store with a few tables for sitting down and eating such fine sandwiches as bison shoulder braised in Schlitz and barbecue sauce on a bun; wild Alaskan sockeye gravlax with pickled ginger, vegetables, and wasabi mayonnaise on a baguette; and an insanely opulent gloss on the traditional Reuben, this one made of hot bison pastrami, caramelized onions, pepperoncini, mayonnaise, and provolone on a crusty hard roll. We also treasure this place as a source of provisions. It is a secure feeling to hit the road with a stack of saltines and hunks of perfumy Lake Superior whitefish and smoked salmon for noshing between meals.

## Tavern on Grand

656 Grand Ave.
St. Paul, MN

651-228-9030
www.tavernongrand.com
LD | $$

There is more to eat than walleye at "Minnesota's State Restaurant Serving Minnesota's State Fish," but the moist white fish is so rare anywhere else that it behooves the culinary traveler to focus on it. Walleye cakes (like crab cakes, served in a spill of Béarnaise sauce) or a basket of deep-fried walleye bites make fine hors d'oeuvres. Many regular customers come for a walleye sandwich—a grilled or fried fillet on French bread. Probably the best way to savor the flaky fineness of the locally loved fish is to have it simply grilled, served on a plate with some vegetables. It comes with tartar sauce, but it's a shame to smother so delicate an eating experience with anything. Surf 'n' turf types can get the Lakeshore Special—a single fillet accompanied by a half-pound sirloin steak. You can even get walleye in the Minnesota fairgoer's favorite configuration, served on a stick like shish kebab. To round out a regional meal, there is wild rice turkey soup.

With interior appointments reminiscent of a hunting lodge in the North Woods (but comfortable!), Tavern on Grand feels like the right place to enjoy a Great Lakes meal. Wherever you sit in the bar, you will have a good view of the TV and whatever game is currently on.

## World's Best Donuts

10 E. Wisconsin St.
Grand Marais, MN

218-387-1345
www.worldsbestdonutsmn.com
BL mid-May–mid-Oct | $

"The only donut that has ever rivaled my late grandmother's donuts," wrote tipster Paul Swindlehurst, attributing the excellence of World's Best Donuts to its frying medium: lard. "Best when warm," Mr. Swindlehurst advised. Heeding his advice, we arrived shortly after the shop opened at 4:30 one spring morning. Amen and hallelujah! Still warm from the fryer, these circular sylphs are donut royalty. We were awestruck by the plain cake donut, a hand-cut beauty that is substantial but in no way leaden, sweet enough and yet with deep, savory satisfaction. Chocolate-frosted and cinnamon-sugar cake donuts are simple and unimprovable, and the locally loved skizzles (similar to elephant ears), which are deep-fried dough discs smothered with sugar, provide a great way to maximize the joy of lard cooking.

Regulars keep their cups on the mug shelf so they can pour their own while waiting in line to place an order. Registered donut eaters (sign up for free) are entitled to a free donut when they return.

## Amighetti's

5141 Wilson
St. Louis, MO

314-776-2855
www.amighettis.com
LD | $

Amighetti's is a serve-yourself sandwich shop that has become a beloved culinary institution on "The Hill," St. Louis's old Italian neighborhood. Eating here is casual and fun, especially on a pleasant summer day. Place your order at the window and wait for your name to be called. Find yourself a seat on the sunny patio, and feast on a legendary Italian sandwich. Next door to the restaurant, Amighetti's bakes its own bread—a thick-crusted loaf with sturdy insides ready to be loaded with slices of ham, roast beef, Genoa salami, and cheese, garnished with shreds of lettuce and a special house dressing that is tangy and a little bit sweet. All kinds of sandwiches are available, including a garlicky Italian hero, roast beef, and a three-cheese veggie sandwich—all recommended primarily because of the bread.

Each sandwich is wrapped in butcher paper secured by a tape inscribed with Amighetti's motto: "Often Imitated, Never Duplicated."

## Arthur Bryant's

1727 Brooklyn Ave.

Kansas City, MO

816-231-1123

www.arthurbryantsbbq.com

LD | $$

Arthur Bryant used to shock reporters by calling his esteemed barbecue restaurant a "Grease House." Although the master of Kansas City barbecue passed away in 1982, his business heirs, bless them, never tried too hard to shed that moniker. The original location of the "House of Good Eats" (another of Mr. Bryant's appellations) remains a cafeteria-style lunchroom with all the decorative charm of a bus station. (There are branches at the Kansas City Speedway, Ameristar Casino, and the airport.)

Because Arthur Bryant and his brother Charlie (who started the smokehouse) hailed from Texas, it makes sense that smoked brisket—a Texas passion—is the best meat in the house. It drips flavor. Have it in a sandwich or if you come as a large party, order a couple of pounds of beef and a loaf of bread and make your own at the table. Pork ribs are wonderful too, glazed with blackened burnt edges and loads of meat below their spicy crust. Skin-on French fries are bronze beauties, and the goopy barbecue beans are some of Kansas City's best.

What makes Arthur Bryant's unique is the sauce. It is beautiful—a gritty, red-orange blend of spice and sorcery that is not at all sweet like most barbecue sauces. It packs a hot paprika wallop and tastes like a strange soul-food curry that is such a nice complement to any meat. Once you've tasted it, you'll understand why this old Grease House is a foodie legend.

## Booches

110 S. 9th

Columbia, MO

573-874-9519

LD | $

A billiard parlor/tavern where the beverages of choice are beer (in a bottle) and iced tea (in a pitcher), or maybe Coke in a paper cup, Booches is a magic name to hamburger aficionados. The hamburgers—known among old-timers as "belly bombers"—are small but juicy, maddeningly aromatic, and served unceremoniously on a piece of wax paper. They are available with or without cheese, and the condiments are onions, pickles, mustard, or ketchup; yet their smoky/meaty flavor is extraordinary from first bite to last. In 1999, Booches won kudos from the *Digital Missourian* as an Earth-friendly eatery, not only because each hamburger is cooked to order (thus, no meat is wasted), but because "no one can leave a Booches burger half-eaten."

Some of the food's charm is no doubt due to the offhand way in which it is served in colorful surroundings. Booches is the oldest pool hall in Columbia, and it is likely that your burger—or good chili dog—will be eaten to the wooden clack of pool shooters as well as the noise of whatever sports event is blaring on the television. Décor is a combination of sports memorabilia, praise from famous artists who have enjoyed the beer and burgers, and some delightful politically incorrect humor, including one sign that advises, "Parents . . . keep your ankle-biting little crumb-gobblers on a leash or I will put them in the cellar to play with the rats."

## C&K Barbecue

| | |
|---|---|
| 4390 Jennings Station Rd. | 314-385-8100 |
| St. Louis, MO | www.candkbbq.com |
| | LD  \| $ |

St. Louis has always been a barbecue town; C&K represents the best of this tradition. It is a small former service station with no seating (all takeout) and late-night hours well suited to after-midnight rib cravings. Ribs, rib tips, chopped meat, even chicken, all bathed in Daryl Brantley's exclamatory sauce, are served in Styro boxes with sweet-potato salad and soft white bread that makes a good sponge for drippy extra sauce. These are extremely messy meals, so we recommend getting extras napkins.

In addition to all the familiar specialties, C&K offers a few rarer items such as snoots (pig snouts baked until crisp and bathed in sauce) and ears (yes, pig ears, cooked until butter-soft and served between two slices of white bread, with or without sauce). These items are for the advanced barbecue connoisseur. First-time visitors should start with a slab of ribs!

## Carl's Drive-In

| | |
|---|---|
| 9033 Manchester Rd. | 314-961-9652 |
| Brentwood, MO | LD (closed Sun & Mon) \| $ |

A sixteen-stool diner on old Route 66, Carl's is the place to belly up for elegant-oily hamburgers and foot-long hot dogs smothered with chili. The burgers are mashed flat on the grill so that their edges turn into a crisp filigree of beef, and they are thin enough that a double or a triple makes good sense, as does the addition of cheese.

Burgers are the main attraction, but Carl's is also a source for three-way chili and tamales topped with chili or sauce. Shoestring French fries are a great companion for any meal, and the thing to drink is house-brewed root beer drawn straight from the barrel, served in a frosted mug. (Milk shakes, available in only two flavors, vanilla and chocolate, are the real deal.)

Expect to wait for a seat at lunchtime, but not too long. The turnover is quick, and it is an amazing thing to watch the staff juggle.


## Crown Candy Kitchen

1401 St. Louis Ave.          314-621-9650
St. Louis, MO                www.crowncandykitchen.net
                             LD | $

The Crown Candy Kitchen is an old-time sweet shop that makes its own chocolate candy and serves all kinds of malts, shakes, sodas, and sundaes. We are especially fond of the chocolate banana malted and the hot fudge malted. The house policy is to give five malts free to anyone who can consume them in thirty minutes (except during the lunch-hour rush).

Other than excellent ice cream treats, Crown has a nice lunch-counter repertoire of sandwiches, tamales, chili, and chili mac. Items of special interest from the kitchen are what the menu calls a Heart Stopping BLT, loaded with bacon and guaranteed to be made with Miracle Whip, and house-made chicken salad, available only on Tuesdays and Thursdays.


## Donut Stop

1101 Lemay Ferry Rd.         314-631-3333
St. Louis, MO                www.thedonutstopinc.net
                             B | $

A stark-white building, the Donut Stop has been earning loyal customers since 1953. Glazed donuts are lightweight beauties, and there are five kinds of fruit-packed fritters, a variety of fried pies, twists, cream-filled long johns, French crullers, and cinnamon rolls. The single item that makes us dream of coming back is what is known as a Cinnamon Glob, a hole-less pastry with egg-rich insides and an exterior with mouth-watering sugar crunch.

## Goody Goody Diner

5900 Natural Bridge Ave.      314-383-3333
St. Louis, MO      www.goodygoodydiner.com
BL | $

Breakfast is served all day (until closing midafternoon) Wednesday and Friday at the Goody Goody Diner, and other days until 11 a.m. The menu is vast, ranging from omelets, pancakes, waffles, and French toast to boneless catfish fillets with eggs and one amazing dish known as the Wilbur. Known in other local diners as a slinger, the Wilbur is an omelet filled with chili, fried potatoes, peppers, onions, and tomatoes.

Goody Goody's chili is stout and salty, made with chunks of beef, and it is the fundamental element in a once-popular but now rare Midwestern diner dish, chili mac. Goody Goody's chili mac is prepared with blunt hashhouse style: well-cooked spaghetti noodles are crowned with chili and a mass of shredded Cheddar cheese.

"We have changed many items on our menu over the years," the Goody Goody credo goes. "But the way we prepare our Certified Angus Beef hamburgers will never change. They're not fancy. Just *Really* Good." We agree. Regulars and doubles, patty melts and cheeseburgers, slawburgers and barbecue slawburgers are all outstanding, available with sides that include onion rings, French fries, cheese fries, and, of course, chili. Each burger is mashed down hard enough on the grill that it becomes a thin, rugged patty with a lacy-crisp circumference.

## Hodak's

2100 Gravois Ave.      314-776-7292
St. Louis, MO      www.hodaks.com
LD | $

Hodak's is a tavern with a full menu, including steaks, frog legs, sandwiches, and toasted ravioli. Most customers come for fried chicken, made from a recipe used by the Hodak family since 1962 (and voted #1 by St. Louisans for decades). Meals come as half chickens, four drumsticks, five wings, or chicken livers. Pay 40¢ extra and you will get an order of Hodak's excellent hot barbecue sauce for dipping.

Nearly everybody waits for a table at mealtimes. Despite its modest appearance and location in a blah neighborhood, Hodak's attracts hordes of hungry families from miles around. If you are having a party, the kitchen offers up to a two-hundred-piece fried chicken package for $236.

## Jess & Jim's

517 E. 135th St.                                816-941-9499
Kansas City (Martin City), MO        www.jessandjims.com
                                                        LD | $$$

Jess & Jim's, a Kansas City landmark that opened in 1938, is all about beef. This is apparent even from a distance, when you spot the huge statue of a bull atop the roof. Steaks arrive from the kitchen exuberantly sputtering, crusty from an iron griddle. The pound-and-a-half Playboy Strip is two inches thick, and unlike the super-tender bacon-wrapped fillets, it demands some chewing. Not that it is tough; but neither is it a cut for milquetoasts. Dense and intense, this is steak lover's steak, which is not to say that the T-bones, porterhouses, and strips are anything less than excellent.

On the side of regal meat, excellent potatoes are essential. There are cottage fries and French fries and immense bakers available, of course, with sour cream, bacon, and shredded cheese as condiments. The sleeper on the menu here is fried chicken. It's a reminder that as much as it always has been Beef Central, Kansas City also is a noteworthy fried chicken town.

Be aware that on weekends especially, this place gets very crowded. Call-ahead seating is available . . . and much advised.


## LC's Barbeque

5800 Blue Pkwy.                          816-923-4484
Kansas City, MO                          LD | $$

LC's sandwiches are presented in little trays because they are too messy for a flat plate. Sauce-sopped meat is piled in outlandish measure onto a puny slice of white bread and topped with another slice. The bread underneath disintegrates before it arrives at your table. Eating is done either with plastic utensils or picking at the sandwich by hand and unrolling plenty of paper towels that are supplied to every table by the roll.

From the barbecue pit behind the counter come beef, ham, turkey, pork, sausage, and ribs, as well as burnt ends. These are luscious nuggets cut from the outside edges of smoked brisket. Many pieces are laced with an obscenely delicious amount of fat; there are chewy pieces and crunchy pieces, the whole shebang fairly glowing with LC's thin, powerfully peppery, celery-seed-accented barbecue sauce. First-rate French fries come alongside.

Luxurious as the food may be, LC's is a stark place, décor consisting of a television set up in the corner of the dining room and a few dusty game-animal heads on the wall. Place your order and pay for it at the counter, and it will be delivered to your table posthaste.

## Niecie's

5932 Prospect  
Kansas City, MO

816-444-6006  
www.nieciesrestaurant.com  
BLD | $

Niecie's is a soul food café opened by Denise Griffin Ward in 1985. Since then it has become a sort of community center, and every morning except Sunday you can expect to see a table with a dozen or more Baptist and Holiness Church pastors gathered for breakfast. As we sat down in a booth one day, a couple nearby were praying over their pork chops before digging in.

We really like the breakfast of chicken and waffles: three jumbo wings, fried with lots of gnarled crisp skin, along with a waffle and a plastic jug of Hungry Jack syrup. Other breakfast choices include pancakes, country ham, and eggs with grits. Roadfood.com's Buffetbuster described Niecie's biscuits as "more like grilled corn cakes." Topped with peppery sausage gravy, he deemed them "simply the best I have ever had."

Among the daily lunch specials are salmon croquettes on Monday, a legendary smothered chicken Tuesday, short ribs Friday, and fried catfish Saturday. If you do have lunch, be sure to reserve enough appetite for dessert. Layer cakes—chocolate or caramel-frosted—are memorable.

The most exotic item on the menu, at least for those of us who don't have easy access to southern Midwest soul-food specialties, is the pig ear sandwich. "You get two ears!" beamed waitress Ms. Myra C., whose badge identified her as having nineteen years of service at Niecie's. Yes, indeed; it is two whole ears in a bun. We got ours with the works: lettuce, tomato, onion, and horseradish. We've got to admit that ears are a little scary, not so much because they're the worst part of the pig—there are plenty of parts far worse even to think about. The problem is that they look exactly like what they are: large, pointy porker ears. Their taste is not objectionable; it's something like the fatty parts of bacon or streak o' lean; but the gelatinous texture is, to say the least, a little weird.

# Riley's Pub

3458 Arsenal St.                      314-664-7474

St. Louis, MO                       LD | $

St. Louis–style pizza is characterized by unleavened, matzoh-thin crust and Provel cheese—a made-in-Wisconsin product that is a combination of provolone, Cheddar, and Swiss. Provel is essential because it tends not to weep oil when it cooks, thus helping keep the crust good and crisp. You can get this pizza at a chain called Imo's, at an Italian neighborhood place called Rigazzi's, and at Riley's Pub. Not exactly the place you'd expect to find memorable pizza, Riley's is a corner bar complete with darts, live music, Tuesday-night karaoke, and half-price pizza Monday and Tuesday.

The pizza is cut into little squares wieldy enough to hold in one hand while grasping a schooner of beer in the other. Completely unlike pies that are thick or chewy, it is easy to eat without worrying about drippage or crust collapse. In fact, it is rather amazing how the fragile-seeming crust stays crisp under toppings that can include sausage, pepperoni, buffalo chicken, and barbecue chicken. If this strange style of pizza is not your cup of tea, Riley's has a full pub menu that includes ribs, steaks, burgers, and sandwiches.

# *Snead's

17101 Holmes Rd.                 816-331-7979

Belton, MO                     www.sneadsbbq.com

                                   LD (closed Mon & Tues) | $$

Of all the many good smoke-cooked meats on Snead's menu, our favorites are beef and/or ham brownies, which are the crusty, smoky chunks stripped from the ends and tips of the meat—the best burnt ends imaginable. They aren't as soft as the ordinary barbecue, but they fairly explode with the flavor of meat and smoke. Sliced pork does not pack the potency of brownies, but it is hugely satisfying and sensuously tender. Beef brisket is shockingly fatless, and sauce is a natural companion. Snead's offers two variations: a slightly sweet mild sauce and a vigorously peppery orange brew that is reminiscent of Arthur Bryant's, not at all sweet. Then there are log sandwiches, named for their shape: tubular mixtures of finely ground barbecued beef, turkey, and ham, all minced together and wedged into a long bun. The result is a salty, powerful mélange reminiscent of a Maid-Rite. On the side: hand-cut, freshly made French fries, barbecue beans, and finely chopped coleslaw that is perfectly suited to brightening a fatigued tongue.

A low, rustic dining room decorated with quilts, farmy pictures, and a small collection of vintage wooden coat hangers, Snead's is way out in the country, where urban sprawl hasn't yet arrived. Opened in 1956 on Bill Snead's farm, it is, in our book, one of the greats, if not the greatest, among Kansas City barbecue restaurants.

## *Stroud's

| | |
|---|---|
| 5410 NE Oak Ridge Dr. | 816-454-9600 |
| Kansas City, MO | www.stroudsrestaurant.com |
| | D Mon-Thurs; LD Fri & Sun (Sat open |
| | from 2 p.m.) \| $$ |

Stroud's location on Oak Ridge Drive lacks the tumbledown charm of the original restaurant Mrs. Stroud opened in the 1930s on the location of the family fireworks stand, but the modern place has its own assets: an expansive frontier farmhouse with dining tables overlooking green grass on the rolling countryside. What better spot on Earth could there be to enjoy the ultimate fried chicken dinner?

The chicken is slow-sizzled in an iron skillet, emerging with a coat of gold that is noisy to crunch and not the least bit bready; there is just enough of it to shore in all the juices. Once you break through, those juices flow down chin and fingers and forearm. Side dishes are straight from heaven's table. Pour some peppery cream gravy onto the thick cloud of mashed potatoes; tear off a piece of warm, buttery cinnamon roll; spoon into chicken soup with homemade noodles. Even the green beans, which left al dente far behind, pack surprising porky sparkle.

Meals are served family-style. Stroud's is hugely popular and most of the time you will have to wait for a table, then wait while your chicken is fried. You will be glad you did.

A second location is at 4200 Shawnee Mission Parkway, Fairway, KS (913-262-8500).

## *Ted Drewes

| | |
|---|---|
| 6726 Chippewa | 314-481-2652 |
| St. Louis, MO | www.teddrewes.com |
| | (closed in winter) \| $ |

For anyone in search of America's most delicious ice cream (and who is not?), here's a name to put on the short list of candidates for greatness: Ted Drewes. Technically, Drewes' product is not ice cream. It is frozen custard, meaning it is egg-rich and ultra-creamy. There's nothing more purely dairy-delish than vanilla, but you can mix it with flavoring agents from chocolate and strawberry to fudge, cherries, cookies, nuts, and candy bars.

The best-known dish in the house is called a concrete, which is a milk shake so thick that the server hands it out the order window upside down, demonstrating that not a drop will drip out. Beyond concretes, there are sundaes, cones, floats, and sodas.

Ted Drewes has two locations (the second is at 4224 S. Grand Boulevard, phone: 314-352-7376), both of them thronged all summer long with happy customers spooning into huge cups. In autumn, the custard operation closes and Ted goes into the Christmas tree business.

If you are far away and seriously crave this superb super–ice cream, Ted Drewes is equipped with dry ice to mail-order its custard.

## Aglamesis Bros.

3046 Madison Rd.                    513-531-5196
Cincinnati, OH                      www.aglamesis.com
                                    LD | $

Anne Mitchell, dining editor of Cincinnati's alt-weekly newspaper *City-Beat,* informed us that Queen City ice cream connoisseurs tend to come down strongly in favor of either Aglamesis or Graeter's. It is her opinion that the decision depends on whether you like maximum butterfat (which Graeter's delivers) or extreme sweetness (an Aglamesis trait). It's a fine difference, and both are so good that we'd be hard-pressed to choose. But since Graeter's is a big chain and there are only a couple of Aglamesis Bros., the latter gets our nod.

Aglamesis's pumpkin ice cream, an autumn-only flavor, is as dark as Indian pudding, a just-right balance of spice and cream. Fresh banana delivers real tropical fruit flavor and can be haloed magnificently by a generous application of house-made bittersweet chocolate sauce. Dense-bodied whipped cream and a hail of chopped pecans complete the picture of perfection.

In addition to being an ice cream parlor (accoutered all in pink), Aglamesis is a complete chocolate shop with cases full of barks, clusters, truffles, and turtles. There is a second location at 9899 Montgomery Road, Cincinnati (513-791-7082).

## *Al's Corner Restaurant

545 W. Tuscarawas Ave.       330-475-7978

Barberton, OH       L Mon-Fri | $

This immaculate storefront luncheonette, open only for weekday lunch, is a treasure trove of blue-plate Hungarian meals at blue-collar prices. Step to the right when you enter and there you'll find a small steam table with all the day's food set out. Beth Gray will put it on a plate and then a tray. Dine either at a table or the long U-shaped counter in the center of the room.

Choices are limited, but we've yet to find a clinker among such Old World stalwarts as cabbage and dumplings, pierogies, stuffed cabbage rolls, and Al's sausages, which are available in two variations—mild Slovene and spicy Hungarian. Made down the street at Al's Quality Market, the sausages are dense and big flavored (even the mild). Paprikash is creamy with a real paprika punch, the chicken falling-off-its-bone tender. For an accompanying starch, the choice is daunting: buttery dumplings, mashed potatoes and gravy, or *halushka,* which is a savory mix of cabbage and noodles. For dessert: beautiful strudel (apple, cherry, or cheese).

## Avril-Bleh & Sons

33 E. Court St.       513-241-2433

Cincinnati, OH       www.avril-blehmeats.com

                         L | $

Avril-Bleh & Sons has been in the pork-packing business for well over a century (house motto: "A Link with the Past Since 1894"), and its display of tube steaks is a postgraduate education in oinky edibles. The curriculum includes bierwurst, bratwurst, knockwurst, bockwurst (spring only), yard sausage (with garlic), tiny links, oatmeal rings, liverwurst, kielbasa, wieners (natural casing or skinless), Cajun andouille, smoked Italian, chorizo, and *metts.* Short for *mettwurst,* a *mett* is a cured, deeply smoked, rugged-grind sausage about twice as large as a regular hot dog, firmly packed inside natural casing. *Metts* are also sold by street carts around town.

While most of what Avril-Bleh sells is meat to take home and cook, the shop does maintain a cook-cart out on the sidewalk as well as a handful of chairs for alfresco dining. The cart's menu is minimal: kielbasa, Italian sausage, chorizo, brats, cheeseburgers, hot dogs, and three kinds of *mett* (regular, hot, and Cheddar), all available in a bun with peppers, onions, kraut, and condiments. The Cheddar *mett* is magnificent. The skin audibly crackles when severed by teeth; its interior, while not oozy, is radiant with sweet pork flavor and a fusillade of spice.

## Babushka's Kitchen

6531 Brecksville Rd.  216-447-9275
Independence, OH  www.babushkafoods.com
        LD | $$

So, so many tempting choices! Do you start with *czernina* soup, a sweet-and-sour brew made with duck, prunes, and dumplings and served in a charming little ramekin with a bird on its lid? Or chicken soup with *kluski* noodles? Or stuffed cabbage soup? Or tomato dumpling soup? Of course, you must have pierogies, but these are so large that two make a meal. Do you have them filled with potato and Cheddar? Roasted sauerkraut? Sweet dry cottage cheese? On the side of dinner, how can one choose a single item from the likes of sauerkraut and dumplings, cabbage and noodles, marinated cucumber salad, and real mashed potatoes with roast pork gravy?

Among Babushka's special dinners, we do highly recommend the Warsaw, which is sinfully tender roast pork mixed with grilled onions, sauerkraut, and gravy sandwiched between potato pancakes with a crown of sour cream. Smoked kielbasa is firm and juicy, well accompanied by kraut and dumplings. Even if you don't particularly like stuffed cabbage, try Babushka's. These *golabki*, enveloped in a rich, sweet-and-sour tomato gravy, set the standard.

Babushka's is a simple place with homespun charm. For those in search of food with a real connection to local culture, it's a gem. The house slogan is "Revive Your Memories and Reunite Your Family."

## Balaton

13133 Shaker Sq.  216-921-9691
Cleveland, OH  www.balaton-restaurant.com
        LD (closed Mon) | $$

Great Hungarian food is one of Cleveland's culinary assets, and there is no better place to enjoy that fact than at a table in the Balaton. We've seen it described as a home-cooking restaurant, and dining here could be like coming home for supper, but only if you were lucky enough to have a mom who cooked brightly spiced and velvety paprikash (chicken or veal), crunch-crusted wiener schnitzel, and potato pancakes energized with a jolt of pepper. No mom we've known makes so magnificent a version of *lecso*—rugged smoked sausage atop a stew of yellow peppers, tomatoes, and onions.

Expert as it is, there really is something motherly about this food. It is so nurturing, so real, so down to earth. The hearty fare is well abetted by the setting, a handsome space that once was a men's clothing store, and by the staff, who all seem to be family (or act like it), including the small boy who was doing his homework at a back table when we stopped in for lunch.

The drink menu includes Hungarian wine as well as tart cherry juice from northern Michigan. You will have to choose dessert from a mouth-watering roster of multilayer *dobos* torte, chestnut cream torte, sponge-cake dumplings tipsy with rum, and *palacsinki,* which are slim crepes rolled around filling of apricot, sweet cheese, walnut, or poppy seed.

## Balyeat's Coffee Shop

133 E. Main St.        419-238-1580
Van Wert, OH        BLD (closed Monday) | $

Fried chicken has starred at Balyeat's since it opened in 1924. Good though it may be, it is just the headliner on a menu that is an honor roll of mid-American square meals. Here is a place to sit down for a plate of roast pork or roast beef, cooked that morning, served hot and large, with piles of mashed potatoes and gravy. Sauerkraut and sausage is on the menu every day but Friday, and you can usually count on a choice from among barbecued ribs, meat loaf, and liver and onions. If mashed potatoes don't ring your chime, how about the fine alternative, escalloped potatoes?

Ahh, dessert! Pie is king, and Balyeat's pies are pastries to behold. There are cream pies, fruit pies, custard pies, and pecan pie; our personal favorite is the one known as "old-fashioned pie" (OF pie). It is like custard, but tawnier, and with a layered effect that happens as its cream rises to the top. It is utterly satisfying: culinary synecdoche for Balyeat's Coffee Shop.

## Belgrade Gardens

401 E. State St.        330-745-0113
Barberton, OH        D | $$

Are you looking for fried chicken that is drippingly juicy with a dense, red-gold crust that crunches and melts into pure savory flavor? If so, come to Barberton, Ohio, where a handful of restaurants in the Akron suburb specialize in what is known as Barberton chicken. Belgrade Gardens, which opened in 1933 and is now a huge, happy function hall, is where this particular kind of chicken first gained popularity, and while the menu is vast—including steaks, chops, seafood, sandwiches, and some really good chicken paprikash—first-time visitors need to get the full chicken dinner. You can get white or dark meat or a combination or a plate of nothing but legs, thighs, backs, wings, or tenders. Each is available small, medium, and large.

The secret of this chicken's appeal is no secret at all: It is fried in lard, and only lard can yield the supersavor that defines it. All the local chicken houses make it the centerpiece of a ritual feast that includes a bowl of spicy tomato-rice hot sauce, sweet-tart coleslaw, French fries, and a basket of white and dark bread.

## *Camp Washington Chili Parlor

3005 Colerain Ave.          513-541-0061
Cincinnati, OH              www.campwashingtonchili.com
                            Always open, except Sunday | $

Camp Washington sets the standard for Cincinnati's unique style of chili—a layered mound of limp spaghetti noodles topped by vividly spiced ground beef, then kidney beans, raw onions, and, finally, a fluffy crown of shredded Cheddar cheese. Oyster crackers are used as a garnish and one traditional side dish is a Coney Island hot dog topped with chili, cheese, and onions.

The other notable Queen City specialty on Camp Washington's menu is the double-decker sandwich, the basic principle of which is similar to five-way chili: stacked ingredients as impressive for looks as for multileveled tastes. Possible double-decker ingredients range from eggs and breakfast meats to roast beef, ham, and cheese. While half of a well-made one can indeed be picked up in two hands, it cannot be eaten like a normal sandwich, with all strata going into the mouth at one time. It must be nibbled at in such a way that some bites are more the top layer and others more the bottom.

While proprietor John Johnson has expanded and modernized the open-all-night restaurant since taking over in 1977, he has—bless his soul—maintained the welcoming, democratic spirit of a great American urban diner.

## Cathedral Buffet

2690 State Rd.             330-922-0467
Cuyahoga Falls, OH         www.cathedralbuffet.com
                           LD | $

If you are neither a devout Christian nor a student of heartland American foodways, you probably won't enjoy dining in this restaurant, which is one part of the vast Ernest Angley Ministries. Before or after eating in the thousand-seat mess hall, one can step into the basement and pay a dollar to walk through the life of Christ as depicted in dioramas at Barbie-doll scale that show his journey from Nativity to Resurrection.

As for the food, it is of the church supper genre. Grab a plate and help yourself to an awe-inspiring multiroom buffet, including a cheerfully named Talk-of-the-Town salad bar area arrayed not only with lettuce and such but with a shimmering, multihued Jell-O mold, butterscotch pudding, and chocolate ambrosia with broken-up cream-filled cookies. (All are considered salad in much of the Midwest.) Of the dozens of other dishes available, we have enjoyed such home-ec masterworks as turkey Tetrazzini, broasted chicken, noodles in broth, and fruit cocktail cake: soul food for squares.

## Crabill's

727 Miami St.  
Urbana, OH

513-653-5133  
www.crabillshamburgers.com  
L | $

Once an accursed branch of hash-house gastronomy, the griddle-fried micropatty known as a slider has become strangely fashionable. We have encountered Kobe beef sliders as hors d'oeuvres in striving restaurants, and most people who eat out have likely come across non-beef, so-called sliders made of barbecue, crab cakes, or tuna tartare. Let us assure you that the sliders you will eat at Crabill's are not trendy or upscale, and they are made of ordinary hamburger beef (and optional ordinary cheese) on spongy little buns. Eating one (that's about two bites' worth) is a unique experience: Cooked in deep oil on the grill, it has an outside surface with formidable crunch, and it is so skinny that there is virtually no interior. Six singles or a trio of doubles make a decent meal, but you might want to try to beat a record, which, last we looked, was thirty-three singles in one sitting (by a man) and nineteen doubles in one sitting (by a woman).

## Eckerlin Meats

116 W. Elder St.  
    (in the Findlay Market)  
Cincinnati, OH

513-721-5743  
www.eckerlinmeats.com  
L | $

Eckerlin is a fairly small retail butcher shop in the very large Findlay Market. Given its modest space, it does booming business. We first were directed to it by Roadfooder Marjorie Solomon, who said it made the best *goetta,*

Cincinnati's beloved pork and pin oats breakfast meat. A man behind the counter said he would be happy to make us a *goetta* sandwich, as long as we had the patience for it to fry.

Even before frying, the preparation of *goetta* is a painstaking process. Eckerlin cooks it a full four hours in a Dutch oven where a bell goes off every twenty minutes to remind a member of the staff to stir it. Once it's done and made into a loaf, slices from the loaf are fried ten or twelve minutes until the outside gets crusty and the inside is cooked through.

Although condiments are available, we took our sandwich plain on buttered white toast and strolled into the market for coffee to accompany it. It is easy to understand why Eckerlin is considered the top of the line among *goetta* connoisseurs. Instead of being made from ignominious by-products—its original provenance as a thrifty dish—it is made from creamy pork shoulder and a rainbow of spice, its meaty intensity cheerily leavened by little earthy bits of oat. It deserves status right up there with ham and bacon as one of pork's glories.

## Flury's Cafe

1300 Sackett Ave.
Cuyahoga Falls, OH

330-929-1315
www.fluryscafe.com
BL | $

This tiny diner seats scarcely over a dozen people and there is nothing revolutionary on the menu, but if you are in greater Akron and looking for a hospitable slice of Americana, we highly recommend it. There is always a pancake of the day—we enjoyed cornmeal and banana-nut—and lunch opportunities include meat-loaf sandwiches and mac 'n' cheese, preceded by proprietor Kim Dunchuck's homemade soup. All the usual milk shake flavors are available, plus blueberry, raspberry, cherry, and peanut butter. For dessert, choose from among Kim's homemade cookies and shortcake laced with blueberries or blackberries.

## G&R Tavern

103 N. Marion St.
Waldo, OH

740-726-9685
www.gandrtavern.com
BLD | $

Since 1962, the G&R Tavern has built its reputation on bologna sandwiches that put pale, thin-sliced supermarket bologna to shame. In this family-friendly sports bar, the bologna is dark and smoky, firm as a knoblewurst salami, and sliced as thick as a good-sized hamburger patty. It is fried until its exterior turns crisp, then loaded into a burger bun with sweet pickles and onion, or your choice of mustard, mayonnaise, or tomato. Fitting side dishes include a variety of deep-fried vegetables and curly fries.

G&R also offers a bologna salad sandwich, and because this bologna is so much better than the spongy packaged stuff, the salad reminds us of something made with ham. The dessert roster includes high-rise, high-calorie chocolate peanut butter cream pie.

## Hathaway's Coffee Shop

441 Vine St. (inside the Carew
Tower Arcade)
Cincinnati, OH

513-621-1332
BL | $

Here's a good Cincinnati breakfast for you: Hathaway's French toast, bright with cinnamon flavor and dusted with powdered sugar and splotched with melting butter. On the side, the locally loved pork-and-pin-oats loaf known as *goetta,* sliced thin and fried crisp. To drink: a bottomless cup of coffee, never allowed below half-full by the watchful waitstaff.

Located on the first level of Carew Tower, Hathaway's is one of a nearly extinct species: the downtown coffee shop. Seating is at one of three U-shaped counters or at a steel-banded dinette table against the wall. In addition to plate lunch, sandwiches, and well-respected hamburgers, there's a full soda-fountain menu of sundaes and banana splits, plus traditional malts and yogurt shakes. These latter include a banana whisk, a pink cloud (made with strawberries), and a crème sickle (orange juice and milk). The yogurt shakes evoke an era when yogurt was an alternative to normal food. The menu touts them as "Healthful Pick Me Uppers," for when one needs that sweet boost in the middle of the shopping day.

## *Henry's

6275 Route 40
West Jefferson, OH

614-879-9321
LD | $

No traveler in a hurry wants to be on Highway 40, the side road parallel to I-70, but anyone with an appetite for home cooking needs to make the detour. Here, set back from the south side of the road is a defunct gas station. The pumps are long gone, but the on-premises restaurant is alive and well—a generous serving of Roadfood at its finest.

The meals are country-style fare: baked ham, hot roast pork sandwiches with mashed potatoes and gravy, creamed chipped beef on corn bread. But it's not the savories that put this unlikely knotty-pine-paneled roadside café on the map. It is pie. Here are some of the best pies in Ohio, in the Midwest, anywhere: peach, banana, chocolate, peanut butter, cherry, coconut, et cetera. The butterscotch pie is thick and dense, full-flavored the way only real butterscotch can be. Custard pie is modestly thin, a sunny yellow wedge dusted with nutmeg. It is melt-in-the-mouth tender. The flavor of the rhubarb pie is as brilliant as bright summer sun, intensely fruity, sweet but just-right tart, supported by a crust that flakes into buttery shards.

## Kennedy's B.B.Q.

| | |
|---|---|
| 1420 7th St. NW | 330-454-0193 |
| Canton, OH | L \| $ |

Relish the relish! Whichever barbecued meat you get in your sandwich at Kennedy's, you must get it topped with cabbage relish. Vaguely similar to the slaw that goes into a pig sandwich in the South, but more pickly than sweet, the relish is bright and refreshing. And oh, what lovely pork this is: Tender with occasional chewy shreds, it is piled so high and huge in a bun that well over half the sandwich must be eaten with a fork or fingers. That much tumbles out if you try to lift it by hand.

Other pit-cooked meat choices are ham (fabulous), beef (yet to be tried), and turkey (not impressive). The rest of the menu is chili and bean soup, plus corn bread and Amish pies. That's the extent of it. The connoisseur's choice, other than a sandwich, is a bowl of bean soup loaded with chunks of pit ham and crowned with crumbled corn bread.

A Canton landmark since 1922, when it opened as Spiker's, the minuscule eatery was bought and renamed in 1960 by Jack Kennedy, who ran it for forty-nine years. After Mr. Kennedy died in 2009, it was taken over by Ernie Schott, proprietor of Canton's superb Taggarts Ice Cream (p. 410). Mr. Schott extended the lunch hour to late afternoon but otherwise made no changes in the time-honored formula.

## Liberty Gathering Place

| | |
|---|---|
| 111 N. Detroit St. | 937-465-3081 |
| West Liberty, OH | BLD \| $ |

"We have girls who come in at four in the morning to make the coleslaw and macaroni salad," a Gathering Place waitress boasted when we asked if the side dishes were good. "Good" turned out to be not a good enough word to describe them, for the little bowl of macaroni salad set before us was inspired: blue-ribbon, church-supper, Independence-Day-picnic fabulous! It was creamy with a pickle zip, dotted with hunks of hard-cooked egg and a few crunchy shreds of carrot, the noodles cooked just beyond al dente but not too soft.

Noodle rapture proved to be a paradigm for the dining experience at what appears to be a typical Main Street café, but is in fact an extraordinary one. During a week we spent in Dayton having suppers at the Pine Club (p. 406), the Gathering Place became our destination lunch stop for moist ham loaf and deep-flavored smoked pork chops sided by mashed potatoes and bread-crumb-enriched escalloped corn. We were astounded by the fried tenderloin sandwich—totally unlike the brittle-crisp, foot-wide 'loins typical of Midwest cafés. Here, the tenderloin is a thick pork steak with only a hint of crust—a slab of meat that is folded over inside the bun so you get a double layer of pork as juicy as a pair of chops. For dessert, we had cool coconut and peach crunch pie, the latter served hot and veined with melted butter.

## Little Polish Diner

5772 Ridge Rd.                440-842-8212
Parma, OH                     LD | $

The name of the Little Polish Diner is not a cute affectation. It is really little: six counter stools and five tables in a space about the size of a walk-in closet. And it is really Polish too: its motto: "Our Food Is Just Like Mom Used to Make." How we wish we had a mom who made such fine pierogies, *golabki* (stuffed cabbage), and pork-and-kraut *bigos* (hunter's stew).

We stopped in on a Wednesday, when the special lunch was a Warsaw Combination Plate, consisting of a crisp breaded boneless pork chop, stuffed cabbage glistening with sweet-tart sauce, a serving of *bigos,* and mashed potatoes. The soup of the day was chicken noodle, which was homey to the nth degree, filled with savory dark meat and spoonfuls of vegetables. We also got what the menu calls a Polish Boy—a length of kielbasa with sauerkraut in a roll; the sausage was bursting with juice and flavor. We want to return on a Saturday, when the special is chicken paprikash.

## New Era Restaurant

10 Massillon Rd.                    330-784-0087
Akron, OH                          LD | $

Since 1938, the New Era Restaurant has been a gathering place for Canton Serbs and others who like Serbian food. The well-weathered old facility was replaced in 2005 by a somewhat sterile, spanking new building; but even if architectural charm is lacking, the staff remain avatars of Old World charm and, more important, the kitchen continues to serve classic Middle European fare of the highest order.

"Where do you get your strudel?" we asked a young waitress when it came time to order dessert. She looked at us like we were crazy and pointed to the New Era kitchen. "We get it from there," she answered. "My grandmother makes it." Its spectacularly flaky dough encloses warm apple compote that is fruit-sweet more than sugar-sweet.

Unlike the more common Hungarian paprikash that is creamy-rich, New Era's is more a thin broth, insinuating its pepper flavor into the little dumplings that surround chicken pieces on the plate. The menu refers to it as "Our 75-Year-Old Signature Dish." We love the *cevapi*, skinless Serbian sausages with a good chaw and a pepper bite. Side them with mashed potatoes and rich brown gravy with a scattering of crisp chopped onion and you have a New Era Old World meal to remember.

## New Sandusky Fish Company

235 E. Shoreline Dr.               419-621-8263
Sandusky, OH                       LD | $

Virtuoso Roadfooders Bruce Bilmes and Sue Boyle turned us on to this little takeout-only shack that offers sandwiches and whole dinners at single-digit prices. Located on Lake Erie's southern shore, it boasts fresh yellow perch and walleye fried to golden-crusted tenderness and piled into buns with abandon, as well as catfish and bass fillets. Frog legs are available at dinner along with fries, onion rings, hush puppies, et cetera.

Many customers are anglers who bring their catch here to have it cleaned (in a building out back) and have a sandwich while they wait. While all business is takeout, travelers who prefer outside-the-car dining will find nice bench seats in a gazebo across the street.

## Perla Homemade Delights

5380 State Rd.  
Parma, OH

216-741-9222  
www.perlahd.com  
B | $

The Cleveland suburb of Parma is a bright star in northern Ohio's firmament of European food. In the neighborhood known as Ukrainian Village, Perla Homemade Delights mostly sells prepared meals to take home and heat—the pierogies are legendary, always winning #1 at the local pierogie festival—but for those of us passing through and demanding instant gratification, there are a couple of tables and an enthralling pastry case. Have a Lady Lock (a cream-filled puff pastry horn), a piece of strudel or nut roll, or, best of all, a slice of supremely refined *dobos torte,* a twelve-layer sponge cake ribboned with chocolate buttercream and capped with caramel.

## The Pine Club

1926 Brown St.  
Dayton, OH

937-228-7463  
www.thepineclub.com  
D | $$$

The Pine Club is a true Midwest supper club, open only in the evening, until midnight on weekdays, 1 a.m. on Friday and Saturday. No reservations, no credit cards, no nonsense. Fantastic steak. You have your choice of filet mignon, porterhouse, or sirloin, each cut and aged on premises and grilled so the outside gets crunchy but the inside is swollen with juice.

Regulars begin a meal with Nantucket Bay scallops—sweet, firm nuggets with a pale light crust and smouldery sea taste. All meals are served with a basket of dinner rolls, and steaks come with a handful of onion straws and choice of potatoes that includes Lyonnaise: a crunchy, plate-wide pancake of shredded spuds woven with veins of sautéed onion. The traditional Pine Club salad is iceberg lettuce—cold, crisp chunks served "red and bleu," which is French dressing loaded with enormous clods of dry blue cheese. Those not wishing to spend $30+ on a cut of beef can get a terrific hamburger for one-third the price. One other favorite sandwich among longtime customers is sardines on rye.

# Price Hill Chili

4920 Glenway Ave.
Cincinnati, OH

513-471-9507
www.pricehillchili.com
BLD | $

Price Hill Cincinnati chili is prudently spiced and perfectly constructed: up to five layers, starting with spaghetti noodles and meat sauce on the bottom. But chili is only a fraction of what makes Price Hill a longtime favorite among Cincinnatians. Other dishes served with high style include Coney Island hot dogs (topped with the same meaty chili), double-decker sandwiches, and *goetta* (a locally preferred breakfast loaf made of pin oats, onions, and pork that is grilled to a crisp). Price Hill will serve *goetta* as a side with any meal or in a sandwich on rye, white, or whole wheat toast.

An amiable, family-friendly diner (with a larger cocktail lounge adjacent), Price Hill is open from dawn to late at night and has a full menu of typical sandwiches, hot dinners, salads, and breakfast omelets. The homemade soup of the day, in our experience (Monday chicken noodle and Tuesday beef barley), is fantastic.

# Putz's Creamy Whip

2673 Putz Pl.
Cincinnati, OH

513-681-8668
www.putzscreamywhip.com
LD (closed in winter) | $

Putz's is a drive-up stand with a menu of hot dogs, foot-long cheese Coneys, burgers, and barbecue, but everybody comes for custard. It is smooth and rich, an ivory-hued soft-serve product that is great swirled into a sugar cone or waffle cone or heaped into a cup and enjoyed for its pure, creamy goodness. Or you can have it whipped up for an extra-thick milk shake or malt or mixed into a soda.

The way we enjoy it most is in a sundae or banana split, the latter made in a long plastic boat that holds three mounds of ice cream, plus all the toppings. Best of all sundaes is the turtle, for which the bottom of a cup is filled with caramel, the caramel is topped with custard, then the custard topped with chocolate syrup. The chocolate syrup is mounded with whipped cream, chopped nuts, and a cherry.

Putz's is just off the highway in a little grove all its own (on a street that was rechristened to honor the longtime favorite destination-dessert place). There are pleasant picnic tables alongside that are an ideal place to spoon into creamy-whip perfection.

## Slyman's Restaurant

3106 St. Clair Ave.
Cleveland, OH

216-621-3760
www.slymans.com
BL (closed Sat & Sun) | $$

A vintage near East Side deli where the corned beef slicing machine never stops, Slyman's is open only for weekday breakfast and lunch, the morning menu including a dandy corned beef, egg, and cheese breakfast sandwich. At lunch, there's a full menu but corned beef stars—on rye, of course. The sandwich is very big, the meat sliced thin. It is extremely tender and somewhat lean, lacking the lasciviousness of fatty corned beef. That is exactly why Slyman's Reuben is so popular. The addition of cheese and sauerkraut, plus a crisp crust of griddled rye, add the reckless luxury that lean beef does not deliver.

On the menu is a lexicon of slang unique to Slyman's sandwich-makers. Mummy = mustard + mayonnaise. Special K = hold the sauerkraut. Cake = mayonnaise + horseradish. Grill Brick = grilled bread only. Waitresses are no-nonsense, and the guys behind the counter are full of joie de vivre. Curiously, the menu is classic Jewish deli, but brochures at the cash register invite customers to know Allah better and the menu includes praise to Jesus in the form of a reference to John 3:16.

## Sokolowski's University Inn

1201 University Rd.
Cleveland, OH

216-771-9236
www.sokolowskis.com
L Mon–Fri; D Fri & Sat | $$

It's a hearty appetite's dream to walk along the cafeteria line of this 1923-vintage tavern and gaze upon pans full of pierogies, kielbasa, sauerkraut, breaded lake fish, and stuffed cabbage. Pierogies are the most famous dish in the house: big, tender pockets filled with cheese and smothered in onions with which they are sizzled in butter until the onions turn caramel-soft and sweet. The kielbasa is as buff as a sausage can be, nearly too muscular for the flimsy cafeteria knife and fork provided, and it delivers megatons of smoky, piggy, spicy flavor. We especially like the balance of Sokolowski's *halushka,* which is a mix of salubrious sautéed cabbage and little squiggles of dumpling. On Friday nights, the menu features beer-battered cod and Lake Erie perch, with live piano music to dine by. Sokolowski's is open for supper only Friday and Saturday nights, when the menu expands to include grilled rainbow trout, prime rib, and chicken paprikash.

To drink, you can pluck a bottle of beer from one of the coolers, domestic and exotic kinds, and there is Vernor's ginger ale on tap. For dessert, we love the egg custard pudding dotted with fat grains of rice.

This is a hale, rollicking place. Our first visit was a few weeks before Christmas, when the sound system throbbed with familiar carols and holiday songs, all with a polka beat. In addition to the usual welcome signs in Polish and countless pictures of the celebrities who have come to enjoy this landmark restaurant, effigies of Santa and his elves were everywhere.

## State Meats

5338 State Rd.
Parma, OH

216-398-0183
www.statemeats.com
L | $

State Meats is a butcher shop and smokehouse, not a sit-down restaurant, but it is a godsend for sausage fans who are hungry and passing through Parma. Located in a shipshape neighborhood known as Ukrainian Village (and not far from swoonful pastries at Perla Homemade Delights [p. 406]), this family-run enterprise has a broad repertoire of kishka, rice rings, kielbasa burgers, Slovenian sausage, pork chops, and cottage hams that are smoked out back, and the porky, beefy, smoky aroma in here is a powerful appetite inducer for anyone of the carnivorous persuasion.

The one hot meal you can get to eat immediately (in your car, for there are no dining tables) is kielbasa. The big, taut, and brightly spiced sausage, complemented by delicious sauerkraut and packed into a hefty bun, is a terrific sandwich, although a challenge to eat without lots of napkins. Proprietor George Salo also gave us a few smokies, which he described as his favorite car snack. Smokies are thin, chewy, garlic-packed salami sticks that were a pleasure to gnaw out of one hand while swilling from a bottle of State Meats–brand root beer with the other (and steering with the third).

## Swensons

18 S. Hawkin Ave.
Akron, OH

330-864-8416
www.swensonsdriveins.com
LD | $

King of the menu at this curb-service drive-in is the Galley Boy, a double cheeseburger dressed with two sauces, one mayonnaisey with bits of onion added, the other zesty barbecue. Optional condiments include ketchup, relish, sweet pickles, horseradish, Worcestershire, Tabasco, cocktail, honey mustard, tartar, and Cajun spice. Garnish choices are tomato, lettuce, olives, grilled onions, hot peppers, bacon, Coney sauce, and coleslaw.

Beyond hamburgers the menu lists a quarter-pound all-beef bologna sandwich, salads, soups, fried chicken, and shrimp. Among the beverages are milk shakes and malts, something called a California (reminded us of Kool-Aid), and half-and-half (iced tea and lemonade). Onion rings are a brittle-crusted joy. French fries, which we didn't try, are listed as "Only Idaho's," the dubious apostrophe apparently having migrated from the restaurant name, which doesn't contain one on the outdoor sign or menu.

Swensons has no indoor seats. Meals to be eaten here are presented on sturdy trays that clip onto the inside of car windows in such a way that it's possible to dine in comfort even when it's raining.

## Taggarts Ice Cream

1401 Fulton Rd. NW                330-452-6844
Canton, OH                        LD | $

Taggarts's hot fudge is the consistency of chocolate syrup, deeply fudgy-flavored, served just warm enough to dramatically pair with cool ice cream. Although Taggarts is an unassuming Midwestern ice cream parlor that goes back to the early twentieth century, there is something sophisticated about this hot fudge. Elegant. Suave. It comes topped with whipped cream and a cherry and perfectly roasted pecan halves salted just enough to create taste-bud buzz with the hot fudge and ice cream. Turtle sundaes and banana splits also benefit from the first-rate nuts.

The signature concoction is known as a Bittner, named for a customer back in the 1930s who dared the mixologists to create a milk shake so thick that a spoon would stand upright in it. Made from three-quarters of a pound of vanilla ice cream and chocolate syrup, it resembles concrete, but comes heaped with those good roasted pecans as well as whipped cream.

Ice cream is Taggarts's claim to fame, but there also is an inviting roster of sandwiches and short-order fare reminiscent of times gone by. We've tried the wonderfully old-fashioned olive-nut cream cheese on toast as well as a grilled cheese sandwich with bacon, and both were great. But it's hard to pay attention to the main course when dessert is so compelling.

## Tucker's

1637 Vine St.                    513-721-7123
Cincinnati, OH                   BL | $

Tucker's opened for business in 1946, and while some things in the humble Over-the-Rhine hash house have no doubt changed since then, its ambience remains more mid-twentieth-century than early twenty-first. Joe Tucker, who runs the place with his wife, Carla, grew up with it, and his ninety-year-old mother is still a significant presence. The day we had breakfast, she sat in a back booth peeling potatoes for the excellent hash browns.

Along with the spuds and a sumptuously loaded vegetable omelet, we had a tile of *goetta*, the only-in-Cincinnati breakfast meat made from pork, beef, onions, pin oats, and spice. Joe slices his loaf of *goetta* thin and grills it a good long while (this is not fast food) until the outside is crunchy and glistening but the interior stays succulent.

Everything Tucker's does is first-class. An omelet comes scattered with eye-opening fresh snips of basil. Biscuits are from scratch; corn bread is Mid-South-style, in the form of a pancake. French toast comes decorated with fresh fruit. Last we looked, Tucker's neighborhood is on the skids, but the restaurant remains a bastion of hospitality.

## White House Chicken

180 Wooster Rd. N.               330-745-0449
Barberton, OH                    www.whitehousechicken.com
                                 LD | $$

White House chicken is for skin lovers. Each piece is enveloped in a chewy, spicy, supersavory coat so thick that the meat inside—white as well as dark—yields no juice until the envelope is breached. While we would hesitate to call any chicken too juicy, the soft, moist meat simply cannot compete with the assertive crust around it. In fact, nice as the meat is, we find that a full plate of this fine chicken with the works, which means French fries, spicy rice, coleslaw, and bread, has so much of that good, red-gold skin on it that we might leave meat behind just to make sure we get all the really good stuff.

What makes White House chicken skin such a marvel is that the frying medium is lard, insinuating every bite with wanton luxe. Like all the Barberton chicken houses, White House cuts its bird the old-fashioned way into wing, drumette, breast, leg, thigh, and back, an economical technique left over from Depression days when cooks tried to maximize the number of pieces they could get from one bird. When you sink your teeth into a piece, you may find meat where you don't expect it or not enough meat where you want it (in the back), but who cares when the additional pieces mean more of that can't-stop-eating skin.

The original location is a big white corner building with a neighborhood-tavern feel; the last time we ate here, a kindly old lady walking out the door smiled at us, poked a finger in our direction, and said, "You found it!" We have yet to visit any of the other Akron-area locations of the White House, which apparently is looking to franchise nationally.

## White Turkey Drive-In

388 E. Main Rd.  
Conneaut, OH

440-593-2209  
www.whiteturkey.com  
LD Mother's Day-Labor Day | $

"If you find yourself along Lake Eerie in the northeast corner of Ohio, pull into the White Turkey, a seriously vintage drive-in." So wrote a Roadfood tipster in a note with no return address and no ID. So we don't really know who to thank for this suggestion, but we sure would like to! This Richardson's Root Beer stand is a fine Roadfood stop along old US-20, offering seats at high stools where you can feel a lake breeze and watch the cars cruise past while you dine on true mid-American, midcentury drive-in fare. Its namesake turkey sandwich is the real thing, loaded with shredded meat. No compressed loaf here! You can get a plain one or a Large Marge, which also includes cheese and bacon. Beyond turkey, there are double and triple cheeseburgers, hot dogs, and chili cheese dogs.

While only vanilla ice cream is available, the variety of soda fountain drinks and desserts is mesmerizing. Of course there are cones, shakes, and malts; there are sundaes topped with pineapple, cherry, chocolate, hot fudge, homemade peanut butter, caramel, butterscotch, or blueberry. You can get a black cow (here, a blend of root beer and ice cream). And the root beer floats are divine, available in sizes from kiddie (80¢) to Super Shuper, created with a quart of root beer and a quantity of ice cream to match.

# Young's Jersey Dairy

6880 Springfield-Xenia Rd.      937-325-0629
Yellow Springs, OH      www.youngsdairy.com
BLD | $

Young's Jersey Dairy, which opened in 1968, is a farm-themed amusement park that includes a goat-petting zoo, a gift shop, a miniature golf course named Udders and Putters, and a summertime art exhibit of statuary cows painted by local artists. A few years back, a gourmet coffee shop with espresso drinks and Wi-Fi access was added. But of all its many attractions, the one that will keep us coming back is ice cream. They blend their own, and at 15 percent butterfat, it is rich but not insanely so. There is a different featured flavor every week of the year, from peaches and cream to espresso chocolate crunch and caramel cookie dough. Of all the ones we have tried, the one distinguishing characteristic is their balance. None is too sweet or overflavored. All are just right for eating multiple scoops.

Milk shakes, made in sizes from Calfshake to Cowshake to Bullshake and Lotsa Bullshake start with French vanilla ice cream and are available extra-rich, with malt powder. Gelato and sorbet also are available. You can eat a meal here: a basic menu of eggs and pancakes from 7 a.m. to 2 p.m. and burgers, hot dogs, soup, salad, and sandwiches for lunch. Plus excellent fresh cheese curds befitting of a real dairy farm.

## Anchor Bar

413 Tower Ave.
Superior, WI

715-394-9747
www.anchorbar.freeservers.com
LD | $

The Anchor Bar is a spare-looking tavern in an industrial non-neighborhood near the Duluth shipyards. The inside is nearly pitch-dark. Customers at the bar and big round tables include rugged-looking seamen having rugged-sounding conversations. The aroma of grilling beef is irresistible. The Anchor Bar is a destination hamburger lovers need to know.

Each burger is a thick, hand-formed patty made of meat fat enough to weep juice into the bun even before you lift it. It is not high-end prime beef, but its stout, blue-collar satisfaction is undeniable. And its proletarian price is irresistible. A single burger, served in over a dozen guises, including topped with cheeses, hot sauces, even pineapple or cashews, costs less than four dollars. A heap of hot-from-the-kettle golden fries—big square, spuddy logs laced with lots of crisp squiggles and burnt bits—adds $1.25 to the price. An amazing five-dollar meal (not counting beer)!

The menu makes fun of the few non-burger items available, noting that the ham sandwich is "great if you like ham" and the BLT is "not blueberries, liver, and truffles."

## Beerntsen's Candy Store

108 N. 8th St.
Manitowoc, WI

920-684-9616
www.beerntsens.com
$

In the back of Beerntsen's, through an elaborately carved archway, handsome wooden booths are occupied by customers who come for such ice cream fancies as a Sweetheart (caramel, vanilla ice cream, marshmallow, crushed nuts) or a Sunset (strawberry and vanilla ice cream, pineapple, marshmallow, crushed nuts). Hot fudge sundaes are served with the fudge in a separate container, allowing customers to pour it on as they eat.

Up front are more than a hundred different kinds of hand-dipped candy, including a chocolate cosmetology set (brush, mirror, hair dryer), smoochies (like Hershey's kisses, but bigger), raspberry and vanilla seafoam dainties, and—the pièce de résistance—a bonbon known as fairy food, which is a two-inch square of brittle spun sugar shrouded in deep, dark chocolate. We are very happy we live nowhere near Manitowoc, Wisconsin, and that fairy food is too delicate to be shipped; otherwise, we'd be addicts.

## Bendtsen's Bakery

3200 Washington Ave.
Racine, WI

262-633-7449
www.bendtsensbakery.com
Closed Sunday | $

Bendtsen's calls its kringle "the world's finest Danish pastry," a claim with which we would not disagree. If you don't know what kringle is, think of an ordinary Danish, like you have with morning coffee. Now imagine its crust buttery and feather-light, almost like a croissant, and fill it with a ribbon of pecan paste and chopped nuts, or a layer of almond macaroon paste, or a tunnel of cherry and cheese. Picture it as big as a Christmas wreath, about a foot and a half across and iced with sugar glaze or flavored frosting. Have it warm with butter melting on top, accompanied by a leisurely pot of coffee. There you have one of the great breakfast (or teatime) treats in America, a dish that has become the signature of Racine, Wisconsin.

Bendtsen's has pictures on the wall that show the time they made the world's largest kringle, but size isn't what makes their pastry so wonderful. Each kringle made here, whether simply filled with apricot jam or fancy-filled with a mash of cranberries and walnuts, is a beautiful sight—a broad oval rather than a perfect circle, quite flat, and ready to slice into small pieces (of which you'll want three or four).

There is no place to eat at Bendtsen's, although samples of kringle are often available for tasting on the counter.

## Benji's

4156 N. Oakland Ave.        414-332-7777
Milwaukee, WI               BLD | $$

Benji's is an old-school Jewish-Midwestern delicatessen. Its menu ranges from corned beef sandwiches on rye to Friday-night fish fries, from blintzes filled with sweet pot cheese to a Cobb salad. We like it because it is one of the few restaurants in the Midwest that serves the old farmhouse meal called hoppel poppel—a griddle-cooked, kitchen-sink breakfast of salami, scrambled eggs, and potato chunks. Super hoppel poppel adds peppers and mushrooms and blankets the whole thing with melted cheese.

Of course, it is a good place for piled-high deli sandwiches, lox-and-bagel platters, sweet-and-sour cabbage borscht, and crisp potato pancakes served with applesauce. For dessert, we recommend noodle kugel (a cheese-cake-rich block of cooked egg noodles and sweetened cheese), served hot with sour cream. And for a beverage to drink with your meal, Benji's offers true melting-pot variety: domestic or imported beer, kosher wine, Dr. Brown's in cans, Sprecher's soda in bottles, and chocolate phosphates (seltzer water and chocolate syrup).

## Charcoal Inn

1313 S. 8th St.            920-458-6988
Sheboygan, WI             www.charcoalinn.com
                          L | $

The Charcoal Inn is a leading source of the great Wisconsin sausage known as a brat (rhymes with "hot," short for bratwurst). It is served as a sandwich, wrapped in wax paper, delivered without a plate. Each brat is slit and flattened before getting grilled, which makes for easy stacking in the bun if you get what many regulars get: a double brat (with pickle chips and raw onions). The sausages are generously spiced and deeply perfumed with the sizzle of a charcoal fire. Thick and resilient but thoroughly tooth-tender, they are as savory as sausage can be, oozing a delectable blend of meat juice and the melted butter with which they are basted.

While brats are the star attraction, burgers are big here too, and although the beef is not prime, it is plenty rich because it also gets basted with butter. A double burger with cheese is plush beyond measure.

For dessert you need a torte. Different days bring different flavors, from Old World poppy seed to modern American Oreo. Each piece is a square about four by four inches wide and two inches high. It is dense and smooth, sitting on a pallet of graham cracker crumbs, tasting like a pint of cream that has been reduced, thickened, flavored, and sweetened. It is similar in texture to a cheesecake, but so pure and rich you'll want to call it cream cake.

## Chili John's

519 S. Military Ave.
Green Bay, WI

920-494-4624
www.chilijohns.com
LD | $

In 1916, "Chili John" Isaac devised a recipe for ground beef cooked with a fusillade of spice. His recipe featured an eye-opening measure of peppery oil, but the way he served it at his little eat place, in concert with spaghetti noodles, beans, and cheese, the heat became part of a well-balanced plate of food. Although some locals still call the multilayered configuration Texas-style chili (an appellation Texas chili-heads no doubt would abhor), variations of the formula are now known throughout the state as Green Bay–style chili, and the chili parlor has become a culinary guiding light.

## Jack Pandl's Whitefish Bay Inn

1319 E. Henry Clay St.
Whitefish Bay, WI

414-964-3800
www.jackpandls.com
LD | $$

Jack Pandl's (since 1915) serves German-flavored Dairyland cuisine in a friendly, wood-paneled dining room with a wall of windows that look out over elegant Lake Drive. Waitresses wear dirndl skirts and there is lots of Old World memorabilia for décor (including a tremendous collection of beer steins), but the menu is at least as Midwestern as it is Middle European. At lunch, when the steel-banded tables are set with functional paper place mats, you can eat a julienne salad or a Reuben sandwich made with Wisconsin cheese, or pork chops, or a Denver omelet. In addition to broiled whitefish ("always purchased fresh," the menu guarantees), there is that lean but luscious local specialty, walleyed pike, filleted and broiled to perfection. This being Milwaukee, Friday is fish-fry night, of course. Pandl's perch is very nice—whole fish filleted so their two halves hold together, encased in a golden crust and accompanied by first-class potato pancakes.

We love *schaum torte* for dessert. That's a crisp meringue dolloped with freshly made custard. On the other hand, we never can resist the German pancake. It's not really a dessert item, and many people have it as their main course, but somehow it makes a grand conclusion to a meal. This gorgeous edible event, a Jack Pandl's specialty, is a big puffy cloud of batter similar in texture to Yorkshire pudding, but slightly sweeter. It arrives at the table piping hot and shaped like a big bowl, its circumference crisp and brown, risen high in the oven, its center moist and eggy. Dust it with a bit of powdered sugar and give it a spritz of lemon, creating a sophisticated syrup, then dig in immediately. It is a big plate of food, maybe enough to share.

## Jake's

1634 W. North Ave.  
Milwaukee, WI

414-562-1272  
www.jakes-deli.com  
L | $

It took us a long time to realize that Milwaukee was a major corned beef city, but if we had any doubts, Jake's erased them. Here is a vintage urban deli where the hand-sliced corned beef is steamy-moist, unspeakably tender, and vivid-flavored.

Proprietor Michael Kassof suggested that one reason for his beef's deliciousness might be that a dozen or more briskets are boiled together, their pot becoming a slurry of spice and beef flavor that reinsinuates itself into the fibers of the meat. Just as the counterman prepares to slice a whole brisket for sandwiches, it is sprinkled with paprika, adding a little jolt to the taste. The beef is sliced medium-thick, then piled into slick-crusted, Milwaukee-made Miller Bakery seeded rye: not an outrageously huge sandwich like you might get in Chicago or New York, but in no way skimpy, either.

There are a few other items on Jake's menu: pastrami, turkey pastrami, hard salami, hot dogs, and soups like Mama should have made, and you can have the corned beef as part of a Reuben with sauerkraut and cheese. But for us, and for generations of Milwaukeeans, Jake's is synonymous with corned beef on rye.

With its pale yellow walls, its tables topped with worn linoleum, its ancient wood booths equipped with out-of-order buzzers once used to summon service, Jake's exudes faded charm. It has been around since 1935, when the neighborhood was mostly Jewish. Original proprietor Reuben Cohen sold it to Jake, who sold it to Michael Kassof's dad in 1967, and now Michael runs the place—the last Jewish business in a neighborhood that is mostly African American. Superlative corned beef is a cross-cultural infatuation.

## Jo's Café

3519 W. Silver Spring Dr.          414-461-0210
Milwaukee, WI                    BL | $

Hoffel poffel (aka hoppel poppel) isn't widely known anywhere in the United States. The few restaurant examples we have found are in Iowa and Wisconsin. It is one gigantic breakfast plate of eggs scrambled with chunks of potato, onions, and, at Jo's, lots of nuggets of spicy salami and, optionally, some cheese on top. The only reason we would recommend not getting it for breakfast at Jo's is that the *other* kind of potatoes—the thin-cut hash browns—are delicious. Cooked in a flat patty until brittle-crisp, they too are available under a mantle of melted cheese. Actually, either sort of potato dish will leave precious little room for Jo's pecan rolls and cinnamon rolls. Nor should one abjure toast. Roadfood warrior Cliff Strutz declared, "No matter what kind of bread you get with your breakfast, you must cover it with the homemade apple jelly sitting out on the counter." (There is a different kind of homemade jelly every week.)

We generally think of Jo's for breakfast, but lunch is good too. Blue-plate cuisine is the order of the day, including such daily specials as meat loaf, beef stew, pork chops, and country-fried steak with real (of course!) mashed potatoes, homemade gravy, and a yeasty fresh-baked dinner roll. Every day you can order barbecued pork ribs or chicken.

## Klinger's East

920 E. Locust                   414-263-2424
Milwaukee, WI                    LD | $

Klinger's East does not look like a promising eatery. It is a shadowy bar and pool hall where you might not expect anything but beer nuts and potato chips, and where, at first glance, you have to wonder if newcomers will be made to feel, shall we say, unwelcome. But in fact, it is a comfy place, even for strangers, and its customers include wholesome-looking families you'd never see dining in such an establishment in other parts of the country. But in Milwaukee, taverns aren't just for drinkers; they are community centers. We recommend it for the Friday fish fry, which is ridiculously inexpensive and unexpectedly good. Of course cod is on the menu, sheathed in a crunchy coat of beer batter. Bluegill sometimes is available. And you usually can get smelt (pronounced "shmelt" hereabouts)—a fish lover's fish with unabashed oily character—crunch-coated two-inch sprats well accompanied by a short stack of silver-dollar-size potato pancakes.

# Kopp's Custard

5373 N. Port Washington Rd.
Glendale, WI

404-961-3288
www.kopps.com
LD | $

Kopp's is a good place to stand and have a cooked-to-order double butter cheeseburger (there are no table seats), but it is better known for custard, not ice cream. You can see it pour in thick cascades from great silver machines behind the order counter. It is ivory-white, rich, and densely flavorful.

Plain vanilla is so, so pure—the true choice of a serious custardhead. No matter what else we get, we always need to dip a spoon into one dish of that. Beyond vanilla, Kopp's makes a new and different flavor every single day of the year. Among our fondest memories are caramel-apple with mixed nuts, Key lime pie, and Snickers chunky cheesecake. The menu also includes a milk shake of the day (mocha coconut frappe, for instance) and a featured sundae. "Magic flavors" are composed of several varieties mixed together, such as Cherry Bomb, a swirl of burgundy cherry, Key lime pie, and passion fruit.

There are two other Kopp's locations: 18880 West Bluemound Road, Brookfield (404-789-9490) and 7631 West Layton Avenue, Greenfield (404-282-4312).

# *Leon's

3131 S. 27th
Milwaukee, WI

414-383-1784
www.leonsfrozencustard.us
$

There is no place to eat at this Eisenhower-era hangout other than in your car or standing in the neon-lit parking lot along with other pilgrims who have come for frozen dessert. Leon's menu is all custard: cones, cups, sodas, sundaes, malts, pints, and quarts. (Hot dogs are available, but irrelevant.)

Milwaukee is fanatical about custard, which is heavy, smooth, and pure—denser than the richest super-premium ice cream and nothing like wan frozen yogurt. As made by Leon's, it is egg-rich, sweet but not cloying, and uncomplicated. No mix-ins, no silly names for flavors, no cookie dough or brownie chunks. Choose vanilla, chocolate, strawberry, or butter pecan. Have it in a cone or cup. Or have a sundae topped with sauce of your choice and delicious toasted nuts: pecan halves that have a wicked crunch, a salty punch, and an earthy flavor that accentuates the superior custard.

## Maggie's

257 Manypenny Ave.                    715-779-5641
Bayfield, WI                          www.maggies-bayfield.com
                                      LD | $$

Snowy whitefish fillets, which come sautéed in butter, seem almost too tender to attack with a fork. On most Friday evenings, Maggie's offers a special
of headless but otherwise whole whitefish with all its bones, skin, and fins.
Even if you've never faced a whole fish like this, getting the meat is a snap.
The waitstaff will show you how to peel back the skin, then start at the top
and easily separate moist forkfuls from the bone. The flavor of whole whitefish is not significantly different from those that are filleted and broiled or
sautéed, but the presentation adds fish-camp fun to the dining experience.

On the subject of fish-camp vittles, how about a plate of whitefish livers? Because it takes a lot of fish to gather a small amount of livers—they're
about the size of a quarter, and a dinner of them might include fifteen or
twenty—mongers who sell to local restaurants and markets traditionally
have thrown them away. But old-time fishermen have long considered them
a delicacy, and in recent years as Bayfield has gone from quiet fishing village
to popular tourist destination, livers have begun to appear on menus of a
handful of plain and fancy restaurants. Like the flesh of the whitefish, the
livers' most distinguishing characteristic is their inland water taste, more
mellow than chicken liver but definitely an organ meat. Maggie's rolls them
in spiced flour and sautés them with peppers, onions, and mushrooms until
their outsides have a crunch and the inside of each turns melting-soft.

Remember that the northern Midwest is apple country. Maggie's apple
cake is not to be missed, especially served warm and à la mode.

## Mazo's

3146 S. 27th St.                      414-671-2118
Milwaukee, WI                         www.mazoshamburgers.com
                                      LD Mon-Sat | $

One of Milwaukee's lesser-known culinary attractions is excellent hamburgers. Many connoisseurs believe Mazo's serves the best. It is a tiny place, now
run by Nick Mazo, whose grandparents started it in 1934, and if you come
at lunchtime, prepare to wait a while once you find a precious seat in the
dining room. These burgers are *not* fast food, but they are worth the wait.
They are normal-sized patties of good ground beef in toasted buns, but
what sends them into orbit is the fact that they are garnished with butter—

the Milwaukee way!—resulting in a confluence of the two most wickedly good fats: meat and dairy. Available toppings include fried onions, sautéed mushrooms, and of course a layer of cheese. Other choices for dressing up the burger are bacon, lettuce, and tomato as well as thousand island dressing. On the side, have coleslaw, French fries, or baked beans.

Bonus: Mazo's is directly across the street from the excellent Leon's custard stand (p. 420).

## *McBob's

| | |
|---|---|
| 4919 W. North Ave. | 414-871-5050 |
| Milwaukee, WI | www.mcbobs.com |
| | BLD \| $$ |

We first came to McBob's for its fish fry. Every Friday, there are three choices: perch, walleye, or grouper; or you can have a combo of perch and walleye, or a super combo of all three. With the fish come American fries or potato pancakes, coleslaw, and bread. Each fish fillet is encased in a highly seasoned, fragile crust. The walleye is light and ephemeral; the grouper is mild with a sweet, oily flavor. The perch is snowy white. If you get the meal with potato pancakes—you must!—the pancakes are fanned out on the plate as a kind of edible trivet for the fish. They are laced with bits of onion and have a potato flavor that perfectly complements the crisp fish.

If you happen to be a Friday fish-fry frowner, do not ignore McBob's! Every day of the week it is a source of A-1 corned beef. Big chunks of steamy-hot meat from a super-tender spiced brisket are piled into a sandwich of plain rye or in toasted rye with sauerkraut, horseradish mustard, and Swiss cheese (a Reuben). The meat is extraordinarily lean and yet dripping with flavor. The ideal condiment is horseradish mustard. The next morning, Mc-Bob's turns the corned beef into some of the best hash we've ever eaten.

## Mr. Perkins' Family Restaurant

| | |
|---|---|
| 2001 W. Atkinson Ave. | 414-447-6660 |
| Milwaukee, WI | BLD \| $ |

Mr. Perkins' is a city lunchroom with a mostly African American clientele. It is a good place to know about even if you don't have a taste for such soul-food standards as neckbones and chitlins. Who couldn't find comfort in this baked chicken with dressing? Fried chicken bears a gorgeous golden crust; meat loaf is firm and satisfying; fried perch, three boneless fillets encased in a sandy cornmeal crust, is amazingly juicy with flavor as lusty as beefsteak.

One of the most delightful aspects of lunch and supper at Mr. Perkins' (which also serves breakfast) is choosing side dishes. Mac 'n' cheese is a duet of tender noodle and crusty edge; fried okra retains tremendous vegetable salubrity; fried green tomatoes are tangy and brittle-crisp; there are pot-likker-sopped turnip greens *or* turnip bottoms, made into an intriguing squashlike mash with butter and sugar. Corn bread is Tennessee-style—that is, a griddle-cooked cake that is buttery, tender, golden-colored, and an ideal tool for mopping gravy and vegetable drippings from a plate. Desserts include luxuriant banana pudding, individually sized fried peach pies, sweet-potato pie, and cool lemon icebox pie. To drink, the beverages of choice are lemonade and iced tea, both served southern-style: *sooo-eeeet!*

## Plaza Tavern

319 N. Henry St.        608-255-6592
Madison, WI         www.theplazatavern.com
                                 LD | $

Some people go to the Plaza Tavern to drink or play pool. We come for the Plazaburger. What makes it different from a regular hamburger (which is also available) is the secret-sauce condiment that drenches the patty to a degree that it seems to seep right into it. Based on a combo of sour cream and mayonnaise, it is thinner than ketchup and its texture reminds us of an odd barbecue sauce, although it has neither vinegar tang nor peppery spice. In addition to infusing the meat with its flavor, it gets deeply imprinted into the dark bun. Connoisseurs have it on their French fries too.

The Tavern menu is an otherwise unremarkable array of sandwiches, plus, of course, deep-fried cheese curds. Beers are sold by the pint and pitcher. Ambience is pure Midwest saloon: long bar, tight booths, and wall murals showing scenic Wisconsin.

## Real Chili

419 E. Wells St.        414-271-4042
Milwaukee WI       www.realchili-milwaukee.com
                                 LD | $

Real Chili, which dates back to 1931, serves an only-in-the-Midwest kind of chili, a layered affair of cheese atop beef atop beans atop spaghetti noodles, with oyster crackers and raw onions on the side. You can get it mild, medium, or hot; you can ask for sour cream on top; and if you are a chili *bec fin,* you can doctor it up with a spritz of sweet or hot vinegar, both of which are supplied on Real Chili's tables.

The déclassé joint that serves this witch's brew is the kind of beanery you once could find in cities throughout the Heartland. With the exception of Cincinnati, the Midwest has lost most of its chili parlors, and although this style of chili gets no respect from purists, it is a culinary adventure you don't want to miss. Uniformed waitresses dole out second helpings at half price, and the preferred beverages are beer or Coke.

There is a second location at 1625 West Wells Street (414-342-6955).

## *Solly's Grille

4629 N. Port Washington Rd.　　　　414-332-8808
Milwaukee, WI　　　　www.sollysgrille.com
　　　　BLD Tues-Sat | $

Hamburgers are a passion in Milwaukee, where butter is the staff of life. Ergo, the butter burger. At Solly's, it is a medium-thin patty of beef, cooked through, served on a bun and saturated with unconscionable amounts of melted butter. Not margarine, not flavored oil: pure, dairy-rich, delicious butter. There is no hamburger we know so wickedly indulgent. You can get a Super Solly Burger (two patties, and a good idea—a single is overwhelmed by its bun) or a Super Special, which adds lettuce, tomato, and mayo to the mix (also a good idea), as well as cheeseburgers and burgers topped with onions, mushrooms, and Monterey Jack cheese. The biggest of all is the Cheesehead—a half pound of sirloin with Swiss and American cheese, stewed onions, raw onion, and mushrooms.

There are other sandwiches on Solly's menu, none of which we've tried, also omelets and fish fries, excellent crinkle-cut French fries, and made-here pie. If you've got a sweet tooth, apply it to a milk shake, which is Dairy State–rich and made in flavors that include chocolate, hot fudge, strawberry, pineapple, vanilla, and the superb fresh banana malt. Another confectionery alternative is a black cow, made with Sprecher's root beer. And, this being a city where ice cream is as beloved as butter burgers, there is a full array of sundaes too.

Seating is at two horseshoe-shaped counters, and the staff of uniformed waitresses go about their business with well-seasoned hash-house élan.

## Speed Queen

1130 W. Walnut St.          414-265-2900
Milwaukee, WI          www.speedqueenbbq.com
LD | $

Speed Queen's neighborhood is iffy, but the barbecue is definitive. Pork, beef, and turkey are slow-cooked and glazed with sauce, either mild—robust and slightly sweet—or hot, which is an explosive, dark-orange emulsion reminiscent of Arthur Bryant's in Kansas City. For many customers, the mild is a little too mild, the hot is too lip-burning, so it is not uncommon to hear orders for "half and half." (Sauce is sold in bottles to take home: *highly recommended*!)

There are two kinds of pork available: shoulder or outside meat. Shoulder is thick slices that are almost chunks, tender as velvet. Outside meat is a motley pile of nearly blackened shreds and nuggets, some of which are tender, some of which are crusty, and some of which quite literally melt on the tongue. It is smokier-tasting than inside meat, like essence of barbecue. A favorite way to eat at Speed Queen is to order a half-and-half plate (ribs and outside, rib tips and shoulder, et cetera) that consists of meat, sauce, a couple slices of spongy white bread (necessary for sopping sauce), plus a cup of coleslaw. Beans and potato salad cost extra. You can also get a sandwich; but beware: these "sandwiches" are lots of meat and sauce piled onto white bread in such a way that it is inconceivable to hold it in your hands.

Everything is delivered at the order window in a Styrofoam container, and while most business is takeout, Speed Queen offers a row of functional booths for dining-in. Décor is minimal, consisting of two identical photomurals of the Wisconsin Dells on opposite walls. While there is a jukebox, it seems seldom to be plugged in or playing. Room tone is a hush punctuated by lip-smacks, sighs of pleasure, and the quietest kind of reverential conversation—the pensive hush induced by good barbecue.


## *Stockholm Pie Company

N2030 Spring St.          715-442-5505
Stockholm, WI          www.stockholmpiecompany.com
L Closed Wed | $

A corner store in a sweet little hamlet on the shore of Lake Pepin, the Stockholm Pie Company has quickly become a Roadfood legend for its cream pies, fruit pies, and savory pies.

Among the savories are sausage apple Cheddar, bacon pear blue cheese, and chicken potpie. They're very good, especially because of the flaky, melting-rich crust. With a locally bottled Spring Grove root beer—not too sweet, very spicy—one such pie is a memorable meal.

Sweet pies are swoonfully good. There are full-sized pies, six-inchers suitable for two, and at least a dozen pies available by the slice. The inventory varies day to day, including such seasonal specialties as mincemeat, pumpkin, rhubarb, and eggnog custard. Among year-round favorites are caramel apple crunch, sour cream apple, peanut butter fudge, banana cream, and a stunning double lemon that is a ribbon of citrus-specked curd atop creamy lemon chess. If you love genuine, from-scratch butterscotch pie and know you are coming to Stockholm, call ahead and they will make one for you.

A snug, very informal place with tote-your-own service. Seats include a few tables and a four-stool counter along the wall. Even if you don't have to use the lavatory, go. It is accessible through a door out back. When you enter, you pass the kitchen, where you can see cooks at work creating pies.

## Three Brothers

2414 S. St. Clair St.      414-481-7530
Milwaukee, WI              D | $$

Branko Radiecevich's Serbian restaurant, which his father named for Branko and his two brothers, is a Milwaukee landmark that attracts eaters from all walks of life and all ethnic groups. Accommodations are polite but humble. Start with lemon-and-wine-marinated rice-stuffed grape leaves served with black olives and firm sticks of nut-sweet *kashkaval* (a goat's milk cheese) or a "Serbian salad" of tomatoes, green peppers, and onions veiled with a web of finely grated *bryndza,* a soft goat's-milk cheese.

One autumn several years ago when we came for supper, Branko reminded us that it was leek season and brought out a savory pastry pie layered with caramelized peppered leeks. He was even more enthusiastic about roast lamb, a Three Brothers signature dish that is basted four hours in its own juices with tomato, pepper, onion, and garlic, and served *just barely* on the bone. Poke it and bite-sized hunks of meat separate from the haunch and fall into the juice. The menu describes it as a must for the lamb lover; but we suspect that even non–lamb lovers might find its refined taste irresistible.

The building in which Three Brothers serves its superlative meals is a corner tavern that was built in 1897 and for decades was owned and operated by the Schlitz Brewing Company. The Schlitz insignia—a globe—still crowns the peak of the roof. There are no longer seats at the old bar, which runs the length of the front room and is now a service area, but the wood-floored saloon retains the warmth of a community gathering place.

## Watts Tea Room

761 N. Jefferson St.    414-290-5720
Milwaukee, WI           www.wattsteashop.com
                        BL Mon-Sat | $

When we wrote the cookbook *Square Meals* in 1984, we described the ritual of ladies' lunch as culinary history. We were wrong. At the Watts Tea Room, on the second floor of George Watts & Son fine china shop, ladies' lunch is alive and well . . . along with afternoon tea and lovely breakfasts of croissant macadamia French toast and hot chocolate, or slightly spicy ginger toast.

Such a pleasant place! At the front door downstairs, you are greeted by a member of the staff and directed to the elevator. Past display cases of Limoges and Wedgwood, you find yourself on the second floor in a broad lunchroom with a window view of Jefferson Street below. The tables are well-worn bare wood, the floral carpet is a muted blue. Coffee is served in Royal Worcester Hanbury-pattern cups, and napkins are white linen. Of course, waitresses wear uniforms.

The lunch we want to return for is Watts's classic chicken potpie, topped with a featherweight puff pastry crown. We also have fond memories of chicken salad Polynesian, for which white meat was mixed with coconut shreds, pecans, and a citrus vinaigrette. Afternoon tea includes finger sandwiches and pastries. And even if none of the above were available, we always will return to Watts for dessert, especially one called filled sunshine cake, made from a decades-old recipe for triple-layer sponge cake with custard filling and seven-minute frosting. From the beverage menu, we recommend a hot or cold Russian, a mix of coffee and chocolate topped with whipped cream.

## White Gull Inn

4225 Main St.     920-868-3517
Fish Creek, WI    www.whitegullinn.com
                  D | $$

When it's summer in Wisconsin, vacation fancies turn to Door County, a slim peninsula of natural beauty that juts into Lake Michigan east of

Menominee and north of Sturgeon Bay. The meal to eat in Door County is a fish boil, and no one does it with more panache than the White Gull Inn. Guests who are staying at the White Gull and visitors who reserve a place well in advance enjoy not only eating a fish boil but watching it being prepared—and that is half the fun. Into a hot-water cauldron over a campfire go small red potatoes, then onions, then fish steaks and salt. As the meal cooks, fish oil rises to the surface of the boiling water, and about ten minutes after the fish goes in, the "master boiler" tosses kerosene on the flames below. The burst of fire is spectacular and causes what is known as a boil-over, spilling unwanted fish oils over the rim and leaving the fish chunky, moist, and flavorful. The whole meal is then bathed in butter and concluded with a slice of cherry pie made, of course, from local cherries.

Andy Coulson, proprietor of the White Gull Inn, points out that for the old-time fishermen who likely invented the ritual, as well as for crowds of contemporary visitors who come north to enjoy the cool breezes that waft in off Lake Michigan every summer, one big appeal of the fish boil is the camaraderie it inspires among large groups of people. The bonfire and boil-over bring strangers together in an ebullient mix of awe and hunger. "As a meal for six, it is inefficient," Coulson says. "But for a dozen or more, it's a thing of beauty. This is Door County's answer to the all-American barbecue."

# Southwest

Arizona

✳

Colorado

✳

Kansas

✳

Nevada

✳

New Mexico

✳

Oklahoma

✳

Texas

✳

Utah

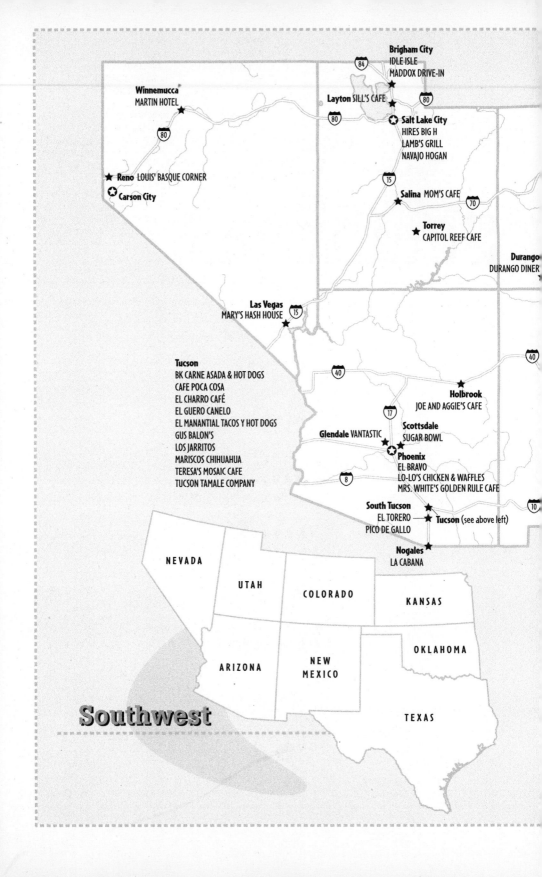

**Winnemucca**
MARTIN HOTEL

**Brigham City**
IDLE ISLE
MADDOX DRIVE-IN

**Layton** SILL'S CAFE

**Salt Lake City**
HIRES BIG H
LAMB'S GRILL
NAVAJO HOGAN

★ **Reno** LOUIS' BASQUE CORNER

✪ **Carson City**

**Salina** MOM'S CAFE

**Torrey**
CAPITOL REEF CAFE

**Durango**
DURANGO DINER

**Las Vegas**
MARY'S HASH HOUSE

**Tucson**
BK CARNE ASADA & HOT DOGS
CAFE POCA COSA
EL CHARRO CAFÉ
EL GUERO CANELO
EL MANANTIAL TACOS Y HOT DOGS
GUS BALON'S
LOS JARRITOS
MARISCOS CHIHUAHUA
TERESA'S MOSAIC CAFE
TUCSON TAMALE COMPANY

**Holbrook**
JOE AND AGGIE'S CAFE

**Glendale** VANTASTIC

**Scottsdale**
SUGAR BOWL

**Phoenix**
EL BRAVO
LO-LO'S CHICKEN & WAFFLES
MRS. WHITE'S GOLDEN RULE CAFE

**South Tucson**
EL TORERO
PICO DE GALLO
**Tucson** (see above left)

**Nogales**
LA CABANA

NEVADA

UTAH

COLORADO

KANSAS

ARIZONA

NEW
MEXICO

OKLAHOMA

TEXAS

**Southwest**

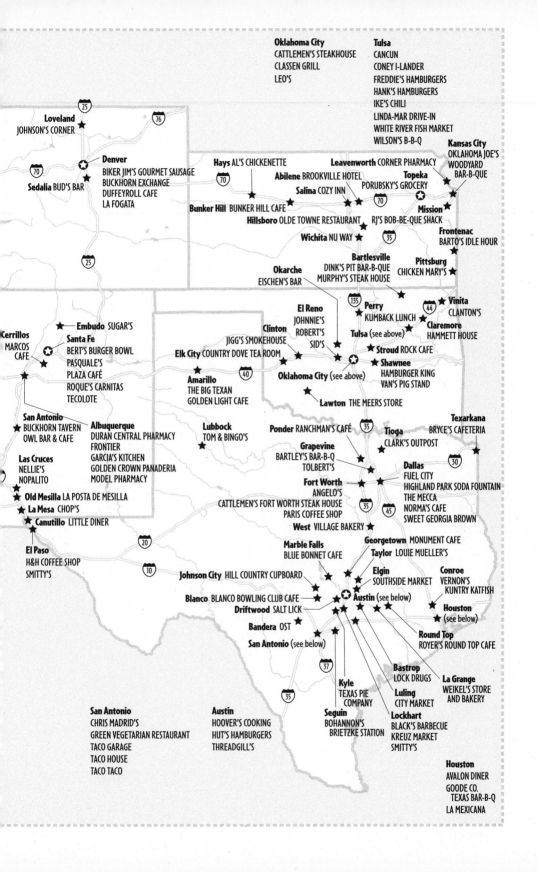

**Oklahoma City**
CATTLEMEN'S STEAKHOUSE
CLASSEN GRILL
LEO'S

**Tulsa**
CANCUN
CONEY I-LANDER
FREDDIE'S HAMBURGERS
HANK'S HAMBURGERS
IKE'S CHILI
LINDA-MAR DRIVE-IN
WHITE RIVER FISH MARKET
WILSON'S B-B-Q

**Loveland**
JOHNSON'S CORNER

**Denver**
BIKER JIM'S GOURMET SAUSAGE
BUCKHORN EXCHANGE
DUFFEYROLL CAFE
LA FOGATA

**Sedalia** BUD'S BAR

**Hays** AL'S CHICKENETTE

**Abilene** BROOKVILLE HOTEL

**Salina** COZY INN

**Leavenworth** CORNER PHARMACY

**Topeka**
PORUBSKY'S GROCERY

**Kansas City**
OKLAHOMA JOE'S
WOODYARD
BAR-B-QUE

**Bunker Hill** BUNKER HILL CAFE

**Hillsboro** OLDE TOWNE RESTAURANT

**Wichita** NU WAY

**Mission**
RJ'S BOB-BE-QUE SHACK

**Frontenac**
BARTO'S IDLE HOUR

**Okarche**
EISCHEN'S BAR

**Bartlesville**
DINK'S PIT BAR-B-QUE
MURPHY'S STEAK HOUSE

**Pittsburg**
CHICKEN MARY'S

**Embudo** SUGAR'S

**Cerrillos**
MARCOS
CAFE

**Santa Fe**
BERT'S BURGER BOWL
PASQUALE'S
PLAZA CAFÉ
ROQUE'S CARNITAS
TECOLOTE

**El Reno**
JOHNNIE'S
ROBERT'S
SID'S

**Clinton**
JIGG'S SMOKEHOUSE

**Perry**
KUMBACK LUNCH

**Vinita**
CLANTON'S

**Elk City** COUNTRY DOVE TEA ROOM

**Tulsa** (see above)

**Stroud** ROCK CAFE

**Claremore**
HAMMETT HOUSE

**Amarillo**
THE BIG TEXAN
GOLDEN LIGHT CAFE

**Oklahoma City** (see above)

**Shawnee**
HAMBURGER KING
VAN'S PIG STAND

**Lawton** THE MEERS STORE

**San Antonio**
BUCKHORN TAVERN
OWL BAR & CAFE

**Albuquerque**
DURAN CENTRAL PHARMACY
FRONTIER
GARCIA'S KITCHEN
GOLDEN CROWN PANADERIA
MODEL PHARMACY

**Lubbock**
TOM & BINGO'S

**Ponder** RANCHMAN'S CAFÉ

**Tioga**
CLARK'S OUTPOST

**Texarkana**
BRYCE'S CAFETERIA

**Las Cruces**
NELLIE'S
NOPALITO

**Grapevine**
BARTLEY'S BAR-B-Q
TOLBERT'S

**Dallas**
FUEL CITY
HIGHLAND PARK SODA FOUNTAIN
THE MECCA
NORMA'S CAFE
SWEET GEORGIA BROWN

**Old Mesilla** LA POSTA DE MESILLA

**La Mesa** CHOP'S

**Canutillo** LITTLE DINER

**Fort Worth**
ANGELO'S
CATTLEMEN'S FORT WORTH STEAK HOUSE
PARIS COFFEE SHOP

**West** VILLAGE BAKERY

**El Paso**
H&H COFFEE SHOP
SMITTY'S

**Marble Falls**
BLUE BONNET CAFE

**Georgetown** MONUMENT CAFE

**Taylor** LOUIE MUELLER'S

**Conroe**
VERNON'S
KUNTRY KATFISH

**Johnson City** HILL COUNTRY CUPBOARD

**Elgin**
SOUTHSIDE MARKET

**Blanco** BLANCO BOWLING CLUB CAFE

**Driftwood** SALT LICK

**Austin** (see below)

**Houston**
(see below)

**Bandera** OST

**San Antonio** (see below)

**Round Top**
ROYER'S ROUND TOP CAFE

**Bastrop**
LOCK DRUGS

**La Grange**
WEIKEL'S STORE
AND BAKERY

**Kyle**
TEXAS PIE
COMPANY

**Luling**
CITY MARKET

**San Antonio**
CHRIS MADRID'S
GREEN VEGETARIAN RESTAURANT
TACO GARAGE
TACO HOUSE
TACO TACO

**Austin**
HOOVER'S COOKING
HUT'S HAMBURGERS
THREADGILL'S

**Seguin**
BOHANNON'S
BRIETZKE STATION

**Lockhart**
BLACK'S BARBECUE
KREUZ MARKET
SMITTY'S

**Houston**
AVALON DINER
GOODE CO.
TEXAS BAR-B-Q
LA MEXICANA

## BK Carne Asada & Hot Dogs

5118 S. 12th Ave.        520-295-0105
Tucson, AZ        www.bktacos.com
      BLD | $

America's most flamboyant wiener, the Sonoran hot dog, starts as a simple beef frank. It gets wrapped in bacon and grilled alongside other bacon-sheathed hot dogs whose grease drippings make the process very much like deep-frying. Bacon flavor melts into the dog, leaving the outside patched with streaks of lean that provide marvelous chewy contrast to the frank they embrace. Stuffed into a substantial, yeasty *bolillo* roll, the frank is topped with tomatoes, pinto beans, onions, mustard, hot green jalapeño sauce, and mayonnaise. On the side comes a roasted guero pepper, which is about the same size, shape, and heat level as a jalapeño, but more yellow than green. At BK, you eat this hot dog on a covered patio and accompany it by cold beer or the refreshing Mexican rice drink known as *horchata*.

While Sonoran hot dogs are the featured attraction, the other part of the restaurant's name requires attention. BK's carne asada is some of the best in Tucson: tender strips of grilled flank steak that are spicy, smoky, and hugely beefy. Order the meat in a taco and it arrives plain in a corn or flour tortilla (your choice), but its flavor is pronounced enough that it flourishes when you dress it to the nines at the copious salsa bar, which includes chunky guacamole as well as salsa verde, chopped tomatoes, pico de gallo, onion, radish, lime, and sliced cucumber.

## Cafe Poca Cosa

110 E. Pennington
Tucson, AZ

520-622-6400
www.cafepocacosatucson.com
LD | $$$

Many years ago when we first came upon Cafe Poca Cosa, it was the dining room of a crappy hotel and its décor was standard-issue Mexican fiesta. It now inhabits ultramodern quarters with objects of Mexican art displayed as in a fine museum. Ambience has turned from fiery to cool. But one thing hasn't changed. Meals still are innovative, unpredictable, and impossible-to-categorize Mexican fare like you will eat nowhere else. There are no printed menus because the kitchen's yield changes as ingredients get used up and new ones come into play. Once you are seated, you will be shown a portable blackboard menu on which nearly every item needs explaining. Nothing chef Suzana Davila makes is familiar; certainly, there are no tacos, enchiladas, or burritos! Neither are there lists of appetizers and side dishes from which to choose. Each dinner is presented on a plate exactly how, and with what, Ms. Davila believes it should be served.

There always are at least a couple of chicken molés, or perhaps the variant of molé known as *pollo en pipian,* for which boneless chicken is cosseted in sauce made from bitter chocolate, crushed red chiles, Spanish peanuts, pumpkin seeds, and cloves. Tamale pie is a menu regular too, and while it is a vegetarian alternative, please do not let your love of meat dissuade you from ordering it. As tender as a soufflé, it comes in many variations. We have had it topped with hot green chile purée, with mango sauce, with curried carrots, and with a zesty tomato paste reminiscent of Italian marinara.

There is shredded beef *(deshebrada)* infused with smoky chili flavor; there are seafood dishes and pork too. Each entree shares its plate with a bright, fresh salad, so that whatever your main course is, it mixes with the greens and makes a happy mess of things. On the side come small warm corn tortillas, and for dessert, there's Mexican-flavored chocolate mousse (is that cinnamon we taste?) and a sultry square of flan, floated on a dish of tremendously sweet burnt-sugar syrup.

# El Bravo

8338 N. 7th St.                      602-943-9753
Phoenix, AZ                          LD | $$

Chuck Henrickson recommended we visit El Bravo for the "best tamale in Arizona." Thumbs-up to that! The chicken and green corn tamales we sampled are earthy, just zesty enough to perk up the taste buds, and impossible to stop eating until appetite has become only a dim memory.

Add to that the other AZ-Mex fare on this merry menu and you have a restaurant that is hard to resist. It's not much for looks: décor is piñatas and beer signs. But who needs mood-making ambience when you can choose from among chiles rellenos, enchiladas, burros and burritos, and a fragile-crusted Navajo red beef popover that are all dishes to remember? On the side come supersavory refried beans. We are especially fond of the *machaca,* aka dried beef, that is available in tacos, burritos, and flautas. For dessert? How about a chocolate chimichanga?

Service is homey, meaning sometimes slow and sometimes brisk. Grandma is friendly, but not cloyingly so.


# El Charro Café

311 N. Court                         520-622-5465
Tucson, AZ                           www.elcharrocafe.com
                                     LD | $$

El Charro is a century-old mission-style home now expanded into a multi-room restaurant, bar, and gift shop, a fortress of Southwestern foodways.

The tostada grande, created here by founder Tia Monica Flin, is a broad cheese crisp like a Mexican pizza. Most people get it with a thin veneer of creamy melted cheese on top; other options include green chiles, guacamole, air-dried beef, and refried beans. El Charro's round-the-world version is a majestic appetizer, served on a pedestal and garnished with fresh basil leaves.

*Carne seca* is a Tucson passion. El Charro's is cured high above the patio in back of the restaurant, where strips of thin-sliced tenderloin hang in an open metal cage. Suspended on ropes and pulleys, the cage sways in the breeze, wafting a perfume of lemon and garlic marinade into the fresh Arizona air. Sautéed after it is air-dried, *carne seca* is customarily served in concert with sweet onions, hot chiles, and tomatoes, making an explosion of flavor like no other food. El Charro has a full menu of tacos, enchiladas, and chiles rellenos, plus such rarer regional specialties as enchilada Sonorese (a patty of fried corn meal garnished with chili) and chalupas (small corn meal canoes filled with chili, meat, or chicken and whole beans). Beyond these hearty meals, the kitchen offers a full repertoire of nutritionally enlightened fare—lo-cal, lo-fat, good-for-you, and good-tasting!

El Charro is noisy and sociable, almost always packed with tourists, Tucsonians, health nuts, and burrito hounds who spoon up fiery salsa picante with corn chips and drink Tecate beer. Mariachi music sets the mood as the sturdy wood floors rumble with the crowds and the air fills with the aroma of hot tostadas grandes. Wall décor is a kaleidoscope of vintage south-of-the-border advertisements, straw sombreros, and years' worth of El Charro calendars, which feature melodramatic scenes of Mexican horsemen (known as *charros*), proud steeds, and pretty maidens all making flirty eyes amid stormy landscapes.

## *El Guero Canelo

5201 S. 12th Ave.
Tucson, AZ

520-295-9005
www.elguerocanelo.com
BLD | $

More than any of the hundred places that sell Sonoran hot dogs in and around Tucson, El Guero Canelo deserves the credit for making it popular. Opened in the 1990s, when the "hot-dog estilo Sonora" was strictly a street-cart affair, it is a happy urban picnic more than a restaurant, its outdoor dining area shaded by a canopy with nozzles all along the rim that rain down mists of cool water to hydrate savage desert air. Hot dogs are assembled at a cart adjoining the patio; other Mexican dishes are cooked in a separate kitchen. After you get your meal but before you take a seat, you can gather condiments from the salsa bar to dress your caramelo, taco, torta, or quesadilla with salsa verde, chopped tomatoes, pico de gallo, onion, radish, lime, or sliced cucumber.

But you do not dress your Sonoran hot dog. That is done by the hot dog man, and it is almost always done exactly the same way. A beef frank, wrapped in bacon and grilled in a trough, is inserted in a big, soft Mexican bun, then dressed with chopped tomatoes, a scattering of pinto beans, grilled or raw onions, a line of yellow mustard, a green ribbon of hot jalapeño sauce, and an artistic squiggle of mayonnaise. On the side comes a roasted guero pepper, which looks like a pale jalapeño (*guero* = "blond") and can be every bit as hot. It would be possible to omit one of the ingredients—onions, beans, or jalapeño sauce, perhaps—but that would be wrong. A Sonoran hot dog with everything is unimpeachable harmony. If you really love the hot dog and bacon duet, El Guero Canelo's cook can make you a Sammy Dog, which is two in one bun, equally well-accoutered—a reasonable idea, considering the dogs are modest-sized and the bun capacious.

## El Manantial Tacos Y Hot Dogs

Park Ave. & 36th St.      520-429-4248
South Tucson, AZ      LD | $

We cannot guarantee El Manantial will be found at Park Avenue and 36th Street in South Tucson. It is a mobile food truck and the location is a vacant lot. If the proprietors find a better location, the truck may relocate. That's the nature of dozens of itinerant vendors who sell good Mexican food in the Old Pueblo. But El Manantial has been in its current spot for quite a while and it seems extremely popular, so if you are on the hunt for one of the city's best Sonoran hot dogs, it is worth seeking out.

Like the more permanent places that sell Sonoran hot dogs, El Manantial is two kitchens: one for tacos, burros, caramelos, tortas, and quesadillas, the other a small adjoining wagon dedicated to hot dogs. The dog is swaddled in bacon, nestled in a fresh bun, and dressed with the full galaxy of condiments—tomatoes, beans, mustard, mayo, and very hot jalapeño sauce. The roasted guero pepper that accompanies all of Tucson's Sonoran dogs is wrapped in smoky bacon. As happens on the wiener, the cooking process glues the bacon to the outside of the pepper, creating a lusty laminate of chewy pork and firm-walled vegetable. The bite of the pepper is offset by a droplet of creamy melted cheese stuffed inside the pod.

Dine at picnic tables with a canopy for protection from the desert sun.

## El Torero

231 E. 26th St.      520-622-9534
South Tucson, AZ      LD (closed Tues) | $$

South Tucson is surrounded by the city of Tucson but is legally and culturally separate. In this part of town, buildings are festooned with brilliant painted tiles, streets hum with low riders cruising in their chopped-roof custom *caruchas,* and at least a dozen different restaurants serve Mexican food that most of us gringos never know.

One of the best is El Torero, a place so inconspicuous that you likely will drive right past it. Once you do walk in, you know you have entered Mexican-food paradise. The jukebox will be belting out party tunes; the bar you walk past to get inside will be occupied by happy people knocking back long-neck beers; at tables in the brightly lit dining room, where the walls are decorated with bullfighter paintings and one large stuffed swordfish, people plow into expertly prepared Sonoran-style food.

Start with a wafer-thin tortilla crisp of cheese and green chile strips, presented on a silver pedestal so all at the table can pull away slices. This crisp is among the thinnest and tastiest in a neighborhood full of excellent crisps. The main menu offers familiar Sonoran Mexican dishes, such as tacos, burros, enchiladas, and chimichangas, plus a few items that are truly special. These include off-the-bone turkey topped with a spicy molé sauce or, on occasion, the similar sauce known as *pipian*, which includes pumpkin seeds. Also noteworthy is the *topopo* salad, named for its resemblance to a volcano. It is a Devil's Tower–shaped mound of lettuce, peas, carrots, et cetera, packed with chicken, *carne seca*, or whatever floats your boat, its sides bolstered by columns of hard cheese.

## Gus Balon's

| | |
|---|---|
| 6027 E. 22nd St. | 520-747-7788 |
| Tucson, AZ | BL \| $ |

Gus Balon's is a cut above in every way. Seemingly ordinary breakfast sandwiches are elevated to excellence by Gus's homemade bun. Eggs come with American fries freckled with crunchy bits from the griddle. The pancakes, which look ordinary, are light and delicious—far better than you'd expect. Gus's sweet roll is outlandishly huge, served warm with a big schmear of butter.

Aside from breakfast and inexpensive lunches served in a bare-bones coffee-shop setting (counter and booths), Gus's is known for first-rate pies. It's hard to choose among them (although the freshly made butterscotch is pretty hard to resist), because they all look so good. A few years back, we took inventory of one single day's list: banana, chocolate banana, chocolate peanut butter banana, chocolate peanut butter, chocolate, coconut, lemon, butterscotch, blueberry, peach, raspberry, peanut butter, pineapple, apple, cherry, raspberry, peach, and raisin. Plus crumb-topped apple-cranberry, peach, raspberry, apple, apple-raisin, cherry, and pumpkin!

Waitresses are diner pros who pour coffee and bring food almost faster than you can speak the words to order it.

# Joe & Aggie's Cafe

120 W. Hopi Dr.                    520-524-6540
Holbrook, AZ                      www.joeandaggiescafe.com
                                   BL | $

Despite the interstate replacing Route 66, Holbrook remains a town where you can get a good feel for what life was like along western roads in the two-lane days. It still has the famous "Sleep in a Wigwam" motel; there are some fascinating pawnshops and Native American jewelry emporia; and at Joe & Aggie's—the oldest restaurant in town, since 1946—you can have a real old-fashioned roadside diner meal.

Tables are outfitted with squeeze bottles of honey for squirting onto sopaipillas (puffy triangles of fried bread), and meals begin with a basket of chips and an empty bowl in which you decant some hot, pepper-flecked hot sauce for dipping. The sign on the front window boasts of "Mexican and American food," but in fact, the menu at Joe & Aggie's is not quite either; it is a blend of Mexican and American that is unique to the Southwest. After the chips and salsa, you move on to such meals as enchiladas made with red or green chili, burros, tacos, or chicken-fried steak with potatoes and hot sopaipillas on the side. Roadfood.com user "icrmg" posted a ravishing photo showing breakfast of green chili–topped huevos rancheros sided by a cake of hash browns and a side of cheese-dripping refried beans.

# La Cabana

840 N. Grand Ave. #12             520-287-3249
Nogales, AZ                        BLD | $

La Cabana is a cozy cantina in a cluster of shops on the main drag. It is outfitted with tables and a couple of comfortable booths. For serious eating, we recommend a booth, where you can lounge like royalty.

Start with made-to-order guacamole. Spruce it up with a dab of the hot salsa provided to every table, as well as a spritz of tiny Mexican limes. The bordertown menu includes corn tamales, enchiladas, corn-crusted tacos, and a beef burrito filled with meat that is moist and pot-roast tender. Chiles rellenos are packed with deep green-chile flavor, oozing melted cheese, and enrobed in crisp-fried crust. Among the most memorable flavors on the table are the simple flour tortillas: warm, delicate, with an earthy wheat flavor so rich they taste pre-buttered.

## Lo-Lo's Chicken & Waffles

1220 S. Central Ave.
Phoenix, AZ

602-340-1304
www.loloschickenandwaffles.com
BLD | $

It wasn't long after Larry White, grandson of the esteemed Mrs. White of Mrs. White's Golden Rule Cafe, opened Lo-Lo's in 2002 that you could barely get in. This soul-food beacon in downtown Phoenix quickly became such a magnet for visiting celebrities as well as locals that there always was a line outside. Mr. White expanded to the current former warehouse, and although there is now a second location (2765 North Scottsdale Road in Scottsdale), you still can expect to wait for a table at either place.

The popularity is well deserved, especially for the signature dish, chicken and waffles. Lo-Lo's waffles are thin and crisp, served hot enough that big balls of butter melt fast into the treads, along with pieces of whatever chicken parts you desire. The dish is most commonly had with gravy and sautéed onions, but some devotees actually use syrup. Beyond chicken and waffles, the menu includes salmon croquettes (which the menu attributes to one Aunt Hattie) and biscuits and gravy (a recipe from "Yo Mama"). There also is a full roster of good side dishes such as peppery collard greens, mac 'n' cheese, candied sweet potatoes, fried okra, cheese grits, and buttered corn.

## Los Jarritos

4832 S. 12th Ave.
Tucson, AZ

520-746-0364
www.losjarritosmexicanfood.com
BL | $

Los Jarritos, a tiny Twelfth Avenue café, always has green corn tamales on the menu, and they are some of the best anywhere, a swirl of sweet corn and hot pepper flavors steamed to a point of opulent harmony. Order at least a couple of them to accompany such classic Sonoran meals as carne asada, *nopalitos con chili* (prickly pear cactus with chili Colorado), and red or white *menudo* available in sizes from a pint to a gallon. Most meals are ordered to take out and most tamales are sold by the dozen, but a couple of tables inside and a few on a small patio out front give regulars the opportunity to linger over long breakfasts of huevos rancheros with house-made chorizo and carry on conversations with one another and with strangers.

Note to alcoholics: Los Jarritos sells *menudo* "ready to cook." For $35 you get the essential fixins needed to make a large vat of the traditional

Mexican hangover cure: eleven pounds of tripe, two beef feet, and five pounds of *nixtamal* (treated corn).

## Mariscos Chihuahua

| | |
|---|---|
| 2902 E. 22nd St. | 520-326-1529 |
| Tucson, AZ | www.mariscoschihuahua.com |
| | LD \| $$ |

Mariscos Chihuahua is a big place with sunlight streaming in picture windows all around, illuminating a tempestuous seascape mural that covers one wall. The staff are friendly, and the sound system belts out Mexican tunes that make every meal feel like a celebration. Seafood stars: oysters raw or cooked, fish grilled or fried, stews and soups. And oh, such shrimp! The menu lists a dozen different styles, including cool cocktails and "drowned raw," meaning ceviche-style—cooked by immersion in a lime marinade.

We are partial to shrimp *endiablados,* which means devilishly hot. They come strewn across a bed of French fries on a broad, fish-shaped plate that also holds a mound of rice, a green salad, and a warm tortilla wrapped in foil. This way of plating the shrimp ensures that whatever they are sauced with, be it garlic butter, soy sauce, oyster sauce, or that wicked *endiablados,* seeps down and flavors the French fries that are their bedding. That means that as you approach the end of your shrimp, you then get to savor crisp fries infused with whatever flavor it was that gave the shrimp their character.

Beverages include excellent presweetened (and lemon-flavored) iced tea as well as *horchata* (sweetened rice milk). A large cooler in the dining area holds bottles and cans of Dos Equis, Tecate, Corona, and Bud and Bud Lite.

There now are eight Mariscos Chihuahuas in Tucson. The Twenty-Second Street shop is the original.

## Mrs. White's Golden Rule Cafe

| | |
|---|---|
| 808 E. Jefferson St. | 602-262-9256 |
| Phoenix, AZ | www.mrswhitesgoldenrulecafe.com |
| | LD (until 3 a.m. Fri & Sat nights) \| $$ |

Here is a soul-food restaurant that attracts a rainbow of customers at lunch. It can get crowded, but waiting a while for a seat is an incredible appetizer. Sniffing the food from this kitchen makes the time joyful. Mrs. White's is one of the best-smelling restaurants we know.

The menu is a soul-food party: fried chicken, catfish, oxtails, and two kinds of pork chops—smothered and simply fried. Other choices include catfish and crunchy-crusted fried chicken, all of them accompanied by corn bread. A list of the day's vegetables is written directly on the wall, which is like a chalkboard. They include sweet yams, black-eyed peas, mac 'n' cheese, and (weekends only) okra gumbo. For dessert, there are sweet-potato pies, layer cakes, and four-star peach cobbler.

Mrs. White's normally closes at 7 p.m., but on Friday and Saturday nights, it reopens at 9 p.m. and stays open until 3 a.m. The late-night menu is streamlined to catfish, wings, hot links, and burgers.

## *Pico de Gallo

2618 S. 6th Ave.  520-623-8775
South Tucson, AZ  LD | $

This informal serve-yourself eatery started as a street-corner taco stand and has grown into several small dining rooms. Nothing about the increase in size has affected its magnificent food. Tacos, constructed in rugged, made-here corn tortillas, are among the best anywhere, available with carne asada and *birria* or more exotic ingredients such as tongue, manta ray, and beef cheeks. We love the *coctel de elote* (corn cocktail), which is not quite the beverage its name suggests. It does come in a large Styrofoam cup, the cup filled with an extraordinary stew of warm corn kernels, drifts of soft melted cheese, hot chili, and lime. Spoon it up like soup; it is corn-sweet and lime-zesty. The menu also lists burros, quesadillas, and tamales by the dozen.

In other regions, "pico de gallo" refers to salsa that serves as a condiment; but here the restaurant's namesake is an astonishing fruit cocktail: chunks of watermelon, coconut, pineapple, mango, and jicama, all spritzed with lime and sprinkled with salt and exclamatory chile powder. The red-hot spice elicits the fruit's sweetness and packs its own lip-tingling punch. It is a heady culinary collusion like nothing else we've ever eaten.

## Sugar Bowl

4005 N. Scottsdale Rd.  602-946-0051
Scottsdale, AZ  www.sugarbowlscottsdale.com
LD | $

Few restaurants are as pure in spirit and intention as the Sugar Bowl, which seems like it might not have changed at all since opening day in 1958. With its pink-upholstered booths and swift young staff who look so cheerful carrying Raspberry Glaciers (Sprite and sherbet), Golden Nuggets (Sprite, sherbet, and ice cream), and Turkish coffee sodas, it is the archetypal ice cream parlor. In particular, we recommend Camelback sodas, made with either vanilla or coffee ice cream, "extra luscious malts," for which glasses are lined with your choice of marshmallow, hot fudge, or caramel sauce, and the tin roof sundae, made with excellent chocolate syrup and a bounty of redskin Spanish peanuts.

There are sandwiches, soups, and salads too, and those we've tasted are very good; but in truth, when we walk into this happy place, we instantly become too obsessed with ice cream to think much about anything else.

## Teresa's Mosaic Cafe

2455 N. Silverbell Rd.      520-624-4512
Tucson, AZ      www.mosaiccafes.com
BLD | $

Teresa's Mosaic Cafe bills itself as Oaxacan, and there are some less familiar Mexican dishes on the menu—chile rellenos stuffed with shredded chicken, marinated pork loin fillets served with squash, and smoked and pickled pasilla chiles that make a spot-on garnish for anything savory—but much of what's offered is familiar border cuisine (tacos, burros, chimichangas, enchiladas). And Tucson's own personality is reflected in such specialties as *topopo* salad and cheese crisps. Corn and wheat tortillas are made at the back of the dining room and arrive at your table griddle-hot. We love the chunky guacamole and mini chimichanga appetizers, and the green corn tamales, dotted with fresh kernels, are classic Sonoran desert fare.

We found this inconspicuous diner thanks to Roadfood.com team members Chris Ayers and Amy Breisch, who proclaimed Teresa's breakfast worthy of exaltation: "Amy dubbed the huevos rancheros the best ever, while Chris made the same claim for the cheese enchilada." The latter is available as part of a combination plate that also includes eggs and a hot tamale. The former, without being outlandish or unique, truly is the model for the way huevos rancheros ought to be: the eggs glistening with butter and perched atop a tortilla that is crisp but also a bit chewy, the salsa hot enough to make you grab for a tortilla from the accompanying basket to tamp your tongue and yet not so hot that the tomato, pepper, egg, wheat, and cheese don't each sing their essential notes loud and clear.

## Tucson Tamale Company

2545 E. Broadway
Tucson, AZ

520-305-4760
www.tucsontamale.com
L | $

Todd Martin is a man on a mission: to celebrate tamales. He makes fine versions of familiar green corn tamales and cheese and jalapeño tamales, but also has invented countless variations on what he sees as an opportunity for invention. Among his creations are vegetarian tamales, vegan tamales, gluten-free tamales, and breakfast tamales such as the Denver (ham, red pepper, onion, cheese) and the Tubac (chorizo, potato, cheese). We love the Arizona tamale—roasted sirloin and smoky chipotle chiles—and the Santa Fe tamale, made with pork loin and green chiles. A few other wonders: the Little Italy tamale, loaded with spicy sausage, pepper, and cheese; the Thanksgiving tamale, which is basically a full turkey dinner enrobed in sage masa; and the New Delhi tamale, which is a cornucopia of carrots, corn, potato, and onions flavored with curry powder and coconut milk. There even is an ode to Tucson's notorious Sonoran hot dog: the dogmale (say "dog-molly"), which is an all-beef hot dog, bacon, beans, and salsa enveloped in corn masa.

"Simplify, Sustain, and Celebrate" is the motto of Martin's sunny little storefront, which vends hundreds of dozens of tamales every week—by mail and takeout for cooking at home and warm for eating on premises at a handful of tables (along with house-made salsas in three heat levels). "People think of the tamale as a Mexican thing," Martin says, "but it goes back to pre-Columbian Mesoamerica, long before the Spanish. So many cultures around the world have their own take on the concept."

## Vantastic

4729 W. Olive Ave.
Glendale, AZ

623-435-2024
BL | $

The formal name of this place is Vantastic Donuts & Bagels. The bagels, baked elsewhere, are not vantastic. The donuts are. Nothing wild and crazy about them; there are creamy-cakey sinkers, sugar-glazed puffy ones, chewy donut holes, apple fritters, and, best of all, crunch-crusted buttermilk bars with a tangy twist that makes their sweetness all the sweeter.

The place itself is a nostalgic mid-twentieth-century coffee shop. In the early morning, it is a locals' hangout for counter coffee klatches.

# Biker Jim's Gourmet Sausage

2148 Larimer St.                 720-746-9355
Denver, CO                       www.bikerjimsdogs.com
                                 LD | $

OMG, what a menu! If, like us, a restaurant with too many tempting choices induces anxiety—which of all of these inviting things should I order?—Biker Jim's could make you catatonic. But what delicious madness! A printed menu does help the decision-making by organizing your thoughts into a step-by-step process. First, choose a dog. The dozen-plus available can be as basic as an all-beef frank or it can be a sausage made of elk, rattlesnake/ pheasant, reindeer, buffalo, or duck. There's a vegan one too.

Having selected a tube steak, you then peruse available toppings: wasabi aioli, New Jersey chili, caramelized apple, roasted cactus, Coke-marinated grilled onions, and so on. Next: side dishes. There are fine homemade fries and hand-cut potato chips, plus mac 'n' cheese, baked beans, and fried green tomatoes. Far be it from us to recommend one combo over another, but we will say that the recommendation of Roadfood.com's Cliff Strutz and Cousin Johnnie made us very happy: a wine-laced pork sausage on a pretzel roll topped with Dijon cream, crunchy squiggles of beer-battered onion, toasted sauerkraut, and a dusting of tomato bacon powder. It's called a Waatlander Dog.

To drink: thick, freshly made milk shakes topped with whipped cream.

And for dessert, how about limoncello sour orange swirl cheesecake with a gingersnap crust?

## Buckhorn Exchange

1000 Osage
Denver, CO

303-534-9505
www.buckhorn.com
LD | $$$

Holder of Colorado Liquor License #1 (issued in 1893), outfitted with a few museums' worth of antique firearms and furniture, and hung with a menagerie of some five hundred game animal trophies shot by former owner Shorty Zietz, the Buckhorn Exchange is no mere frontier-themed restaurant for tourists. It happens to be a fine place to eat the cuisine of the Rockies.

At lunch, hamburgers, salads, and sandwiches are consumed without ado by a cadre of regular customers inured to the stare of a thousand glass eyes and the creak of wood floors where Buffalo Bill once trod. Tourists like us cannot help but gape and wonder . . . and then tuck into a seriously carnivorous meal. Those who want to eat really Wild Western fare can start with Rocky Mountain oysters (deep-fried calf testicle) or rattlesnake marinated in red chile and lime. Less daunting hors d'oeuvres include the Buckhorn's legendary bean soup and smoked buffalo sausage with red chile polenta. For the main meat you can choose buffalo tenderloin, elk medallions, Colorado lamb, beefsteaks, baby-back ribs, or Gramma Fanny's Pot Roast, made from a recipe that dates back to 1893. If there's more than a single passionate meat-eater at the table, the dish to have is the Big Steak, carved tableside. It's a strip steak available in sizes from one and a half pounds (for two) to four pounds (for five). The latter sells for $199.

Top it all off with a broad slab of hot crumb-topped apple pie with cinnamon rum sauce, and you will have eaten a true-West meal.

## Bud's Bar

5453 Manhart St.
Sedalia, CO

303-688-9967
LD | $

Bars tend not to be great places to look for excellent food, but if it's a hamburger you seek, they're worth putting on the hit list. For a rewarding bar burger, we suggest heading south on Highway 85 out of Denver to the town of Sedalia and finding a mid-twentieth-century watering hole named Bud's. Here is served what tipster Mindy Leisure described as "one of the best burgers you will ever eat." It is juicy with a good crust, modest-sized, nothing fancy. You have a choice of a single or a double with or without cheese. Pickles and onion are the only garnishes available. There's no deep-fryer on premises, so the menu advises patrons, "We don't have no damn fries." Instead, you get a bag of potato chips.

As you might guess by the extremely limited menu—there's nothing to eat other than burgers—Bud's attracts a lot of people for whom the hamburgers are a side dish to the main course, which is beer.

## Duffeyroll Cafe

| | |
|---|---|
| 1290 S. Pearl St. | 303-753-9177 |
| Denver, CO | www.duffeyrolls.com |
| | BL \| $ |

Colorado is rich in cinnamon rolls. The most famous is the enormous, plate-sized megaroll at Johnson's Corner truck stop up in Loveland (p. 448). The most elegant is the one at the Duffeyroll Cafe in Denver. Actually, there are several Duffeyrolls available—crisp-edged swirls of dough drizzled with maple, orange, even Irish cream frosting, but it's our firm belief that such drippy indulgence, while a welcome addition to big, doughy rolls, overwhelms the fragile texture of a plain Duffeyroll. Oh, we do like pecanilla crunch and English toffee, which are applied judiciously and add a nice extra note. But the regular roll is so perfectly sugary and cinnamony and buttery that we are loath to adulterate it.

If you do need something denser and more substantial, have a pecan sticky bun, stuck with a thick blanket of nuts. Sandwiches, wraps, soups, and salads are available at lunch.

There are two other locations: in Denver, 4994 East Hampden Avenue (303-753-9177) and in Englewood, 5198 South Broadway (303-996-5900).

## Durango Diner

| | |
|---|---|
| 957 Main Ave. | 970-247-9889 |
| Durango, CO | www.durangodiner.com |
| | BLD \| $ |

It was pancakes that made us fall in love with the Durango Diner—plate-wide pancakes, preferably with blueberries, glistening with butter and running rivers of syrup. We branched out to other breakfasts, and liked them plenty, especially the "half and half" plate of biscuits with gravy and green chile, and the big warm cinnamon roll. You will share breakfast in this Main Street hash house with some locals who claim to have been having coffee an' at these seats since opening day in 1965.

If you are a connoisseur of hamburgers, put Durango on your treasure map, for its Bonus Cheeseburger Deluxe: one-half pound of meat under a mantle of melted Swiss cheese and diced green chiles, French fries on the side. We love the Durango Diner's bacon double cheeseburgers almost as much as we love the chiliburgers (available red or green), and although some customers combine all these toppings on one mound of meat, we must confess that bacon and chili together atop a cheeseburger is just too much for our delicate palates.

## Johnson's Corner

2842 SE Frontage Rd.          970-667-2069
(Exit 254 off I-25)           www.johnsonscorner.com
Loveland, CO                  Always open | $

A favorite truckers' stop along Highway 87 between Denver and Cheyenne since before there was an interstate, Johnson's Corner serves breakfast (and lunch and supper) around the clock, and is famous for its colossal cinnamon roll. The roll is OK—probably the most bang for your buck, but when we seek maximum flavor along with maximum calories, we prefer Johnson's chicken-fried steak with eggs, crunchy hash browns, and a biscuit with gravy. The breakfast menu contains all the usual suspects—omelets, pancakes, corned beef hash—as well as buffalo sausage and a breakfast burrito. Non-breakfast highlights include pot roast dinner, hot turkey sandwich, steaks, and pork chops. A full-service soda fountain offers shakes, floats, malts, and one heck of a handsome banana split.

Recently remodeled, the dining area sports hugely spacious booths and counter service. And for truckers and other travelers who want to stay connected, it is a Wi-Fi hot spot.

## La Fogata

5670 E. Evans Ave.            303-753-9458
Denver, CO                    www.la-fogata.com
                              BLD | $

La Fogata means "the bonfire," however the green chile bowl (available with or without pork) served in this bilingual establishment isn't really all that hot. But it is quite delicious: zesty, glowing with sunny chile flavor, and packed with the punch of cumin. If you are looking for excellent Mexican food in Denver, this is the place to be.

Many items on La Fogata's menu are nationally familiar Tex-Mex staples—enchiladas, chiles rellenos, tamales—expertly made and served in abundance, but this is also an opportunity to be adventurous. If you are blasé about beef in your taco, you can order tacos filled with crisp-roasted pork (wonderful!), tacos with beef tongue (spicy!), or ceviche tostadas; or you can spoon into the bowl of the tripe and hominy stew known as *menudo*. To drink, there are imported beers, plenty of tequila cocktails, and the true-Mex non-alcoholic favorite, *horchata,* which is sweet rice milk.

This is a fun place to dine, where the crowd is equal measures downtown business executives, blue-collar beer drinkers, and foodies who appreciate a taste of high-quality but unpretentious Mexican food.

Two other locations: 8090 East Quincy Avenue, Denver (720-974-7315) and 16600 Washington Street, Thornton (303-252-5530).

## Al's Chickenette

700 Vine St.                     785-625-7414

Hays, KS                         LD | $

If you are traveling in western Kansas along I-70 with any degree of appetite as you approach Hays, do yourself a favor and find Al's. It will be especially easy to find if it's after dark, for this sixty-year-old eatery has a beautiful vintage neon sign glowing outside. Indoors, the walls are covered with evocative pictures of Kansas railroad history and a huge collection of chicken figurines.

Of course, the thing to eat is chicken. Fried. You can buy it by the quarter or half bird, tenders or nuggets, a breast fillet or a giblet dinner of livers and/or gizzards. This is not fast-food chicken. It will take a while for your order to cook, which is one reason it is so good. As your teeth crack through the chicken's crunchy skin, aromatic steam erupts into the air. It is delicious plain, but the way Al's customers know to eat it is to drizzle some honey across the crisp skin (as well as on the excellent French fries). The honey's sweetness sings mellifluous harmony with the chicken's salty crust.

# Barto's Idle Hour

210 S. Santa Fe St.                   620-232-9834

Frontenac, KS                        D | $$

Even before goofball TV found its way to the fried chicken restaurants in and around Pittsburg, Kansas, and made a big deal of the rivalry among them, food writers tended to concentrate only on the big two: Chicken Mary's (p. 452) and Chicken Annie's. Considering they are within spitting distance of each other and they were the first to specialize in full-bore chicken dinners, the concentration made sense. But in fact there are six restaurants in the area that specialize in fried chicken, and to many of those who have tried them all, Barto's Idle Hour stands supreme.

It is relatively new, opened as a music hall in the 1950s and finally taking up the fried-chicken gauntlet in the 1960s. When Roadfood.com's Chris Ayers and Amy Breisch visited in 2010, this is what they had to say: "The fried chicken skyrocketed to the top of our list, having exceeded all necessary criteria from the crispy-without-being-overly-greasy skin to the melt-in-your-mouth juiciness of the meat. Pieces of white and dark meat can be ordered individually, but to do so would mean missing out on the traditional sides that are inextricably tied to chicken dinners in this region. As opposed to the mayonnaise-laden potato salads and coleslaws most familiar to the American palate, local menus offer these side dishes German-style (vinegar and oil–based). The result is nothing short of *wunderbar,* as both sides are both delightfully zesty and highly addictive. Those looking to emphasize the 'fried' in fried chicken dinner are encouraged to pay the supplemental charge and add a side of homemade onion rings to the mix. Their fragile crusts make these rings indeed unforgettable. Each table also gets a basket of bread freshly baked by the Frontenac Bakery, which services all of the chicken restaurants in the area."

Chris and Amy, who have been to nearly all the great Roadfood restaurants coast to coast, concluded their review by saying that Barto's "ranks among our most memorable Roadfood stops of all time."

# Brookville Hotel

105 E. Lafayette Ave.              785-263-2244

Abeline, KS                    www.brookvillehotel.com

                                         LD | $$

Buffalo Bill slept at the Brookville Hotel in the small town of Brookville, as did untold numbers of drovers when Kansas was the end of the line for trail drives up from Texas. It was opened in 1870 and has built a reputation for its bountiful family-style chicken dinners since 1915.

It was a sad day when it closed in 1999 and moved to Abeline. While the new setting lacks the charm of the old railhead town of Brookville, great pains were taken to make the building look like the old facility. Even if it is more like a theme park than a century-old restaurant, the Brookville Hotel continues to serve the meal that has made it a destination for generations of hungry Kansans who think nothing of driving two hours each way for Sunday supper. As always, fried chicken is the main attraction—a half a bird, skillet fried and served with mashed potatoes and cream gravy, with creamed corn, cottage cheese, baking-powder biscuits with sweet preserves, sweet-and-sour coleslaw, and ice cream for dessert.

## Bunker Hill Cafe

609 Elm St.      785-483-6544
Bunker Hill, KS      D Weds-Sat | $$$

Located in a blink-and-you-miss-it crossroads community, the Bunker Hill Cafe is a rugged limestone building that opened as a drugstore then became a pool hall. Today it is a destination steak house, open for supper only Wednesday through Saturday. It's a small place, no more than a dozen tables, with a menu that includes shrimp, catfish, and chicken, although nearly everybody comes for steak. Filet mignon is available in sizes that range from two to sixteen ounces, sirloin from four to sixteen. There's also bacon-wrapped ground beef and, on occasion, Kansas elk and buffalo. Our sirloins were laden with juice, tender but not at all tenderized, a joy to slowly savor. It was late summer, and on the side came beautiful, full-flavored tomatoes and corn on the cob, as well as the house specialty, honey bread (available for purchase by the loaf).

Décor is Plains rustic: lots of mounted trophies and naturalist pictures on the wall and a couple of wood-burning stoves for warmth in cool weather. As seating is limited, reservations are advised.

## Chicken Mary's

1133 E. 600th Ave.      620-231-9510
Pittsburg, KS      D | $$

The narrow lane off Highway 69 between Frontenac and Pittsburg, Kansas, is known as the Chicken Dinner Road, home of two flourishing restaurants—

Chicken Mary's and Chicken Annie's—that specialize in nearly identical dinners of deep-fried chicken.

Mary and Annie have long ago gone to their reward, and many years ago Mary's son—no spring chicken himself—explained to us that in the hard times of the 1930s, his father and Annie's husband both worked in a nearby mine. In 1934, Annie's husband lost a leg in a mine accident. To make ends meet, Annie opened a little restaurant and served her specialty, fried chicken. Only a few years after that, Mary's husband had to quit work too, because of a bad heart. "There were three of us kids to feed," the old man recalled. "And my mother could see how well Annie was doing selling chicken dinners out here. She took a hint and opened her own place, Chicken Mary's, just down the road."

A tradition was begun. The rivalry has made this unlikely farm road a chicken lover's mecca for six decades. The meals are ritualized family-style feasts, centered on chicken that arrives glistening with grease. The skin is chewy and luxurious, the meat below moist and tender. You can order whichever parts you want in whatever quantity: dark, white, wings, backs, even livers, gizzards, or hearts. On the side you want German potato salad and/or coleslaw. Poultry frowners can order chicken-fried steak.

Note: Chicken Annie's is a few hundred yards up the road, at 1143 East 600th Avenue (620-231-9460). We've never eaten at both in the same trip, nor have we done enough research to rate one place above the other.

## Corner Pharmacy

429 Delaware St.                    913-682-1602
Leavenworth, KS                     BL | $

Located in a well-tended Victorian building that dates back to the beginning of the twentieth century, the Corner Pharmacy really is a pharmacy. It hosts a soda fountain that serves breakfast all day (to 6 p.m., closing time) and classic lunch-counter single-digit-priced meals.

The countertop is faux marble, but the food is real. Watch the mixologist create a Green River or a phosphate and see milk shakes assembled scoop by squirt, then whirled in the multi-wand mixer and served in their ice-frosted silver canisters. Hamburgers are lunch-counter-thin and just greasy enough to leave a savory imprint on the bun. A plate of biscuits and gravy is one of the best dollars-for-calories deals in the nation.

## Cozy Inn

108 N. 7th St.  
Salina, KS

785-825-9407  
www.cozyburger.com  
LD | $

When the McDonald brothers opened their first hamburger restaurant in California after World War II, the Cozy Inn had already been around a quarter century. This is one of America's original hamburger stands, and although its management has changed over the years and it was threatened with extinction (but saved by a consortium of local hamburger patriots), it serves burgers that are pretty much the same as they were in 1922.

They are archetypal sliders. The first great thing to praise about them is their smell. As you approach the diminutive diner, the scent of grilling onions and beef with a hint of dill pickle tickles your senses like exotic hash-house perfume. There is a window for takeout orders, but for full enjoyment, sit inside at the counter on one of six stools. Here, the ten minutes to have lunch of maybe a half dozen sliders and a bag of potato chips will ensure that the Cozy aroma will saturate your clothes and stay with you the rest of the day. Freeze a bag of Cozies, heat them in the microwave oven six months later, and their scent will billow out.

The second exceptional thing about them is their taste. These are no Salisbury steaks or quarter-pounders. They are thin-as-a-nickel, one-ounce patties in little buns that somehow form a perfect combination with pickle, mustard, and ketchup. It is a configuration so consecrated that, according to Cozy Inn folklore, some years ago when a Cozy cook tried to put a piece of cheese on his own personal burger, he was fired on the spot.

## Nu Way

1416 W. Douglas Ave.  
Wichita, KS

316-267-1131  
www.nuwayburgers.com  
L | $

We don't know of another American food with as many names as loosemeats. That is what Heartland eaters call a sandwich of spiced, unpattied, and unsauced beef that usually is served in a bun with pickle and onion, sometimes with cheese, and sometimes mustard (but never ketchup). Its native habitat is Iowa, where it also goes by the brand name Maid Rite; up in Siouxland, you'll find it listed as a Tavern, Charlie Boy, Big T, or Tastee.

In Wichita, Kansas, the sandwich is called a Crumbly Burger or, eponymously, a Nu Way, after the place that serves it. Nu Way's Nu Way is available medium or large (twice the amount of crumbly burger on a big bun), arriving wrapped in wax paper and already cut in half for easy eating without too much of the beef falling out when you pick it up. The meat is moist with temperate beefy taste, well abetted by onion, pickle, and mustard.

While the beef tends toward bland, Nu Way's garlic salad is alarmingly flavorful, a creamy slaw with garlic pungency that tastes nearly radioactive. If you don't love garlic, you won't like it, and even if you do love garlic, it can be overpowering. You definitely do want Nu Way onion rings, which are big hoops crusted with fragile batter, and sweet, dark, brewed-here root beer. Limeade, regular or cherry-flavored, is squeezed to order.

There now are six Nu Ways in Wichita. The West Douglas Avenue location is the original, dating back to 1930. It was opened by Tom McEvoy, who came to Kansas from (no surprise) Iowa.

## Oklahoma Joe's

3002 W. 47th Ave.
Kansas City, KS

913-722-3366
www.oklahomajoesbbq.com
LD | $

A gas station, convenience store, and cafeteria-style barbecue restaurant, Oklahoma Joe's offers traditional KC barbecue by the pound and sandwich as well as such specialty sandwiches as the Z-Man, which is brisket and provolone cheese topped with onion rings, and Hog Heaven, which is pulled pork *and* sliced sausage.

Unless you are a purist, you might want to try the fine Smokie Joe, which is a combo sandwich of beef and pork. While the plain pulled pork is great sauceless—sweet, juicy, and radiant with smoke flavor—Joe's peppery, slightly sweet sauce makes the meat duo sing.

Tables are outfitted with paper towels, and myriad banners celebrate the victories of OK Joe's barbecue men in competitions far and wide.

## Olde Towne Restaurant

126 N. Main St.  
Hillsboro, KS

620-947-5446  
BL Tues-Sat; D Fri and Sat; Sun supper  
| $$

In a big old limestone building on Main Street in downtown Hillsboro, Olde Towne Restaurant really is olde! Located in what was built in 1887 as the town's bank (with a vault in the basement), it served for many years as an egg factory, where women candled, sorted, and crated eggs. Lower-story décor includes vintage egg crates made of wood as well as antique farm implements and a mural of old Hillsboro.

Olde Towne is the one nice restaurant in Hillsboro, and so it has a menu with something for everyone, from sandwiches, soups, and hamburgers every day at lunch to an all-you-can-eat Mexican smorgasbord on Friday nights and a Saturday-night Low German buffet. Hillsboro is the heart of America's Mennonite community, and many of today's three thousand citizens descended from Germans who came to the USA (some via Russia). One of those who upholds the culinary heritage is Linden Thiessen, proprietor of Olde Towne, a man who makes a point of serving such melting-pot dishes as *verenika* (cottage cheese dumplings), zwieback bread, German sausage, and the beef-and-cabbage-stuffed pastry meal known as a *bierock* (here spelled *bierrock*). Dessert measures up to grandmotherly standards and includes an array of cream pies, bumbleberry pie, hot fruit cobbler, and cream puffs.

## Porubsky's Grocery

508 NE Sardou  
Topeka, KS

785-234-5788  
L Mon-Thurs | $

For more than half a century, customers have been coming to the Little Russia neighborhood of North Topeka to eat Porubsky's chili (during chili season only—October to March) and cold-cut sandwiches. Regulars include a blue-collar crowd, traveling trenchermen, and politicians who want to be photographed in a setting that makes them look like normal people.

The sandwiches are no big deal—ordinary lunch meats on regular bread—but the extras are outstanding. The most famous of these are Porubsky's pickles. They are big, firm discs that start as dills but are then infused with horseradish, mustard, and hot peppers to become an eye-widening garnish guaranteed to snap taste buds to attention. They are a favorite complement, along with crumbled saltine crackers, atop a bowl of

Porubsky's chili. Before the hot pickles are applied, the chili is a fine bowl of Heartland comfort: ground chuck cooked with a measure of chili powder and other spice, then added to a battered old pot of simmering beans.

## RJ's Bob-Be-Que Shack

5835 Lamar Ave.                913-262-7300
Mission, KS                    www.rjsbbq.com
                               LD (breakfast on weekends) | $$

There was a time when burnt ends were nothing but bits, scraps, and shreds gathered from the cutting board after barbecued brisket had been sliced. A duet of rugged crunch and melting fat, these traditional burnt ends, once a delicacy known only to barbecue devotees, are now a smokehouse menu staple. The meal that used to be debris has become so popular that contemporary barbecue restaurants cut tidy little chunks off the edge of the brisket so that burnt ends can be a regular, everyday menu item. That's not necessarily a bad thing; modern burnt ends, although leaner and therefore less lascivious, can still deliver tremendous flavor. RJ's Bob-Be-Que Shack proves the point. Available here as pork or beef burnt ends, these nuggets of meat are available in a sandwich, on a platter, and—Saturday and Sunday only—as the anchor of burnt-end hash, a tangle of pork or brisket with onions, peppers, mushrooms, and bacon.

RJ's menu beyond burnt ends is vast, including four kinds of ribs by the rack (spare, St. Louis, baby backs, and lamb ribs), barbecued chicken, Polish sausage, and a butt burger. That last one is a half pound of ground pork butt, pattied and smoked. Interesting side dishes include a cheesy corn bake and potato chips drizzled with truffle oil and balsamic vinegar.

## *Woodyard Bar-B-Que

3001 Merriam Ln.               913-362-8000
Kansas City, KS                www.woodyardbbq.com
                               LD | $$

The Woodyard is in fact a woodyard selling hickory, cherry, pecan, and applewood logs to pitmasters and backyard barbecuists. It is also a restaurant that serves first-rate Kansas City barbecue, which you can enjoy at tables inside a country wood-frame house or on a patio built around an open-air smoker. From the smoker emerge splendid baby-back ribs sheathed in meat that pulls right off the bone in big, juicy ribbons.

Smoke profoundly infuses the Woodyard's burnt ends (tips, squiggles, shreds, and nuggets of barbecued meat), which are available in a sandwich or on occasion as the topping for multi-bean chili. Burnt ends are powerful stuff. For those less extreme in their barbecue lust, the pulled pork here is nothing short of magnificent, just-right smoky and so full of juice and flavor that sauce is entirely optional. Other items on the menu include hot legs— like wings, but meatier—and a Friday special of pecan smoked salmon.

## Louis' Basque Corner

301 E. 4th St.  
Reno, NV

775-323-7203  
www.louisbasquecorner.com  
LD | $$

We ate at Louis's Basque Corner on our first trip across the USA in the early 1970s. At the time, the place was five years old—Mr. and Mrs. Louis Erreguible, who had only recently come to Reno from southern France, were ebullient hosts in their new-world dining room. After supper, we walked out utterly inspired, thinking that *someone* really ought to be writing about marvelous local restaurants in unlikely places across the country. We've been writing about such restaurants ever since, and Louis' Basque Corner continues to serve what Mrs. Erreguible described long ago as "simple food cooked to perfection."

By average-American-meal standards, the food at Louis' is far from simple. What you eat at the long, family-style tables are copious feasts that start with soup, salad, bread, and beans, then move on to a plate of beef tongue, paella, oxtails, lamb stew, or Basque chicken. That's the *first course*! After that comes the serious eating: an entree of sirloin steak, paella, pork loin or pork chops, lamb chops, or a fish of the day.

Louis's is a colorful place with waitresses outfitted in native attire and walls decorated with travel posters of the Pyrenees as well as pottery from Ciboure. Its clientele is a mix of travelers passing through for whom a meal here is a special treat as well as plenty of locals who make Louis' a regular part of their regimen.

## Martin Hotel

94 W. Railroad St.
Winnemucca, NV

775-623-3197
www.themartinhotel.com
LD | $$

Bring plenty of appetite if you plan to eat dinner at the Martin Hotel, which has been serving Basque feeds to locals for well over a century. The copious meals start with soup, salad, herbed carrots, Basque beans, garbanzo beans with sausage, garlic mashed potatoes, and bread, all accompanied by basso profundo burgundy wine. Next, you have a steak, lamb shank, pork chops, pork loin, sweetbreads, or salmon, accompanied by excellent French fries cut from local potatoes. There is good bread pudding for dessert, and you must also consider a glass of Picon Punch, the bittersweet Basque digestif.

The hotel is a humble stucco building that still has hitching posts outside. Dining is at long communal tables that seat up to a dozen people. At lunch, normal-sized plates of food are served.

## Mary's Hash House

2605 S. Decatur, Ste. 103
Las Vegas, NV

702-873-9479
www.hashhouse.com
BL | $

If we were sticklers for our own rules, one of which defines Roadfood as fare of the region where the restaurant is located, Mary's Hash House would not be included in this book. It's in Las Vegas and boasts of serving Midwestern food. But because Las Vegas is a city where normal rules of life don't apply and, more important, because it is a city with a dearth of normal restaurants (what is native Las Vegas cuisine, anyway?), we include it here as a service to hungry travelers in search of something other than an all-you-can-eat buffet or yet another celebrity chef's high-priced eating shrine. (Please, do not confuse it with Hash House A Go Go at the Imperial Palace on the Strip.)

We'd never have found it were it not for the intrepid appetites of Roadfood.com's Bruce Bilmes and Sue Boyle, who wrote, "The simple, unflashy home-cooking, served in a simple, unflashy room, plays well in mega-flashy Vegas." They noted that it really is a hash house, its breakfast-all-day menu featuring corned beef hash, ham hash, roast beef hash, and chicken hash, as well as Super Hash, which blends them all. A good-sized portion, including a couple of side dishes (fried potatoes, grits, fresh fruit, toast) will get you change from a ten-dollar bill: one of the city's true dining bargains. Bruce and Sue emphasized that just about everything at Mary's is made right here: The hash, of course, which you can have with or without peppers, onions, mushrooms, or even eggs scrambled in, but also an amazing array of jellies and jams, including hot habanero, not-quite-as-hot jalapeño, peach, strawberry, and watermelon.

The menu extends far beyond hash. Omelets, pancakes, waffles, eggs Benedict, Alaskan salmon, and perch with eggs for breakfast; soup, salad, sandwiches, fried chicken, and hamburgers for lunch.

## Bert's Burger Bowl

235 N. Guadalupe                    505-982-0215

Santa Fe, NM                        LD | $

Bert's says it invented the green chile cheeseburger. We cannot confirm the claim, but we can tell you that the one made here is a doozy. Patties of beef are sizzled on a grate over charcoal, from which flames lick up and flavor not only the meat but also the bright orange cheese laid upon it. Dollops of fiery minced green chiles are mounded atop the cheese from a bucket near the fire, and unless you say otherwise, your burger will come dressed with mustard, pickle, lettuce, onion, and tomato. Experienced customers, who dine under umbrellas on a sun-drenched patio overlooking Guadalupe Street, gradually peel back the wax paper in which the sandwich is wrapped as they eat, thus avoiding too much spillage.

Other popular burger configurations include BBQ and mayo/relish, and if the normal quarter-pounder seems insufficient, a half-pound hamburger is available. Anyone who eats four half-pound burgers in thirty minutes gets them free. The menu also lists taco carnitas, *flautas de pollo,* chile dogs, and Fritos pie.

Everything at Bert's is cooked to order, so even though it is informal and efficient, you will wait for your food. A sign on the cash register advises: "All our food at Bert's is specially made for you and the approximate wait is 12 minutes once order is placed."

## Buckhorn Tavern

68 US Hwy. 380                575-835-4423
San Antonio, NM          LD | $

Buckhorn Tavern's green chile cheeseburger is a swirling combination of beef, melted cheese, hot green chile, lettuce, tomato, and pickle chips on a broad, tender bun. There are more elegant GCCBs in New Mexico and there are some that are beefier or oozier; this one earns kudos for harmony.

Buckhorn's Fritos pie is another example of multiple-ingredient poise, the corn chips an agreeable medley of tamale-soft and hard-breaking crisp. Chile cheese fries are also a good ensemble idea, but the ones we ate were limp and not cooked through. Maybe it was just a bad deep-fryer day, or perhaps our arrival at the very start of lunch hour meant the cooking oil wasn't yet hot enough.

Buckhorn Tavern got a lot of attention on TV food shows a few years ago, meaning that even though San Antonio, New Mexico, is in the middle of nowhere, it usually is so crowded that you will wait in line for a seat. The place opens at 11 a.m.; a 10:45 arrival puts you in the first wave.

## Chope's

16145 S. Hwy. 28          575-233-3420
La Mesa, NM              LD | $

You'd expect this kitchen's work with chiles to be good; many of its regular customers are planters whose business is to grow the legendary New Mexico peppers. There is no better way to taste the long greens of the Mesilla Valley than as Chope's chiles rellenos. Stuffed with mild cheese, battered, and crisp-fried, the fleshy walls of the pod have a strapping vegetable punch.

As for red chiles, their quintessence can be tasted in the cream-thick, bright vermillion purée that is scrupulously handmade in the kitchen. It is pretty darn hot, the kind of lip-searing hot that any restaurant outside New Mexico would warn customers about. But in this area, it's normal. The really hot stuff on the table is green salsa, made entirely from Mesilla Valley jalapeños. Chope's will oblige those who insist on maximum heat by offering special four-alarm chile in a bowl or on enchiladas. The chilecentric menu also includes gorditas, tacos, plates of chile con carne, tamales, and green chile-draped cheeseburgers.

## Duran Central Pharmacy

1815 Central NW
Albuquerque, NM

505-247-4141
www.durancentralpharmacy.com
BL | $

One of our favorite views in the scenery-rich Southwest is from a stool at the lunch counter in Duran Central Pharmacy. To the right is the kitchen, where you can view one of the staff using a dowel to roll out rounds of dough into broad flour tortillas that are perfect tan circles. Straight ahead is the grill where they are cooked. To see them puff up from the heat and blister golden-brown, then to smell the warm, bready aroma filling the air, is to know for certain that good food is on its way.

These superlative tortillas, available plain or glistening with butter, come on the side of most lunches, including the wondrous Thursday-only *carne adovada*. They are used to wrap hamburgers and as the base of quesadillas. We like them best as a dunk for Duran's red or green chile, which is available either plain (nothing but chiles and spice) or loaded with your choice of ground beef, beans, potatoes, or chicken. The green is hugely flavorful, hot and satisfying with an earthy character; the red is pure essence of plant life, liquefied with a full measure of sunshine.

Duran, by the way, is a full-service pharmacy.


## *Frontier

2400 Central SE
Albuquerque, NM

505-266-0550
www.frontierrestaurant.com
5 a.m.–1 a.m. daily | $

The Frontier boasts that it is "home of the latest in broiled food and the Frontier sweet roll." We're not up on broiled food trends, and the famous Frontier sweet roll, while awesomely sized, is not on our top ten list. Nevertheless, we love this place—not only because it is cheap, informal, and open twenty-one hours a day, but because the New Mexican food is first-rate.

At breakfast, huevos rancheros are available with a choice of four toppings: salsa, green chile stew, red chile, and green chile. The last one is the hottest, with a full-tilt chile punch, giving the plate a roasted, earthy aroma that is insanely appetizing. Cheddar cheese should not be left out of this big platter that looks like a mess but eats like a dream. On the side comes a puffy, just-cooked flour tortilla (you can watch the man make them behind the counter) that is almost too hot to handle. Orange juice is fresh-squeezed. Quart carafes of coffee are available for $2.

The lunch menu includes such Land of Enchantment specialties as a *carne adovada* burrito, green chile stew, and, naturally, a chile cheeseburger, here dubbed the Fiesta Burger. Homemade lemonade is available to drink.

One thing that makes dining at the Frontier fun is its breakneck pace. Because meals are ordered fast, cooked fast, and served instantaneously, you are guaranteed that things that are supposed to be hot are piping hot; we've gotten hamburgers still sizzling from the grill. Although many customers linger over coffee, it is possible to be in and out, with a good meal under your belt, in five minutes. The system is serve-yourself. While you wait in line, study the overhead menu and make your decision. When the green light flashes, indicating someone is ready to take your order, step up to the counter and say what you want. Approximately two minutes later, you are carrying your meal to an open table.

## Garcia's Kitchen

1113 4th St. NW
Albuquerque, NM

505-247-9149
www.garciaskitchen.com
BLD | $

Garcia's Kitchen has been around since 1975 and there now are seven locations in Albuquerque. All are bright and gay, from Fiestaware dishes to colorful murals on inside and outside walls. The menu is big, including such New Mexico signature dishes as blue corn enchiladas, green chile cheeseburgers, and stuffed sopaipillas. There are Tex-Mex chili con carne and true-Mex *menudo,* as well as a full array of burritos available "chili in," "chili and cheese over" or "smothered."

Whatever else you get, we highly recommend a bowl of *chicharrones,* which are a bacon lover's fantasy: whole nuggets of crisp fried pork rind that are about half-meat, half-fat—unbelievably delicious when eaten still melt-in-the-mouth warm, still irresistible as we devoured the last of them at the end of the meal, appetite only a memory but taste buds still ravening. It was especially fun to tear off a small piece of sopaipilla, insert a single *chicharrone,* then drizzle on some honey: sweet, wheat, and meat all in one!

Glorious *carne adovada:* hunks of pork saturated with sunny chile flavor and bathed in red purée—so much purée that the yolks of two sunnyside-up eggs on the plate barely poke up through the chile. On the side come good fried potatoes and lard-rich refritos. Huevos rancheros is an equally overabundant plateful. You get your choice of red or green chile; say "Christmas" and you get both—two soupy brews that magically arrive perfectly separated on the plate but then swirl together as soon as you attack with a fork. A huge breakfast burrito is available similarly dressed.

## Golden Crown Panaderia

1103 Mountain Rd. NW
Albuquerque, NM

505-243-2424
www.goldencrown.biz/shoppingcart
BLD | $

Not far from Albuquerque's Old Town, the Golden Crown is a full-service bakery making everything from *biscochitos* cookies (the official state cookie of New Mexico) to bread loaves shaped like turkeys. Artisan pizzas are available on regular "peasant dough" or on a New Mexico green chile crust. The toppings roster includes green chiles and jalapeños.

Aside from fascinating pizza, must-try breadstuffs include green chile bread. It is made with bits of tomato, green onions, cilantro, grated cheese, and ribbons of smoke-scented roasted green chile pods. Hot stuff . . . but not ferocious. Chris Ayers and Amy Breisch of Roadfood.com said that this bread, toasted and buttered, is so good that "time may actually stand still."

Other menu notables: fruit-filled empanadas, sugary flautas, and cinnamon-sugared tostadas.

## *La Posta de Mesilla

2410 Calle de San Albino
Old Mesilla, NM

505-524-3524
www.laposta-de-mesilla.com
LD | $$

La Posta is one of the grand old Mexican-American restaurants of the Southwest. Opened in 1939 by Katie Griggs, and now run by her descendants, it is a sprawling, multiroom place that attracts a lot of tourists and is well worth the trip for anyone with a hankering for authentic regional food.

When we say authentic, we mean *tostadas compuestas,* a dish that became a standard throughout the Southwest after it was invented here. It is a crisp-fried corn tortilla cup into which is ladled red chili con carne, beans, cheese, lettuce, and tomato. Other expertly made native dishes include folded and rolled tacos, flautas, green chile enchiladas, sunset-hued *carne adovada,* and steak smothered in green chile and melted cheese. No matter what you order, you will get a basket full of warm sopaipillas for mopping up every last good bit of food off the plate.

## Model Pharmacy

3636 Monte Vista Blvd. NE
Albuquerque, NM

505-255-8686
L | $

You enter this neighborhood pharmacy past the drug counter, navigate among perfumes, soaps, and sundries, then find the little lunch area: a few tables and a short marble counter with a Pueblo-deco knee guard of colorful enamel tiles. If you are like us, your attention will be drawn to the right of the counter, where the cobblers are displayed under a spotlight. Three or four are made every day—geological-looking strata of flaky crust atop syrupy tender hunks of apricot, peach, blackberry, or a mix thereof—and they are available warm or with a globe of ice cream melting on top.

The soda fountain is impressive: a fully stocked armory of milk-shake mixers, syrup dispensers, and soda nozzles, plus a modern espresso machine (so you can get an espresso milk shake—mmm). As for lunchtime entrees, locals love the walnut chicken salad, and some come to eat hamburgers and cold-cut sandwiches, but we'll choose green chile stew every time. It is more a soup, actually, chockfull of carrots, tomatoes, and bits of green chile with good flavor and alarming heat.

## Nellie's

1226 W. Hadley Ave.
Las Cruces, NM

575-524-9982
BL | $

Inside this snug, cozy cinder-block and glass-brick restaurant, a sign on the wall clearly declares the kitchen's priorities: "A day without chile is like a day without sunshine." Danny Ray Hernandez, Nellie's son, makes vivid salsas using five to seven different types of chile and specializes in such eye-opening breakfasts as huevos à la Mexicana (scrambled with jalapeños) and eggs with chile and meat. For the latter you can get red or green or the combination of both, known as Christmas. The red tastes of pure pod; the green is hot enough to require tongue-tamping with the kitchen's pulchritudinous sopaipillas.

Years ago, Nellie's and its offspring, Little Nellie's Chile Factory, served dinner. Today it is strictly a breakfast-and-lunch eatery.

## Nopalito

310 S. Mesquite St.　　　　　　575-524-0003
Las Cruces, NM　　　　　　　　LD | $

Las Cruces is in the heart of chile-growing country and Nopalito is a family-run restaurant (actually two restaurants; the other is at 2605 Missouri Avenue) where you can count on excellent chile-based food. It is neither Tex-Mex nor Arizona-Mex nor California-Mex nor Sonoran Mex but the unique cuisine of New Mexico. That means that nearly every meal poses the question: red or green chile? There is no rule about which is hotter. The day we came to Nopalito (which means "little cactus"), the waitress assured us that green was the hot stuff but that red was more delicious. What to do? "Christmas!" she replied, which is the term for a dish topped with both.

Before the main course come crisp, warm tortilla chips and a set of salsas, red and green. The green is served hot (temperature-wise), but is fairly mild. The red is served cool but is very, very hot. To tamp down tongue fires, there's practically nothing better than a tall glass of the rice milk drink called *horchata*. Nopalito's is smooth and just-right sweet.

The building that houses Nopalito originally was built as a church. Its mission décor and spacious dining room provide a broad, comfortable environment well suited for quiet contemplation of commendable local food.

## Owl Bar & Cafe

77 Hwy. 380　　　　　　　　　575-835-9946
San Antonio, NM　　　　　　　BLD | $

The Owl Bar is a watering hole to which many customers come first thing in the morning to start their day with cans of Bud. It also just might be the place where the green chile cheeseburger was invented. The story is that when the atom bomb was being tested at nearby White Sands, scientists would repair here for after-work drinks and thermonuclearly hot hamburgers. Whether or not that's true, the Owl Bar's green chile cheeseburger is a good one, built upon a crusty patty of beef covered with only moderately hot chopped green chiles, then bright orange cheese that melts down to blanket everything. Raw onion, lettuce, tomato, and pickle chips are the standard-issue condiments. Monomaniacal chiliheads can accompany their GCCB with a plate of French fries smothered with chopped green chiles.

## Pasquale's

121 Don Gaspar Ave.
Santa Fe, NM

505-983-9340
www.pasquales.com
BLD | $$

Pasquale's looks like a modest corner café and in some essential way it is. But the food is too good to be modest and while breakfast or lunch won't break the bank, dinner for two can cost north of $50. At any mealtime in the crowded, split-level dining room, you are lucky to find a seat at a small table or at the large shared one, where a local or a stranger from just about any part of the world might break bread with you.

At breakfast, we love the chunky corned beef hash, the pancakes, the blue and yellow cornmeal mush, big sweet rolls, and giant bowls of five-grain cereal with double-thick cinnamon toast on the side, accompanied by immense bowls of latte. And for lunch, we can never resist the expertly made soups. Little things mean so much: fresh bread for sandwiches, flavorful chiles on quesadillas; even the coffee is a tasty surprise.

## Plaza Café

54 Lincoln Ave.
Santa Fe, NM

505-982-1664
www.thefamousplazacafe.com
BLD | $

Although many of the businesses that now surround Santa Fe's plaza are trendy and high-priced, the Plaza Café, established in 1918, is what it's been all along—a three-meal-a-day town café frequented by locals as well as travelers, who come for dishes that range from American cheeseburgers to Greek souvlaki to New Mexican green chile stew. The sopaipillas that come with the stew are hot from the fry kettle, perhaps the best in town, and please have the quesadilla, a griddled tortilla sandwich filled with soft, shredded pork and little nuggets of caramelized garlic.

## Roque's Carnitas

San Francisco St. & Old Santa Fe Tr.,
   on the Plaza
Santa Fe, NM

No phone
L (closed in winter) | $

Roque's is a jolly little chuckwagon that serves a sandwich folded inside a sturdy flour tortilla that has been heated on a grate over a charcoal fire. Inside the warm tortilla is succulent beef, and plenty of it—top round steak thinly sliced and marinated, sizzled on a grate along with onions, chiles, and fiery jalapeño salsa. As soon as you peel back the foil and try to gather up the tortilla for eating, chunks of salsa tumble out, meat juice leaks, onions slither, and plump circles of earth-green chile pepper pop free. In the past, customers dined standing over open garbage cans to catch the spillage, but recently Roque has started bringing little yellow stools where people can sit and take advantage of having a lap to catch all that drops. There also are dining facilities in the form of park benches in the Plaza.

If you are allergic to beef, chicken carnitas are available, as are green chile-cheese tamales (vegetarian) and pork red chile tamales.

## San Marcos Cafe

3877 NM 14
Cerrillos, NM

505-471-9298
www.sanmarcosfeed.com/cafe.htm
BL | $

The San Marcos Cafe is a popular destination eatery and feed store that is a convenient stop for folks on their way to Cerrillos or Madrid. Cinnamon rolls are taller than they are wide, and rather than being dense and doughy like so many others, they are lightweight, almost croissant-like in character. Other dandy breakfast items are "eggs San Marcos," which is a large serving of scrambled eggs wrapped inside a tortilla and sided by beans, chili, and guacamole under a mantle of melted cheese; biscuits topped with spicy sausage gravy; and *machaca* (beef and eggs with pico de gallo).

A cozy, charming ranch house decorated in country-kitchen style (old enameled stoves, wooden cupboards, knickknacks galore), the café also happens to be a veritable bird jungle. Peacocks and peahens, wild turkeys, and roosters all cavort around the front and back, and while they are not allowed inside the restaurant, there are pictures of the most famous chicken of them all, a leghorn rooster named Buddy who served long tenure as unofficial maître d'. Dressed in black tie, Buddy cheerfully greeted guests and crowed through the breakfast hour. Years ago, when Buddy passed away, customers mourned. Although a few other roosters have been named to take his place, none has ever shown the people skills that Buddy had.

# Sugar's

1799 State Rd. 68                      505-852-0604
Embudo, NM                             LD | $

Fusion cuisine: Texas and New Mexico. The Texas part is brisket: thick flaps of juice-heavy beef so painfully tender that they fall apart when handled, pervaded by sweet smoke and rimmed with an edge that is blackened, crisp, and succulent. The New Mexico contribution is roasted green chiles with sunny flavor and the kick of capsicum. Intertwine these two items with cheese that melts because of the meat's heat and roll them inside a soft, flaky flour tortilla and you have a magically delicious burrito that is a prototypical wrap.

Eat this superb sandwich at a picnic table adjoining the tin-sided trailer that is Sugar's kitchen, or ensconced in your vehicle. There are no indoor seats at this remote Land of Enchantment gem. Sugar, by the way, was a bulldog bitch whose progeny you might see in the yard to the left of the tin trailer. Sugar's picture adorns the wall-mounted menu, which is a roadside roster of burgers and green chile cheeseburgers, corn dogs, burritos, and of course, Fritos pie.


# Tecolote

1203 Cerrillos Rd.                     505-988-1362
Santa Fe, NM                           www.tecolotecafe.com
                                       BL | $$

Santa Fe has many places that serve good breakfast. Breakfast is Tecolote's raison d'être. Our favorite thing to eat is pancakes made with blue cornmeal and studded with roasted piñon nuts. Pale blue inside with a faintly crusty exterior from the grill, each cake is ethereally fluffy, and gosh, what joy it is to bite into a little lode of those roasty-rich nuts! There are blueberry pancakes too, made with a similar, from-scratch batter, Toll House chocolate chip pancakes, fresh strawberry pancakes, and plain ones that are anything but plain—each available singly, as a short stack (two), or a full stack (three).

Of course, there are omelets galore and eggs of every kind, including shirred on a bed of chicken livers; as the crown of corned beef hash; rancheros-style—fried on a corn tortilla smothered in red or green chile and topped (at your request) with cheese. One nontraditional meal we hold dear at Tecolote is a gallimaufry called "sheepherder's breakfast"—new potatoes boiled with jalapeño peppers and onion, cooked on a grill until crusty-brown, then topped with two kinds of chile and melted Cheddar cheese.

## Cancun

705 S. Lewis Ave.
Tulsa, OK

918-583-8089
www.eatatcancun.com
LD (closed Weds) | $$

Cancun is a neighborhood Mexican restaurant where English is a second language. It is a welcoming little place with a handful of tables, those along the front window offering a view of the bumpers of cars in the parking lot. We plowed into a super burrito stuffed with carnitas (shredded pork), rice, and beans; smothered with shredded cheese and warm salsa; and decorated with dabs of sour cream and guacamole. It's a grand meal, the savory roast pork packing heaps of flavor. On the side you can have *horchata,* the cool, sweet rice beverage that is so refreshing with spicy food; Jarritos-brand mandarin orange soda; or, of course, beer.

The menu is frustrating for anyone with time for only a single meal. Beyond the big burrito, choices include tacos filled with a wide range of ingredients from spicy pork to tongue, cheek meat, tripe, fish, chicken, and goat. Other temptations: enchiladas, chile verde and chili Colorado, fajitas, and chimichangas. Seafood specialties include *camarones al Tequila* (shrimp with green salsa and tequila) and *pescado frito* (whole fried fish).

## *Cattlemen's Steakhouse

1309 S. Agnew
Oklahoma City, OK

405-236-0416
www.cattlemensrestaurant.com
BLD | $$

The neon sign outside says "Cattlemen's Cafe," and yes, indeed, this is the café to which people who work in and around the Oklahoma stockyards come for a 6 a.m. breakfast of calf brains and eggs (or, of course, steak and eggs). It is also a top-end steak house, serving some of the best cuts of beef you will find in the West. Top-of-the-line is a big, boneless prime sirloin that comes from the kitchen alone on a white crockery plate, surrounded only by a puddle of its translucent pan juice. It is charred on the outside, but not drastically so, and you can see by its glistening, pillowy form—higher in the center than around the rim—that this hefty slab has been seared over a hot flame. Cattlemen's provides each customer a wood-handled knife with a serrated blade. The blade eases through the meat's crust and down into its warm red center—medium-rare, exactly as requested.

If you are an adventurous eater, you probably want to know that Cattlemen's makes a specialty of lamb fries—that is, nuggets of deep-fried testicle. They are served as an appetizer: a mound of them on a plate with a bowl of cocktail sauce for dipping and half a lemon to squeeze on top. They are earthy-tasting inside their golden crust, the exquisite organ meat quivery and moist, with nut-sweet savor.

While you easily can spend $50 on a steak dinner, lunch can be one-quarter of that price. We like the steak burger in particular. It is juicy and radiant with big beef flavor. Dinner patrons tend to be a dress-up group, but the crowd at lunch is a mix of ranchers in $1,000 beaver hats and fancy boots, huge blue-collar guys in overalls, and skinny blue-haired ladies out with their friends.

## Clanton's

319 E. Illinois
Vinita, OK

918-256-9053
www.clantonscafe.com
BLD | $

Clanton's makes its chicken-fried steak by dipping a well-tenderized cube steak in a mixture of egg and buttermilk, then dredging it once and only once (any more and you will smother the beef with crust). Cooked in vegetable oil until crisp and palomino gold, it is tender enough that a knife is superfluous. The edge of a fork is all you need to sever a mouthful. With the steak comes a globe of mashed potatoes smothered with peppery cream gravy and a side of palate-refreshing coleslaw. There are many other good things on Clanton's menu—we love the chicken and sage dressing, but whatever else you eat, save room for pie: chocolate cream, coconut cream, or banana cream, all poised atop the most fragile foundation of crust.

Route 66 sightseers often find their way to Clanton's, which is one of the oldest continuously operating restaurants along the old Mother Road. (It's not the original building, though. That burned down and was rebuilt.) When Sweet Tater Clanton opened for business in 1927, most of the highway was not yet paved, and it is said that to attract customers Mr. Clanton used to walk out the front door and bang a pot and pan together when he spied someone about to drive past.

## Classen Grill

5124 S. Classen Cir.                    405-842-0428
Oklahoma City, OK                       BLD | $

We love to start the day at Classen Grill with a glass of fresh-squeezed orange juice and a plate of *migas*, the Mexican egg scramble that includes strips of tortilla, chunks of tomato, nuggets of sausage, and a mantle of melting shredded cheese. Chinook eggs are salmon patties topped with poached eggs and accompanied by a block of cheese grits. Taquitas are tortilla-wrapped packets of eggs, cheese, and vegetables. The chicken-fried steak is nearly as big as its plate. It is tender enough that the knife provided seems irrelevant. When we arrive with insatiable appetites, we go for "biscuits debris"—two big ones split open and smothered with gravy chockablock with ham and sausage chunks, cloaked with melted Cheddar cheese.

On the side of breakfast, enjoy significant potatoes—either home fries or the specialty known as Classen Grill potatoes, which are mashed, seasoned with garlic and rolled into little balls, then deep-fried until brittle gold on the outside. The result is a kind of prairie knish—but not so heavy.

The place is an ultra-casual, one-room café with paintings of fruit and other gastronomical items posted on its pink stucco walls. Early during Sunday breakfast, nearly half the customers sit at tables reading the morning paper while leisurely enjoying their meals. By brunchtime, the place is too crowded for casual reading.

## Coney I-Lander

7462 E. Admiral Pl.          918-836-2336
Tulsa, OK                    LD | $

Dating back to 1926, Tulsa's Coney I-Lander (of which there are a few outlets in the city) is among the nation's first Coney Island restaurants, specializing in plump little hot dogs in steamed buns, dressed with mustard, onions, and a finely ground, elaborately spiced, but ultimately mild meat sauce. At some point in hot dog history, shredded orange cheese became a popular addition, and here in Tulsa, many folks get theirs with a sprinkle of cayenne pepper. The dogs are small enough so that one or two are a snack, four or six a meal. It is not uncommon to see a runner from a nearby business walk out with dozens to take back for lunch with colleagues.

Ambience is fluorescent-light divey. Service is immediate. The menu is minimal. Coney I-Lander's one dandy alternative to a hot dog is the Southwest's beloved hot lunch, a Fritos pie.

## Country Dove Tea Room

610 W. 3rd                   580-225-7028
Elk City, OK                 L | $

The recognized glories of Oklahoma cuisine tend to be rugged, manly, and beef-centric. Country Dove Tea Room is something else. A charming little destination, it is an opportunity to enjoy heartwarming examples of that bygone genre known as ladies' lunch, served with grace and good manners in an old country home. Creamed soups are accompanied by heart-shaped muffins and honey butter; little squares of Jell-O are known here as "Jell-O salad," presented on a lettuce leaf. The house specialty is chicken-avocado salad, which is the two elements pulverized together with mayonnaise and served on either a croissant or grilled wheat bun.

It is such a nice, polite repertoire of dishes . . . until you get to dessert and French silk pie, which is a powerhouse: lasciviously chocolaty, smooth, dense, topped with a frothy ribbon of whipped cream and mounted on a plush nut crust. Proprietors Glenna Hollis and Kay Farmer, who opened the tearoom over a quarter century ago, blush when they recall the author who came through many years back and later wrote that he wasn't sure if he should eat the pie or smear it all over his body.

Glenna and Kay are kind hosts who made us feel like we had come to a family reunion. They delighted in showing off their kitchen, which is little more than the original home kitchen, including the four-burner electric stove. Beyond two small dining rooms, the first and second stories of the house serve as a Christian bookstore and country décor emporium.

## Dink's Pit Bar-B-Que

2929 E. Frank Phillips Blvd.

Bartlesville, OK

918-335-0606

www.dinksbbq.com

LD | $$

Dink's barbecue selection is broad. Hickory-cooked pig dinners (pork loin), ham, turkey, chicken, sausage, spare ribs, brisket, and back ribs all are available, and while the menu advises that brisket is the specialty, we like pork better. The brisket can be dry—not a horrible problem, considering that Dink's red-orange sauce beautifully revives it and adds a welcome tangy punch. The spare ribs were so good that we left only bare bones on the plate, and the pig dinner is succulence squared. Each dinner comes with a choice of two side dishes from a roster that includes baked beans, fried okra, pinto beans, green beans, coleslaw, curly-Q fries, baked potato, potato salad, and cottage cheese, plus bread, pickles, green onion, and sauce.

A Bartlesville fixture since 1982, Dink's is a family-friendly, multiroom establishment with buckaroo décor: steer horns, pictures of hunters, cowboys, and Indians, and displays of the "Barbed Wire that Fenced the West."

A second Dink's in Bentonville, Arkansas, is at 3404 Macy Road (479-657-6264).

## Eischen's Bar

108 N. 2nd Ave.

Okarche, OK

405-263-9939

LD (closed Sun) | $$

Opened in 1896 and touted as the state's oldest bar, Eischen's is a Wild West destination a half hour northwest of Oklahoma City. The brick-front bar is patronized by locals at lunch and is almost always crowded with pilgrims at suppertime, especially weekend nights when it is not uncommon for strangers to share the big tables in the back dining room. Everybody comes for fried chicken of succulent meat and bacon-rich skin that is made to be eaten by hand (plates and silverware are nonexistent). The chicken comes with pickles, onions, and bread as well as fried okra. The beverage of choice is cold beer from the tap. The only other thing on the menu is chili-cheese nachos, another no-utensil food.

Classic road-trip tunes blare from the jukebox, and when you wait for a seat, avail yourself of one of two available pool tables to pass the time.

## Freddie's Hamburgers

802 S. Lewis Ave.        918-585-3544

Tulsa, OK        LD | $

The complex of condiments, the audacity of magnitude, and the quotient of fat in Freddie's bunned hamburgers put all the national chains to shame. You don't have to get the Double Jumbo, which is a pair of one-third-pound patties, to see what we mean. Take the Double Deluxe basket: two quarter-pound patties that are dripping cheese, garlanded with a bouquet of lettuce, tomatoes, pickles, fresh onions, fried onions, and mustard (plus mayonnaise if requested), all stacked in a soft, oversized bun. It is a challenge to one's burger-handling skills. When you first pick it up, you instantly become aware of just how tender and pliable the bun is—a wonderful textural note in the whole package. But its very feel foreshadows catastrophe: The glistening patties want to slide out whichever side of the bun your fingers aren't gripping, lettuce shreds start to fall, pickles and onions slip and squiggle, mayo oozes. It is an outstanding burger-eating adventure, one of the best in Tulsa, which is one of Oklahoma's several nuclei of hamburger greatness.

The place itself has personality to spare. At first glance, it looks a bit disreputable and, indeed, the counter in the front room does tend to attract fringy types; counter seats also guarantee that you will smell of grilling beef and onions for hours afterward. But around to the right are a series of little dining rooms—spare places that double as storage areas—where tables and chairs are set up for a more gracious mealtime experience. Here we saw nice couples and families downing the mighty burgers (and also Fritos pies and Coney dogs). "Delicious as usual!" chirped one white-haired granny as she and a couple generations of her family exited, politely returning their emptied plastic baskets to the burger makers up front.

## Hamburger King

322 E. Main        405-878-0488

Shawnee, OK        www.hamburgerkingshawnee.com

                                         LD (closed Sun) | $

We love the look of this 1927 lunchroom with its tall ceiling and long rows of tables, each equipped with a direct phone line to the open kitchen. The menu refers to this as the "electronic order system." On the walls are pictures that show the history of Oklahoma in general and Hamburger King in particular, the showstopper being a blown-up photo of founder George

Macsas flanked by King of Western Swing Bob Wills and movie star Jack Hoxie. Wills once wrote a song to celebrate his favorite eatery:

*When you're feelin' blue, and hungry too*
*Here's a tip to make you sing.*
*Pick up your hat, close your flat*
*Go down to the Hamburger King.*

Right up front behind the counter and cash register where broad, medium-thick burger patties sizzle on the grill, you can watch each one being assembled by a cook skillful enough to bun, dress, and garnish one faster than it takes to name its components. The result is a classic lunch-counter hamburger: not too thick, not thin, oily enough to flavor the bun with juice, crusty enough to provide textural contrast to the lettuce, tomato, and pickle on top.

## Hammett House

1616 W. Will Rogers Blvd.     918-341-7333
Claremore, OK     www.hammetthouse.com
     LD | $

Thanks to intrepid Roadfooders Howard Baratz, Cliff Strutz, and Cousin Johnnie for clueing us in to the pies at Hammett House. In Cliff's words, the banana cream pie "had wonderful real banana flavor, plus lots of small cut-up bits of banana. The filling was thick but still airy and just about the perfect texture. All housed in a buttery, flaky crust: a high-quality slice of pie." As for peanut butter chocolate chip, Cliff described it as "smooth, airy, with strong peanut butter flavor"; sour cream raisin pie struck "that perfect balance between the sweet and sour"; and buttermilk chess ("the best of the best") was "soft [with] buttermilk tang, plus a strong cinnamon taste."

Other choices in the pie repertoire include coconut cream (Hammett House's bestseller), chocolate cream, lemon pecan, and sour cream cherry. But suppose you are in the mood for something pre-pie? Chili is available with and without beans; "pamper-fried" chicken, served with cream gravy, is a specialty; and testicle lovers have their choice of lamb fries or turkey fries or a combo plate of both. There are steaks and chops and sandwiches and salads and a menu of half-pound hamburgers, plus child-sized sliders.

Last we looked, Wednesday was cinnamon roll day. The first hundred customers in the door after opening at 11 a.m. get one free.

# Hank's Hamburgers

8933 E. Admiral Pl.          918-832-1509
Tulsa, OK                    www.hankshamburgers.com
                             LD | $

Burger central: have a single, a double, a triple, a Big Okie (four patties), or a Hank's Burger, which is a single half-pound patty. While the heft of a Hank's Burger is impressive, we prefer the multiple-patty configurations. The interleaved meat and cheese provide a textural adventure that a large single patty cannot. Standard condiments are mustard, pickle, grilled onion, raw onion, lettuce, and tomatoes.

Hank's is a tiny place with just a few booths around the counter, which is high enough that no seat affords a good view of Mr. Felts, chef and owner, orchestrating events at the griddle. We recommend standing up, or going to the walk-up to-go window at the front, because watching him create his burgers is short-order ballet. Onions are pressed hard onto the surface of each patty before it hits the hot surface so that as the burger cooks under a heavy iron, the onions caramelize and virtually become one with the hamburger itself. When the iron is lifted and the burger is flipped, Felts sprinkles on some of his secret seasoning, then cheese. If he is creating a double, triple, or quadruple, he applies the bun top to one patty, uses a spatula to lift it onto another, and so forth until the pile is ready to be placed onto the bottom half of the bun, which has been arrayed with all other condiments.

"Please allow us a few minutes to prepare your order for you because we don't cook ahead," the menu asks. "Please call early and tell us what time you would like your order. We will try our BEST to have it ready for you right on time and FRESH off the grill." A sign above the counter advises, "We will call your name & bring your food to you as fast as possible . . . Hank's a lot."

# Ike's Chili

5941 E. Admiral Pl.          918-838-9410
Tulsa, OK                    www.ikeschiliius.com
                             L | $

According to a 1936 article in the *Tulsa Daily World,* reprinted on the back of Ike's menu, "When the original Ike Johnson established his first modest little 'parlor' down by the old Frisco depot twenty-five years ago, there was no lowlier food than chili. . . . It was openly sneered at by the Social Register and the hot dog was much higher up on the social scale." To this day, chili maintains a plebeian aura, and there's no better place to savor that aura, and a classic bowl of chili con carne, than Ike's. We thank Tulsan Jim Oakley for tipping us off to this excellent Southwestern chili parlor.

Made from a recipe supposedly secured from a Hispanic Texas employee named Alex Garcia, Ike's chili is a viscous dish of ground beef and a peppery jumble of spice. It comes plain in a bowl, with spaghetti noodles, or three-way, meaning with noodles and beans. Cheese, jalapeño peppers, and onions are extra-cost options, but even a double three-way with everything is scarcely more than five dollars. Chili is also the star of Ike's Fritos pie and Coney dog, described as being built upon a "large Oscar Meyer."

## Jigg's Smokehouse

Exit 62 off I-40
Clinton, OK

580-323-5641
www.jiggssmokehouse.com
L Tues-Sat | $

Jigg's beef jerky is one tough chaw, and that's the way it is supposed to be. Slices of loin as big as a handkerchief are desiccated in a dry mix of brown sugar, garlic, and cayenne pepper, then slow-smoked over coarse-ground hickory sawdust for up to twenty-four hours. The result? Gnarled burnt-sienna-colored patches that pack a resounding harmony of beef, pepper, and smoke. Chew, chew, chew: The waves of flavor are relentless.

Unlike the mighty jerky, Jigg's barbecue is tenderness incarnate, although some of the specialty sandwiches are a real challenge to eat. The Wooly Burger, for example: thirty-one ounces of smoked ham and summer sausage, Cheddar cheese, chowchow relish, mayonnaise, and barbecue sauce. The menu calls it "2 lbs of fun!!!" Jigg's pigsickles, which are slabs of rib meat (no bones) with Cheddar cheese and sauce, come as doubles and triples. Normal-sized sandwiches also are available; sausage and beef brisket are exemplary. Sides are beans, potato salad, and potato chips.

Accommodations in the weather-beaten Okie snack shack include a front porch where you can sit in the shade and interior dining rooms decorated with countless business cards, portraits of meat-eating heroes John Wayne and Marty Robbins, and—noted on a recent visit—a Christmas wreath made of green and red shotgun shells.

# Johnnie's

301 S. Rock Island                    405-262-4721

El Reno, OK                         BLD | $

A sphere of beef is slapped onto a hot griddle. Onto the beef goes a fistful of ultrathin-sliced yellow onions—about the same cubage as the beef. The grill man uses a spatula to flatten the onions and the meat together, creating a broad circular patty with an uneven edge; he presses down three or four times, slightly changing the angle of attack with each press, and pressing only one-half to two-thirds of the patty each time. The ribbons of onion get mashed deep into the top of the soft, raw meat, which assumes a craggy surface because of the uneven, overlapping use of the spatula. Once the underside is cooked, the burger is flipped. The air around the grill clouds with the sweet steam of sizzling onions. After another few minutes, the hamburger is scooped off the grill with all the darkened caramelized onions that have become part of it and it is put on a bun, onion side up. Lettuce, tomato, mustard, and pickles are all optional if you like them, but no condiment is necessary to enhance this simple, savory creation.

Johnnie's also makes a great El Reno–style Coney Island hot dog, topped with meaty chili and a strange, soupy slaw that local epicures hold dear. (Some customers get this slaw on their burger too.) We also like breakfast at Johnnie's, when the little place is packed with locals eating Arkansas sandwiches (that's a pair of pancakes layered with a pair of eggs) and all-you-can-eat platters of biscuits and gravy. It was at breakfast one day that we decided we had to stick around El Reno for a midmorning pie-break, for as we were finishing our coffee, in walked Everett Adams, Johnnie's baker, wedging his way through the thirty-seat restaurant toting a battered tray above his head on which were set the coconut meringue pies and Boston cream pie he had made that morning for the lunch crowd.

# Kumback Lunch

625 Delaware                     580-336-4646

Perry, OK                          BLD | $

Kumback Lunch was founded in 1926 in a town created by the 1893 Cherokee Strip land run. Its walls are covered with pictures and memorabilia of "Perry Heroes," including local athletes, several governors of the state, and Oklahoma Highway Patrol officer Charlie Hanger, who captured Oklahoma City bomber Timothy McVeigh and brought him to the county jail in Perry.

History and beautiful art deco façade aside, Kumback Lunch is a swell place to eat. And everyone in the town of Perry (and beyond) seems to know that fact, because the place always is crowded with happy eaters and coffee drinkers. For breakfast, we recommend blueberry and pecan pancakes, swirly warm cinnamon rolls, biscuits and gravy, egg-stuffed burritos, and crisp-crusted chicken-fried steak. That steak also makes a fine lunch or supper, or you can choose from among a dozen different hamburgers, barbecued ribs and brisket, and a selection of Mexican meals that includes a baked potato stuffed with seasoned beef, cheese, and salsa.

## Leo's

3631 N. Kelley Ave.                405-424-5367
Oklahoma City, OK                  LD | $

Leo's barbecue beef is coarsely hacked so that a portion of it, on a platter or sandwich, contains some outside chunks with crunchy blackened edges and others that are soft and dripping natural juice. Sauce is dark and spicy with a vinegar punch, good not only on the meat but on the buttery baked potato half that can be had with sandwiches and entrees. Leo's also offers magnificently meaty pork ribs, hot links that are seriously hot, and a locally favored treat, bologna. Before you dismiss barbecued bologna as a smokehouse aberration, you need to try it here. This is not bubble-gum-colored supermarket lunch meat; it is a thick-sliced slab with wicked zest—dense and smoky. We don't like it better than the beef or ribs, but it *is* interesting.

Undecided types can order meals that combine all meats and a couple of side dishes (sweet and porky beans and cool potato salad are recommended), but such bet-hedging does run the risk of discovering that you love the ribs (or links, or brisket) most of all, and you are getting only a partial portion thereof. Meals come with dessert: a slice of wonderful frosted yellow layer cake topped with bananas, strawberries, and a sweet sugar glaze.

Located in an old gas station, Leo's looks a little scary, but the people inside are as friendly as can be. You do need to be careful, though. "Due to high humidity, please watch your step," a sign on the front door warns. The humidity, a good portion of which comes from years' worth of fatty meats cooking over smoldering coals, makes the floors slick and slippery the way Arthur Bryant's of Kansas City used to be.

## Linda-Mar Drive-In

1614 W. 51st St.                 918-446-6024
Tulsa, OK                        LD | $

*The Andy Griffith Show* plays continuously on a TV in the corner of the dining room, which is decorated with NASCAR mementoes. The crowning piece of Americana comes from the kitchen and is known as the Westsider. Named for the neighborhood in which this quick-eats joint is located, it is two seared quarter-pound beef patties, each topped with cheese, served between a couple of slabs of buttered and grilled-crisp Texas toast, preferably with the works, which means chopped lettuce, sliced tomato, grilled onion, mustard, pickle chips, and—if requested—mayonnaise. It is a two-fisted, fat-glistening sandwich, the kind of wanton pleasure that anhedonic nutrition prigs abhor and robust eaters find immensely satisfying.

Bunned singles, doubles, and triples also are available, as are Fritos pie and Coney dogs. O-rings and fries are nothing special, but if you are on a burger-eating mission, Linda-Mar deserves attention.

## The Meers Store

26005 Hwy. 115                   580-429-8051
Lawton, OK                       www.meersstore.com
                                 LD | $

*Tulsa World* magazine once declared the hamburger at the Meers Store the best burger in Oklahoma, which is a bold pronouncement. Border to border, Oklahoma is crazy for all kinds of interesting and unusual burgers, including the unique giants—seven inches across—known as Meersburgers.

A Meersburger is special not only for its size but because it is made exclusively from Longhorn cattle that are locally raised. Longhorns are less fatty than usual beef stock and supposedly have less cholesterol than chicken, and yet the meat has a high-flavored succulence. In addition to Meersburgers, Meerscheeseburgers, and Seismic Meersburgers (topped with bacon, cheese, jalapeño peppers, relish, mustard, pickles, tomatoes, onions, and lettuce), the Meers Store has a menu of steak, chicken-fried steak, prime rib, and barbecue, plus a salad bar.

The town itself is a sight. In the southwest corner of the state, it sprung up in the wake of a gold strike in the 1890s but is now populated by exactly six citizens—the Maranto family, who run the Meers Store. The Store is the only open business, located in what was once a mining-camp emporium.

Its walls are blanketed with antiques, memorabilia, pictures of famous and not-so-famous customers, and business cards left behind by happy eaters.

## Murphy's Steak House

| | |
|---|---|
| 1625 SW Frank Phillips Blvd. | 918-336-4789 |
| Bartlesville, OK | LD \| $ |

What Roadfooder could resist a menu whose motto is "Gravy Over All"? When you tell the waitress you want a hot hamburger, that is what she will ask: "Gravy over all?" The correct answer is yes.

Gravy is what makes Murphy's signature dish, the hot hamburger, special. Nothing like a regular bunned burger, a hot hamburger is in fact more like a Springfield, Illinois, horseshoe sandwich: a real plateload. Its foundation is a couple of slices of toasted white bread. Atop the bread goes a hamburger been hacked up into chunks of beef. Atop the deconstructed burger go French fries. And the whole shebang is crowned with a spill of dark, velvety gravy. It's a transcendent combination: crisp logs of fried potato softened where the gravy blankets them, imbibing a rich, beefy savor for which squiggles of onion (an optional component) are an ideal accent. Even people who come for steak get a side dish of fried potatoes with gravy.

Don't let the words "steak house" lead you to think that Murphy's is in any way high-end. It is in fact more like a diner, complete with counter, bare-topped tables, a walk-up window for carry-out orders, and reasonable prices. (A hot hamburger is under $10; a T-bone is under $20.)

## Robert's

| | |
|---|---|
| 300 S. Bickford Ave. | 405-262-1262 |
| El Reno, OK | BL \| $ |

El Reno is a hub of hamburger culture in Oklahoma, which has a higher hamburger consciousness than any other state. Of its several burger joints, Robert's is the oldest, dating back to 1926, and it is a virtual museum piece—the sort of eatery that makes Route 66 such an interesting trip. The menu does not list an onion-fried burger, but burgers cooked with onions are such a pillar of local gastronomy, that is what you automatically will get: a burger melded with a tangle of caramelized onions. The cook forces the onions right into the patty by squishing them down as the burger sizzles.

In addition to serving what may be the best onion-fried burger in Oklahoma (and therefore the best on Earth), Robert's makes a wicked Coney

Island—the El Reno way, of course, which means the chili sauce is topped with a spill of coarse, pickly coleslaw.

## Rock Cafe

114 W. Main St.     918-968-3990

Stroud, OK      www.rockcafert66.com

          BLD | $

The Rock Cafe opened in 1939 when the last stretches of the Oklahoma section of Route 66 were paved. So much of the historic road from Chicago to Los Angeles has vanished, as have the colorful tourist courts, service stations, and short-order diners that once made it a bonanza of highway kitsch, but this solid little restaurant is a vision out of the past. Even a devastating fire in 2008 couldn't keep it down. Left with little more than its four rock walls, proprietor Dawn Welch re-created it once again.

Just as those heavy sandstone walls endured the fire, so did the café's original grill, named Betsy, which cook and proprietor Dawn Welch describes as having been "seasoned for eternity." She credits the old grill—one of the very first made by Wolf—with the shattering-crisp crust that hugs her chicken-fried steak as well as with the dripping moistness of the thick ribbon of beef inside. "The moment you put something in a deep fryer [the typical way to make a bad chicken-fried steak], you can see the juice start coming out of it," she says, adding that the traditional version, made with beef, shares the menu with a similar dish, made with pork. Although it sounds similar to the tenderloins popular in the Midwest, this one is thicker and spicier and fathomlessly juicy, sporting a complex bouquet of flavor from its tenure on the venerable grill. Dawn told us that she graces everything possible with a spell on the grill: chili to top burgers, ham for ham and beans, even sauerkraut and spaetzle to accompany the no-beef, all-pork chicken-fried steak.

Dawn says that several years ago a rich woman from New York offered to buy the grill so she could bring it back east with her. The offer was generous, big enough to buy a modern replacement, but Dawn refused what she considered a Faustian bargain. The soul of the Rock Cafe was not for sale.

## Sid's

300 S. Choctaw
El Reno, OK

405-262-7757
BLD | $

Sid's is one of El Reno's legendary hamburger restaurants, where onion-fried burgers are cooked so that onions mashed into the patty of meat get charred from their time on the grill, giving the sandwich a sweet and smoky zest. Burgers are available regular and king-sized, with cheese, bacon, chili, slaw, lettuce, tomato, and jalapeño peppers. Non–burger eaters get two or three Coney Islands, which are bright-red weenies topped with chili and a super-fine slaw that is sweet but also packs mustard punch. Milk shakes are thick enough to require a spoon as well as a straw.

Sid's is noteworthy for its amazing interior décor, which is a virtual museum of El Reno history. Using eleven gallons of clear epoxy to seal some 450 pictures onto the top of the counter and the tops of tables, proprietor Marty Hall has arranged his gallery in chronological order starting at the far left of the restaurant. Here are pictures of the Oklahoma land lotteries and cowboys on horseback, as well as ephemera from the early days of car culture, when El Reno was a major stop along Route 66. No matter where you sit at Sid's, images of olden days in Oklahoma will surround you.

## *Van's Pig Stand

717 E. Highland
Shawnee, OK

405-273-8704
www.pigstands.com
LD | $$

This rustic, wood-paneled eatery, where tables are outfitted with rolls of paper towels and sheaves of toothpicks and woodwork covered with volumes of graffiti, is the oldest barbecue in Oklahoma, and one of the best anywhere. It offers a large menu of smoked meats, hamburgers, and Sunday chicken dinners, but the essential thing to eat is pork, either as ribs that are crusty with glaze and packed with flavor, or in a pig sandwich, which is vividly sauced hacked hunks of pork in a bun with Van's own zesty relish. Superb sides include "Curlie Q fries," which are a variegated tangle of honeytone twigs, and a bacon-flavored, twice-baked potato invented by the current Van's grandma and listed as "Vanized" on the menu.

"The pie lady goofed," said the girl taking our order at Van's counter. "She put coconut meringue on the chocolate pie and regular meringue on the coconut pie." This heinous error—which, in fact, made the chocolate pie extra-good—was the worst thing that happened during a magnificent meal at one of the great barbecue outposts of the Southwest. Opened in 1928 in Wewoka, Van's has four locations in Oklahoma, including one in Norman, one in Moore, and another in Shawnee.

## White River Fish Market

1708 N. Sheridan
Tulsa, OK

918-835-1910
www.whiteriverfishmarket.com
LD | $$

Surrounded by light industry and warehouses, the White River Fish Market is not where anyone would expect to eat well. Outside, it looks like a hardware store in a strip mall; there is no printed menu—just a posted list of items on the wall above the counter where customers stand in line to place orders. Meals come at fast-food speed to boomerang-pattern Formica tables, some of which are private, some communal; the brightly lit dining room sounds like a rowdy factory mess hall, occupied by blue collars and Oxford shirts, blacks and whites and native Americans. For all its indecorous democracy, this outpost is an aristocrat among seafood restaurants.

At the order counter just inside the front door is a long glass case with trays of raw sea scallops from Boston, catfish live-hauled from Arkansas, rainbow trout from Idaho, red snapper, frogs' legs, colossal shrimp and popcorn shrimp, salmon steaks, tilapia, orange roughy, perch, and whole Gulf Coast flounders. Select the item you want and tell the server your preferred cooking method. If you want it fried, the piece or pieces you have chosen are immediately dipped into salted cracker meal; if it is to be broiled, your selection is put directly onto a broiling tray. The ready-to-cook order is then handed through a large pass-through portal straight to the kitchen. Meanwhile, you pay and find a seat. The servers will make note of where you've gone, and by the time you're comfortable and sipping sweet tea, the meal will be carried from the kitchen trailing wisps of savory smoke.

The dish at the top of our must-eat list is broiled flounder. It is one big fish, weighing over a pound and wider than a large dinner plate. Its flesh is scored in a diamond pattern, making the display of several raw ones on ice in the glass case resemble a shimmering ocean jewel box. When broiled, the flesh firms up and forms a pattern of bite-sized diamonds of meat arrayed neatly atop the skeleton. The tail, hanging over the side of the large oval plate on which it is served, is blackened by flame and provides its own smoked scent; each juicy nugget you lift—using the gentlest upward pressure of a fork—has a delicate ocean sweetness that disallows fancying up.

## Wilson's B-B-Q

1522 E. Apache
Tulsa, OK

918-425-9912
www.wilsonsbar-b-que.com
LD | $

A recording of Chicago blues floats into the parking lot at Wilson's on East Apache, a Tulsa street that sports a handful of interesting barbecue parlors. Inside the door, the blues are louder, but another rhythm is even more compelling: the whack-thud-whack of a meat cleaver hacking hickory-cooked beef into shreds. "U Need No Teeth to Eat Our Beef" is one of Wilson's several mottos (others being "U Need a Bib to Eat Our Ribs" and "U Need No Fork to Eat Our Pork"), and sure enough, that hacked-up beef is preposterously tender. Moist, velvet-soft shreds are interspersed with crusty strips from the outside of the brisket. Wilson's sauce is tongue-stimulating hot with vintage savor that reminded us of fine old bourbon.

Hot links are terrific: snapping-taut, dense, and peppery. Another house specialty is a huge smoke-cooked spud that is presented splayed open and lightly seasoned, available "plain" with just butter and sour cream, or stuffed with your choice of brisket, cut-up hot links, or bologna.

Wilson's is a modern two-room eat place with wood-paneled walls, table service, and a counter where people come for takeout orders. Décor includes signs that read, "Our cow is dead. We don't need no bull" and "The bank and I have an agreement. They will not sell bar-b-que and I will not lend money or cash checks." Tulsa law enforcement officials who dine at Wilson's are entitled to a 10 percent discount for their public service.

## Angelo's

2533 White Settlement
Fort Worth, TX

214-332-0357
www.angelosbbq.com
LD | $

Angelo's, which dates back to 1958, has become one of the most respected barbecue parlors in the Metroplex. It is a large dining hall with a remarkable exhibition of game-animal trophies, including big fish and brown bears, one of which wears a souvenir T-shirt.

When you stand at the order counter, you can watch brisket being carved. As the knife severs the dark crust and glides into the meat's tender center, each slice barely stays intact enough to be hoisted onto a Styrofoam plate, where it is sided by beans, potato salad, coleslaw, a length of pickle, a thick slice of raw onion, a ramekin of sauce, and two pieces of the freshest, softest white bread in America. Tote your own meal to a table.

The hickory pit also yields pork ribs with meat that slides easily off the bone, as well as hot link sausages, ham, and salami. In the relatively cooler months of October through March, Angelo's serves chili. It is an unctuous soup/stew of ground beef and plenty of pepper. Most people get an order to accompany a rib or beef plate or sandwiches . . . along with a few of Angelo's huge, cold mugs of beer.

## Avalon Diner

2417 Westheimer            713-527-8900
Houston, TX                www.avalondiner.com
                           BL | $

Although it is in the deluxe neighborhood of River Oaks and extravagantly manicured ladies come to lunch, the Avalon Diner isn't the least bit fussy. Eating here is a taste of lunch-counter democracy.

It is the place to get to know Texas drugstore chili or to sample such Dixie delights as smothered pork chops, chicken-fried steak, or a pimiento cheese sandwich. Hamburgers are short-order classics, just thick enough that a hint of pink remains in the center, their crusty outsides glistening with oil from the griddle. The configuration is deluxe, meaning fully dressed with tomato, lettuce, pickle, onion, mustard, and mayonnaise, and the bun has been butter-toasted crisp on the inside but is ineffably soft outside.

Avalon serves elegant, small-tread waffles, all the better to hold countless pools of swirled-together syrup and melted butter. Not-to-be missed beverages include vibrant squeezed-to-order lemonade and milk shakes served in the silver mixing can.

Note: There are two other Avalon Diners, in Stafford, at 12810 Southwest Freeway (281-240-0213) and at 8823 Katy Freeway (713-590-4377).

## Bartley's Bar-B-Q

413 E. Northwest Hwy.      817-819-9191
Grapevine, TX              www.bartleysbbq.com
                           LD | $

The sight of Bartley's, in a strip mall next to a Laundromat, will not set anyone's Roadfood radar beeping. This house of meats has none of the visual charisma of the tumbledown pits of the barbecue belt east of Austin. But inside the door, the air is righteously perfumed by smoke and the decorative theme is Mythology of the West: horseshoes, steer horns, Navajo rugs, a saddle or two, and a portrait of John Wayne.

Service is cafeteria-style, and the selection of meats is broad: brisket, ribs, hot links, Polish sausage, and thick slices of bologna. Tell the extremely friendly guy at the cutting block what you want—specify how fatty you like the brisket, whether you want the ribs severed or slabbed—and he accommodates, all the while keeping up a nice conversation with customers.

If we had a quibble with the food at Bartley's, we would say that the ribs might be *too* tender, not quite buff enough to reward a good chew. Brisket, on the other hand, feels just right, and while it tends toward dry when sliced, application of the house's good sauce fixes that instantly. Side dishes include giant baked potatoes (stuffed or not), collard greens, and braised cabbage. For dessert, pecan cobbler is richer than the richest bread pudding—without doubt the perfect food for anyone seeking to grow a huge ass.

## The Big Texan

| | |
|---|---|
| 7701 E. Hwy. 40 | 800-657-7177 |
| Amarillo, TX | www.bigtexan.com |
| | LD \| $$$ |

While it does not fit any reasonable definition of a Roadfood restaurant, the Big Texan is an experience that every traveler should have at least once. It is brash and touristy, and although the featured meal is a gimmick worthy of P. T. Barnum, the steaks are really good!

The Big Texan's trick is that if a single person eats a seventy-two-ounce sirloin in an hour—along with a shrimp cocktail, salad, a baked potato, and a dinner roll with butter—it is free. More than forty thousand people have tried since the offer began in 1960, and fewer than one in five has succeeded. You don't just sit at your table and eat it. You go onstage, where other diners get to watch you eat it. In other words, you become the evening's entertainment. Even if that is acceptable to you, the big problem is that among the four and a half pounds of red meat is enough marbling so that even if you could devour, say, three pounds of steak in a single sitting, you also must consume a pound of fat. Not that there's anything wrong with fat. It is what makes this steak, as well as the Big Texan's normal-sized cuts, taste good. A while back, when one of us Sterns took the challenge, he got rather close to consuming all the best parts of the steak, but there had to be a couple of pounds left on the plate that became a beefy Waterloo.

## Black's Barbecue

| | |
|---|---|
| 215 N. Main St. | 512-398-2712 |
| Lockhart, TX | www.blacksbbq.com |
| | LD \| $ |

Black's, since 1932, boasts that it is Texas's "oldest and best major BBQ restaurant continuously owned by the same family." Whatever its provenance, of this we are certain: It is one of the top destination barbecue parlors in the heart of Texas and therefore one of the great barbecues in this solar system. Its pit-cooked sausage rings veritably burst with flavor and its brisket is unspeakably succulent.

Black's differs from the other exalted barbecues in Lockhart because it actually has quite a menu beyond meat. Stroll through the short cafeteria line and choose among hard-boiled eggs stuck on toothpicks, little garden salads in bowls, and fruit cobbler for dessert. There are pit-cooked potatoes loaded with chopped meat; there even is sure-enough Lone Star chili. It is possible to have the man behind the counter put your meat into a sandwich and your sandwich on a plate—a deluxe presentation unheard-of in more traditional barbecues where meat is sold by the pound and accompanied by a stack of white bread or saltine crackers. Furthermore, Black's dining room has décor—another smoke-pit oddity—in the form of game trophies and pictures of the high school football team on its knotty pine walls.

Black's will ship ribs overnight to most places in the United States. Although the cost of sending them is about the same as the ribs themselves, this is a good emergency source to know about when the craving strikes.

## Blanco Bowling Club Cafe

310 4th St.  
Blanco, TX  

830-833-4416  
www.blancobowlingclub.com  
BLD | $

The Blanco Bowling Club Cafe menu offers a nice selection of burgers, sandwiches, tacos, chalupas, and enchiladas, and a recent visit at breakfast time featured huge warm biscuits. But it's for the pies that we will be returning, especially for the meringues that rise three times as high as the filling they top. And the fillings are delicious. Coconut pie has an indescribably creamy flavor, accented by little bits of toasty coconut scattered across the top of the meringue. Fudge pie is dense, rich, and super-chocolaty. If you are a pie fancier, put this bowling alley on your must-eat list.

It really is a bowling alley where the nine-pin league rolls at night. During the day the alleys are curtained off, although customers in the back dining room do enjoy such décor as bowling trophies, racks of balls, and ball bags piled atop league members' lockers. Accommodations are basic: wood-grain Formica tables set with silver wrapped in paper napkins. There is a short counter in the front room with a view of the pass-through to the kitchen and one big table where locals come and go for coffee and cinnamon buns and glazed donuts all morning.

## Blue Bonnet Cafe

211 Hwy. 281             830-693-2344
Marble Falls, TX         www.bluebonnetcafe.net
                         BLD | $

The Blue Bonnet Cafe can satisfy any sort of appetite, whether it's for a modest salad or an immodestly large plate of chicken-fried steak or pot roast. With big meals come choices from a roster of such sides as fragile-crusted fried okra, pork-rich pinto beans, and butter-sopped leaf spinach. Lunch and supper begin with a bread basket that includes four-by-four-inch yeast rolls with a bakery sweetness that perfumes the whole table as soon as you tear one apart. With the rolls are rugged corn-bread muffins. At breakfast (served all day), eggs are accompanied by hash brown potatoes or grits and your choice of thin toast, biscuits, or double-thick Texas toast.

The only problem with eating breakfast at the Blue Bonnet Cafe is that the pies may not be ready to serve until after 11 a.m., and in this place it behooves diners to heed the sign posted on the wall that implores "Try Some Pie!" Eight or ten are available each day, plain or à la mode, and while we enjoy the apple pie and pecan pie, the one we'll come back for is peanut butter cream. Smooth and devilishly rich, topped with a thick ribbon of white cream, it is accompanied by a small paper cup full of chocolate sauce. It is up to you to decide whether you want to pour the chocolate all over the slice or to dip the pie into the cup, forkful by forkful.

Monday through Friday from 3 p.m. to 5 p.m., the Blue Bonnet Cafe features "pie happy hour" at which a slice and a cup of coffee go for $3.50.

## Bohannon's Brietzke Station

9015 FM 77              830-914-3288
Seguin, TX             BLD | $

"If you think you have already experienced pie bliss, you haven't yet experienced one of Mutsie's pies," Cheryl Speakman wrote to us. She said that the next time we visited Texas, we had to visit Bohannon's Brietzke Station, where the pies are served, and which she described as "a foodie's dream."

To say Brietzke Station is an inconspicuous eatery hardly does justice to its humble looks. Driving past, you might think it was just a gas station; but a small sign on the wall outside says "Cafe." Opened in 1977 by John and Mutsie Bohannon, it is a town gathering place, where citizens come for coffee and homemade biscuits every morning, and for chicken and dumplings, steak and gravy, and fish specials every Wednesday and Friday night.

Mutsie's cream pies are modest but masterful. The one that made us swoon was chocolate: not spectacular to look at and not at all sinfully fudgy, but totally satisfying in an old-fashioned milk-chocolate way.

## *Bryce's Cafeteria

2021 Mall Dr. (I-30, Exit 222)    903-792-1611
Texarkana, TX    www.brycescafeteria.com
    LD | $

Here is cafeteria quintessence, featuring more vegetables than most Yankees see in a year: purple-hulled peas, fried green tomatoes, red beans, turnip greens cooked with chunks of ham, and a full array of potatoes, ultracheesy macaroni casseroles, rice casseroles, buttered cauliflower, sauced broccoli, pickled beets, et cetera, et cetera. . . . Main course highlights include fried chicken that is stupendously crunchy and big slabs of sweet ham sliced to order. There are roast beef and gravy, chicken and dumplings, turkey with all the fixins, fried and broiled fish. Among the multitude of pies, we like Karo-coconut pie and chess. Excellent alternatives include hot fruit cobbler and traditional banana pudding made with meringue and vanilla wafers.

Bryce's has been a Texarkana landmark since it opened downtown in 1931. Now in modern quarters with easy access from the interstate, it remains a piece of living culinary history. They don't make restaurants like this anymore! Among amenities are a smartly uniformed dining-room staff (to carry your tray and place all dishes from it on the table when you arrive at your chosen place) and servers who address men as "sir" and ladies as "ma'am." Bryce's also offers drive-through service, which, although convenient for travelers in a hurry, eliminates the joy of browsing along one of the nation's most appetizing cafeteria lines.

## Cattlemen's Fort Worth Steak House

2458 N. Main St.    817-624-3945
Fort Worth, TX    www.cattlemenssteakhouse.com
    LD | $$$

Portraits of monumental Herefords, Anguses, and Brahmans decorate the walls at Cattlemen's Fort Worth Steak House, located in the historic stockyards district since 1947. At the back of the main dining area, known as the Branding Room, raw steaks are displayed on a bed of ice in front of a charcoal fire where beef sputters on a grate. Before placing a dinner order, many customers stroll back toward the open broiler to admire the specimens on ice and compare and contrast rib eye and T-bone, demure filet mignon and ample porterhouse, KC sirloin strip and pound-plus Texas strip.

Texas sirloin is the steak lover's choice, a bulging block of aged, heavy beef with a charred crust and robust opulence that is a pleasure simply to slice, and sheer ecstasy to savor. About the Heart O' Texas Rib Eye the menu warns, "Not to be ordered by those who object to heavy marble." Sweet dinner rolls make a handy utensil for sopping up juices that puddle onto the plate. Start with a plate of lamb fries—nuggets of testicle sheathed in fragile crust, get the zesty house dressing on your salad, plop a heap of sour cream into your baked potato, and accompany the big feed with frozen margaritas, long-neck beers, or even a bottle of Texas's own Llano Estacado Cabernet Sauvignon. It's one grand cowtown supper.

## Chris Madrid's

1900 Blanco Rd.  210-735-3552
San Antonio, TX  www.chrismadrids.com
LD | $

An efficiency expert might blow a gasket looking at Chris Madrid's, a chaotic, multiroom tavern/burger joint where the modus operandi makes no sense but works beautifully. First, squeeze into a line that heads toward the order counter, where you tell the lady what you want and pay for it. You are given a vibrating pager, and while the food is being cooked, you hunt around for space at a table (outdoors or in). When the pager vibrates, return to the pick-up counter and carry trays full of burgers back to the dining room.

Madrid's hamburgers are broad and beautiful, not too thick, but juicy enough to ooze the moment finger pressure is applied to the big-domed bun that holds them. Several variations are available, including a flaming jalapeño burger, a Porky's Delight layered with bacon, and a super-goopy Cheddar Cheezy, but the house specialty, not to be missed, is a Tostada Burger. Silky refried beans and massive amounts of Cheddar cheese form a luxurious crown for the big hamburger, also layered with a sheaf of tortilla chips that offer earthy corn flavor and intriguing chewy crunch. The great condiment is salsa, to which customers help themselves near the pickup window. French fries are fresh-cut and delicious. Among wine, beer, and cocktails, a favorite among many customers is Madrid's mango margarita.

Chris Madrid's is loud, boisterous, and colorful, something like a cross between a frat party and a family reunion. Décor is beer signs and signed T-shirts; when it's really crowded (it usually is), strangers share tables.

## City Market

633 E. Davis St.

Luling, TX

830-875-9019

www.lulingcitymarket.com

LD | $

The dining area at the City Market in Luling is cool and comfortable. To fetch the food, however, you must walk into hell. A swinging door leads into a back-room pit—a shadowy, cavelike chamber illuminated by the glow of burning logs in pits on the floor underneath the iron ovens. It is excruciatingly hot, but apparently at ease in their sweltering workplace, pit men assemble meats on pink butcher paper with gracious dispatch. They take your money, then gather the edges of the paper together so it becomes a boatlike container you easily can carry back into the cool, pine-paneled dining room.

The brisket is terrific, as are pork ribs, but City Market's great dish is a sausage ring. Even when the long communal tables are crowded and a dozen conversations are in full sway all around, you cannot help but hear the crunch and snap as diners' teeth bite into the unbelievably taut casings of a City Market sausage ring. These horseshoe-shaped, string-tied guts are a lean, rugged grind with only the echo of pepper laced through their mineral-rich muscularity.

Uncharacteristically (for Texas), the City Market also makes significant barbecue sauce—a spice-speckled, dark-orange emulsion so coveted by customers that signs above every booth implore "Please Leave Sauce Bottles on Tables."

## Clark's Outpost

101 Hwy. 377 (At Gene Autry Dr.)

Tioga, TX

940-437-2414

www.clarksoutpost.com

LD | $$

Clark's fame is built on brisket, slow cooked for days until it becomes beef and smoke laced together in exquisite harmony that defies description. Rimmed with a crust of smoky black, each slice is so supple that the gentlest fork pressure separates a mouthful. The warm barbecue sauce, supplied on the side in Grolsch beer bottles, is dark, spicy, and provocatively sweet. Pork ribs are another treasure, rubbed with a seasoning mix and cooked until tender. Rib dinners arrive at the table severed into individual bones, each one lean and smoke-flavored, glistening with its own juice but also begging for some of that good sauce.

Country-style side dishes include crisp-fried okra, jalapeño-spiked black-eyed peas, and French fried corn-on-the-cob, the last a length of corn, unbattered and unadorned, that has been dipped in hot oil just long enough for the kernels to cook and begin to caramelize. The result is corn that is quite soft with a mere veil of a crust, and is astoundingly sweet. Each piece is served with blacksmith's nails stuck in its ends to serve as holders.

Despite success and renown, Clark's is deliciously rustic. Located in a town that is little more than a farmland crossroads, it is a small agglomeration of joined-together wood buildings surrounded by a gravel parking lot and stacks of wood for the smoker, with the flags of Texas and the United States flying above.

## Fuel City

801 S. Riverfront Blvd.  
Dallas, TX

214-426-0011  
www.fuelcity-tacos.com  
BLD | $

We do not recommend Fuel City only because it is a takeout window in a gas station, open twenty-four hours a day, seven days a week. Neither is our enthusiasm for the tacos prejudiced by the longhorn cattle out back or the cart outside serving delicious cups of warm corn mixed with cheese, sour cream, and hot sauce. Yes, the ambience is sensational, but it really is the tacos that make Fuel City worth a visit.

Between 5 a.m. and 10 a.m., tacos are available filled with eggs, along with bacon, chorizo, and/or potatoes. Non-breakfast varieties include picadillo (spicy ground beef with diced potatoes), beef or chicken fajita (sautéed with onions), *barbacoa* (roast beef), and *pastor* (pork). Standard garnishes include chopped raw onions, cilantro, hot sauce, and a wedge of lime. They are modest-sized so that three or four make a meal.

Even if they were served on fine china in a linen-table dining room at $5 apiece with a wine list instead of beer, we would give the thumbs-up to these tacos. Their authenticity goes beyond the no-nonsense setting. The cilantro is fresh and overwhelmingly green-flavored; onions are crisp and sweet. *Barbacoa,* cooked so long it has lost all resistance, delivers baritone beef satisfaction with a sweet-meat edge; *pastor,* which is chunky and chewier than *barbacoa,* is sneaky-hot, creating ecstatic mouth glow; picadillo is as consoling as Mom's casserole.

## Golden Light Cafe

2908 W. 6th Ave.
Amarillo, TX

806-374-9237
www.goldenlightcafe.com
LD Mon-Sat | $

The Golden Light really does glow in the afternoon light along old Route 66. The oldest restaurant in Amarillo, it originally opened as a hamburger joint and although the menu has expanded, burgers are still the big allure. They are not hoity-toity burgers, mind you. The medium-thin patties come off the vintage grill cooked through but still juicy enough, at their best when topped with cheese and chiles (hot jalapeños or milder greens) and sided by thin-cut French fries. An alternative is to have the burger wrapped in a giant tortilla along with hot sauce and sour cream. We are also big fans of the Fritos pie (here known as Flagstaff Pie)—a large oval plate of Fritos chips topped with the stout house red chili, cheese, and onions. What's great about Fritos pie is how different every chip is, depending on how close it gets to the chili. Those corn ribbons that are totally smothered turn to soft, salty cornmeal; some remain untouched and crisp; most are half-and-half crisp and tender, or on their way to delicious disintegration.

Next door to the café is the Golden Light Cantina, a live music venue that features Texas red dirt band music.

## Goode Co. Texas Bar-B-Q

5109 Kirby Dr.
Houston, TX

713-522-2530
www.goodecompany.com/
restaurantbbq1
LD | $$

To Houstonians, Goode Co. means good food. Driving south on Kirby from the city center, you pass Goode Co. Seafood and Good Co. Taqueria, and there is another branch of Goode Co. Bar-B-Q on Katy Freeway. The place on Kirby is a large eating barn (with a nice covered outdoor patio) surrounded by stacks of wood and the perfume of smoldering mesquite. Inside, there's always a line leading to the cafeteria-style counter. The line moves fast because nearly everyone knows exactly what they want. Once you've eaten at Goode Co. barbecue, chances are good you will return for more.

Long-smoked brisket is velvet-soft and so moist that sauce is superfluous. You can get the beef as part of a platter with superb, slightly sweet baked beans, potato salad, and jambalaya, or you can have it in a sandwich. While blah bread is de rigueur in most great barbecue parlors, Goode Co.

offers a fantastic alternative: thick slices of fresh, soft jalapeño corn bread that make a first-rate mitt for the smoky beef. Brisket frowners (if there are such creatures in Texas) have the option of getting pork sausage, pork ribs, ham, chicken, duck, or turkey. Brazos Bottom Pecan Pie is legendary.

GFRAP (the Gluten Free Restaurant Awareness Program) has given its blessing to many of the items on Goode Co.'s menu, including most of the meats and many side dishes. Rubs and seasonings are certified gluten-free. The special menu does advise, "Ask to have the cutting board wiped with a clean cloth before they cut your meat!"

## Green Vegetarian Restaurant

200 E. Grayson St., Ste. 120      210-320-5865
San Antonio, TX                   www.greensanantonio.com
                                  BLD (closed Sat) | $

For eating meat, San Antonio is hard to beat. Soul-food barbecue and bordertown *barbacoa, menudo* at the taquerias and macho burgers at Chris Madrid's (p. 495), Tip Top chicken-fried steak and Barn Door T-bone: It's a carnivore's delight. And so it was that after four days of doing our damnedest to deplete the population of Texas cows, we actually found ourselves craving a moo-less meal. As far as we could discover, there is one game in town—Green Vegetarian Restaurant—and it is a doozy.

The day's special veggie drink was a Ginger Bomb of apple juice, carrot juice, beet juice, and ginger. When he saw our waitress bring it, co-owner Chris Behrend came by the table to remind us that it needed to be shaken or stirred before every pull on the straw because the juices almost instantly want to separate. Momentarily forced together, they sure sing a happy tune.

At lunch or supper, you can have gluten-free sushi vegetable rolls, grilled portobellos that are designed to remind you of steak, even chicken-fried steak made of "wheat meat." Chili, available as a side with other meals, does a yeomanly job of impersonating real chili, albeit not authentic *Texas* chili, as it contains beans. But the spices are right and it is extremely hearty.

Among pseudo meats, few are weirder than wham, a ham substitute that has a smoky flavor and texture something like tender pastrami. It's the star of a tremendously satisfying sandwich named Mike (for chef and co-owner Mike Behrend), which contains jaw-stretching strata of avocados, cucumbers, sprouts, spinach leaves, tomato slices, purple onion, sliced tomato, and jalapeño jelly—all on thick slices of fresh, rugged-grained bread.

There is a second location of Green at 10003 Northwest Military, Suite 2115, San Antonio (210-233-1249).

## H&H Coffee Shop

701 E. Yandel                                915-533-1144
El Paso, TX                                  BL | $

If you are hungry and your car is dusty from traveling Southwest roads, the place to go is the H&H Coffee Shop, where table seats in the little café afford a view of the adjoining car wash where your vehicle gets scrubbed and dried. We prefer counter stools with a vista of chiles rellenos getting battered and fried and huevos rancheros being topped with a curious buttery gravy flecked with onions and hot peppers. Artemisa, who has been a waitress here for years, frequently conjures up her own special salsa, which capsicum addicts know to request. "It will hurt you," warns proprietor Kenny Haddad, who offers curious visitors a few spoonfuls in a saucer. It is flecked with seeds and pod membrane (the hottest parts) and glistens seductively. Artemisa, who is normally a stern sort of person, broke into a broad grin when she watched us wipe the last of it up with warm tortillas, then wipe the beads of perspiration from our brow with napkins.

Not everything posted on the H&H wall menu is four-alarm. You can eat ordinary eggs for breakfast or a hamburger for lunch (the café closes at 3 p.m.). Burritos are available seven ways: stuffed with chile rellenos, egg and chorizo sausage, picadillo, red chile, green chile, *carne picada*, or beans. Specials include chicken molé, red and green enchiladas, and—always on Saturday—*menudo*, the tripe and hominy stew renowned for its power to cure a hangover.

Hospitality at the well-worn cookshop is enchanting. If you speak Spanish, so much the better: you will understand the nuances of the chatter. But if, like us, you are limited to English, you will still be part of the action. The day we first visited, many years ago, we were wearing ten-gallon hats, so we soon became known to one and all as the cowboys. *"Vaqueros,"* called a waitress as we headed out the door, *"vaya con dios."* With our car newly cleaned and the radio tuned to the rollicking Mexican polka rhythms of Tejano music, we highballed north along the Rio Grande.

## Highland Park Soda Fountain

3229 Knox St.                               214-521-2126
Dallas, TX                                  www.highlandparksodafountain.com
                                            BL | $

Whereas the Highland Park neighborhood of Dallas is sleek and swanky, the Highland Park Soda Fountain, located in the Highland Park Pharmacy, opened in 1912, is a humble relic. Perhaps only a very well-heeled community has the luxury of letting such low gross-income real estate remain unexploited. Whatever the reason, this timeworn eatery that takes up more than one half of a working drugstore continues to serve inexpensive, unfashionable food to fashion-conscious shoppers, nearly all of the distaff persuasion. The menu posted above the counter lists grilled pimiento cheese sandwiches, hot dogs and chili dogs, chicken salad sandwiches on white or whole wheat, and a full battery of soda fountain drinks, fizzes, and sundaes.

In the second decade of the twenty-first century, how many eateries in upscale locations do you know that offer a choice of a phosphate, a cooler, a freeze, a float, or a soda? This is one of the few places we know that serves what chili guru Frank X. Tolbert used to refer to as drugstore chili: thick and meaty, just a bit pepper-hot, eager to be complicated with shredded cheese and raw onions or to serve as the soul of a Fritos pie.

Chocolate sodas are expertly concocted: First, chocolate syrup is squirted into a tall glass; then a stream of soda gets jerked in, hitting the syrup hard enough that no spoon is needed to mix it; finally the whole foamy brew is topped with a couple scoops of vanilla ice cream. The Highland Park Soda Fountain business card boasts that its lunch counter is "home of the best milk shake in Dallas."

## Hill Country Cupboard

101 S. Hwy. 281                830-868-4625
Johnson City, TX              www.hillcountrycupboard.com
                              BLD | $

Chicken-fried steak is bedeviling. There are so many bad ones that a person could lose faith. But then you come across one such as that served at the Hill Country Cupboard and you are a believer once again. This big barn of a restaurant claims to serve the world's best. Two sizes are available: regular and large, the latter as big as its plate. Neither requires a knife; a fork will crack through a golden-brown crust that is rich and well spiced, a perfect complement to the ribbon of tender beef inside. Alongside the slab of crusty protein comes a great glob of skin-on mashed potatoes and, of course, thick white gravy blankets the whole kit and caboodle.

Beyond chicken-fried steak, Hill Country Cupboard has a full menu of Southwest eats: barbecued beef, sausage, turkey, and ribs; catfish fillets; grilled chicken with jalapeño cheese sauce. There are even salads, available topped with hunks of chicken-fried steak or chicken-fried chicken!

## Hoover's Cooking

2002 Manor Rd.
Austin, TX

512-479-5006
www.hooverscooking.com
LD | $$

Chef Hoover Alexander says, "I am an Austin native with deep central Texas roots that run from Manchaca and Pilot Knob to little o' Utley, Texas. All of the recipes we use here were inspired by both my mother Dorothy's good cooking and the styles and spices native throughout Texas itself. I grew up on home cooking—nicely seasoned vegetables, smoked foods, pan-fried dishes, and spicy foods with a nod toward Tex-Mex and Cajun. I also have never forgotten eating a lot of Mom's fresh-baked rolls, corn bread, and desserts. . . . After you've had one of our freshly made meals and washed it down with a nice cool beverage, you'll understand why I like to call the restaurant my Smoke, Fire, and Ice House!"

Hoover's has its own smokehouse, perfuming the parking lot outside, from which come pork ribs, Elgin sausage, highly spiced Jamaican jerk chicken, and lesser-spiced (but nonetheless delicious) regular-spiced barbecue chicken. In addition to smoked fare, the menu lists chicken-fried steak (perhaps the best one anywhere), meat loaf, catfish, and an array of sandwiches that range from a meatless muffuletta (made with a portobello mushroom) to half-pound hamburgers. On the side of any meal, choose from a large selection of vegetables that include chunky mashed potatoes, mac 'n' cheese, black-eyed peas, sweet and hammy mustard greens, crisp-fried okra, and jalapeño-accented creamed spinach.

## Hut's Hamburgers

807 W. 6th St.
Austin, TX

512-472-0693
www.hutshamburgersaustin.com
LD | $

Hut's is a burger joint with nineteen different varieties of hamburger listed on its menu (not to mention the options of buffalo meat, chicken breast, or veggie burgers), each one topped with a different constellation of condiments that range from hickory sauce (delicious!) to cheeses of all kinds to guacamole to chipotle mayonnaise. We recommend the Buddy Holly Burger (American cheese, mayo, mustard, onions, pickles, lettuce, tomato), the double-meat Dag Burger (also with the works), and the Mr. Blue (blue cheese dressing, Swiss cheese, bacon, lettuce). Monday nights, meat frowners can get two veggie burgers for the price of one. French fries are very good, available on a half-and-half plate with onion rings that have a peppery zest: a joy to overeat. There are other sandwiches, a different blue-plate special every day (chicken-fried steak, meat loaf, catfish, et cetera), and beverages that include cherry Coke, pink lemonade, and a root beer float.

Decorated to the rafters with neon beer signs, team pennants, and clippings celebrating its long-standing fame—since 1939—it is a small place that is always overstuffed with people, with noise, and with a spirit of fun. You will likely wait for a seat in the small vestibule or on the sidewalk outside, but once seated, the food comes fast.

## Kreuz Market

619 N. Colorado
Lockhart, TX

512-398-2361
www.kreuzmarket.com
LD | $$

Kreuz (rhymes with "bites") started as a downtown meat market more than a century ago, and it was one of the places that defined Texas barbecue. Several years ago, owing to a complicated family feud, it moved out of town to an immense roadside dining barn with all the charm of an airplane hangar. Ambience notwithstanding, one cannot deny that its fatty—OK, we'll say "well-marbled"—slabs of pit-cooked prime rib are among the most carnivorously satisfying foodstuffs on Earth. And despite the modern facilities, Kreuz has maintained the pit-cook tradition of tote-your-own service from a ferociously hot pit where meat is sliced to order and sold by the pound. While the prime rib is a splurge (at nearly $20 per pound), the more familiar meats (priced about half that) are superb in their own right: beef brisket and shoulder, pork chops, ribs, ham, and sausage rings. In a nod to convenient dining, there is a separate counter where ice cream can be purchased and small servings of banana pudding are available for dessert.

## La Mexicana

1018 Fairview St.
Houston, TX

713-521-0963
www.lamexicanarestaurant.com
BLD | $$

La Mexicana started more than thirty years ago as a corner grocery store and now offers sit-down meals in a festively decorated dining room and bar as well as takeout meals from a cafeteria line, and all sorts of interesting pastries from the in-house bakery. In fact, this is a good place for breakfast, starting at 7 a.m. In addition to baked goods, the choices include all sorts of huevos rancheros, eggs scrambled with chorizo (Mexican sausage), *migas* (a sort of tortilla omelet), and, on Saturday and Sunday only, *menudo,* which is a bowl of stewed honeycomb tripe. *Menudo* is Mexican folklore's hangover cure. Every morning from 7 a.m. to 9 a.m., customers are welcome to "jump start happy hour" with $3 mimosas and $8 jumbo margaritas.

When you sit down for a lunch or dinner, a waiter (outfitted in white shirt and tie) brings a basket of thin, elegant tortilla chips, still warm, along with a mild red sauce and a hotter, lime-tinged green pepper sauce. The chips are large and somewhat fragile; if you eat your way through half the basket so that only smaller, broken half-chips remain, the old basket is whisked away and a new one of full-sized, warm chips takes its place.

The menu is huge, including fajitas à la Mexicana, for which the beef is stewed rather than grilled, tacos, flautas, tamales, enchiladas, and chiles rellenos. We love the fish tacos, made not the typical way with fried fish but with succulent strips of grilled mahimahi. They are light, refreshing, and hot (if you ask for them that way), the fish, cabbage, tomato, and cilantro laced with little nuggets of tongue-searing pepper. Alongside come Mexican rice and a bowl of creamy-smooth, blue-black refritos.

No matter how much we eat, it is hard to pass up the likes of chocolate cake topped with flan, or at least a few fudge-coated coconut macaroons. For the road we always take a bag of heart-shaped cinnamon-sugar cookies.

### *Little Diner

7209 7th St.  
Canutillo, TX

915-877-2176  
www.littlediner.com  
LD | $

Lourdes Pearson's Little Diner, also known as the Canutillo Tortilla Factory, is far off I-10 in an obscure residential neighborhood north of El Paso, but her crisp-skinned gorditas (stuffed cornmeal pockets) are worth getting lost to find. The normal filling is ground meat, but the great one is chili con carne. Tender shreds of beef become an ideal medium for the brilliant red chile that surrounds them with a walloping flavor of concentrated sunshine. You can also get the chili con carne in a bowl—one of the few classic "bowls of red" still to be found in all of Texas. Its flavor is huge, and you wouldn't think of adding beans or rice to this perfect duet. Of course, you do want to tear off pieces from Lourdes's wheaty flour tortillas to mop the last of the red chili from the bottom of the bowl.

We love everything about this friendly diner, where you step up to the counter and place your order before sitting down. The tortilla chips that start each meal have an earthy corn character and are scarcely salty—all the better to taste the essence-of-red-chile salsa served with them. Flautas are crunchy little fried tortilla tubes (like flutes, which is what the name means) packed with moist shreds of chicken or succulent pot roast. The last time we visited, the green chili was even hotter than the red (this varies with the harvest); it adds potatoes and onions to the basic meat-and-chiles formula.

The broad Tex-Mex menu includes burritos, enchiladas, tapatias, and tacos. Tamales—red chili pork, green chili cheese, green chili chicken, and green chili chicken cheese—are generally made once a week, but Lourdes told us that in December, they are a menu item every day.

## Lock Drugs

1003 Main St.
Bastrop, TX

512-321-2422
www.lockdrugs.com
L | $

Texas food fans know Route 183 as a critical detour off I-10 between San Antonio and Houston into the town of Lockhart, which is to Lone Star barbecue what Milwaukee is to Dairy State butter burgers: source of the best. Of Lockhart's world-class smoke pits, which include Kreuz Market (p. 503), Smitty's (p. 511), and Black's (p. 491), only Black's offers meaningful dessert (hot cobbler), so we recommend travelers save their sweet tooth for a half-hour drive northeast to Bastrop, where you will find Lock Drugs.

It isn't as old as it looks, despite the display of patent medicine remedies in exquisite carved wood fixtures. Opened in Bastrop in 1970, Lock Drugs is a Roadfood landmark for its dedicated soda fountain (no sandwiches or hot meals). The menu warns that "malts and shakes cannot be made with ice cream that has nuts, as it will break our machine," but that's fine, because we're ordering a magnificent black-and-white soda (topped with crunchy fresh chopped peanuts) and an item we've seen nowhere else, a frosted Coke. The latter is built just like a milk shake with an ice cream of your choice (smooth ice cream, please!) and flavored syrup, but blended with Coca-Cola instead of milk. The result isn't as thick as a regular shake, but it is rich, effervescent, and candyland sweet—essence of soda fountain.

## *Louie Mueller's

206 W. 2nd                          512-352-6206
Taylor, TX                          www.louiemuellerbarbecue.com
                                    LD | $$

Several years ago, Louie Mueller's, which we have long considered the best of all Texas barbecue parlors, added a modern dining room that lacks the smoky patina of the original brick-walled restaurant; but no matter where you eat in this august temple of meat, the flavor is historic. Here is a restaurant where beef brisket (as well as sausage, ribs, and mutton) are cooked and served the way Texas pitmasters have been doing it for decades. Step up to the counter that separates dining tables from the smoke pits. Place your order by pound or plate. Carry it yourself to a table.

The brisket is a thing of beauty. It is sliced relatively thick, each individual slice halved by the ribbon of fat that runs through a brisket, separating the leaner, denser meat below from the more marbled stuff on top. Wayne Mueller, Louie's grandson, and now master of the barbecue domain, told us that no spices go into or onto his briskets other than salt and pepper. Add time and smoke to those two elements, plus a pitmaster who knows how to move the meat around in the pit to take maximum advantage of hot spots, cool spots, and drafts, and the result is brisket that is impossibly juicy and huge-flavored. By comparison, prime sirloin and Wagyu kobe filet mignon are wimpy. There is sauce reminiscent of jus, but it is irrelevant. Meat is what you want to eat: brisket, with perhaps a side of all-beef sausage.


## The Mecca

5815 Live Oak St.                   214-352-0051
Dallas, TX                          www.themeccarestaurant.com
                                    BL | $

The Mecca's cinnamon roll is immense, filling most of a dinner plate, slathered with frosting, oozing melted margarine, stuffed with cinnamon and sugar, tall enough that excavating from top to bottom takes knife and fork through strata that range from doughy to syrupy. Elegant it is not.

And elegant is not what Mecca tries to be. But for appetites that demand potent appeasement, this place cannot be beat. The egg and tortilla medley known as *migas* is hugely hearty, loaded with (optional) chorizo. Refried beans that come alongside are laced with strips of pork, mostly fat, that melt into a piggy slurry. Chicken-fried steak comes with thick pepper-cream gravy. Biscuits are almost as significant as the cinnamon roll.

# *Monument Cafe

500 S. Austin Ave.
Georgetown, TX

512-930-9586
www.themonumentcafe.com
BLD | $$

Three meals a day are served at the Monument Cafe, and we have enjoyed everything from a grilled cheese sandwich to chicken-fried steak; but it is breakfast we like best. The kitchen's *migas* are perfect: eggs scrambled with cheese, diced tomatoes, and small ribbons of tortilla that variously soften and turn crisp depending on where they are in the pan, giving the dish an earthy corn flavor. On the side come peppered bacon and refried beans, plus red salsa to heat it up if desired. Pancakes and waffles are of the highest quality, as are the big squarish biscuits. The pastry we'd kill for is sour cream coffee cake, its top blanketed with sugar and frosting, its inside layered with local pecans.

"We make our own desserts, from scratch, every day," the menu notes. "And we use only real ingredients: real whipping cream, real butter, real yard eggs." Of these boasts, you will have no doubt if you order a piece of cream pie. Here is some of the best pie in Texas, some of the best *anywhere*! Chocolate pie with a toasted pecan crust is inspired and devilishly chocolaty. Coconut cream pie is equally amazing, but angelically light, silky, fresh, and layered on a flaky gold crust.

Oh, one more thing: lemonade, limeade, and orange juice are *fresh*.

# Norma's Cafe

1123 W. Davis
Dallas, TX

214-946-4711
www.normascafe.com
BLD | $

An overarching 1950s consciousness and the house slogan, "Life Is Short—Eat Dessert First," suggest that Norma's Cafe is trying awfully hard to be a down-home diner. It needn't try; it is the real deal. It dates back to 1956; modern website notwithstanding, it remains a sprung-spring-booth and worn-counter hash house with cop and blue-collar clientele, breakfast with gravy over everything, and no-bull waitresses pouring bottomless coffee.

Biscuits arrive all warm and friendly, fairly reeking buttermilk tang, needing neither the margarine nor jelly that are supplied, and just right for mopping up cream gravy. Loaded with gnarled chunks of sausage, the gravy is light on pepper and heavy on cream.

A sign hanging over Norma's dining room proclaims "Pie Fixes Everything." If you eat nothing else in this place, you must eat some, for these pies are made by masters. Peanut butter chocolate is an exquisite balance of those two oh-so-complementary elements that make Reese's candy right, neither layer hogging attention, both cool and silky, their frothy white crown dotted with enough nutmeat to provide happy crunch. The crust is sturdy and serviceable, more like a cookie than the flaky pastry of aristocratic pies.

While there are plenty of booths, counter seats provide an opportunity to kibitz with the staff and also to look into the kitchen's pass-through window, where cooks are busy cutting up fatback for cooking vegetables, icing cinnamon buns, and seasoning pots of soup and gravy destined to be lunch.

There is a second Norma's Cafe in North Dallas at 17721 Dallas Parkway (214-946-2101). Another Norma's, in Farmer's Branch, is not related.

## OST

305 Main St.  
Bandera, TX  

830-796-3836  
BLD | $$

OST (Old Spanish Trail) has been Bandera's town café since 1921, and its roomy cypress booths and barstools made of western saddles make it an especially appealing destination for hungry travelers in search of cowboy culture. One whole room is devoted to images of John Wayne; its spur collection includes rowels dating back to frontier days; and the buffet is set out under a downsized covered wagon. The buckaroo trappings make a lot of sense in Bandera, which is surrounded by dude ranches and has proclaimed itself the Cowboy Capital of the World.

The number one cowboy dish in these parts is chicken-fried steak, and OST makes a good one: a tantalizing balance of crunch and tenderness with gravy that is cream-soft but pepper-sharp. The menu highlights include such Tex-Mex stalwarts as enchiladas, fajitas, and chiles rellenos. Old-fashioned buttermilk pie is the great dessert; blackberry cobbler is excellent too.

## Paris Coffee Shop

700 W. Magnolia  
Fort Worth, Texas  

817-335-2041  
www.pariscoffeeshop.net  
BL | $

The day starts early in cattle country, so it should be no surprise that Fort Worth has always been a good breakfast town. By 7 a.m., the Paris Coffee Shop is bustling. A convivial, wood-paneled room with a counter, booths, and tables, it smells delicious in the morning, its air fragrant with the piggy perfume of sausages, bacon, and pork chops, as well as biscuits smothered with gravy. Beyond biscuits, breadstuffs include soft, glazed cinnamon rolls and a choice of eight-grain, sourdough, or sun-dried tomato toast.

The Paris Coffee Shop is also a legendary lunchroom (since 1926), known for meat loaf, fried chicken, and chicken-fried steak with mashed potatoes and gravy, as well as one of the best bowls of chili in the Metroplex. The café's signature dish is an Arkansas Traveler: hot roast beef on corn bread, smothered with gravy. Such Lone Star comfort fare is accompanied by your choice from a wide variety of southern-style vegetables such as turnips and/or turnip greens, pole beans, and butter beans.

Any meal *must* be followed by a piece of Paris pie. One morning, when we spotted a single piece of custard pie we wanted behind the counter and ordered it for breakfast, the waitress warned, "It's not today's." (Today's pies were still in the oven.) But then she agreed with our choice, declaring, "Hey, yesterday's egg custard pie is better than no pie at all!"

## Ranchman's Café (aka Ponder Steak House)

110 W. Bailey St.  
Ponder, TX

940-479-2221  
www.ranchman.com  
LD (reservations advised) | $$$

In a sleepy encampment by the train tracks at the northern fringe of the Dallas/Fort Worth Metroplex, the Ponder Steakhouse (actually named Ranchman's Café) has been a meat-eaters' destination since 1948. Indoor bathrooms were added many years ago, but the steaks are still hand-cut, and the ambience is Lone Star to the core.

The menu ranges from quail quarters and Rocky Mountain oyster hors d'oeuvres to fabulous made-from-scratch buttermilk pie. It is big, glistening steaks that motivate us for the drive. Porterhouse, T-bone, club, rib eye, and sirloin are sizzled on a griddle until they develop a wickedly tasty crust. Although tender, they are steaks of substantial density that require a sharp knife and reward a good chew with tides of flavor. French fries come on the side, but if you call ahead, they'll put a baked potato in the oven and have it ready when you arrive. Pies, made from scratch, include apple, strawberry-rhubarb, buttermilk, chocolate, coconut, and pecan.

## Royers Round Top Cafe

On the Square              1-877-866-7437

Round Top, TX         www.royersroundtopcafe.com

LD | $$

Bud Royer has described his menu as "contemporary comfort food" but no single category of cuisine begins to describe his kitchen's boundlessly creative bent. Yes, there are familiar square meals: filet mignon, rack of lamb, a fourteen-ounce pork chop, and Sunday's garlicky, buttermilk-battered fried chicken, but nearly everything has a Royer twist. Grilled pork tenderloin is topped with a peach and pepper glaze, quail comes stuffed with shrimp and wrapped in bacon, Bud's salad includes both grilled beef and bacon.

If you know Royers Round Top, you know we haven't yet mentioned its flagship dish: pie. Bud (who goes by the moniker Bud the Pieman) offers big country-style classics with ribbons of baked fruit oozing out over the edge of knobby crusts as well as several pies of his own design. We believe the pecan pie, made with giant halves of Texas-grown nuts, is the best anywhere—a perfect balance of toasty nut flavor and syrupy sweetness. And the chocolate chip pie, loaded with pecans and super-chocolaty—really more a huge, thick cookie than a pie—is nothing short of devastating.

Royers is so deeply into pies that the menu threatens to charge customers 50¢ extra if they do not get it à la mode. "It is so wrong to not top your pie with Amy's ice cream!" (Amy's is an Austin brand started in 1984 by Amy Miller, who earned her chops working at the legendary Steve's in Boston.) If you come with a group, you can order a pie sampler for dessert: four different kinds à la mode. Those who cannot come should know that Royers is set up to ship pies anywhere in the United States, and pie devotees can enroll in one of the café's Pie-of-the-Month plans. They range from six pies delivered every other month for a year to Pie-for-Life!

## Salt Lick

18001 FM 1826          512-725-8542

Driftwood, TX 78619     www.saltlickbbq.com

LD | $$

Our first review of the Salt Lick, in the earliest edition of this book, described a place that began with neither four walls nor a restroom—just a smoke pit and makeshift tables on Thurman and Hisako Roberts's six-hundred-acre ranch. My, how it's grown! Located in the Hill Country west of Austin, it has become a theme park of barbecue with seats for two thousand, its limestone buildings surrounded by rough-hewn log fences, the air smelling of slow-smoked meats. Compared to the region's back-of-the-butcher-shop barbecue parlors, it's a refined place with ambience you might call Rustic Deluxe. There is a printed menu, there is waiter service, and the kitchen's repertoire includes all sorts of side dishes and dessert.

One other element that separates the Salt Lick from the primal parlors: sauce. Unless you ask to have your meat dry, it comes already painted with sauce. Not that the meat needs it—it's moist and full-flavored—but it does happen to be really tasty sauce, a tangy-sweet glaze with perhaps a hint of mustard. In fact, the sauce is good enough to use as a between-meat dip for the slices of good white bread that come alongside the meal. The sausage is smoky and rich, made from equal amounts of pork and beef. Brisket, slow-smoked for sixteen hours, is lean and polite (unless you request fattier slices), and if it lacks a certain succulence, Salt Lick sauce is an instant fix. Pork ribs drip juice from the tender meat at the bone and deliver a stupendously concentrated smoke-pit flavor in the chewy burnt ends.

Among the worthy side dishes are an intriguing cabbage slaw flecked with sesame seeds and cool, German-style potato salad. And of course, pickles and sliced raw onions are available with every meal.

## Smitty's

| | |
|---|---|
| 6219 Airport Rd. | 915-772-5876 |
| El Paso, TX | LD \| $ |

Smitty's is a kick-ass barbecue favored by soldiers stationed at Fort Bliss, and it makes an easy quick stop for people on their way to or from the El Paso Airport. (Takeout orders are a specialty, as is custom barbecue: "You bring it, we'll BBQ it!") The spacious dining room smells of smoke from the pit; décor is a combination of beer signs and Wild West imagery; and the background music is just right for knocking back longnecks and engaging in full-volume palaver with table mates.

The meat selection is vast: regular beef or lean beef, corned beef or lean corned beef, ham, turkey breast and turkey sausage, chicken, sliced pork and chopped pork, pork chops, pork ribs, and beef ribs. Most of these items can be had on a lunch plate or larger dinner plate (with German fried potatoes, slaw, and beans); in a sandwich or stuffed into a burrito; or on the "high-protein special" plate, which is meat accompanied by a Styrofoam cup full of Smitty's opaque sweet sauce and a few slices of soft white bread. That sauce is valuable for adding moistness to the beef, chicken, and sliced pork, which need a kick. The sausage needs nothing to make par.

Tea (unsweetened) is presented to each table in a large pitcher so you can constantly replenish your glass as you dine.

## Smitty's

208 S. Commerce       512-398-9344
Lockhart, TX       www.smittysmarket.com
      LD | $$

The atmosphere at Smitty's backroom barbecue is tangible: eye-stinging clouds of smoke rise from wood fires around the indoor pit where you order meat by the pound. It is cut and assembled and wrapped in butcher paper so you can carry it to a communal table in the dining room. The pork chop is swell, but the Texas beef is definitive. Brisket is indescribably tender. Barbecued boneless prime rib (cut extra-thick, please) has got to be the ultimate in pit-cooked luxury, pink in its center, saturated with juice, and giddy with carnivorous energy. The sausage rings are insanely succulent, so loaded that if you plan to snap one in half, you must be sure to push out and away from you, lest its juices splatter your shirt.

Smitty's operates from the oldest barbecue facility in Lockhart, the building in which Charles Kreuz opened his grocery store more than a century ago. In 1948 Kreuz sold the business to the Schmidt family, but several years back, a feud split the Schmidts and sent the Kreuz Market out to a big new building (p. 503). Smitty's retains a charismatic historic feel; to walk in off Commerce Street through the age-burnished dining room with its benches along the wall is to see a virtual museum of Texas foodways. The room, now idle, was still in use when we first dined at Smitty's in the 1970s. The long counters were equipped with sharp knives attached by chains long enough for customers to cut their meat but too short for a knife fight.

## Southside Market

1212 Hwy. 290       512-281-4650
Elgin, TX       www.southsidemarket.com
      LD | $

In the geography of American sausage, no town holds more respect than Elgin (with a hard g, as in "gut"), known for hot beef sausages ever since the Southside Market fired up its smoke pit in 1882. One hundred and ten years after opening day, the sawdust-floored house of meats moved to a huge, spanking-clean, barn-sized building on the outskirts of town. While the new place lacks the charm of a well-aged and dilapidated barbecue parlor, it maintains a working butcher shop, and it still smokes sausage and beef brisket the old-fashioned way, in big iron pits over slow-smoldering post oak wood. Order your meat by the pound and carry it to a table.

The sausage is some of the best anywhere, a crazy-moist balance of spicy pyrotechnics and stalwart beef. Beyond the signature sausage, this is a good place to eat such Lone Star smoke-pit standards as brisket (regular or lean), and one of four kinds of rib: mutton, pork, beef, and baby back. Bread is sold by the slice (10¢) or loaf ($1.99); jalapeño peppers cost 39¢ apiece.

## Sweet Georgia Brown

2840 E. Ledbetter Dr.      214-375-2020
Dallas, TX      LD | $$

Mac 'n' cheese alert! Toothy elbow noodles are bound in a dense emulsion that is far from soupy, but more like custard. It is thick mac 'n' cheese that you actually chew, albeit barely. If you request or happen to receive a portion with reefs of edge and topskin, you seriously will chew it, for these elastic sections do require jaw work. In return they provide intense cheesy satisfaction.

Sweet Georgia Brown is a soul-food restaurant serving mostly African Americans. It is best known to its corps of loyal customers for barbecue. Here you will eat brisket and ribs, hot links and Polish sausages that are deliriously fatty and inescapably delicious. With a meal of one, two, or three of these meats, or with catfish, smothered chicken, meat loaf, or beef tips, each customer selects from an array of about a dozen different side dishes, macaroni being one of them. Other choices include collard greens, sautéed corn, fried okra, braised cabbage, beans and peas of various size and color, and a broccoli casserole in which pieces of the vegetable exist only to provide something firm amidst a dish that is really all about melting cheese.

Do bring plenty of appetite to Sweet Georgia Brown. A full meat-and-three meal weighs more than five pounds and will serve at least two large hungry people, meaning that the $10–$15 price is a bargain. (BBQ sandwiches also are available at about $7; they too are big.)

## Taco Garage

8403 Broadway

San Antonio, TX

210-826-4405

www.tacogarage.com

BLD | $

With plenty of open space and, one trusts, good ventilation, an old service station garage makes a nice restaurant dining room. At San Antonio's Taco Garage, once a Break Check shop, the automotive theme endures in the form of front door handles that are little chain-link steering wheels. Out back, a forlorn VW microbus echoes hippie times with faded flowers painted on its body panels. The front of the menu advertises "Tex-Mex Cruizine."

There is a connection between custom cars and tacos—both are fields in which Mexican craftsmen excel—but once you are seated in this place, the food commands serious attention while the car stuff seems like fluff. As soon as you sit down, salsa is brought to the table. Dark and smoky, hot enough to make sure every taste bud is wide-awake, it keeps you eating as long as there are chips in the basket, or until meals arrive. Made with corn tortillas that have been rolled out and cooked just moments earlier, the tacos are sure proof of San Antonio's hegemony in the taco world. Cooked either flat or puffy (the latter quickly deep-fried), they can be filled with crisp-broiled shrimp and cabbage, ground beef, or chicken and cheese, or, for breakfast, huevos à la Mexicana. In fact, the menu lists twenty-six different kinds of taco, plus enchiladas, nachos, flautas, fajitas, and even hamburgers.

Drinks include "high horsepower" margaritas as well as "unleaded" (non-alcoholic) Mexican sodas.

## Taco House

6307 San Pedro Ave.

San Antonio, TX

210-341-3136

BL | $

In some places, breakfast tacos are a novelty. In San Antonio, they are a staple, served in dozens of little eateries all over the city. The best of the taquerias use tortillas that are rolled out and griddle-cooked on the spot, just minutes before construction. Taco House, which has been a destination for decades, offers more than a dozen different kinds, from bacon and egg to *carne guisada* (gravy-sopped beef) and *lengua* (tongue). Fresh, chewy flour tortillas make a big difference, delivering even the most plebeian filling with high honors. But Taco House's plebeian fillings are far from drab. Eggs are buttery; bacon is thick and smoky; nuggets of potato are cooked to a perfect point of inside creaminess and outside crunch.

If you're going to have only one breakfast, consider chorizo and eggs, which, per local custom, is not eggs with a side order of chorizo sausage but rather eggs scrambled with ground-up sausage to become an entirely new and different food: juicy, spicy, and cream-rich. It's great on a plate with refried beans and potatoes or as the filling of a taco.

Lunch is a full roster of Tex-Mex fare, including tacos, enchiladas, flautas, and chicken molé. If you order chili, you will be asked whether or not you want beans. Say no and you are presented with an enormous bowl of true chili con carne, a minimalist dish of meat and red chile. Fajitas, like tacos, are available with crisp or puffy tortillas, the latter another San Antonio fave—quickly fried so they blow up like a flat sopaipilla.

## *Taco Taco

145 E. Hildebrand Ave.      210-822-9533
San Antonio, TX      www.tacotacosa.com
     BL | $

Service is swift at Taco Taco, but if you come at peak hours for breakfast or lunch, you will have to wait for a table. The goodness of its tacos is no secret among San Antonio Tex-Mex aficionados, who have a huge number of excellent taquerias from which to choose. As in all the good places, Taco Taco rolls out its tortillas by hand and griddle cooks them. This means yours will be warm and fresh—delicious to eat with no filling whatsoever.

It is customary for local taquerias to offer *barbacoa* on the weekend, and it's hard to imagine a more delicious version than Taco Taco's. It is the tenderest, most unctuous smoky beef imaginable, slowly roasted and loaded into the taco in heaping shreds that audibly ooze when bitten. No other ingredients are warranted in this taco, as opposed to a chicken taco where a layer of refritos and a sprinkle of cheese are a nice complement, or a potato and egg breakfast taco gilded with the kitchen's marvelous salsa. Puffy tacos, a San Antonio passion, also are available—the same ingredients but enveloped in a tortilla that has been fried just enough to swell and soften. Specialty tacos are made on tortillas that are double-wide. El Norteno contains sizzled chicken (or beef) with beans, slices of avocado, cheese, peppers, and onions. Fiesta is fajita-grilled chicken with chunky pico de gallo.

Meals begin with excellent tortilla chips and that house salsa—impossible to stop eating until all chips are gone or the main course arrives. Beyond tacos, the menu offers weekend *menudo* and such fine borderland dishes as chicken molé enchiladas, gorditas, and flautas.

## Texas Pie Company

202 W. Center St.
Kyle, TX

512-268-5885
www.texaspiecompany.com
L | $

There is no chance you will miss the Texas Pie Company if you drive through Kyle along West Center Street. Looming over the roof that shades the sidewalk is an immense 3-D sculpture of a slice of cherry pie. Behind that, the house motto is written in bright red letters: "Life Is Short. Eat More Pie!"

This dessert-focused café is especially convenient for travelers just passing through because it makes single-serving mini pies as well as big ones. Crusts are terrific—not all that pretty, but light and savory. Lemon chess pie radiates dazzling citrus flavor with a buttermilky cushion; coconut is supremely toasty, its fleshy white shreds packing full nutty richness; and the nuts that crowd the top of the pecan pie taste fresh enough to have just come out of their shell. We also highly recommend strawberry cake, which is delectably moist and crowned with a heap of fruit-flavored frosting.

In addition to dessert, the Texas Pie Company sells simple lunches to eat here, including sandwiches and salads, and sells hot meals to take home. Among the latter is that Texas home-ec specialty of chicken and canned soup, King Ranch casserole.

## Threadgill's

6416 N. Lamar
Austin, TX

512-451-5440
www.threadgills.com
LD | $$

In the years we've been eating at Threadgill's, portions have gotten noticeably smaller. Now one full meal is big enough to feed only a couple of people. Still, this boisterous restaurant remains a bonanza for endless appetites, particularly appetites ravening for southern and/or Texas cooking.

Side dishes are vital here, from virtuous (okra with tomatoes) to wicked (garlic cheese grits). Many fans come to Threadgill's to eat *only* vegetables, accompanied by big squares of warm corn bread. If you choose right, a meal of five vegetable selections is, in fact, every bit as satisfying as a few pounds of beef. Among the excellent choices from the regular list are the San Antonio squash casserole, turnip greens, and crisp-fried okra.

As for entrees, we tend to go for chicken-fried steak or an impossibly rich plate of fried chicken livers with cream gravy. Those of lighter appetite can choose a very handsome (albeit gigantic) Caesar salad piled with grilled chicken, and there are a couple of unfried fish items.

Aside from big, good food, Threadgill's is worth visiting for its history (the Austin music scene started here; Janis Joplin used to be a waitress) and its Texas-to-the-max ambience. Although the original beer joint/gas station that Kenneth Threadgill opened in 1933 burned down twice and virtually none of it remains, the restaurant today has the feel of an antique: creaky wood floors, wood-slat ceilings, and a devil-may-care floor plan that gives the impression the sprawling space just kept growing through the years. The decorative motif is beer signs.

## Tolbert's

423 S. Main St.  
Grapevine, TX

817-421-4888  
www.tolbertsrestaurant.com  
LD | $$

Downtown Grapevine is like a large living-history museum, populated with antiques stores and western-themed specialty shops. Among the reliquaries is a restaurant called Tolbert's. Named for the late Frank X. Tolbert, author of *A Bowl of Red,* the definitive book about traditional Texas cooking, it is run by his daughter and son-in-law. Tolbert's is one of the few places we know that serves a bowl of true chili con carne.

What is chili con carne? Literally, it is chili with meat. Texas loyalists will accept nothing else as genuine. No add-ins or add-ons are allowed. No beans, no tomatoes, no bell peppers or Yukon golds or ground turkey or soysage. Chili con carne, as served at Tolbert's, is a muscle-bound duet of beef and heat. It comes with tortilla chips on the side, as well as shredded cheese and chopped raw onions to sprinkle on top, but the diehard Texas chilihead can ignore those things and spoon into delicious purity.

Beyond chili con carne, Tolbert's offers a full menu that ranges from chicken wings and ballpark nachos to steaks, seafood, burritos, and chocolate mousse cake. You can even get a sacrilegious bowl of chili, made with pinto beans. On the menu, it is titled "North of the Border."

## Tom & Bingo's

3006 34th St.  806-799-1514
Lubbock, TX  L | $

A wood-slat shack surrounded by a parking lot, Tom & Bingo's serves tender, moist beef brisket in a bun. Everybody comes for the brisket; the only alternatives are a ham sandwich and a burger. Gluttons can get a sandwich of all three: brisket, ham, and burger on a bun. Side dishes are chips by the bag, pickles, and onions. Sauce is good, but hardly necessary to enhance brisket so succulent after its long hickory-smoke bath. Seating is spare, at school desks along the wall.

Whole briskets are available if you order in advance, and Meg Butler, who tipped us off to this place, reported that after she and her husband shared four sandwiches at Tom & Bingo's, they bought one to carry home. "Security screeners at the airport didn't blink," she said.

## Vernon's Kuntry Katfish

5901 W. Davis  936-760-3386
Conroe, TX  www.kuntrykatfish.com
LD | $

Hugely popular—you will wait for a table any weekday at lunch—Vernon's Kuntry Katfish serves not only Mississippi-raised catfish, but also a passel of country-style vegetables every day. Mustard greens or turnip greens, northern beans, field peas, fried okra, mashed potatoes, and cheese-enriched broccoli are some of the selections; and crunchy, dark-cooked hush puppies, studded with bits of onion and jalapeño pepper, are accompanied by bowls of pickled green tomatoes. If catfish is not your dish, try the chicken-fried steak. It's one to make Texans proud, gilded with pepper gravy and served with biscuits or corn-bread squares on the side.

Dessert is significant: fruit cobbler, banana pudding, or an item known as Good Pie, which is a uniquely American pastry edifice of pineapple chunks, bananas, cream cheese, nuts, and chocolate syrup.

## Village Bakery

108 E. Oak St.  254-826-5151
West, TX  B | $

The *kolache*, brought to Texas by immigrants from central Europe, has become a morning pastry more popular than donuts in some towns. It is like a fruit-filled Danish, but made with sweeter dough that is so delicate, you need to hold it tenderly lest you compress it with brutal fingers. For some of the best *kolaches,* go to the town of West, Texas, just off I-35, and visit the Village Bakery. "Kolače [Czech spelling] are sold warm from the oven," assures the movable-letter menu above the counter. Apricot, prune, and poppy seed are standard-bearers from the old country. More modern variations are fruitier, filled with apple, strawberry, or blueberry preserves. A recent special contained espresso-chocolate and cream cheese filling.

The Village Bakery added a Texas twist to tradition in the early 1950s when baker Wendell Montgomery asked his mother-in-law to come up with a snack-sized version that included the sausage links that are another passion of Eastern Europeans who settled the heart of Texas. Her creation was a gloss on Czech *klobasniki,* which are customarily made with ground sausage. Purists still refer to them as that or, possibly, as pigs in blankets, reserving the term *kolache* for those filled with fruit, cheese, or poppy seeds. Savory *klobasnikis* are now popular wherever *kolaches* are sold. The Village Bakery makes regular and hot sausage versions.

More a bakery than a full-service restaurant, this welcoming little shop will sell you a cup of coffee and offers three small dining tables and one circular ten-seat table occupied by gabbing townsfolk most mornings.

## Weikel's Store and Bakery

2247 W. State Hwy. 71　　　　979-968-9413
La Grange, TX　　　　　　　　www.weikels.com
　　　　　　　　　　　　　　　BL | $

A Danish-like pastry with Czech lineage, the *kolache* has become a tasty symbol of the Eastern European roots that have helped make this part of Texas such a culinary adventureland. One of the least likely places to find superior *kolaches* is Weikel's, a convenience store attached to a gas station by the side of the highway. While it might at first look like any other quick-shop highway mart, bakery cases toward the back tell a different story. Here are handsome cakes, rolls, and cookies, plus several varieties of *kolache* from a house repertoire of about a dozen. Prune, cream cheese, apricot, and poppy seed are fluffy-crumbed superior coffee companions.

You know Weikel's is serious about its *kolaches* when you consider the house motto: "We Got'cha Kolache." In addition to its pastry treasures, one other house specialty worth sampling is the house-made pig-in-a-blanket. It is a taut-skinned, rugged-textured kielbasa sausage fully encased in a tube of tender-crumb bread that is finer than any hot dog bun we've ever eaten.

## Capitol Reef Cafe

360 W. Main St.
Torrey, UT

435-425-3271
www.capitolreefinn.com
BLD | $$

At the west end of the town of Torrey in the wilds of south-central Utah, the Capitol Reef Cafe is an oasis of good food and elevated cultural consciousness. It is not only a restaurant: It is an inviting (and inexpensive) motel with hand-hewn furniture in the rooms; it is a bookstore featuring practical and meditative volumes about the west; and it is a trading post with some intriguing Native American jewelry and rugs.

The restaurant serves three meals a day and appears to be as informal as any western motel dining room, except for the fact that you are likely to hear the gurgle of an espresso machine in the background and Bach played to set the mood. The house motto is "Local, Natural, Healthy," and while you can have a fine breakfast of bacon and eggs, you can also choose to have those eggs accompanied by smoked local trout, or you can have an omelet made with local cheeses . . . with fresh-squeezed juice to drink.

The Capitol Reef dining room is a blessing for traveling vegetarians. A few notable meatless menu items include spaghetti with marinara sauce (also available with meat), fettuccine primavera, and plates of steamed, stir-fried, or shish-kebab vegetables. Beef, chicken, and seafood are always available for vegetable frowners (that trout, broiled with rosemary, is what we recommend), and desserts include a hot fudge sundae and apple pie.

## Hires Big H

425 S. 700 East
Salt Lake City, UT

801-364-4582
www.hiresbigh.com
LD | $

Ever since the success of nickel-a-glass root beer at A&W stands during Prohibition, "the temperance beverage" has been an axiomatic drive-in drink. At Hires Big H, with three curb-service outlets in the Salt Lake City area, it comes in five sizes, from "kid" to "large," and of course there are root beer floats. Or you can sip a limeade or a marshmallow-chocolate malt. Lemon, lime, cherry, vanilla, and chocolate can be added at no charge.

The juicy quarter-pound Big H burger is available plain or topped with bacon, ham, pastrami, Roquefort cheese, grilled onions, or a trio of crunchy onion rings, and it is brought to the car in a wax paper bag that makes a handy mitt. The bun is gentle-tempered sourdough with a floury top (as opposed to what the combative menu describes as "some preservative-enhanced, wilted crust studded with obnoxious seeds"), and French fries and onion rings are served with fry sauce, reminiscent of French dressing. Correspondent Mel Fullmer informed us that Utah fry sauce was invented at the Arctic Circle Drive-In in 1948. It has since become a thing of pride among burger joints as far away as California, Oregon, and Washington.

Other locations: 835 East Fort Union, Midvale (801-561-2171) and 2900 West 4700 South, West Valley City (801-965-1010).

## Idle Isle

24 S. Main
Brigham City, UT

435-734-2468
BLD | $

Ahh, idleberry pie! A sultry, dark extravaganza that resonates with the booming fruitiness of blueberries, blackberries, and boysenberries, all packed into a crust that complements the berries with savory luxury, this pie is so complete that even à la mode seems superfluous. That's the one dish for which we always will love Idle Isle.

But we love Utah's third-oldest restaurant (since 1921) for all sorts of other things, and not just the food that is served. This is the sort of cordial town dining room once found on Main Streets everywhere. In the twenty-first century, its charm is a rarity to treasure.

You can have a burger and a malt at the marble and onyx soda fountain, and there is a slightly more boisterous back room with oilcloth-covered tables where regulars congregate at noon, but the choice seats, at least for us travelers, are in polished wood booths up front, each outfitted with a little ramekin of Idle Isle apricot marmalade for spooning onto fleecy rolls. The rolls come alongside dinners that are blue-plate fundamentals, including divinely tender pot roast with lumpy mashed potatoes shaped like a volcano crater to hold gravy as well as such daily specials as Wednesday braised beef joints, Friday trout, and Saturday prime rib.

## Lamb's Grill

169 S. Main St.                          801-364-7166
Salt Lake City, UT                       www.lambsgrill.com
                                         BLD | $$

Utah's oldest restaurant hasn't changed much since we first ate here some three decades ago, at which point it was celebrating sixty years in business. Liquor is more readily available (although you still have to make a special request to see the booze menu), but it remains a house of family-friendly, meat-and-potatoes classics, some of which have all but vanished from modern restaurants' repertoires. Poached finnan haddie, anyone? Beef tenderloin à la Stroganoff? None of it is self-consciously old-fashioned. These simply are dishes that never have been dropped from a menu that has indeed changed with the times to include the likes of Cajun salad with blackened chicken breast and portobello mushroom ravioli.

Still, it's the old-fashioned dishes we like to see on our plate at this well-aged diner/coffee shop in the heart of Salt Lake City: broiled chicken with lemon caper sauce, triple lamb chops, mountain trout, or chicken-fried steak with garlic-tinged whipped potatoes. Meals come with sesame-seeded Greek bread, which is at once wispy and chewy—great to use for mopping gravy or for eating with or without butter.

If Utah has one distinguishing culinary characteristic (other than scones and fry sauce to accompany French fries), it is a love of sweets. You will appreciate this at Lamb's in the dark, chocolaty five-layer cake thick with icing, in the homey baked apple, and in the unusually al dente rice pudding blanketed with powdered cinnamon.

## Maddox Drive-In

1900 S. Hwy. 89
Brigham City, UT

435-723-8545
www.maddoxfinefood.com
LD | $

The Maddox Drive-In, attached to the Maddox Steak House, serves lots of hamburgers but specializes in another drive-in delight, the chicken basket: fried chicken and French fries piled into a woven plastic trough. The beverage of choice is known as "fresh lime," which tastes something like lime-aided Sprite with extra sugar. The long, covered tramway where you park at Maddox is festooned with enthusiastic signs apparently meant to stimulate appetites: "We serve only grain-fed beef . . . We invite you to visit our entire operation." What we remember best is the huge sign high above the restaurant, where futuristic letters boast of MADDOX FINE FOOD.

There used to be a feed lot right in back, allowing customers at the adjoining steak house to look out the window at future steaks on the hoof as they dined. Today the cows are gone, but pound-plus T-bones remain the order of the day, accompanied by a basket of crunchy corn pones and glasses of pure drinking water drawn from Maddox's own well..

## Mom's Cafe

10 E. Main St.
Salina, UT

435-529-3921
BLD | $

Salina is a dusty old cowboy town with a few thousand citizens; Mom's is on its Main Street, serving blue-plate meals since 1929. We included this place in the very first edition of *Roadfood* (1978), giving it only one star out of four because there was no Mom in evidence, and service, by a gaggle of goofy teenagers, was sloppy. But the hamburgers were hand-formed and the coconut pie was fine, and, frankly, there weren't a whole lot of other dining options in central Utah. "Next time around," we wrote, "we'll peek in the kitchen first. If Mom is there, we'll give it another try."

About fifteen years later, we didn't have to look in the kitchen because the current Mom oversaw the operation from a desk right out in the dining room. Carolyn Jensen ran a tight ship. We were impressed by the efficiency of coffeepot-armed waitresses who wore blue uniforms that matched the aqua-blue upholstered booths, and more important, we had learned enough about Southwestern food to better appreciate a truly regional meal. Chicken-fried steak with pepper-cream gravy, biscuits with gravy . . . heck, nearly everything with gravy was (and remains) first-rate. Pies at Mom's are

Roadfood paradigms: lovely apple and cherry and custards, blueberry sour cream that is extraordinary, and, on occasion, cherry sour cream too.

It was on that return visit to Mom's that we first tasted the kind of scone that is unique to Utah. Completely unlike the dense, English-ancestored quick-bread scone, a Utah scone is a flat disc of puffy fry bread—pliable, crisp-edged, and tender within. It is no doubt related to the sopaipilla of New Mexico, but customarily it is made with sweeter dough. All meals at Mom's come with kettle-hot scones accompanied by the Beehive State's favorite condiment, honey butter.

## Navajo Hogan

447 E. 3300 South
Salt Lake City, UT

801-466-2860
www.navajohogan.com
LD | $

Few foods served in modern restaurants actually are native to America; nearly everything we eat is the product of immigrants bringing their recipes (and sometimes their seeds, livestock, and spices) and mixing them with what's available across the fruited plains. Navajo Hogan's tacos are, in fact, exactly the sort of melting-pot dish that characterizes our nation's cuisine at its most exuberant: Mexican, New Mexican, and Utahan, with a measure of fast-food brio.

The Navajo taco, popular throughout the Southwest, is built upon fry bread: excellent stuff here, made using flour and cornmeal that gets slid into a pan of hot oil and fried into a pliable disc ready for anything. Atop the bread goes your choice of ingredients, ranging from what the menu calls "traditional" (beans, beef, lettuce, tomato, shredded cheese, and sour cream) to dessert versions topped with honey butter or cinnamon sugar. You can get green or red chili from New Mexico, vegetarian toppings, or grilled chicken. That is the extent of the menu, except for Saturday-only mutton stew, a true Navajo dish that goes back at least a millennium.

Roadfood.com contributor Dale Fine, whose screen name is Wanderingjew, noted that Navajo Hogan is the sort of place "you're likely to pass by without realizing it's there": a windowless cinder-block bunker with fabric signs hung outside. We thank Mr. Fine for discovering it.

## Sill's Cafe

335 E. Gentile St.                    801-544-7438

Layton, UT                            BLD | $

We wouldn't suggest making a special trip to Sill's Cafe to eat fabulous food. The one unique-to-Utah item on the menu, a scone, is very good— especially so because the deep-fried disc of dough, vaguely reminiscent of a monstrous beignet, comes with a cupful of fine honey butter that melts immediately from the freshly fried scone's heat. Another notable specialty of the house, albeit not exclusive to the Beehive State, is the peppery SOS—a thick sausage gravy that is especially welcome as the blanket for a plateload of hash-brown potatoes. The cinnamon rolls are large and gooey, and there are pancakes and eggs for breakfast and hot beef sandwiches with drifts of mashed potatoes, burgers, and such for lunch and supper.

If the meals are not necessarily tripworthy, the place is. Roadfood.com's Dale Fine nailed its appeal by noting that it is a restaurant that is very much part of its community. For more than fifty years now, Sill's has attracted a cadre of regulars who are served by a staff of professional waitresses in an interactive daily encounter that is the spirit of Layton. There are no bells and whistles (except maybe for that outstanding scone), but there is true satisfaction for the traveler in search of traditional small-town foodways.

# Great Plains

Idaho

Montana

Nebraska

North Dakota

South Dakota

Wyoming

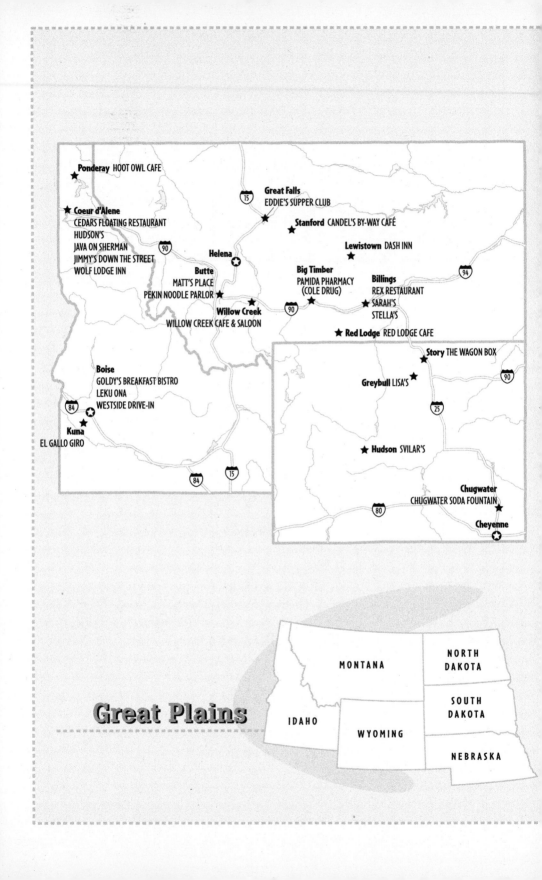

Ponderay  HOOT OWL CAFE

Great Falls
EDDIE'S SUPPER CLUB

Stanford  CANDEL'S BY-WAY CAFÉ

Coeur d'Alene
CEDARS FLOATING RESTAURANT
HUDSON'S
JAVA ON SHERMAN
JIMMY'S DOWN THE STREET
WOLF LODGE INN

Lewistown  DASH INN

Helena

Butte
MATT'S PLACE
PEKIN NOODLE PARLOR

Big Timber
PAMIDA PHARMACY
(COLE DRUG)

Billings
REX RESTAURANT
SARAH'S
STELLA'S

Willow Creek
WILLOW CREEK CAFE & SALOON

Red Lodge  RED LODGE CAFE

Story  THE WAGON BOX

Boise
GOLDY'S BREAKFAST BISTRO
LEKU ONA
WESTSIDE DRIVE-IN

Greybull  LISA'S

Kuna
EL GALLO GIRO

Hudson  SVILAR'S

Chugwater
CHUGWATER SODA FOUNTAIN

Cheyenne

Great Plains

NORTH
DAKOTA

MONTANA

SOUTH
DAKOTA

IDAHO

WYOMING

NEBRASKA

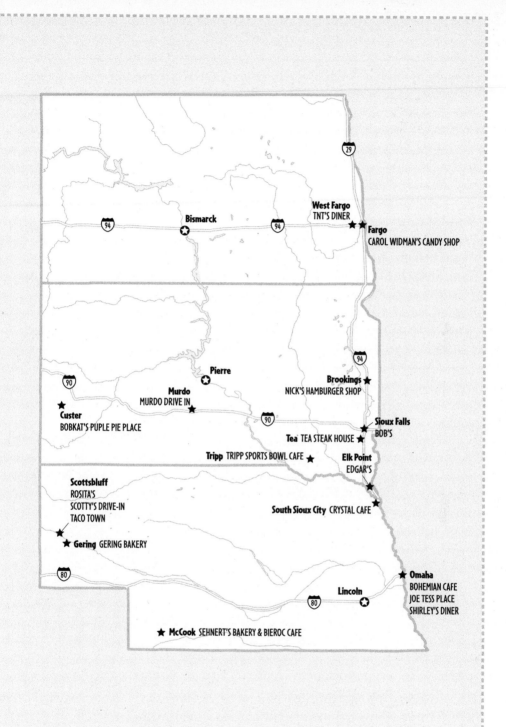

West Fargo
TNT'S DINER

Bismarck

Fargo
CAROL WIDMAN'S CANDY SHOP

Brookings
NICK'S HAMBURGER SHOP

Pierre

Murdo
MURDO DRIVE IN

Custer
BOBKAT'S PUPLE PIE PLACE

Sioux Falls
BOB'S

Tea TEA STEAK HOUSE

Tripp TRIPP SPORTS BOWL CAFE

Elk Point
EDGAR'S

Scottsbluff
ROSITA'S
SCOTTY'S DRIVE-IN
TACO TOWN

South Sioux City CRYSTAL CAFE

Gering GERING BAKERY

Omaha
BOHEMIAN CAFE
JOE TESS PLACE
SHIRLEY'S DINER

Lincoln

McCook SEHNERT'S BAKERY & BIEROC CAFE

## Cedars Floating Restaurant

1 Marine Dr. (Blackwell Island)    208-664-2922
Coeur d'Alene, ID    www.cedarsfloatingrestaurant.com
D | $$$

Rugged as it is, the landscape of northern Idaho can be irresistibly romantic—especially when appreciated at dinner hour from a table in Cedars Floating Restaurant, which is one of the few eateries that takes full advantage of the city's auspicious setting at the north end of Coeur d'Alene Lake. In fact, Cedars is located *in* the lake, moored about a hundred yards out at the head of the Spokane River and reachable by a walk down a long, narrow gangplank from the parking lot. Permanently berthed on three hundred tons of concrete, the dining room does not bob with the waves (as the original structure did in the 1960s!), but the window tables are virtually on the waterline. Our first visit was on a drizzly September evening when the lake was steel-gray, low clouds creeping down over a forested horizon.

A crackling fire and the lively sounds of an open kitchen set the mood in the spacious circular dining room, where every seat affords a view of waterfowl skimming over waves and the distant rocky shoreline. Cedars specializes in fish from Pacific waters. Salmon, ahi, sea bass, halibut, shark, and mahimahi are some of the frequently available choices; they are cut into thick fillets and charcoal-broiled, served with a choice of clear lemon butter caper sauce, tropical fruit salsa, or cucumber dill sauce.

We started our meal with a pound of steamed clams lolling in a garlicky wine broth and accompanied by toasted French bread and a plate of fresh-seared calamari with garlic aioli and red pepper remoulade. Our fillet of Hawaiian wahoo was well over an inch thick: firm and sweet-fleshed with a savory crust from the grill. French fries are guaranteed to be Idaho russets. On a subsequent visit, we were thrilled by a one-pound prime rib, slow-roasted and rubbed with herbs. A marinated "biergarten" filet mignon was deliriously tender . . . if somewhat painfully priced (currently $42).

The dessert list is short, and it includes huckleberry cheesecake and Cascade Creamery huckleberry ice cream.

## El Gallo Giro

482 W. 3rd St.
Kuna, ID

208-922-5169
www.elgallogirokuna.com
LD | $

A cheerful restaurant whose name translates as "the fighting rooster," this Treasure Valley gem southwest of Boise and just a few minutes from I-84 serves superb true-Mex food. Start with *pozole* (hominy-pork soup), *campenchana* (octopus and shrimp in a garlic-lime marinade) or freshly made guacamole accompanied by chips and salsa. Quaff a Mexican beer or creamy-sweet *horchata* (rice milk), then move on to a beautiful plate of chicken molé blanketed with intense chile-chocolate sauce or fish tacos on soft tortillas. *Molcajetes*, served in lava rock bowls, are a dining event. Even the refried beans are extra-good, sprinkled with crumbled cotija cheese.

From what we could see on other people's tables, the more familiar Tex-Mex meals are mighty tempting: enchiladas, chimichangas, fajitas, et cetera. El Gallo Giro's little tacos, selling for a dollar apiece, are local legend. You can have them filled with steak, pork, goat, cheek, tongue, chicken, or tripe.

One reason people return again and again, other than the food, is the hospitality of Enrique Contreras, who is known for circulating around the dining room to say hello to old friends and welcome new ones.

## Goldy's Breakfast Bistro

108 S. Capitol Blvd.
Boise, ID

208-345-4100
www.goldysbreakfastbistro.com
BL | $$

Who couldn't love Goldy's "Create Your Own Breakfast Combo"? Select a main course, which can be eggs, chicken-fried steak, or a salmon fillet, then take your pick from long lists of meats, potatoes, and breads. Among the not-to-be-missed meats are habanero chicken sausage, Basque chorizo, and pork sausage infused with sage. The potato roster includes not only hash browns and sweet-potato hash browns but also red-flannel hash (spuds, beets, and bacon) and cheese grits. Among available breads are fresh-baked biscuits, sourdough, and cinnamon raisin walnut.

Hollandaise sauce is fantastic: smooth and fluffy with an ethereal lemon perfume. It comes on several variations of eggs Benedict. There's eggs Blackstone (Black Forest ham and tomato); a dilled salmon fillet blanketed with slivers of cucumber and sauce; even a veggie benny, which is sauce over broccoli, asparagus, and tomato. Other choice breakfast items: frittatas, breakfast burritos, cinnamon rolls, and sticky buns.

A stylish little place with an open kitchen, Goldy's can be maddeningly crowded, making meal service less than speedy, and on weekends expect to wait for a table. But if your goal is having the best breakfast in Boise, this is the place to go.

## Hoot Owl Cafe

30784 Hwy. 200         208-265-9348
Ponderay, ID            BL | $

Looking for a unique local drink? Have a huckleberry lemonade at the Hoot Owl Cafe. Looking for a really hearty breakfast? Biscuits, made each morning, are served plain to go with eggs and such, or as a meal, smothered with sausage gravy. They also are the foundation for Redneck Eggs Benedict, in which sausage patties substitute for Canadian bacon and gravy replaces hollandaise. (Note: The day's supply of biscuits can be gone before lunch.)

Hoot Owl's rib-sticking gravy is also available atop an order of hash browns. If you want something seriously filling, consider Hash Browns Supreme: spuds and scrambled eggs, onions, peppers, tomatoes, mushrooms, spinach, zucchini, and chopped fresh garlic, with salsa on the side.

This is a made-from-scratch sort of place where nothing is trendy but everything is a cut above: fresh corned beef hash sizzled as crusty as you request, plate-wide pancakes, gnarled chicken-fried steaks. Vegans can order Hash Browns Supreme made without eggs.

The Hoot Owl opens at 5 in the morning, shortly after which it is populated by locals drinking coffee and enjoying one another's company.

## *Hudson's

207 Sherman Ave.                   208-664-5444
Coeur d'Alene, ID                  L | $

"Pickle and onion?" the counterman will ask when you order a hamburger, a double hamburger, or a double cheeseburger at Hudson's, a counter-only diner that has been a Coeur d'Alene institution since 1907, when Harley Hudson opened a quick-eats lunch tent on the town's main drag.

Your garnish selection is called out to grill man Todd Hudson, Harley's great-grandson, who slices the raw onion to order, using his knife blade to hoist the thin, crisp disc from the cutting board to the bun bottom; then, deft as a Benihana chef, he cuts eight small circles from a pickle and arrays them in two neat rows atop the onion. When not wielding his knife, Todd hand-forms each burger, as it is ordered, from a heap of lean ground beef piled in a gleaming silver pan adjacent to his griddle. All this happens at warp speed as customers enjoy the mesmerizing show from the sixteen seats at Hudson's long counter and from the small standing area at the front of the restaurant, where new arrivals await stool vacancies.

Each patty is cooked until it develops a light crust from the griddle but retains a high amount of juice inside. One in a bun makes a balanced sandwich. Two verge on overwhelming beefiness. Chef Hudson sprinkles on a dash of salt, and when the hamburger is presented, you have one more choice to make: which condiment? Three squeeze bottles are deployed adjacent to each napkin dispenser along the counter. One is hot mustard, the other is normal ketchup, the third is Hudson's spicy ketchup, a thin orange potion for which the recipe is a guarded secret. "All I can tell you is that there is no horseradish in it," the counterman reveals.

There are no side dishes at all: no French fries, no chips, no slaw, not a leaf of lettuce in the house. And other than the fact that a glass case holds slices of pie for dessert, there is nothing more to say about Hudson's. In the last century it has honed a simple perfection.

## Java on Sherman

324 E. Sherman Ave.               208-667-0010
Coeur d'Alene, ID               www.javaonsherman.com
                                 BL | $

Years ago during a week in Coeur d'Alene, we started every day at Java on Sherman, and fell in love with it. We sampled breakfast at other cafés and diners around town, but none were as compelling as this stylish storefront coffeehouse, where Seattle-level caffeine connoisseurship combines with muffin mastery. All the usual drip-brewed and espresso-based beverages are expertly made, supplemented by house specialties that range from the Hammerhead (coffee with a double dose of espresso) to the sublime Bowl of Soul, which is a balance of coffee and espresso with a tantalizing sprinkle of chocolate and cinnamon served in a big ceramic bowl.

Java offers a repertoire of hot breakfasts, including bulgur wheat with apples and raisins, non-instant oatmeal, and eggs scrambled then steamed at the nozzle of the espresso machine; but it's the baked goods that have won Idahoans' hearts: handsome scones, sweet breads, and sour-cream muffins, plus a trademarked thing known as a lumpy muffin—big chunks of tart apple with walnuts and raisins all suspended in sweet cinnamon cake. Considerably more top than base, this muffin breaks easily into sections that are not quite dunkable, but are coffee's consummate companion.

## Jimmy's Down the Street

1613 E. Sherman Ave.  
Coeur d'Alene, ID

208-765-3868  
www.jimmysdownthestreet.com  
BL | $

For a hearty breakfast in Coeur d'Alene, you can't beat Jimmy's Down the Street. Locals congregate at this welcoming counter-and-table town café for such rib-stickers as a chicken-fried steak skillet with chunky fried potatoes and cheese and a couple of eggs, plus oversized biscuits and cream gravy. Pecan rolls are big, flat mesas of cake-rich dough, topped with a slurry of caramel glaze and chopped nuts. French toast, made with sourdough bread, can be had stuffed with sweet cream cheese and topped with berries and whipped cream. The day we went, it was Meat Lovers Scramble Day—a scramble made with three eggs, bacon, ham, and sausage, topped with cheese.

Breakfast is served all day, and lunch begins at 10 a.m. There are seven-ounce burgers, including a summer-only chili cheeseburger and patty melt on grilled rye. The signature dish is chicken and dumplings, which is copious although fairly bland. A more exciting choice among gigantic lunch possibilities is the John Wayne sandwich, which is a half foot of chicken-fried steak, bacon, fried dill pickles, onion rings, and a bunch of condiments. Not a lot of finesse here, but plenty of flavors!

For dessert you can have a bowl of ice cream, an individually sized apple or pecan pie, or a deep-fried pecan roll.

## Leku Ona

117 S. 6th St.

Boise, ID

208-345-6665

www.lekuonaid.com

LD | $$$

Located on what Boisians know as the Basque Block, Leku Ona is both a five-room boutique hotel and an adjoining restaurant celebrating the hearty, high-spiced cuisine of the people of the Pyrenees. Unlike many of the region's Basque restaurants, which serve only groaning-board, family-style meals, this Old World ode offers a regular menu from which each customer is free to choose an appetizer (perhaps Urdaiazpikoa, aka Serrano ham), a soup (red bean and chorizo, please), and an entree, which can range from whole squid cooked in its ink to honeycomb tripe or lamb shank. Prices are high on the Roadfood scale (dinner entrees in the $20+ range); service is suave and each dish is exemplary.

For those who want the more traditional Basque-hotel experience, Leku Ona does offer family-style feeds of soup, salad, and hot bread, followed by battered codfish and chef's paella, French fries, and your choice of lamb stew, pork chops, or roast chicken, sirloin steak, pork loin, or meatballs. Drink choices include Pagoa (a Basque beer) in lager, red ale, and stout. There's also a *pinxtos* (aka tapas) bar featuring small portions of such savories as leek pancakes, beef tongue, and cod croquettes. For dessert: *madari egosiak*, a lurid dish of sweetened pears poached in red wine.

## Westside Drive-In

1939 W. State St.

Boise, ID

208-342-2957

LD | $

A drive-in owned by "Chef Lou" Aaron, who has a regular cooking segment on Boise's KTVB and is the creator of a dessert called the Idaho Ice Cream Potato, Westside is a place people come to eat (off their dashboards or on the patio's picnic tables) and to take home such Chef Lou specialties as prime rib, pastas, and salads. The drive-in fare includes crisp-fried shrimp and fish and chips and a roster of extraordinary made-to-order hamburgers that are thick and crusty and juicy inside, nothing like franchised fast-food junkburgers. There are doubles, deluxes, Cajun burgers, guacamole burgers, and Maui burgers. We like a good ol' cheeseburger, preferably with lettuce and tomato. It comes wrapped in wax paper for easy eating. With French fries, you get the sweet dip called fry sauce . . . which many like on burgers too.

In honor of his home state, Chef Lou offers "the biggest bakers in the valley," which are one-pound Super Spuds available simply saturated with butter or loaded with chili, cheese, and onions. To drink, there are fine milk shakes, including huckleberry and black raspberry.

## Wolf Lodge Inn

12025 E. Frontage Rd. (Exit 22 off I-90)
Coeur d'Alene, ID

208-664-6665
www.wolflodgecda.com
D | $$$

Here are meat-and-potatoes meals of Homeric scale. A vast red barn-board roadhouse just yards from the highway, this exuberant Wild West domain features oilcloth-clad tables and walls festooned with trophy animal heads, bleached bovine skulls, antique tools, old beer posters, and yellowing newspaper clippings of local-interest stories. It is a sprawling place with miscellaneous booths and dining nooks in several rooms; at the back of the rearmost dining area is a stone barbecue pit where tamarack firewood burns a few feet below the grate. On this grate lie sizzling slabs of beef, ranging from a ten-ounce filet mignon to the Rancher, which is forty-four ounces of porterhouse and sirloin. (Seafood is also available, cooked over the wood.)

Cowboy-cuisine aficionados start supper with a plate of "swinging steak"—sliced and crisp-fried bull testicles, served with cocktail sauce and lemon wedges. We relished a bowl of truly homey vegetable beef soup that was as thick as stew with hunks of carrot, potato, beef, green pepper, and onion. Dinners come with saucy "buckaroo" beans, a twist of *krebel* (fried bread), and baked or fried potatoes, the latter excellent steak fries, each of which is one-eighth of a long Idaho baker that has been sliced end-to-end and fried so that it develops a light, crisp skin and creamy insides.

There is a second Wolf Lodge Inn in Spokane, Washington.

## Candel's By-Way Café

36619 U.S. Highway 87          406-566-2992

Stanford, MT          BLD | $

Candel's pies won't win any beauty contests. They are too delicate to stay intact for long. That's OK with us! The sour cream raisin pie here is one of the best anywhere, with a wicked tangy-sweet character. The crust underneath a slice of warm peach pie we got one morning before it cooled was so melt-in-mouth good that we wound up hunting stray little slivers on the empty plates. "Why are these pies so good?" we called out from our counter seats, quite literally ecstatic from finding them. Sheila Candelaria, who runs the place with her husband, Mike, credited them to her mother, from whom she learned to bake growing up on a ranch seventeen miles south of town. But pies aren't the only reason we love this place.

"We cut the steaks, we make our seasoning mixes, even our chicken fingers are from scratch," Sheila told us, singing especially high praises of the chunky, garlic-studded salsa that accompanies the Mexican food Mike makes. At this point, post-pie lunch seemed essential.

Mike's beef-and-bean burrito is smothered with orange-hued chili Colorado that tastes like pure peppers and spice. We could hear our chicken-fried steak getting pounded tender through the pass-through window to the kitchen, and rather than coming sheathed in the typical thick batter coat and smothered under gluey gravy, this one has a thin, brittle crust. It sits atop a puddle of refined white gravy with a pepper punch.

Sitting at a table where the view out the front window is the fronts of parked pickup trucks, a few everyday customers told us just how much they appreciate this place. Everyone in Stanford comes here to eat and to meet and linger over coffee and conversation. As we paid our bill at the cash register we noticed a book of blank, non-personalized checks from the Basin State Bank: for customers who don't have cash.

## Dash Inn

206 NE Main St.          406-535-3892
Lewistown, MT            LD | $

Long before foodies knew about paninis, the Dash Inn made its reputation on a burger known as the Wagon Wheel: a beef patty that gets cooked and put between slices of bread, then grilled until the bread gets crisp. There are singles, doubles, cheese Wagon Wheels, and Western Wagon Wheels; there also are regular bunned hamburgers, twin burgers, triple burgers, and pizza burgers. If for some reason you are not in the mood for a hamburger, the Dash Inn also serves many other sandwiches, including the Montana-born Pork Chop John sandwich and a Sourdough Dash that is Swiss cheese, bacon, tomato, and mayonnaise on grilled sourdough bread. Fried chicken is sold by the piece and bucket.

On the side, choose from among tater tots, French fries, curly fries, and potato wedges, and while there are smoothies, milk shakes, and floats to drink, do consider soda pop. Offering both Coke and Pepsi products, the Dash Inn will doctor up your favorite drink with flavored syrup, including lime, chocolate, and cherry. Blythe Butler, who first alerted us to this jolly place, wrote that the most popular potation was Coke with Hot-N-Tot, which is cinnamon syrup. She also suggested rum syrup in Mountain Dew.

The Dash Inn is strictly drive-through, all food served in paper bags. There is plenty of space around the restaurant to park and eat.

## *Eddie's Supper Club

3725 2nd Ave. N.
Great Falls, MT

406-453-1616
LD | $$

Eddie's is supper-club dining at its finest, patronized since 1944 by generations of Montanans who come to have cocktails and steaks in comfort.

There are two halves to it: a coffee shop, which is lighter-feeling, more casual, and with a menu that includes sandwiches, and the more serious restaurant, which has a big-deal menu of beef and seafood.

We like sitting in the supper club if only for its décor: large, handsome pictures of horses, all kinds of them: trotters in action, a bucking horse tossing a cowboy, western horses at work tending cattle. The picture at the back of the room, which has a horse's head in the foreground and a herd of cows in back, is especially beguiling. "We call him Mr. Ed," our waitress said. "His eyes follow you all around the room."

Booths are comfortable, lights are low, and the staff are able pros. Steaks are grand. "Tastes just like that old Marlboro Cowboy cooked it over the campfire," advises the menu. Our waitress told us that the secret of the steaks is not the fire, but the house's special wine marinade. This seeps into the meat and gives it a special tang, also coating the surface so the exterior of the steak develops a crunchy, caramelized crust as it cooks. The T-bone we ate was spectacularly good. And an off-the-menu hamburger, which has the marinade folded into the meat, was wild.

## Matt's Place

2339 Placer St.
Butte, MT

406-782-8049
LD | $

A virtual time machine, Matt's of Butte, Montana, looks like it might not have changed at all since opening in 1930. The state's oldest drive-in has a short, curved counter and a bright-red, waist-high Coke machine from which you fetch your own bottle from icy waters. Hamburgers sizzle in the back kitchen; milk shake mixers whir, and soda jerks ply seltzer and syrup dispensers to brew effervescent potions. If you are not in the mood for a pork chop sandwich (Montana's passion) or an ordinary hamburger, Matt's offers custom burgers, including one topped with fried eggs and a "nutburger" spread with mayonnaise and a fistful of chopped peanuts.

## Pamida Pharmacy (Cole Drug)

136 McLeod St.                    406-932-5316

Big Timber, MT                    L | $

More than a decade ago, cruising through the quiet town of Big Timber, we could not resist stopping at the lunch counter of what was then the Cole Drug Store. Although the place locals continue to call Cole Drug has become a Pamida Pharmacy, its menu remains the same as it was back when we first faced the challenge of a Big Timber sundae (nine scoops of ice cream and all the toppings in the house). During a more recent visit, we ate more modestly and enjoyed a perfectly made black-and-white soda and a huckleberry sundae. Huckleberries are big in the Plains states, and their intense fruity flavor makes for an ideal ice cream topping. We were also impressed with the good crunch of the nuts on top.

It is a quiet, soul-satisfying pleasure to sit at the boomerang-pattern Formica counter and chat with the soda-fountain mixologists as well as customers who walk in for sodas and sundaes or to avail themselves of the house blood pressure monitor. We can't imagine anyone's blood pressure getting too high in this nice place in a nice town in a very nice part of the world.

## Pekin Noodle Parlor

117 S. Main                       406-782-2217

Butte, MT                         D | $

Pekin Noodle Parlor is a relic of Butte's boom days as a mining town, when the small street out back was known as China Alley. An ancient sign on the wall says, "Famous Since 1916." Climb a small dark staircase to the second floor and you will be escorted to your own curtained dining cubicle. The setting suggests exotic intrigue, like an old Montana version of the *Shanghai Express*. When the food comes from the kitchen, it is announced by the rumble of the waitress's rolling trolley along the wood-plank floor; the curtain whisks aside, and behold! Here is a vista of foreign food the likes of which most devotees of Asian cookery forgot about fifty years ago.

Chop suey and chow mein are mild, thick, and harmless; fried shrimp are girdled by a pad of breading and served on leaves of lettuce with French fried potatoes; sweet-and-sour ribs drip pineapple-flavored syrup; and the house specialty—noodles—come in a shimmering clear broth with chopped scallions on top. Get the noodles plain or accompanied by strips of pork, beef, or chicken served on the side in a little bowl with half a hard-boiled egg.

The after-dinner drink menu that time forgot includes Separators, Stingers, White Russians, and Pink Squirrels. The thing to drink before a meal is a Ditch—Montanese for whiskey and water.

## Red Lodge Cafe

16-18 S. Broadway          406-446-1619
Red Lodge, MT             BLD | $

Come for breakfast and you can have a jumbo omelet, ham steak, or blueberry buckwheat pancakes and sip coffee long enough to eavesdrop on the conversations of locals and passers-through. Lunch is such stalwart items as country-fried steak and potatoes and buffalo burgers, as well as deluxe hamburgers. For dessert, everybody has pie: apple or berry pie or, best of all, banana cream pie, so jiggly that it eats better with a spoon than a fork.

The Red Lodge Cafe is eager to please with all modern facilities, yet ingenuous like a mid-twentieth-century tourist stop. It has a western theme, but there is something for everyone from morning to night: keno, weekend karaoke, and the strangest-shaped pool table we've ever seen. Lighting fixtures above the dining room are made of wagon wheels, the ceiling is stamped tin, and the walls are bedecked with painted wooden totem poles and spectacular murals of scenery along the 11,000-foot Beartooth Highway that leads from here to Yellowstone. The two-lane highway is closed by snow in the winter, but once it's open, it is a spectacular trip.

## Rex Restaurant

2401 Montana Ave.         406-245-7477
Billings, MT              www.therexbillings.com
                          LD | $$

Montana Avenue in Billings has become a restaurant row with a handful of trendy places drawing people back downtown for dinner. One of the old reliables in the area is the Rex, a vintage hotel dining room that has been cleaned up but not drastically modernized to be one of the city's most respected upscale eating establishments. Unless you sit on the breezy patio, accommodations are dark and clubby, all varnished wood, brass, raw brick, and cut glass under an old stamped-tin ceiling.

Start with immense, thick-cut onion rings or a hunk of iceberg lettuce blanketed with blue cheese or thousand island dressing. Then move on to beef. Prime rib is a beauty: thick, juice-laden, and full-flavored. For those not intent on ingesting maximum red-meat protein, the broad menu includes pizzas made to order, sandwiches and big salads, shrimp, crab, salmon, and lobster. Lunch can be as inexpensive as a $10 half-pound bar burger or an $8.50 Caesar salad; beef dinners range to near $40.

We were introduced to the Rex many years ago by a local saddle maker whose doctor had told him he needed to eat less beef, so he ordered cream-sauced pasta, which looked to us like it was richer than a rib-eye steak!

## Sarah's

310 N. 29th
Billings, MT

406-256-5234
www.sarahsmexfood.com
BLD | $

Sarah's is a little hard to figure out, but worth the effort for some of the best Mexican food in the Plains. Here's the way it works. Upon entering, go to the back of the room to an order window. At the right of the window is a large posted menu. Choose your burritos, tacos, or enchiladas and tell the nice lady who steps out of the kitchen what you want. Then go to the cash register and pay for it. Now move over to the condiment bar and help yourself to Styrofoam cups full of hot sauce or mild sauce, onions, or jalapeños to carry to a table, where a basket of chips is set out along with lots of napkins. When you are halfway through the chips, the meal arrives.

We especially love the taquitos, which would be called flautas in much of the Southwest: tightly wrapped, crisp-fried tortilla tubes containing moist shredded beef. They are served with a cup of garlicky guacamole. The red smothered beef burrito is a mighty meal, loaded with big hunks of beef. Our one complaint is that the plastic forks provided are only barely up to severing the tortilla wrap and beef inside.

## Stella's

110 N. 29th St.
Billings, MT

406-248-3060
BL | $

The back of Stella's is a large bakery that supplies breads, cakes, cookies, bagels, and rolls to local restaurants and stores, but if you're in town for breakfast, why not eat at the source? Stella's cinnamon rolls are monumental, each one bigger than a softball. The rolls are made fresh each day, but when you order one, it is microwaved so a big glob of butter set atop it is melting when the roll arrives at the table. Heating also tends to give the caramel glaze on top a chewy texture that makes it a fork-and-knife pastry. Even bigger than the cinnamon roll is Stella's giant white caramel roll—fourteen ounces of sweet dough served with a small tub of whipped butter.

Everything is large at Stella's, especially pancakes, which are known as monster cakes. "You've got to see 'em to believe 'em," the menu boasts. Each one is a good twelve inches, edge to edge, and yet they have a nice light texture that makes it easy to eat a couple, or maybe even three. You have your choice of buttermilk or wheat batter, and if you can polish off four of them in a single sitting, you get a free cinnamon roll! We are especially fond of the very small print underneath the pancake listing on the menu: "Diet Smuckers jelly & syrups available upon request." So these would qualify as diet food?!

There are normal-sized breakfasts at Stella's: omelets, hot cereals (oatmeal, seven-grain, and Stella's homemade grits), and egg sandwiches; the lunch menu includes such regular-sized items as club and sub sandwiches, chili by the bowl, and a French dip, as well as hamburgers that range up to the half-pound Ziggyburger, served on an outsized bun to match.

For dessert? Bread pudding made with Stella's homemade breads, please.

## Willow Creek Cafe & Saloon

21 Main St.                             406-285-3698
Willow Creek, MT                        D (reservations advised) | $$

Reservations advised? In Willow Creek, population 209?

You bet. Here is a way, way out-of-the-way restaurant that attracts customers from Three Forks and Manhattan, MT, even Bozeman, some fifty miles away. They come for pillowy beef steaks and chicken-fried steaks, hamburgers and homemade soups, pies and cakes made that day, even such upscale suppers as pork marsala and saltimbocca. There's always prime rib on weekend nights, but the one never-to-miss meal is barbecued ribs, anointed with a brilliant honey-mustard glaze that teases maximum flavor from the pork. A chalkboard lists the day's specials and featured wines, which oenophile friends tell us are a good deal.

The place itself is a hoot: a sunflower-yellow house that started life in 1912 as the Babcock Saloon and has been a pool hall, barber shop, and a butcher shop. Dining facilities are small indeed, with room for only a few dozen customers at a time. The old-fashioned print wallpaper and antique wood fixtures make it feel like a trip back in time. If you're heading for Willow Creek, don't worry about finding it. It is the only business in town.

## Bohemian Cafe

1406 S. 13th St.          402-342-9838
Omaha, NE                 www.bohemiancafe.net
                          LD | $$

The Bohemian Cafe is an immensely cheerful place, a vast, multiroom eating hall decorated with colorful old-country woodwork and pictures of men and women in traditional peasant attire; tables are patrolled by veteran professional waitresses in bright-red dirndl skirts. "*Vitáme Vás,*" meaning "We welcome you," is the house motto of this 1924-vintage Omaha landmark. Whether you are an old-timer who came with your parents decades ago or a visiting fireman who wants a fun-time meal with polka music setting the beat in the dining room, you will feel welcome.

The traditional way to begin a meal is with a cup of liver dumpling soup, which is homely and homey; we also love the plain-dumpling, chicken-stock soup that is often available as an alternate. Every meal also begins with a basket of chewy sour rye bread. The big menu includes American-style steaks and seafood, a quartet of specials every day, and traditional Czech specialties. Foremost among the kitchen's accomplishments is roast duck— half a bird with crisp skin and flavorful meat that pulls off the bone with ease. We are fond of the sauerbraten, which is a stack of pot-roast-tender hunks of beef that are a joy to pull apart with the tines of a fork. We also like the Czech goulash, a vivid red, smoky pork stew. There is a large choice of side dishes, but the two for which the Bohemian Cafe is best known are dumplings and kraut. The former is a pair of saucer-sized slices of doughy matter covered with whatever gravy your main course demands; the latter is a fetching sweet and sour mix, thick as pudding, dotted with caraway seeds. Whatever entree you choose, it will come flanked by dumplings and kraut—an awesome presentation that is a challenge to all but the mightiest appetite.

Paper place mats remind diners that this restaurant is home of the Bohemian Girl Jim Beam commemorative bourbon bottle (there is a huge collection of Jim Beam commemoratives in the entryway), and the mats also list the lyrics to the house song, which has been used in radio advertisements:

> *Dumplings and kraut today*
> *At Bohemian Cafe*
> *Draft beer that's sparkling, plenty of*
> *parking*
> *See you at lunch, OK?*

## Crystal Cafe

4601 Dakota Ave.      402-494-5471
South Sioux City, NE      Always open | $

At 8:30 in the morning at the Crystal Cafe, men and women who are starting the day (and some finishing a long night) converse about issues that include jackknives, deadheading, log books, and speed traps. They are professional truckers; the Crystal Cafe is where they come not only to eat but for fuel and over-the-road supplies. It is an open-all-night truck stop just west of the Missouri River.

Each place is set with a coffee cup and a water glass. The waitress flips your cup right-side up and pours coffee and refills throughout breakfast. The cuisine is haute highway: big food, served in abundance. Plate-wide buttermilk pancakes, chicken-fried steak with a patty of oily hash browns, sausage gravy on big, crumbly biscuits are some of the morning specials. The morning item we especially like is the caramel sweet roll, which is thick and goopy. At lunch, you can have a breaded pork tenderloin, a bowl of chili, or a ten-ounce king-of-the-road Texaco Burger. Crystal Cafe's sour cream raisin pie is one of the Midwest's best: dense, creamy, and sweet, crowned with ethereal meringue.

# Gering Bakery

1446 10th St.          308-436-5500

Gering, NE          www.geringbakery.com

BL | $

A small sign in the window of the Gering Bakery advertises cabbage burgers. Considering that we were in Nebraska, home of the *runza* and the *bierock*—bread pockets stuffed with ground beef, cabbage, and spice—the sign caused us to come to a sudden halt and investigate. *Runzas* and *bierocks* are nineteenth-century immigrant fare, but in the mid-1950s, the name Runza was trademarked and is now the lead item at the eponymous restaurant chain. Runza's Runzas are OK, but the monotony of the identical restaurants makes us depressed.

Gering Bakery, on the other hand, is the real deal. Sure enough, the advertised cabbage burger is a non-corporate *runza,* bigger and more delicious. Available in bulk or singly, heated up by the kind lady behind the counter, they are fully enclosed pillows of tender bread inside of which is a spill of juicy beef and peppery bits of cabbage and onion. Delicious, real comfort food.

Our hearts won over by the cabbage burger, we had to sample some of the good-looking sweet pastries on the bakery shelves. We liked the crisp-edged old-fashioned cake donuts and fell instantly in love with something called a peanut butter pretzel. That's a twisted piece of pastry dough generously frosted with sweet peanut butter icing.

Most business is takeout, but Gering Bakery offers a few window tables as well as help-yourself coffee and a cooler full of soda.


# Joe Tess Place

5424 S. 24th St.          402-733-4638

Omaha, NE          www.joetessplace.com

LD | $

Roadfood warriors Bruce Bilmes and Sue Boyle pointed us to Joe Tess Place (no possessive apostrophe), which bills itself as "Home of the Famous Fish Sandwich." It is a restaurant, tavern, and fresh seafood market on the south side of Omaha that serves a fish little known on dining tables outside the region: carp. Like the herring that swim upriver in North Carolina, carp are fish-flavored fish that get deep-fried long enough that their fine bones become part of the soft, juicy flesh underneath the crunchy batter crust. The fried pieces of carp are available on rye in the famous sandwich or doubled up in the double fish sandwich. (The connoisseur's condiment is hot pepper sauce.) Or you can have a dinner-sized portion bedded on rye on a plate with coleslaw and discs of fried potato, the latter known here as jacket fries. Catfish is another specialty. Like the carp, mudpuppies are trucked in live from Minnesota and you can see them swim in the tanks of the live fish market. For those with a less adventurous palate, the Joe Tess menu offers chicken (white or dark), grilled salmon, and fried shrimp.

There is a full bar's worth of beverages to drink, plus the western working man's version of a Bloody Mary, known as red beer: beer and tomato juice. Bruce and Sue noted, "Any restaurant that serves upside-down cake gets bonus points from us." Besides pineapple upside-down cake larded with pecans, the dessert menu includes a swell cream cheese bundt cake.

Ambience is all-fish, all the time and everywhere. The bar is shaped like a boat and walls are decked with taxidermied fish of every size and shape as well as pictures, posters, and nautical memorabilia.

## *Rosita's

1205 E. Overland      308-632-2429
Scottsbluff, NE      LD | $

Here are great corn chips, nearly as three-dimensional as a sopaipilla, fried so they puff up and become airy triangles with fragile skin. An order arrives almost too hot to handle; they come plain or as the foundation for the house specialty called panchos—a circle of them topped with frijoles, melted cheese, guacamole, and jalapeños. Panchos are like nachos, but the chips' refined texture and their perfect poise between breakable and bendable give panchos character far more satisfying than any bar grub.

The same quick-fry technique makes Rosita's taco shells an ideal crispy-chewy wrap for beef or chicken with plenty of garnishes; flat tostadas are made the same way, and even taco salad includes the fine, fluffy chips.

Proprietor Rosemary Florez-Lerma credits her mother-in-law with the recipes that make this friendly Mexican café a standout in an area with an abundance of Mexican restaurants (the legacy of fieldworkers who came to pick beets). The cinnabar-red, garlic-charged salsa that starts every meal and chunky pico de gallo that dresses up any dish with a stunning spicy punch are especially memorable. We also are fond of Rosita's garlicky *menudo*, thick with puffs of *posole* and strips of tripe, sparkling with fresh lemon.

## Scotty's Drive-In

618 E. 27th St.                    308-635-3314
Scottsbluff, NE               LD | $

Scotty's menu features a picture of an anthropomorphic serving of French fries talking to an equally humanoid beverage, the scene captioned, "This spud's for you." These are indeed very good potatoes: thin and crisp-edged. They're an ideal companion for burgers that range from singles to bacon-double-cheese to quarter-pounders and half-pounders and a Bluff Burger that is three meat patties, cheese, and all appropriate condiments.

The menu lists lots of sandwiches beyond burgers, including fish, chicken, pork, and shrimp. The most interesting alternative is Scotty's Tasty Tavern, a sloppy joe that echoes the passion of neighboring Iowa's Siouxland for ground meat sandwiches. Scotty's Taverns are small (and cheap, at about $1 each); we saw a group of large local boys each ingesting a half dozen of them along with a family pack of French fries for supper.

Roadfood.com contributor Buffetbuster, whose sweet tooth is infallible, says that his favorite items at Scotty's are the extremely thick milk shakes.

## Sehnert's Bakery & Bieroc Cafe

312 Norris Ave.                 308-345-6500
McCook, NE                 www.bieroccafe.com
                              BL | $

Sehnert's is a full-service bakery with donuts, crème horns, apple fritters, cinnamon buns, peanut-butter-frosted sweet rolls, and bread by the loaf. Just before Christmas, fruited stollens are a specialty, available by mail order.

Locals are the clientele; they come to chat 'n' chew, drink coffee and espresso, and eat such sandwiches as the Apple Planter (turkey, bacon, provolone, and apples with honey mustard on focaccia bread) and the Happy German (a Reuben, available in a lettuce wrap as well as on rye). For Roadfood devotees in search of unique regional specialties, the star attraction is a unique Great Plains pocket meal known as a *bieroc*—a packet of soft bread enclosing seasoned ground beef and your choice of either sauerkraut or cabbage. In the same genre as an Upper Peninsula pasty, a Cajun meat pie, and a Mexican empanada, the *bieroc* is moist and satisfying—truly homey.

Sehnert's also is a live music venue. For an up-to-date schedule of performers, visit their website.

## Shirley's Diner

5325 S. 139th Plz.　　　　　402-896-6515
Omaha, NE　　　　　　　　www.shirleysdineromaha.com
　　　　　　　　　　　　　BLD | $

If you haven't spent some time in Omaha, or if you are not a devoted visitor to Roadfood.com, you might not know about a specialty unique to cafés and diners in eastern Nebraska known as the Frenchie: a cheese sandwich that is batter-dipped and deep-fried. At Shirley's it is spelled Frenchy, and the batter dip includes crumbled cornflakes, adding extra crunch to what becomes a crisp coat surrounding an interior of Texas toast and a molten mix of jack and American cheese. Frenchys are available for breakfast as well as lunch and dinner.

The rest of the menu is familiar heartland fare: pork tenderloin sandwiches, hot beef and hot turkey sandwiches, and an "atomic" chicken-fried steak, so named because it gets a hot-sauce dip. Desserts include deep-fried Oreos. Breakfast at Shirley's is a big deal, featuring hash browns that can be ordered country-style, topped with sausage gravy.

This restaurant is completely uninviting from the outside: a bland storefront in Millard Plaza. Inside, it is a hospitable town café with nostalgic 1950s décor.

## Taco Town

1007 W. 27th St.　　　　　308-635-3776
Scottsbluff, NE　　　　　　LD | $

Since the mid-twentieth century, Taco Town has been a favorite gathering place for locals, many of whom are descendants of the Mexican families who settled here to work on the vast beet farms surrounding Scottsbluff. While the inside seats are frequently buzzing with table-to-table conversations (a sign outside boasts "We're the Tac-O the Town!"), many customers simply drive through and pick up food at the window just as one would do at any humdrum junk-food franchise.

Despite a corporate appearance, Taco Town definitely is not Taco Bell. Pork chili, sold by the pint and quart, is a full-flavored homey stew. There are handsome plates of burritos, enchiladas, and flautas, and for $6.75 you can have a combo meal with all of the above plus rice and beans. The regular taco is a simple delight, its earthy corn shell audibly crisp but pliable enough that it doesn't shatter, loaded with a heap of ground beef filling that is creamy-rich and peppery. Each taco comes wrapped in paper that is twisted tight at both ends to keep it secure until you've found a parking place and are ready to unwrap it and dine off the dashboard. Soft-shell and super-soft-shell tacos also are available.

## Carol Widman's Candy Shop

4325 13th Ave. S.　　　　　　701-281-8664
Fargo, ND　　　　　　　　　www.carolwidmanscandy.com
　　　　　　　　　　　　　　$

Widman's has been the big name in Red River Valley candy for more than a century. It is especially well known for its unusual chocolate-covered savories that represent some of North Dakota's crops: wheat nuts, soybeans, sunflower seeds, and—best of all—potato chips. The chocolate-covered chips are called chippers, and they are an unlikely but compelling harmony of sweet and salt, melting chocolate and crunchy fried potato. Chippers are available enrobed in milk chocolate or semisweet dark chocolate, as well as strawberry, peanut butter, and butterscotch.

It is a joy to stop into the candy store in Fargo to inhale its chocolaty aroma and sample some of everything. If you are not coming to Fargo, Widman's will mail chocolates by the pound and gift-box. Because chocolate melts in hot weather, mail-order sales are available only between October 1 and May 1. As the lady behind Widman's counter told us, "If you are comfortable, the candy will be too."

## TNT's Diner

405 Main Ave. W.
West Fargo, ND

701-277-7062
BL | $

Thanks to Roadfood explorer Dale Fine for discovering TNT's Diner off the beaten path in West Fargo. Dale made special note of *klub,* a dish that was new to us: large potato dumplings served two-by-two with a ramekin of butter for dipping or pouring and a choice of either bacon or ham. Other menu highlights in this friendly small-town café are hot beef and hot turkey sandwiches with real mashed potatoes and gravy, cabbage rolls, Swedish meatballs, and *knoephla* (dumpling) soup every Friday.

And then there is dessert: at least a half-dozen homemade pies every day, among them that upper Midwest favorite, sour cream raisin, which Dale described as "slightly more sour than sweet . . . loaded with nutmeg, vanilla, and raisins." There are cookies and cheesecakes, brownies and fruit crisps, rice custard, and—most tempting of all—bread pudding blanketed with caramel sauce.

## Bobkat's Purple Pie Place

19 Mt. Rushmore Rd.        605-673-4070

Custer, SD        LD (closed in winter) | $

Yes, the restaurant is shockingly purple. And yes, pie is its specialty—really good pie. Sour cream raisin comes with a Cool Whip top, but once that's pushed aside, it's a just-right balance of sour cream and the sweetness of raisins and custard. Sturdy-crusted fruit pies are available filled with rhubarb, apple, and berries of all kinds; there is one called bumbleberry, which is a crazy-good mix of pretty much all the fruit in the house. Of course, fruit pies are better à la mode—maybe with huckleberry ice cream, when available. Better still if they are warm, which is achieved by briefly nuking a slice—not the best crust conditioner, but not a disaster, either.

Pie's the thing here, but there is a dining room in back and a pre-pie menu of sandwiches, soup, chili, and barbecue.

## Bob's

1312 W. 12th St.        605-336-7260

Sioux Falls, SD        www.bobscarryout.com

                                  BLD | $

Bob's was known as the Pickle Palace when it opened in 1944. Having gained fame as a hamburger destination, it became Ray's Drive-In, then finally Bob's in 1951. In 2000, Bob sold the business to Ben Weiland, who kept the name, which now in the twenty-first century is as well known for broasted chicken as it is for burgers.

Hamburgers start as round balls that get placed on the griddle then flattened with a spatula—but not too hard—to form thick patties with a good crust and a load of juice. If you are very hungry, you'll want to know about the Mega Bob Meal, which is a three-quarter-pound hamburger, along with three-quarters of a pound of French fries, a twenty-ounce soda, and a couple of cookies. You can buy broasted chicken by the piece, in a basket with spuds, slaw, and a roll, or as a 250-piece order to feed a hundred. Anyone who eats an entire chicken platter in an hour gets the meal free, plus a Bob's T-shirt and a $50 Bob's gift certificate. A platter is sixteen pieces, five potatoes, and rolls, along with a pint of gravy.

Breakfast is swell, especially when enjoyed from a stool at the curvy counter with a view of the grill. Of special note is a meal called Hash Browns Delight, which augments the crisp-fried spuds with steak, peppers, onion, mushrooms, and cheese. Thursday (and only Thursday) is caramel roll day.

## Edgar's

107 E. Main St. (Bus. Rt. 29)   605-356-3336
Elk Point, SD       www.edgarssoda.com
            L | $

With its pink-and-white tin ceiling, vintage wood booths, and steel-rod chairs for a scattering of tables, Edgar's is a charming little sweetshop where mixology is an art. Order a soda and observe: First, syrup is combined with a dab of ice cream at the bottom of a tulip glass, forming a sweetshop roux; next, soda is squirted in and mixed vigorously; penultimately, a globe of ice cream is gingerly floated on top; finally, a crown of whipped cream is applied and, to that, a single cherry. It's a beautiful sight, and while much of the soda will drip down the sides of the glass as soon as it is touched by a spoon, one cannot help but admire the confectionery perfectionism.

The same high standards apply to sundaes, malts, and shakes, and a long roster of more elaborate and daring delights that range from the relatively familiar turtle sundae (vanilla ice cream with hot caramel, chocolate syrup, and pecans) to the Rocket—an astonishingly vertical banana split that the menu promises "will send you for a blast!"

Edgar's menu includes practical how-to articles taken from the 1906 *Standard Manual of Soda and Other Beverages*. Among the suggestions are that a soda fountain attendant "should never stand watching the patrons drinking," and "should study each customer's desire and endeavor to remember the particular way in which he likes his drinks mixed and served." The year all this was written, the *Centerville Journal* declared Edgar's soda fountain one of the finest in the state, and over a century later, it has no peers.

## Murdo Drive In

| | |
|---|---|
| 212 Kennedy Ave. | 605-669-2972 |
| Murdo, SD | www.murdodrivein.com |
| | LD (summer only) \| $ |

Just a hop off Interstate 90 in the relatively food-barren middle of South Dakota, this eat shack serves nothing that is especially regional, but the burgers, chicken, and turtle ice cream are definitely worth a stop.

The menu is emblazoned with these watchwords: "We are not fast! We are good. We are cheerful. We are courteous. But we are not fast. For fast, go to Chicago. Here we are north of the 'tension line.' So relax." If you order broasted chicken, you will have a good twenty minutes to relax, because it is cooked to order and arrives at your place still sizzling hot. Likewise, burgers are not from pre-pressed patties, and the dessert/drink cyclones, which are something like milk shakes, are actually made with real fruit when available. Hans Bauman, who reviewed the friendly place at Roadfood.com, noted that his rhubarb cyclone was "delicious, from its creamy substrate to the tangy threads of freshly harvested rhubarb." Less crop-dependent cyclone flavors include banana split, banana pudding, Oreo, chocolate-covered cherry, and peanut butter crunch.

## Nick's Hamburger Shop

| | |
|---|---|
| 427 Main Ave. | 605-692-4324 |
| Brookings, SD | www.nickshamburgers.com |
| | LD \| $ |

Nick's is a Roadfood landmark for the itty-bitty hamburgers it has served since the early days of the slider, in 1929. The price of a Nickburger has gone up from a nickel to well over a dollar in the last fourscore and five years, and the restaurant, officially listed on the National Register of Historic Places, has gotten bigger; but the burgers are still buy-'em-by-the-sack lovelies, hand-formed and cooked on a grill with so much oil that they are virtually deep-fried. Onions are part of the formula, so the burger as well as Nick's itself is perfumed with the sweet smell of them caramelizing. They're small and wieldy enough that plates are extraneous; Nickburgers are presented on wax paper. We'd say three to five or a couple of doubles makes a nice meal. The ingestion record is thirty-four in a single sitting, set by a student from South Dakota State. Whoever beats the record eats free.

## Tea Steak House

215 S. Main St.
Tea, SD

605-368-9667
www.teasteakhouse.webs.com
LD | $$

The cushiony pound-plus T-bone oozes juice at the first poke of a knife. It's a good thing to order hash brown potatoes on the side to soak up the beef's seepage; crisp and oily, they are fine potatoes in their own right (much better than the foil-wrapped baked potato or uninteresting French fries). We also ordered filet mignon, which came splayed open and wrapped in bacon, and it was amazing just how different these two cuts of beef were: each excellent, but while the T-bone had a vivid, almost gamey smack and tight-knit texture that rewarded serious chewing, the filet was cream-gentle in flavor and wanted to melt on the tongue.

The Tea Steak House serves more than steak. You can eat chicken or ham, halibut, perch, lobster tails, or a Saint & Sinner supper of one lobster tail and one small sirloin. Don't ask us how any of that stuff tastes. When we're in Tea, we'll eat beef. Dessert is limited to cheesecake and ice cream.

The restaurant motto: "We're Glad You Brought Your Sugar to Tea."

## Tripp Sports Bowl Cafe

210 S. Main St.
Tripp, SD

605-935-6281
L | $

Tripp, South Dakota, population 631, is a small town in big country. A short jog off the highway takes you to Main Street, where the bowling alley and town café are one. We love this place where the locals eat (few travelers pass through Tripp at all), and where décor includes not only the bowling alleys themselves but trophies won by the likes of Doug Janssen (a 300 game!) and Dorothy Schnabel (267). The day we visited, a blackboard in the dining area listed the day's special as creamed chicken on toast—quintessential comfort food—but we were also intrigued by an item called the Dakota Burger.

The Dakota Burger turned out not to be a hamburger at all—at least if you define hamburger as a patty of ground beef—but rather, Tripp's version of that upper Midwest pleasure, hot beef. Junellia Meisenhoelder, chef and proprietor at the Sports Bowl Cafe, didn't tell us why the sandwich is known as a burger, but there is no point quibbling about labels; it is swell. Hot beef served with mashed potatoes and gravy is a frequent daily special at the Sports Bowl Cafe, and the Dakota Burger is a somewhat more wieldy variation on the theme: chunks of ultra-tender roast beef, warm enough to melt a slice of bright orange cheese placed atop them, piled into a grill-warmed bun. Simple and excellent!

## Chugwater Soda Fountain

314 1st St.                                 307-422-3222
Chugwater, WY                        www.chugwatersodafountain.com
                                                BLD | $

The year 2014 marks the hundredth anniversary of the storefront that houses Chugwater Soda Fountain, which lays claim to being the oldest operating soda fountain in Wyoming. A seat at the counter affords a view of Wendell the Elk (a trophy dating back to the 1940s) and an assortment of vintage milk-shake mixers, plus the opportunity to enjoy silver-beaker shakes and malts, sundaes, sodas, flavored Cokes, and ice cream served in cones and cups.

The town of Chugwater, population 244, has gained some fame as the home of Chugwater chili. Made from a Wyoming State Championship recipe purchased in 1986 by a group of townsfolk, there are two varieties available at the soda fountain: red and green. Both are more soup than stew, the red a mild mix of ground beef and beans in cinnabar broth, the green made with chicken in a bisquey liquid that does pack a half-alarm of heat.

Chugwater Soda Fountain also has a summer beer garden and a small package store.

## Lisa's

200 Greybull Ave.　　　　　　　307-765-4765
Greybull, WY 82426　　　　　　www.lisaswesterncuisine.com
　　　　　　　　　　　　　　　BLD | $$

As you travel west out of the Big Horn Mountains—or prepare to head east into them—the town of Greybull offers all sorts of attractions. These include a sprawling Museum of Flight and Aerial Fire Fighting with decommissioned airplanes on display, a museum of taxidermy, and Lisa's.

"In Wyoming when we say hearty, we mean hearty!" Lisa's menu crows. But it isn't so much the generous size of meals that makes this a worthwhile stop; it is the taste. Breakfasts include chunky corned beef hash, warm biscuits with luxurious sausage gravy, "puff scrambles," which are eggs stuffed into puff pastries and topped with hollandaise sauce, and side orders of crisp Indian fry bread. Breakfast Charlotta is a tortilla stuffed with potato hash, scrambled eggs, cheese, and pico de gallo, sided by beans and hash browns.

Lunch features such Southwest and Tex-Mex dishes as fajitas, enchiladas, chimichangas, and chiles rellenos, plus a catalog of sandwiches, half-pound hamburgers, salads, and a soup of the day.

We love the watchwords on Lisa's menu: "The original chefs of the Big Horns were of course the Native Americans. Cattle drives brought more South American influences such as pinto beans and peppers. At Lisa's, aromas of the past prevail . . . paying tribute to our Western Plains heritage and original chefs. Not all chefs live in the city!" Décor includes Navajo rugs, Mexican tiles, and walls of stucco and wood; a tree-shaded outdoor patio offers the opportunity to dine in crisp mountain air.

## Svilar's

173 Main St.　　　　　　　　307-332-4516
Hudson, WY　　　　　　　　D | $$$

Hudson, Wyoming, is hours from any interstate on the south edge of Wind River Reservation, where shaggy horses graze the flatlands by the Little Popo Agie River and derelict oil works are strewn across the hills. It is nothing but a short strip of bedraggled buildings with businesses that look to be defunct. But in the evenings, Friday and Saturday in particular, the old Main Street comes alive. A sign in one parking lot boasts "Welcome to Hudson: World's Finest Food." An overstatement, perhaps, but High Plains folk who travel the two-lanes through the land of the Arapahoe to dine at

Svilar's gladly attest to the fact that the little community is home to the finest beef in the Cowboy State.

Svilar's, a supper club that has been a culinary High Plains magnet since the middle of the last century, serves a full-course dinner that starts with relish tray and salad, then moves on to a hot-appetizer course of ravioli and stuffed cabbage (Serbian-style). Although chicken, shrimp, and lobster tails are available, the only appropriate entree is red meat, either steaks available in cuts from wee filet to multipound rib eye or great mesas of prime rib large enough to overhang a dinner plate. Maybe there's dessert, maybe not. We've never bothered to inquire, figuring that if we have any appetite at the end of the meal, we probably didn't order a large-enough piece of cow.

### The Wagon Box

103 N. Piney
Story, WY

307-683-2444
www.wagonbox.com
LD | $$$

A rustic inn with cabin accommodations, The Wagon Box also is a restaurant that attracts beef eaters from miles around. Start with a salad dressed with huckleberry vinaigrette, then plow into such big cuts of cow as prime rib up to a pound, filet mignon wrapped in bacon, and rib-eye steaks served with sautéed garlic and mushrooms. On the side, you can have potatoes your way: baked, mashed, baby reds, French fries, or made-to-order chips. There are all kinds of surf 'n' turf options and beef frowners can choose from a menu of shrimp, salmon, lobster tails, and crab legs. Whatever else you get, we highly recommend starting with prime rib mushroom soup when it is available. Cousin Johnny of Roadfood.com said it reminded him of beef Stroganoff in a bowl.

Dining facilities include a big stone fireplace and a cool outdoor patio surrounded by fragrant Ponderosa pines. Lunch can be had for $10–$15. Dinner tends to be north of $25.

# West Coast

California

*

Oregon

*

Washington

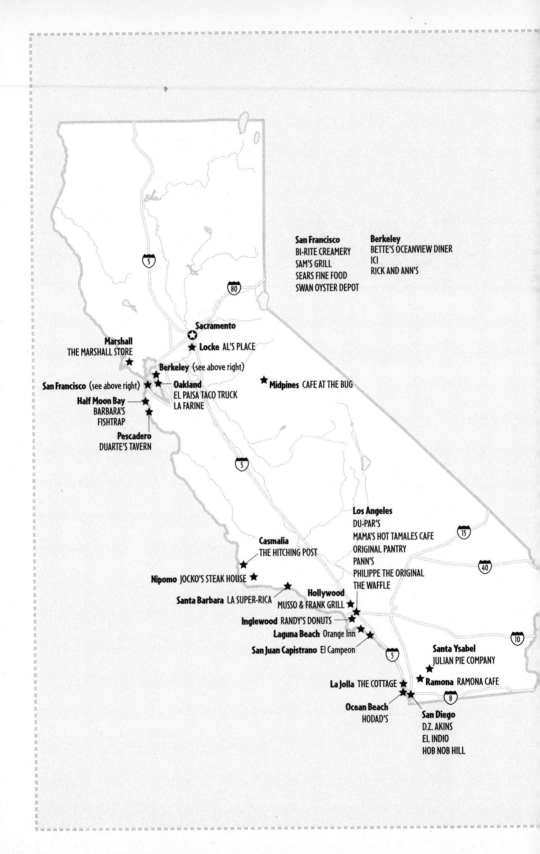

San Francisco
BI-RITE CREAMERY
SAM'S GRILL
SEARS FINE FOOD
SWAN OYSTER DEPOT

Berkeley
BETTE'S OCEANVIEW DINER
ICI
RICK AND ANN'S

Sacramento

Marshall
THE MARSHALL STORE

Locke  AL'S PLACE

Berkeley (see above right)

San Francisco (see above right)

Midpines  CAFE AT THE BUG

Oakland
EL PAISA TACO TRUCK
LA FARINE

Half Moon Bay
BARBARA'S
FISHTRAP

Pescadero
DUARTE'S TAVERN

Casmalia
THE HITCHING POST

Los Angeles
DU-PAR'S
MAMA'S HOT TAMALES CAFE
ORIGINAL PANTRY
PANN'S
PHILIPPE THE ORIGINAL
THE WAFFLE

Nipomo  JOCKO'S STEAK HOUSE

Santa Barbara  LA SUPER-RICA

Hollywood
MUSSO & FRANK GRILL

Inglewood  RANDY'S DONUTS

Laguna Beach  Orange Inn

San Juan Capistrano  El Campeon

Santa Ysabel
JULIAN PIE COMPANY

La Jolla  THE COTTAGE

Ramona  RAMONA CAFE

Ocean Beach
HODAD'S

San Diego
D.Z. AKINS
EL INDIO
HOB NOB HILL

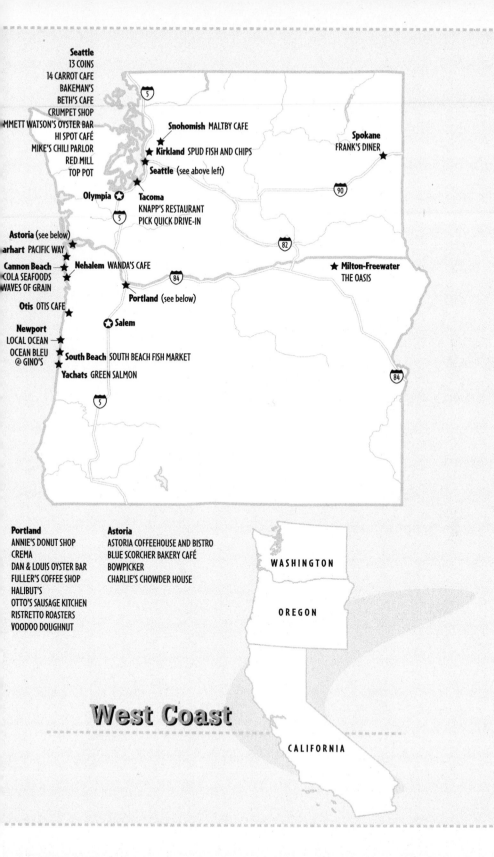

**Seattle**
13 COINS
14 CARROT CAFE
BAKEMAN'S
BETH'S CAFE
CRUMPET SHOP
MMETT WATSON'S OYSTER BAR
HI SPOT CAFÉ
MIKE'S CHILI PARLOR
RED MILL
TOP POT

**Snohomish** MALTBY CAFE

**Spokane**
FRANK'S DINER

**Kirkland** SPUD FISH AND CHIPS

**Seattle** (see above left)

Olympia

**Tacoma**
KNAPP'S RESTAURANT
PICK QUICK DRIVE-IN

**Astoria** (see below)
arhart PACIFIC WAY

**Cannon Beach**
COLA SEAFOODS
WAVES OF GRAIN

**Nehalem** WANDA'S CAFE

**Milton-Freewater**
THE OASIS

**Portland** (see below)

**Otis** OTIS CAFE

Salem

**Newport**
LOCAL OCEAN
OCEAN BLEU
@ GINO'S

**South Beach** SOUTH BEACH FISH MARKET

**Yachats** GREEN SALMON

**Portland**
ANNIE'S DONUT SHOP
CREMA
DAN & LOUIS OYSTER BAR
FULLER'S COFFEE SHOP
HALIBUT'S
OTTO'S SAUSAGE KITCHEN
RISTRETTO ROASTERS
VOODOO DOUGHNUT

**Astoria**
ASTORIA COFFEEHOUSE AND BISTRO
BLUE SCORCHER BAKERY CAFÉ
BOWPICKER
CHARLIE'S CHOWDER HOUSE

WASHINGTON

OREGON

**West Coast**

CALIFORNIA

## Al's Place

13936 Main St.
Locke, CA

916-776-1800
www.locketown.com/als.ht
LD | $$

Built by Chinese immigrants early in the twentieth century, the old levee community of Locke was once notorious for its gambling halls, brothels, and last—maybe least—of its pleasures, Cantonese food. Locke's weathered Main Street of wood-plank sidewalks and swayback second-story balconies remains a magical sight. In the middle of it is Al's Place.

The building housed a regular Chinese restaurant from 1915 to 1934, when Al Adami, fresh out of prison as a convicted bootlegger, came up the river and took over. Al had no menu—he asked you how you liked your steak, which was the only thing to eat amid the slot machines and card tables in the dining room behind the front-room bar. Legend says that at some point in time, a hungry crop duster came in with jars of peanut butter and marmalade and asked Al for some toast. Al liked the idea, and started putting peanut butter and marmalade on every table, a tradition that endures.

Al's Place still feels illicit. You enter past the beer and shooter crowd who occupy a dimly lit bar hung with dusty game trophies and memorabilia, into a backroom dining area lined with worn laminate tables equipped with shared benches instead of chairs.

The menu remains simple, now including hamburgers, cheeseburgers, steaks, and one amazing steak sandwich. It is amazing because it is only barely a sandwich. In fact, what it is, is a sandwich-sized steak on a platter accompanied by a second plate of toasted pieces of sturdy Italian bread. Horseradish and minced garlic are available to spread on the meat. Most people put the peanut butter or jelly on their toast, but the management informed us that some use it to garnish their steaks.

## Barbara's Fishtrap

281 Capistrano Rd.          650-728-7049
Half Moon Bay, CA          LD | $$

Barbara's makes fish and chips with rock cod, aka Pacific snapper, that is cut thick enough to remain extremely moist, its natural sweetness underscored by a gold coat with light, oily crunch. You get four large tiles, hot from the fryer, accompanied by thick fried potatoes. Tartar sauce is unnecessary with fish so flavorful, and ketchup for the fries is irrelevant. (Malt vinegar is supplied for the spuds too, but why moisten their crisp skin?)

To precede fish and chips, you want a cup or bowl of clam chowder. This is good stuff, its heartiness very much of the Pacific variety, meaning it is creamless but nearly fork-thick, loaded with large pieces of tender clams as well as potatoes and celery: a winning balance of elements.

Barbara's menu is big, including linguine served with your choice of clams, mussels, prawns, or calamari, as well as full-bore cioppino with Dungeness crab. There are shrimp and/or crab Louie and vegetable plates that come steamed, sautéed, or tempura-fried. Meals begin with baskets of fresh, chewy sourdough. At a little over $10, fish and chips is the most affordable meal on the menu. Most entrees are in the $20 range.

Barbara's is casual with a charming nautical dishevelment about the décor, and it is small enough always to seem crowded. It offers a pleasant view overlooking the boats in Pillar Point Harbor. But windows remain closed. It became obvious why, when, mid-meal, we watched a very large seagull swoop down and perch on a rail just outside. It seemed all too clear that he had come to watch us with his beady, greedy little eyes.

## Bette's Oceanview Diner

1807 4th St.                    510-644-3230
Berkeley, CA                    www.bettesdiner.com
                                BL | $

We first found Bette's Oceanview Diner while looking for macaroons at Bette's to Go, the bakeshop next door. Aside from the magnificent macaroons and trompe l'oeil chocolate espresso Twinkies (the finest snack cake on earth), the bakery shelves' delights include pecan-topped red velvet cake and twin-layer lemon bars (creamy on top, crunchy below).

Anyone with an appetite and a functioning olfactory system would be hard-pressed to visit the bakery without being seduced by aromas from the diner next door: potato pancakes grilling to a crisp, waffles pried fresh from the irons, and eggy, oven-baked pancakes.

All these and a full menu of diner classics are dished out in a restaurant that is a savvy gloss on the vintage diner. We usually are skeptical about retro restaurants, diners in particular. Even if their heart is in the right place, all too often the food is not. But a first meal at Bette's disabused us of all prejudice. Here is a modern diner with classic values . . . and really good buttermilk pancakes, usually available in a special flavor each day. For our first visit, around Christmas, the day's pancake (and waffle) was eggnog. Mm-mm-good. The extra egginess was quite subtle, adding an intangible richness to the cakes, all the better when drowned with real maple syrup.

Another compelling breakfast highlight is scrapple, which is some of the best anywhere, including the Delaware Valley. Part of a "Philadelphia breakfast" with poached eggs, it is made from pork butt and hock meat, cornmeal, sage, and plenty of pepper, and sliced thick enough that while the outside gets nice and crisp, the interior virtually melts into nothing but flavor. If you get a fruit salad, fruits are cut and peeled to order. Muffins are available . . . made with donut batter: genius!

## Bi-Rite Creamery

3692 18th St.                   415-626-5600
San Francisco, CA               www.biritecreamery.com
                                LD | $

We've never had a banana split we did not like. And we've never had one in the same league as the one made at Bi-Rite Creamery. The vanilla ice cream is a shocking reminder that it is, in fact, chilled cream, suffused with liquor of vanilla beans. The chocolate sauce is cocoa turned to liquid velvet; the bananas are caramelized in amber syrup; the whipped cream—out of Straus Family Dairy cows that graze on grass above Tomales Bay—is as dense as crème fraîche. Dazzling!

Boasting that it makes "small-batch, artisanal ice creams," Bi-Rite offers such unusual flavors as salted caramel, strawberry balsamic, and honey lavender, as well as a sundae made with bergamot olive oil(!), and a lemon-gingersnap pumpkin ice cream sandwich. Still, we recommend you start with vanilla ice cream . . . and the best banana split in the universe.


## Cafe at the Bug

6979 Hwy. 140          209-966-6666
Midpines, CA           www.yosemitebug.com/cafe.html
                       BLD | $

If you are coming to Yosemite to hike, bike, swim, or savor the wilderness, but want to stay in a room or tent cabin for the evening, you won't do better than the Yosemite Bug Mountain Resort. And if you're looking for a nice place to eat other than around a campfire, the Cafe at the Bug is swell.

It's a three-meal-a-day place with outdoor patios and a glassed-in deck for scenic dining and a menu with choices that range from carnivorous to vegan. You can start the day with a giant buckwheat pancake (available vegan or not), muesli, eggs, or tofu egg substitutes. And while you are having breakfast you can have the kitchen prepare a boxed lunch for the trail. We relished our dinner of stuffed trout with rice and seasonal vegetables and a handsome sirloin steak with potatoes. We were especially fond of the chocolate cake served for dessert; while we cleaned the last of it from our plates, we listened to neighbors rave over their cheesecake.

Service is casual, semi-cafeteria-style. Order at the counter and pick your table. It is customary for customers to bus their own tables.


## *The Cottage

7702 Fay Ave.          858-454-8409
La Jolla, CA           www.cottagelajolla.com
                       BL | $$

Here is Southern California at its brightest: fresh and casual and delicious. On a quiet corner in the village of La Jolla, the Cottage offers vibrant meals in either a sun-drenched dining room or on the breezy patio outdoors.

Breakfast is especially wonderful. As you walk in the door, look right. There's the bakery case holding the nut-topped cinnamon rolls, muffins, and buttermilk coffee cake with cinnamon and walnut crumb topping. The pastries are superb . . . but so are hot meals. In particular, we recommend Cottage Irish oatmeal, served with a full complement of brown sugar, sliced bananas, raisins, milk, and a dish of sensational sticky-crunchy caramelized walnuts. Also grand are meat-loaf hash crisped with cottage-fried potatoes and topped with eggs, French toast stuffed with strawberry compote and mascarpone, and crab Benedict, which is like eggs Benedict, but heaped with pure rock crab instead of Canadian bacon. Cottage granola is extra-special—dark and toasty, a delightful chew.

Lunch is an opportunity to taste a high-tone version of San Diego's favorite fast food, the fish taco, here built around grilled mahimahi, dressed with cilantro-avocado sauce and accompanied by bowls of creamy black beans and chunky papaya relish. The pork and beef chili has a true Southwest pepper zest, and the hamburger is a SoCal classic, served with an abundance of Cheddar cheese, tomato, lettuce, onion, and mayo. The BLT, augmented with avocado, reigns supreme.

The restaurant is in a bungalow that was built early in the twentieth century and served as a private home in the days when La Jolla was a little-known community of sun-and-surf worshippers. It still exudes edge-of-the-continent charm that once made California so appealing.

## Duarte's Tavern

202 Stage Rd.               650-879-0464
Pescadero, CA               www.duartestavern.com
                            BLD | $

We weren't yet driving around looking for Roadfood in 1894 when the Duarte family opened a tavern in Pescadero (neither were there any automobiles to drive around in; it was a stage stop); but we can tell you that the rugged old tavern hasn't changed much at all since we first happened upon it in the mid-1970s. It is still a place where locals come for coffee and three square meals a day at mismatched tables and chairs in a knotty pine-paneled dining room or at the short counter opposite the kitchen.

Travelers have come to know it for its artichokes, which are farmed just south of Pescadero around Castroville, and which grow into gorgeous globes in the Duarte family's abundant garden behind the restaurant. The pick of the backyard crop is available simply steamed—you won't believe how much flesh you can scrape off each petal—and you can have artichokes stuffed with fennel sausage, in breakfast omelets, or as the foundation of blissful cream of artichoke soup.

Most of the menu is down-home dining, California-style: pork chops with homemade applesauce and chunky mashed potatoes, chicken and dumplings, roast turkey with sage dressing. Even the house salad—a perfunctory gesture in so many restaurants—comes topped with beets and tomatoes that come directly from the family garden. The kitchen's respect for its provender's seasonal correctness rivals that of any highfalutin bistro in wine country. Ron Duarte, who took over the business in the 1950s from his parents (and whose kids, Kathy and Tim, now run it), cannot hide his happiness as Dungeness crab season starts in November, because that means the restaurant's legendary cioppino will be at its best. "We don't buy frozen or precooked," he says. "We like to get them live."

To conclude any meal at Duarte's, you must have pie. We are gaga over the one made using olallieberries from nearby Watsonville; but they have a short season early summer, so after that, they are replaced by marionberries from farther north. The last time we visited, Ron showed off a big box of just-picked pears and a handsome pie the kitchen staff had made from them.

## *Du-par's

6333 W. 3rd St.  
Los Angeles, CA

323-933-8446  
www.du-pars.com  
Always open | $

There's a lot of fashionable cooking in Los Angeles, but if you are looking for a place that reflects California cuisine when the Golden State was the end of the rainbow, you won't find a more perfect example than this coffee shop in the Farmers Market (and a few other locations).

It is always open, 24/7/365, offering a menu of such comfort food as savory potpies, Welsh rarebit, corned beef hash, turkey with all the trimmins, and meat loaf. Desserts are wonderful, including pecan, lemon, and coconut custard pie as well as several puddings. Regular customers time their lunch visits according to the immemorial daily specials: Monday fried chicken, Tuesday turkey, Wednesday pot roast, Thursday liver and onions, Friday meat loaf—all accompanied by freshly mashed potatoes.

Breakfast is best of all, especially the pancakes. You can get a single, a short stack (three) or a full stack (five). These are some of America's finest flapjacks, fairly thick but not heavy, sizzled on a slick grill so they develop a glistening, fragile crust. They come with plenty of syrup as well as a good-sized pitcher of melted butter. The 'cakes already are buttery; pour on the extra butter, swirl in some syrup, and you're in breakfast paradise.

The meals are served in spic-and-span surroundings by professional uniformed waitresses who see your half-full cup of coffee as half-empty.

## D.Z. Akins

6930 Alvarado Rd.
San Diego, CA

619-265-0218
www.dzakinsdeli.com
BLD | $$

As folks who frequently complain that urban delis aren't what they used to be, we were thrilled several years ago the moment we walked into D.Z. Akins. The air was perfumed with spiced beef and the bakery shelves up front held a handsome array of ryes, pumpernickels, bagels, hard rolls, and challahs, plus countless macaroons and cookies, all baked right here. The sandwiches we got were fantastic: hot, fat-striated corned beef radiant with flavor, cut thick and piled between slices of old-fashioned deli rye, soft inside with a sour smack and a tough, savory crust. Roast beef was presented in a poppy-seed-spangled hard roll. At breakfast you can feast on matzoh brei, blintzes, or bagels and lox. Nothing is short of excellent.

The full-service restaurant also features a soda fountain, the menu of which includes sundaes and sodas of all kinds, from a traditional banana split to one called Prenatal Silliness: chocolate ice cream and pickles, with your topping of choice!

## El Campeon

31921 Camino Capistrano #12
San Juan Capistrano, CA

949-489-9767
www.elcampeon.com
LD | $

Located in a nondescript Orange County shopping center, El Campeon is a large, bustling cafeteria, bakery, and fresh juice source specializing in sleeves-up Mexican food. The menu is displayed on the wall above a service line where meats and garnishes are arrayed in pans, ready to be stuffed into tacos, tortas, or burritos. Options include *cabeza de res* (beef head), *birria* (goat meat), and more familiar meats such as carnitas (roasted pork), *barbacoa* (sauced roast beef), chicken, and ham. Burrito fillings include red or green chili (along with arroz, frijoles, *cebolla,* cilantro, and ensalada).

The carnitas are moist and robust, especially well complemented by hot green salsa available at a serve-yourself bar in the center of the dining area. *Barbacoa,* in the form of massive shreds, delivers big beef flavor, sopped with spicy sauce. Carne asada, sprinkled with cilantro (which the server does not apply unless you give him the green light) can be rather dry, a condition beautifully remedied by an application of vivid red salsa. To drink: *horchata* (rice milk), cinnamon-sweet and perfumy.

Seats are limited to counter stools, so some customers simply dine while standing either indoors or on the shopping-center sidewalk. A lot of business is takeout.

## El Indio

3695 India St.
San Diego, CA

619-299-0333
www.el-indio.com
BLD | $

Meals are served on Styrofoam plates with throwaway utensils at this cafeteria-style taqueria adjacent to Interstate 5. There are a few seats at a counter and some tables to the side of the order line, but many people choose to eat on the fenced-in patio across the street. Here, one is serenaded by vehicles passing on the raised highway.

The menu is Cal-Mex. An on-premises tortilla press turns out warm, wheaty ones for burros and chimichangas; there are freshly fried, hot corn tortillas and deliciously crunchy taquitos, and there are all sorts of combo plates topped with gobs of sour cream. El Indio's fish taco is a hefty meal served in a foil wrapper along with a wedge of lime. When the foil is pulled back, you find a double layer of warm corn tortillas loosely wrapped around a log of crisp-fried cod with a golden crust. The fish sits on a bed of ruggedly shredded cabbage, a few tomato shreds, and a faintly peppery pink sauce. Give it a spritz or two from the wedge of lime provided—an ideal complement for the sweet meat of the white fish and its savory crust.

Above the windows where you order your food at El Indio are portraits of fierce Mayan gods, including the god of war, the gods of rain and wind, and the god of Mexican food, who, according to this portrait, goes by the name of El Indio. We are not up-to-date on our Mayan theology, but one cannot deny that El Indio is indeed a deity in San Diego's food scene.

## El Paisa Taco Truck

2900 International Blvd.
Oakland, CA

510-384-5465
LD | $

Oakland's International Boulevard is well populated with taco trucks. Tacos el Paisa is the one to know. Proprietor Abel Lopez and his staff offer a wide array of fillings that include chicken, carne asada, beef tongue, head, and brain. There is spicy pork *(al pastor)* and pork carnitas, the latter crusty-edged, big-spiced, and juicy nuggets of fried meat. Tacos are built in double-layer corn tortillas and garnished with parsley and pink salsa chopped so fine it looks like caviar. Surrounded by crisp radishes, hot peppers, and slices of tomato, these are some of the most beautiful of all street-served tacos. The good carnitas also are available as the stuffing of a quesadilla, which is a superthin flour-tortilla sandwich containing not only the pork but also melted cheese, bits of onion, and tomato.

This is great food, and at the right price. Whether you get a couple or three tacos or a quesadilla cut into five good-sized triangles, you'll be hard-pressed to spend more than $5 for a meal. El Paisa has no formal seating, just a few available curbs in the lot where the truck parks.

## The Hitching Post

3325 Point Sal Rd.  805-937-6151
Casmalia, CA  www.hitchingpost1.com
D | $$$

Unlike barbecue in the South and Southwest, where meat is cooked for hours in the smolder of hardwood coals, Santa Maria barbecue is always done in the open on a grate over flaming red oak logs. While much of it is served from mobile cookeries in local parking lots, the best restaurant source is the Hitching Post, where T-bones, sirloins, and filet mignons anchor full dinners that start with a relish tray and shrimp cocktail and include a head lettuce salad, garlic toast, and potatoes either baked or French fried (the latter are wonderful). The meat glows with the flavor of the fire and with the piquant smack of a wine vinegar and oil marinade applied as it cooks. "The trick is in how the steaks are handled," proprietor Bill Ostini explained. "You've got to know how to cook which steak which way—some are made to be cooked rare, some well-done; it depends on the marbling and how much age they have. It takes two to three years to train a cook to do it the right way."

Ambience in this old, family-run roadhouse evokes a forgotten California, when the Golden State was cattle country and its people were frontier types. Above the bar, a TV is always playing; the mirror is plastered with decals from NASA, *Voyager,* and the Army Corps of Engineers; a bison head on one wall wears a Buffalo Bills cap. In the dining room, which affords a view of the kitchen, there are mounted deer heads and old black-and-white family photos of the proprietors on hunting and fishing trips. The hallway that leads to the restrooms is lined with cattle hides.

# Hob Nob Hill

2271 1st Ave.  
San Diego, CA

619-239-8176  
www.hobnobhill.com  
BLD | $

The California coffee shop is a unique style of square-meal restaurant, but there aren't a lot of them left. Hob Nob Hill pretty much defines the genre: a three-meal-a-day place where the food is homey, the service fast, and the prices low. You may have to wait in line, especially at breakfast. But the line moves quickly, and once you are seated you are set upon by a team of waitresses who could not move faster if they flew through the aisles—taking orders, filling coffee cups, making sure everyone is happy.

The kitchen's offerings are broad, and there isn't a clinker on the menu. Breakfast items include pecan waffles, pigs in blankets (buttermilk pancakes rolled with ham, sausage, and sour cream), blueberry hotcakes, grilled smoked pork chops, et cetera—plus a bakery's worth of coffee cakes, muffins (try carrot), and a not-to-be-missed pecan roll. Even the little amenities are special: syrup is served warm; jelly comes in hollowed-out orange halves; coffee is strong and rich.

At dinner, it's meat-and-potatoes time: leg of lamb with sage dressing and mint jelly, chicken and dumplings, roast tom turkey with giblet gravy, corned beef and cabbage, pot roast and buttered noodles. There are turkey croquettes with cranberry sauce, a nursery-nice breast-of-chicken curry, and baked ham with fruit sauce and yams on Thursday. Accompaniments are such comfort-food side dishes as warm applesauce (homemade, of course), marinated bean salad, and puffy yeast rolls.

# *Hodad's

5010 Newport Ave.  
Ocean Beach, CA

619-224-4623  
www.hodadies.com/home  
LD | $

There isn't a restaurant more casual than Hodad's, where a sign notifies patrons: "No Shirt, No Shoes, No Problem." The place throbs with wave-riders' music and its walls are plastered with hundreds of decommissioned vanity license plates, their meanings ranging from silly (Texas OI VEY) to provocative (California I LUV SX). Hodad's has no silverware and no written menus; the one hot meal cooked in its kitchen is a hamburger.

Oh, what a hamburger: the most awe-inspiring one we have ever seen, a paragon of SoCal burger culture, a joy to behold and an adventure to eat.

Nothing casual or slapdash about this bunned beauty! The burger itself is swell—good and juicy with a savory crust—but it's the way it's built that puts it in a class by itself. It comes with the works, unless you say otherwise, and that means mayo, mustard, raw onion, ketchup, pickle slices, sliced tomato, and shredded lettuce, plus bacon and/or cheese if desired. All these elements are piled high and handsomely to create a sandwich so strapping that no human jaw could possibly enclose it top to bottom.

Beautiful hamburgers aside, we love Hodad's for its infectious joie de vivre. Seating includes not only booths and one long communal table where stoked bros congregate and swap great-wave stories, but also an entire front section of a VW Microbus with seating for two and a table where the dashboard used to be, plus a counter up front where the stools offer a ringside view of Newport Avenue. A latter-day Haight-Ashbury, this amped artery of Ocean Beach includes surf shops, head shops, bead shops, and juice bars. This off-the-wall burger joint fits right into the high-attitude avenue.

## Ici

2948 College Ave.  
Berkeley, CA

510-665-6054  
www.ici-icecream.com  
$

First, a warning: If you want an ice cream cone or cup, you almost surely will wait in line at Ici. The line moves slowly because once a person gets to the head of it, he or she is allowed—even encouraged—to try little spoonfuls of different kinds of ice cream before committing to one. This is a very good thing, because so many of Ici's flavors are ones you would likely never have tried, such as mocha salted almond, sesame praline, Santa Rosa plum, and peach habanero sorbet. If that is off-putting, we have an insider's tip: Those with ice cream hunger so great that it precludes waiting can bypass the line and step right up to the counter, where they are free to buy and instantly consume an ice cream sandwich, such as fudge-streaked vanilla ice cream between two devil's food cookies or lemon ice cream sandwiched in tiles of gingerbread.

Still, the weird and original flavors are good enough to wait for. And they demand slow savoring. As much as we like ice cream cones (Ici's are particularly nice: homemade, of course, with a nugget of rich chocolate in the point at the bottom), we suggest getting your chosen flavor in a cup. That allows for very slow licking—an unnatural act that is well worth practicing, for as this ice cream warms, its flavors blossom.

## Jocko's Steak House

125 N. Thompson Ave.          805-929-3565
Nipomo, CA                    BLD | $$

We found Jocko's many years ago while we were students at Gary Leffew's bull-riding school north of Santa Barbara. When the week of riding was over, cowboys who hadn't broken too many bones and had some jingle in their jeans headed for Nipomo to eat beef at Jocko's on Saturday night.

When you walk into this place, you might have to remind yourself that yes, you are in California. For this is a California very different from the sad, broke, troubled cities and suburbs in the news. It is a California populated by country folk whose idea of fun is to come to this tavern, quaff beers under taxidermized animal heads, and eat red meat. Although the steaks are first-class, the experience of dining at Jocko's is absolutely nothing like a meal in one of the high-priced, dress-up steak house chains. Wear your jeans and boots and Stetson or farm cap and you'll be right at home.

Beef, pork, and lamb are what there is to eat. (One Roadfooder wrote to us suggesting that this must be the place where bad vegetarians go when they die, for it truly is a kind of beef frowners' hell, where smells of roasting meat permeate the air.) Shockingly thick steaks and hefty lamb chops and pork chops are cooked on an open pit over oak wood and served Santa Maria–style, accompanied by tiny pinquita beans and salsa. It's a great, filling meal, and even if you get a relatively modest-sized filet mignon, chances are you'll be taking meat home in a doggie bag.

## Julian Pie Company

21976 Hwy. 79                 760-765-2400
Santa Ysabel, CA             www.julianpie.com
                             $

Apple pie is the specialty of the Julian Pie Company, a sweet oasis at the base of Volcan Mountain, where the climate is perfect for growing tasty apples. The handle on the front door advises, "Begin Smelling." Indeed. Walk in and you will be bowled over by one of the best smells there is: apple pies baking in the oven. You can watch the pies being made behind the counter; you can buy whole pies to take home; or you can get a single slice and a cup of coffee and find a seat at the counter and indulge.

There are many different variations available, including Dutch apple, strawberry apple, and apple rhubarb. Non-apple pies include peach, blackberry, and pecan. But for us, it's basic apple pie every time. It is perfect, with a flaky crust and filling that is big-flavored and very sweet—fruit-sweet more than sugar-sweet.

One other item we love at this place: pie crust. Yes, crust, just crust. These are heart-shaped morsels made from dough that is baked in a veil of cinnamon sugar to become cookies that fall into flakes as you bite.

The other store is at 2225 Main Street in Julian (760-765-2449).

## La Farine

6323 College Ave.          510-654-0338
Oakland, CA                www.lafarine.com
                           B | $

A French pastry shop in *Roadfood*? We debated whether to include La Farine, and we are not listing it here for its fruit tarts and frangipanes or brandy cherry truffle tortes . . . although all of those things are drop-dead good, as is the flaky morning bun. No, it earns its place in the Roadfood pantheon because it is a super source of the signature bread of San Francisco: sourdough. Available as a baguette, petit pain, or bâtard, with or without Kalamata olives laced into the dough, it is fantastically chewy with a crisp crust. Sour but not overwhelmingly so, this is bread that asks no condiment or complement whatsoever.

Nearly all business is takeout, but there is a large round table inside where customers can sit and nosh on bread and pastries and sip coffee. A great perk of sitting here is that the staff frequently brings out plates of little samples of the bakers' work to try.

Three other locations in the East Bay: 3411 Fruitvale Avenue, Oakland (510-531-7750); 1820 Solano Avenue, Berkeley (510-528-2208); and 4094 Piedmont Avenue, Oakland (510-420-1777).

## La Super-Rica

622 N. Milpas St.          805-963-4940
Santa Barbara, CA          LD | $

La Super-Rica is barely a restaurant. It is a taco stand where service is do-it-yourself and customers are expected to clean their own place when they're finished eating. All plates and utensils are disposable, and seating is at wobbly tables on a semi-alfresco patio.

Using made-here tortillas, tacos can be had with beef, with green chile and cheese, or as a "chorizo especial" of spicy sausage, melted cheese, and tomato. We are especially fond of the taco *adobado* (grilled pork) and the frijol Super-Rica (chorizo and pinto beans with bacon and chile). In addition to tacos, La Super-Rica makes gorditas, quesadillas, cheese-stuffed pasilla peppers, and what Julia Child once proclaimed to be her favorite tamales. Each of the three kinds of salsa is excellent: chunky tomato, spicy red chile, and even spicier green chile. Beverages include *horchata* (sweet rice milk), hibiscus, and Mexican beer.

Since Isidoro Gonzalez opened for business in 1980, this extremely modest eatery has built a huge reputation, meaning you will wait in line at mealtime. In one way, the line is a good thing: La Super-Rica has no signs outside, so the crowd of people you see on North Milpas Street is the sign that lets you know you have arrived.

## Mama's Hot Tamales Cafe

2124 W. 7th
Los Angeles, CA

213-487-7474
www.mamastamales.com
L | $

Gracias to Chris Ayers and Amy Breisch, the endlessly adventurous team who sign their Roadfood.com reviews "ayersian," for tipping us off to Mama's Hot Tamales Cafe in general and Mama's Mexican mocha in particular. The tamales reflect cuisines of South America and Central America beyond Mexico. Some come wrapped in banana leaves or avocado leaves rather than corn husks; there are sweet ones as well as savories. All together, the kitchen's repertoire includes fifty varieties, about a dozen of which are available at one time.

Any day, you can step back to the coffee bar and order Mexican mocha, which is latte made from syrupy, licorice-dark espresso and chocolate infused with steamed milk and shot through with a full measure of cinnamon. There's no better beverage for after a multi-tamale meal, or as a companion to a guava tamal from Colombia or a peach tamal from El Salvador.

Mama's Hot Tamales is a community center that hosts art shows and adjoins Bohemia Books, where you can buy Latino literature and art. Bohemia's gallery of work by local artists changes every month, and the bookstore hosts an open-mike "Street Dialogue" night once each month.

## The Marshall Store

State Rt. 1
Marshall, CA

415-663-1339
www.themarshallstore.com
L | $$

The Marshall Store, which gets provender from the Hog Island Oyster Company up the road, brushes just-opened oysters on the half shell with butter and cooks them on a grate only until they are warm. They are then dabbed with barbecue sauce and served with garlic toast. There are few simple pleasures as right as this, the experience amplified by the casual magic of the dining facilities, which are boards set out on wine barrels where the Tomales Bay breeze wafts over your meal.

There is more on the Marshall Store menu, including raw oysters on the half shell, chowder (dip your own), sandwiches, and salads. It's those barbecued oysters that will keep us coming back.

## Musso & Frank Grill

6667 Hollywood Blvd.
Hollywood, CA

213-467-7788
www.mussoandfrank.com
LD | $$

When Musso & Frank opened for business in 1919, Hollywood was young and fresh and Hollywood Boulevard was a magic address. The boulevard went to honkytonk hell in a handbasket and is now trying to rebirth itself with entertainment complexes and shopping malls that compete for attention with hookers' wig shops, but the moment you step inside Hollywood's oldest restaurant, the battle of the lifestyles is left behind.

In fact, whenever meat and potatoes are decreed by food oracles to be having a renaissance (perhaps once every seven years), this vintage eatery almost seems trendy. Musso is known for dowdy kinds of meals: thin flannel cakes (for lunch), Welsh rarebit, chicken potpie on Thursday, classic corned beef and cabbage every Tuesday, lamb shanks, baked ham, chiffonade salads. Ten different kinds of potato occupy the menu, from mashed and boiled to Lyonnaise and candied sweet. Steaks and chops—cooked on an open broiler where those sitting at the counter can watch—are splendid. From the dessert list, note bread and butter pudding, and its deluxe variant, diplomat pudding—topped with strawberries.

Many adventurous gourmets of our acquaintance do not understand the appeal of Musso & Frank. They compliment its antique Tudor décor and comfortable red leather booths but complain that the food is ordinary. Yes, indeed! It is some of the tastiest ordinary food anywhere.

## Orange Inn

703 S. Coast Hwy.                949-494-6085
Laguna Beach, CA                BL | $

Whether or not the smoothie was invented at the Orange Inn is debatable. The goodness of its smoothie, however, is indisputable. The Pacific Coast Highway shack, first opened in 1931, does put a trademark sign in superscript next to the listing on its menu. More important, this smoothie tastes like the original intent. Nothing about it is outlandish or exotic, at least by twenty-first-century standards. It is elemental, a blend of strawberries, bananas, dates, juice, and ice, topped with a sprinkle of bee pollen. It tastes quite healthful and it is refreshing in two ways: first for its cool, fruity flavor, but also for its simplicity. The date shake is another old-time drink made here without folderol.

Beyond whirled drinks, the Orange Inn serves fine coffee with or without espresso and has an inventory of beguiling pastries. Among the latter are gnarly muffins with tops that are chewy and dense. On the counter above the morning muffins, we spotted a tray of brownies that were billed as "extra-chewy [with] a thick crispy edge . . . baked in Great-Grandma's glass baking dishes." God bless Great-Grandma and whoever makes these dark-brown monuments today. Taste in brownies varies tremendously; some like them light and feathery-textured, others want them as intense as a chocolate truffle. We think Orange Inn's are a perfect balance: powerfully chocolaty and offering serious tooth resistance but more like cake than fudge.

The one other item we need to recommend is granola. Like the smoothie, it contains nothing surprising, but it is a masterful mix of nuts, grain, and fruit, just barely sweet and perfectly complemented by a dab of plain yogurt.

## Original Pantry

877 S. Figueroa St.              213-972-9279
Los Angeles, CA                 www.pantrycafe.com
                                Always open | $

Not far from the Staples Center, the Original Pantry is a choice stop for fans after Lakers games. Never having closed its doors since opening in 1924, this round-the-clock temple of honest eats is renowned for hotcakes and full-bore egg breakfasts accompanied by sourdough toast, thick slabs of bacon, and piles of excellent hash brown potatoes. OJ is fresh-squeezed and the coffee keeps coming. At supper, you can't go wrong with a steak platter or such stalwarts as roast beef or short ribs, and the favorite dessert is hot apple pie with rum sauce. Sourdough bread and coleslaw are served with every meal.

When the Original Pantry was threatened by developers in 1980, former mayor Richard Riordan bought it, and Hizzoner's aura helped make it a destination for city politicians, bigwigs, and wannabes, especially at breakfast, when people-watching is a sport. A relatively small place, it is always bustling and service, by hash-house pros, is nearly instantaneous.

## Pann's

6710 La Tijera Blvd.
Los Angeles, CA

323-776-3770
www.panns.com
BLD | $

Pann's is like the polymorphous Flubadub on the old *Howdy Doody* TV show: a single entity composed of wildly different characters. In this case, the culinary crazy quilt is part medieval grotto (ponderous stone walls), part spaceship-boomerang panache, and part tailfin automobile upholstery. In other words, it is a perfect example of what is known as Googie-style, aka Do-Wop design, that thrived in mid-twentieth-century America.

Like the place itself, the menu is a nostalgic wonderland of such coffee shop classics as roast turkey with corn-bread stuffing, liver and onions, chicken and waffles, mile-high layer cakes, and tapioca pudding. Beverages include milk shakes and malts, strawberry lemonade, and root beer floats. If you order coffee, a uniformed waitress will top it off approximately every ninety seconds.

Fried chicken is a house specialty. It comes enveloped in a dark-gold crust as unctuous as crisp bacon. Mashed potatoes are available with white gravy, brown gravy, or country sausage gravy. Pann's is proud of its buttermilk biscuits, served with butter and bubble packs of honey. Unlike fluffy southern-style biscuits, these are dense and heavy. But we don't mean that in a bad way. Their avoirdupois is a style unto itself.

## Philippe the Original

1001 N. Alameda St.  
Los Angeles, CA

213-628-3781  
www.philippes.com  
BLD | $

Genesis, according to Philippe's: One day in 1918 Philippe Mathieu was preparing a beef sandwich at his proletarian eat place when the roll fell into gravy. Fetched out with tongs, the drippings-sopped bread looked good enough that an impatient customer said, "I'll take it just like that." And so the French dip sandwich was created.

Philippe's moved to its current location in 1951, but it remains a sawdust-on-the-floor, people-watcher's paradise. Place your order with a carver at the counter, then carry it to a communal table, where your dining companions will range from tourists to refugees from the nearby courthouse to SoCal creative types seeking a dose of old-fashioned reality.

Dips are made from pork, beef, ham, lamb, or turkey. The beef is soft and tender, the pork even tenderer. The sliced meat of your choice is piled into a fresh roll and sopped with gravy that is radiant with protein. You can get cheese on top, which we consider superfluous; but you must apply some of Philippe's hot mustard, a roaring-hot emulsion that is meat's best friend. Beyond the famous dips, there is a full menu of breakfasts, salads, sandwiches, and two soups each day. The price of coffee remains 9¢ per cup.

## Ramona Cafe

628 Main St.  
Ramona, CA

760-789-8656  
BLD | $$

Here is a menu that respects potatoes. No mere side dish, Ramona Cafe's glistening chunks of home-fried potato are the underpinnings of whole breakfasts piled into ceramic skillets. Design your own, selecting toppings from a list that includes ham, bacon, taco meat, chorizo sausage, four kinds of cheese, crushed garlic, and jalapeños. Or choose the Kitchen Sink, which is a panful of hunky home fries loaded with some of everything, including sausage gravy and a couple of eggs, and sided by an immense squared-off biscuit. If you want a meal that is less complicated but perhaps even more filling, consider Ramona Cafe's cinnamon roll: a half-pound circle of hot, sweet pastry veined with cinnamon sugar and accompanied by two paper cups of butter. It's really enough for two, or three, or four.

Among the many omelets available, of special note is the Gilroy Omelet, named for the California town that has proclaimed itself the garlic capital of the world: ham, bacon, mushrooms, Cheddar, and jack cheese, plus lots and lots of garlic.

Lunch is big too. There are good-sized cheeseburgers, hot meat loaf sandwiches with good mashed potatoes and gravy, turkey potpie, and fried chicken that is crusted with breading made from the café's breakfast biscuits. If you are looking for pie (and who is not?), the list of pies is a long one, including boysenberry crunch and apple crunch, coconut cream, and chocolate peanut butter cup.

## Randy's Donuts

805 W. Manchester Ave.　　　310-645-4707
Inglewood, CA　　　　　　　www.randys-donuts.com
　　　　　　　　　　　　　　　Always open | $

With a two-story-tall donut perched upon its roof, Randy's has long been a favorite location for movies and TV shows that want a background of roadside kitsch. It is a good example of what became known in the mid-twentieth century as vernacular architecture, a term that, in the world of gastronomy, refers mostly to buildings that are shaped like the food they serve.

Architectural significance aside, Randy's also happens to be a fine place to get donuts at any time of day or night. Varieties include honey-glazed, chocolate-covered, jelly-filled, powdered, frosted, and filled with crème. Glazed twists and sugar twists are lighter than the standard sinkers, and the maple bars are superb. Randy's also offers very good cinnamon rolls, apple fritters, and bear claws.

Note to those arriving at LAX: Randy's is a five-minute drive from the airport.

## Rick & Ann's

2922 Domingo Ave.　　　　　510-649-8538
Berkeley, CA　　　　　　　 www.rickandanns.com
　　　　　　　　　　　　　　　BLD | $$

Rick & Ann's is not Bay-Area hip, so we really like it. Hey, what's not to like about a place proud of fried chicken supper with mac 'n' cheese and corn bread?

We are not its only fans. Crowds come to this spot across from the Claremont Hotel, especially on weekends. (There is a communal table that is great for singles or those in search of conversation.) Breakfast is the beacon meal, featuring gorgeous red-flannel hash made with sweet and new potatoes and enough beets to turn it brick-red. With eggs and toast, it is part of a breakfast known as the Northeast, but you'd be hard-pressed to find red-flannel hash this good in New England. As devoted waffle folks, we heartily endorse the thin, crisp gingerbread-corn waffles (regular buttermilk waffles also are available), and on a return visit, we swooned over the fragile, flavorful lemon ricotta pancakes. For dinner, if fried chicken is not your idea of comfort-food bliss, how about chicken potpie or meat loaf with mashed potatoes?

Rick & Ann's website changes each day to list such specials as shrimp tacos, summer caprese salad with heirloom tomatoes, and springtime crepes with roasted artichokes, fava beans, asparagus, portobello mushrooms, and goat cheese. And let's have a plum strawberry tart for dessert!

## Sam's Grill

374 Bush St.
San Francisco, CA

415-421-0594
www.belden-place.com/samsgrill
LD Mon–Fri | $$$

Food trends come and go, and hot restaurants appear and fizzle. Sam's never seems to change. Tracing its history back to the 1860s, it is at once deluxe and informal, featuring high-priced, top-quality groceries prepared simply. It looks the way you want a great old California restaurant to look: outfitted with yards of thick white linen, brass hooks for coats, and private wooden dining booths for intimate meals.

The daily printed menu is divided into such enticing categories as "Fish (Wild Only)" and "From the Charcoal Broiler," and the big rounds of sourdough bread brought to table at the beginning of the meal are among the best anywhere. The menu lists so many things that are intriguing, from the unknown (what is chicken Elizabeth? what are prawns Dore?) to such bygone classics as hangtown fry and mock turtle soup to ultra-exotica (fresh abalone meunière). It is possible to order charcoal-grilled steaks and chops, sweetbreads done three ways, short ribs of beef with horseradish sauce, or just bacon and eggs, but nearly everybody comes to Sam's for the seafood. Our favorites have all been sole: rex sole fillets glistening with butter (perhaps the tenderest seafood we've ever slid onto the tines of a fork), charcoal-broiled petrale sole, and delicately fried fillets.

Sam's is open only on weekdays, only until nine at night, hours aimed at customers who work downtown and come every day for lunch, or for an early dinner before heading home. At noon, it is mobbed with successful-looking types jockeying for a table, or crowding three deep against the bar. Once you are seated, it is an immensely comfortable place to eat. The impeccably dressed waiters are consummate professionals, treating out-of-towners in jeans with as much respect as high rollers in business suits.

## Sears Fine Food

439 Powell St.

San Francisco, CA

415-986-0700

www.searsfinefood.com

BLD | $$

It was worrisome late in 2003 when it looked like Sears was about to vanish from the San Francisco landscape. While not the most exciting or innovative restaurant in town, nor an undiscovered gem, this comfortable storefront facing the cable cars on Powell Street has been Old Reliable since it opened in 1938, especially for breakfast. In fact, three meals a day are served and the lunch and dinner menus are extensive; but like most other tourists who find their way here, when we think of Sears we think of little Swedish pancakes served eighteen to a plate, sourdough French toast as tender as custard, non-Belgian waffles (from an old Fannie Farmer cookbook recipe) and thick, crisp bacon or plump sausage links alongside.

Happily, reports of Sears's death were greatly exaggerated, and while new owners took over in 2004, the traditional specialties remain reassuringly unchanged and the vintage dining-room décor sets a cozy tone.

## *Swan Oyster Depot

1517 Polk St.

San Francisco, CA

415-673-1101

L | $$

Swan's is an urban seafood shack that is a combination oyster bar and storefront market. Seating is limited to a nineteen-seat counter, where your chances of finding a seat at mealtime are near zero. It is relatively expensive, uncomfortable, and noisy. And yet somehow its inconvenience is part of its charm (as is the ebullience of the Sancimino family, who have run the lunch counter since 1946). For devotees, it is simply the best place in San Francisco to eat fresh seafood. Fans have been crowding in for nearly a century to feast on oysters from the East and West Coasts, whole lobsters, salads of shrimp or crab, and smoked trout or salmon. Also, New England–style chowder, which is so right with hunky sourdough bread. The marble counter is strewn with condiments: Tabasco sauce, lemons, oyster crackers.

Dungeness crab is served in season (generally, mid-November through May), available "cracked," meaning sections of cooked, cooled claw, leg, and body ready to be unloaded of their sweet meat. Crab Louie is a regal dish in which large chunks of crab are cosseted in a condiment made from lemony mayonnaise spiked with relish and olive bits, enriched by hard-cooked egg.

## The Waffle

6255 W. Sunset Blvd.
Los Angeles, CA

323-465-6901
www.thewafflehollywood.com
BLD | $

The Waffle stays open past midnight on weekends. Apparently the square-ness of its menu has garnered a retro-chic admiration society. But you'll see little stylin' if you arrive at what most people consider normal breakfast time. After the sun comes up and before the cool crowd wakes up, this place could pass for a regular diner. Coffee is presented with a stirrer already in the mug, and it gets topped off with hash-house regularity.

The Waffle's waffles are big Belgian rectangles but light and crisp rather than doughy, and they have the eggy flavor that morning meals want. Each comes with a couple of little butter tubs, and although the butter is soft, there is no way to easily spread it on a tile with treads so big. Some holes get more, others less or none. Each trough holds massive amounts of syrup. All sorts of waffles are available, two to an order, including ones with pecans or bacon baked in, multi-grains, gluten-frees, a red velvet waffle, and a rather ridiculous sticky-bun variation, which is a plain waffle topped with the sort of goo that adorns Cinnabons: unjustifiable by any meaningful culinary or nutrition standards, but good to eat.

There are plenty of non-waffle breakfasts as well as a full menu of sand-wiches, soups, and milk shakes. Vegan and vegetarian options are available.

## Annie's Donut Shop

3449 NE 72nd Ave.  
Portland, OR

503-284-2752  
B | $

There's been a donut renaissance in the Pacific Northwest. Seattle and Portland are bonanza cities for sinker lovers, especially those who like their morning pastry with excellent coffee. For all the new, fashionable, retro, vegan, and Goth donuts available in both cities, we have a soft spot for traditional ones that cost less than a dollar and go so well with morning coffee (not latte!). These you will find at their best at Annie's. They are fresh and the variety is tremendous. Old-fashioned cake donuts have the double-circle crown profile so popular in the Northwest that provides twice the crunchy exterior of a simple round one. Glazed and maple-frosted OFs are especially swell, and although the price is plebeian, the taste and mouth-feel are aristocratic. Cream puffs are light and impeccably fresh-flavored, the only way a cream puff ever should be. The wickedest variety we sampled was a raspberry fritter—unctuous, super-sweet, slightly fruity, and monumentally filling. And if you need something really outrageous, try Annie's chocolate-glazed peanut-butter fritter.

Annie's has none of the amenities of upscale coffee and donut shops: no art on the walls, no Wi-Fi, no couches or lounge chairs and, of course, no baristas. You sit in molded plastic booths that look out on the parking lot and are served by a staff with no attitude other than pride in the donuts.

## Astoria Coffeehouse & Bistro

243 11th St.  503-325-1787
Astoria, OR  www.astoriacoffeehouse.com
BLD | $$

Coffee hounds know that America's caffeine consciousness is at its zenith in Seattle, Portland, and throughout the Northwest—all the way to Anchorage, which has more coffee shops per capita than any other American city. One nice piece of evidence is the Astoria Coffeehouse & Bistro in the northwesternmost part of Oregon. The coffee poured is Caffé Vita–brand from Seattle, and in addition to all the usual espresso drinks are such exotic lattes as lavender vanilla, cardamom mocha, salted caramel, and maple brown sugar.

Actually, the food at breakfast wowed us more than the coffee. Smoked salmon hash is a mélange of bite-sized salmon, potatoes, and peppers, topped with eggs and sided by a buttermilk biscuit. We savored an almond paste–filled croissant and a slice of moist chocolate cake. There are *aebleskivers* (Danish pancakes), cardamom bread French toast, and biscuits topped with bacon gravy.

You can have an over-$20 meal for supper, which the menu describes as "neo-regional cuisine using direct caught seafood, all natural meats and wild local produce 'foraged' from the area." These items include Cajun oysters, chickpea and tabouli salad, pork molé, paella, steak frites, French dip, sushi rolls, and pad Thai. We are a little confused about the concept of neo-regionality, but the goodness of the salmon hash and freshness of the rhubarb scones make us want to discover exactly what it means.

## Blue Scorcher Bakery Café

1493 Duane St.  503-338-7473
Astoria, OR  www.bluescorcher.com
BL | $

Operating as a workers' collective with noble principles that include the use of actual cloth napkins and non-disposable flatware to minimize waste, gluten-free Fridays for people who are allergic, and a seasonal-local vegetarian menu, the Blue Scorcher has some of the best pastries anywhere. To wit: chocolate babka cupcakes, Irish brown butter cake with mascarpone filling, and mixed-fruit ginger custard tartlets.

Must eat: extremely moist chocolate chip applesauce cake, full of little melting chips. Must eat #2: chocolate gingerbread that delivers sharp ginger snap as well as a tsunami of chocolate flavor. The intensity of the latter could easily induce taste-bud overload were it not for the palliating globe of pure (organic) whipped cream offered on top.

We were so busy eating cakes and drinking good espresso that we did not even think to order from an interesting breakfast selection that includes house-made Northwest cherry hazelnut granola, the Breakfast of Wonder (poached eggs on greens with tempeh and toast), frittatas, and "huevos scorcheros." Lunch items include pizza and calzones, veggie burgers, soups, and salads. Based on the goodness of the pastries, these are all worthy of a return visit. We did manage to come away with a loaf of asiago sourdough bread that was memorably delicious.

## *Bowpicker

| | |
|---|---|
| 1634 Duane | 503-791-2942 |
| Astoria, OR | www.bowpicker.com |
| | LD \| $ |

Bowpicker is not a building but a former fishing vessel now landlocked and serving some of the best fish and chips anywhere on the West Coast. It is a small craft, scarcely more than a kitchen and cash register. There is no indoor seating and only a couple of picnic tables around it. Most customers get their meal to take somewhere else, if only to the dashboard of a car.

We highly recommend eating your meal soon after you get it. The gossamer beer-batter crust on this fish demands immediate indulgence. Enveloped inside are trapezoidal hunks of albacore tuna dense with seafood-richness (as opposed to the more typical fried-fish oily-crust richness). French fries are very good, but we found ourselves pretty much ignoring them, not wanting to use up any appetite while there was still superlative fish to eat.

By the way, the first syllable of the restaurant's name is pronounced "bough," like the front of a boat off of which fish are picked from the net.

## Charlie's Chowder House

| | |
|---|---|
| 1335 Marine Dr. | 503-325-2368 |
| Astoria, OR | LD \| $$ |

At the northernmost end of Route 101 in Oregon, the city of Astoria lacks the pristine beauty that defines so much of the state's coast, but it has a gritty, seaside-city appeal that is hard to resist. Charlie's Chowder House is a good example, where the word "eclectic" does not do justice to the ambience and décor. Every table is arrayed with a different salt-and-pepper set and a diorama in the window shows a Barbie Doll mermaid hovering over a pile of pirates' bones while a school of sharks swims close.

All that is immaterial to the fact that Charlie's chowder is terrific. Its identity at first seems ambiguous, listed on the menu as "Astoria's own" but on the wall as "New England clam chowder"; one bite tells you the former is true. This chowder is thick and peppery, enriched not by cream but by massive amounts of bacon. Its bounty of chopped clams is so tender and savory-sweet that sometimes you think you have hit a nugget of bacon when in fact you are enjoying a morsel of clam. After the taste-bud rapture of this chowder, everything else we ate, while perfectly fine, lacked punch. If you must have something beyond chowder, we recommend the grilled mahimahi tacos.

## Crema

2728 SE Ankeny St.
Portland, OR

503-234-0206
www.cremabakery.com
BL | $

Crema is among the crème de la crème of Portland coffeehouses. It features French-press coffee brewed so strong that hot water is available for those who need to weaken it. The espresso is thick and syrupy, black as licorice, and among the fancy drinks is a dazzler called Spanish latte, which is made with sweetened condensed milk, adding extra body and luxe. Were the espresso not so strong, the supermilk might be overwhelming, but the two extremes form an infinitely satisfying yin-yang morning beverage. As gilding for this lily, the baristas at Crema know how to add the foam on top in exquisite patterns, making each drink a potable work of art.

We also like this large, enthusiastically caffeinated coffeehouse for its pastries. Among the wide assortment of sweet ones are Mexican chocolate cupcakes, green tea cheesecake, orange cinnamon buns, cranberry-caramel pecan bundt cake, chocolate bread pudding studded with bananas, and a double-chocolate, powdered-sugar-dusted earthquake cookie complete with fault lines. There are all sorts of savory breakfast pastries made with eggs and veggies, our favorite being the ruggedly handsome Cheddar corn biscuit, a squat circle that is all crusty and chewy with baked cheese and dotted with sweet corn kernels.

## Dan & Louis Oyster Bar

208 SW Ankeny St.                    503-227-5906
Portland, OR                         www.danandlouis.com

LD | $$

Oyster stew at Dan & Louis is little more than warm milk, melted butter, and lots of small Yaquina oysters, which are sweet and mild and ideal
participants in a bowl full of warm comfort. If we are really hungry, we'll
follow stew with a plate of pan-fried oysters. Yaquinas fry up beautifully
with a toasty golden crust. They are sent to the table with ramekins of tartar
sauce and thousand island dressing, as well as a pile of lettuce shreds heaped
with small shrimp and a length of chewy sourdough bread.

Among non-oyster items on the menu, we are fond of the dowdy
creamed crab on toast, a dish that one might expect to have been served in a
department store lunchroom seventy-five years ago. You'll also find cracked
Dungeness crab, shrimp Louis, and halibut fish and chips.

The interior of Dan & Louis is mesmerizing, its handsome sailing-ship
wood walls bedecked floor to ceiling with an inexhaustible accumulation
of nautical memorabilia and historical pictures, notes, and maps that tell of
Portland since Louis started serving food here.

## Ecola Seafoods

208 N. Spruce                        503-436-9130
Cannon Beach, OR                     www.ecolaseafoods.com

LD | $$

Cannon Beach is one of the most picturesque places on the Oregon coast,
known for the awe-inspiring haystack-shaped rock just offshore. It is a quiet
hamlet and a grand destination for eaters because of Ecola Seafoods (named
for nearby Ecola State Park). Ecola is total Roadfood—extremely casual
and extremely local, a no-frills seafood market and restaurant where fresh is
all. We love simply browsing the cases of Dungeness crab, oysters, scallops,
and flat fish that we seldom see back east. For those who arrive with a good
appetite, what fun it is to choose from a broad menu of "fish and chips,"
the former part of the equation including Willapa Bay oysters, Oregon Albacore tuna, razor clams, or troll-caught Chinook salmon. Plus Pacific cod,
halibut, jumbo prawns, and ocean scallops. Each is available as a lunch or
dinner (bigger portion), and you can get the cod, halibut, salmon, or oysters
fried up and put into a toasted, buttered bun with lettuce, tomato, and a
couple of lemon wedges.

We feasted on a crab cocktail, which was cool, pearly meat in a bowl along with zesty red cocktail sauce. And we liked the chowder too: fine-textured and creamy, its ocean savor highlighted by a jolt of pepper.

The market's own *F/V Legacy* brings in wild salmon that can be had in the form of a grilled salmon taco, a salmon burger (a couple of big chunks in a bun), topped with mango salsa, or encased in crusty batter on a fish and chips plate. Smoked Chinook salmon is dense and heavy, falling into moist, bite-sized forkfuls as fully satisfying as prime aged beefsteak. A sign on the wall warns, "Friends don't let friends eat farmed salmon."

For picnickers, sandwiches and whole ready-to-eat dinners are available to go, as are all manner of cook-it-yourself fish.

## Fuller's Coffee Shop

136 NW 9th
Portland, OR

503-222-5608
BL | $

Off the tourist path but loved by locals, Fuller's is the sort of high-quality urban hash house now nearly vanished from most American cities. A man sitting near us at one of the two U-shaped Formica counters mopped the last of some yolk off his plate with a forkful of pancake and declared that he used to eat at Fuller's nearly every day thirty-two years ago, and as far as he could see, nothing's changed but the prices. "This is a diner where they know how to fry bacon!" he declared. Yes, indeed. An order of bacon is four medium-thick ribbons that are crisp but retain enough pliability so they don't break at first bite. And the hash browns are a short-order delight, fried so they are a mix of golden crust and soft, spuddy shreds of buttery potato. The pancakes are good too, and the cinnamon roll, baked fresh each day, is yeasty and tender.

Our favorite thing at Fuller's is the bread. It's not artisan bread; it's not fancy at all. You get white or whole wheat. These slices are simple and perfect, especially so when toasted and buttered and accompanying a well-rounded breakfast. Jelly and marmalade are set out along the counter.

Lunch is such short-order classics as chicken-fried steak, French dip, hot beef and gravy (on the good bread), and ham and/or cheese sandwiches. There always is interesting seafood: salmon steaks in season; batter-dipped fish and chips; fresh-fried oysters; and big, slightly scary (but easy to eat) egg-battered, fried razor clams with French fries and coleslaw.

## Green Salmon

220 Hwy. 101 N.         541-547-3077
Yachats, OR         www.thegreensalmon.com

BL | $

The Green Salmon serves great coffee and espresso, but that's just the beginning. How about a Cafe Oregonian with hazelnut milk, a Cafe Mexico with pepper, brown sugar, and cocoa, or a Kopi Jahe, which is a double-strength brew infused with the sparkle of ginger and sweetness of cane sugar?

Good coffee, great pastries. Muffins, scones, and croissants are all hale and hearty. Breakfast opportunities include a panini-grilled Sicilian egg sandwich on multigrain bread, granola baked with maple syrup and moistened with steamed milk, and a wide-bodied croissant frosted with a thick glaze of maple (the Pacific Northwest is crazy for the flavor of maple). On a recent visit, we enjoyed a sensational (if irregular) plate of lox and bagel: gorgeous, glistening-pink ribbons of smoked Pacific salmon accompanied by a whole-wheat bagel and cream cheese infused with matcha tea. Plus, of course, capers, tomatoes, and chopped onions.

Crowded and sociable, the Green Salmon is more for lingering than for a quickie coffee. Partly, this is because drinks and hot dishes all are made to order; but also because the place is infused with the life-savoring rhythms of the slow food movement . . . despite all the caffeine consumed on premises.


## Halibut's

2525 NE Alberta         503-808-9600
Portland, OR         www.halibuts.squarespace.com

LD | $$

The best fish and chips in the west? This place is on the short list for that honor. When we walked in, owner Dave Mackay was at the left side of the restaurant behind the counter where the row of fry kettles are, proclaiming aloud the beauty of a particular side of salmon. It was vivid pink with dense, heavy flesh fairly dripping fatty savor. While broiling or grilling it would be grand, this restaurant's deep-fry skills are equally brilliant, encasing the kingly meat in a thin, fragile crust that is amazingly grease-free and only enhances the essential taste of the fish within. Dave cut the side of fish with aplomb, creating chunks about 2 x 2 x 4-inches for frying.

Halibut also makes for great fish and chips. You get four heavy blocks that are moist and sweet, big white hunks of their flesh flaking off with pieces of crust when you hoist them from the basket that also contains crunch-crusted French fries. If you don't want fried fish, you can have Dungeness crab cakes, which are nicely spiced with a red-gold crust. The restaurant's subtitle is "Fish/Chips and Chowder," and the chowder is thick with clams and potatoes and a surfeit of rich pig meat. You can get it plain or make a super meal of it by ordering it ballasted with shrimp.

Halibut's is a casual bar with raucous blues playing on the speakers (performed live many nights). There is a happy hour menu and a long list of such whoop-de-doo cocktails as the Ultimate Margarita, a Mai Tai, and a Lemon Drop that is made with fresh-squeezed lemons, Absolut Citron, Triple Sec, Bacardi Limon, sweet-and-sour and sugar and served in a goofy-stemmed martini glass.

## Local Ocean

213 SE Bay Blvd.  
Newport, OR

541-574-7959  
www.localocean.net  
LD | $$

Local Ocean is a loud and lively place staffed by a crew who are fully aware that they are operating what is the cutting-edge seafood place on Bay Boulevard. The attitude is more one of confidence than arrogance, so we won't hold it against them; neither will we be bothered by fairly high prices. The fact is that you get your money's worth here: some of the finest seafood meals in a region replete with really fine seafood meals.

Dungeness crab soup glows warm with roasted garlic; crab cakes come with crunchy fennel slaw; a handsome crab po' boy is dressed with green chile avocado purée and is sandwiched in a loaf crusted with parmesan cheese. Fish tacos, which include a wild pickly hot salsa, are made with the catch of the day; it was ling cod when we last stopped in: white, smooth, and flaky. Salads may be enriched by house-smoked salmon and toasted Oregon hazelnuts, or you might want a halibut panzanella salad made with crisp-grilled ciabatta bread and roasted vegetables. Dessert is nothing short of sensational: lemon shortcake smothered with local berries and whipped cream.

Local Ocean also is a seafood market, each kind of raw fish in the case marked with a placard that tells which vessel caught it, using what fishing technique.

## The Oasis

85698 Hwy. 339                                541-938-4776
Milton-Freewater, OR                           BLD | $$

A short detour off the main road at the Washington State line leads to the Oasis, a sprawling roadhouse that seems to have expanded room by room over the last seven decades. It is a favorite destination for locals in search of meat and potatoes, live music on the weekends, and Texas Hold 'Em.

Sirloin steaks come branded with crosshatch char marks on their surface. These are cuts of beef with chaw, available in all cuts and sizes, eclipsed in their beefiness only by the kitchen's grandiose prime rib. Many customers who come from afar to dine at the Oasis make a special night of the occasion by treating themselves to the most celebratory of all restaurant meals, surf and turf, which is such a house specialty that an entire section of the menu is devoted to its various permutations. Prime rib or sirloin is available alongside a lobster tail or with prawns, scallops, or grilled oysters.

Breakfast at the Oasis is a roll-your-sleeves-up kind of meal, served all day with the exception of pancakes and biscuits, which are available only until 11 a.m. The biscuits are extraordinary, a single order consisting of three behemoths and a cascade of thick gravy. This is a meal of caloric content suited to the eater who plans to flex muscles all day.

## Ocean Bleu @ Gino's

808 SW Bay Blvd.                               541-265-2424
Newport, OR                                    www.oceanbleuseafoods.com
                                               BLD | $$

Newport's harbor is filled with fishing boats. Bay Street, along the waterfront, abounds with good restaurants that serve what they catch. One such place is Ocean Bleu @ Gino's, which is one of the few harborside eateries that serves three meals a day.

Although a person can breakfast on perfectly fine fried eggs, French toast, or pancakes (accompanied by house-smoked bacon), locavores will pay more attention to the likes of smoked salmon Benedict, grilled razor clams with eggs, and the Ocean Bleu scramble, which includes pink shrimp and/or cracked Dungeness crab. To drink: locally roasted coffee, hot apple cider, or a variety of adult beverages that includes Bloody Marys, mimosas, and that Northwest fave, red beer, which is tomato juice and Coors.

The lunch and dinner menu is a bonanza of coastal specialties. Fish-and-chips is available with everything from rockfish and wild salmon to popcorn shrimp and local tuna. Onion rings are made from sweet Walla Wallas. Tiny Yaquina oysters are harvested just upriver; black cod, salmon, and sable are smoked in-house; Dungeness crabs are kept live in a seawater tank. Newport being the Dungeness Crab Capital of the World, it behooves visitors to tuck into Ocean Bleu's "sea pups," which are cornmeal fritters like Yankee clam cakes but laced with cracked crab and jack cheese. (*Sea Pup,* by the way, is the restaurant's own fishing vessel.)

As for the name of the place, it began as a fish market called Gino's. It remains a market as well as a restaurant, the house motto: "Live Free, Love Often, Eat Wild."

## Otis Cafe

1259 Salmon River Hwy.      541-994-2813
Otis, OR      www.otiscafe.com
      BLD | $

The Otis is an undersized roadside diner serving oversized meals. Located next to the post office, featuring a picnic-table patio as well as counter-and-table seats inside, the modest eat place has received national acclaim for great pies, and lumberjacks' (or more accurately in this case, fishermen's) breakfasts. Sourdough pancakes have a tang beautifully haloed by lots of melting butter and a spill of syrup. Eggs come with hash browns, the potatoes blanketed with melted cheese and green onions (known as German potatoes), and excellent homemade black molasses bread or a jumbo cinnamon roll.

One great lunch is the BLT made with full-flavored slices of beefsteak tomato, plus a bonus layer of cheese. We also recommend the one-third-pound cheeseburger, a goopy affair on a hefty bun with Otis's homemade mustard. On the side come dreamy griddle-fried potatoes or potato chips. (Otis Cafe does not have a deep-fryer; hence, no French fries.)

Pies are gorgeous, especially the West Coast rarity, marionberry. A more intense, supremely aromatic blackberry, the marionberry was made to be put in a pie. The crust here is crisp and aristocratic, making it all the more excellent a dessert.

## Otto's Sausage Kitchen

4138 SE Woodstock Ave.          503-771-6714
Portland, OR                    www.ottossausage.com
                                L | $

While it is a full-scale meat market and smokehouse with cold cuts and sausages of all kinds to take home and cook, Otto's is also a dandy place to eat lunch—either deli sandwiches (the Reuben is grand) or hot dogs. Whether you choose an ordinary beef-and-pork frankfurter (with snap to its skin that is far from ordinary) or an extra-large sausage made from chicken or pork, you might just find yourself amazed by just how much better these fresh, homemade tube steaks taste than factory-made ones. The progeny of Otto Eichentopf, who opened this neighborhood meat market in 1927, maintain the highest standards of Old World sausage making. The beauty of the links they make for lunch is that you really taste the meat of which they are made. Spices are used to accent rather than overwhelm the primary ingredient. Served with a choice of onions, kraut, relish, mustard, or ketchup for you to apply yourself, Otto's sausages can be enjoyed with a beverage chosen from a cooler full of local soft drinks and interesting beers.

Dining facilities are nothing more than a bunch of wooden tables arranged on the sidewalk outside, as well as a handful of places to sit indoors. It's a neighborhood picnic every lunch hour.

## Pacific Way

601 Pacific Way               503-738-0245
Gearhart, OR                  www.pacificwaybakery-cafe.com
                              BLD | $$

Pacific Way actually is two places: a friendly little bakery where locals hang out every morning sipping espresso drinks and eating muffins, croissants, and casual breakfasts, and a restaurant for sit-down, multicourse meals next door. The restaurant starts things off with a terrific bread basket—slices of Cheddar-basil onion, oatmeal molasses, and French bread—and we liked the restaurant's pear and gorgonzola salad. As for Dungeness crab pizza, the crab gets outshouted by sun-dried tomatoes and sweet, creamy cheese.

It's the coffee shop that won our hearts—a cozy spot with a couple of chairs and a few counter stools, plus outdoor tables under and around which customers' dogs goof off and hunt crumbs. Conversations fly through the air at this perpetual town party, and when we stood at the counter trying to decide which pastry to get with our coffee, a flash of group consciousness arose among the indoor diners, who determined it must be the multi-fruit Danish—a bouquet of Oregon berries on a pallet of flaky crust. On a coast rich with first-rate pastries, this one really stood out. Gearhart, incidentally, is the town where culinary Zeus James Beard was raised.

## Ristretto Roasters

3520 NE 42nd St.      503-284-6767
Portland, OR      www.ristrettoroasters.com
     BL | $

Ristretto Roasters coffee is brewed and sold in several places throughout the Portland area, and it is available by mail order, but there is nothing like drinking at the source. There now are two other Ristretto Roaster Cafes. The original location, on Northeast Forty-Second Street, is a small storefront, yet in a city with more than its fair share of excellent coffee sources, there is a line of caffeine-hungry Portlanders all morning long, waiting for cups of the city's best, made from beans roasted right here.

Espresso is no sledgehammer. Rather, it is a perfect balance of caffeinated punch and smooth, chocolaty flavor; the regular coffee has a civilized demeanor too. You want to be able to drink a lot of this coffee because Ristretto offers peerless pastries made by Kim Boyce (author of *Good to the Grain*). Kim's pastries are intriguing: figgy buckwheat scones, sweet and salty cookies, corn and gruyère muffins, and such seasonal selections as boysenberry scones in the summer, raspberry crumble bars in the fall, and Italian prune-plum tarts for Christmas.

## *South Beach Fish Market

3640 South Coast Hwy.      541-867-6800
South Beach, OR      www.southbeachfishmarket.com
     L | $$

South Beach is a picnic-style café and fish market attached to a convenience store where you can buy a souvenir T-shirt that tells the world, THE 2ND AMENDMENT IS MY GUN PERMIT. The store sells some scary food: movie-theater hot dogs kept warm on rolling dowels for who-knows-how-long, sports-stadium nacho trays, and Crock-pot chili, plus an immense inventory of energy drinks and beer. Honky-tonk it may be, but the restaurant on premises serves magnificent seafood. Dungeness crabs are cooked in cauldrons by the highway out front; chunks of their cooled meat are piled into a cup with no adornment other than a wedge of lemon (and, if you wish, horseradish hot sauce) to become an impeccable Pacific cocktail. Salmon, tuna, sturgeon, mussels, oysters, and sable are marinated and smoked using hickory and alder wood. Wild Chinook king salmon is made into "candy" by glazing nuggets of smoked pink meat with pepper and brown sugar. Each firm, moist piece packs a provocative sweet and savory punch.

South Beach fried seafood, veiled in tempura batter laced with garlic, has few equals anywhere. Jumbo wild prawns offer two levels of crunch: first, the crackle of the crust that surrounds them, then the dense snap of the meat itself. Salmon, tuna, oysters, and calamari all are available as fish and chips, as is snow-white halibut. While the French fries are fine, we highly recommend paying a few dollars more for onion rings too. Along with perfect O-ring circles, each basket also contains frail squiggles of batter that are merely onion-flavored and several hoops of onion with hardly any batter: It's all good. Dishware at South Beach is paper and plastic, and you may have to dispose of not only your own trash but also of that left behind by the last people who used the picnic table you claim for yourself.

## Voodoo Doughnut

22 SW 3rd Ave.  
Portland, OR

503-241-4704  
www.voodoodoughnut.com  
B | $

When Roadfood.com regular Mr. Chips wrote to tell us that Voodoo Doughnut, a block away from the estimable Dan & Louis Oyster Bar (p. 593), was a "great place to view Portland's strong Goth culture as well as sample tasty donuts," we were intrigued. We generally don't think of Goth culture as a source of good eats, and while we cannot say for sure if the ambience of this brick-walled ex-warehouse indeed is true Goth, we can tell you with certainty that the donuts are swell.

There are beautiful old-fashioned cake donuts with crunchy crust and creamy insides, puffy raised donuts, one glazed behemoth as big as a pizza labeled a Tex-Ass donut (if you can eat it in eighty seconds or less, your money is refunded), and donuts topped with powdered sugar, multicolored jimmies, and all sorts of flavored glazes. The menu lists such lunacies as a No Name donut, a Dirt donut, a Cock-N-Balls donut, a Dirty Snowball, and a Diablos Rex. One time when we visited, the menu above the counter listed a Nonexisting Fritter, its cost nil. We suspect that may be Goth humor.

The one pastry we shan't forget is a bacon-maple bar. It is a substantial raised yeast long john frosted with maple glaze and festooned with strips of bacon that somehow, magically, retain a welcome crunch.

Two other locations: 1501 Northeast Davis Street, Portland (503-235-2666) and 20 East Broadway, Eugene (541-868-8666).

## Wanda's Cafe

12870 H St.  
Nehalem, OR

503-368-8100  
www.wandascafe.com  
BL | $$

Decorative diversity rules at Wanda's. A few details: souvenir plates all over the walls, vintage radios and toasters on display in every nook and cranny, old vinyl record album covers tacked up among the plates, a few hundred different salt-and-pepper sets on shelves throughout the main dining area, one corner of which is occupied by a dinette set with steel-banded double-leaf table and matching canary-yellow chairs as well as a mid-twentieth-century television set.

If all that doesn't wake you up, have a cup of Oregon-excellent Sleepy Monk espresso. Irish coffee or a Bloody Mary will open your eyes, as will a Laughing Wanda, which is vodka with orange juice and peach nectar.

Cookies, scones, coffee cakes, brownies, and biscotti all are alluring, but we went for the hot-breakfast menu and a plate of huevos rancheros: beans, eggs, cheese, and chopped onions crowned with spectacularly fresh salsa. Oregon being biscuit country, we also ordered biscuits and gravy. The biscuits are huge, dense, and delicious; the gravy is rib-sticking thick, loaded with hunks of spicy sausage.

We arrived at Wanda's on a weekday, just after opening at 8 a.m., and were seated right away, but there can be a long wait for a table, especially on weekends. Lunch also is served (Wanda's closes at 2 p.m.), the menu featuring sandwiches made on multigrain, sourdough, rye, or polenta bread.

## *Waves of Grain

3116 S. Hemlock St.  
Cannon Beach, OR

503-436-9600  
www.wavesofgrainbakery.com  
BL | $

We don't know too many bakeries where the proprietors' family grows the wheat from which breads and pastries are made. In fact we know just one: Waves of Grain, in the achingly scenic oceanside community of Cannon Beach. Jason and Hillary Fargo buy their wheat out Pendleton way from Hillary's second cousin, Fritz Hill, who is a fourth-generation farmer.

The Fargos will tell you that it's the wheat, a variety known as dark

Northern, that gives character to their biscuits, breads, muffins, sticky buns, and cheese sticks. It's also talent and passion, all of which result in the most delicious baked goods north of the San Francisco Bay. During a long visit to Cannon Beach, we had breakfast here every morning and managed to nab focaccias and quiches for lunch, followed by dessert of chocolate buttermilk cupcakes and blueberry cream cheese bars. As local berries ripen, they make their way into and onto custard tarts, scones, tiramisu, and muffins.

Of particular note is the big Tillamook cheese biscuit with its crisp edges and creamy inside, the crusty cheese sticks, and the elegant sticky bun (which, if you get here early enough, will still be hot from the oven). Good coffee and espresso drinks are made from organic, fair-trade beans roasted in town by an outfit called Sleepy Monk.

## 13 Coins

125 Boren Ave.
Seattle, WA

206-682-2513
www.13coins.com
Always open | $$

At 13 Coins, you can spend $15 for breakfast or $150 for dinner and fine wine, and you can do either 24 hours a day, 7 days a week, 365 days a year. Opened over forty years ago, this favorite haunt of journalists from the nearby *Seattle Times* is not for trend seekers or effete gourmets. But if you appreciate a square meal composed of quality ingredients cooked and served by pros, there's no finer place north of Hollywood's Musso & Frank (p. 581).

Décor is a jaw-dropping anomaly of Tudor weight with mid-twentieth-century frivolity. Booths have upholstered backs that soar toward the ceiling; counter seats are not stools but rather huge padded thrones that swivel to make for easy conversation with a neighbor and provide full-access vision of the short-order chefs at work in the open kitchen. It is a pleasure to watch the cuisiniers shuffle sauté pans on the stove, poach eggs, grill meats, and griddle-cook potatoes.

The menu is gigantic, ranging from a grilled cheese sandwich to surf 'n' turf, including likeable versions of the West Coast specialties Joe Special (ground sirloin, spinach, and eggs topped with shredded Parmesan cheese) and Hangtown Fry (oysters, bacon, and eggs, here cooked frittata-style). The one must-eat dish, whatever else you get, is hash brown potatoes. They are cooked on the griddle with plenty of clarified butter in cakes thick enough for the outside shreds to turn hard and chewy while the inside softens but doesn't become mush. Other allures from the multipage menu include French onion soup, a Joe special made with sausage, Dungeness crab Louie, chop-chop salad, and smoked Cheddar and prosciutto macaroni.

## 14 Carrot Cafe

2305 Eastlake Ave. E.  
Seattle, WA

206-324-1442  
www.14carrotcafe.com  
BLD | $

Casual and comfortably disheveled, nutritionally enlightened, and perfumed inside and out by coffee, here is an echt-Seattle dining experience. Although lunch includes excellent salads and soups as well as vegetarian plates and no-beef hamburgers, most fans of the 14 Carrot Cafe consider it a breakfast place. Omelets are big and beautiful, served with good hash browns and a choice of toast, English muffin, or streusel-topped coffee cake. The coffee cake itself is something to behold: a moist crumble-topped block, served with a sphere of butter as big as a ping-pong ball. Other notable breadstuffs include blueberry muffins and cinnamon rolls. The latter, described as "large and gooey" by our waiter, is a vast doughy spiral with clods of raisins and veins of dark sugar gunk packed into its warm furrows..

One of the best-known specialties of the house is Tahini toast, gilded with a thin layer of sesame butter. Hotcakes come sourdough or regular, with sliced bananas, apple slivers, or blueberries, with bacon on the side or cooked into the 'cakes. If you are in a cereal mood, you can get homemade granola or hot oats with soy milk, dates, and cashews.

## *Bakeman's

122 Cherry St.  
Seattle, WA

206-622-3375  
www.bakemanscatering.com  
L Mon-Fri | $

A working-class cafeteria with a menu that is pretty much limited to soup, sandwiches, and salads, Bakeman's is open only for lunch, 10 to 3, Monday through Friday. Its claim to fame is the turkey sandwich on white or whole wheat. The bread is homemade, stacked up at one end of the cafeteria line. It is not artisan bread, just good sandwich bread: tender slices that come to life when spread with mayo, mustard, cranberry, and/or shredded lettuce, then heaped with turkey or—almost as wonderful—slabs of meat loaf.

The meat loaf is tightly packed but tender, gently spiced, and with a delicious aroma. As for turkey, get it any way you like, because this is superb, *real,* carved-from-the-bird turkey with homey flavor. The dark meat is lush; the white meat is moist and aromatic; either variety has an occasional piece of skin still attached, a nice reminder of just how real it is. The way we like it is, in the words of the countermen who hustle things along "white on white; M & M," which means white-meat turkey on white bread with mustard and mayonnaise. Turkey sandwiches get no better than this!

Bakeman's offers three or four good soups each day, such as turkey noodle or beef vegetable, plus a nice chili, or, on one memorable occasion, Chinese eggflower—an egg-drop variation. There are other sandwiches—tuna, egg salad, baked ham, et cetera—and a few salads, but they aren't all that interesting. Dessert can be wonderful—carrot cake, cookies, or cake of the day, such as lemon poppy seed cake, sliced like bread.

## Beth's Cafe

7311 Aurora Ave. N.
Seattle, WA

206-782-5588
www.bethscafe.com
Always open | $

Are you hungry? Really hungry? If so, eat at Beth's. Order the twelve-egg omelet. Yes, that's an even dozen, served not on a puny plate but on a pizza pan. If you're only half-hungry, Beth's offers six-egg omelets. Each comes piled onto a heap of hash brown potatoes and, if desired, bacon strips that have been cooked under a weight so they arrive flat and fragile. Biscuits-and-gravy is another of Beth's monumental meals, but if you arrive with only a tiny appetite, the menu offers mini breakfasts that are merely a single egg with hash browns and your choice of bacon or sausage.

The flagship meal at lunch is a half-pound Mondo Burger with cheese, bacon, lettuce, and tomato, fries on the side. There's a big Reuben sandwich as well as normal-sized burgers, BLTs, and French dips.

Beth's is open 'round the clock and is not a place to please the fastidious epicure. It is what some have called an "alternative greasy spoon," attracting wee-hours diners from the fringes of city life. And in Seattle, those fringes are pretty far out!

## Crumpet Shop

1503 1st Ave.
Seattle, WA

206-682-1598
BL | $

At the entrance to the Pike Place Market, the Crumpet Shop is a small café that serves crumpets for breakfast, brunch, and lunch. A crumpet is thick like an English muffin but poured out and cooked on a griddle, coming off chewy and rich-flavored with a craggy-textured surface that begs to be spread with butter and fruit-clotted marmalade. You can have one simply buttered, with butter and maple syrup, or with your choice from among nearly two dozen different sorts of sweet and savory toppings, including honey, Nutella, local jams, ham, cheese, and smoked salmon. On the side, have espresso, cappuccino, or, better yet, imported tea. If crumpets are not your cup of tea, the Crumpet Shop also bakes terrific loaves of bread, including a rugged groat bread that is an apt foundation for a hefty sandwich.

## Emmett Watson's Oyster Bar

1916 Pike Pl., Ste. 16
Seattle, WA

206-448-7721
www.emmettwatsonsoysterbar.com
LD | $$

For leisurely enjoyment of oysters, clams, and mussels, or fish and chips, or wonderful chowders, this brash little place is a Seattle treasure. There is a sunny, flower-adorned courtyard behind the building for warm-weather dining at rickety tables, and an indoor area with small booths.

Happy hour starts at 3 p.m., and for many regular customers, Emmett Watson's is a place where drinks are the main course and oysters—raw or broiled—are the side dish. A relatively secluded spot tucked away from the bustle of the Market, it is an ideal setting for long afternoons of grazing. Soups are notable, including a spicy shrimp soup "Orleans," Puget Sound salmon soup, and a classic cioppino stew of cod, shrimp, clams, and mussels. Meals are accompanied by slices of French bread and butter, and there is good Key lime pie for dessert.

# Frank's Diner

1516 W. 2nd Ave.

Spokane, WA

509-747-8798

www.franksdiners.com

BLD | $

Located in Seattle from 1931 to 1991, then trucked to its current location in Spokane, Frank's really did start life as a railroad car. For the last several decades it has served as a hash house with a traditional counter providing a view of the short-order cook at work.

The breakfast menu includes waffles, blueberry muffins, French toast, Benedicts, corned beef hash, and what the menu assures are "authentic fried green tomatoes" topped with hollandaise sauce. Omelets are especially handsome. Our fave is the Italianate meal known as a New Joe Special, which is three eggs scrambled with seasoned beef, sausage, spinach, and onion, flavored with Parmesan cheese.

We were clued in to Frank's Diner by a Washington State tipster named Charlie, who told us that breakfast is the best meal to eat at Frank's; but lunch has never let us down. It includes a terrific hot turkey sandwich, made from turkey roasted in Frank's kitchen, as well as a grilled meat loaf sandwich on Texas toast, turkey potpie, and giant-sized burgers made with assorted combinations of cheese, bacon, and even pineapple.

A second Frank's Diner is located at 10929 North Newport Highway in Pinewater Plaza, North Spokane (509-465-2464).

# Hi Spot Café

1410 34th Ave.

Seattle, WA

206-325-7905

www.hispotcafe.com

BL | $$

Upon entering this popular neighborhood café, glance right. Here you see the pastries, which are a primary Hi Spot attraction: huge flavor-packed scones, huger buttermilk biscuits, and ridiculously huge cinnamon rolls that are crammed with sugar and slivered nuts. Attractive as the jumbo breadstuffs may be, it's the omelets that won our hearts, especially El Pacifico, which is full of smoked salmon, dill cream, capers, and scallions and topped with more dill cream. The Round-Up is another winner, built of chicken sausage, goat cheese, tomatoes, and basil. Both come with home fries and toast. Egg dishes are served until closing at 2:30 p.m. The lunch menu, which becomes available at 11:30 a.m., includes soups and salads and sandwiches on superb Macrina Bakery rolls.

Among the attractive drink options are freshly squeezed limeade, mimosas, and Fonte coffee. Fonte is a local microroaster; the espresso we had was chocolaty, dark, and smooth.

## Knapp's Restaurant

| | |
|---|---|
| 2707 N. Proctor | 253-759-9009 |
| Tacoma, WA | BLD \| $ |

All kinds of people give us suggestions of places to eat; but when one of the nation's great restaurateurs tells us where to go, we pay special attention. It was Hap Townes, who for many years ran a grand lunchroom in Nashville, Tennessee, who tipped us off to Knapp's. "It's your kind of place," Hap said with assurance born of watching us eat many of his fine meals.

The setting of Knapp's in the Proctor district helps create an aura of small-town charm in the midst of big-city life. Walking into the old brick building is like going back in time. (Knapp's dates back to 1933.) The dining room is patrolled by teams of waitresses—pros who refill coffee and replace needed silverware with the grace of a four-star sommelier.

The menu is nostalgic too. This is a place to have a platter of liver and onions or turkey with sage-flavored dressing and a pile of mashed potatoes with a ladle of gravy on top. Every Tuesday, Knapp's serves corned beef and cabbage; every Wednesday, roast pork loin. Weekend dinner specials include roast pork and dressing, old-fashioned pot roast, and Sunday fried chicken. Begin your meal with homemade soup (clam chowder on Friday) and top it off with homemade peach pie. It is an all-American experience, not necessarily for the fussy epicure, but a treasure for aficionados of square meals.

## Maltby Cafe

| | |
|---|---|
| 8809 Maltby Rd. | 425-483-3123 |
| Snohomish, WA | www.maltbycafe.com |
| | BL \| $ |

If ever we write a book called *Really Big Food,* the Maltby Cafe would be featured for breakfast. Its cinnamon roll is less a roll than a loaf—a massive circular coil of sweet, walnut-enriched pastry smothered with drippy icing that comes on a dinner plate, which it fits edge-to-edge. It is a couple of breakfasts unto itself.

While other items on the menu are not so flabbergastingly immense, they are satisfying in the extreme. The Maltby omelet, for example, is another plate filler, loaded with ham, beef, peppers, and onions. The Maltby prime rib omelet includes plenty of beef, plus mushrooms, peppers, onions, tomatoes, olives, and two kinds of cheese: Cheddar and Swiss. The Whole Hog omelet features bacon, sausage, and ham, plus Tillamook Cheddar. Oatmeal is served with melted butter running all over the top of the bowl; the French toast is double-thick; and, lest we forget, the strawberry jam on every table is homemade and especially delicious when liberally spread on a big, oven-warm biscuit along with—are you ready?—crème fraîche.

Lunch is big too, especially the half-pound burgers. There are French dips, chicken-fried steak with mashed potatoes and biscuits with sausage gravy, and a prime rib stir-fry. Desserts include hot apple strudel, pie à la mode, and a Maltby sundae, which is a Maltby Bar (oatmeal, chocolate chips, walnuts) with ice cream, chocolate sauce, and whipped cream.

Maltby is a nostalgic little town with an allegedly haunted cemetery. Its cafe is located in a former school gym and cafeteria built in 1937.

## Mike's Chili Parlor

1447 NW Ballard Way      206-782-2808
Seattle, WA      LD | $

Outfitted with a billiards table, video games, an ATM station, and pull-tab lotto, decorated with beer signs and festooned with announcements warning that only cash is accepted and touting such specials as a Big Ass Bowl of Chili, Mike's is an in-your-face chili parlor. Seats are available at a couple of communal tables in the center of the room, at the counter, and in a few booths. Customers are a tough bunch, and the staff can seem tougher. In fact, among the "extras" listed on the menu, such as jalapeño peppers (25¢) and onions (25¢), is "abuse" (free). You must be twenty-one to enter.

The chili is a he-man brew of coarse-ground beef with bright Greek seasonings, saturated with enough grease that when it is served by the bowl, your spoon will slide through a glistening layer on top before it hits meat. (Oyster crackers are provided, and they are the connoisseur's way to soak up the oil.) Beans are optional, as are grated cheese and chopped onions.

You can have this stout stuff in a cup or bowl, as the dressing for burgers, hot dogs, and steak, and in concert with spaghetti noodles. You also can buy it by the gallon (at about $50), but for that you must bring your own container.

## Pick Quick Drive-In

4306 Pacific Hwy. E.　　　　253-922-5599
Tacoma, WA　　　　　　　　www.pick-quick.com
　　　　　　　　　　　　　　L (closed Dec 1–Feb 1) | $

Here's a roadside blast from the past (1949, to be precise), especially alluring when you can sit outside and enjoy a nice double bacon cheeseburger deluxe, chili fries, and chocolate malt . . . all of that for well under $15.

The hamburgers are medium-thin, crisp-edged, modest-sized, and of uniform shape with a moist savor from the well-aged grill that imprints itself into the toasted bun. Grilled onions are a popular topping. For 20¢ extra, the deluxe version includes lettuce, tomato, onion, pickle, and Pick Quick sauce. French fries, made from spuds cut right here, are very good, and the milk shakes can be extraordinary, as they are made from fresh fruit in season—strawberries, blueberries, blackberries, cherries, raspberries.

Pick Quick is a minuscule establishment that originally served as the canteen for a now-defunct drive-in movie theater. There is plenty of dining room in the great outdoors with picnic tables of all shapes and sizes.

There is a second Pick Quick at 1132 Auburn Way North, Auburn (253-248-1949), which is open year-round.

## Red Mill

1613 W. Dravus St.　　　　206-284-6363
Seattle, WA　　　　　　　　www.redmillburgers.com
　　　　　　　　　　　　　　L | $

There was a diner called the Red Mill in Seattle for thirty years starting in 1937. Twenty-seven years after it closed, a new Red Mill opened in Phinney Ridge, and a hamburger legend was born. No doubt, Seattle is a significant burger city, and many of its connoisseurs believe Red Mill's rate near the top. Flame-broiled to a smoky savor, they come in many configurations, including patties topped with blue cheese, barbecue sauce, and/or peppery bacon. You can get a double—that's a half pound of meat—and you even can get a meatless garden burger. We are fond of the verde burger with roasted green chiles, jack cheese, red onion, lettuce, tomato, and the Red Mill's proprietary sauce. Condiments and dressing are applied in abundance, so while the meat patty itself is good, the extras put it over the top.

On the side, onion rings are essential. They are big crunchy rounds with thick ribbons of sweet, caramelized onion inside. And there is a whole menu of milk shakes and malts, plus fresh-squeezed lemonade.

As if burgers, O-rings, and shakes weren't enough to love this place, we should also add that it has a strict *no cell phone* policy, allowing all of us to dine well and in peace. If you do need to take or make a call, there's a Starbucks right next door.

Seattle's first Red Mill is in Phinney Ridge at 312 North Sixty-Seventh Street (206-783-6362).

## *Spud Fish and Chips

9702 NE Juanita Dr.    425-823-0607
Kirkland, WA    www.spudfishandchips.com
LD | $

When he found out we were in the Seattle area, Roadfood.com contributor Wanderingjew sent us an urgent note advising we head to Kirkland for fish and chips. We now pass along this advice to anyone eager for cod, halibut, shrimp, scallops, or oysters hand breaded and fried in fresh oil until crisp, served alongside first-rate French fries. Spud Fish and Chips, a local destination since 1935, has a limited menu, with salad and chowder just about the only non-fried items, but you can be sure these folks know how to fry. The crust on each piece of fish is thin and crunchy; the cod is cream-moist; the halibut falls into elegant flakes; the shrimp snaps. Onion rings also are excellent: individual circles with severely crunchy exteriors holding ribbons of onion that have caramelized to tender sweetness. You will pay extra for tartar sauce (25¢), but it's worth the splurge; this homemade stuff is studded with al dente bits of pickle. While the iced tea and lemonade are fine, we also recommend the milk shakes, which are too thick for a straw.

Service is do-it-yourself. Place your order at the counter, pay, then wait until the order is put on a tray and ready for you to carry it to a booth inside or to the exterior counter and picnic tables. Signs atop each napkin dispenser ask customers to please bus their own tables when they've finished.

## Top Pot

2124 5th Ave.    206-728-1966
Seattle, WA    www.toppotdoughnuts.com
$

Top Pot has grown into a Seattle-area empire of fourteen cafés, but conspicuous success has in no way diminished the excellence of its donuts. They remain some of the nation's best. First and foremost, there's the crunch of the skin on the old-fashioneds—crisp enough to feel like your teeth are breaking something, after which they slide into the creamy cake interior just below the golden crust. Now, encase the top half with silky dark chocolate, maple frosting, or a glistening thick sugar glaze, and these modest-sized circular pastries become ecstasy.

The kitchen has a repertoire of forty different kinds, not all of which are always available. Some of our favorites are the cinnamon old-fashioned, the maple bar, and the apple fritter, which is chockfull of hunks of caramelized apple. However they are dressed, even with multicolored jimmies or coconut shavings, there is nothing froufrou or pretentious about these lovelies. They are good ol' donuts, the kind you want to have with morning coffee. By any meaningful standard—taste, texture, heft, even good looks—they are world-class, far superior to any of the national chains, as well as to their doppelgängers sold around the country.

# NEW ENGLAND

## Connecticut

Abbott's Lobster in the Rough   Noank, 5
Al's Hot Dog Stand   Naugatuck, 6
Big Dipper   Prospect, 6
Blackie's   Cheshire, 7
Carminuccio's   Newtown, 7
Clamp's   New Milford, 8
Coffee An'   Westport, 8
Colony Grill   Stamford, 9
Denmo's   Southbury, 9
Doogie's   Newington, 10
Dottie's Diner   Woodbury, 10
Dr. Mike's   Bethel, 11
Frank Pepe Pizzeria Napoletana   New
    Haven, 12
Harry's Drive-In   Colchester, 12
K. LaMay's   Meriden, 13
Kitchen Little   Mystic, 13
Lakeside Diner   Stamford, 14
Laurel Diner   Southbury, 14
Lenny & Joe's Fish Tale
    Restaurant   Madison, 15
Lenny's   Branford, 15
Letizia's   Norwalk, 16
Lobster Landing   Clinton, 17
Louis' Lunch   New Haven, 17
The Lunchbox   Meriden, 18
Mamie's   Roxbury, 18

Modern Apizza   New Haven, 19
Pizzeria Lauretano   Bethel, 20
Rawley's Drive-In   Fairfield, 21
Ridgefield Ice Cream Shop   Ridgefield, 21
Roseland Apizza   Derby, 22
Sally's Apizza   New Haven, 22
Shady Glen   Manchester, 23
Stanziato's   Danbury, 24
Super Duper Weenie   Fairfield, 24
Sycamore Drive-In   Bethel, 25
Ted's   Meriden, 26
Zuppardi's Apizza   West Haven, 26

## Maine

Beal's Lobster Pier   Southwest Harbor, 28
Becky's   Portland, 28
Bet's Famous Fish Fry   Boothbay, 29
Bob's Clam Hut   Kittery, 30
Cindy's Fish & Chips   Freeport, 30
Clam Shack   Kennebunkport, 31
Cole Farms   Gray, 31
Colucci's Hilltop Market   Portland, 32
Congdon's Donuts   Wells, 33
Dolly's   Frenchville, 33
Doris's Café   Fort Kent Mills, 34
Five Islands Lobster Co.   Georgetown, 34
Flo's   Cape Neddick, 35
Harmon's Lunch   Falmouth, 36
Harraseeket Lunch & Lobster   South
    Freeport, 37

Helen's  Machias, 37

Hodgman's Frozen Custard  New Gloucester, 38

Jordan's Snack Bar  Ellsworth, 38

Lobster Shack  Cape Elizabeth, 39

Long Lake Sporting Club  Sinclair, 39

Maine Diner  Wells, 40

Moody's Diner  Waldoboro, 41

Nunan's Lobster Hut  Kennebunkport, 41

Pemaquid Lobster Co-Op  Pemaquid, 42

Portland Pie Co.  Portland, 42

Rock's Family Diner  Fort Kent, 43

Sea Basket  Wiscasset, 44

Shaw's Fish & Lobster Wharf  New Harbor, 44

Shaw's Ridge Farm  Sanford, 45

Waterman's Beach Lobster  Thomaston, 45

Young's Lobster Pound  Belfast, 46

## Massachusetts

Betty Ann Food Shop  East Boston, 47

Christina's Homemade Ice Cream Cambridge, 47

Clam Box  Ipswich, 48

Donut Dip  East Longmeadow, 49

Durgin-Park  Boston, 49

Essex Seafood  Essex, 50

Graham's Hot Dogs  Fall River, 50

Hartley's Original Pork Pies  Fall River, 51

J.J.'s Coney Island  Fall River, 51

Kelly's Roast Beef  Revere, 52

The Liberal Club  Fall River, 52

Marguerite's  Westport, 53

Marty's Donut Land  Ipswich, 54

Marzilli's Bakery  Fall River, 54

Mee Sum Restaurant and Lounge  Fall River, 55

Nick's  Fall River, 56

Nick's Famous Roast Beef  North Beverly, 57

Red Skiff  Rockport, 58

R.F. O'Sullivan & Son  Somerville, 58

Santarpio's  East Boston, 59

Toscanini's  Cambridge, 59

Turtle Alley  Gloucester, 60

The Village Restaurant  Essex, 60

The White Hut  Springfield, 61

Woodman's of Essex  Essex, 61

## New Hampshire

Bishop's  Littleton, 63

Brown's Lobster Pound  Seabrook, 64

Gilley's PM Lunch  Portsmouth, 64

Hart's Turkey Farm  Meredith, 65

The Ice House  Rye, 65

Polly's Pancake Parlor  Sugar Hill, 66

Rye Harbor Lobster Pound  Rye, 67

Sunny Day Diner  Lincoln, 67

## Rhode Island

Allie's Donuts  North Kingstown, 68

Bocce Club  Woonsocket, 69

Champlin's Seafood Deck  Narragansett, 69

The Commons Lunch  Little Compton, 70

Evelyn's Drive-In  Tiverton, 70

Flo's Clam Shack  Middletown, 71

Gray's Ice Cream  Tiverton, 72

Haven Brothers  Providence, 72

Jigger's Diner  East Greenwich, 73

Johnny Angel's Clam Shack  Charlestown, 73

Mike's Kitchen  Cranston, 74

Olneyville N.Y. System  Providence, 74

Stanley's Famous Hamburgers  Central Falls, 75

Wein-O-Rama  Cranston, 75

Wright's Farm  Harrisville, 76

## Vermont

Al's French Frys  South Burlington, 77

Art of the Chicken  Ludlow, 78

Baba-À-Louis  Chester, 78

Blue Benn Diner  Bennington, 79

Chelsea Royal Diner  Brattleboro, 79

Curtis' All American Bar B Q  Putney, 80

Miss Lyndonville Diner  Lyndonville, 80

Mrs. Murphy's Donuts  Manchester, 81

P&H Truck Stop  Wells River, 81

Papa Pete's  North Hero, 82

Up For Breakfast  Manchester, 83

Wayside Restaurant  Berlin, 83

# MID-ATLANTIC

## Delaware

Charcoal Pit  Wilmington, 89

Countrie Eatery  Dover, 90

Helen's Sausage House  Smyrna, 90

Sambo's Tavern  Leipsic, 91

Woodside Farm Creamery  Hockessin, 91

## District of Columbia

Ben's Chili Bowl  Washington, D.C., 93

Florida Avenue Grill  Washington, D.C., 94

## Maryland

Bear Creek Open Pit BBQ  Callaway, 95

The Breakfast Shoppe  Severna Park, 96

Chick & Ruth's Delly  Annapolis, 96

Chubby's Southern Style Barbeque  Emmitsburg, 97

The Cove  Crisfield, 98

Ruby & Ketchy's   Morgantown, 224
Stewart's Original Hot Dogs   Huntington, 224

Singleton's Seafood Shack   Mayport, 258
T-Ray's Burger Station   Fernandina Beach, 258
Whitey's Fish Camp   Orange Park, 259

## DEEP SOUTH

### Alabama

13th Street Bar-B-Q   Phenix City, 231
Bob Sykes Bar B-Q   Bessemer, 232
Bogue's   Birmingham, 232
The Brick Pit   Mobile, 233
Dew Drop Inn   Mobile, 233
Greenbrier Restaurant   Madison, 234
Martin's Montgomery, 234
Niki's West   Birmingham, 235
Waysider   Tuscaloosa, 236
Wintzell's Oyster House   Mobile, 236

### Arkansas

AQ Chicken House   Springdale, 238
Catfish N   Dardanelle, 239
Charlotte's Eats & Sweets   Keo, 239
Cotham's Mercantile   Scott, 240
Craig's Bar-B-Que   DeValls Bluff, 240
Ed & Kay's   Benton, 241
Family Pie Shop   DeValls Bluff, 241
Feltner's Whatta-Burger   Russellville, 242
Franke's   Little Rock, 242
Grapevine   Paris, 243
McClard's   Hot Springs, 244
Mickey's BBQ   Hot Springs, 244
Rhoda's Famous Tamales   Lake Village, 245
Stubby's Bar-B-Que   Hot Springs, 245

### Florida

Barnacle Bill's   St. Augustine, 247
Beach Road Chicken Dinners   Jacksonville, 248
Blue Heaven   Key West, 248
El Siboney   Key West, 249
Ernie's Bar-b-que & Lounge.   Fort Lauderdale, 249
Havana   West Palm Beach, 250
JB's Fish Camp   New Smyrna Beach, 250
Jenkins Quality Barbecue   Jacksonville, 251
Jerry's Drive-In   Pensacola, 252
Keys Fisheries   Marathon, 252
La Teresita Cafeteria   Tampa, 253
Louie's Backyard   Key West, 254
Old Spanish Sugar Mill Grill   De Leon Springs, 254
O'Steens   St. Augustine, 255
Pepe's Café & Steakhouse   Key West, 255
Saltwater Cowboys   St. Augustine, 256
Schooner's Seafood House   St. Augustine, 257

### Georgia

Barbecue Kitchen   College Park, 260
Blue Willow Inn   Social Circle, 261
Buckner's Family Restaurant   Jackson, 261
Bulloch House   Warm Springs, 262
The Colonnade   Atlanta, 262
Community BBQ   Decatur, 263
The Crab Shack   Tybee Island, 263
Dillard House   Dillard, 264
Dinglewood Pharmacy   Columbus, 265
Don's Famous Bar-B-Q   Pooler, 265
Edna's   Chatsworth, 265
Hot Thomas' Barbeque   Watkinsville, 266
Mamie's Kitchen   Conyers, 266
Mary Mac's Tea Room   Atlanta, 267
Matthews Cafeteria   Tucker, 268
Mrs. Wilkes' Dining Room   Savannah, 268
Nu-Way Weiners   Macon, 269
Old South Bar-B-Q   Smyrna, 269
Peachtree Cafe   Fort Valley, 270
Sconyer's Bar-B-Que   Augusta, 270
Silver Skillet   Atlanta, 271
Skipper's Fish Camp   Darien, 271
Smith House   Dahlonega, 272
Varsity Drive-In   Atlanta, 272

### Louisiana

Acme Oyster House   New Orleans, 274
Bon Ton Café   New Orleans, 274
Boudin King   Jennings, 275
Bozo's   Metarie, 276
Brenda's Diner   New Iberia, 276
Café des Amis   Breaux Bridge, 277
Café du Monde   New Orleans, 277
Casamento's   New Orleans, 278
Central Grocery   New Orleans, 278
Champagne's Breaux Bridge Bakery   Breaux Bridge, 279
D.I.'s   Basile, 280
Domilise's Po-Boys   New Orleans, 280
Don's Specialty Meats   Scott, 281
Dwyer's Café   Lafayette, 281
Earl's   Lafayette, 282
Galatoire's   New Orleans, 282
Hansen's Sno-Bliz   New Orleans, 283
Jerry Lee's   Baton Rouge, 284
Johnson's Boucanière   Lafayette, 284
Lasyone's Meat Pie Kitchen   Natchitoches, 285
Lea's Lunchroom   Lecompte, 286
Middendorf's   Akers, 286

## Wisconsin

Anchor Bar   Superior, 414
Beerntsen's Candy Store   Manitowoc, 415
Bendtsen's Bakery   Racine, 415
Benji's   Milwaukee, 416
Charcoal Inn   Sheboygan, 416
Chili John's   Green Bay, 417
Jack Pandl's Whitefish Bay Inn   Whitefish
     Bay, 417
Jake's   Milwaukee, 418
Jo's Café   Milwaukee, 419
Klinger's East   Milwaukee, 419
Kopp's Custard   Glendale, 420
Leon's   Milwaukee, 420
Maggie's   Bayfield, 421
Mazo's   Milwaukee, 421
McBob's   Milwaukee, 422
Mr. Perkins' Family Restaurant   Milwaukee,
     422
Plaza Tavern   Madison, 423
Real Chili   Milwaukee, 423
Solly's Grille   Milwaukee, 424
Speed Queen   Milwaukee, 425
Stockholm Pie Company   Stockholm, 425
Three Brothers   Milwaukee, 426
Watts Tea Room   Milwaukee, 427
White Gull Inn   Fish Creek, 427

# SOUTHWEST

## Arizona

BK Carne Asada & Hot Dogs   Tucson, 433
Cafe Poca Cosa   Tucson, 434
El Bravo   Phoenix, 435
El Charro Café   Tucson, 435
El Guero Canelo   Tucson, 436
El Manantial Tacos Y Hot Dogs   Tucson,
     437
El Torero   Tucson, 437
Gus Balon's   Tucson, 438
Joe & Aggie's Cafe   Holbrook, 439
La Cabana   Nogales, 439
Lo-Lo's Chicken & Waffles   Phoenix, 440
Los Jarritos   Tucson, 440
Mariscos Chihuahua   Tucson, 441
Mrs. White's Golden Rule Cafe   Phoenix,
     441
Pico de Gallo   South Tucson, 442
Sugar Bowl   Scottsdale, 442
Teresa's Mosaic Cafe   Tucson, 443
Tucson Tamale Company   Tucson, 444
Vantastic   Glendale, 444

## Colorado

Biker Jim's Gourmet Sausage   Denver, 445
Buckhorn Exchange   Denver, 446

Bud's Bar   Sedalia, 446
Duffeyroll Cafe   Denver, 447
Durango Diner   Durango, 447
Johnson's Corner   Loveland, 448
La Fogata   Denver, 448

## Kansas

Al's Chickenette   Hays, 450
Barto's Idle Hour   Frontenac, 451
Brookville Hotel   Abilene, 451
Bunker Hill Cafe   Bunker Hill, 452
Chicken Mary's   Pittsburg, 452
Corner Pharmacy   Leavenworth, 453
Cozy Inn   Salina, 454
Nu Way   Wichita, 454
Oklahoma Joe's   Kansas City, 455
Olde Towne Restaurant   Hillsboro, 456
Porubsky's Grocery   Topeka, 456
RJ's Bob-Be-Que Shack   Mission, 457
Woodyard Bar-B-Que   Kansas City, 457

## Nevada

Louis' Basque Corner   Reno, 459
Martin Hotel   Winnemucca, 460
Mary's Hash House   Las Vegas, 460

## New Mexico

Bert's Burger Bowl   Santa Fe, 462
Buckhorn Tavern   San Antonio, 463
Chope's   La Mesa, 463
Duran Central Pharmacy   Albuquerque, 464
Frontier   Albuquerque, 464
Garcia's Kitchen   Albuquerque, 465
Golden Crown Panaderia   Albuquerque,
     466
La Posta de Mesilla   Old Mesilla, 466
Model Pharmacy   Albuquerque, 467
Nellie's   Las Cruces, 467
Nopalito   Las Cruces, 468
Owl Bar & Cafe   San Antonio, 468
Pasquale's   Santa Fe, 469
Plaza Café   Santa Fe, 469
Roque's Carnitas   Santa Fe, 469
San Marcos Cafe   Cerrillos, 470
Sugar's   Embudo, 471
Tecolote   Santa Fe, 471

## Oklahoma

Cancun   Tulsa, 472
Cattlemen's Steakhouse   Oklahoma City,
     473
Clanton's   Vinita, 473
Classen Grill   Oklahoma City, 474
Coney I-Lander   Tulsa, 475
Country Dove Tea Room   Elk City, 475
Dink's Pit Bar-B-Que   Bartlesville, 476

Eischen's Bar   Okarche, 476
Freddie's Hamburgers   Tulsa, 477
Hamburger King   Shawnee, 477
Hammett House   Claremore, 478
Hank's Hamburgers   Tulsa, 479
Ike's Chili   Tulsa, 479
Jigg's Smokehouse   Clinton, 480
Johnnie's   El Reno, 481
Kumback Lunch   Perry, 481
Leo's   Oklahoma City, 482
Linda-Mar Drive-In   Tulsa, 483
The Meers Store   Lawton, 483
Murphy's Steak House   Bartlesville, 484
Robert's   El Reno, 484
Rock Cafe   Stroud, 485
Sid's   El Reno, 486
Van's Pig Stand   Shawnee, 486
White River Fish Market   Tulsa, 487
Wilson's B-B-Q   Tulsa, 488

## Texas
Angelo's   Fort Worth, 489
Avalon Diner   Houston, 490
Bartley's Bar-B-Q   Grapevine, 490
The Big Texan   Amarillo, 491
Black's Barbecue   Lockhart, 491
Blanco Bowling Club Cafe   Blanco, 492
Blue Bonnet Cafe   Marble Falls, 493
Bohannon's Brietzke Station   Seguin, 493
Bryce's Cafeteria   Texarkana, 494
Cattlemen's Fort Worth Steak House   Fort
   Worth, 494
Chris Madrid's   San Antonio, 495
City Market   Luling, 496
Clark's Outpost   Tioga, 496
Fuel City   Dallas, 497
Golden Light Cafe   Amarillo, 498
Goode Co. Texas Bar-B-Q   Houston, 498
Green Vegetarian Restaurant   San Antonio,
   499
H&H Coffee Shop   El Paso, 500
Highland Park Soda Fountain   Dallas, 500
Hill Country Cupboard   Johnson City, 501
Hoover's Cooking   Austin, 502
Hut's Hamburgers   Austin, 502
Kreuz Market   Lockhart, 503
La Mexicana   Houston, 503
Little Diner   Canutillo, 504
Lock Drugs   Bastrop, 505
Louie Mueller's   Taylor, 506
The Mecca   Dallas, 506
Monument Cafe   Georgetown, 507
Norma's Cafe   Dallas, 507
OST   Bandera, 508
Paris Coffee Shop   Fort Worth, 508
Ranchman's Café   Ponder, 509

Royer's Round Top Cafe   Round Top, 510
Salt Lick   Driftwood, 510
Smitty's   El Paso, 511
Smitty's   Lockhart, 512
Southside Market   Elgin, 512
Sweet Georgia Brown   Dallas, 513
Taco Garage   San Antonio, 514
Taco House   San Antonio, 514
Taco Taco   San Antonio, 515
Texas Pie Company   Kyle, 516
Threadgill's   Austin, 516
Tolbert's   Grapevine, 517
Tom & Bingo's   Lubbock, 518
Vernon's Kuntry Katfish   Conroe, 518
Village Bakery   West, 518
Weikel's Store and Bakery   La Grange, 519

## Utah
Capitol Reef Cafe   Torrey, 520
Hires Big H   Salt Lake City, 521
Idle Isle   Brigham City, 521
Lamb's Grill   Salt Lake City, 522
Maddox Drive-In   Brigham City, 523
Mom's Cafe   Salina, 523
Navajo Hogan   Salt Lake City, 524
Sill's Cafe   Layton, 525

# GREAT PLAINS
## Idaho
Cedars Floating Restaurant   Coeur d'Alene,
   531
El Gallo Giro   Kuna, 532
Goldy's Breakfast Bistro   Boise, 532
Hoot Owl Cafe   Ponderay, 533
Hudson's   Coeur d'Alene, 534
Java on Sherman   Coeur d'Alene, 534
Jimmy's Down the Street   Coeur d'Alene,
   535
Leku Ona   Boise, 536
Westside Drive-In   Boise, 536
Wolf Lodge Inn   Coeur d'Alene, 537

## Montana
Candel's By-Way Café   Stanford, 538
Dash Inn   Lewistown, 539
Eddie's Supper Club   Great Falls, 540
Matt's Place   Butte, 540
Pamida Pharmacy   Big Timber, 541
Pekin Noodle Parlor   Butte, 541
Red Lodge Cafe   Red Lodge, 542
Rex Restaurant   Billings, 542
Sarah's   Billings, 543
Stella's   Billings, 543
Willow Creek Cafe & Saloon   Willow
   Creek, 544

## Nebraska

Bohemian Cafe  Omaha, 545
Crystal Cafe  South Sioux City, 546
Gering Bakery  Gering, 547
Joe Tess Place  Omaha, 547
Rosita's  Scottsbluff, 548
Scotty's Drive-In  Scottsbluff, 549
Sehnert's Bakery and Bieroc Cafe  McCook, 549
Shirley's Diner  Omaha, 550
Taco Town  Scottsbluff, 550

## North Dakota

Carol Widman's Candy Shop  Fargo, 552
TNT's Diner  West Fargo, 553

## South Dakota

Bobkat's Purple Pie Place  Custer, 554
Bob's  Sioux Falls, 554
Edgar's  Elk Point, 555
Murdo Drive In  Murdo, 556
Nick's Hamburger Shop  Brookings, 556
Tea Steak House  Tea, 557
Tripp Sports Bowl Cafe  Tripp, 557

## Wyoming

Chugwater Soda Fountain  Chugwater, 559
Lisa's  Greybull, 560
Svilar's  Hudson, 560
The Wagon Box  Story, 561

# WEST COAST

## California

Al's Place  Locke, 567
Barbara's Fishtrap  Half Moon Bay, 568
Bette's Oceanview Diner  Berkeley, 569
Bi-Rite Creamery  San Francisco, 569
Cafe at the Bug  Midpines, 570
The Cottage  La Jolla, 570
Duarte's Tavern  Pescadero, 571
Du-par's  Los Angeles, 572
D.Z. Akins  San Diego, 573
El Campeon  San Juan Capistrano, 573
El Indio  San Diego, 574
El Paisa Taco Truck  Oakland, 574
The Hitching Post  Casmalia, 575
Hob Nob Hill  San Diego, 576
Hodad's  Ocean Beach, 576
Ici  Berkeley, 577
Jocko's Steak House  Nipomo, 578
Julian Pie Company  Santa Ysabel, 578
La Farine  Oakland, 579
La Super-Rica  Santa Barbara, 579
Mama's Hot Tamales Cafe  Los Angeles, 580

The Marshall Store  Marshall, 581
Musso & Frank Grill  Hollywood, 581
Orange Inn  Laguna Beach, 582
Original Pantry  Los Angeles, 582
Pann's  Los Angeles, 583
Philippe the Original  Los Angeles, 584
Ramona Cafe  Ramona, 584
Randy's Donuts  Inglewood, 585
Rick & Ann's  Berkeley, 585
Sam's Grill  San Francisco, 586
Sears Fine Foods  San Francisco, 587
Swan Oyster Depot  San Francisco, 587
The Waffle  Los Angeles, 588

## Oregon

Annie's Donut Shop  Portland, 489
Astoria Coffeehouse & Bistro  Astoria, 590
Blue Scorcher Bakery Café  Astoria, 590
Bowpicker  Astoria, 591
Charlie's Chowder House  Astoria, 591
Crema  Portland, 592
Dan & Louis Oyster Bar  Portland, 593
Ecola Seafoods  Cannon Beach, 593
Fuller's Coffee Shop  Portland, 594
Green Salmon  Yachats, 595
Halibut's  Portland, 595
Local Ocean  Newport, 596
The Oasis  Milton-Freewater, 597
Ocean Bleu @ Gino's  Newport, 597
Otis Cafe  Otis, 598
Otto's Sausage Kitchen  Portland, 599
Pacific Way  Gearhart, 599
Ristretto Roasters  Portland, 600
South Beach Fish Market  South Beach, 600
Voodoo Donut  Portland, 601
Wanda's Cafe  Nehalem, 602
Waves of Grain  Cannon Beach, 602

## Washington

13 Coins  Seattle, 604
14 Carrot Cafe  Seattle, 605
Bakeman's  Seattle, 605
Beth's Cafe  Seattle, 606
Crumpet Shop  Seattle, 607
Emmett Watson's Oyster Bar  Seattle, 607
Frank's Diner  Spokane, 608
Hi Spot Café  Seattle, 608
Knapp's Restaurant  Tacoma, 609
Maltby Cafe  Snohomish, 609
Mike's Chili Parlor  Seattle, 610
Pick Quick Drive-In  Tacoma, 611
Red Mill  Seattle, 611
Spud Fish and Chips  Kirkland, 612
Top Pot  Seattle, 612